Toddler 411

Clear Answers & Smart Advice for Your Toddler

Denise Fields and Ari Brown, M.D.

Copyright Page and Carbon Neutral Snack Mix

Moog, clavinet and lead guitar by Denise Fields
Drums, programming and interior layout by Alan Fields
Cover/interior design and keyboard solo by Epicenter Creative
Catering, trade show roadie by Mark Brown
Backing harmony vocals and hand claps by Andy and Julia Brown
Percussion and Wurlitzer synths by Ben and Jack Fields
Index by New West Indexing
Band photography by Jim Lincoln and Tracy Trahar

Distribution to the book trade by Ingram Publisher Services.

To order this book, order online at Toddler411.com or call 1-800-888-0385. Questions or comments? Please call the authors at (303) 442-8792. Or write to them at Windsor Peak Press, 436 Pine Street, Boulder, CO 80302. E-mail us at authors@Toddler411.com.

The latest info on this book is online at Toddler411.com

Library Cataloging in Publication Data

Brown, Ari, M.D.
Fields, Denise
    Toddler 411: Clear Answers & Smart Advice for Your Toddler / Ari Brown, M.D. and Denise Fields
    544 pages.
    Includes index.
    ISBN 1-889392-38-3.
    1. Toddlers—Care. 2. Child rearing. 3. Mother and infant—Popular works.

    649′.122′0296—dc20. 2011.

Version 3.0

Do you have an old copy of this book? Check our web site at Toddler411.com make sure you have the most current version (click on "which version?").

TODDLER 411 MEDICAL ADVISORY BOARD

PRAISE FOR TODDLER 411

"Toddler 411 delivers evidence and experience-based recommendations in a format and language that is exceedingly practical and user-friendly. Like Baby 411, I will give a copy to each family."

- Jason V. Terk, M.D., FAAP
Pediatrician

"Dr. Ari Brown knows her stuff! Her new book, *Toddler 411,* is an easy-to-use, authoritative guide for parents. The question and answer format is perfect for busy parents who want expert advice, but don't have the time to wade through pages of text to find the one nugget of information they are looking for. She covers everything parents need to know about their toddler and gives parents the tools to handle almost any problem. Brown's book is more than just a book full of practical tips—though it is chock full of them. It conveys an attitude of love, and the joy that parents experience when they know what they are doing."

- Ted Huston, Ph.D.
Professor of Human Ecology, Professor of Psychology
University of Texas at Austin

"Just as I did when I read *Baby 411,* I felt as if someone was reading my mind answering all of my questions and concerns as a parent. Dr. Brown tackles all of the issues facing parents of toddlers, and has a unique ability as both a pediatrician and a parent. It is a wonderful book to read as well as a useful reference guide to consult over and over again."

- Helen Gilbert, mother of toddler

"Finally, a manual on a two year old! Every household needs this book in every room of the house (& car). We have four children from ages 1 to 6 and this addresses many of the situations that we have endured and gives you sensible advice. It's easy to reference answers on all our toddler dilemmas!"

- Lisa and Karl Shackelford, parents of four

"This book needs to be read by all parents of toddlers! It not only covers all the essential topics related to this developmental stage, but it is so easy to read and understand. Dr. Brown's style of writing will keep any parent engaged…and most importantly, this book does an excellent job of translating the written words into the practice of parenting."

- Allison K. Chase, Ph.D.
Clinical Psychologist

"This book is exactly what I asked Ari Brown to write for the follow up to *Baby 411*—I had a toddler going through the "terrible twos" at the time. It gives clear concise information and sound advice in an easy to read format. It is also made more believable by the fact that she has been through it herself and shares some of those experiences."

- Sandi Treybig, M.D., FAAP
Pediatrician and mother of a 4 year old

OVERVIEW

How do you plant the seeds of discipline with a toddler? This part of the book explores the nuts and bolts of toddler discipline, including picking your battles, surviving the public tantrum and more. Next, it is milestones: is your toddler hitting his milestones? Learn how a toddler grows, physically, socially and emotionally. What behaviors are normal? And what things should concern you?

How can you stimulate your child's development with play? We've got the low-down on play, enrichment programs, preschool and other activities.

What is autism? We'll discuss how to spot autism, plus explore the other challenges parents might face with their toddlers, including sensory processing disorder and more.

Then it's on to toilet training—can you really toilet train your child in one day? Which day? We'll give the inside scoop on how to leave those diapers behind forever.

What about sleep? We'll discuss what's normal when it comes to toddler sleep—and when to move a toddler to a big kid bed. Plus learn how to deal with sleep disruptions and fix bad habits.

Finally, we'll talk about picky eaters—how do you introduce a new food to a toddler? What should a toddler be eating anyway? We'll discuss the food tricks and treats to make sure your toddler is getting all the nutrients she needs.

How do you care for your toddler's skin and hair? This section of the book explores basic toddler hygiene as well as everything you wanted to know about your toddler's poop and pee! Exciting, we know.

Learn the tricks to avoiding the wait at your doctor's office—and what regular visits you'll be making to your toddler's doctor. We'll also discuss which vaccines your toddler needs.

In this part of the book, we'll explore what can make your toddler sick: both infections and diseases. You'll get the 411 on strep throat, rashes, allergies and more!

Finally, it's time for first aid—learn how to handle the top 10 toddler emergencies, from vomiting to broken bones.

This section includes detailed information on medicines, alternative therapies, lab tests, more info on infections, the glossary, references and footnotes.

ACKNOWLEDGMENTS

If you actually have time to read this page you are a) ignoring a tantrum or b) avoiding doing the laundry while your toddler is taking a nap.

Because you will soon be whisked away to reality, I'll be brief. And, it's probably more important for you to read the section on keeping your child from using spaghetti sauce as finger paint.

But this is my page to thank all the people who have helped me, motivated me, and put up with me through this experience.

To Mark, the love of my life. Thanks for believing in me and believing in this "little" project. Your spoken and unspoken support carried me through times I contemplated why the heck I ever decided to write books. As if having a full-time job and raising a family wasn't enough to do!

To The Fields, thanks for taking chances. I owe you some BBQ for our late-night, pre-vacation editing session.

To Mrs. Morini, my AP English teacher. Thanks for making me write a descriptive paragraph about capers. If I could make capers sound interesting, I knew I could write a medical book and not put my readers to sleep.

To my patients and their parents. You have been and continue to be my inspiration to write. The countless conversations and experiences I have shared with you fill the pages of this book

Other encouraging folks, friends, and spiritual advisors to whom I am eternally grateful:

The entire community of Austin, Texas. There are too many of you to thank individually!
The physicians and staff at Capital Pediatric Group.
The staff at Parents Magazine and Parents.com.
The communications department of the American Academy of Pediatrics.
Texas Pediatric Society.
National Association of Medical Communicators.
The University of Texas at Austin Child and Family Lab School.
Banyan Productions and The Learning Channel. Thanks for having me on Surviving Motherhood and not on What Not To Wear.
C.S. Lewis & Co.

Finally, I dedicate this book to Andy and Julia. Thanks for letting me share some of your stories to help other moms and dads. I am so proud to be your mom, it goes beyond words. All my love, Mom.

- Ari Brown, M.D.

TABLE OF CONTENTS

Chapter 4

IS THIS NORMAL?

Chapter 5

PLAY & PRESCHOOL

Chapter 6

CHALLENGES

SECTION TWO: THE POTTY, SLEEP & FEEDING

Chapter 7

TOILET TRAINING

Chapter 8

SLEEP

Chapter 9

GROWTH

Chapter 10

NUTRITION

Chapter 11

FOOD TRICKS & TREATS

PART TWO: TODDLER HEALTHWATCH

Chapter 12

HYGIENE

Chapter 13

THE OTHER END

Chapter 14

YOU & YOUR DOC

Chapter 15

VACCINES

Chapter 16

COMMON INFECTIONS

Chapter 17

COMMON DISEASES

Chapter 18

THE ENVIRONMENT & YOUR TODDLER

Chapter 19

FIRST AID

PART THREE: THE REFERENCE LIBRARY

ICONS

 Helpful Hint

 Reality Check

 Bottom Line

 Red Flags

 Feedback from the Real World

 Old Wives Tale

 Insider Secrets

 New Parent 411

 Age-specific Advice

INTRO
Why read this book?

WHAT'S IN THIS CHAPTER

◆ MEET THE AUTHORS

◆ NO ADS? NO PLUGS?

◆ SHOW US THE SCIENCE

◆ THE 3 TRUTHS ABOUT PARENTING A TODDLER

You've juggled the 2400 diaper changes . . . the 3am feedings . . . the modern Olympic record for spit-up . . . that's all history now.

Congratulations! You've survived the first year of parenthood!

As a seasoned pro, you can handle anything, right?

Welcome to the toddler years—where the fun is just beginning!

As a parent of a newborn, you probably had pages of questions for your pediatrician. By the time you reach the one-year check-up, your questions fit on a Post-It note.

Yet even though you've mastered the feeding, bathing and basic care of your baby . . . your newborn has now morphed into a toddler. While you've been growing more confident, so has your child. He's been studying your every move, your tricks. Now, he's ready to launch into full toddler mode.

It reminds us of a quote from one of our favorite movies, *Galaxy Quest*:

Sure, they're cute now, but in a second they're gonna get mean, and they're gonna get ugly somehow, and there's gonna be a million more of them.

Okay, the actor in this scene was talking about aliens. But you get the picture.

Here's a little secret no one tells you about toddlers: the "Terrible Two's" start well before age two . . . and last until age four, or longer!

Let's see if you recognize this child:

Every tooth brushing is a wrestling match.
Bribery is required to get him into his car seat.
You can rate and name his tantrums like tropical storms.
And he only eats beige colored food.
Will he survive toddlerhood? Will you?

That's where we come in: your tour guides to making those "special" years between ages one and four more enjoyable. No, we don't do babysitting. And outsourcing your parenting duties to a call center in India isn't going to happen either. (Yes, we have all entertained that idea on occasion.)

Here's what we *can* do:

The goal of this book

Our #1 Goal is to help you understand your toddler—well, at least a little bit. We will share tried and true tricks from parents and pediatricians on how to get your child to eat something other than chicken nuggets and Cheerios. We'll prepare you for toilet training—yes, some day soon, you will change your last diaper.

And of course, we hope this book provides you the most up-to-date medical information about toddlers and preschoolers. With this knowledge, you should gain insight, patience, and appreciation for your little person.

And we want to hear from you. While we've tried to answer the most common questions parents have about toddlers, we know you might have additional questions. Pop over to our web site Toddler411.com and drop us an email. Yes, we read and answer all of them! (How many other parenting authors can you actually email? Go ahead and ponder that. We'll wait right here).

In case you haven't read our other books (see the back of this book for details), let's take a second to introduce ourselves. We'll also explain this book's no-ad policy, our "show us the science" mantra and more.

Meet the new authors, same as the old authors

This book was created by the same team that brought you *Baby 411*— Denise Fields & Dr. Ari Brown. Yes, Denise Fields is the same author who penned the best-sellers *Bridal Bargains* and *Baby Bargains* (if you've read our wedding books in addition to our baby books, we owe you lunch).

But who is Dr. Ari Brown?

More than a mere co-author, Dr. Brown has written the majority of this book . . . especially the detailed medical advice. An award-winning pediatrician in private practice in Austin, TX, Dr. Brown graduated from the Baylor College of Medicine. She did her pediatric residency at the renowned Children's Hospital in Boston, under the auspices of legendary pediatrician T. Berry Brazelton. In short, Dr. Brown knows her stuff.

As an official spokesperson for the American Academy of Pediatrics, medical advisor to *Parents* magazine and children's health expert for WebMD, Dr. Brown is a trusted voice on children's heath issues.

Denise Fields brings her 15 years of experience as a consumer advocate to *Toddler 411*—as the co-author of *Baby Bargains* and *Toddler Bargains*, Fields has been featured on Oprah, The Today Show and Good Morning America as well as in articles in the *Wall Street Journal* and *New York Times*. For *Toddler 411*, Denise adds in her experience as both a mom and author—many of the questions we get on our message boards hit the same hot button issues you'll see here.

As always, the secret sauce to our books is reader feedback. First, you'll notice readers of our previous books contributed to several sections of this book—you'll see their "Real World Feedback" when it comes to topics like nutrition, potty training and more. Second, look at the questions we list in each chapter. These are the frequent, real-world questions asked by patients of Dr. Brown. . . and the same questions that most parents of toddlers ponder.

Yes, both of the authors of this book are also mommies. They have four children between them. Best of all, we are from your generation—we know you want detailed info, the latest research and trends, plus handy web resources. We know you want to go online to get the latest updates, so we've created a special web site for this book (Toddler411.com). There you can read any breaking news on our blog, swap stories with other parents on our message boards and sign up for a free newsletter that will provide even more insight.

How to use this book

Instructions: Open cover. Start reading.

Just kidding! We realize you know how to read a book, but let's go over a few details on how to get the most out of *Toddler 411*.

First, let's talk about BIG UGLY LATIN WORDS. You can't discuss child's health without whipping out the Latin. To keep the jargon from overwhelming you, we have a handy glossary at the end of this book. When you see a **BIG UGLY LATIN WORD** in bold small caps, turn to the back to get a quick definition.

Second, if you flip through the chapters, you'll note boxes with Dr. B's opinion. As it sounds, these are her *opinions* on several hot button issues. Feel free to disagree with these thoughts, but they are based on years of seeing real-world patients and talking with parents. Unlike some other parenting books, we think readers deserve to know where the line is drawn between fact and opinion. You can then decide what works for you and your family.

Finally, let's talk footnotes—we've tried to footnote the sources used throughout this book. These references are in Appendix F.

INTRO

? ?

No ads? No plugs?

Yes, that's true—as with all our books, this guide contains ZERO ads, spam and commercial plugs. No pharmaceutical or formula company has paid the authors to plug their products in this book. Dr. Brown does NOT go on all-expense paid junkets to Aruba to learn about the latest drug or medical research (although she could use a beach vacation after writing this book). The opinions in this book are those of Denise Fields and Dr. Brown—in the latter case, based on her training and experience in the practice of pediatric medicine.

Full disclosure: the publisher of this book does offer a "custom publishing" program for this and our other titles. That means a company or non-profit organization can purchase a special run of books, putting their logo on the cover and customizing the title page. These groups then give away the book as a gift to their customers, employees or clients. Of course, these companies have no influence over the editorial content of the book. See the contact page at the end of this book if you'd like more information on this program.

iPhone app, Facebook, Twitter, Blog

Toddler 411 is more than just a book—we have all sorts of interactive goodies and online extras. Let's review.

If you'd prefer to read this book on your Kindle or iPad, we have handy ebook versions of *Toddler 411* for your viewing pleasure. Search Toddler 411 on the Kindle ebookstore or the iBookstore.

For the latest news and research studies on toddler health, check out our blog at Toddler411.com. Download our free iPhone app (search Baby 411 on the iTunes store) to read the blog on the go, as well as watch videos on kid health news and see the latest news on our Facebook page.

Did we mention Facebook? Yep, if you have a second, please pop over and fan us at Facebook.com/Expecting411. Our Facebook page includes all the latest goings on our books, media appearances and more. And you can follow our Twitter feed at Twitter.com/Baby411.

Show us the science!

The goal of *Toddler 411* is to provide you with the most up-to-date medical info on your child. We're talking state-of-the-art when it comes to your toddler's health and nutrition.

So, in the age of Internet rumors and 24/7 cable news, let's take a moment to talk SCIENCE.

When it comes to your child's health, our mantra is SHOW US THE SCIENCE! Before we recommend a particular treatment, parenting method or medicine, we expect there to be good science behind it.

What is good science? Good scientific research is conducted by reputable researchers and published in a major medical journal, like the *New England Journal of Medicine*. Good science is based on a large enough sample to be statistically significant—and verified by peers before it is published.

Contrast this to junk science. Much of what you see online is, unfortunately, junk science—"research" done by questionable individuals who are usually trying to sell a miracle cure along with their theories. Junk science is often based on flawed studies that use too-small samples to be relevant. Example: just because four of your friends have babies with blue eyes does not mean there is an epidemic of blue-eyed babies on your block.

Much of the junk science you see online or read in the media is there to push a political agenda. Sure, these zealots are well meaning, but they harm their cause by hyping some obscure study from a doctor in Fiji as medical "truth."

Of course, this isn't always so black and white—sometimes good science is "spun" or hyped by groups who want to push their cause.

To put this in perspective, let's look at an example: a 2008 study from Cornell University compared the rates of autism and the amount of rainfall in a community. Researchers took a weak hypothesis (spending excessive time indoors would increase the chances of having autism), performed mathematical acrobatics and presto! Rain = autism. If you live in a rainy area, the study declared your child has an increased chance of autism. Researchers speculated, without any supporting evidence, that time spent indoors (Watching TV? Video games? Not getting enough Vitamin D? Inhaling carpet cleaning chemicals?) caused autism.

Bottom line: this was a flawed study that never should have been published in the first place. Why? Just because two things are seemingly related (towns like Seattle have more autistic kids) doesn't mean that rain CAUSES autism.

Of course, that didn't matter to the media. Outlets like *USA Today* and MSNBC reported that rainfall and autism were linked. And some autism advocacy groups used this study as *proof* that indoor environmental toxins were surely the reason for their children's diagnoses. None of which is true.

Clearly this study was junk science—but this is an example of how "research" takes on a life of its own as it winds its way through the meat-grinder of the 24/7 media and online culture these days.

As your guides in Toddler Health Land, we hope to steer you toward the good science when making decisions for your baby.

Disclaimer our lawyers wanted

Yes, no medical book about children is complete without that ubiquitous legal disclaimer . . . so here's ours:

The information we provide in this book is intended to help families understand their child's medical issues. It is NOT intended to replace the advice of your doctor. Before you start any medical treatment, always check in with your child's doctor who can counsel you on the specific needs of your child.

We have made a tremendous effort to give you the most up-to-date medical information available. However, medical research is constantly providing new insight into pediatric healthcare. That's why we have an accom-

INTRO

? ?

panying website at Toddler411.com to give you the latest breaking updates (and why you should also discuss your toddler's medical care with your child's doc).

What's new in this edition

For the third edition of Toddler 411, you'll find the latest studies on toddler nutrition, development and topics like autism.

Readers of our last edition asked for more help in solving their toddler discipline challenges. So we've completely revamped and expanded the discipline chapter, now chock full of specific tips on what to do and say when it comes to typical toddler behavior. To make this section easy to use, new icons point out which ages you're likely to see these unpleasant behaviors. That will help you adjust your game plan as your child progresses through the toddler years!

In fact, these new age-specific icons are scattered throughout the entire book. That way you can focus on specific tips based on your toddler's age.

The three truths about parenting a toddler

1 **YOU CAN'T MAKE A KID EAT, SLEEP, OR POOP ON THE POTTY.** Yes, toddlers have a will all their own—and if they don't want to do any of the above, darn it, that's the way it is. Nope, you have to come well-armed with a series of clever strategies and tricks to work some magic. We'll give you the spells over the next 400 pages.

2 **PARENTING IS THE GREAT EQUALIZER.** No matter whether you're a CEO or a working stiff, parenting a toddler puts us all in the same place. We all have to deal with the same anxieties, concerns and frustrations. And yes, even the experts (ahem) have had their toddler throw a tantrum when its time leave the playground.

3 **MONKEY SEE, MONKEY DO.** Long gone are the days when you could behave badly and have your little newborn look up at you with a blank stare. Nope, your toddler is studying all your moves . . . so if you expect your toddler NOT to throw a tantrum or utter curse words, you have to set the example.

So, enough intro already! Let's get rolling and enter the Wild World of Toddlers.

Toddler 411

Part One

Tantrums, Picky Eaters and What's Normal

Toddler Discipline, Nutrition and More

Toddler 411

section one

Discipline & Development

DISCIPLINE
Chapter 2

"You can learn many things from children. How much patience you have for instance."
~ Franklin P. Jones

Have you hit the PIZ? You know, the Parent Insanity Zone—that exact moment when you question WHY you had a child in the first place. Yes, every parent has multiple PIZ's . . . as parents of four kids altogether, we feel your pain. Really!

While we agree that parenting is the most admirable job in the world, we also agree that living with a toddler sometimes makes a parent consider selling their child on eBay . . . or paying big money to hire a full-time, live-in babysitter.

No matter how many parenting books you read, the actual parenting of a toddler is more like a prizefight than a classical ballet. In this corner, we have your toddler, weighing in at 27 lbs. Don't let his size fool you, he'll go ten rounds with an adult nine times his size and get a TKO. In the other corner, we have...you, the parent.

In Vegas, we'd be betting on your toddler with 2:1 odds. It's not that we don't have faith in you, it's just that we know how resilient toddlers can be—by sheer determination, they figure out how to wear their parents into submission. Don't be embarrassed; we have all been there.

Here's an important point: Kids are not born with social skills. It is animal nature (and that includes us humans) to be born with a "survival of the fittest" mentality. It's what helped us survive as cavemen before we owned SUV's and had a Home Depot and McDonald's on every corner. It's our job as parents to TEACH our children social skills and self-discipline, while preserving self-esteem. Yes, it is akin to breaking a wild horse. But you won't break your child's spirit if you do it correctly.

The goal of this chapter is to teach you how to manage your toddler and preschooler so they learn how to act appropriately, safely, and confidently . . . both when you are around and when you aren't. Your job is to implant a "good citizen" memory chip in your child's brain that will remind your child how he is supposed to act.

Here is the take-home message: *the seeds of discipline you plant now will blossom later and you will be thankful for the fruits of your labor.* We also think you will enjoy your child more if you don't feel that you spend 90% of your day yelling at him.

So let's get started by talking about your child's temperament. You'll need to understand who your child is, and how he views the world, before you can implement a discipline approach that will work specifically for him.

Next, we'll discuss parenting styles . . . are you running a dictatorship or democracy in your house? Your style impacts your toddler's behavior, so we'll go over how this fits in the puzzle.

Finally, it's the nuts and bolts of discipline. Join us as we recite the 20 Commandments for Toddler Discipline. (Yes, Moses just had ten, but he was traveling on business most of the time). Then we'll discuss Intervention 411: what you need to do when things go wrong, including advice on dealing with public tantrums (you know, in the cereal aisle of the grocery store). Finally, we'll give you specific tips on how to deal with common toddler "challenges," like the biter, the nudist and the shop-a-holic.

Whew! That's a lot of stuff. So, let's get the ball rolling.

Temperament

Q. What is temperament?

You've heard all the clichés: this toddler is a "difficult child" while this other one is "easy." Some kids are cautious, while others have no fear . . . and so on. But when you get down to it, temperament is just the way your child approaches his world. It starts on Day One of life and continues through a person's lifetime. No matter how much we try, we can't change anyone's temperament (much as we would like to at times)—we are born with it. However, parents can positively impact the way a child learns to deal with his world. It's that old nature vs. nurture debate—both have an influence on a person's behavior.

Figuring out what type of temperament your child has will help you anticipate how he will react to certain situations. And you will have a better idea of how to make everyone's world more pleasant.

Q. When will I be able to figure out my child's temperament?

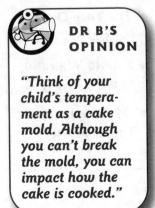

DR B'S OPINION

"Think of your child's temperament as a cake mold. Although you can't break the mold, you can impact how the cake is cooked."

By the time a child hits age one, most parents have their number . . . they have a good idea of the baby's temperament and what might happen in the toddler years.

And here's something that won't shock you: some temperaments are more difficult to live with than others. But all have their strengths. When you are frustrated with your toddler, just think about how successful he will be with those traits as an adult!

Here are seven questions that help determine the temperament of your child.[1]

1. **Adaptability.** How does your child respond to change or new situations?
2. **Regularity.** Does your child follow a schedule with sleep and mealtimes?
3. **Mood.** Is your child's attitude positive or negative about life?
4. **Persistence.** Does your child persist at activities or give up easily?
5. **Intensity.** Is your child intense or easy going?
6. **Sensitivity.** Is your child sensitive or oblivious to environmental changes (that is, noises, smells, tastes, lights)?
7. **Energy.** Is your child energetic or quiet?

See the box on the next page for our take on the seven types of toddlers!

Q. My first child was so easy. My second one is much more of a challenge. Does birth order have anything to do with this?

Maybe, maybe not.

Temperament is in the genes. However, many environmental influences play a role in how those "genes" are worn. Birth order, age between siblings, sex of siblings, and parenting style all have an impact on temperament.

In general, firstborn kids are more likely to be cautious rule-followers. Youngest children are more flexible and easy going (probably because they get carted around everywhere). And we've all heard about middle children—they are the rule breakers who vie for attention.

But besides birth order, something else is different the second time around—your parenting style. Whether you like it or not, you cannot devote as much time to your second child as you did with your first one. The positive: your second child is more independent. The negative: your second child may act up more to get your attention.

Take home message: Give your second child attention when he is being good and he may have fewer outbursts. Stay tuned for more on this subject later in this chapter.

Parenting Style

Q. I hate to admit it, but my toddler is driving me nuts! Why do I feel this way?

Welcome to the club. This phase in your child's life can be very chal-

NEW PARENT 411: SNOW WHITE & THE 7 TODDLERS

Here is a rundown of the top temperaments and who these little ones turn out to be as grown-ups!

◆ **Grumpy**: (a.k.a. The Difficult Child) This is the kid with the attitude. His cup is always half empty and everyone will hear about it. He resists change and gets frustrated easily. He's still not sleeping through the night because Mom and Dad are afraid to deal with the protest. Transitioning from one activity to the next is a challenge, for the same reason. Potential future job: he'll be a lawyer that scares the dickens out of opposing counsel. Very successful, but also very intimidating.

◆ **Sleepy**: (a.k.a. The Sleeper) Don't sell this kid short just because she is slow to warm up and low in energy. She will quietly play, often independently. She does better with gradual transitions to new activities and thrives on routines. As a grown up, she'll be a tech support guru for Dell. She'll do great things, but she'll do them quietly behind the scenes.

◆ **Dopey**: (a.k.a. The High Spirited Child) Don't take the name the wrong way. He's a really sweet child who aims to please. He's full of energy and is the life of the party. Future career: pharmaceutical rep. Socially, very charming. And that charm makes for career success, too.

◆ **Doc**: (a.k.a. The Intense Child) She's the persistent, intense, serious kid. Yes, she'll be very successful in life, but may not be the life of the party. The Intense Child is a little slow to warm up, but very nice once you get to know her. She is a little sensitive to new situations and environmental change. True to the name, she'll be a successful doctor. People respect her passion and perseverance.

◆ **Sneezy**: (a.k.a. The Sensitive Child) He wants to be easy going, but he's sensitive to environmental changes. He's quietly intense. The Sensitive Child would rather pick up interesting rocks on the playground than run around. He cries over spilled milk. Unfortunately, this child is easy prey for a bully. This grown-up forges his own path and gravitates towards independent rather than large group projects. Potential future job: forest ranger, archeologist.

◆ **Bashful**: (a.k.a The Slow to Warm Up Child) This little one takes a while to warm up to new situations and change. He will hide in his shell when he is faced with someone or someplace new . . . and he prefers quiet activities to loud, high energy ones. This is your future accountant. Again, very successful at occupations that avoid the limelight.

◆ **Happy**: (a.k.a. The Easy Child) This kid is easy going and very adaptable. He rolls with the flow. He's willing to play with anyone. He will persevere and has good problem solving skills. He is socially savvy and well liked. Forecast: class president and future small business owner. This is the successful adult that knows everyone in the neighborhood.

Dr. B's opinion. We wish we all had Happy for a child. But life wouldn't be nearly as interesting if everyone was Happy. It would be like living in The Truman Show. And most of the time, we are blessed with a child who has a mixture of more than one temperament.

lenging. His job is to try to be independent. Your job is to set limits on his behaviors. As you might guess, those two occupations are in direct conflict.

But there is good news: after the toddler phase, you enter the blissful "I Want To Please You" zone. This happens around four or five years of age—go ahead and put that in your calendar to look forward to! From there, you get about six years of good behavior before the teen years start . . . and then the water gets choppy once again.

But back to the present tense and those toddler years. Here's another reason why you feel so frustrated—your child's temperament may be too much like yours! Sometimes you see a reflection of yourself in your child. For instance, an intense mom and an intense child can be the recipe for some real fireworks! If you are spending more time being annoyed with your child than being happy with him, it's time to take a step back and look at the situation. Think about what is working and what is not. Actively try to modify your approach. Pretend you are a fly on the wall in your living room and listen to your interactions with your child. If you think your family would qualify to be on "Supernanny" it's time to change your tactics.

Q. My spouse and I argue about handling situations with our toddler. Help!

You and your partner have had a year to develop a particular parenting style. By style, we mean the way you approach child rearing and parenthood. Doubtless, you and your partner have gotten to know each other more than you did before. A friend once said, "You're not really married until you have children." You've probably had your share of discussions about whose approach is right. These discussions are healthy for both your marriage and your toddler. Have these meetings on a regular basis—not just when one of you is feeling frustrated. We suggest these meetings take place without your child around.

While we won't take sides on which parent is the winner, we do have some tips for perfecting your parenting style.

1. **Figure out what works and roll with it.** What intervention produces the desired outcome you are trying to achieve? Fine-tune that strategy as your child grows (and catches on to you).

2. **Listen to your partner's advice.** Sometimes you need a bit of distance to get a fresh perspective on a parenting dilemma. A spouse that works outside the home may be able to offer a good solution to a toddler "challenge." Reflect upon your partner's *constructive* criticism, learn, and perhaps try a new approach.

3. **Be consistent.** Arrive at decisions you are both happy with and implement them consistently.

A few caveats: blended families have more complex issues with parenting styles, as there are more parents in the mix. It will be harder to come to a unified plan, but try to take the emotional piece out of it for your child's sake. Single parent households rely on other relatives or friends for parenting advice and help. Whatever your family situation is, it's always a good idea to take a step back periodically and look at your parenting techniques in an objective way.

DISCIPLINE

? ?

Q. **We are divorced. How do both parents (and stepparents) enforce a consistent discipline plan?**

For the sake of your child(ren), rise above your own problems getting along. If you must, get a mediator like a social worker or counselor to help you accomplish this. Inconsistent messages leave a child confused *and* rebellious. Come up with a plan you can agree on—even if it is just a few major offenses that everyone decides should be disciplined.

Q. **My husband and I agree on our parenting style. How do I convince my mother/mother-in-law to follow our approach?**

You don't. Our parents have their own ideas of how to raise kids (that is, their way). And their parents did the same thing to them. But let's face it, our parents must have done something right. We turned out okay, didn't we? You may find a few of their parenting strategies actually work. Respect their opinions, but follow your own instincts.

Here are some suggestions to keep the peace:

1. **House rules are universal.** There are some rules that should never be broken, regardless of which adults are around. These involve safety or health hazards. For example: your child will always ride buckled up in a car seat.

2. **Grandparents are special.** Grandparents let grandkids do things they can't get away with at home. Your child's relationship with you will always be different. We know you feel like the heavy because you are trying to enforce the rules. When you get back

BEHIND THE SCENES: THE 3 STYLES OF PARENTING

Yes, there are basically three different types of parenting styles.[2] And with each one, comes a different approach to discipline. Although you may naturally gravitate to one or more of these styles in a given situation, it's a good idea to take a more critical look at what you are doing.

◆ *Dictatorship* (a.k.a. "Authoritarian" Parent). Parents value absolute power in this household. They use negative forms of discipline like physical punishment or taking away privileges for poor behavior. "The beatings will continue until you behave." This is the 1950's mentality of parenting. Father knows best, right? Most experts do not recommend this approach as it breaks the horse and its spirit. Bottom line result: Kids have poor self-esteem and poor relationships.

◆ *Anarchy* (a.k.a. "Permissive" Parent). Parents prioritize free thinking and self expression. They give children too many choices and thus, give the power to the child. "Do whatever you want, honey." This

to your house, remind your toddler that the "usual rules" are back in effect.

3. **Look at the big picture.** While it is important to enforce house rules on some things, others not nearly as critical in the grand scheme of things. An extra snack or a slightly later bed time is not a big deal.

4. **Tell them your doctor suggested it.** Kids haven't changed in the past thirty years, but what we have learned about them has. It is hard for you to explain that to grandparents, so feel free to say that you are following your doctor's advice on whatever topic you are discussing. Or, buy an extra copy of this book for them!

If there is a grandparent who is serving as a caretaker while you are working outside the home, you should discuss parenting styles more formally. See the box on the next page for some suggestions.

The Big Picture on Discipline:

Discipline is teaching your child to learn self-control and with that, comes confidence and self-esteem. Repeat after us: discipline is the underpinning of many issues in your child's life.

Now, we aren't just talking about teaching your toddler to be nice to the dog, but much more: he's capable of falling asleep on his own; he can't eat chicken nuggets for every meal; and so on. It's important to be consistent and follow through with your plan in all of these situations. You will see more specific tips that are really "discipline moments" throughout other

is the 1970's free love approach to parenting. Are you sure you want your three-year old going to Woodstock? Most experts do not recommend this approach, as it does not teach children to have boundaries. And let's face it, the real world has boundaries. Bottom line: Kids lack self-discipline and cause trouble.

◆ *Democracy* (a.k.a. "Authoritative" Parent). Parents value mutual respect. They encourage cooperation by listening to their kids. Kids feel like they share power and have a vested interest in working within their boundaries."I respect your ideas. Let's figure out a way to make this work and we'll both be happy." As you can probably tell, this is the style that most experts recommend. Make your home a democratic society and everyone wins. Actually, in the real world, most parents don't run their households as democracies—they are more like constitutional monarchies. That is, there is democratic feedback up to a point . . . and then King and Queen have final say! Bottom line: Kids have high self-esteem and self-discipline.

THE SECRET LIVES OF YOUR MOTHER-IN-LAW

If a grandmother is serving as your child's caretaker while you are at work, it's a touchy issue to ask her to follow your discipline style (especially if your viewpoints differ!)

We realize you are treading on thin ice because you are indebted to your mother for taking care of your child. And it's extremely difficult not to put your mom or Mother-in-law on the defensive. Tell your mom, "I need your help in managing my child's behaviors. She seems to respond to these (fill in blank) approaches. What are you seeing when she is with you?" This should help open up the discussion, make her feel like you value her opinion, and not put the blame on her. Then, close with your sales pitch: "Let's try these approaches when she is with both of us and see if her behavior improves."

Getting her a gift certificate to a day spa will also go a long way!

chapters in the book. But the message remains the same: *have a plan and stick to it.*

The take-home message: being a parent is not a popular job. You will not always be your child's friend or buddy. View the screaming, whining, and tantrums as signs that you are doing your job as an effective parent. And yes, at some point in your child's life, she will say the dreaded words, "I hate you." That's because you are doing something to protect her by setting a limit she dislikes. That's okay. Your child will always love you, no matter what. And she will thank you someday for guiding her to become the best person she can be.

If you let your toddler call the shots, you will be in trouble down the road. The offenses that your toddler has right now may seem minor. But the lack of limits may come back to haunt you—as your child gets older, the stakes will be higher.

When your child demands candy in the grocery store checkout line, are you going to give in just to keep the peace? And when your teen asks for the car keys to go to a party where the kids are drinking underage, are you going to hand them over? These are two sides of the same discipline coin.

Ultimately, discipline is all about learning personal responsibility. Children need to learn that there are natural consequences for their behavior. Their behavior impacts them and others. Let's face it, that's what the real world is like. If we act like jerks at work, our co-workers don't want to talk to us or help out with a project—we might just lose that job. And when a child behaves poorly, he should see (in a safe way) the natural consequences of his actions.

Discipline Nuts and Bolts

Before we delve into the 20 commandments of discipline (see later in this chapter), we need to go over a little lingo so we're all on the same page.[3]

discipline

Helpful Hint: Discipline lingo

And now, as promised, a bit of jargon. Lather. Rinse. Repeat.

◆ *Reward Good Behavior.* Think about Pavlov's drooling dogs here. Pavlov trained his dogs to drool when they heard the dinner bell ringing. The dogs associated the bell noise with food because Pavlov consistently fed them after ringing the bell. Here's how it equates to human behavior: if you praise your child (positive reward) every time he cleans up his toys, he's more likely to clean up his toys. You can give artificial rewards like praise, stickers, or special activities with mom or dad until your child clues into the natural reward for good behavior: a sense of accomplishment.

◆ *Avoid Rewarding Bad Behavior.* Parents unknowingly reinforce behaviors that they want to stop. For example: your toddler has nightly tantrums when you are trying to cook dinner. You respond by leaving the kitchen and screaming back at him. In your child's view: mission accomplished. He got your attention, which was exactly what he wanted. Even though it was negative (your screaming), it was attention (a valuable reward). Check mate. The same scenario applies to sleep issues. If your child protests every night until you bring him into your bed, you've just rewarded the behavior you want to stop. The child learns that if he protests, he gets a ticket to your bed. More on this in Chapter 8, Sleep.

◆ *Limit Setting.* Setting limits shows your child how far he can go with his behavior. Sounds cruel? Not really—you are letting your child explore and experience the world . . . but in a way that is safe for himself and others around him. Of course, limits may be both physical and verbal. One and two-year-olds may need physical limits (putting the potted plant out of reach, for example). With three and four-year-olds, words should be enough ("Don't touch that plant, honey").

◆ *Active Listening.* This is more than inserting a few "uh-huhs" into a conversation with your child. You take the time to listen and actively move conversation's direction. Don't just jump in with your commentary—you are validating someone's feelings and opinions when you actively listen. It works wonders with your child (and with your spouse). With toddlers, you give them the words to express themselves. With preschoolers, you can get them to really open up and tell you more of what is on their minds. Here's an example: Pretend you are a sportscaster describing a sporting event to the TV audience. If your one to three-year-old is frustrated, say, "It looks like you're really mad." "It looks like you are having trouble with that puzzle." With a four-year-old child, you can pretend to be a journalist and ask "who, what, when, where and why" questions if your child is upset about something. The goal is to avoid lecturing your child at every moment.

◆ **Problem Ownership.** This isn't a bad real estate investment. We're talking about avoiding the "blame game." Instead of accusing your child of making a mess (and having her react defensively), consider approaching the problem more diplomatically, giving her an opportunity to "own up" to the problem and help solve it. For example, don't say, "YOUR playroom is a mess. Clean it up." Instead, say, "I have a problem with the messy playroom. Let's clean it up together…"

◆ **"I" Messages**. Nope, it's not some new text messaging system from Apple. It's another way to prevent your child from feeling he is to blame for your frustration. Use the word "I" to start a sentence instead of saying "You". For example, don't say, "You made us late for preschool again." Instead say, "I need you to help me get moving in the morning so we don't miss school."

Q. When should we start to discipline our child?

Now.

Here's the bottom line: children can respond to discipline techniques by *nine months of age*. That's about the time they start testing the waters with you to see if they can get away with activities you have already said "no" to. You know the drill—your child cruises over to the coffee table and throws the remote control at the dog. But before he does it, he turns his head and looks over at you with a devilish grin on his face. That's because you've already told him, ten times, this is not okay.

If you have seen this played out in your living room, you know that your

---

THE CATEGORY 5 TANTRUM

Just for fun, as parents of a toddler, we rated our son's temper tantrums using the Saffir-Simpson scale for measuring hurricanes. Hence, there were minor episodes at toy stores when he didn't want to leave . . . these were your tropical storms and Category 1 tantrums. And yes, there were the more rare, yet far more intensive Category 5 melt-downs—you know, like Hurricane Katrina.

So, here's a true Fields story of a Cat 5 tantrum: we took our oldest son to a model train show when he was 18 months old. He loved Thomas the Tank Engine, so we knew the show would be right up his alley. . . until it was time to leave. We figured we'd visit the show in the afternoon about an hour or so before it closed. That way, we'd have an excuse to leave. And dutifully, after an hour of non-stop train fun, we reported to our toddler that it was time to go.

That's when it happened. The Category 5. Our wonderful angel started screaming from the time we walked out the front door and didn't stop for an hour. Yes, a whole hour. As we sat there in a parked car, we realized we needed to leave the vehicle and let him scream it out. So there we were, standing outside our car as our child wailed and wailed.

So, how did it end? He exhausted himself and fell asleep. His mom and dad, however, needed some serious cocktails.

DISCIPLINE

child cannot plead insanity to this offense. It was pre-meditated. And if your child is smart enough to figure out this human behavior, he is more than ready to be disciplined for it.

There are different discipline techniques that work for different age groups, and we will talk about a variety of strategies as you read on.

Q. When do the Terrible Two's start?

Around 15 months.

You've heard all the stories of the "Terrible Two's" from other parents. What no one tells you, however, is the Terrible Two's start closer to your child's FIRST BIRTHDAY (again, around 15 months), not at midnight of your child's second birthday. That leaves many parents shocked and unprepared for the events to come.

Funny but true story: I had a patient's mom call me because her previously well-behaved 18 month old had a fit while they were at the grocery store. She was truly concerned that there was something medically wrong with her daughter. She had no idea this was normal. Now, several tantrums later, this mom is an expert at navigating shopping trips.

The take home message: be prepared for this new phase. Yes, you've reached that time where your kid behaves so poorly that you are embarrassed to take her out in public. Or, claim her as one of yours.

To get through this ugly phase, it's time to change your perspective. As Dr. T. Berry Brazelton would say, toddlers are simply making a "Declaration of Independence." (Dr. Brazelton views every situation as the cup is half-full). And knowing *why* your child is acting like this helps you know *how* to respond to it.

Q. When do the Terrible Two's end?

When they leave for college.

Okay, it's not that bad. But this phase can last for a *long* time, so don't be surprised by that. Some children's behavior will settle down by age three. Some kids will torture their parents for an extra year and improve by age four. Just think of it this way, the Terrible Two's will give you a lot of practice for when your child becomes a teenager! The behaviors are strangely similar (and both phases are in the name of independence).

Since this is a long time to endure, and there aren't any toddler boarding schools that we know of, you will need to have a consistent management plan with all caregivers (parents, grandparents, babysitters) to survive the next couple of years.

BOTTOM LINE

Consistency is the key to making a discipline plan work. If there is an adult (a.k.a. the Softy) who ignores a behavior that other adults reprimand, the behavior will continue. Grandparents are usually the worst in this department—and kids know it. It's like having a substitute teacher.

DR B'S OPINION

"Remember, you are planting the seeds of discipline. Don't expect a tree to grow overnight. You won't see the fruits of your labor for a very long time!"

DISCIPLINE

? ?

BOOKMARK THIS PAGE! THE 20 COMMANDMENTS OF

You can't say we don't give you value here at *Toddler 411*. Here are 20 commandments (suggestions, really) for toddler discipline. Sadly, your child didn't get the memo on this and can't read yet, so it's up to you to spread the word.

These strategies are applicable to all discipline moments. Whether it's running in the street, or negotiating about bedtime, the underlying issue is usually the same. And the strategies work across the board. See later in the chapter for specific ways to apply these gems.

1 *Use a prevent defense.* Apologies for the football cliché, but this one is easy. Make your house kid friendly and be realistic about your expectations. If you take your Swarovski crystal figurine collection off the coffee table, your toddler won't be tempted to fling it at the TV set. If the family is eating out, go early so you won't have to wait for a table.

2 *Don't back down to avoid conflict.* We all hate conflict. No one wants to be the party pooper. But you cannot give in merely to avoid having a showdown in the grocery store aisle. If you decide that your child cannot have the sugar-coated cereal he saw on TV, stick to your guns. Later, you'll be happy you did.

3 *Anticipate conflicts.* There are certain times of the day and certain events that are always going to bring about bad behaviors. Prime suspect #1: transitions from one activity to the next (going to bed, stopping play to eat dinner, etc). Give your child a head's up so she is more prepared to make a transition. "Five minutes and we will be having dinner, Boo Boo."

4 *Anticipate attention-seeking behavior.* Yes, your little angel will act up when your attention is diverted (making dinner, talking on the phone, nursing a baby, etc). Prepare for this by providing your toddler with some entertainment (a favorite toy, a quick snack, etc). True story: my son ate dog food once while I was answering a patient call. Take home lesson: if you don't provide something for your toddler to do when you are busy, he will . . . and the results may not be pretty.

5 *Act immediately.* Don't wait to discipline your child. He won't remember why he is in trouble more than five minutes after he did the dirty deed.

6 *Be consistent.* This is the key to any discipline plan. When your child knows what is in store when he pulls on the cat's tail, he will stop doing it. But be aware that it may take numerous "lessons" to eliminate that undesirable behavior.

7 *Pick your battles.* Saying "No" twenty times a day loses its effectiveness. Prioritize behaviors into large ones, medium ones, and those too insignificant to bother with. In Starbucks terms, there are toddler Venti, Grande, and Tall screw-ups.

8 *Make your comments short and sweet.* Speak in short sentences, such as "No hitting." This is much more effective than, "Chaz, you know its not nice to hit the dog." Believe us, you lost Chaz right after "you know".

9 *Focus on the behavior, not the child.* Be sure to state that a particular behavior is bad. NEVER tell your child that HE is bad.

10 *Remind your child that you love her.* It's always good form to end your discussion with a positive comment. This shows your child you are ready to move on and not dwell on the problem. It also reinforces the reason you are setting limits—because you love her.

DISCIPLINE

TODDLER DISCIPLINE!

11 ***Don't yell.*** But change your voice. It's not the volume but the tone of your voice that gets your point across. Remember *The Godfather*? He never needed to yell.

12 ***Show respect.*** Use active listening and don't interrupt. And whatever you do, don't laugh.

13 ***Be a good role model.*** If you are calm under pressure, your child will take the cue. And if you have a temper tantrum when you are upset, expect that your child will do the same. He's watching you, always watching.

14 ***Catch your child being good.*** Praising good behavior reduces the amount of attention-seeking bad behavior that you will see. Think of praise as fertilizer for that super-ego.

15 ***Use age-appropriate and temperament-appropriate techniques.*** No matter how much advice we give you, you have to tailor it to your own child. And what worked at 15 months won't work when your child is two. He's read your play books and watched the films. You have to adjust your strategy over time.

16 ***Don't treat your child like an adult.*** Your child really doesn't want to hear a lecture from you. Nor does he understand it. Much as you would like to have a man-to-man talk, so to speak, it won't work; so don't waste your time or energy. But toddlers do understand consequences. Next time your toddler throws his spaghetti on the wall, don't break into the "You Can't Throw Your Food" lecture. Calmly evict him from the kitchen for the night. (See more about Cause and Effect in the section below.)

17 ***Lower your expectations.*** A lot of parent frustration stems from setting the bar too high. If you expect less from your child, you'll be pleasantly surprised when you get more. Read the Development section beginning with Chapter 3, Milestones.

18 ***Take emotion out of the equation.*** We give kudos to Dr. Thomas Phelan, author of the book, *1-2-3 Magic* for pointing out parents' two biggest mistakes: "Too much talking, too much emotion." Your kids enjoy the fight. If your toddler can get you to raise your voice and stomp your feet, he has just won Round One. The less you react and talk during an intervention, the better. (It feels really empowering, by the way, when you don't get sucked in—probably because your blood pressure isn't sky high).

19 ***Don't negotiate or make false promises.*** This isn't Capitol Hill, it's your living room. Avoid hearing yourself say, "If you behave, I will buy you that doll you want." We'd never suggest that you resort to this tactic. Otherwise, you'll create a three-year old whose good behavior will always come with a price tag. Think Veruca Salt from *Charlie & The Chocolate Factory*.

20 ***Remember to take a step back.*** Don't get sucked into the vortex. Instead, take a longer view of what is happening. You'll have a better idea of what manipulative behaviors your child is using and get a fresh perspective on how to change your approach.

DISCIPLINE

???

Insider Secret:
Discipline and intellectual development

To implement an effective discipline strategy, you should be realistic about what your child understands. This will make more sense as you read through common discipline struggles later in this chapter. But here is an example: when you say, "Be nice," your 15 month old may not understand what "nice" means. You have to demonstrate what you mean by "nice," like showing her how to pet the cat instead of grabbing his tail.

Another point: You can't just tell a child to quit an ugly behavior and expect him to stop doing it. Your child may be acting that way because it is the only way he knows how to get your attention or play with another child. You may need to show him HOW to appropriately approach a social situation. To get the attention of a potential playmate, a toddler might simply bite the other child's arm.. Besides saying, "You bit that child and hurt him," you also need to say, "Did you want to play with him? This is what you can do next time…"

TODDLER INTERVENTION 411

What happens if your toddler breaks a rule? Yes, you too can have an intervention right in your own family room. Here's how to play the board game at home.

◆ *Ignore.* If it's not a major infraction, ignore the behavior. If your child doesn't get a rise out of you, she will stop doing it. For example, your child screams whenever you read your email. Either ignore the screaming, or check email after Junior goes to bed.

◆ *Redirect.* Move your child to a different activity. Kids will repeat the inappropriate behavior to see if they can get away with it. Often, it takes several times and consistent redirection of the same misbehavior to eliminate it. Don't give up. For example, your child unrolls the entire toilet paper roll for the tenth time today. Calmly move your child out of the bathroom and close the door.

◆ *Use humor.* It works beautifully with power struggles. Instead of digging in your heels and holding your ground, change to an upbeat approach. Your child will do the same. For example, your child refuses to eat his peas . . . so pretend you are going to eat his share if he doesn't.

◆ *Time out.* Yes, it really works. Call it The Naughty Room, Solitary Confinement, The Penalty Box, or whatever you like, but here is the premise. Your child is removed from his play and must sit out for a period of time—without your attention. Losing attention from you is the most effective way to get your message across. Your child gets docked one minute for every year of age. Kids under age two rarely sit in a corner or in a chair. They are on the floor kicking and scream-

24   TODDLER 411   ???

Q. Is it okay to spank my child?

Many parents recall being threatened or actually spanked in their childhood. We've all heard these phrases come out of our own parents' mouths.

"Just wait until your father gets home."

"I'm getting the soap to wash your mouth out."

"I'll take out my belt if you don't behave."

While most of us turned out okay despite corporal punishment, child development experts do not recommend regularly beating your child into submission. There are many more effective ways to get your message across. You are your child's role model. So if you think about it, using physical force is the least desirable behavior that you want your child to imitate (for example, spanking your child for hitting or kicking you is only reinforcing the message that it's okay to express your frustration by force.)

A study published in Pediatrics in 2010 supports this theory. The study looked at about 2500 kids who were spanked at three years of age. At age five, the spanked group showed a whopping 50% more aggressive behavior than the non-corporal punishment group.

ing. That's fine, just make the time out location a safe one. Time out is reserved for particularly inappropriate behaviors and it should be used every time that behavior occurs. For example, your child takes a bite out of his friend's arm. He goes immediately to Time Out City. More details on time out to come (see section below).

◆ *Positive Reinforcement.* Children thrive on attention from their parents. Although they prefer positive attention (hugs and praise), they'll also accept negative attention (screaming and yelling). Heck, they'll take what they can get. So, if you praise your child for good behavior, you'll see more of it. For example, your child cleans up his toys because he gets big hugs from you when he does it.

◆ *Give choices.* Choices make a child feel he has a vote—remember the democratic parenting style? Just make the options all the things you want to accomplish. And be careful to avoid giving too many options to kids. They get overwhelmed, just like I do when we go outlet shopping. For example, "you have a choice—you can put your shoes on first. Or your coat."

◆ *Teach consequences.* Your child should learn the natural consequences of the behavior he chooses—otherwise known as Cause and Effect. Instead of getting into a power struggle, let your child pick the consequences of his actions. For example, if your child insists on picking out his pajamas (which may take an eternity), then he is choosing not to read books before bed. Cause: Prolonged PJ choosing = Effect: No time to read. Next time, he will make his PJ selection more quickly or let you pick them out.

Of course, one might argue this is a "chicken or the egg" dilemma. In other words, do already aggressive kids get spanked more often? The study authors say they accounted for that question. But they did report that parents tended to spank children who were considered to be more "defiant" and "easily frustrated."

When a child is "defiant," it really means he is seeking independence and control. When a child is "easily frustrated" it means he needs help solv-

NEW PARENT 411: THE TIME-OUT PRIMER

Time out is a tried and true technique that really works if it is done correctly and consistently. Just like any other discipline strategy, it will need to be implemented several times to be effective. Of course, we realize parents have many questions on how to do time outs. We'll answer some of the questions below. However, remember there is no one correct way to approach time out. The only requirement is consistency. Here's a Q&A:

At what age can we start doing time out?
Around nine months of age. Time outs can begin as soon as your child understands his actions and behaviors.

How long do I put my child in time out?
The general rule of thumb: one minute for every year of age.

Where should I put my child in time out?
Your child needs to be someplace where he cannot get hurt if he throws a fit (which he probably will). Popular locations are the dining room, guest bedroom, and even the utility room if it's clean.

Is my child's crib or his room an acceptable place?
There is some disagreement here about the answer to this one. Some experts feel that the crib or a child's room is his safety zone and he should NOT go there to be punished. Others feel that the purpose of time out is to be removed from the location that the child currently is in—so any place in the house is okay.

Can my child have toys to play with during time out?
Again, there's some wiggle room here. Purists argue that time out is punishment and kids need to do solitary confinement without entertainment. Others contend that time out is a way to blow off steam. Moving a child away from the parent is punishment enough . . . even if a child is playing with a toy during time out.

Can I be in the time out room with her?
While it's preferable to have the child be alone, sometimes it is not practical. If you must be in the room with the child, do not pay any attention to her for the duration of the time out. For certain situations, you may need to have the child restrained on your lap, facing away from you for the time out.

I've tried time out and it doesn't seem to work. Does she really care?
Yes, she cares. She's just acting like she doesn't. It's a clever kid strategy (adults do it too). Don't let her fool you. It takes about twenty times to sink in, that's all. Kids will continually test the limits

ing a problem. Getting a spanking for trying to find your place in the world teaches just one thing—FEAR. It teaches a child that his parent will hurt him to keep him in line. It doesn't teach the child why the line is there (the natural consequence for behavior that goes unchecked), or an alternative solution to a situation (problem-solving skills).

The bottom line: raising children is the toughest (and most satisfying) job you will ever have. Take the time to learn why your child is acting this

to see if they can wear you down. Just keep plowing ahead in a calm and consistent way.

My child destroys her room when she goes to time out. Help!
Either try a different location or remove any objects she can throw. You can leave the mess for her to clean up later. That's a natural consequence of the destructive behavior she has selected.

My child never stays put in time out. What should I do?
The child's age, size, and strength will determine how to manage this one. You are allowed to put a safety gate on the door or even lock the door to the room your child is in. It's only a few minutes. Alternatively, you can be in the room where your child is to ensure he stays put as long as you don't pay attention to him.

Should I put my child in time out for a tantrum?
Your child has put himself into time out if he resorts to a tantrum. He is no longer communicating with you. (We'll discuss more on this below.) You can ignore the tantrum and in effect, create a time out wherever the tantrum is occurring. Alternatively, with a three or four year old child, he can be excused to his room until he can pull himself together. Say, "I see you are having a tantrum right now and you know that is not okay. Let me know when you are done." Then, calmly walk away.

If my child has a tantrum in time out, do I start the count after she settles down?
Many kids will have tantrums when they are put in time out. And the tantrums can outlast the length of the time out. Once the allotted time has expired, you can tell your child time out is over. If he needs more time to settle down, he can remain in the time out place until he is settled, with freedom to leave at any time.

Is there a time out equivalent if we are out in public?
This one's always a challenge and kids know it! Yes, you need to discipline your child even if it's in front of the entire world. Find an acceptable place, like your car and institute the time out in a timely manner. Waiting until you get home ruins the effectiveness.

Given how my toddler acts, I fear she will be in time out all day. Is this all right?
No. Time out is reserved for absolutely unacceptable behavior. That usually means something that will endanger your child or somebody else. You have to make the call. There are other methods of discipline that work well for ugly, but less serious offenses—we'll discuss that shortly.

way instead of resorting to a poor parenting choice.

So, the next time you think about spanking your child…please consider what you want your child to learn from your behavior. We know you may be tempted at times, but remember that you are the grown-up. Don't resort to acting like a child.

Q. My 18 month old hits me, and then he laughs about it. Should I hit him back?

No. And you also shouldn't hit back if your toddler lashes out at you when he is having a tantrum.

If you can predict when the hitting is going to occur, steer clear! If you've just been hit, move your child away from you so he is no longer in striking distance.

Sternly but calmly say, "NO hitting." Put your child in a safe place, away from you. He learns that hitting will lose your attention, not gain it. You win.

However, like any other ugly behavior, it will take about 20 times for your discipline technique to sink in.

Feedback from the Real World

One of the best quotes I've heard about school discipline came from my son's kindergarten teacher. "If I'm doing my job, I don't have to discipline them!"

Reality Check: When you lose your cool

You cannot be a good role model if you have a temper tantrum yourself. If you feel like you have lost control of the situation, take a step back, take a deep cleansing breath, and then return to the issue at hand once you have calmed down.

Q. Do sticker charts work?

Sticker charts and other reward systems give kids an incentive (positive artificial reinforcement) to perform certain behaviors or not perform others. Use a chart to track your child's success in accomplishing his goals. This gives you and your child a good visual way to assess progress.

So, how can you make a sticker chart work for you and your toddler? Here the details:

1. **Post the chart someplace visible.** It is meant to be a constant reminder. For example, post a chart in a playroom to encourage a toddler to clean up his toys.
2. **Focus on one behavior for each chart.** For example, your child gets a sticker *each time* he cleans up his toys. That may earn him more than one sticker a day.
3. **Cash in for larger incentives**. When your child collects three stickers, he gets to do a special activity with Mom or Dad (like going to the library).
4. **For a limited time only.** Use the chart for two to four weeks at the most. It loses its novelty after that. Next, move on to natural reinforcements (your toddler should be proud of his accomplishment).

DISCIPLINE

ENDING WHINING AS WE KNOW IT

Every child, at some point in his career, will resort to whining. It's as painful to listen to as nails being scratched on a chalkboard . . . and it's effective because you just want the noise to stop.

Our advice: be strong.

If you respond to your child when he whines or has a tantrum, you have just validated this juvenile form of communication (remember unintentional reinforcement?). If you ignore it, it stops because your child realizes it doesn't work.

Alternatively, you can discipline this behavior to eliminate it. This also works. Your child can have three chances to stop. So, here's how it goes: start counting. If you reach three, he has bought himself a time out. That's the approach in *1-2-3 Magic* (Phelan), a best-selling guide to child discipline. We really like this book's no-nonsense attitude. If you are pulling your hair out, we highly recommend *1-2-3 Magic* before you go bald.

Q. Can I give my child an allowance and use it the same way as a sticker chart?

A child who is school aged may respond to having an allowance that is dependent on good behavior, but don't back yourself into a corner. Remember, you don't want a child who only performs well for a price.

And if you choose to give your child an allowance, don't make household chores part of the bargain. Your child should do these without being paid! Being part of a family means ALL members must do chores . . .no payment required.

For kids under age five, having an allowance will not get you very far because they have no concept of the value of money. They are simply collecting pretty coins. Stickers are much cheaper!

Q. A friend suggested that I use a kitchen timer for discipline. What do you think?

Ages 1-4 Kitchen timers are a great way to redirect your child's anger away from you. Your child can scream at the timer all he wants and it won't flinch. It makes the disciplining moment more diplomatic. You can set the timer for your child's time out. When the timer goes off, he knows he is done.

Also, use the timer when your child is having trouble sharing a toy with another toddler. Each child can have a few minutes with the toy and when the timer goes off, it's time to hand it over. The timer can be set for other transitions as well. For example, your child he has to get ready for bed when the timer goes off.

Feedback from the Real World

A kitchen timer is a great way to encourage your child to play independently while you get dinner ready. Explain to your child

DISCIPLINE

SURVIVING THE PUBLIC TANTRUM: OUR TIPS

No matter how hard you try, your toddler is going to throw a temper tantrum in public some day. Be prepared for the stares, the glares and the whispers. And then have a plan.

Most parents know when a tantrum is likely. Your child is tired, bored, hungry, you name it. And something little will set her off. So have in mind what you will do. Here are some ideas for dealing with public tantrums:

◆ *Walk away.* We always tried to put a few feet between us and our screaming toddler in full melt-down mode. Yes, be prepared for well-meaning adults who think your child has been abandoned and needs to be comforted. Sometimes we wish we had portable orange safety cones we could set out by our child to warn off other adults.

◆ *Stop what you're doing and leave.* Even if it means you won't have anything for dinner because you have to leave the grocery store. Order in some pizza and go back tomorrow. Sometimes pulling the pin is the best course.

◆ *An ounce of prevention.* While all public tantrums can't be prevented, remember that you as a parent can sometimes push things over the edge. Example: too many errands. While it might be tempting to make just one more stop to pick up the dry cleaning, remember that the fuse on most toddlers who are hungry/tired/bored is very short. Get that cranky toddler home and do that last errand tomorrow.

that you will play together when the timer goes off. ("In a minute" loses its meaning when it's really ten minutes...and toddlers cannot keep time anyway.)

Pop Quiz! Test your toddler discipline smarts—29 examples

Now that you are a discipline pro, let's put your skills to the test. Here are some classic disciplinary challenges, and what to do about them. We've taken our 20 discipline commandments (page 22-23) and seven intervention strategies (page 24-25) and applied them to real situations. These are divided into three categories: general challenges, specific ones, and special situations. And within each category, we have organized these situations in the way most parents will encounter them. You'll be referring back to this section over the next three years.

General challenges

Ages 1-4

DR JEKYLL AND MR HYDE (ANGEL IN PUBLIC AND TERROR AT HOME)
Be thankful she has a wonderful public persona. People will think you are a terrific parent (which you are) for having such a

DISCIPLINE

well-behaved child.

Here's what is happening in grown up terms: You have a terrible day at work—you lost an important client, have to work late on a project, and to top it off—you didn't eat lunch. When you get home at the end of the day, you pick a fight with your spouse. It's not your spouse's fault, but you've held it together all day and you can't help but unload on the person you love the most. So....when your child has a terrible day at preschool, be

> ### DR B'S OPINION
>
> *"If you have appropriate expectations of your toddler, you will be less frustrated with him!"*

prepared. And be flattered that she loves you the most.

Another reason kids turn into Mr. Hyde around mom and dad is the difference in how we respond to them. Children learn very quickly what their parents' buttons are and how to push them. They know they cannot get away with nearly as many things at preschool because the teacher simply will not put up with it.

What to do and say:
- ◆ Act more like a preschool teacher. Set up the house rules and then abide by them. (Kids act out when they know their behavior changes your mind.)
- ◆ Be a good listener—and a good hugger. That's what makes you feel better when you've had a bad day, right?
- ◆ If your child is having a full-blown tantrum, let her get it out of her system before attempting to have a conversation. You can take some deep cleansing breaths while you patiently wait for the storm to pass.
- ◆ To a 1-2 year old, say, "It seems like you had a bad day. Let's go play together (that is, move on)."
- ◆ To a 3-4 year old, say, "Did you have a bad day? Do you want to tell me about it?"

THE BREATH-HOLDER
Some kids will hold their breath when they get angry. Parents usually worry that something dire will happen as a result (and so they give in to whatever the child demands). Don't worry. At worst, he will faint. If your child holds his breath long enough, he will lose consciousness and start breathing spontaneously. This sounds really cruel, but a **BREATH-HOLDING SPELL** is potent ammunition for a little kid to get his way.

What to do and say:
- ◆ If you want to win the battle, you cannot give in. Follow through with your plan.
- ◆ If your child passes out, so be it. Just make sure to catch him before his head hits the coffee table!

Insider Tip
If your child has numerous breath-holding spells, check in with your doctor. Believe it or not, this can be related to iron-deficiency anemia.

DISCIPLINE

Ages 1-3

CRYING OVER SPILLED MILK

Toddlers are all about independence and control. Your child may have a laundry list of things that didn't go his way today. He did not want to get ready for school, but you made him. He did not want to wear a long sleeve shirt, but you made him. He wanted his toast cut in rectangles, not triangles. Then, you commit the unthinkable…you tie his shoes the wrong way. This may seem like such a minor thing to you, but it's the twentieth thing that did not go his way and it throws him into a Category 5 Temper Tantrum.

What to do and say:

◆ Say, "Tell me (or 'show me' for a child who isn't speaking yet) what you need/want."

◆ Say, "I'm sorry you are frustrated. Can I help you?"

◆ Sometimes it isn't what you say, but what you do that helps. Give your child a warm, reassuring hug instead of a lecture.

◆ If your child is already in full-blown tantrum mode, say, "You are having a tantrum. That's not okay. Let me know when you are done." Period. Do not try to communicate.

Ages 1-3

STUBBORN AS A MULE (PICKING YOUR BATTLES)

You will have to decide what are important issues to you and your child. Remember you are planting those seeds of discipline. While it may seem easier to avoid conflict than take these issues on, you will pay for your approach later when the stakes are higher. Planting those seeds will prepare you for the day you hear, "Why can't I shave my head? All my friends are doing it!"—or worse. Here are some classic toddler battlefronts:

What to do and say:

◆ **Tooth brushing.** Not negotiable. Cavities are expensive and unpleasant. Just do it.

◆ **Diaper changing.** Changing a wet diaper while your toddler is standing up instead of sitting may be negotiable (depending on your diaper changing skills). Changing a poopy diaper standing up is not negotiable. Offer a special toy to play with that is only available during poopy diaper changes.

◆ **Taking medicine.** Not negotiable. Say, "If you can't take your medicine, you will feel bad/not get to play/ or worst of all…you could need a shot!" See Appendix A, Medicines for more sneaky ideas too. Worst-case scenario: one adult holds the child securely and the other gives the medicine. If you need to, you can hold your child's nose to get him to open his mouth. Yes, it can be a real pain—especially if the medication needs to be given three times a day for a week or two! But if you always follow through, your child will stop protesting. (Ask your child's doc for a once a day medication if you have a particularly stubborn toddler.)

The common thread to all of these scenarios is that you must do all of these activities, as ugly as they are. And when your child realizes that you mean business, he will eventually give in.

DISCIPLINE

discipline

COPING WITH THE AFTER DAYCARE MELTDOWN

Q. My husband and I both work all day. After we pick up our 18 month old at daycare, she does okay on our 45-minute car ride home. But once we get home she doesn't want to do anything on her own. She wants us to hold her until dinner. If we don't, she screams. She is a very stubborn child. Suggestions?

Your toddler may be stubborn, but we prefer to say "confident and strong willed." And she probably is tired and hungry—which is why you see the outbursts before dinner.

Face it. She has a long day at childcare. She is busy "working" when you are at work. For her, play is work. She's had to put up with other toddlers vying for attention of childcare providers, toys, etc. and having to sort through all those emotions. Then, she gets a boring 45-minute ride home and she is probably hungry too. She most likely only gets one nap at daycare (if it is the typical toddler classroom) but she might still be a two-nap girl. Bottom line: perfect set-up for a meltdown.

The solution: offer a snack in the car ride home. Have dinner partially prepped on the weekend, so you can get dinner on the table pronto when you get home. Let her tantrum if she must while you do your thing. Then, after dinner, aim for an early bedtime so she isn't exhausted every day. More sleep and a full tummy lead to better behavior!

Q. I have a very sweet, yet very bossy four-year-old daughter. She has a clear sense of right and wrong and feels it is her job to correct everyone. It is starting to affect her friendships. She gets so mad when they won't play the way she wants them to. Then she hurts her friends' feelings. The only playdates that go "well" are those with a passive friend who does everything she says. How do I change this behavior so she doesn't become a bully?

All personalities need a little tweaking from time to time. Your daughter has some great leadership qualities, but she needs to work on brainstorming and compromising.

In preschool terms, that means that everyone gets to take a turn in choosing what to play—and people won't want to play with you if they don't ever get a turn. Kids do a great job of policing each other's behavior (because they simply won't put up with it) and your daughter will quickly learn this on the playground or in preschool/kindergarten when kids reject her for acting that way. But pointing this out to her will help her down that road.

Before a playdate, you should pretend to have a playdate with her. Model appropriate play skills (taking turns, asking for ideas, accepting others' ideas). At the real playdate, you can remind her of the things you all practiced. After the playdate is over, discuss what went well and what didn't.

Ages 1½-3

THE BOSS (NOT BRUCE SPRINGSTEEN): IT'S HER WAY OR THE HIGHWAY!
This probably describes just about every toddler. Disciplining this behavior is a fine balancing act between fostering your child's independence and self-confidence . . . and staying in charge. *Note to self: you are not your child's buddy. Thus, there are times when you have to put your foot down.*

The key to building your child's self-esteem: make him feel that his opinion counts.

What to do:
◆ Be a good listener. While you may not implement the plan he has in mind, you respect him enough to listen.
◆ The Boss likes to win. (So does the Negotiator—the next character in our discipline hit parade.) As often as you can, let your child choose from a variety of options that are all what you'd like him to do anyway. Example: "We can't eat ice cream for breakfast,

---

DRAWING A LINE IN THE SAND

If you have decided that something is not negotiable, make sure you a) have the determination to follow through and b) haven't backed yourself into a corner. In this case, the corner turned out to be a bathroom....

One family, who will remain nameless, shared this story of a father versus a strong willed two-year old. Here's the overview:

The battle: Taking an antibiotic. Guess who wins?
Scenario: The child refuses to take her morning dose of medicine.
Dad: Decides this is not negotiable (You go, Dad).
Discipline strategy: Dad decides that he and the child will stay in the bathroom until child takes the medicine. (That's a fine idea unless you have a really smart, strong willed toddler).
Child: Instead of deciding that the bathroom is boring and seeing the light . . . .she decides she will just play in the bathroom with nothing more than her imagination until lunchtime.
Dad: Misses half a day of work in the name of drawing the line in the sand. (Well, we like that he followed through, but perhaps a different strategy would have gotten him out of the bathroom and to work sooner. And he had finished reading the newspaper and his Diet Coke after the first hour.)

One thing I learned early on in medical school while studying psychology is never to put the patient between you and the door. That way, if the patient gets out of control, you have an exit strategy. This dad had no exit strategy. If he let her out of the bathroom, she won the battle.

We are all about giving choices, and teaching consequences (like not being able to go to preschool until she takes her medicine). But at the end of the day, if something is truly not negotiable, you open the child's mouth and shoot the medicine in—even if there is a protest. Because....this child needed 18 more doses of that antibiotic!

but do you want yogurt or bananas?"

◆ Say, "I like your idea. I like hearing what you have to say." That doesn't mean you have to follow through with it, though.

Reality Check

Some parents will go to extremes to avoid confrontation with the child who is the boss. Here's a story of one mom we'll call . . . Rapunzel. True to the name, this mom had long, beautiful hair. But being a mother of three children under age five, she often wore it up in a ponytail (because what mom has that much time to lavish on hair care in the morning?).

Well, her toddler daughter decided she only liked mom's hair loose. She would scream and protest every time mom wore a ponytail. You can guess where this is going . . . instead of putting her foot down, Rapunzel sacrificed some of her already few hours of precious sleep to do her hair every morning.

Rapunzel had her fourth baby recently. She came into the office the other day sporting a very cute bob haircut. She'd donated her hair to Locks of Love. This was certainly one solution to the problem, but I might have suggested other alternatives. The take-home message: you should be able to decide how you want to wear your hair. And while this may seem like an extreme scenario, many of the concessions that parents make to keep the peace are equally as ludicrous.

Reality Check
The Power Play, otherwise known as "How Your Child Gets To Yes"

Humans can be very manipulative—particularly the littlest ones. Don't let their charm and cute cheeks beguile you. As a guide for parents, we've included the most popular manipulation methods from the secret guide book, *The Tipping Point: How Little Things* (a.k.a. kids) *Can Make a Big Difference* (in what their parents decide to do)…with apologies to author, Malcolm Gladwell. You will see these methods emerge in your two to four-year-old, and they will continue indefinitely (so get used to it).

> **Stormin' Norman.** Have a tantrum and watch the parents cave. Home version works; public version is even more powerful.
> **The Black Widow.** Draw your prey into the web and force a fight.
> **The Negotiator.** Deal or no deal?
> **The A Factor.** Annoy parent until they give in just to shut you up.
> **The Guilt Card.** Works really well with working moms and single parents.
> **The Sting.** Set one parent up to unknowingly disagree with the one you've already asked.

Key point: your child may employ one or more of these clever tricks and resort to them time and again IF you cave and give in. Why wouldn't they? So, the person's behavior that needs to change is yours. Stop letting these tactics get to you and your child will stop using them!

Ages 2-4

THE NEGOTIATOR.

Some preschoolers just have a knack for wearing down their parents to get what they want. When your child is on the high school debate team, it will be a blessing. Right now, it feels like a curse. If you find yourself giving in to your child's every whim, this section is for you.

Frequently, parents "give in" because they are sick of hearing their child whine, or they want to avoid conflict. The path of least resistance is to let the kid have what he wants.

Think about why your child is acting like this. She has figured out that this tactic works. She knows that you will give in to avoid the fight. Some things simply are not worth the time or energy to argue about (wearing mismatched socks, for example). But there are certain situations where you should stand your ground—even if it happens in public. You'll have to decide where to draw your line in the sand, but once you do, stick to it.

What to do and say:
- ◆ If you see your child trying to make a deal with you, try using some humor to lighten the mood and move on.
- ◆ Negotiators like to win. Give them choices of all the things you want them to do anyway. Then you both win.
- ◆ Pick your battles. Sometimes you have to simply say, "No." And stick to it!

Q. What do I do if my child has a tantrum in public?

Ages 1-4

THE PUBLIC TANTRUM.

Parents are always bothered by their child acting up in public. And let's face it, these tantrums are embarrassing.

Here's the truth about public tantrums: every other parent has been there and really doesn't think you are a bad parent—they are just relieved it's not their kid making the noise!

Again, think about the world from your toddler's point of view. Kids realize they are smaller than most people in their world, so they need to be louder to be seen and heard. They want to be in charge, but cannot control when you plan to leave the grocery store . . . especially if there is a line at checkout.

So what are they going to do to get what they want? You got it—they will yell!

What to do and say:
- ◆ Keep your composure.
- ◆ Don't back down just because you are in public.
- ◆ See the box on page 30 specific tips.

Ages 1-4

TROUBLE SHIFTING GEARS: TRANSITIONS.

There is no question that some of your child's worst behaviors will occur as you are changing from one activity to the next. These are called "transitions." When your child is playing, he won't want to stop to eat dinner. The same goes for transitioning from dinner to bath time, bath time to bed time, and so on. Toddlers get focused and involved on a certain activity and don't want to stop (especially if it means going to bed for the night).

If you haven't experienced this yet, teachers have a real knack at mobilizing a group of children when we parents can't even get one child going. Here are a few things I learned when I was a preschool student teacher in college (besides parenthood, it was the most tiring job I ever had):

What to do and say:

◆ First and foremost, do not get frustrated!

◆ Have realistic expectations of your child's ability to switch gears. If you know it will take ten minutes in the morning for your child to move from the breakfast table to the car seat to get to childcare, then give him ten minutes. Giving him only five minutes and then yelling at him will not make the process go any faster.

◆ Speaking of yelling…resist the temptation. In fact, whispering or lowering your voice makes your child stop what he is doing to hear what you are saying to him.

◆ Get your child's attention by turning off the lights, or ringing the "clean up" bell.

◆ Get on your child's eye level and give him instructions.

◆ Give clear instructions. Say, "Which toys should we clean up first?" Choosing not to clean up is not one of the choices. They get to decide which toys go first, and you get the playroom cleaned up before dinner.

◆ Be consistent. Kids thrive on routines.

◆ Kitchen timers work very well for transitions. Set that kitchen timer so your child knows it is time to stop playing and get ready for dinner. It keeps you from boiling over.

◆ Make toy clean up a game as a way to transition out of playtime to cleanup time. When it seems like fun, your child will be more inclined to participate.

◆ Give your child a place to keep his unfinished work…like a puzzle, art project, or block tower. (How would you feel if your mom made you stop working on a novel you were writing, or worse—walked over to your computer and deleted it. Think about it!)

Reality Check: The morning rush

No doubt, you will feel the most frustrated with your toddler's dilly-dallying when you have someplace you need to be. Consider these five ways to ease the transition from home to work and childcare for the day:

◆ *Start earlier.* Then, you don't have to rush.

◆ *Prepare ahead of time.* Have everyone's clothes (your and your child's) picked out for the morning. Have lunches prepared the night before. Have keys, and any other necessities ready to go at the door.

◆ *Smile.* Start the day with a smile on your face. Stress is counterproductive.

◆ *Incentivize.* Let your child have a special toy or doll that only gets played with in the car.

◆ *Distraction.* Talk about what the day holds instead of talking about

DISCIPLINE

? ?

why you are frustrated with your child's inability to get moving. (I call this the gynecologist's trick—ever notice how she gets you talking about something else while performing your internal exam?)

THE SHORT-FUSE.
There is an art to problem solving. Some kids are naturally gifted in this department, while others need to be taught how to do it. Kids who are easily frustrated, difficult to calm down, or give up easily, need help.[4]

What to do and say:

◆ Say, "You're unhappy. Let's figure out a different way to build this Lego tower/color the picture/etc." Don't give your child the answer, but help guide him to think outside the box.

◆ Teach your child the skill of problem solving. It will reduce the amount of frustration and therefore, the number of tantrums. The basic idea: you can role play problem-solving skills so that your child is prepared to put them into action when the situation arises. Teach the Four P's: Practice, Praise, Point Out, and Prompt.[5] This works well for two to four-year-olds.

As an example, let's take a look at "taking turns":

◆ *Practice:* Pretend you want the same toy as your child does.

◆ *Praise:* Say, "I'll set the timer so both of us will get a turn." Then say, "I'm really proud of you for sharing with me."

◆ *Point out:* Show your child how everyone takes turns, like when you check out at the grocery store.

◆ *Prompt:* At the beginning of a playdate, give your child a little reminder. Say, "Remember to take turns with Zoe."

Reality Check
It will seem easier for you to just step in and solve the problem. Your child will learn a more valuable skill, though, if you help

---

GETTING BEYOND "NO!"

Here are some other tips to get beyond "No!" and "Mine!" These work well for three to four year olds:

1. *Clarify the problem.* Use "I" messages and active listening. "I see that you and Parker are having a problem sharing the toy."
2. *Define the problem.* "What do you need?"
3. *Problem ownership.* "You both want a turn. How can we solve this?"
4. *Neutral zone.* "I'll hold onto the toy until you decide what to do."
5. *Brainstorm.* "What do you think is fair?"
6. *Make a plan.* "Let's listen to both of your ideas."
7. *Action.* "You get the toy for five minutes. Parker gets the toy when the timer goes off."
8. *Feedback.* "You did a great job sharing."[6]

DISCIPLINE

them to think it through and let *her* solve the problem.

Ages 2-4

CAN YOU HEAR ME NOW?

I have had more than one parent come into my office requesting a hearing test for their toddler. Is it a medical problem or is it just "selective hearing loss"? Some children choose to ignore their parents when they are engrossed in an activity. It may be because the activity is so much fun, or because the child doesn't want to hear what you have to say (like, "It's time to clean up").

Since we've pointed out that ignoring a behavior is a useful discipline strategy, you can view this approach from your kid as turning the tables!

What to do and say:

- ◆ Get onto your child's eye level, make eye contact, and speak directly to him.
- ◆ Don't lecture. Just make it clear what you need to communicate.
- ◆ Remind him of the natural consequence for his procrastination (usually the motivation to ignore mom or dad). Example: Say, "If you continue playing with your trains, there won't be time to read books before bed."
- ◆ If it truly seems that your child cannot hear or respond to you even when you say, "Want to go get some ice cream?" you should definitely check in with your child's doctor.

Specific challenges

Ages 1-3

THE BITER. Yes, it's embarrassing to be labeled as Dracula's mother. But toddlers bite or hit as a form of communication. They express themselves physically because their language skills are poor. They bite or hit to show they are frustrated, confronted, or simply looking for attention.

Put yourself in your toddler's shoes. The whole world is bigger than you. You understand what people are saying to you, but you can't talk back. You think people can read your mind. You want complete independence. So when another child takes away the toy you wanted to play with, how would you respond? Hitting, biting, and kicking are survival of the fittest tactics and they are a normal part of child development.

What to do and say:

- ◆ **Don't bite back.** Remember, you are the grown up. Your child watches you as her role model. If you are the one bitten, remove your child from your body. Calmly and sternly say, "No biting. Time out." Short and sweet—no lectures. She gets a minute for each year of age.
- ◆ **Play man-to-man defense.** Whenever your child is playing with other children, you need to be your child's shadow. Catch up with your friends later. When your child is a biter, you don't have time to socialize. That way, you can prevent the biting from happening.
- ◆ **Automatic time out.** If your child takes a bite out of a friend,

DISCIPLINE

? ?

offer to pay the doctor's bill (well, at least apologize profusely). Then immediately remove your child from the situation and implement a time out. She may return to play afterwards. If she bites again, go home. It teaches consequences for the behavior.

◆ **Take a closer look.** Many times, kids will only bite or hit at daycare when they are feeling threatened or forced to defend their territory (that is, toys). So, when the daycare personnel suggest to a parent to discuss biting with their child at home, it is often futile since that is not where the behavior is occurring. If you are going through this, do an observation at school to see what is happening. There may not be enough supervision of the biting child. Caregivers need to pay closer attention to the physically aggressive kid to head them off at the pass.

And don't forget to be consistent! Biting is ALWAYS disciplined, no matter what the time or scene of the crime.

MR. ANNOYING CELL PHONE GUY: RUDE MANNERS. Babies are not born with manners or social skills. So you'll need to teach your child how to get along with others. In the age of "Mr. Annoying Cell Phone Guy," it's no wonder that our kids grow up thinking that rudeness is acceptable. Change that trend, one child at a time.

Your child is already getting informal manner training, just by watching you. Be on your best behavior! We can't expect miracles overnight, so have reasonable expectations and pick certain battles (like keeping elbows off the table) for a later day. For now, be happy if your kid uses utensils!

We know toddler etiquette sounds like an oxymoron, but here are four scenarios your little one can learn from some 20th century icons:

Scenario #1: John Belushi.
(Throwing food) "Food Fight!" Whether or not your child has mastered the fork yet, it is NEVER okay to throw food. Most of the time, when a child hurls his food, he isn't hungry and is just looking for attention or entertainment.

What to do and say:
◆ If your child breaks this rule, he is excused from the table. That's the natural consequence for the behavior. You'd get kicked out of Chili's if you threw your food, right?
◆ Say, "Throwing your food tells me you are done eating."
◆ If your child likes to use his sippy cup as a shot put, say, "If you cannot hold your drink, I will hold it for you." If your child really wants to be in charge of things, he has to be responsible enough not to throw them.

Scenario #2: Rodney Dangerfield.
(Interrupting) "I get no respect." Kids instinctively will interrupt you and others when you are trying to have a conversation. Whether it's an important phone conversation, a discussion with the doctor at your child's well check, or a chat with your spouse at the dinner table, the motivation to interrupt is the same. Your child wants your atten-

tion to be directed at him. He also feels he has something to contribute.

What to do and say:

- ◆ Teach your child to respect others by respecting your child.
- ◆ Be a good role model. When it is his turn to talk, listen to him. Don't interrupt.
- ◆ Then, when it is your turn to talk, remind him to show you the same respect.
- ◆ If you must take a phone call, give your child something to do to entertain himself. If your child is bored, he will definitely vie for your attention. And keep the length of the call to a minimum! You've got to have realistic expectations of your child's attention span.
- ◆ Say, "When I am done talking on the phone, it will be your turn to talk to me." Then, stick to it! If your child tries to interrupt your conversation, ignore her.

Reality Check

I frequently rescue moms in my office desperately trying to have a conversation with me while their antsy toddler vies for their attention. I'll hand the child some paper cups to stack, cotton balls to put in and out of those cups, or even a crayon to color on the exam table paper. It doesn't take that much creativity to get five minutes to speak with another adult!

Scenario #3: Jerry Springer. (Using force instead of words) No chair throwing—or using physical force to express ourselves.

What to do and say:

- ◆ Safety related offenses always deserve a time out.
- ◆ Say, "No _____ (hitting, throwing, biting). Time out."

Scenario #4: Barney and Emily Post. (Manners 101) "Please and thank you, they're called the magic words. If you want nice things to happen they're the words that must be heard." That pretty much sums it up. And what ever happened to the art of thank-you notes?

What to do and say:

- ◆ Model good behavior. Say please and thank you yourself!
- ◆ Practice at home. Say, "Say "please" and I will get you a drink." Then, wait until your child says "Thank you" before you hand it over.
- ◆ If your child receives a gift, have him "write" a thank you note (or at least scribble a nice picture in appreciation).

THE KID WHO PULLS OFF HIS DIAPER. This one always gets to parents. Maybe it's the smell. Or maybe it's the toddler using poop as fingerpaint.

? ?

DISCIPLINE

What to do:

And the answer is . . . DUCT TAPE. We're not kidding on this one. Several families have successfully secured the diaper tabs with duct tape when their toddlers go down for nap and bedtime. Believe us, it's much more effective than having a rational conversation with your toddler about why playing with poop is a bad idea. Skip the lecture and head to Home Depot.

THE STREAKER. Lady Godiva is a little more challenging than poop art. While it's okay to be naked around the house, you cannot really duct tape the clothes on a toddler to go out in public.

What to do for kids 1-4 years old:

◆ Sew a few stitches from your child's zippers to her clothes to keep her dressed. (This was my sister-in-law's trick!)
◆ Limit public appearances while your child goes through this phase!
◆ Offer naked time. Every night after bath, you give your child X minutes to run around the house naked. Having a scheduled naked time may prevent your toddler from spontaneously streaking.

What to do for kids age 4 and up:

A lesson in natural consequences: I told a five-year-old clothing-challenged patient recently that she could not play outside without clothes on because it was either too cold or the sun would burn her skin. So, if she chose to be naked, she would have to stay indoors all day long. After mulling over her options, she decided to wear clothes and has ever since!

REBEL WITHOUT A CAUSE. If this sounds like your child, you have probably already visited your local emergency room for stitches or a cast. This is the toddler who repeatedly scales the kitchen cabinets and dances on the dining room table. There's no malice here. This child simply enjoys challenges and testing limits.

Unless you've got a padded cell in your house, your child may manage to get into perilous situations even if he is contained in your living room.

What to do and say:

◆ *Every* time he starts to climb, you need to follow through and redirect his play. You may want to temporarily store the dining room chairs elsewhere until this phase passes. That works particularly well for a child under two years of age.
◆ If he is doing something that truly puts him or someone else in danger, he gets a time out (under your supervision, of course).
◆ Say, "No swinging from the chandelier (or whatever the risky business is). Time out."

THE RUNAWAY. If you have given serious consideration to buying your child a leash, read on. Some kids love to run. While it's great exercise, it's not so great when he runs into the street or out of your reach in a public place.

What to do and say:

◆ The natural consequence (getting hit by a car), isn't the best result!

DISCIPLINE

So, the more preferable natural consequence is to say, "If you cannot stop running into the street, you cannot play outside." Your child learns that his behavior (running into the street) has consequences—he cannot play outside. If he wants to play outside, he remembers not to run in the street.

◆ And encourage your child to try out for the track team in the future.

THE SLOB. Does your child's playroom or closet look like a tornado blew through? Do you feel like a maid? Right now, you bear most of the responsibility for cleaning up, but that doesn't mean your child is off the hook. Plant the seeds now so your child learns that if he makes the mess, he's in charge of cleaning it up. It's called taking personal responsibility, and that is a big lesson your child needs to learn.

What to do and say:

◆ Make clean-up a part of spending time together.
◆ Play a clean-up game or sing a clean-up song.
◆ Give lots of praise—especially if your child initiates it without you nagging her to do it!
◆ Say, "I like how you started cleaning up all by yourself! Great job!"
◆ As your child gets older (age four and up), the natural consequence of leaving a mess is that things get thrown away if they are on the floor (or taken away for a period of time). That usually encourages the child to put things away where they belong.

THE KID WHO HATES HIS CAR SEAT. You are driving along and suddenly your four year old decides he doesn't want to be in his car seat. Before you have a chance to say "boo!," your child is unbuckled and roaming the back seat. What do you do?

What to do for kids 2-3 years old:

This can be a discipline challenge complicated by the fact that big toddlers are growing out of their harnessed, convertible car seats too soon. Ideally, keep your child in a harnessed seat as long as possible (it is harder to MacGyver your way out of a five-point harness). See our book *Baby Bargains* for harnessed car seats that work to 70 pounds.

What to do for kids age 4 and up:

Older kids need to understand how CRITICAL it is to stay buckled up in a moving vehicle. So this is a non-negotiable rule: get out of the car seat and the vehicle will come to a stop (pull over safely, of course). There is no playdate, lunch or wherever you were going unless he gets BACK in the seat, pronto. For a four-year-old, stress the no-belt, no-go rule. A fun suggestion: reinforce that message by having a police officer explain the law to your child and what will happen if they break it.

THE GRAFFITI ARTIST. While parents should encourage self-expression, it's not okay to paint or color on the walls. We know that you can't watch your child's every move, every minute of the day. And this type of behavior will most likely happen when you are letting the dog out or answering a phone call.

What to do and say:

- The obvious prevention: put all arts and crafts under lock and key.
- If you have to take a phone call on your watch, get your child set up with an activity to do while you are on the call. Then, he won't resort to drawing on the walls for attention.
- If your child does draw on the walls, make your comments short and sweet. Say, "No drawing on the walls" and redirect him to the art supplies he is supposed to use.
- Natural consequence: your child gets to help you clean up the walls.
- If your child is a habitual wall artist, this is your cue to keep a closer eye on him.
- Catch him being good. Give plenty of praise for artwork that ends up on paper. Say, "I like how you drew that picture on the art paper."

THE SHOP-A-HOLIC. The shop-a-holic child demands the purchase of trinkets or gum for each errand. If she leaves the store empty handed, she pitches a fit. Note to self: If you have to bribe your child to get out of Home Depot, you have a problem.

While errands are seldom fun for small children, they are a fact of life. As long as you don't have unrealistic expectations of how many errands you will run or how long the trip will take, you should be able to take your child out with you instead of hiring a babysitter so you can go buy light bulbs.

What to do and say:

- Stick to your guns and do not buy something to pacify your child. It is opening Pandora's box.
- Involve your child in the experience. Say, "Can you help me pick out some good light bulbs?"
- If you must resort to bribery, use it sparingly. Getting a shot at the doctor deserves something special. Going to the gas station does not.

THE FASHION PLATE. Some children (okay, mostly girls) decide early in life that they want to pick out their attire for the day. Welcome this as a sign of self-expression. At least it's less costly than the Graffiti Artist.

It's okay if the outfit doesn't match, really. No one is going to criticize your parenting skills because your child is wearing white shoes after Labor Day.

What to do and say:

- Ignore it.
- Pick your battles. If your child is truly dressed inappropriately, then say "you can wear the princess heels after you get home from preschool." (It's hard to climb on the playscape in princess heels.)

THE BULLY. There's no doubt, if your child is the bully, you need to nip this behavior in the bud. Both the bully and the bullied have self-esteem issues. First and foremost, figure out why the child feels the need to have a pecking order. Your child may be feeling inadequate and frustrated about something.

DISCIPLINE

discipline

7 SECRETS TO RUNNING ERRANDS WITH A TODDLER IN TOW

- ◆ **Plan ahead**. Make a list of things you need to reduce the amount of time you are in a store.
- ◆ **Follow the "Two Stop" Rule.** Getting in and out of your car with a toddler is an experience itself. With our kids, we always had a two stop rule for Saturday errands—that is, if you have to stop the car more than twice to do errands, you are asking for trouble. Take advantage of drive-through windows for the bank, dry cleaners and so on to avoid moving your child in and out of the car.
- ◆ **Involve your child.** Let your child put the fruits or veggies on the scale, or place the items on the checkout belt.
- ◆ **Find freebies.** Our son used to love getting the free used car magazines at the grocery store. We had him convinced that we had to pay for them, so he would give it to the checkout clerk to run through the scanner. He was thrilled to get a new magazine every time. Coupons can be used in a similar way (your child can "cash them in" at checkout). Another idea: schedule your visit when a store is handing out free samples (such as warehouse clubs on the weekend).
- ◆ **Go without the child.** If one parent can baby-sit while the other goes to the mall, everyone will probably be happier.
- ◆ **Shop online.** Even if you have to pay for shipping, the additional cost may be worth avoiding the headache of going shopping with a toddler. And savvy shoppers know they can avoid online shipping charges by taking advantage of online coupons and free shipping offers when you buy $X worth of items.
- ◆ **Don't push it.** Don't go shopping at nap time or late at night with a toddler.

What to do and say:

- ◆ Dr. Allison Chase, a child psychologist, suggests the following: "Even if the bullying child feels bad, it does not excuse him from facing the music."
- ◆ Ask him to draw an apology picture and deliver it to the child he bullied.
- ◆ Discuss the natural consequences: Say, "If you hurt someone's feelings, you won't have friends to play with."
- ◆ Work on those problem-solving skills. Your child is resorting to bullying to get what he wants. Empower him with more positive methods. Say, "Why don't you try it this way instead?"

Ages 3-4

IF EVERYONE ELSE IS JUMPING OFF A BRIDGE . . . That's another golden oldie phrase that haunts all of our childhoods. As children enter preschool, they may experiment with behaviors they witness in other kids. Sometimes, the ringleader at school will model good behaviors (yay!), or sometimes not-so-good behaviors (yikes!). If the ringleader gets the other kids to laugh at his antics, you can be certain your child will test out the same thing at home to see your

HOW CAN I PROTECT MY CHILD FROM BEING BULLIED?

A child's temperament may make him a target for a bully. Bullies prey on children who are the most likely to be bothered. Kids who are bullied tend to have poor self-esteem because they feel threatened and vulnerable.

Use those active listening skills. Let your child be heard. Then, teach him how to problem solve. This doesn't mean enrolling him in karate class. It means role-playing these situations and teaching him how to ignore or walk away from the bully. When bullies realize that their tactics aren't working, they move on. *Most importantly, remind the sensitive child how special he is.*

response. As with many of these scenarios, it may be a relatively innocuous behavior now, but the risks get bigger as your child gets older. Today it may be putting a playground rock up her nose. Tomorrow it may be snorting a controlled substance.

You don't want your kid to be the follower. You want her to make her own decisions, based on your principles of right and wrong. This is the foundation of self-esteem.

What to do and say:

◆ Say, "I really like it when you make your own decisions."

◆ Say, "I am very proud of you being a leader. You are very good at making the right choices."

◆ When she makes those good choices, reinforce that behavior by giving lots of praise.

◆ Remind her that her teachers, parents and caregivers can help her make decisions if a friend suggests an idea that maybe isn't the best one.

◆ Opening the lines of communication now will serve you well as your child grows up and encounters more complex social situations and pressures.

◆ Most importantly, tell your child that a true friend will still be a friend even if your child decides not to follow her idea.

THE POTTY MOUTH. "You're a poo-poo head!" Yes, those words will come out of your preschooler's mouth someday. That deteriorates into other expletives we need not mention here. The first time is funny, because it gets a rise out of Mom or Dad. Your reaction is what leads to the 20th or 100th time later on.

What to do: Ignore it. If it doesn't get a rise out of you, your child will quit saying it.

LIAR, LIAR. All children go through a phase of lying. Sometimes they just make up stories since fantasy and reality can be the same world for a toddler. That's a part of normal development (see more on this in Chapter 3, Milestones). Other times, they do it to avoid being disciplined. You'll have to figure out

DISCIPLINE

the motivation in each individual situation.

You have to be very careful how you discipline for lying. (The same goes for stealing, by the way). The dilemma: you cannot punish your child twice.

You need to choose which offense you are going to discipline: the misdeed they are covering up or the lying, but not both. If you get your child to fess up to the crime, you have to be willing to respect your child for being honest and not punish him for the act. Think about it. Why in the word would your child be motivated to tell you he lied next time if he knows he's going to get punished for it?

Here's a scenario that explains this double discipline dilemma. Okay, it's a dog story, but it is still a good example. Our neighbors had an invisible fence for their dog. If you are not familiar with invisible fencing, the dog wears a collar that gives him an electrical shock if he goes past the boundary line of the "fence." Well, this cute little dog loved to play with our dogs, so he routinely escaped from his home to come over to ours. He was willing to take the "zap" to come and play.

But here's the rub with an invisible fence: that electrical charge fires no matter which direction the dog is going—in *or* out of his yard. The point: that dog had no desire to go back home because he would be punished again with a second "zap."

We don't encourage invisible fencing for your child—and we don't recommend that he get zapped twice for lying. Once is enough to get your child to understand that lying is wrong.

What to do and say:

◆ Say, "Tell me what happened."

◆ If you suspect your child is fibbing, say, "You won't be in trouble for _____ (drawing on the walls, etc.) if you can tell me what really happened." If your child confesses, say, "I'm proud of you for telling me the truth. It's important to always tell the truth. Now let's clean up that wall together."

◆ If your child persists in telling his whopper, say, "I know you were afraid to tell me the truth, but no one else uses crayons in this house. We have to trust what we tell each other." Then, remove the crayons for the day and clean up the walls together. (Even though it is tempting, it's pointless to say, "Why did you lie to me?).

◆ Be sure to tell your child that it is bad to lie, but that doesn't mean he is bad.

Special Situations

SQUIRMY AT CHURCH. Well, let's think about this. You are asking a one to four-year-old to sit still and be quiet. If you bring a very large bag of quiet activities, you might last about twenty minutes with your average two year old. But . . . the average Protestant service lasts about 45 minutes. And the typical Jewish service is about two to three *hours*. Lower your expectations, and you won't be frustrated.

Do what you feel comfortable doing as a family. Just take your toddler's attention span into account.

What to do and say:

◆ Don't expect your child to sit still and stay quiet. Some congregations offer family rooms where children can climb around and talk while parents can still hear and see the service.

◆ Stay as long as your child can handle it (and don't get frustrated if you need to take a break and walk around the lobby).

◆ Before services begin, remind your child of appropriate behavior in a house of worship. Say, "Remember to be quiet and sit still so everyone can pray."

◆ Or consider putting your little one in the nursery or babysitting area if you want to pray without distraction!

Feedback from the Real World

One family suggests sitting in the front pew at church with their little ones. Sounds crazy, since you'd think the best place is in back where you can sneak out if your kid starts acting up. But they find their kids are much more attentive in front row seats where they can see the action on the pulpit.

THE NEW KID ON THE BLOCK: HAVING ANOTHER CHILD. While there is no one "right time" to have another baby, experts suggest spacing children two and a half to three years apart. This gives you more time to spend with each child and promotes strong sibling relationships.

Also, from a medical standpoint, experts suggest waiting at least 18 months between pregnancies to give mom's body time to recuperate. If you get pregnant sooner than 18 months before the last baby was born, there is a higher risk of premature birth and low birth weight.

When that new baby arrives, it doesn't matter what your oldest child's age is . . . he will resent having to share the limelight! It takes about two months for the older child to forgive you for not leaving that screaming baby at the hospital. We discuss this issue in more depth in Chapter 4, Is This Normal?

What to do and say:

Here are some practical tips to survive the first couple of months at home and beyond.

◆ **Special attention.** Catch the older child being good. Your child will seek out attention from you. Whether it is positive (reading books with you) or negative (getting chewed out by you), it is still attention focused towards him and away from the baby. Say, "You are doing a great job on that puzzle." Or "Let's read a book together while the baby is eating."

◆ **Special time.** Set aside special time for the older child. No matter how many other family members offer to spend time with your older

DR B'S OPINION

"Out of sheer necessity, your parenting style will change when you have more than one child to care for. Sometimes, that's a good thing. Your older child will take on more responsibility and independence."

DISCIPLINE

discipline

THE TERRIBLE THREE'S: DR. B'S TRUE STORY

My first child was an absolute angel—when he was two. We thought we had made it through toddlerhood without tantrums or protests, thanks to our wonderful mastery of parenting. Well, that was before our daughter was born. Our son was a little over three years old when his sister arrived and rocked his world. We stopped patting ourselves on the back and considered hiring an Exorcist.

In the first six weeks of our daughter's life, our son made his grandmother cry by telling her that she did not love him anymore, called 911 and got a friendly police officer to visit our home (the officer had a knowing look in her eye when she spied the newborn), and acquired a blood-curdling scream that could wake the dead.

Our kids are now best friends, and our son cannot imagine life without his sister (except when she messes with his baseball cards). He cannot even remember his life pre-sister. Take home message: There's really no perfect time to have another baby. It just takes some time for everyone to adjust.

---

child while you care for the baby, it's not time with you. Hand the baby over to the family and take your older one out to the park.

◆ **Special jobs.** Give your older child special jobs and praise him. Make him feel he has an important role in the family. A two-year-old can hand you a clean diaper during diaper changes. A four-year-old can help feed and bathe the baby. Say, "You are such a great helper! You are a terrific big brother/sister!"

◆ **Special privileges.** Allow your child to have special toys that are his alone. The older child is always the one who is expected to share. Pick out those toys that aren't safe for infants (like Legos) and let your older child play with those in his room. Say, "You have some special toys that are only for you. Let's pick those out together and keep them in a safe place."

◆ **Discipline both kids.** Discipline the younger child as well as the older one. As your little one gets older, she will know exactly how to quietly antagonize her big brother *and* make him get in trouble. It doesn't matter who started the fight—both kids get in trouble. That motivates both of them to have good behavior.

◆ **Play fair.** Frequently, the younger child's needs get priority. And sometimes that's unavoidable—like going home for an earlier bedtime. The older child starts to blame the younger child for things he doesn't get. Be a good listener and have a family meeting to address everyone's needs.

Ages 1-4

HAVE TODDLER, WILL TRAVEL. Traveling with a toddler can be challenging. Don't expect perfect behavior. Toddlers have short attention spans and like moving around. Thus, airplane or car travel may be unpleasant if it is more than just a short trip.

What to do:

◆ Regardless of travel mode, be sure to bring along a bag of

DISCIPLINE

? ?

tricks—full of toys your child has never seen before. That usually buys you a few extra minutes for the novelty factor.

◆ Music is both entertaining and soothing. Bring an iPod full of kid-friendly songs.

◆ Try to travel off peak to avoid delays and crowds.

◆ Be realistic about your expectations. Adjust your travel plans accordingly. You may want to get into Disney World when the gates open and stay until 10pm closing . . . but your toddler may poop out by 3pm. If your toddler is unhappy, you can guarantee everyone else will be, too.

For air travel, here are some tips.

◆ Get a seat for your child under age two if you can afford it. Not only is this the safest option, but everyone will appreciate the extra space. Some airlines will discount the child's seat.

◆ To equalize pressure in a toddler's ears, drink some water during takeoff and landing. (Bring your own so you are not waiting on a flight attendant.) Yawning can also help.

◆ What about drugs? Parents often ask about giving Benadryl (diphenhydramine) to make their child fall asleep. If the flight is over six hours long, it's a consideration. But check with your doctor first.

If you are the one with the screaming child at 30,000 feet, apologize and buy your fellow passengers a round of drinks.

DON'T MAKE ME STOP THIS CAR! Yes, this happens to all of us….the day we turn into our moms. If you've got more than one kid, it's pretty much guaranteed that there will be fighting in the backseat (unless you have a three-row SUV or minivan).

If you are driving the car, it's hard to know exactly which child started the problem. Often, the instigator is the younger child, not the older one.

What to do and say for a two to four year old:

◆ If it is just bickering, take a step back, ignore it, and see if the kids can work out their differences on their own. It's an opportunity for them to learn problem-solving skills!

◆ If you must intervene, change your tone of voice—you know which one that is.

◆ If the action gets out of hand, both kids get disciplined. And yes, it's okay to pull over to the nearest parking lot or shoulder until the fighting stops. The natural consequence is that their poor behavior keeps everyone from getting to their destination.

◆ Calmly say, "Let me know when you are done." You can step out of the car if you need to escape the screaming in the backseat.

Reality Check

This also falls into the sibling rivalry category. Siblings know just the right buttons to push to annoy each other. An older child may tease the younger one by touching, poking, or grabbing toys. Some of this is motivated by the older child trying to assert dominance and say, "This is my space." If possible, doing occasional special activities with each child separately helps diffuse this need to have a pecking order in the house.

BOTTOM LINE

Final word: In all discipline situations, your child needs to know the behavior is unacceptable, not him. On one hand, you need to teach your child safe limits for behavior, nutrition, sleep, you name it. On the other hand, you don't want your child's self esteem to suffer because he begins to think you don't like him or he cannot do anything right in your eyes. Mr. Rogers said it best, "I like you just the way you are." Remind your child of that everyday!

Helpful Hints: Suggested further reading

Consider these books as good bedtime reading for you and your spouse:

1-2-3 Magic: Effective Discipline for Children 2–12. Phelan, TW. 3rd edition. Glen Ellyn, IL: ParentMagic, Inc. 2004.

Becoming The Parent You Want to Be. Davis, L., et al. New York: Broadway Books, 1997.

The Explosive Child. Greene, R. New York: HarperCollins, 2005.

Now that you've learned all the tricks to disciplining your toddler, next we'll dive into development. What are the milestones your toddler should be hitting? We'll discuss that and more in the next chapter.

MILESTONES
Chapter 3

"Like the legendary explorer, an 18-month old will repetitively scale a forbidden sofa 'because it's there.'"
~ Mel Levine, M.D.

Welcome to the development section of Toddler 411, where we try to answer that age-old question, "Just what the heck is normal?" And if something isn't, how do we fix it?

Let's start with a discussion of milestones. This chapter will focus on *what* your toddler should be doing and *when* . . . from when your toddler learns to drink from a cup . . . to the day he can properly configure a Bluetooth device to sync to your computer. (Answer on that last one: sooner than you think).

This chapter will also discuss HOW your toddler learns, plus what to expect when it comes to social and emotional growth. Along the way, we'll cover issues like when toddlers start to show a hand preference and how to adjust development milestones if you have a preemie.

In the chapters to follow, we'll tackle other issues, like how to super-size your child's smarts (technical term: developmental stimulation) and what happens when things go wrong (concerns, questions, disorders, etc).

But first, let's explore just what is normal. Get that highlighter ready, as we'll first launch into milestones.

? ?

MILESTONES

Normal Development & Milestones

We've all been there—sitting on a park bench with other parents while our kids run around on the playground like Energizer bunnies. Invariably, the parent sitting next to you strikes up a conversation. "Which one is yours? How old is he? Really? Well, my child was doing advanced calculus at just six months of age!"

Don't you just want to slap that parent? While you try to figure out a polite way to leave the park bench, a little voice inside you wonders if your child is developing normally.

Unless you are a child development expert, that little voice may create a lot of undo stress and anxiety. Here are the Three Golden Rules when it comes to being a parent of a toddler.

> **Rule #1:** Trust yourself. Unless the park bench parent IS a child development expert (odds: slim to none), ignore him/her.
>
> **Rule #2:** Do not obsessively compare other siblings or random children at the playground to your child.
>
> **Rule #3:** Read this chapter and find out what children are really *supposed* to be able to do. If your child is not where he should be, talk to your doctor.

Before we get to the nitty-gritty details, here is the big picture of what your child will look like over the next few years. You'll want to bookmark this entire section so you can refer back to it periodically!

A snapshot of your child, by age

Wondering what your child should be able to do at a certain age? Here's the 411. Your child's doc will ask about these milestones at well-child visits. Watch what your child is doing and take notes. We'll give you the doctor's question list at the end of this chapter so you will be prepared.

12 Month Old

A 12 month old gets around the house by crawling, cruising, or walking. He explores everything, using less of his mouth and more of his hands. He will feed himself, using his hands (and make a mess).

He understands much of what is said to him and communicates mostly non-verbally. He will say "mama" and "dada" intentionally, but probably will only say one more word beyond that. He will make eye contact to get someone's attention and respond when someone calls his name. If you point to an object, he'll look to see what you are pointing at. If faced with a new situation, he will look to his parents for approval.

He will imitate some of your activities, like talking on the phone or using the remote control.

MILESTONES

15 Month Old

A 15 month old is unstoppable. She walks and climbs, and maybe even runs away from you. She is curious, and will test her boundaries for the sake of figuring out where they are. She's all about doing things herself (and her way).

She likes routines and will be rigid about sticking to them. (This continues for several months to years, by the way).

She is increasingly verbal, and may speak entire sentences in a language you cannot understand. On average, she'll have at least three words you understand (nobody else will, though). A 15 month old communicates her needs very effectively by pointing and grunting. But she understands much more than what she is able to say. She can follow simple directions (such as, "Bring me the cup.")

She will copy or imitate activities she sees you doing—cleaning up, turning pages of a book, trying to cook. She has separation anxiety, and may be fearful of strangers. (Visits to the doctor can be a real challenge—fair warning!)

18 Month Old

An 18-month-old child resembles a bull in a china shop. And you will get your share of exercise in the name of damage control. He will continually test your patience as he demands more autonomy. Tantrums are common—hopefully more from your child than from you. Ugly and embarrassing behaviors like hitting, biting, and kicking are also common. Fun times!

The good news—he will start to use more words to express himself. There is an explosion of language just around the corner. While he may not have more than a handful of words, he understands most of what you say to him. Whether he chooses to follow directions or not is another story!

An 18 month old is able to use his hands more to explore and maneuver things. He will play with toys purposefully—pretending that trains go on the track or babies are fed and put to bed. He will be able to use utensils, although he may still prefer to use his hands to feed himself.

2 Year Old

A two year old is fairly bossy. It's her way or the highway. And armed with a full compliment of vocabulary words, she will tell you how she feels. "No" and "mine" are the top two vocabulary words used most often. She'll put together two word sentences (such as, "Mommy go."), and have at least 50–200 words that she can come up with on her own (not just imitating you). If things don't work out the way a two year old has planned, be prepared for a melt down.

A two year old usually loves the playground, since she can run, jump, climb up and down steps, and slide down a small slide. She also likes figuring out puzzles and coloring. Besides "no" and "mine", "why?" is also a favorite word. Don't get annoyed by it, she is trying to make sense of her world.

She also likes to pretend. She will watch what other kids are doing, and will play beside another child (**PARALLEL PLAY**). But two year olds will not know how to or try to play together.

Most two year olds are not toilet trained at their second birthday, nor are they even remotely interested in the potty. But this milestone is on the

MILESTONES

? ?

to-do list for many kids later in the second year.

She may be very fearful of things she cannot control, like loud noises. She has trouble separating fantasy from reality, and may be fearful of monsters and the dark.

3 Year Old

A three year old can have a conversation with an adult, if he is not too shy. Most of his language should be understandable to strangers. He can say his name and what he likes to play with. He can tell you whether he is a boy or a girl.

He loves to pretend and play with other kids. He is not the best at sharing, but he's capable of taking turns (with some encouragement). If you have a girl, she is probably toilet trained. If you have a boy, it's less likely. But even most boys are toilet-trained during the day by three and a half. He can climb stairs, ride a tricycle, throw and kick a ball. He can draw more meaningfully (not just scribble), get dressed with a little help, and wash his hands. He might even be able to brush his own teeth (but probably not very well). Don't let him fool you, he can help clean up and put away his toys.

He may still be afraid of things he cannot control or anticipate.

4 Year Old

A four year old will have no trouble talking with an adult, if she is comfortable. She can say what she likes to do and knows (and can name) her friends. She uses pronouns correctly, and most of her speech is understandable to everyone (not just you). Some kids will still make some articulation errors (for example, *w*abbit instead of *r*abbit).

She will play well with other kids. She may play chase or tag on the playground, or create a make-believe story with several children (acting out roles). And sometimes, she will prefer to play by herself, creating art projects or building with Legos. Most four year olds will happily play with other kids (**ASSOCIATIVE PLAY**) and play alone (**SOLO PLAY**).

She will know a few colors, and perhaps recognize some letters and numbers. She might be able to write her name. She can draw stick figures. And she can jump, hop, throw balls overhand, and climb stairs with alternating feet.[1]

She can follow directions and help with some household chores (YES!)

If these little vignettes do not describe your child, talk to your child's doctor. And read Chapter 6, Challenges for details on developmental differences.

Now, let's get into the nitty-gritty details of your toddler's milestones.

Q. What does development mean anyway?

Development is the way a child masters his brain and body. It includes his/her muscle skills (large and small muscles), language skills, social and emotional skills, and intelligence (cognition). Development is different from the term "growth" which refers to physical body changes. Here are some key terms to keep in mind when it comes to development:

MILESTONES

1 **GROSS MOTOR DEVELOPMENT.** Using large muscle groups to function (that is, arms, legs, torso—or your "core" for you Pilates people). Milestones include: crawling, climbing, walking, running, throwing, and kicking a ball.

2 **FINE MOTOR DEVELOPMENT.** Using small muscle groups (fingers) to function. Milestones include: picking up objects, feeding oneself, maneuvering food utensils, holding writing utensils, scribbling, and writing.

3 **ORAL MOTOR DEVELOPMENT.** Using and maneuvering mouth and tongue muscles. Milestones include: chewing, talking, and whistling (I still can't do this one).

4 **LANGUAGE DEVELOPMENT.** Communicating with others. Language development is subdivided further into the ability to understand language (receptive language) and the ability to speak language (expressive language). Milestones include: understanding spoken language, following directions, expressing needs, speaking words, and knowing body parts. Language breaks down into three areas:

◆ *Receptive language skills*: This is the language "input." Older babies and toddlers understand what you are saying to them (including "No") long before they say anything back to you. Don't let your toddler fool you!

◆ *Expressive language skills*: This is language "output." Frequently this is what most parents think of when we refer to language delays (that is, the child isn't talking yet).

◆ *Nonverbal communication skills*: This is the ability to communicate without words. Kids as young as 12 months old can tell (demand) what they want by pointing, grunting, or taking a parent by the hand.

If there is a concern for ANY language delay, your child should be checked to ensure that there is not a receptive language problem, a hearing problem, or a problem processing information that is heard (see **AUDITORY PROCESSING DISORDER**).

5 **SOCIAL-EMOTIONAL DEVELOPMENT.** This is how a child adjusts to his world. Milestones include: engaging with another person, making eye contact, expressing needs, imitating others, anxiety towards strangers, anxiety about being separated from loved ones and seeking independence.

People are not born with social skills—they are learned. And parents are the most important influence on their children.

Temperament plays a big role in how children adapt and interact with others. See Chapter 2, Discipline for details about temperament.

6 **COGNITIVE (INTELLECTUAL) DEVELOPMENT.** This refers to how a child figures out his world. Let's compare this to a computer. Newborns start with a basic hard drive and create their own software programs (at an exponential rate).

Kids take in vast quantities of information on a daily basis, and make sense of it based on strategies that have worked in the past for them (those software programs). Toddlers create new strategies when faced with new situations—this is that trendy term "developmental stimulation" you'll hear in parenting circles.

Milestones include: knowing how to get someone's attention, understanding cause and effect (for example: if I push the buttons on the remote control—the TV turns on—AND mommy grabs the remote from me), and knowing how to problem solve (such as: if the cube doesn't fit in the circle, try the square opening).

Q. How do I know that my child is developing normally?

First of all, continue reading this chapter! We will give you the entire range of what is normal and what is not.

Then, you visit your child's practitioner at regularly scheduled well child visits and touch base. That is the time to bring your concerns up—don't be shy. Your doctor won't laugh at you.

If a delay is detected, the child may be watched more closely for a period of time to see if he/she catches up; or a referral may be made to a specialist in that particular field (See Chapter 6, Challenges for details on specialists and developmental delays.)

Pediatricians rely on parents to be Developmental Detectives. We may not see everything your child is doing or not doing in an office visit. We utilize a developmental milestone checklist and information from you to identify a problem.

Reality Check

The earlier a developmental problem is diagnosed, the sooner a child gets help—and the better the outcome for the child. *Early intervention makes the greatest impact in lifelong outcomes.*

Q. What does the term "developmental milestones" mean?

These are the individual skills your child masters as she grows physically, emotionally, and intellectually. Key point: there is a *wide range* of time for when milestones are achieved. So don't freak out when your best friend's kid outpaces your own. Just take your child in for his check ups. Those well-child visits help you and the pediatrician make sure your child is hitting his marks.

Q. My child was born prematurely. How do I adjust the developmental checklist for his age?

Premature babies catch up in most of their physical growth in the first year of life. But it may take up to two years for a preemie grad to catch up *developmentally*. Use their **adjusted age** to track their progress.

MILESTONES

DEVELOPMENTAL CHECKLISTS: 7 THINGS TO KNOW

We know checklists like this can become an obsession for some folks. So before any panic sets in when it appears your child might have "missed" a milestone, keep these points in mind:

1. The checklist is not perfect—but it is a helpful guide for doctors to screen for developmental delays.

2. You must promise not to tape it to your child's bed frame and check off his accomplishments!

3. There is a very low hurdle to "pass" a test . . . so that kids with normal skills are not falsely considered delayed.

4. Because children accomplish milestones at a range of ages, mastery of a particular milestone varies over a period of time. The cutoff for "normal" is at the level where over 90% of kids have achieved a milestone.

5. If a child "fails" a *series* of test items, it is quite likely he has a developmental delay in a certain area.

6. If a child "fails," his doctor will either do a further assessment in the office or refer the child to a developmental specialist.

7. For kids who were born prematurely (born before 36 weeks of gestation) and are still under two years of age, subtract the number of months missed in pregnancy from the child's current age and check the milestones at the *adjusted age*. See the discussion on the previous page for more info.

Once a child is over two years of age, however, he should be meeting the milestones of his peers. If that is not the case, he may need professional help to catch up (for example, physical therapy).

Even if your child is following the milestone checklist, you should continue to monitor her progress closely. Children who are born significantly early and/or significantly small (less than three pounds at birth) are at increased risk of subtle developmental, behavioral, and learning differences that become more apparent as a child enters school.[2]

For more information regarding early intervention programs, check out Chapter 6, Challenges.

Without further ado, see the next two page for the big milestone checklist.

???

Bookmark this page! Toddler Development Checklist

And now, as promised, the toddler development checklist! Please take a second to read the caveats on the previous page. What if you have a preemie? See the question on the previous page before this chart for info on adjusting these benchmarks.[3]

Fine Motor (small muscles)	Age achieved:
Bangs objects together	7 to 12 months
Mastery of pincer grasp*	9 to 14 months
Drinks from a cup	10 to 16.5 months
Puts block in cup	10 to 14 months
Scribbles	11 to 16 months
Uses spoon or fork correctly	13 to 20 months
Makes tower of two cubes	13 to 21 months
Makes tower of four cubes	16 to 24 months
Makes tower of six cubes	19 months to 2.5 years
Makes tower of eight cubes	2 to 3.5 years
Hand preference	18 months to 4 years
Wiggles thumb	2.5 to 3.5 years
Can copy a circle drawing	3 to 4 years
Can draw a person with three body parts	3.5 to 4.5 years
Can copy a cross drawing	3.5 to 4.75 years
Can copy a square drawing	4 to 5.5 years
Can draw a person with six body parts	4 to 5.5 years
Writes name	4 to 5 years

Pincer grasp refers to the ability to grab a small item between the thumb and forefinger

Gross Motor (big mucles)	Age achieved:
Walks holding onto furniture (cruises)	7.5 to 12.5 months
Stands alone briefly	9 to 13 months
Stands alone	9.5 to 14 months
Walks alone	11 to 14.5 months
Runs	13 to 20 months
Walks up steps (both feet on each step)	14 to 27 months
Kicks ball	16 to 24 months
Throws ball overhand	17 months to 3 years
Jumps	22 months to 2.5 years
Balances on each foot for one second	2 to 3 years
Walks up stairs alternating feet	3 years
Rides tricycle	3 years
Hops	3 to 4.25 years
Balances on each foot for five seconds	3.5 to 5.5 years
Skips	5 years
Rides bicycle without training wheels	6 to 7 years

Language/Communication:	Age achieved:
Comprehension	
Follows simple directions	12 to 24 months
Follows two part instructions	18 to 24 months
Points to pictures when named	18 to 24 months
Knows six body parts	18 to 25 months
Understands in, on, under	3 years
Recognizes some letters of alphabet	3 to 4 years
Expression	
Says Mama and Dada and means it	9.5 to 13.5 months
Indicates wants non-verbally (Point/Grunt)	10.5 to 14.5 months
Says three words besides Mama/Dada	11.5 to 20.5 months
Says six words besides Mama/Dada	14 to 21 months
50 to 200 word vocabulary	2 to 2.5 years
Speaks two word sentences	21 months to 2 years
Speaks three to four word sentences	3 years
>500-1000 word vocabulary	3 years
Uses pronouns (I, you, we)	2 to 3 years
Can say name, age, gender	3 years
Speaks four to five word sentences	3 to 4 years
Speech	
Speech half understandable to strangers	17 months to 3 years
Speech all understandable to strangers	2 to 4.5 years
Normal dysfluency (stuttering)	3 to 4 years

Social/Intellectual development	Age achieved:
Plays pat-a-cake / "high five"	7 to 13 months
Can shake head to say "no"	9 to 12 months
Plays ball with someone	9.5 to 16 months
Finds hidden item child has watched move	12 to 18 months
Feeds a doll (symbolic play)	15 to 24 months
Brushes teeth with help	16 months to 2.75 years
Washes and dries hands	19 months to 3 years
Plays next to another child (parallel play)	2 years
Puts on a t-shirt	2.25 to 3.25 years
Names a friend	2.25 to 3.25 years
Recognizes and names one color	2.5 to 3.75 years
Plays board/card games	2.75 to 5 years
Brushes teeth without help	2.75 to 5 years
Understands taking turns	3 years
Gets dressed without help	3 to 4.5 years
Counts one block	3 to 4 years
Can tell which line is 'longer'	3 to 5.5 years
Recognizes and names four colors	3 to 5 years
Prepares cereal	3 to 5 years
Plays with another child (associative play)	3 to 4 years
Counts five blocks	4 to 5.5 years
Counts to ten	5 years

Q. What does it mean if my child fails some of his milestones?

We have a whole chapter (Ch. 6, Challenges) devoted to this question later in this book, but the short answer is—maybe something or maybe nothing.

A child may have an isolated delay in one particular developmental area (that is, a gross motor delay, or expressive language delay, etc). With a little help and encouragement, these children catch up with their peers and you might not notice a problem later on. For others, it may always be an issue. For instance, a child with a gross motor delay may always be clumsy or he may turn out to be a Heisman trophy winner. A child with an expressive language delay may turn out to have a learning disability or she may become valedictorian. It just may take a little more motivation for that particular kid to succeed in that particular area.

The children we are most concerned about are those with delays across the board, called "global developmental delays." These kids are at risk of never catching up to their peers. If children continue to have global developmental delays by the age of three, they are ultimately diagnosed with an intellectual disability (formerly known as mental retardation). There is a range from mild to severely affected. If a child has global developmental delays, an extensive medical workup is in order that includes *metabolic* (the way the body breaks down certain chemicals) and *genetic* testing (inherited chromosome defects).

With autism in the news lately, no doubt you may have concerns that *any* developmental delay is a sign of autism. It's not. To help spot those early clues, see Chapter 6, Challenges. Here's what's important to remember: a child who fails milestones in both social and language development should be assessed for an autism spectrum disorder.

Q. My child mastered some milestones, yet now he is no longer performing them. It seems like he is regressing. Do I need to worry?

When kids are working on a new skill, they may abandon one they already know how to do. This is not unusual unless a child is losing skills across all developmental areas.

Kids will also do this when faced with stressful situations—like a new baby in the house. Kids see that babies get attention . . . and quickly conclude that acting like a baby might get attention too.

Some parents of children with autism will report that their child had normal language milestones then suddenly lost their ability to speak. We will discuss this further in Chapter 6, Challenges.

Now that you've seen the overall milestones, we're going to go over some key child development theories. Don't fall asleep here—it's important to know this stuff so you can understand your child's cognitive (intellectual) and social/emotional development.

How Your Child Learns

How does your child learn all the amazing things she does? Dr. Jean Piaget, the father of cognitive (intellectual) development theory, believed that a child's brain processes and understands information in different ways at different ages. As a parent, it's helpful to know what "stage" of brain development your child is at, because *your child's reasoning will be different than yours*. And if you understand where your child is, you can have a meeting of the minds.

It's also fascinating to see how your child figures things out. Anyone who believes "child's play" is just for fun, has never really watched a child playing. Their "play" is pretty hard work! It's like a parent installing a car seat . . . with directions in Swedish.

So, here is the general idea, stage by stage:[4]

Sensory-Motor: Age birth to two years
Key Goal: Infants and toddlers learn by hearing, feeling, tasting, smelling, moving, and manipulating (i.e. using their Five Senses).

Birth to 12 months: Babies are born with a clean slate, with little more than primitive neurological reflexes (sucking, rooting, grasping) to explore their world. They rapidly start to test out items with their mouths and hands. They use their memory of what worked in the past to approach new situations by eight to 12 months old. And they learn that objects still exist even if they disappear (e.g. a toy, or Mom and Dad) by the time they reach a year of age; this is called **object permanence**.

12 to 18 months: Toddlers have more sophisticated problem solving skills, believe it or not. They experiment systematically, with a trial and error method of attack. They explore more with their hands than mouths. And they can follow directions (it's a matter of whether they CHOOSE to or not).

18 to 24 months: As children approach age two, they fine tune trial and error strategies for more complex situations (e.g. doing puzzles). They figure out *causality*—their actions produce a desired effect (that is, winding up a toy to make it move).

Pre-operational: Age two to seven years
Key goal: Children master the concept that symbols represent things—like written words and pretend play.

But their level of reasoning is based on *their* viewpoint. They are not capable of taking someone else's perspective. So don't be shocked if they lack empathy for a child whose toy they just stole.

They have very basic or "pre-logical" thinking. For example, a full four-ounce juice cup will look like it has more in it than a half-full 12 ounce water glass.

They also live in a fantasy world. Santa Claus and Tinkerbell really exist. But so do monsters. Understandably, kids this age have a number of unrealistic fears.

Reality Check
Babies and young children are *egocentric*, meaning that they think the world revolves around them. They continue to think this way until about age six or seven. Some grown-ups still think this way!

Concrete Operational: Age seven to eleven years

Key goal: Children can think logically. But everything is black and white—there is no gray zone.

Your child will become the moral police officer, reporting on misbehavior of other children. He will also be bothered if you deviate a hair from the rules of a game.

Formal Operational: Age 12 to adulthood

Key goal: Teens become capable of abstract reasoning and can finally think outside the box. A teen should be able to interpret a hypothetical situation and reason it out.

Your child's social and emotional growth

Do you want to know how your child learns to cope and find his place in the world? Look no further than Erik Erikson, one of the most influential psychologists of the 20th century. He says that your emotional growth depends on how you deal with a series of conflicts or "stages." Your sense of identity is based on how you resolve these conflicts. If you don't overcome a conflict, the unresolved issue sits there and festers the rest of your life (giving new meaning to the phrase "you've got issues").

SANTA CLAUS AND THE TOOTH FAIRY

I love old holiday movies. It's my annual December ritual to watch those classics. One of my favorite lines is from *Miracle on 34th Street.* "Faith is believing when common sense tells you not to." That line has become more meaningful after seeing my own little ones outgrow the days of believing in Santa Claus, the Tooth Fairy, and Cinderella.

We took our daughter to Disneyworld when she was five. It was priceless to see her meet Cinderella—live, and in person. Our daughter asked for a personal tour of her bedroom! Of course, Cinderella could not oblige, but she was very gracious about it.

But that same magical thinking of childhood has its downsides . . . my husband and I also got to check our children's rooms for monsters under the bed for a while! It's very normal for young children to have fears—monsters, loud noises, shadows, people in costume (really, is there anything scarier than a clown?).

The lines between fantasy and reality are blurred to a child under six or seven years of age—and that's why some things are so scary to them.

Until your child overcomes his magical thinking, you might as well use it to your advantage. Let your child think his teddy bear has magical powers that will protect him from things that go bump in the night. Tell your child he can scare away the monsters just by saying, "Go away!" Play along and empower your child while you do it.

So, when should you fess up about Santa Claus and the Tooth Fairy? Never. "Faith is believing when common sense tells you not to." Let your child decide if he wants to continue believing or not. And you just keep eating Santa's cookies and the reindeers' carrots....

MILESTONES

According to Erikson, people also regress to prior stages during times of stress (for example: a four year old returns to Terrible Two antics when a baby sister is born).

So, here are the conflicts faced during childhood (we'll save the adulthood conflicts for a Dr. Phil show):

Trust vs. Mistrust: Birth to 18 months
Key goal: Infants and young toddlers learn to trust their parents (and caretakers).

They learn that the adults in their lives will take care of their needs. They feel comfortable investigating and exploring because they have a sense of security.

In short, babies form important attachments to adults during this critical period. As that bond grows, a child gets upset if he is separated from that person. That's why kids this age have *separation anxiety* and *stranger anxiety*. (These terms describe a child who has a panic attack every time you leave to go to the bathroom or the one who spies an unfamiliar person and tries to climb up your leg). Babies who do not form appropriate bonds are distrustful and apprehensive around others. It's a red flag for developmental delay, family dysfunction, or child neglect/abuse if a child lacks an attachment to an adult by 18 months of age.[5]r

Autonomy vs. Doubt: 18 months to three years
Key goal: Children seek independence and try to gain confidence in their abilities.

This happens at the same time that parents are trying to set limits on inappropriate behaviors. This is why this age group can be such a challenging one to a parent! Your goal to create boundaries is in direct conflict with your toddler's goal of breaking them down.

With that in mind, let your child have some autonomy to learn self-reliance, or she'll begin to doubt herself. And here's the essential trick of parenting a toddler: *let a child think HE is calling the shots, when in fact YOU are!*

Initiative vs. Guilt: Three to six years
Key goal: Children thrive on decision-making and accomplishments.

If parents do not support these experiences, the child feels guilty for trying to be independent.

Hang finger-paintings on your refrigerator and beam over your child's mismatched choice of clothing for the day.

Industry vs. Inferiority: Six to twelve years

DR B'S OPINION

"You can't make a toddler eat, sleep, or poop on the potty. And if you try, it will inspire the toddler do exactly the opposite!"

Children gain confidence in their skills and want to learn. With failure or lack of support, children feel inferior to others.

MILESTONES

Identity vs. Role Confusion: 12 to 18 years

Simply put, teens either figure out who they are and what they want (sense of self) or they are confused and reliant on their peers.[6]

Specific Developmental Questions, by Age

Q. My 14 month old isn't walking yet. Should I be concerned? How can I help to teach him?

No, you don't have to be concerned. Only 50% of kids have mastered walking by their first birthdays. But 90% of toddlers take those big first steps by the time they are 15 months old. Your child is normal.

Many toddlers have the physical ability to walk, they just have to get over a mental hurdle to be confident enough to do it. If this describes your child, here are a few tips:

◆ Gently hold her hand while walking until she gains more confidence.

◆ Give her a walking toy (like a pretend lawn mower or shopping cart) to play with. She'll soon forget that she is walking!

◆ If you are really anxious about it, try a gadget called Walking Wings (upspringbaby.com; sold at major baby store chains) that makes your child think you are holding onto him while he is cruising around.

◆ Just wait it out for a few weeks.

If your child can't walk because he can't support his weight on his legs, then you need to check in with the pediatrician.

Q. My 15 month old won't let me leave her sight. Help!

Does your 15 month old blow a gasket if you step into the kitchen just to check on the casserole in the oven? The official term is **SEPARATION ANXIETY**. What's all the fuss about?

Take it as a complement—he likes hanging out with you and is comforted by your presence. Your toddler also has no concept of time. So, if you leave your child's sight, he doesn't know if you are leaving for a minute, an hour, or for a lifetime. That would make anyone a little anxious, right? And how dare you leave playtime on the living room floor to go to the bathroom, or worse—leave him at daycare to go to work. Egocentricism, baby. It's totally about him, and not about you.

Don't try to outsmart your toddler by sneaking out the door when he starts playing with the sitter or daycare provider. This is the wrong solution. It can actually make separation anxiety worse. If your child takes his eyes off of you, and then you disappear, he will be very hesitant to leave your arms. Your child needs to know that you are leaving.

What's the best strategy to survive this phase? Here are some tried and true tips:

◆ *Always say goodbye.* Talk to your toddler. Tell him you are going to make dinner now, use the restroom, or whatever it is that takes you away from him. Tell him you are coming back soon.

◆ *Make your exit short and sweet.* Lingering does no one any good.

◆ *Don't feel guilty.* Yes, your child might cry, but he will quickly move on to his next activity.

The good news: separation anxiety only lasts a month or two…or three.

Q. My 15 month old cries every time my mother-in-law comes over. What should I do?

Remember when your baby would smile and go to anyone who opened their arms to him?

Not anymore. Now your toddler (usually 12-18 month old) will cling to any of your available body parts when another person looks at him. And he will look to you for approval of this person. This is called **STRANGER ANXIETY.**

Look on the bright side: your child is gaining more awareness of his sur-roundings and wants to be sure a stranger is okay before letting him enter his space. The downside: sometimes that stranger is a grandparent or loved one who doesn't visit every day. That can be awkward when your toddler has no desire to be held by someone who has made a special trip just to visit him!

It's also a challenge if your child is in the throws of stranger anxiety when you start a new childcare situation. You may wonder if it's just a nor-mal phase or if your childcare provider is not a good fit for your child.

Here are a few tips to get through these situations:

◆ Give your toddler some time to check out the stranger before expecting him to go to this person.

◆ Have a friendly conversation with the stranger. This shows your child the stranger is someone who you are familiar with and like.

◆ Warn the grandparents before their arrival that your child is not so keen on new people.

◆ If you are in a new childcare setting, see how your child does over several days. Once she knows and gets used to a new care provider, she should smile or show you she is happy to see this person. (She still might protest when you leave though, thanks to separation anxiety). Kids who do not like their childcare providers will tell you without words. No need to buy a nanny cam!

◆ Lower your expectations and be patient. This too shall pass.

What isn't normal? It's unusual for a child to continue his play or exploration and not seek approval of his parents (like he is in his own world). It's also a red flag if a child does not desire to be comforted by a parent in a new situation with new people.

Bottom Line

You are your child's security blanket. That's why he will stick to you like glue when a stranger appears.

MILESTONES

? ?

Q. My 18 month old only has a few words. All my relatives tell me not to worry because he is just a "late talker" like his uncle. Should I worry?

It's normal if your child only says five or six words plus "mama" and "dada." It's abnormal if your child has only a word or two and no words to call for mom or dad. And while your Uncle Harry may have been a late talker and turned out just fine, that does not mean it is normal.

Look for an explosion of language in the next two or three months. When language development takes off, it really takes off. The light suddenly turns on and a child will pick up a new vocabulary word every day. If you don't see this happening, you need to contact your pediatrician. Don't wait until your child's two-year well check to tell his doctor that your toddler only has a handful of words.

See more about language disorders in Chapter 6, Challenges. See more about red flags below.[7]

Q. Is it true that boys talk later than girls?

Yes. Research shows that girls have a developmental advantage over boys in the language department. We just start talking and never stop!

So, we will cut your son a little slack if he doesn't hit those language milestones as quickly as his big sister. But regardless of sex, there are red flags that should always be addressed (see below).[8]

RED FLAGS:
Late Talkers[9]

See more on this issue in Chapter 6, Challenges.
Here are the red flags for when to get help:

◆ 12 months old: No babbling, pointing, or gesturing
◆ 16 months old: No single words
◆ 24 months old: No two-word sentences (example: "Mommy go.")
◆ Loss of language skills at any age

Q. I have 18 month old twins. Is it normal for their language development to be lagging?

Yes, and there are many reasons why this happens. It's that nature vs. nurture thing. First, many twins are born prematurely and/or with low birth weights. Both of these factors are a set-up for developmental delays, although most kids catch up to their peers.

But there appear to be environmental factors too. Twins get less one-on-one conversation time with their parents or caretakers. Instead, it's usually a three-way conversation. This may interfere with promoting language skills. And twins learn to communicate with their own twin language, called "idioglossia." They have less motivation to speak like their parents because they create their own.

In the long run, twins do just fine. But don't hesitate to get help if either or both kids are significantly behind in their milestones. Early intervention makes a difference.

MILESTONES

Q. My two year old hears two languages in our household. Will he talk later than normal?

The official term is bilingualism. It is true that early language skills are complicated by learning two languages at once. Two year olds often mix vocabulary and grammar from both languages. But by age three, kids are usually fluent in both languages.[10]

Q. I'm the only one who can understand what my two year old is saying. Is this okay?

Yes. A child should master most language sounds by age five. Prior to that, here is the rule of thumb:

Two years old: language is about half understandable to strangers
Three years old: about three-quarters understandable to strangers

Bottom Line
If no one understands what your two year old is saying, that's okay. If no one understands your four year old, that's a problem. Note: it is okay for a four year old to still have some trouble with certain sounds like "r" and "th."

Q. My two year old doesn't play with other children in playgroup. Is this normal?

Short answer: yes, it is very normal. Your child will test the waters for quite a while before he is ready to play together with another child.

Two year olds will play side by side; this is called **PARALLEL PLAY**. The kids will notice each other, but they will not work on things together (and they definitely will not share). If one child is interested in an item that the other one has, he will likely grab it away or wait until the object is left unattended—whether or not a fight breaks out depends on his or her temperament (see Chapter 2, Discipline for that). Yes, it is survival of the fittest.

Three year olds are capable of taking turns with items, although they may not be happy about it. Setting a timer for the length of time one child may play with an item is a good way to teach fairness.

By the time your child is three or four, she will finally play with another child (called **ASSOCIATIVE PLAY**). Often this play involves pretend scenarios where each child has a role to act out.

Q. My two year old doesn't know his colors yet. Could he be color blind?

At this age, it is unclear. While some kids know all their colors when they are two, many kids do not know them until they are four or five. So, color-blindness is not something your child's doctor can test for before five years of age. For details on color-blindness, see Chapter 17, Diseases.

Bottom: there is a broad age range when kids reach this milestone.

Q. My two-and-a-half year old suddenly started stuttering. Should I worry?

MILESTONES

Most of the time, yes. A child may have relatively fluent speech and then lapse into stuttering for several weeks. Or, he may only stutter when he is trying to say something important or quickly. Stuttering begins around two to four years of age and can run in families.

The good news—75% of kids who stutter will outgrow it on their own. Although it happens equally among boys and girls, boys are more likely to need help to overcome it.

The term "speech fluency" describes the ability to put sounds together correctly and flow words together into sentences. Stuttering is considered a "dysfluency." There are two categories of dysfluencies:

Between Word Dysfluency	Example
Interjections	Where, um, where is she going?
Phrase repetitions	Is she going…..is she going to the store?
Revisions	She is going to…..I think she left.

Within Word Dysfluency	Example
Repetition of sound/syllables	W-w-where is she going?
Prolonged sounds	Wwwwwhere is she going?
"Blocks"	[silent pause]…Where is she going?

RED FLAGS: Stuttering

How do you know whether your child will outgrow it or not? Here are the red flags for when to get help:[11]

◆ Stuttering more than six months without improvement.
◆ Stuttering begins after age three.
◆ Another family member stutters/needed therapy to improve.

Here are some resources for more info:

◆ American Speech Language and Hearing Association (asha.org)
◆ Friends: The Association of Young People who Stutter (friendswhostutter.org)
◆ National Stuttering Association (nsastutter.org)

Q. When is my child old enough to help with chores?

Around two years of age. You can give your child more complex chores as she gets older, but your child can be an active participant in your family starting right now. Chores give your child a sense of accomplishment and it gives you some help around the house. Warning: don't expect perfection. Just be satisfied with task-completion!

What chores are age-appropriate? Here's a quick list:[12]

Age two:
◆ Pick up toys.
◆ Wipe off the coffee table.
◆ Fold napkins for dinner.

Age three:
◆ Feed the pets.

- Match up the socks in the clean laundry.
- Set the table (silverware, plastic dishes and cups).
- Stack magazines and books.
- Sort dirty laundry into a pile of whites and colored clothing.

Age four:
- Make the bed.
- Fold laundry and put it into drawers.
- Help wash the car.
- Pulling weeds or planting in the garden.
- Water the plants.
- Help put groceries away.
- Help unload the dishwasher.
- Help clear the dinner table.

Q. My three year old isn't potty trained yet. Should I push him to do it?

Nope. Toilet training, like walking and talking, is a developmental milestone and your child is going to achieve it when he is ready. But you can certainly encourage it and cheer him on! See Chapter 7, Toilet Training, for a complete run-down.

Q. My three-and-a-half year old doesn't have a hand preference yet. Is this okay?

Yes, it's okay.

Kids usually develop a hand preference between 18 and 24 months. They will preferentially use one hand over the other to hold a fork, spoon, or writing instrument. Some kids use both hands interchangeably up to age four, and this is still normal.

What's not normal is for a child under a year of age to have a dominant hand. That's a red flag for a weakness of the non-dominant side (see **CEREBRAL PALSY**).

Putting it all together

You've seen the developmental checklists, and you've had the crash course in Child Development 101. Now you are ready to put it all together. Here are the real questions the pediatrician will ask you at each well child visit to see if your child is tracking where he should.

12 month old

You should answer yes to most of these questions. It is okay if your child has not accomplished a few of these milestones yet.

Large Muscle
Can your child stand, holding on to something?   Yes No
Does your child crawl, scoot, or walk holding onto furniture (cruise)? Yes No

Can your child stand alone?	Yes No
Can your child take steps or walk alone?	Yes No

Small Muscle

Does your child feed himself (without utensils)?	Yes No
Does your child hold his own cup?	Yes No
Does your child pick up small items between his thumb and index finger (pincer grasp)?	Yes No
Does your child bang objects together?	Yes No
Can your child put objects into a container?	Yes No

Language/communication

Comprehension:

Does your child respond when you call his name?	Yes No
Does your child understand what you are saying to him?	Yes No
Does your child look where you point when you say, "Look at the _____."	Yes No

Expression:

Does your child say "mama" or "dada" and mean it?	Yes No
Does your child say one word besides mama or dada?	Yes No
Does your child babble like he is speaking a foreign language that you cannot understand?	Yes No
Does your child take turns "talking" to you, as if you are in a conversation?	Yes No
Does your child try to get your attention?	Yes No
Does your child communicate his needs without words?	Yes No
Can your child shake his head to say "no"?	Yes No

Social/intellectual

Does your child play pat-a-cake with you?	Yes No
Does your child imitate you (e.g. pretend to talk on the phone, clean up, or use the remote control)?	Yes No
Does your child wave bye-bye?	Yes No

Autism Screening Questions
You should answer no to all of these questions. Inform your child's doctor if any of your answers are yes.

Does your child have constant repetitive behaviors, like flapping of the hands?	Yes No
Does your child have a unusual preference for a hard object, like preferring to carry a phone around instead of a doll or blanket?	Yes No
Does your child avoid eye contact?	Yes No
Does your child act like he is in his own world?	Yes No
Is your child bothered by cuddling?	Yes No

? ?

MILESTONES

15 month old

You should answer yes to most of these questions. It is okay if your child has not accomplished a few of these milestones yet.

Large Muscle
Can your child walk alone?   Yes No
Can your child run?   Yes No
Can your child climb up stairs?   Yes No
Can your child walk up stairs?   Yes No

Small Muscle
Does your child feed himself (without utensils)?   Yes No
Does your child hold his own cup?   Yes No
Can your child scribble?   Yes No

Language/communication

Comprehension:
Does your child follow simple instructions?   Yes No

Expression:
Does your child say "mama" or "dada" and mean it?   Yes No
Does your child say 3 words besides mama or dada?   Yes No
Does your child try to get your attention?   Yes No
Does your child point/grunt to communicate his needs?   Yes No

Social/intellectual
Does your child imitate you (e.g. pretend to talk on the
phone, clean up, or use the remote control)?   Yes No
Does your child pretend when she plays (e.g. feed a doll)?   Yes No
Can your child play ball with you?   Yes No

Autism Screening questions
You should answer no to all of these questions. Inform your child's doctor if any of your answers are yes.

Does your child have constant repetitive behaviors, like
flapping of the hands or rocking obsessively?   Yes No
Does your child have an unusual preference for a
comfort object, like a cell phone instead of a doll or blanket? Yes No
Does your child avoid eye contact?   Yes No
Is your child bothered by being held or kissed by you?   Yes No

18 month old

You should answer yes to most of these questions. It is okay if your child has not accomplished a few of these milestones yet.

Large Muscle
Can your child walk alone?   Yes No
Can your child run?   Yes No
Can your child climb up stairs?   Yes No
Can your child walk up stairs?   Yes No
Can your child walk backwards?   Yes No
Can your child push and pull items?   Yes No

Small Muscle

Does your child feed himself with a spoon or fork?	Yes No
Does your child hold his own cup?	Yes No
Can your child scribble?	Yes No
Can your child take off his shoes and socks?	Yes No

Language/communication

Comprehension:

Does your child follow simple instructions?	Yes No
Can your child point to pictures of words he knows?	Yes No

Expression:

Does your child say "mama" or "dada" and mean it?	Yes No
Does your child say six words besides mama or dada?	Yes No
Does your child try to get your attention?	Yes No
Does your child point/grunt or use words to communicate his needs?	
	Yes No

Social/intellectual

Does your child imitate you (e.g. pretend to talk on the phone, clean up, or use the remote control)?	Yes No
Does your child pretend when she plays (e.g. feed a doll)?	Yes No
Can your child play ball with you?	Yes No

Autism Screening Questions: See M-CHAT, Autism Screening Checklist in Chapter 6, Challenges.

Two year old

You should answer yes to most of these questions. It is okay if your child has not accomplished a few of these milestones yet.

Large Muscle

Can your child run?	Yes No
Can your child climb up stairs?	Yes No
Can your child walk up stairs?	Yes No
Can your child walk backwards?	Yes No
Can your child push and pull items?	Yes No
Can your child kick a ball?	Yes No

Small Muscle

Does your child feed himself with a spoon or fork?	Yes No
Does your child hold his own cup?	Yes No
Can your child scribble?	Yes No
Can your child take off his shoes and socks?	Yes No
Can your child turn the pages of a book?	Yes No
Can your child build a tower with four blocks?	Yes No

Language/communication

Comprehension:

Does your child follow simple instructions?	Yes No
Can your child point to pictures of words he knows?	Yes No
Does your child know at least six body parts?	Yes No

Expression:

Does your child say at least 50 words?	Yes	No
Does your child speak in two or three word sentences?	Yes	No
Is his speech half understandable to strangers?	Yes	No
Does your child try to get your attention?	Yes	No
Does your child use words to communicate his needs?	Yes	No

Social/intellectual

Does your child imitate your activities (e.g. cooking, cleaning, working on the computer?)	Yes	No
Does your child pretend when she plays (e.g. feed a doll)?	Yes	No
Does your child show affection and accept affection from you?	Yes	No
Will your child play next to another child?	Yes	No

Autism Screening Questions: See M-CHAT, Autism Screening Checklist in Chapter 6, Challenges.

Three year old

You should answer yes to most of these questions. It is okay if your child has not accomplished a few of these milestones yet.

Large Muscle

Can your child walk up stairs, with alternating feet?	Yes	No
Can your child jump up and down?	Yes	No
Can your child balance on one foot for a second?	Yes	No
Can your child throw a ball overhand?	Yes	No
Can your child ride a tricycle?	Yes	No

Small Muscle

Does your child feed himself with a spoon or fork?	Yes	No
Can your child draw a circle?	Yes	No
Can your child put his shoes on?	Yes	No
Can your child turn the pages of a book, one at a time?	Yes	No
Can your child open a door?	Yes	No
Can your child wash and dry his hands?	Yes	No
Can your child build a tower with six blocks?	Yes	No

Language/communication

Comprehension:

Does your child follow two-part instructions?	Yes	No
Does your child understand in, on, under?	Yes	No

Expression:

Does your child say at least 500-1000 words?	Yes	No
Does your child speak in three to five word sentences?	Yes	No
Is his speech half understandable to strangers?	Yes	No
Can your child say his name, age, and gender?	Yes	No
Does your child use pronouns? (I, you, we)	Yes	No

Social/intellectual

Does your child imitate your activities (e.g. cooking, cleaning, working on the computer?)	Yes	No
Does your child pretend when she plays (e.g. play doctor)?	Yes	No

Does your child show affection and accept affection from you? Yes No
Does your child understand taking turns?   Yes No
Will your child play with another child?   Yes No

Four year old

You should answer yes to most of these questions. It is okay if your child has not accomplished a few of these milestones yet.

Large Muscle
Can your child balance on one foot for a second?   Yes No
Can your child throw a ball overhand?   Yes No
Can your child ride a tricycle?   Yes No
Can your child hop up and down?   Yes No

Small Muscle
Does your child feed himself with a spoon or fork?   Yes No
Can your child draw a cross or an X?   Yes No
Can your child draw a person with three body parts? Yes No
Can your child put his shoes on?   Yes No
Can your child get dressed without help?   Yes No
Can your child brush his teeth?   Yes No
Does your child have a hand preference?   Yes No

Language/communication

Comprehension:
Does your child follow multiple-part instructions?   Yes No
Does your child recognize some letters and numbers? Yes No

Expression:
Does your child speak in four to five word sentences?   Yes No
Is his speech completely understandable to strangers? Yes No

Social/intellectual
Does your child pretend when she plays (e.g. play doctor)?   Yes No
Does your child recognize and name a few colors?   Yes No
Does your child show affection and accept affection from you?   Yes No
Does your child play well with other children?   Yes No

Now that you know the theories behind how children learn and develop, you are probably wondering how to apply that knowledge. We have a whole chapter devoted to that (See Chapter 5, Play & Preschool). We'll give you tips on how to foster your child's development for each age and stage. But coming up next, we'll look at all those quirky toddler behaviors that will have you scratching your head and wondering . . . is this normal?

Is this Normal?
Chapter 4

"You can only be young once. But you can always be immature."
~Dave Barry

What's in this Chapter

- ◆ Odd behaviors
- ◆ Imaginary Friends
- ◆ Stuttering
- ◆ Late Talkers
- ◆ Fears & Anxiety
- ◆ Special Situations

O dds are, there will be a moment when you wonder if your toddler is an alien. And we're not talking about one of those friendly ET-type aliens. Nope, we talking about bizarre behavior that might have you speed-dialing your local genetics lab to make sure your DNA really does match.

So, when your child decides to eat shag carpeting, who you gonna call? Us, your toddler wacko-behavior myth-busters. We'll discuss all those odd behaviors that your toddler might do, from eating dirt to sucking one's toes. What's normal and what should you be concerned about? This chapter also will give you advice on when your toddler's imaginary friend decides to move in and file a W-2. Plus we'll cover androgynous play (cue the Boy George soundtrack). Finally, this chapter will also discuss toddler fears (such as separation anxiety) and what happens when you bring home a new baby.

Odd behaviors, rituals, and play by ages

Q. My child eats _____ (carpet pile, dirt, etc). Is this dangerous? Is it normal?

Ages 1-3

Well, it's a bit eccentric, but it most likely is NOT harmful.

Is it normal? Probably. Some children demonstrate compulsive behaviors when

? ?

NORMAL?

they are stressed. It's a coping mechanism much like hair twirling or pencil chewing in an adult. However, if your child is spending more of her day doing odd behaviors than normal ones, it's time to discuss this with your child's pediatrician. You'll need to figure out what is triggering this behavior. Kids with iron deficiency may obsessively eat nonfood items or ice chips. This disorder is called *pica*. And kids who have other unusual behaviors plus eating the carpet pile should definitely be evaluated.

Q. My toddler bangs her head when she is upset. My son used to rock his body. Are these behaviors normal?

Ages 1-3

Most likely, yes. 20% of all kids rock their bodies and 6% bang their heads. These behaviors start around six months of age and continue through toddlerhood. Believe it or not, kids find these repetitive movements soothing. And we promise, in most cases, toddlers won't bang their heads hard enough to do any permanent damage. (If they do, they really might have a psychiatric disorder and should be evaluated by a professional!)

Body rockers usually start moving as they are falling asleep or waking up. They also do it to music. Most kids stop doing this by age three or so, but a few will continue to do it into their teens.[1]

Q. My child has specific rituals for playing with items, getting ready for bed, etc. If we deviate from these rituals, he gets very upset. Is this normal?

Ages 1-4

Kids thrive on situations where they are in control. They also like things to be predictable—it gives them confidence in what they are doing. With that said, a child may like his trains lined up a certain way and get very upset if they are moved. Or a child may throw a fit if you brush his teeth before putting on his pajamas. These are normal behaviors.

There are extreme obsessions or compulsions, however, which do deserve to be checked out. Here are some red flags:

♦ *Rituals interfere with activities of daily living* (child prefers lining up trains to eating or interacting with humans).
♦ *Rituals that cause harm to the child or others.*
♦ *Infinite number of rituals.*

Q. My child still has a pacifier. When is the right time to get rid of it?

Ages 1-3

Remember you (the parent) are in control of the pacifier. You can decide when it disappears. The good news: infants suck to soothe themselves, but toddlers have many more strategies. For more info on this, check out Chapter 12, Hygiene.

This is yet one more opportunity for a discipline moment. You are setting a limit on your child's behavior to promote a healthy lifestyle. Older kids who use pacifiers may have tooth alignment issues and are at greater risk of ear infections. They also tend to continue putting other items into their mouths instead of exploring them with their hands. Be strong and

NORMAL?

ODD, BUT NORMAL BEHAVIORS

We know some of these behaviors will disturb you, but they are nothing to worry about unless your child spends a substantial portion of his day only doing these things.[2]

Infant onset (0-1 year)

Sucking behavior	Thumb and finger-sucking
Lip sucking and lip biting	Toe-sucking
Foot kicking	Rocking and rolling
Body rocking	Head rolling
Head banging	Teeth grinding

Toddler onset (after 1 year of age)

Nail biting	Nose picking
Scratching/picking	

make the break. Your child will move on more quickly than you think he will—like in a day or two. Really.

Q. My child still sucks her thumb. Do I need to discourage this?

It depends on the age of the child. The bad news about thumb-suckers is that you have no control since you cannot take the thumb away. The vast majority of kids won't be sucking their thumbs in kindergarten. See an in-depth discussion of this issue in Chapter 12, Hygiene.

Q. My toddler bites her nails. What can I do about it?

Nail biting is a coping mechanism. Kids will do it when they are tired, threatened, or just plain bored. On the plus side—at least she isn't banging her head or eating carpet pile.

There are a few strategies to limit nail biting:

♦ *Offer a more positive way to reduce stress*—like a stress ball to squeeze. Or give your child a small swatch of satin fabric to keep in her pocket. In stressful moments, she can sneak her hand into her pocket to get her fix.

♦ *Make the child count to ten* before she can bite. It breaks the cycle.

♦ *Allow nail biting to only occur in the child's room.* She must stop her activity and take a break in her room if she needs to bite.

♦ *Do a manicure.* Girls respond well to this one. The only way to keep the pretty polish on is to stop biting.

♦ *Try a polish to stop the biting.* Bitter nail polish formulas are sold in drug stores and work the same way as the thumb-sucking remedies we discuss in Chapter 12, Hygiene.

Is this normal?

Q. My child plays with his genitals—constantly. Is this normal?

Ages 1-4

It's quite normal for a child to explore his or her own body. And boys are NOT the only ones who do it. I had a female patient who used to "ride" the highchairs at restaurants. Needless to say, the family didn't eat out much!

Preferably, body exploration happens in the privacy of your own home and not out in public. A non-judgmental way to approach this: tell your child that you know it feels good to touch his body, but it is something he can do in his own room—it's not okay to do it in public or in your living room.

Helpful Hint: **Naming embarrassing body parts**
Parents come up with cute words for their children's genitals because they themselves are uncomfortable saying the anatomically correct words. Let's face it folks, we all either have a penis or a vagina. And our kids are fascinated with these areas.

While it is acceptable to say "private parts" or "genitals," we also think your child deserves to know the real names of them. And eventually, you will have to tell them what all those parts do (that discussion is beyond the scope of this book, phew!). For your toddler or preschooler, explanations can be given out on a need to know basis.

Here is a true story. My daughter, who was four at the time, was examining her genitals in the bathtub one night. She said, "Mommy? My urethra is where the pee-pee comes out and my anus is where the poop comes out. But my vagina is only used when the baby comes out?" I said, "That's right. Just for when the baby comes out." Like I said—need to know basis.

P.S. While you are having these conversations, it's a good opportunity to remind your child that these areas are private. No one else should be seeing or touching them besides Mom, Dad, or the doctor. For more information on when your child should stop seeing *your* private parts, see Chapter 12, Hygiene.

Q. My daughter demands to pick out her own clothing. She wants to wear crazy combinations or her dress-up clothes. Should I allow her out of the house dressed like this?

Ages 2-4

Yes. It's called independence and self-expression. As we discussed in Chapter 2, Discipline, this is a classic case of picking your battles. Bottom line: it won't hurt your child if her shirt doesn't match her pants.

Q. My daughter has an imaginary friend who joins her everywhere she goes. Is this normal?

Ages 2-4

Yes.
An imaginary friend is someone a child can talk to who never disagrees and always listens. Think about what your child hears everyday—"Don't touch that," "Not now, sweetie," "We're not buying that." You get the idea. When a child doesn't get his way for the twentieth time, he may want to boss someone else around.

Sometimes, the child is the good Dr. Jekyll, and the imaginary friend is Mr.

Hyde. It lets the child play out bad behavior without consequence. But occasionally, a child will do something bad and use the friend as a scapegoat.

Kids may also use imaginary friends to practice social situations before doing something with a live playmate.

It is normal for kids to have imaginary friends. They eventually move on from this phase on their own. If you have imaginary friends as an adult, medical attention is suggested!

Q. My child gets carried away with pretend play. Normal?

I had a patient who pretended she was a kitten. She came into the office on numerous occasions wearing her cat ears headband and meowing. At every appointment, her mother asked me if this was normal behavior, and I reassured her that it was. After about a year, the toddler came to visit without the ears on. I asked her if she was still a kitten and her mother said, with a sigh of relief, "We've moved on."

In my practice as a pediatrician, I have also had guest appearances by Spiderman, a lion, and several firefighters.

As a parent, I would only be worried about pretend play if your child is incapable of having moments of being him/herself . . . or suddenly has a case of hairballs.

Q. My son likes to paint his fingernails. Is it okay?

It's called androgynous play–when girls play with trucks and boys play with dolls. Does this type of play confuse a child? No, but this behavior almost always drives dads nuts. Fathers, much more than mothers, will offer sex-appropriate toys to their child in infancy and react in a negative way when their preschooler plays with gender specific toys of the opposite gender.[3] But is this play abnormal? No. So, a quick memo to Dad: chill out.

Q. My three year old has started lying to me. Is this normal?

Yes. Don't be shocked when your child starts fibbing. He has his reasons. For starters, kids want to avoid punishment and embarrassment at all costs. They also learn early in life what earns praise from adults . . . and giving parents what they want sometimes involves lying!

Tall tales also count as lying. Kids have wonderful imaginations. And remember their intellectual development will not help them sort out fantasy from reality until after age five or so. Until then, a child's wishes or fantasies may be revealed in the stories they tell.

If your child is habitually lying, try to discuss the issue of truth and lies without making the child feel guilty about it. For more tips, see Chapter 2, Discipline.

Tears and Fears

Q. My toddler gets extremely anxious about certain activities. Is this normal? What should I do about it?

Kids are afraid of things they cannot control—such as going to the doctor or getting their haircut. Why? Someone else is calling the shots . . . and they don't know what to expect. This fear extends to loud noises, animals, the dark and so on. Remember, fantasy and reality blur together for a young child (read the section about "how your child learns" in Chapter 3 Milestones).

You must respect the fear, even if it seems irrational. Fears don't go away just because *you* don't think your child needs to worry. Your child will still worry and then not share his feelings with you. Instead, he will internalize the fear and you may see unwanted consequences of this, such as sleep disruption or avoidance of pleasurable activities.

Take-home tips:

1. **Prepare your child for situations when you can**. "I have to turn on the vacuum now."
2. **Empower your child.** Whip up a spray bottle of Monster Be-Gone (really, just water).
3. **Face fears**. Take your child to the petting zoo or pet store to get used to animals.

Q. My child is afraid of birthday parties. Should we cancel the festivities for her?

No, just keep it simple and small. You don't have to invite the entire neighborhood. Loud music, lots of kids running around, and being the center of attention can be overwhelming to a young child.

Think of the party from your child's perspective. You are used to comfortable, predictable routines. Without warning, you enter a tribal ceremony. Many strangers gather around you, touch you, and chant around you. You are forced to sit in front of something with fire on top of it. For all you know, you might be the main course.

Some tips: Limit the number of guests, and follow your child's cues for when he has had enough.

P.S. The same rules apply for Halloween. People in costume can be very scary to little ones. When I was three, I panicked when I saw my mother dressed in cap and gown for a graduation ceremony. Just imagine what a witch looks like to a little one.

Q. My son still cries about everything. Is this okay?

My husband still cries every time he watches *Field of Dreams*. Yes, it's okay for a child of either sex to cry to express his or her feelings. By the time your child is five or six, he'll start pulling it together and won't cry over spilled milk. Some of this is maturational and some of it is peer pressure.

If you think your child is overly emotional, check in with your doctor.

Q. As a Dad, my son and I used to have a wonderful relationship. Now he only wants to hang out with Mom and I might as well not exist. What happened?

We couldn't do a child development chapter and leave out Dr. Freud. Little boys fall in love with their mommies and little girls fall in love with their daddies. Freud coined these concepts the Oedipus Complex and the Electra Complex. For those of you who forgot your Greek mythology, Oedipus fell in love with his mother and killed his father. Don't worry, your son won't be coming at you with a butter knife.

Preschoolers enter a love affair with the parent of the opposite sex for a while as they are sorting out their sex roles. Eventually, kids repress these feelings and begin to identify with the parent of the same sex.

Bottom line: be patient. Don't assume your child has rejected you because of these feelings.

Special situations

Q. Our toddler's behavior has changed dramatically since we brought our newborn home from the hospital. Is this normal and how long will we have to endure it?

Think about it this way. If you lived in the limelight and suddenly had to share it, you would be upset too.

I view this behavior much like the five stages of grieving when someone loses a loved one. That loved one, in this situation, is the old relationship with Mom and Dad. For a toddler version of these stages, see below.

We can tell you not to feel guilty, but we know you won't listen to us. Your child will forgive you, and, someday, thank you for bringing a new friend for him into the world.

FYI: it usually takes about six to eight weeks for a child to reach a point of acceptance.[4]

Stage 1: Denial
That baby is nice, but can we give her back to the hospital now? This isn't really happening, right?

Stage 2: Anger
How dare you bring this baby home! This is all your fault, Mom and Dad! Tantrum, tantrum, tantrum. Excuse my while I go demolish my room.

Stage 3: Bargaining
If I act really nice, can the baby go live with Grandma? See what I can do? Please pay attention to me.

Stage 4: Depression
I am so sad that Mommy and Daddy brought this baby home. I just want to play alone in my room.

Stage 5: Acceptance
Okay, this baby isn't so bad. She sleeps a lot and she is kind of cute when I can get her to smile at me. Maybe I will forgive Mom and Dad for turning my world upside down.

See Chapter 2, Discipline for more discussion on having a second child.

Q. We just had a death in the family. How do I explain that to my toddler? And should I take her to the funeral?

Your approach to the situation depends on your child's level of understanding and her relationship with the person who has passed away.

No one ever likes having discussions about death, but you should talk to your child about it—hopefully before you are faced with a family member who has died. Other things die that are a part of a child's world—like flowers, bugs, pet goldfish. Take advantage of these times to bring up the topic.

Remember where preschoolers are developmentally; they are not even concrete in their thinking yet. They can have some irrational concerns and fears about death. Help relieve those fears by talking about death in ways they will understand.

Deciding whether your toddler should attend a funeral is never an easy call. It really depends on the child. Sometimes the visual is too traumatic for the child. Sometimes it helps provide closure. If you do decide to bring your child, be sure to explain what will happen BEFORE you get there.

Here are some tips for dealing with the death of a loved one:[5]

- ◆ *Don't say death is "going to sleep."* Your child won't ever want to sleep again!
- ◆ *Do explain that not everyone who is sick will die.*
- ◆ *Do explain that the child had nothing to do with the person's death.* Preschoolers often think they did something wrong to cause the event.
- ◆ *Don't give a toddler too many details.*
- ◆ *Do let them grieve.* Let the child keep a special item to remember the loved one.
- ◆ *Don't hide your grief.* It's okay to let your child see you cry.
- ◆ *Do stick to your child's routine as much as possible.* Travel and funeral arrangements can make it difficult, but kids are more comfortable when they follow their schedules.

Here are a few good books to read to your child about death:

The Tenth Good Thing About Barney (Viorst, Judith)
Nana Upstairs and Downstairs (DePaola, Tommy)
The Jester Has Lost His Jingle (Saltzman, David)
When Dinosaurs Die (Brown, Marc and Laurie)

Coming up next: let's talk play and preschool. How can you stimulate your toddler's development? And what is the difference between daycare and preschool? We'll discuss this and more next.

DR B'S OPINION: FEARS

I completely relate to kids being afraid of things they cannot control. I absolutely hate turbulence when I fly. I never liked scary rides at the amusement park, and I really don't enjoy the feeling of having my stomach in my mouth, especially when I don't expect it. So, when your child fears a new activity, what should you do? The key advice: give your toddler as much notice as possible.

On a recent flight, the pilot came on to the overhead speaker and said, "Folks, we are about to go through a choppy patch right about…..now (just as the plane dropped)." Although I still had white knuckles holding on the armrests, I felt much better about it. Really.

PLAY & PRESCHOOL

Chapter 5

"You can lead a boy to college but you can't make him think."
~ Elbert Hubbard

To a toddler, play is not trivial. It's hard work! Children learn how to fine tune their skills and figure out the world through play. So, making play time a priority gives your child many opportunities to learn. Of course, that doesn't mean spending an amount equivalent to Peru's GDP on fancy "developmental" toys. It means that you should give your child time, space, and items that will encourage him to play.

We'll guide you through this maze with some practical suggestions. First, we'll discuss HOW your toddler plays at different ages and explore the world of toys, with specific suggestions and advice. You'll get help on how to find safe, un-leaded toys. Then, we'll go over how you can make the most of playtime with your toddler. Next, we'll discuss language and your toddler, including a recommended reading list of the best books for tots. Finally, we'll discuss enrichment programs, preschools and other activities like play classes. How do you best prepare a child for preschool? What do you look for in a preschool to begin with? We'll answer these questions along with advice on music lessons, computer use and more.

Stimulating Your Toddler's Development

Play

Q. Do children play differently at different ages?

Yes. And it's helpful for you to understand these stages so you can encourage your child to learn through his play. Here's how it breaks down:

◆ *12-18 month old:* A young toddler explores through her senses and manipulates items with her hands. She experiments with how one action produces another (such as, dumping out all the toys in a bucket just to see how they fall). Your house is her playground as she uses her new ability to walk, run, and roam. Her play is loose and unstructured, but she'll look to an adult for guidance. She needs help because she is just beginning to fine-tune her eye-hand coordination, large muscle skills, and finger control.

◆ *18-24 month old:* As large and small muscle skills improve, a toddler places items where he wants them to go and uses trial and error to problem solve (example: mastering a simple wooden puzzle with knobs). He'll run and climb. He pretends more and acts out activities he sees grown-ups doing. He plays by himself, or with an adult. But he won't play with other children yet.

◆ *Two years old.* A two-year old loves to pretend. She acts out a story or situation with toys or props (such as pushing race cars or taking a baby doll for stroll). Adults help by taking a role or providing the play-by-play of the event. Her improved small muscle skills let her manipulate objects, draw and paint. She can start to build things. A two-year old plays next to another child and takes note of what that child is doing. However, two-year olds don't play together.

◆ *Three years old.* A three-year old has better small muscle skills. This, and his improved reasoning skills let him do some pretty sophisticated play. He may sequence or order items, string beads, or figure out a more complex puzzle. He is more coordinated now, which means he will enjoy more activities on the playground. And three-year olds like to play together (finally, you can take a break from being your child's only playmate!).

◆ *Four years old.* A four-year old actively plays with other kids—and much of that is imaginative play. Each child has a role to play in make-believe scenarios. He'll love the playground and early sports games because he has good large muscle skills and decent coordination. A four-year old *might* have terrific small muscle skills and can begin writing letters and cutting with scissors. Others are still working on those skills.

DON'T BE A HELICOPTER PARENT

Helicopter parent. n. *The term used to describe a parent who hovers over her child.*

A study done at Penn State University[1] showed that parents who were over-involved with their kids not only drove their kids nuts but also themselves! These parents based their self-worth on their children's successes. While it's normal to feel badly when your child fails at something, it's not normal to let it take over your life.

Providing your child with developmentally stimulating experiences is one thing—just don't go overboard. Learn how to let go and watch your child fly.

Q. What are some good toys or activities for my child, based on his age?

Before we get to specifics, remember this key piece of advice: you don't have to buy all of this stuff to win parent-of-the-year award. Yes, we've seen parents that have outfitted their house with every expensive developmental toy they can find online. And we understand their motivation—but no, you don't have to spend a fortune turning your living room into a preschool classroom.

Our suggestions are tried-and-true sources of fun and learning, and have been classics for several generations of kids (some may bring back memories of your own childhood!).

Here are the general types of play and their corresponding toys. You may own several of these items already. If you are purchasing items, look for toys that are multi-functional, with numerous ways to play.

THE VALUE OF MAKE-BELIEVE

Do you remember playing dress up or cops and robbers as a little kid? Of course, you do. Kids love to pretend, if given the opportunity. Why the heck do kids do this? And why is it important that we give them the opportunity?

Kids like to pretend because it gives them the chance to work out situations they experience in real life. This is part of normal development. And as you will see in the next chapter, it's a red flag if a child *doesn't* pretend, imitate, or have "symbolic" play.

Psychologists think pretend play helps kids develop critical thinking skills and something called "self-regulation." A self-regulated child controls his behavior and emotion. Self-regulated kids not only do better in school, with lower dropout rates, but they succeed on all levels of development.

Some researchers feel that the changes in the way children have played over the past 60 years has taken its toll on children's emotional and intellectual development. As kids play more with structured toys and less with just their imaginations, self-regulation has declined. Translation: lots of expensive "developmental" toys aren't necessary a good thing.

When kids play independently and pretend, they make up their own rules and follow them. They talk to themselves about what they are doing. That inner voice equates to self-regulation. As a child gets older, he has more elaborate pretend play with other kids. He has to act out his role, remember what the other actors are doing, and improvise on the plot twists. That requires self-control.

As one developmental researcher, Dr. Adele Diamond, points out, we might have fewer kids diagnosed with ADHD if more kids learned self-regulation as toddlers and preschoolers.

The message: just let your kid keep on pretending…and give him the free time to do it.[2]

PLAY

DO IT YOURSELF: RECIPES FOR SENSORY ACTIVITIES

Nope, you don't have to spend a fortune on toys and other toddler play activities. Here are recipes for do-it-yourself fun:

Slime[3]

2 cups white glue
2 cups water
liquid food coloring
1 tsp borax (powdered laundry starch)

1. Pour glue into mixing bowl. Slowly add one and a half cups of water and several drops of food coloring.
2. In separate bowl, dissolve borax in half cup of water.
3. Add borax to glue mixture. Knead for 10 minutes until the slime separates between fingers.
4. Refrigerate overnight to let slime firm up before use.
5. Knead slime to soften before each use.
Lifespan: two weeks, stored in airtight container.

Play dough

2 cups flour
2 cups water
1 cup salt
2 Tbsp cooking oil
4 tsp cream of tartar
liquid food coloring

1. Mix ingredients in heavy pan.
2. Cook over moderate heat for three minutes, stirring constantly.
3. Remove from heat, but continue to stir until dough gets stiff.
4. Cool on waxed paper.
5. Add food coloring.
Lifespan: several weeks, stored in sealed plastic bags in refrigerator.

Silly Putty

1 cup white glue
1 and 1/2 cups liquid laundry starch

1. Add glue to the starch.
2. Stir and the glue will congeal.
3. Drain off excess liquid.
4. Store in airtight container in refrigerator.

Bubbles[4]

1/4 cup liquid detergent (Joy works best)
1 1/4 cup water
1/4 cup glycerine (found in pharmacy section of grocery store)

Mix together to make rainbow hued bubbles.

Of course, as with any toy purchase, safety is a key concern. For example, if your child is still putting everything in his mouth, he's probably not
ready to play with finger-paint or small objects that can be choking hazards. (We have toy safety tips later in this chapter).

◆ *Sensory play:* These are activities that encourage creativity and
use the five senses. Examples: water or sand in a dish tub with
measuring cups, plastic cups, a sieve, or beach shovels. We have
recipes to make your own play dough, silly putty, and slime earlier in this chapter.

◆ *Manipulatives:* These improve finger-muscle and eye-hand
coordination. Examples: stringing wooden beads on yarn, shape
sorters, puzzles, building blocks.

◆ *Books:* Books encourage vocabulary and early reading skills.
(Our favorite reading list is found later in this chapter.)

◆ *Art:* Arts and crafts projects stimulate creativity, small muscle
groups, eye-hand coordination, and self-expression. Examples:
finger paint, sidewalk chalk, non-toxic crayons. Tip: offer large
blank sheets of paper to draw on (not coloring books). It reduces
frustration and encourages creativity.

◆ *Dramatic play (pretend play):* Pretending helps with social skills,
social experimentation, and creativity. Examples: kitchen set (old
pots, pans, wooden spoons), doctor kit, dolls, dress up clothes
(old scarves, chunky jewelry, hats, ties, shirts, sunglasses).

◆ *Floor play:* Designate an area in your home for your child to
spread out and play. This area can be a perfect place for building roads and cities with large wooden blocks, train tracks, or
dancing to music on a rainy day.

◆ *Outdoor play:* The playground or backyard are ideal locations to
work on large muscle groups (arms and legs) and burn off energy!
Examples: large balls for throwing, kicking, and bouncing.

Specific suggestions for play by age

Fun for a 12 month old:
◆ Sensory play: rattles, free standing musical table, nursery rhymes
CD's and books.
◆ Manipulatives: nesting cups, stacking rings, pots and pans/wood-
en spoon, plastic containers.
◆ Books: *Pat the Bunny* and other board books (they have a dual
role as teething toys).
◆ Art: thumbprint art.
◆ Floor play: playing catch (rolling a beach ball).
◆ Other games: play peek-a-boo, hide and seek, "This Little Piggy
Went to Market."

Fun for a 15 month old:
◆ Sensory play: bathtub toys while bathing or used in a water-filled
basin, maracas, tambourine, bells.

PLAY

? ?

- Manipulatives: shape sorter, soft building blocks.
- Books: *Goodnight Moon, Barnyard Dance*.
- Art: stamping.
- Dramatic play: pretend phone, remote control.
- Floor play: Beach ball/Nerf ball and "basket" (trash can, laundry basket, or a small hoop), Toy lawn mower, toy shopping cart/ play food, toy stroller/crib and baby doll.
- Outdoor play: play tunnel.
- Other games: sing the body parts song: "Head, shoulders, knees, and toes."

Fun for an 18 month old:

- Sensory play: Sandbox (or sand table) with beach toys/shovel or with cups, measuring spoons, strainer, funnel.
- Manipulatives: Small nesting/stacking boxes, fabric activity books.
- Books: *Big Red Barn, Brown Bear Brown Bear, First Words* photo board books.
- Art: Crayons, fingerpaint.
- Dramatic play: Plates/utensils, picnic blanket, picnic basket, tea cups and teapot, Little People toysets (farm, garage, school bus), dollhouse (not the collector's kind).
- Floor play: Construction vehicles (dump truck, front loader, etc), emergency vehicles (police car, ambulance, fire truck).
- Outdoor play: Blowing bubbles—catching, popping, stomping them, sidewalk chalk, small slide with a climb up unit.
- Other games: fingerplays— "Itsy Bitsy Spider", Songs: "On our Way to Grandpa's Farm" or "Old McDonald", "Wheels on the Bus".

Fun for a 2 year old:

- Sensory play: Playdoh and rolling pins/cookie cutters, flash-light/shadow play.
- Manipulatives: Simple wooden puzzles with knobs, big Legos, Duplos.
- Books: *Barnyard Dance* (and any other rhyming books), *Very Hungry Caterpillar*.
- Art: Sponge painting, Dot Art paints.
- Dramatic play: Community helpers dress up (fire, police, doc-tor/nurse, mail carrier).
- Floor play: Mini sports sets: Basketball net, T-ball, golf, balloon volleyball, bean bag throw.
- Outdoor play: Scavenger hunt/nature walk (collect rocks, leaves, snails, pine cones), Big Wheel (or plastic tricycle).
- Other games: Letter and number magnets on the fridge, Play "I spy", "Red light, Green light."

Fun for a 3 year old:

- Sensory play: Flour in a plastic tub with cups, funnels, sifters, sing-a-long songs (personal favorites: Hap Palmer, Greg and Steve, Joe McDermott).
- Manipulatives: Stringing wooden beads/cooked tube pasta/fruit loops, Sorting with puff craft balls and muffin tins.

PLAY

◆ Books: *Chicka Chicka Boom Boom, Mama Do You Love Me?, It Looked Like Spilt Milk.*

◆ Art: Watercolor painting.

◆ Dramatic play: Puppets (bought or homemade), felt story boards/storytelling puppets, dress up.

◆ Floor play: Wooden train set, wooden block set.

◆ Outdoor play: Tricycle (and a helmet).

◆ Other games: matching games, sorting games.

Fun for a 4 year old:

◆ Sensory play: shaving cream, uncooked beans, or rice in a plastic tub with cups/spoons, musical instruments (xylophone, drums, triangle, rhythm sticks).

◆ Manipulatives: Simple cooking projects (making pizza, bread), cutting coupons or magazine clippings (modified I Spy), smaller Legos, Lincoln Logs, building sets.

◆ Books: *Sheep in a Jeep, Jamberry, Five Little Monkeys, Old Woman Who Swallowed a Fly.*

◆ Art: Etch-a-Sketch or doodling pad, painting easel.

◆ Dramatic play: Dress up characters (ballerina, super hero, chef, pilot, cowboy).

◆ Outdoor play: Gardening, hopscotch, small swing set, wiffle ball/T-ball, races with an obstacle course (sports cones).

◆ Other games: Counting games, Go Fish, Candy Land, Simon Says, Bingo.

Ideas for your dress up/props box

◆ Doctor's office (patient chart, eye chart, stethoscope, reflex hammer, mini-flashlight).

◆ Pet Vet (stuffed animal, patient chart, stethoscope, reflex hammer, mini-flashlight).

◆ Restaurant (pots, pans, plates, utensils, menus, order pad, pretend money, chef's hat, apron).

◆ Grocery Store (plastic foods, empty cereal boxes, shopping cart, cash register, pretend money).

◆ Tea party/picnic (teapot, teacups, napkins, plates, utensils, pretend food, blanket, basket).

◆ School-teacher/students (books, chalkboard, paper, pencils, stuffed animals for students).

◆ Construction site (pretend tools, tool belt, hard hats, orange cones, safety tape, construction vehicles).

Helpful Hint: Teacher supply stores

Look for teacher supply stores in your community for a larger selection of products than your local toy store. Lakeshore Learning Materials (web: lakeshorelearning.com) is one popular haunt among teachers that also sells products online. While you probably won't find any bargains at these stores, you will find anything and everything you are looking for!

Insider Tip: Words and Music
Can't remember some of those golden oldie kid classics that you loved? Here is a free website to help you out: theteachersguide. com/childrenssongsatog.htm. Voice lessons are not included.

Q. How do I play with my child?

Parents often ask this question. Here is the simple answer: you just do it. We know how you feel. You may be a defense attorney who is at home in a courtroom battle, but you get the jitters having a tea party with your two year old. It's really not that hard, though. Here are some tips for the play-challenged parent:[5]

◆ **Have fun**. Even if you are having tea with the queen (that is, your daughter), don't look like a stiff. Kids can tell when parents aren't having fun.

◆ **Kids rule.** The idea of play is for your child to use his brain. Let him come up with the ideas for how to draw something or make a puzzle piece fit. It's your job to be the assistant if he gets stuck. If your child is getting frustrated, help him troubleshoot. But let him come up with the solution.

◆ **Know when to stop.** Playing is hard work. Move on to other activities before your child wigs out.

And when you do get on the floor to play, make sure your head is in the game. Here are a few reasons why you can't fake it:

1 **SELF-ESTEEM.** Kids are really savvy. They figure out quickly that their parent "isn't into it." While you cannot always be available to be a playmate, showing that you are interested goes a long way to supporting your child's self esteem and confidence in social situations. Just think about how you'd feel if your spouse had no interest in what you did with your time!

2 **PROBLEM SOLVING.** Kids do need to learn how to problem solve and find creative strategies to make toys work or make something fun to play with, but sometimes they need a little nudge or some guidance. Racing through a project or just telling your child the answer is not a learning experience for him.

3 **ROLE MODEL.** Your kids are watching you—always watching. If you rush through something just to complete the task, what have you taught them? If you take pleasure in the process, so will they.

Reality Check: Teaching moments
An interesting study looked at the effects of toddlers (ages 18-30 months) with autism and parents who worked with them using "play-based" learning techniques. Half of the children received therapy by professionals. The other group had therapy with professionals and their parents, who learned how to use specific teaching strategies at home. The professional-only group had a seven point increase in IQ

points two years later. The group of kids who had both professionals and trained parents working with them saw a 17.6 point increase in IQ points.[6]

While this study specifically addressed children with autism and parents who were taught how to play with their kids, consider the broader implications. You may think that sitting down with your child to have a tea party or build a Lego tower is just playtime. But to a child it is an important moment to learn social skills, communication skills, eye-hand coordination, spatial relationships, counting, and ordering. You can help guide your child's play to make him consider these things. Those are called teaching moments, and they are critical for every child.

Q. My toddler always wants to play with me. Is it okay for her to play alone every once in a while?

Yes. There is great value in playing independently. Kids have to figure things out on their own and learn how to entertain themselves. And it provides valuable time to use their imagination and creativity.

Remember when our parents said, "Go play outside"? We did. Somehow we were able to figure out something to do to entertain ourselves.

Kids today seem to have less opportunity to play independently. Obviously, there are several factors at work here. First, there is myriad of kiddie entertainment available today that wasn't around in 1979. Second, there is the perception that society is more dangerous today than it was "back then." Our parents never worried that someone would abduct us from the front yard.

Despite all these reasons and excuses, our point here is this: young children are not learning how to play independently. This is an important skill for problem solving and confidence building. Make sure to give your child some time everyday to play alone.

Language

Q. How can I teach my child to communicate with me?

Before your toddler has an extensive vocabulary, it can be frustrating for everyone to communicate. Here are some practical tips:

1. **Talk on her level (eye to eye)**. Bend your knees and look into each other's faces. That's her cue to listen. If you are speaking over her head physically, you are probably speaking over her head literally, too.

2. **Talk on her level (age appropriately)**. Make your sentences shorter, or even just use single words to describe things. For instance, instead of saying, "Honey do you want the cup?", say, "Cup?" Some experts even suggest saying the child's name before the word to get the child's attention (e.g. "Susie's cup?").

3. **Speak in the present tense.** Kids need to be able to follow along. If you have already done something and then start talking about it, your child will have no visual aid to understand what you are referring to.

4. **Think out loud.** Yes, it feels silly having a monologue at the grocery store or at a restaurant, but it helps your child learn words. Your child will learn more vocabulary words in the produce section than by sitting down with a set of flash cards.

5. **Peat and Repeat.** Use the same word several times in a row when you show an item to your child.

6. **Play dumb.** Some kids are hesitant to use their words. They have mastered the point and grunt and get their demands met. Thus, they lack motivation to resort to speaking. If you think your child is capable, pretend you don't understand what your child is pointing to and see if he speaks up!

Q. Do you think sign language is beneficial?

Imagine being a toddler. It's like living in a foreign country and just trying to find out where the bathroom is—everyday. It's easy to understand why kids get frustrated and have tantrums.

Sign language is a very trendy approach to solving this age-old problem.

Children are capable of understanding language and communicating non-verbally long before they have the ability to speak. So, teaching a toddler hand gestures to communicate makes sense. Is there scientific proof that signing is beneficial? Yes. One study found that infants and toddlers

THE BEST BOOKS FOR TODDLERS

As a first-time parent, you know you need books for your toddler. But where do you start? Here are our top picks. This list is organized with the easiest books first, in order to encourage beginning readers.[7]

Read-to-me books
Big Red Barn, Goodnight Moon, Runaway Bunny (Brown, Margaret)
Barnyard Dance, Moo Baa, La La (Boynton, Sandra)
1,2,3 to the Zoo, The Very Hungry Caterpillar (Carle, Eric)
Jamberry (Degan, Bruce)

Alphabet books
26 Letters and 99 Cents (Hoban, Tana)
Chicka Chicka Boom Boom (Martin, Bill)
Alligators All Around (Sendak, Maurice)

Counting books
Five Little Monkeys Jumping on the Bed (Christelow, Eileen)
Arlene Alda's 1 2 3: What Do You See? (Alda, Arlene)
26 Letters and 99 Cents (Hoban, Tana)
Rain Dance (Appelt, Kathi)

Labeling books*
*Refers to easy vocabulary word accompanied by pictures
Richard Scarry's Best Little Word Book (Scarry, Richard)
Richard Scarry's Just Right Word Book (Scarry, Richard)

who were "sign talkers" spoke earlier and performed slightly better on IQ tests at age eight than their non-signing peers.[8]

But let's talk about the real world here: even if you make an intensive effort to teach your baby to sign, the average toddler will learn only a few words. However, sitting down with your child to learn any new skill has its merits, so we won't be too critical when it comes to baby sign language. For kids who truly have *expressive* language delays, however, sign language is an extremely useful way to communicate.

If you choose to teach your child sign language, you can create the hand gestures on your own—you don't need to buy a book. Formal programs which use ASL (American Sign Language) are really only helpful if you plan on your child learning sign language as a second language.

If you choose not to teach your child sign language, don't fret too much. Regardless of race, sex, or nationality, most kids master the universal "point and grunt" skill to express themselves before they can speak.

Q. Should I teach my child a foreign language? I hear that kids learn a lot better than adults.

An article in *Newsweek* several years ago reported that kids who learn a second language before age ten speak more fluently than those who learn when they are older (like in high school). Couple that fact with the news that kids who have at

Books with few words
　　Hop On Pop, Green Eggs and Ham (Seuss, Dr.)
　　Brown Bear, Brown Bear, What Do You See? (Martin, Bill)
*Wordless books**
　　* Books that contain pictures only. Children create their own story.
　　Good Dog, Carl (Day, Alexandra)
　　The Snowman (Briggs, Raymond)
Easy readers
　　Madeline (Bemelmans, Ludwig)
　　Are You My Mother? (Eastman, PD)
　　Go, Dog, Go (Eastman, PD)
　　Danny and the Dinosaur (Hoff, Syd)
　　The Carrot Seed (Krauss, Ruth)
　　If You Give A Moose A Muffin (Numeroff, Laura)
Must Have Classics
　　The Snowy Day (Keats, Ezra Jack)
　　Make Way for Ducklings (McCloskey, Robert)
　　The Rainbow Fish (Pfister, Marcus)
　　Curious George (Rey, H.A.)
　　Where the Wild Things Are (Sendak, Maurice)
　　Cat in the Hat (Seuss, Dr.)
　　The Giving Tree (Silverstein, Shel)
　　Caps for Sale (Slobodkina, Esphyr)

least four years of foreign language education score better on the verbal portion of the SAT[9] . . . that makes every parent want to run out and buy the deluxe Swahili For Toddlers DVD collection.

While those reports are interesting, we urge parents not to get carried away with this. Yes, some schools and even preschools now offer foreign language in their curriculums. If it is something that appeals to you, check it out. But don't feel guilty if your child hasn't mastered three romance languages by age ten.

Q. Can I teach my child how to read?

You set the stage, and your child does the rest. How? Reading to your child on a daily basis makes books a constant part of her life. Reading time is a chance to bond and promote language development simultaneously. When your child is interested and ready, she will learn to read on her own.

One of the most critical pre-reading skills is understanding how single letters or letter combinations make certain sounds (the $10 term here is "phonemic awareness"). Next, kids memorize certain words that they see all the time (like "and" or "the")—those are called sight words. Here's how kids put it all together: they decipher words by breaking down sounds and recognize familiar words by sight.

The key to success? Having fun. Don't push it. Your child does not need to know how to read when he starts kindergarten.

Here are some easy things to do to encourage reading:

◆ *Read to your child every day.* Repetition is the key.
◆ *Label your child's possessions* (that is, write "blocks," "Legos," "dolls" on storage boxes)
◆ *Have your preschooler keep a diary.* He can sound out words and write them the way that they sound.
◆ *Play "I Spy" with road and store signs.*

Reality Check: Toy Safety

Toys are meant to be fun. Yet sadly, there are over 200,000 toy-related emergency room visits and ten deaths per year in the U.S. Obviously, no parent wants her child to end up in the emergency room.

And who can forget 2007, when just about every time you turned on the TV, another massive toy recall was announced. Lead and magnets were two main culprits of toy recalls, but many parents focused their ire on China, which makes about 80% of all toys sold today.

So, how can you tell if a toy is safe? Do we only need to worry about choking hazards and lead exposure? Is there anything else dangerous lurking in our kids' toys? Doesn't the government regulate these items to make sure they can't harm children?

We'll answer these questions later in this section, but let's take a second to look at what the government is (or is not) doing with toy safety.

Unfortunately, just because a toy is on the market does NOT mean it has been safety tested or even meets federal safety standards. Yes, the federal government has toy safety rules (for example, all toys with small parts must be labeled as "not appropriate for children under age three"). But that doesn't mean unsafe toys are kept off store shelves—witness the large number of toy recalls each year. With only a handful of staff devoted to toy testing, it's no surprise the Consumer Product Safety Commission (CPSC) has failed to adequately do its job.

So the take-home message is EDUCATE yourself on toy dangers. And if you purchase toys online, know that only one-third of online retailers display toy safety warnings such as choking hazards. The Consumer Product Safety Commission does not require online retailers to provide this info.

Since most toys are purchased during the winter holiday season, here's a good way to remember how to weed out dangerous toys for your toddler: ELF STEW.

E **ELECTRICAL TOYS.** These toys can cause electrical shocks or burns. Opt for a battery-powered toy instead.

L **LOUD NOISES.** Some toys will be "intended for outdoor use only." This is the secret code that means *this toy is REALLY LOUD*. Prolonged exposure to sounds at 85 decibels or higher can cause hearing damage. Several toys on the market exceed 100 decibels when they are measured at close range. For example, kids play with toy pistols close to their ears—that can be a problem if they emit a loud noise.

F **FLYING OBJECTS.** These items may accidentally fly into a child's eye or head and cause injury.

S **SHARP EDGES.** Poorly made toys may have hard pieces of plastic or pins that stick out, which can cause cuts and abrasions.

T **TINY PARTS.** Young children swallow small toy pieces, creating a choking hazard, or may put them in other interesting body parts like the nose or ears. A good rule to follow: if the toy is smaller than the diameter of a toilet paper roll, it is too small to be in your toddler's house.

E **EMOTIONAL HAZARDS.** Violent videos or games can have a significant emotional impact on your child. Snow White's evil stepmother can be pretty darn scary to a young child, or even an adult!

W **WRONG TOY FOR THE AGE OF THE CHILD.** Even if your child is a prodigy, it's a good idea to follow the intended-age use for a product. Otherwise, you may be setting yourself up for potential injury.

And even if a toy seems safe, be sure to supervise your toddler while he is playing. Children find creative, unintended, and dangerous uses for toys. (Look at Chapter 19, First Aid for what to do when your toddler sticks a toy up his nose or in his ear!)

Red Flags: Lead & Toys

Now, let's talk lead. In 2007, there were at least 29 separate toy recalls due to lead contamination. Here is a brief Q&A on lead and toys:

Where is the lead coming from? Some recalled toys were painted with lead paint. Lead is also a plasticizer, so it's added to vinyl or plastic to make it softer. And then there's metal jewelry that may have a veneer of brass or nickel. Unfortunately, this jewelry sometimes contains lead, which

PLAY

? ?

is especially troubling if kids put it in their mouths. Over 175 million pieces of novelty jewelry were recalled in 2007 for lead contamination.

Where's the regulation? Well, the CPSC allows a very small percentage of lead (600 parts per million) by weight of the toy. But many recalled toys exceeded this limit despite the safety rules. And in the case of costume jewelry, products that are sold to adults (and then given to children) are not regulated by the CPSC at all.

How do kids get exposed to lead in toys? While some kids move on from their "oral phase" of exploring everything with their mouths after their first birthday, many kids do not. Toddlers are the highest risk group of children because they like to play by putting toys into their mouths. Teething also leads some toddlers to chew their toys. So kids who are putting lead-laden toys into their mouths (especially if the toy is chipped or cracked) are at risk. And just licking costume jewelry (or worse, eating it) can be a hazard.

So, what's a parent to do other than talk to her congressperson or volunteer to work at the CPSC? Here are some practical tips from Dr. Michael Shannon, the former co-director of the Pediatric Environmental Health Center at Children's Hospital, Boston[10] (along with a few tips of our own):

◆ *DO* buy brand-name only toys. Yes, we realize big companies like Mattel have had problems—but we still think they are a safer bet than off-brands for toys. Why? These brands have a huge stake in making sure they aren't linked to lead recalls.

◆ *DON'T* buy toys from discount or dollar stores. Most sell cheap imported toys that are NOT brand names—a red flag.

◆ *DON'T* buy used toys from resale shops or garage sales. They may be cracked or chipped already.

◆ *DON'T* buy costume jewelry for toddlers. If your daughter insists on being accessorized, buy her a nice hat and purse.

◆ *DON'T* buy toys with magnets. Toddlers have been hurt when magnets detach and are swallowed.

◆ *DO* consider buying toys from web sites like Amazon. Why? Amazon will send you an email notice if one of your toy purchases is recalled.

If you are worried that your child may have been exposed to lead toys, your doctor can do a simple blood test. Note: there is no actual "safe" level of lead exposure. Even low levels of lead may have subtle lifelong impacts on learning and development. If your child's blood lead level is elevated, identify and remove the source of lead—ask your doctor for help in this process. For more information on lead exposure, see Chapter 17, Diseases.

We will also discuss plastic toys and their potential chemical hazards in Chapter 18, The Environment & Your Toddler.

Media & Kids: TV, computer and more

Q. When can my child watch educational TV and DVD's?

The American Academy of Pediatrics says two years of age, and we agree with them.

Our kids are fortunate to live in a world that offers so many ways to learn. Educational television programs and DVD's can capture a child's attention and actually teach them something.

However, television is a passive form of learning. You will always be able to teach your child more by working with him one on one. And your child's brain is more stimulated by figuring out what to do with some free time and say, a cardboard box. It's not okay to leave your child in front of the TV all day just because the channel is tuned to PBS.

A true but scary stat: today's children, by the age of 70, will have spent 7 years of their lives parked in front of the TV.[11]

The American Academy of Pediatrics (AAP) recommends holding off on "screen time" (TV, computer, DVD) until age two. We know that many educational videos target age groups younger than this. We also know that parents resort to popping in an educational DVD in hopes of getting in a shower or fixing dinner. And admit it, driving in the car is so much quieter if your child's eyes are glued to the tube.

Before you chastise the AAP for being out of touch with today's electronic world, let's take a moment to consider the rationale for their recommendations:

- ◆ *TV is not educational.* Under age two, kids don't learn from TV or DVDs—even when such content is labeled as "educational." Studies show that children have trouble deciphering the content of television programs compared to having a live person demonstrate the same information. One study aired a Teletubbies episode both forwards and backwards to 18 to 24 month olds. They laughed either way! While some kids over 18 months of age might "get it," most kids do not. So, do not be fooled by programs that claim to be educational or developmentally stimulating for toddlers. Entertaining yes, educational no.

- ◆ *TV is distracting.* Background television is distracting. Even if the TV is showing one of "your shows," young children play and interact less (perhaps because your attention is distracted from your child). Kids are learning language by listening to you, not Oprah. Having the TV on while your little one is around is a missed learning opportunity.

- ◆ *TV displaces playtime.* When kids are watching a television program or DVD, they are not doing something really important with their brains (such as problem-solving or using their own imaginations). And do not underestimate the importance of play. That is how kids fine-tune skills that they need in this world.

- ◆ *TV may be harmful.* Recent studies have looked at the impact of heavy television use on language development (kids aged eight to 16 months old). But we need more research in this area to prove a consistent adverse effect. While the jury is certainly still out, pediatricians tend to follow the precautionary principle. When in doubt, why not avoid a potential hazard?

Once your child enters the media world, there is no turning back. Set up some ground rules:

- ◆ *No TV or computer in your child's bedroom.* You want to monitor what and when your child is watching.[12] There's also a certain level of social isolation that occurs when family members retreat to their own media space. Also: falling asleep in front of the TV is associated with sleep problems.

♦ *Limit total daily screen time to two hours a day for kids over age two.* Screens include TV, computers, smart phones, and kiddie electronic toys (from V Tech toys, Nintendo DS, etc.).

♦ *Have your child watch pre-recorded programs (on a TiVo, for example) to skip over the commercials. Also: DVD's are commercial-free.*

♦ *Sit and watch with your child.* Discussing the content of the show makes the experience a teaching moment.

Q. When can my child start using a computer?

Our opinion: age two.

Toddlers as young as age two can master the mouse and learn letter and number recognition on the keyboard. And there are many educational software programs designed for toddlers and preschoolers. Obviously, you are in charge of monitoring the content of the programs. We don't want your preschooler bidding for used Elmos on eBay. Make it a house rule that surfing the net is allowed only with an adult nearby.

Just remember that computer time is a sedentary activity. The American Academy of Pediatrics recommends no more than two hours of TOTAL "screen time" (computers, DVD's, TV) for kids per day over the age of two.

Q. Can my toddler play with my iPhone or iPad?

It depends how much you trust your toddler with an expensive piece of equipment…and how desperate you are to entertain him. In my experience, once the cat is out of the bag, your child will be as addicted to it as you are.

Because it technically qualifies as a "screen," I suggest waiting until your child is two to use a smartphone or iPad. And by then perhaps he'll be more capable of sharing it with you!

THE ENTERTAINED GENERATION?

If you go to a family-oriented restaurant these days, it's hard NOT to find a zillion kids plugged into a portable game player, cellphone game or even a DVD. Call it the Entertained Generation—these kids think any free moment of time must be spent plugged into a gadget.

Call us crazy, but wouldn't kids be better off if they actually talked with parents, counted sugar packages or played eye-spy?

No matter where you are, here is a key point to remember: play-time is extremely important to your child's development. Active play requires your child to think, problem solve, and use his imagination. Your child can actively play with you, another child, or alone. Limit passive play that allows the toy (or electronic gizmo) to do the thinking for him. Your child doesn't always need to be entertained. His imagination is limitless. Resist the temptation to make your child another casualty of the Entertained Generation.

PLAY

Enrichment programs, preschools, other activities

Q. **My toddler goes crazy if she is cooped up in the house all day (and so do I). Any ideas?**

Get out of your house! Start networking with other families who have young children. Look for other parents in your neighborhood, religious community, local library, and community center. Join a playgroup or start one yourself. Seek out "Parent and Me" programs—you can find out about these gems from other parents or listings in local parenting magazines. There are a multitude of enrichment programs that provide you and your toddler relief from captivity.

Reality Check

The point of enrolling your child in an enrichment program is *not* to give him a competitive edge in kindergarten. The point is to get the two of you out of the house. Some programs are more enriching for the parents than for the child, and that's okay. You may find it a therapeutic place to share parenting challenges. These programs may also give you ideas for fun activities to replay at home. Even if you are not a stay-at-home parent, you may find enrichment programs a great way to spend time with your little one.

Here are some programs that are available nationally (and some, internationally).

♦ **Gymboree Play and Music** (web: gymboreeclasses.com) *True story: the first time I heard parents talking about Gymboree, I thought everyone was going shopping.* Classes are divided by age group and topic. Programs include: music, art, sports, and school skills.

♦ **Little Gym** (web: thelittlegym.com) Gymnastic classes focus on large motor skill development:
Here is a sampling of their classes:
Developmental Gymnastics for four months to 12 years old.
Dance for three to 12 years old.
Cheerleading for three to 12 years old.
Karate for four to 12 years old.
Sports skills for three to six years old.
An added bonus: They offer a Parents' Survival Night class for three to 12 year olds (parent drop off).

♦ **Kindermusik** (web: kindermusik.com) These programs promote language development and music appreciation. They encourage fine and gross motor skills by playing with musical instruments, dancing and sign language.
Here is a sampling of their classes:
Kindermusik Village for newborn to 18 months old.
Kindermusik Sign and Sing for 6 months to three years.
Kindermusik Our Time for 18 months to three years.
Imagine That, and Music Box programs for three to five years old.
Kindermusik Family Time for newborns and up.

Here are some other programs to check into:

- **Mother's Day Out.** These programs, usually sponsored by religious or community groups, offer half-day childcare for infants and toddlers once or twice a week. The environment is often a nurturing one, but with no structured curriculum. Contrary to what the name implies, parents drop off their child for only a couple of hours (not the entire day).

- **Mommy and Me.** (or "Parent and Me") These programs can be found at religious or community centers and offer structured activities with both the parent and the child present. These are often useful resources for ideas to try at home.

- **Playgroups.** Independently formed parent and child circles that get together on a semi-regular basis to play (and maintain sanity) in people's homes. Some groups get very sophisticated with the level of planned activities and field trips. Other groups are more casual. You may get invited to join an existing group; or be bold and start your own.

- **Storytime.** Check your local library or bookstore for periodic children's book readings. And while you are at the library, get your child his own library card. He will carry it proudly and, hopefully, be inspired to use it.

Reality Check: Playgroup etiquette.

It's a good idea to set up some ground rules so parents don't get offended and then feel uncomfortable speaking up. Here are a few tips:

1. **Don't bring a sick child to playgroup.**
2. **Don't bring an older sibling to a group** with little ones, unless everyone feels comfortable doing it.
3. **Don't feel compelled to serve a three-course meal** at your hosted event. The last thing you need to be doing is cooking something elaborate with a toddler under foot.

Q. Does my child need to be in preschool?

No, your child does not NEED to go to preschool. Will it help your toddler keep up with other kids when they start kindergarten? Yes.

Kids under the age of three do just fine having one-on-one time with a nurturing caring adult. They don't need to be around other children for developmental stimulation. If you choose to enroll your child earlier than age three, that's fine—just have reasonable expectations of what you want your child to get out of the program (such as, having new toys to play with or simply just getting out of your house).

Kids under three years of age do not play together. They do something called *parallel play*, meaning they play side by side and occasionally observe one another. When they do engage, it is often to vie for a coveted toy in a toddler version of "Survivor." Around the age of three, kids engage in *associative play*. Now is the time your toddler can develop into a socialized and civilized human being . . . really! Learning to share and respect others are reachable goals for this age group. And in an instructional setting like preschool, toddlers can also learn some important pre-academic skills such listening, paying attention, early phonics, and counting.

Will your child still have a shot at an Ivy League school if he doesn't go to preschool? You bet. You just make the most of your time together and capitalize on those teaching moments. No, this does not mean you drill him on flash cards or buy the entire Baby Einstein library. It means you get down on the floor with your child and take advantage of learning opportunities. For example, when your child is building a tower of blocks, count how many you can stack up before it falls.

Q. What is the difference between preschool and childcare?

There is a big difference, although the line between the two is starting to get a bit fuzzy.

Preschool programs have structured curriculums that include academic skills, learning through play, independent learning, and so on. Preschool, in its purest form, is a half-day program that meets two, three, or five days a week.

Childcare, on the other hand, is intended to provide a nurturing and developmentally stimulating environment for kids while a parent is unavailable (that is, usually working). The schedule of the day depends on the age group of the classroom but usually includes both structured and unstructured playtime. Because many childcare programs are full-day programs, meals and naps are uniformly scheduled for the group.

Of course, the real world isn't so black and white. In recent years, we've seen hybrids where preschools have added childcare services . . . and vice versa. Many preschools now offer extended hours similar to childcare programs and include lunch, nap, and free play (that is, very little structure). And many childcare programs are adding structured preschool curriculums to augment their services.

Q. Is there any benefit to sending my child to preschool?

Yes. There are numerous studies to show that children who attend preschool have long-term positive benefits. Below are just a few examples. Preschool grads are:

◆ More likely to finish high school and get a job.
◆ Less likely to need special education services or to repeat grades.

PRESCHOOL CURRICULUMS: LOOK BEYOND THE NAME

There are several types of preschool curriculums. Some are well-known, like Montessori. Even if you are familiar with a particular program, though, experts say you should still kick the tires of any school. Since schools implement curriculums in such a varied manner, "you cannot predict what the experience is for children by the name alone," according to Carol Armga M.S., Retired Director of the University of Texas at Austin Child and Family Lab School.

The take-home message: what's most important is to consider how a program individualizes the curriculum for the needs of each child.

◆ Less likely to get into trouble with the law or have unwanted pregnancies.

And you just wanted your child to learn how to share!

Reality Check: Universal pre-k education?

There is a movement afoot to offer pre-kindergarten education to all children. I know what you are thinking: our public schools are already under-funded, how can our tax dollars pay for another year of school for everyone? Looking at the long-term benefits, however, pre-kindergarten saves society money.

We think Libby Doggett, Ph.D., executive director of Pre-K Now said it best: "High quality, voluntary pre-k for all children not only improves the K-12 education system, it actually saves money too. When children enter kindergarten more prepared to succeed, schools and society at large benefit through costs savings associated with greater academic success."

Helpful Hints: Preparing for preschool

Children who have spent a majority of their lives with a parent around may have fears about leaving the nest. Here are some practical tips to help them fly.

Preparing your CHILD for preschool:

◆ *Make a dry run.* Show her where the school is. Take a tour if you can.
◆ *Meet and greet.* Set up a time for your child to meet her teacher and see the classroom.
◆ *Calm fears.* Ask her about any fears. Explain that other kids feel the same way and that's fine.
◆ *Be comforting.* Reassure your child she will have fun and believe it yourself.

Preparing YOURSELF for preschool:

◆ *Keep informed.* Touch base with your child's teacher regularly.
◆ *Get involved.* Participate in school functions.
◆ *Be positive.* Even if your child had a bad day, find one thing she enjoyed.
◆ *Have a routine.* Preschool helps regulate schedules for naps, bedtime, and wake up times.
◆ *Have a Plan B.* Prepare to have a child who cries or melts down at preschool. Ask your teacher if it is okay to bring a comfort

DR B'S OPINION:
PLAYGROUP ANXIETY

A playgroup can take on a life of its own. While discussions with other parents can be supportive and thought provoking, they may deteriorate into comparing children (and pediatricians' advice). If you leave the playgroup more anxious than relieved, find a new playgroup.

PLAY

object. (A good book to read to your toddler: *The Kissing Hand* by Audrey Penn, Child & Family Press). And find out if there is a safe place in the classroom for your child to go to if he needs to calm down.

◆ *Shots for tots.* Regulated preschools abide by state vaccination requirements for school entry. Make sure your child's shots are up to date. (See Chapter 15, Vaccines for more info).

Insider Tip: Easing the transition

"Programs of high quality provide for a period of transition at the start of school to introduce the child to the new environ-ment and adults. This might include the teacher doing a home visit, a school visit to allow the child and parents to freely explore togeth-er, as well as modified starting days where parents may stay with the child." *Carol Armga M.S, Retired Director of the University of Texas at Austin Child and Family Lab School*

Q. What should I look for in a preschool program?

The National Institute for Early Education Research (NIEER) has created a ten-item checklist to rate preschools across the country. Here is their list:

1. Check curriculum standards: Does the learning plan cover lan-guage, math, science, social skills, cognitive skills, health and phys-ical development? See more about curriculums in the box earlier.
2. Does the lead or head teacher have a bachelor's degree?
3. Does the lead teacher have special training in pre-kindergarten education?
4. Does the assistant teacher have an associate's degree?
5. Do the teachers attend at least 15 hours of continuing education classes annually?
6. Is the maximum class size 20 children or less?
7. Is the staff/child ratio 1:10 or less?
8. Is a periodic health screening performed?
9. Are parent support services available?
10. Are meals/snacks provided?

FYI: You can see how your state measures up in the quality of preschool programs by going to www.nieer.org.

Other items we might add to this list include those we discuss later in this chapter. We also suggest determining how the school's curriculum will fit with your child's temperament or learning style. Visit several programs.

Helpful Hints: Doing an observation

When you visit a potential preschool to do an observation, look for the following:

STAFF-CHILD INTERACTIONS. How is discipline managed? Is the staff taking advantage of teaching moments or letting the children play independently and merely supervising?

PLAY

2 **ACTIVITY LEVEL.** Is it chaos in the room or is play organized?

3 **PHYSICAL SPACE.** How is the space divided? Look for a combination of spacious areas, small nooks, tables for group activities and places for pretend play. The room should be well lit and inviting.

4 **TOYS.** Are the toys developmentally appropriate? Are there plenty of books?

PARENT 411: GIFTED & TALENTED—DO'S & DONT'S

Gifted children are those who have outstanding abilities in one or several of these categories: general intelligence, academic skill, creativity, leadership, visual/performing arts, or reasoning.[13]

Gifted and talented testing can be performed at public school once your child is age five. Each school district varies on how programs are implemented for these students. Some favor accelerated workloads, and others lean towards separate curriculums. Regardless, it is clear that these children benefit from enrichment programs.

Before your child is age five, here are some practical tips:

DO offer enrichment. Identify interests that your child has and roll with them. If your child loves learning about animals, go to the zoo often. Enrich that experience by asking for a tour guide if one is available. Go to the library and select books about animals. If you are tech savvy, do an Internet search on animals and create a Powerpoint presentation together.

DON'T be pushy. Don't over-schedule your child with too many programs. All kids, gifted or not, learn through play. All kids also need down time. While you may be tempted to enroll your gifted child in several activities, he may do better in just one that he really enjoys.

DO treat the child like a normal kid. Kids will be kids. If you treat a gifted child as unique or different, he will begin to feel the pressure of being in the limelight. It also creates a strain on sibling relationships (who cannot measure up to their "special" brother or sister).

DON'T be afraid to say, "I don't know." Gifted kids ask a lot of questions—some you probably won't be prepared for or know the answer to. When your four year old worries about world hunger, it's okay to say you don't know all the answers to complex problems. But you can learn about these things together.

DO find other gifted kids. Some (but not all) gifted kids may be square pegs when it comes to socializing with other kids. They have different concerns and priorities compared to their peers, and as a result, have trouble finding anything in common. Eventually, gifted kids will find each other. But until that day happens, you may need to identify potential playmates for your child.

DON'T pressure the child to succeed. Most gifted kids do a fine job of pressuring themselves to be over-achievers. Having parents add to this pressure only makes a failure that much more devastating.[14]

PLAY

5 **VARIETY OF ACTIVITIES:** Are there small group activities, large group activities, opportunities for solitary play and quiet time? Is there a balance of structured and unstructured time?

6 **PLAYGROUND EQUIPMENT.** Is it safe? What is underneath it? The "fall zone" is where most injuries occur.

BOTTOM LINE

Research has shown that high-quality childcare programs have positive effects on a child's intelligence, language, and school readiness, particularly for kids who have developmental delays.[13] And no surprise here, good teachers use the same tricks good parents do— warmth, responsiveness, and the ability to let a child be independent.

Do your homework. Check out several preschool programs. Ask the director about teacher-student ratios and teacher certification. Once your child attends the school, be sure to visit. If it doesn't feel like a good fit, be flexible and move on.

Reality Check:
Some interesting preschool stats[15]

In 1965, 5% of three year olds and 17% of four year olds attended preschool.

In 2002, 40% of three year olds and 66% of four year olds attended preschool.

The largest group of children enrolled have parents whose salaries range from $50,000 to $80,000 annually.

The second largest group have parents whose salaries are less than $40,000 annually. These children qualify for Headstart programs.

The lowest enrollment group? Kids whose parents make $40,000 to $50,000 annually— presumably because they cannot afford the cost of preschool or qualify for Head Start.

Q. When should my child start taking music lessons?

It depends on what type of program you are talking about. If the goal is music appreciation, there are both national and local programs that are terrific for infants and toddlers.

In general, most experts recommend starting to teach a child how to read music and learn a musical instrument around seven years of age. Why age seven? As you remember from our discussion of intellectual development in the previous chapter, this is around the age kids develop logical thinking.

Shinichi Suzuki, who created the Suzuki method of music education, disagreed with this notion. In his opinion, Suzuki believed that children as young as age three can learn to play a musical instrument the same way that they learned to speak—by memorization. Suzuki once said, "There is no such thing as talent…the secret is repetition." There are music programs in the U.S. who follow the Suzuki method if you are interested in checking it out. Be aware that it takes discipline on both the part of the child and the parent (yes, parents get homework assignments too with Suzuki).

Bottom line: there are few children who truly have a gift AND will sit still to learn a musical instrument as a toddler or preschooler. However, for the

PLAY

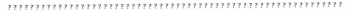
? ?

vast majority of kids, save your money and start music lessons when your child is school-aged.

Whether you choose formal music lessons or not, we do encourage you to promote a love of music. Here are a few easy and inexpensive tips:

- ◆ Buy cheap maracas, tambourine, or a drum.
- ◆ Make your own instruments out of old pots, pans, wooden spoons.
- ◆ Sing songs together.

Reality Check: A real-life piano lesson story

When my daughter, Julia, was four years old, a friend invited her to join a group piano lessons class. I always thought my kids would take piano lessons when they were older, but the class sounded terrific, and I thought she would have fun with her friend.

My husband was so excited that he went out and bought the electric piano that the music store recommended for the class. You can see where this one is going….

The class was great, but Julia refused to practice and began to complain about going (which brought back memories of my own piano lesson

OLD WIVES TALE: THE MOZART MYTH

Does listening to classical music create smart kids?

That bit of lore has entered mainstream culture in the past ten years, as a myriad of products, videos and CDs aim to boost childrens' IQ with doses of Mozart.

Where did this notion come from? And is it true?

In 1993, researchers at the University of California, Irvine set off the Mozart Effect craze by publishing a study that purported to show college students got an IQ boost from listening to classical music before a test. The same researchers announced in 1997 that piano instruction helped improve kids' abstract reasoning.

Overnight, an industry was born. Media coverage whipped parents into a frenzy and companies rushed to roll out Mozart box sets, toys with classical music, videos, DVD's and more. Even the government got in on the action: in 1999, Florida required toddlers in state-run preschools to listen to classical music tapes every day.

All this would be great if the Mozart Effect was real. Sorry to report folks: it isn't.

Numerous follow-up studies by researchers tried to confirm the Mozart Effect . . . but to no avail.[16]

No matter, the Mozart baby industry rolls on, churning out all manner of IQ-boosting music-enhanced products. The Mozart Effect has achieved mythical status. Our favorite take-off: the Incredibles movie scene where the babysitter plays Mozart for the super-human offspring of the title characters. Be sure to watch the results (it's in the Bonus Material)!

So, is it a bad thing to play classical music for your toddler? Of course not. Expose your child to music. We prefer Barenaked Ladies . . . but feel free to pick whatever genre lights your fire.

experiences). We dropped out after the first month. We are still proud piano owners, however. Hopefully, it will get used someday!

Take home message: Sometimes you are ready for your child to have a great learning experience, but your child is not.

Q. When should my child start team sports?

Many communities offer T-ball and soccer for children as young as age four. Should you sign up? It depends on whether or not your child is ready. Here are some points to consider: Can he keep up with the other children physically? Is he afraid of being in a pack of children all trying to kick the ball (and kicking each other instead)?

Encouraging physical activity is an important part of nurturing a healthy lifestyle. But if your child is spending more time picking the weeds in the outfield than paying attention to the batter, you should probably wait a few more seasons. Pick less organized sporting activities like playing hide and seek, riding bikes, or even walking the dog together.

Balancing Work/Family & Childcare Options

This may seem like an odd topic in the play chapter, but childcare is an integral part of fostering your child's development. *Who* you choose to care for your child (and *what* they do with your child during this time) is obviously important. And many parents worry (and feel guilty) about how those decisions will impact their child's well-being.

Q. Any tips on balancing work and family obligations?

"Balance" is really an unachievable goal. "Rising above chaos" is more realistic.

Raising a family is a full time job: accomplishing anything beyond that (running for Congress, solving world poverty, launching a world tour to promote your new album) is sure to create stress and anxiety. If you and your partner both work full-time outside the home, you should try to split up home obligations as evenly as possible.

Ha! We hear the guffaws from halfway across the country now! Okay, let's get real. Moms clearly get stuck with a greater number of household duties than dads. Of course, nothing in your marriage is 50-50 and it is unrealistic to think a child would change that.

Keep in mind one key word: delegate. Many moms (authors included) have trouble delegating responsibility and instead just resort to being chronically exhausted. Ask for help and accept it when it's offered—and don't be overly critical of the results. Okay, so maybe the laundry isn't folded exactly the way you like . . . or the chicken is a little overcooked. Get over it and move on.

And dads, you know life is not an episode of Bewitched. Gone are the glory days of coming home from work to find your slippers, newspaper and martini waiting for you next to the recliner. Whether your spouse has a job outside the home or is a full-time mom, your help is needed to make family life work.

Families are increasingly finding creative ways of juggling work and fam-

play & preschool

ily. Yes, that might mean DAD stays at home while Mom works at an outside job. Our message: keep an open mind and consider all the alternatives.

Q. I feel so guilty going to work and leaving someone else to care for my child. Should I?

Short answer: no.

Long answer: *"quality"* time is more important than the sheer number of hours you spend together. Let's look at the research. Kids do better when their parents *focus* their attention, engaging and responding to them. Positive interactions have measurable effects on children's social behavior, language, and even intelligence.[17]

Getting down on the floor and playing with your child is crucial, whether you work outside the home or not. And turn off the TV or the Blackberry while you are doing this.

There is a hidden bonus to working outside the home for some women: The satisfaction women derive from their careers can be beneficial—happy parents lead to happy children.

BOTTOM LINE: Want to know the secret sauce of parenting that kicks a child's development up a notch? Responsiveness, warmth, acceptance, and encouraging a child's independence.[18]

Q. I have chosen to stay at home with my toddler but I feel like I have lost some of my identity without a career. Any suggestions?

Like the Chinese curse says, may you live in interesting times. Today's generation of women have been taught that they can do anything a man can do and should strive for the same goals. Reality is, women are still the ones who get pregnant and frequently, make concessions with their careers if they have a family. When women "give up" that career, some feel they have lost part of their identity along the way. For past generations, most women established their identities raising children—that was satisfying enough. While that is still an admirable goal today, some women do not feel complete when their career is solely in the home.

Our advice: instead of grieving over your "identity theft," enjoy your parent-at-home career and be proud. It is the most demanding, rewarding, and underpaid job you will ever have. And if you feel like you need to do something to maintain your sense of self, pick your favorite cause and volunteer. Get your preschooler to help, too. Your philanthropic efforts will rub off.

Q. What are my options for childcare?

Your baby stays at home with someone, goes to someone else's home, or goes to a licensed childcare facility. Note: As your child grows, his needs change. Be sure your childcare situation fulfills your child's current needs. What was a perfect situation for your baby may not be so perfect for your toddler or preschooler. We discuss your options below.

PARENT AT HOME. This option gives you complete control over caring and nurturing your child. You will never regret being there to watch your child grow. As we have already stated, it is the quality of the

PLAY

time you spend with your child, and not necessarily the quantity that has the most positive impact.

The cost of staying home is the loss of one parent's salary. But when you factor in the hidden costs of outside childcare (more doctor's visits, dry cleaning bills, gasoline, etc), it may not be such a financial loss to stay at home.

As your child gets older, you may choose to occasionally enroll her in an enrichment program or "Mother's Day Out," which offers new experiences for her and some freedom for you.

Here are some considerations:

Is one parent willing to stay at home and be happy with that decision? Can you afford a single-earner household?

2 **FAMILY CARETAKER.** This option is for those lucky enough to have a relative who cares for your child while you go to work. It gives you the comfort of knowing exactly who your childcare provider is and you usually get them at a discount price! Another bonus: your child will develop a very special relationship with that person.

Here is the downside: it is usually easier to discuss your parenting strategies with someone you employ than with a family member who is doing you a favor—especially if that person is the parent who raised you. Also be aware that keeping a busy toddler out of trouble all day is exhausting. Be mindful of that if your family member has some health issues.

Here are some considerations:

Is a family member willing to take on this job?
Are you willing to avoid micro-managing?
How will the child's day be structured?
Is your family member willing to drive your child to activities?
Can your family member get down on the floor with your child and get back up?
What is your backup plan if your family member is ill?
What is your backup plan when your family member wants a vacation?

WHY GOOD CHILDCARE IS HARD TO FIND

According to 2005 study in *Pediatrics*, almost 50% of childcare centers in the US rate poor, failing to meet minimum childcare standards.[19] With 50% of children needing some form of childcare outside the home, you would think we could make quality childcare a priority.

Here is one of the biggest challenges: pay. the average salary for a childcare provider was $17,630 a year (2006 figures). Who would be attracted to a job that pays less than working at a fast food restaurant and is twice as exhausting? Poor salaries deter better-educated providers from the job, create higher staff-to-student ratios, and lead to high turnover rates. In short—low quality childcare.

So what's the solution? Frankly, we don't have the answer. Some think there should be expanded government subsidies or additional regulation. Others suggest a market-oriented approach with tax credits to help parents pay for better care.

As parents, we urge you to get involved in this issue and advocate in your community for the best-quality care for our children.

PLAY

? ?

3 **NANNY/AU PAIR.** This choice is the priciest form of childcare. Nannies/Au Pairs give consistent care and your child develops a close relationship with another adult. Because you are paying this person and she isn't your mother-in-law, you have more freedom to demand that your parenting guidelines be implemented.

While you don't need a Nanny-cam, it is always a good idea to do a background check (police record, credit check, reference check) and set up a trial week or two before hiring the person. Use your instincts and your child's. Your toddler/preschooler will definitely tell you who she likes and who she doesn't!

There are various ways to find a nanny: word of mouth, newspaper ads, bulletin boards at local colleges, or formal nanny locator services. One bit of advice: be sure you pay taxes on your employed childcare provider. You don't want to ruin your chances for being a Supreme Court justice someday.

Remember that your child's needs change as he grows. Some childcare providers are more comfortable with certain age groups. If your child has outgrown your current nanny, you may do better moving on to another one.

Here are some considerations:

Does the provider have any teaching or early childhood certification?
Does the provider have previous experience as a nanny?
How will the child's day be structured?
Is the provider willing to implement your parenting requests?
Is the provider willing to drive your child to activities?
Is the provider flexible if you are running late to get home?
What is the backup plan when the provider is ill?
Will the provider take vacation time when your family does?

Reality Check: Parenting the Au Pair

Au pairs can be a great experience for both your family and the young woman who is visiting from a foreign country. Be mindful, though, that these are young women. You may be taking on a dual role of parenting your toddler and a teenager.

4 **IN-HOME DAY CARE.** This option puts your child in the home of another loving family while you are at work. This can be a wonderful way for your child to interact with kids of varying ages, and, often, the older kids enjoy playing with the little ones.

The cost is modest compared to a licensed childcare facility. And depending on the provider, you may be able to go to work, even if your child is ill.

Just be sure this is the family you want your child to be a part of. Often, meeting the provider's children is just as important as meeting the provider.

Here are some considerations:

What are the ages of other children in the program?
What is the provider's backup plan if she is ill?
How will the child's day be structured?
Does the provider have any formal teaching/early childhood background?
When does the provider go on vacation?
What is the policy if you are running late to pickup your child?

PLAY

5 **LICENSED DAY CARE FACILITY.** This is the most popular option for working parents. Although the cost varies, this can be a moderately priced choice for childcare. There is also a sense of security knowing that centers have licensing requirements, and you can always drop in unexpectedly to check on your child.

However, all licensed facilities are not created equally. Federal standards are minimal and do not guarantee a quality program. Do your homework and constantly reevaluate.

What you can expect in the toddler room: structured activities, group meal times, and *one* universal naptime—usually on floormats, not in cribs. You'll need to consider whether your young toddler will tolerate this style and frequency of napping.

Helpful Hints:
**Finding a high-quality daycare program—
15 Questions to Ask.**

1. Is the program NAEYC (National Association for the Education of Young Children) approved?. While this doesn't guarantee anything, these programs strive for higher standards than federal guidelines. You can do a search for programs NAEYC's web site (naeyc.org) based on your zip code.

2. Are parents in the program satisfied? The program director will give you a list of parents to contact who undoubtedly will sing the praises of the program. Try to ask another parent or two who is picking up or dropping off a child at the program. You may get a more honest appraisal.

3. How approachable are the director and teachers? Will these providers be open to hearing your concerns? Look for a program that is receptive to making modifications for individual needs.

4. What is the level of training for the staff and director? While level of education does not guarantee a better provider, it does lead to a lower turnover rate. The director should have a college degree (or beyond) in early childhood education or development. The head teachers are not required to have college degrees, but it is certainly a bonus. They may have a child development associate degree. Aides may have no degree at all. However, all providers should be taking continuing education courses annually.

5. What are the staff-child ratios? Here are the federal guidelines for ratios of children and group sizes (but regulations by states vary):[20]

Age	Max Staff: Child Ratio	Max Group Size
0-12 months	1:3	6
13-30 months	1:4	8
31-35 months	1:5	10
3 years	1:7	14
4 and 5 years	1:8	16

6. Can you observe in the classroom? Does the program welcome "surprise" observations once your child is enrolled? The program should have an open-door policy. FYI: Visits can be disruptive, so you may not get an accurate picture of your child's experience. Some pre-schools now offer live web cams that let you peer into classrooms via the 'net.

7. How do the teachers handle discipline issues? Is the style similar to your approach? Will the style fit your child's temperament?

8. Do the teachers get down on the floor and play? This is not babysitting. You are paying good money for a program that will provide developmental stimulation and a nurturing environment for your child.

9. Are the kids and the adults having fun? The sign of a great program is that your child won't want to leave! If you are jealous of the fun your child is having without you, you have found the right place.

10. How is infection control managed? Are providers washing their hands after diapering, before food preparation, and after handling body fluids? Are children washing hands after using the restroom and before mealtime? How often are toys washed?

11. What is the menu for prepared meals and snacks? Some programs provide full-service meals for toddlers and preschoolers. It can be very convenient for busy families, but find out what is being offered. Some programs are more health-conscious than others.

12. How are special needs addressed? Are rules in place to protect a child with food allergies from accidental exposure? Can the program identify children with developmental differences? How are they equipped to handle such challenges?

13. What are the sick child policies? Are kids running around the class with pink eye or are they sent home if they have a temperature of 98.7? There are programs that fall at both ends of the spectrum. While you want a program that ensures your child is not playing in a sick ward, you also want him to stay at school if he is not ill. And beware, some programs are so strict that they require a doctor's note to return to school after an illness.

14. What are the injury prevention policies? Does the program provide safe, developmentally appropriate play equipment and playgrounds? Do they keep poisons/cleaning equipment out of reach?

15. What is the turnover rate of the teaching staff? Children thrive when they have a trusting relationship with an adult. If your child's provider changes as frequently as the weather, your child may have a sub-optimal childcare experience.

Here are some great websites to find more info about childcare programs: childcareaware.org, zerotothree.org, healthychildcare.org.

Reality Check: The Hidden Cost of Daycare
There is a hidden cost of daycare—medical bills for your child's sick visits. If your toddler is a seasoned daycare attendee, he has probably already had his share of illnesses. But he is still in for the other 182 viruses he has never seen before. The good news: by the time he is in kindergarten, he will be immune to most of the germs in your town.

Next up in our discussion of your toddler's development: challenges. What is ADD? Autism? We'll discuss these behavioral disorders, along with cognitive, genetic, sensory and motor disorders. Most importantly, we'll discuss how to get help, what to look for in an assessment and more.

CHALLENGES
Chapter 6

*"I'd like to think the best of me is
still hiding up my sleeve."*
~ John Mayer

You've heard it at the park, at gymnastics lessons, even out shopping at the grocery store: parents diagnosing other people's kids with Attention Deficit Disorder, Autism, Sensory Processing Disorder and so on. But what are these disorders? Could your child have one of them?

Autism Spectrum Disorder has made the headlines in recent years, as increasing numbers of children are diagnosed. That's raised awareness among all parents, which is a positive step—the more awareness, the more likely kids with developmental differences will be able to get crucial help at an earlier age.

In this chapter, we'll walk you through a variety of developmental delays and disorders so you can learn how to spot any concerns. We will present tips and advice on how to get help—what types of help to ask for, as well as advice on the latest therapies. The key message throughout this chapter: if you think something is wrong, seek help.

Behavioral/Social Disorders

Attention Deficit Disorder

Q. **My preschooler can't sit still. Does he have ADHD?**

Ages 3-4 Attention Deficit Hyperactivity Disorder (ADHD) is a diagnosis

CHALLENGES

? ?

made based on a combination of inattention, impulsivity, and hyperactive behaviors. These behaviors impact learning in a traditional school setting, socializing with family and peers, and having good self-esteem. And many kids with ADHD continue to have it through adulthood.

The disorder seems to run in families, and often a parent will realize he has the disorder when his child is being tested for it.

ADHD is usually not diagnosed until a child enters school (that is, at least six years old). Why? Because all preschoolers have trouble paying attention and sitting still! So, don't be alarmed if your three year old doesn't want to sit down for story time at the library.

However, there are a small number of preschoolers with extreme hyperactivity who will ultimately be diagnosed with ADHD.[1]

FYI: Attention Deficit Disorder can also occur without the hyperactivity. It's called ADD. Kids with ADD are diagnosed even later—typically, age eight or nine, because they have fewer behavior problems. ADD kids show signs of trouble when the level of schoolwork requires more focused attention.

Red Flags: What should I be looking for if I am worried about ADHD?

Here are some red flags to be looking for in an ADHD child:[2]

◆ *Hyperactivity*:
Constantly fidgets with hands or body
Always on the go
Trouble sitting in seat (at school or at the dinner table)
Trouble playing quietly
Always talking
◆ *Impulsivity*:
Trouble taking turns
Blurts out answer
Interrupts other's activities
Rejected by peers
◆ *Inattention: (later signs seen around age eight or nine)*
Disorganized
Not detail oriented
Forgetful
Poor task completion

Q. I think my child has ADHD. Any advice?

Here are some suggestions:

◆ *Be sure of the diagnosis.* Other learning disorders (dyslexia, etc.) and sleep problems can create attention problems in school. (See obstructive sleep apnea and sleep disordered breathing in Chapter 9, Sleep and Chapter 17, Diseases).

◆ *ADHD and other disorders can occur together.* Some ADHD kids also have learning disorders, depression, anxiety, and conduct disorders. Get a complete assessment done (which may require more than one specialist).

◆ *Learn about treatments.* Yes, medications can help control the symptoms of ADHD . . . for kids who truly have this disorder. But drugs are not the only answer when it comes to treating ADHD;

therapy can help as well. Kids need to learn how to use their other strengths to work around attention problems and channel that energy in a positive way.

◆ *Know your childrens' rights.* Public schools are required to provide specialized curriculum for children with special needs. Be a strong advocate for your child.[3]

Reality Check

Some parents find it useful to hire a private "student advocate" to help navigate the maze of special education in public schools. These advocates (usually learning specialists or educational psychologists) offer their own evaluations, assessments, and recommendations. The advocate can also be present when parents sit down with the school district to discuss a child's individualized educational plan (IEP). Of course, this is money out of your own pocket. Your public school system is required by law to provide testing and recommendations free of charge. However, it may be worthwhile to hire an outside advocate to verify the school is on the correct path.

As more public schools offer preschool education, this issue may come up well before kindergarten. Learning how to navigate your school district's special education system can be challenging even for the most diligent parent—that's why getting some outside advice is prudent.

Q. Does changing a child's diet reduce symptoms of hyperactivity?

This theory has been around since the 1970's, when allergist Benjamin Feingold penned the book *Why Your Child is Hyperactive.* Feingold's theory was this: by eliminating food additives, sugars, and salicylates (contained in many fruits and vegetables), children's behaviors would improve.

The book's popularity and its subsequent diet (cleverly called the Feingold Diet) led many parents to seek out additive-free foods for their hyperactive kids. But there was only one problem with Feingold's research: there was no scientific proof that this restrictive diet actually worked. And other researchers failed to get the same results. So his ideas fizzled out.

This issue came back to the forefront in 2007, when a study in England took a fresh look at whether food additives cause hyperactivity. Researchers gave 300 kids (half the group were three year olds; the balance were ages eight and nine) a drink containing yellow and red food coloring and a commonly used food preservative, sodium benzoate. Other kids drank a sugar containing drink. While the sugar did *not* have an impact on the child's behavior, the food coloring and preservative did. Not all kids showed a response, but statistically, more kids were overactive, impulsive, and inattentive in the group who drank the food coloring and preservative.

While this diet may not be the solution for every kid with ADHD, it probably doesn't hurt to try it. Avoiding food coloring and processed foods isn't a bad idea anyway—whether it makes your kid hyper or not. We'll have more on this issue in Chapter 18, the Environment.[4]

Old Wives Tale
Sugar makes kids hyper. FALSE.

Q. My child has ADHD and I am wondering if he can take medication for it. Is it approved for preschoolers?

Currently, these medications are FDA approved only for kids over six years of age.

Why? The National Institute of Health completed the first long term study on preschoolers and Ritalin (methylphenidate) in 2006. The study showed that some preschoolers with severe ADHD respond to low doses of stimulant medication. However, this age group seems to be more likely to suffer the adverse side effects of the medication (such as lack of appetite, slowed growth rates, weight loss, insomnia).

Autism Spectrum Disorders (ASD)

Q. What is autism?

Ages 1-4 Autism Spectrum Disorder (ASD) is really a collection of several disorders that have three abnormal areas in common: social skills, communication skills, and repetitive or obsessive traits. There's a broad range from mildly to severely affected. Specialists use the terms ASD and Pervasive Developmental Disorders (PDD) interchangeably. And to get even more confusing, Asperger's syndrome, and "pervasive developmental disorder, not otherwise specified" (PDD-NOS) are other categories that fall under the ASD heading. Here is a brief explanation of each:[5]

Autism Spectrum Disorder (ASD) or Pervasive Developmental Disorder (PDD): These terms describe the entire group of conditions that include autism, Asperger's Syndrome, and PDD-NOS.

◆ *Autism:* These children are the most severely impaired. They have little or no social and communication skills and have repetitive, obsessive behaviors.

◆ *Asperger's Syndrome:* These children have normal intelligence and language development but have trouble reading social cues and making conversation. Asperger's kids often obsess about certain interests.

◆ *PDD-NOS* (Pervasive Developmental Disorder—Not Otherwise Specified) is the default diagnosis for a child who has problems with social and communication skills, but does not fit into either of the above categories.

Autism affects one in 110 children. It is four times more common in males, and seems to run in families.[6]

Q. I've heard autism is on the rise. Why?

The first question we have to ask is, do we really have an epidemic or are more children just being diagnosed? Is it better detection due to better awareness? Are we displacing one diagnosis for another? Here are some explanations for the large rise in autism:

CHALLENGES

1 **DISPLACING ONE DIAGNOSIS FOR ANOTHER.** In previous generations, many children were diagnosed with mental retardation, schizophrenia, or some other psychiatric disorder. Today, many of these same kids are diagnosed with severe autism.

For example, in 1996, 1 in 63 kids were diagnosed with mental retardation (measured by an IQ score of under 70). Yet, in 2000, that number DROPPED to 1 in 83. Why? Were there suddenly much fewer kids with mental retardation? No, many of these kids are now diagnosed with autism instead of mental retardation.[7]

In other words, autistic kids were there in the 80's and 90's—we just didn't call them autistic.

In 1991, the Individuals with Disabilities Education Act (IDEA) required children with developmental disabilities to receive school services and be integrated into a mainstream classroom setting as much as possible. Autism was added as a new diagnosis for which a child could be eligible to receive educational services. In 1993, two years after this code was added, the Department of Education reported a 23% rise in autism. Prior to the coding change, kids with autism were often labeled with non-specific developmental delay, brain dysfunction, or mental retardation.

2 **CHANGING CRITERIA, BROADER DIAGNOSIS.** The definition of autism has changed over the years. The Diagnostic and Statistical Manual of Mental Disorders (DSM) is the authoritative bible for psychiatric disorders in the U.S. The first two editions never even listed autism as a disorder.

Dr. Leo Kanner first diagnosed Autism in the 1940's. Yet it was not until 1980 when psychologists recognized autism. That's when the DSM for the first time listed criteria for the diagnosis of autism.

The autism diagnosis broadened again in 1994 when several more disorders were officially added to the DSM: Pervasive Developmental Disorder (PDD), PDD-NOS (not otherwise specified), Asperger's Syndrome, Childhood Disintegrative Disorder, and Rett's Disorder.

By expanding the definition of autism, suddenly many more kids were declared autistic. Case in point: looking at recent autism diagnoses, up to 75% of these kids are high-functioning children with PDD-NOS or Asperger's.

Unfortunately, many states don't break out where kids are on the autism spectrum. California's autism rate is often cited in the media as example of the "autism epidemic"—yet California doesn't break out where kids are on the autism spectrum, so it's hard to get solid numbers.

Not long ago, kids who were smart but socially awkward had no diagnosis. Today, those kids are often diagnosed with Asperger's Syndrome.[8]

3 **BETTER AWARENESS, BETTER AND EARLIER DIAGNOSIS.** Popular diagnoses rise and fall like skirt lengths. Think about it—ten years ago, had you ever heard of Restless Leg Syndrome?

When it comes to autism, this newfound awareness is actually a positive step. More people—parents and doctors alike—are on the lookout for children with autism.

Making a diagnosis and starting therapy earlier in life improves kids' longterm outcomes. But it also looks like autism is on the rise. Why? Because kids were previously diagnosed with autism after age five or six. Today, kids are diagnosed as early as 18 months of age. This adds many more kids to the rolls . . . but is autism really increasing? Or is there just an earlier diagnosis?

4 **WHY DOES THE U.S. HAVE SO MANY AUTISM CASES?** Autism is not just an American disease—it happens worldwide. But why do the U.S. and United Kingdom have such high autism rates? That's because the U.S. and U.K. have done the lion's share of research and studies into autism.

Other countries are just starting to look into autism. For instance, in South Korea, kids are diagnosed with Reactive Attachment Disorder (RAD) . . . which is really what we call Autism Spectrum Disorder (ASD) here in the U.S. We suspect that South Korea will report an alarming rise in autism when they figure out their RAD kids are the same as our ASD kids.

And counting autistic kids is a relatively recent phenomenon. Before recent legislation led to schools labeling more kids as autistic, researchers just looked at either medical or school records to determine autism rates. This was imprecise to say the least.[9]

5 **PREVALENCE VS. INCIDENCE.** If you've ever taken a statistics class (or tried hard to forget anything you learned if you did), here is a little review. Most of what we know about autism rates are based on *prevalence* studies: these are a *sampling* of a population at one point in time used to estimate overall rates. By contrast, *incidence* studies identify the ACTUAL number of autism cases over a period of time. The only way to know if autism is really an epidemic is to see a rise in the *incidence* of autism.

Unfortunately, there are very few incidence studies of autism. That's because it is extremely difficult to do this research. Only one incidence study on autism is available—that 2005 report found that rates of PDD in the 90's were unchanged. So even though PREVALENCE studies seem to show autism is increasing, the incidence proof is lacking.[10]

6 **SOCIAL ACCEPTANCE.** We've come a long way since autism was first identified as a disorder. Originally, experts though autism was caused by poor parenting—namely, the mother. These "Refrigerator Moms" were blamed for rejecting their kids, causing the kids to have social problems.

Of course, this was WRONG.

What we've learned over the past 70 years is that autism is not the mom's fault. But in the old days, no mother wanted their kid labeled autistic since that would imply HER guilt.

Today, we realize it is not mom's fault—and thus parents are more willing to accept an ASD diagnosis. And the diagnosis now allows for special education services, which many parents realize can help their child.

7 **OVER OR MISDIAGNOSIS?** There is so much awareness now of Autism Spectrum Disorders, that perhaps clinicians are overdiagnosing it. One reputable study suggests that kids who actually have anxiety disorders, obsessive compulsive disorders, and personality disorders may be misdiagnosed now with ASD.[11]

These are possible explanations for the "autism epidemic"—but we don't have all the answers yet. The bottom line: in the 1980's, one in 10,000 kids were diagnosed with autism. Today, it's one in 110. The U.S. is not the only country seeing this trend. Australia, Canada, Denmark, Finland, Iceland, Japan, and Sweden also report a disconcerting rise.

Q. What is Asperger's Syndrome?

Contrary to many people's impressions of autism, kids with Asperger's Syndrome function well with good language skills. But . . . they are socially awkward, and seem out of sync with social cues that come naturally to most kids. And they may take interest in activities to the point of obsession.

Kids with Asperger's generally get diagnosed later in life . . . when they enter preschool or even grade school (or later!). That's because they can talk. But if you have a CONVERSATION with an Asperger's kid for more than a few minutes, you'll realize that he has very limited interests. Asperger's kids also has trouble engaging in "reciprocal" conversation—that is, he doesn't seem to care what you want to talk about. He may be an expert in Pokemon and have all 200 characters memorized. But that's the only topic he'll discuss.

Asperger kids also seem to lack empathy for others. That's part of their social disconnect.

Boys with Asperger's Syndrome outnumber girls by 10 to 1—we don't know why.

Reality Check

Let's not sugarcoat this one—there is a very small (but vocal) group of activists who believe vaccines cause autism. Then there is the rest of the world (many autism-affected families, medical providers and researchers) who believes the scientific and clinical evidence showing there is no link between the two.

We'll be clear: we are in the NO vaccine link camp. We don't buy the argument of government cover-ups, evil pediatricians, or greedy pharmaceutical companies who seek to profit by selling tainted vaccines. As we discussed in the introduction, our emphasis in this book is on scientific research. And the science shows vaccines do NOT cause autism.

Stay tuned for details on this explosive topic in Chapter 15, Vaccines.

Q. Okay, so what causes autism?

The million-dollar question. There appear to be four chief suspects:

DR B'S OPINION: VACCINES & AUTISM

If the scientific data doesn't convince you that vaccines are safe, just take a look at the autism rates in the U.S. since 2001 (the year all childhood vaccinations became mercury-preservative free). If mercury-containing vaccines were the cause, the number of kids being diagnosed with autism should be going DOWN.

Sadly, it is not. Not here, nor anywhere else in the world.

For more information on this subject, go to Chapter 15, Vaccines.

1 **GENETICS.** We know genetics plays a role. Studying twins is an obvious way to detect genetic disorders. If one identical twin has autism, up to 96% of the time, so will the other twin. And siblings of ASD kids have a 5% risk of having an autistic disorder.[12] To date, the exact gene has not been identified, but it may reside on the X chromosome, which may explain the prevalence of autism in boys.[13] In fact, there is a genetic syndrome (called Fragile X) that is one known cause of autism.

(A quick genetics primer: boys only carry one X, girls have 2 X's. So when there is a defect on the X chromosome, boys are more at risk of being affected by it. Girls are protected from a defect manifesting itself since they have a backup X.)

In 2008, researchers identified a specific gene in some kids with autism. This gene is involved in controlling brain cell communication.[14] It appears that a mutation in this gene causes a risk of autism within families.

Other researchers have found abnormalities on several different chromosomes in autistic kids, leading to genetic defects. What causes these abnormalities? Researchers haven't quite figured out the puzzle yet.[15]

One study has shown that dads over the age of 40 have SIX times greater risk of having a child with an autistic disorder than dads who are younger than 30.[16] And moms who are over the age of 40 have a 50% greater chance of having a child with autism than ones who conceive between ages 25 and 29. (Moms over 40 have a 77% greater chance of having an autistic child than moms who give birth under age 25). Hence, autism has eerie similarities to Down Syndrome, a genetic defect that is more common when a mother is of "advanced maternal age" (over age 35).

All of these studies show that genetic defects are a strong suspect in autism.

2 **ABNORMAL BRAIN GROWTH.** Although the cause is unknown, autistic children have problems with brain growth. Babies are born with immature brains that grow rapidly and make nerve connections called synapses…like an information superhighway. In the normally growing brain, some branches of this superhighway get "pruned." In the autistic child's brain, the pruning process is defective. This may explain why babies with autism have abnormally rapid head growth under one year of age. Boys with ASD seem to have higher levels of hormones (insulin-like growth factors), which may contribute to the larger head size, weight, and body mass index.[17]

3 **ENVIRONMENTAL TRIGGER.** Is there some environmental exposure that sets off abnormal brain development in a genetically predisposed baby? Maybe. And that exposure may happen at or shortly after conception—before a mother even knows she is pregnant. There is a critical period of fetal brain development that occurs at 20-24 days after conception where the brain is most sensitive to injury.

Here are just a few theories that scientists are exploring as a cause for autism: flu exposure during pregnancy, and folic acid levels in Dad-to-be's sperm (possibly a too-high level can lead to problems). Studies done by the Environmental Working Group have found about 280 environmental toxins in umbilical cord blood—could one of these be a trigger?

There is also a growing body of evidence that newborns who are later diagnosed with ASD already have abnormal levels of certain proteins in their brains. So, having an environmental trigger in the womb during a critical period of brain development seems a plausible explanation for autism.

What about vaccines? There has been much talk about this theory, specifically that trace amounts of mercury used as a preservative in many vaccines *prior to 2001* caused a spike in autism. We discussed this issue in depth in *Baby 411*, but just to sum up: the scientific evidence does not support this theory. Research during the past ten years has taken a long hard look at vaccines and found conclusive evidence that vaccine exposure is NOT the turn-on switch for autism.[18] And no, despite what you might read online from fringe groups or personal injury lawyers, there is no conspiracy among pharmaceutical companies to inflict autism on unsuspecting children.

4 **PREMATURE BIRTH.** A recent study in *Pediatrics* found that premature, very low birth weight babies (under three pounds) have a 25% chance of developing an autism spectrum disorder.[19]

BOTTOM LINE
Researchers don't know what causes autism, although the above factors provide clues. The goal is to find a way to PREVENT autism . . . but we aren't there yet.

Insider Tip: Be a developmental detective
Pediatricians only get a snapshot of a child in a brief 15 to 20 minute well check visit. Full developmental assessments are often three to four hours in a specialty referral center. We rely heavily on parents to point out their concerns. Parents and doctors can both miss early signs of autism spectrum disorders in the first year of life. This is one of the key reasons why the American Academy of Pediatrics recommends screening specifically for autism at every well child visit.

Reality Check: The road less traveled
When your baby is born, you envision what road your child will take and where you will go with him. Sometimes life puts you and your child on a different path—having a child diagnosed with autism is an obvious example. It's not a bad road, it's just one you didn't expect to drive on.

The first thing a parent does is to wonder if they were responsible for somehow taking a wrong turn. In the classic movie, *Parenthood*, Steve Martin finds out his child has emotional problems. He proceeds to blame his wife, "It's your fault! You smoked so much pot in college I thought you were going to join some reggae band!" It's only natural to blame yourself or your spouse. It's also only natural to have a great deal of family stress when so much energy is placed into helping a child with a chronic medical disorder or developmental disability.

Our advice: The road less traveled may give you a better view of the trees and forest than the road you expected to drive on. Take time to look around. And don't lose sight of the others riding in the car with you.

CHALLENGES

? ?

Q. When do the signs of autism appear?

Although autism is usually diagnosed by age two or three, the clues to the diagnosis are apparent much earlier. Because language delays are one of the key components of autism, the diagnosis is made when lack of language is apparent (usually after 18 months). But there are other clues that are apparent as early as age one. The CDC and the American Academy of Pediatrics encourage professionals to make a diagnosis sooner because early intervention/therapy with these children has proven to be effective.

Some of the early clues by one year of age are:
1. Lack of eye contact.
2. Failure to respond to name.
3. Constant repetitive behaviors (hand flapping, etc.).
4. Preference for unusual comfort objects (that is, not a doll or blanket).
5. Lack of symbolic play or imitation.
6. No babbling by 12 months.
7. No gesturing by 12 months.

Clues from 12-24 months of age are:
1. No words by 16 months.
2. Lack of social skills (for example, not trying to converse, play, or engage).
3. Not following simple commands (for example, "Give me the ball.")
4. Not pointing to show you something.
5. Not looking when you point at something.
6. Not pretending or imitating (for example, feeding a baby, talking on the phone).
7. Seems disconnected, living in his own world.
8. Seems not to hear his name called, seems deaf.
9. Does not feel pain, fearless.
10. No interest in toys or plays inappropriately with them (for example, looking at the wheels instead of making the train go on the track).
11. Keen interest in inanimate objects (for example, repeatedly opening and closing cabinets).

If you have concerns about your child's behaviors, one great resource is a website called FirstSigns.org. The website, started by a mother with an ASD child, posts several videos of children developing normally and those

DR B'S OPINION: NEW AUTISM TREATMENTS

The National Institute of Health funds a collaborative group of researchers called the Autism Center for Excellence. This group recruits volunteers to participate in research studies across the country and includes the results in the National Database for Autism Research.

If you have a child with an autism spectrum disorder, consider volunteering to participate in research studies. You may help your child and many others.

with autism.

Unfortunately, there isn't a simple blood test doctors can do to test for autism spectrum disorders. The diagnosis is based on a clustering of behaviors and developmental differences. We've all got to be detectives here, looking for clues.

The AAP published an expansive report on autism in 2007. The recommendation to pediatricians: screen specifically for autism at all well child visits and screen with a standardized autism checklist at the 18-month and two-year-old well-child visits. Your doctor should hand you a form to fill out at both of these checkups. But in case you want to be ultra-prepared for the test, you can fill it out ahead of time.

Here is the Modified Checklist for Autism in Toddlers (M-CHAT). It is a reliable test for children who have autism. However, know that some kids with Asperger's Syndrome or PDD-NOS will pass this test.[20]

Please fill out the following about how your child USUALLY is. Please try to answer every question. If the behavior is rare (for example, you've seen it once or twice), please answer as if the child does not do it.

1. Does your child enjoy being swung, bounced on your knee, etc? *Yes No*

2. Does your child take an interest in other children? *Yes No*

3. Does your child like climbing on things, such as up stairs? *Yes No*

4. Does your child enjoy playing peek-a-boo/hide-and-seek? *Yes No*

5. Does your child ever pretend, for example, to talk on the phone or take care of dolls, or pretend other things? *Yes No*

6. Does your child ever use his/her index finger to point, to ask for something? *Yes No*

7. Does your child ever use his/her index finger to point, to indicate interest in something? *Yes No*

8. Can your child play properly with small toys (for example, cars or bricks) without just mouthing, fiddling, or dropping them? *Yes No*

9. Does your child ever bring objects over to you (parent) to show you something? *Yes No*

10. Does your child look you in the eye for more than a second or two? *Yes No*

11. Does your child ever seem oversensitive to noise (for example, plugging ears)? *Yes No*

12. Does your child smile in response to your face or your smile? *Yes No*

13. Does your child imitate you? (for example, you make a face—will your child imitate it) *Yes No*

14. Does your child respond to his/her name when you call? *Yes No*

15. If you point at a toy across the room, does your child look at it? *Yes No*

16. Does your child walk? *Yes No*

17. Does your child look at things you are looking at? *Yes No*

18. Does your child make unusual finger movements near his/her face? *Yes No*

19. Does your child try to attract your attention to his/her own activity? *Yes No*

20. Have you ever wondered if your child is deaf? *Yes No*

21. Does your child understand what people say? *Yes No*

22. Does your child sometimes stare at nothing or wander with no purpose? *Yes No*

23. Does your child look at your face to check your reaction when faced with something unfamiliar? *Yes No*

Answer key: all answers should be YES, except for questions 11, 18, 20, 22.

Q. Is it normal for a child to play alone?

Yes and no. It depends on the age of the child and how he plays.

Once a child is three (and definitely by four years old), they will play with other children, if they have the opportunity. Here are some red flags for unusual "solitary" play (playing alone).

◆ Playing with unusual objects for toys (like knobs).
◆ Avoiding play with other children.
◆ Difficulty moving on/playing obsessively with a certain thing.
◆ Lack of playmates by age four.

Q. My child was diagnosed with autism. What are the treatment options?

There are several therapies available for kids with autism. Some are backed by scientific research, some are not. Here is what we know: early intensive therapy with developmental specialists has the most positive impact on ASD kids. There is not a cure for autism spectrum disorders. But there are things you can do to help your child thrive and progress.

Be careful of unproven (and possibly dangerous) therapies that promise a cure. Parents of ASD kids are prey for unscrupulous folks selling snake oil.

As a parent (Denise Fields) who has an ASD child, we know the feeling—you are willing to try anything to help your child. But rather than choosing therapies on a random basis, let's try a more rational approach. Below is a how-to guide to treating ASD kids, complete with pitfalls to avoid.

Of course, there is no one-size-fits-all solution to autism. Because autism is a spectrum (comprised of several disorders), different kids need different treatments.

While autism advocates may argue about which treatment works best, there is one truth about autism therapies: most insurance companies don't cover them. While there are some government-based aid programs (state, local, non-profits), most parents of autism kids pay for therapies out of their own pockets. And that can be extremely expensive.

There are four basic categories of autism therapy:[21] Behavioral/communication, pharmacologic, alternative (biomedical/dietary), and complementary therapy. Each has its own specialists you will encounter. Let's look at them:

1 **BEHAVIORAL AND COMMUNICATION THERAPY.** Intensive behavioral and communication therapy is widely believed to be the most effective treatment for ASD kids. By intensive, we mean at least 25 hours a week, year round. The best programs provide plenty of one-on-one time with the child and the therapist and include other family members.

Early Childhood Intervention (ECI) is a government funded program that is a good starting point to find other services in your community. Because of funding issues, ECI does not provide the intensive therapy ASD kids need, but they are a great resource for children under age three. Once a child turns three, he is automatically eligible for developmental services through his public school system.

2 **PHARMACOLOGIC TREATMENT.** There are prescription medications that can be used to treat some of the symptoms seen with ASD's. Only two medications (risperidone and aripiprazole, see below) are FDA-approved specifically for autistic children ages five to 16. Other medications are used for behaviors that accompany autism but fit into other diagnosis categories.

For hyperactivity/impulsivity like ADHD: methylphenidate, clonidine, guanfacine
For aggressive behaviors: risperidone, olanzapine, aripiprazole
For self-injurious behavior, irritability: risperidone, aripiprazole
For anxiety: fluoxetine
For sleep disturbance: melatonin

3 **ALTERNATIVE (BIOMEDICAL AND DIETARY THERAPY).** Most of these treatments are generally not prescribed by conventional doctors. The reason? They have not been studied or researched to prove effectiveness and safety.

New treatments for autism are constantly coming in the market, yet often lack any solid scientific proof they work. Worse, some are based on pseudoscience. As a doctor, I want to offer any therapy to my patients that works—but no one wants your child to be a guinea pig. So below are treatments you'll have to discuss with your doctor.

92% of families affected by autism will try some complementary or alternative therapies. Even if you do this without your doctor's blessing, it is important to keep the communication lines open so that you can continue to work together.

Here are some common autism therapies—and what science there is to support them:

Gluten-Free, Casein-Free Diet

Gluten is a protein found in grains like wheat, rye and barley. Basically, gluten is what makes bread chewy. Casein is the protein found in milk and cheese.

One of the unproven theories of autism is called "leaky gut"—autistic kids supposedly have digestive tracts that can't properly process gluten or casein. These proteins then "leak" out of the gut and head directly to the brain, causing an opiate-like effect (spaciness, etc). Hence, autistic kids become addicted to gluten and casein, craving large amounts of these foods to further the drug effect (or so the theory goes).

Gluten-free and casein-free (GFCF) diets seek to break that cycle of addiction.

So, where's the proof that GFCF diets work? Unfortunately, the science is lacking: eight recent studies looked at the diet but found no effect.[22]

The lack of scientific proof for GFCF contrasts with the diet's considerable following among some in the autism community (parents and even some psychologists). Fans of GFCF say the diet promotes more social interaction and less autistic behaviors.

And it's much easier to go on a GFCF diet today—stores like Whole Foods stock gluten-free bread, cookies, casein-free cheese and other foods that were unavailable just a few years ago.

Here are the caveats to GFCF:

◆ *There is no way to test to see if this diet will work with your child.* Some alternative nutritionists and clinicians will do a urine test on ASD kids to look for abnormal elimination of "urinary peptides." Unfortunately, there is no scientific basis for this test.[23]

◆ *It is darn expensive.* While it's great that organic grocers carry many gluten and casein-free foods, Whole Foods isn't called Whole Paycheck for nothing—it can be very expensive to go on this diet. And traveling for vacation can make it challenge to stay on the diet.

◆ *Kids with ASD are already picky eaters*—this special diet may make it even more challenging for kids to get their nutritional requirements. If your ASD child craves cheese pizza, taking it away creates a dilemma: what does your child eat now? That's why we strongly recommend you try a GFCF diet only under the supervision of a nutritionist and pediatrician. A nutritionist can monitor your child's weight and suggest supplements if need be.

◆ *Gluten and casein is all or nothing*—you must eliminate ALL the gluten and/or casein, report parents of autistic kids who've tried this approach. There is no such thing as a low gluten or casein diet.

◆ *The diet is NOT a cure for autism.*

So if the leaky gut theory doesn't hold much water, what accounts for the anecdotal reports of success with gluten and casein free diets? It could be the placebo effect—parents want to see the diet work, so they imagine certain improvements that aren't there. Another factor: as autistic kids mature, some symptoms improve . . . diet or not.

Food sensitivities/allergy avoidance

Some naturopathic doctors and nutritionists do food allergy tests to look for food sensitivities that may worsen behaviors with ASD. These tests look for certain markers, called IgG4.

Talk to any board-certified allergist and she will tell you that IgG4 levels are NOT helpful in identifying a food allergy. Why? These tests are likely to cause falsely positive results and are not linked to any disease.

Board-certified allergists use a different blood test (IgE levels) when looking for food allergies. IgE levels require significant quantities to indicate a food allergy. By contrast, IgG4 levels are measured down to a very small quantity.

Hence, you might go to a conventional allergist, do a food allergy blood test and find nothing . . . only to then go to an alternative-medicine doctor and suddenly find all sorts of food allergies. We think the standard test (IgE) is much more accurate—beware results using IgG4 levels.

Omega 3 fatty acids

Do fish oil pills help autistic kids? Almost a third of autistic kids take fish oil pill supplements (which contain Omega 3 fatty acids), according a recent survey. So, does it work? A few studies point to a benefit for hyper-activity symptoms (ADHD), but the jury is still out on whether fish oil helps other autistic behaviors.[24]

Vitamin B6 and magnesium

Taking B6 and magnesium supplements have NOT shown to have any benefit, according to several studies.[25] And here's one general warning about vitamins: if you choose to give your child vitamin supplements, do not use more than the recommended daily intake. Megadoses of anything is never a good idea. Instead, work with your pediatrician and/or nutri-tionist to discuss correct doses of vitamins.

IVIG, Hyperbaric oxygen

On the highly controversial end of autism treatment, intravenous immunoglobulin (IVIG) and hyperbaric oxygen (HBO2) are two expensive options. HOWEVER, both therapies lack any statistically significant science to show improvement in autistic symptoms.

One autism website we found remarks that the cost for hyperbaric oxy-gen treatments average $100 to $300 per session and 40 sessions are rec-ommended to see a benefit (hence, as much as $12,000). Alternatively, par-ents can invest in their own hyperbaric chamber to have in the comfort of their own living room for a mere $20,000.[26] Yikes! The national organiza-tion for hyperbaric medicine currently has no policy statement endorsing HBO2 for autism.

We'd avoid these unproven therapies until someone can show us real benefit and safety.

Chelation

We want to warn parents about another alternative therapy we believe is dangerous: chelation therapy. What is that? Chelation removes heavy metals like mercury from the body through either oral or intravenous trans-fusions with highly-potent chemicals. Sadly, an ASD child died recently while undergoing chelation therapy. Bottom line: we don't buy the theory that autism kids are overloaded with mercury. As a result, we believe chela-tion is dangerous and not recommended.[27]

4 **COMPLEMENTARY THERAPY.** Yes, there are many other purported therapies for autism, from music and art to swimming with dolphins to medical marijuana. Whether or not they help ASD children is debatable.

Beware of overnight success stories. Yes, we realize that alternative therapies offer something vital to families going through this maze: hope. And we know how powerful that feeling is—but it's important to have a healthy dose of skepticism when it comes to miracle autism cures you read online.

Whether a family chooses traditional or nontraditional therapies, here's an encouraging statistic: about 30% to 40% of kids with ASD improve and can function in a regular classroom.

OTHER AUTISM SPECIALISTS
Gastroenterologist and Nutritionist
Some ASD kids get tummy aches from constipation. This is probably due to their very picky (low fiber) diets.

Since autism is at its core a communication/social disorder, it may be hard for an ASD kid to express a problem with their tummies. As a result, some ASD kids' behaviors improve when their stomachaches disappear.

Bottom line: it's helpful to check in with a pediatric gastroenterologist if your child has bowel problems or severe changes in his behavior.

Nutritionists usually work hand in hand with gastroenterologists—it's helpful to look at both issues at the same time.

Neurologist
Some ASD kids will have seizures. Again, this shows that Autism Spectrum probably represents a variety of disorders.

Six to eight percent of kids with mild ASD have seizures. That number goes up to 42% if an ASD child has severe intellectual disabilities, or family history of seizures. That's where a neurologist comes in to help.

Sleep disturbances are also common for ASD kids. They may have an abnormality in the way they regulate melatonin. Neurologists can also help with sleep disorders.[28]

Helpful Hint: Where to get more info on autism
The Centers for Disease Control: cdc.gov/actearly
American Academy of Pediatrics: aap.org
Autism Science Foundation: autismsciencefoundation.org

Other Behavior Disorders

Q. My child doesn't listen to me and is very defiant. Is there something wrong with him?

There are a couple of diagnoses that you may want to consider. Most of the time, kids are just trying to test boundaries and see what they can get away with. However, see if either of these disorders sound like your child:

CONDUCT DISORDER: These kids intentionally break the rules. They try to harm people and animals, destroy property, and steal. If your three-year-old tries to set the cat on fire, he has a problem.

OPPOSITIONAL DEFIANT DISORDER (ODD): These are children who are beyond the "cup half empty" level of negativism. They disobey authority, and have at least four of the rest of the qualities we list below. A child with Oppositional Defiant Disorder often:

Loses temper.

Argues with adults.

Actively defies or refuses to follow adults' requests or rules.

Deliberately annoys people.

Blames others for his or her mistakes or misbehavior.

Is touchy or easily annoyed by others.

Is angry and resentful.

Is spiteful or vindictive.

We know when you read this that every toddler, by definition, has ODD! However, if these behaviors cause a real problem in school and social settings, that's a red flag.[29]

If your preschooler has made it through the Terrible Two's and still has an attitude that is above and beyond the manageable zone, you should get it checked out by a professional.

A great resource for parents on this subject: *The Explosive Child*, by Ross Greene, Ph.D.

Cognitive/Intellectual Disorders

Mental Retardation (Intellectual disability)

Q. My child has developmental delays in all of his milestones. Is he mentally retarded?

Children under three years of age with delays in all areas of development are considered *globally developmentally delayed.* If these children do not catch up to their peers and continue to have delays beyond age three, it is likely they will be diagnosed with an intellectual disability (formerly referred to as mental retardation).

In the strictest terms, intellectual disability is based on the results of intelligence quotient (IQ) testing. Kids who fall more than two standard deviations below the mean test scores have an intellectual disability. So, a child with mild intellectual disability will have an IQ of 52-67.[30]

Q. My child is intellectually disabled. My doctor is sending us to several specialists. Do I need to put my child through all this?

Although a cause is not always found, some treatable disorders may be diagnosed. Or a genetic defect may be uncovered, which may be important for future children in your family. The most important thing is for you not to feel guilty.

Some of the diseases that ultimately cause intellectual disability include:

◆ Inborn metabolism problems (trouble processing certain foods), for example **PHENYLKETONURIA**.

CHALLENGES

? ?

◆ Genetic and chromosome defects (for example, **DOWN SYNDROME, NEUROFIBROMATOSIS, FRAGILE X**).
◆ Complications of pregnancy (prematurity, alcohol/drug use in pregnancy, severe jaundice).
◆ Head trauma.
◆ Serious infection (meningitis, encephalitis, HIV).
◆ Other rare syndromes (there are entire textbooks devoted to this category).

The good news: many of the reversible disorders are being detected by newborn metabolic screening tests. And some disorders are being prevented by better prenatal care and education.

For more information on these disorders, check out the section on genetic defects in this chapter or the handy glossary in the back of the book.

Sensory Disorders

Hearing Disorders

Q. My child had her hearing tested in the hospital when she was a newborn. I don't need to worry about hearing problems anymore, right?

Well, you're not completely out of the woods, but it is reassuring to have a normal hearing screen at birth. Newborn hearing tests look for a specific type of hearing loss called **CONGENITAL SENSORINEURAL HEARING LOSS.** In English, this means docs are testing to be sure the hearing nerves are working properly.

However, nerve injuries that occur later in life due to trauma or infection, for instance, can result in hearing loss. This is called **ACQUIRED SENSORINEURAL HEARING LOSS.**

And there are hearing problems that are related to the transmission of sound waves through the eardrum and middle ear bones, rather than the functioning of the hearing nerves. This is called **CONDUCTIVE HEARING LOSS.**

Audiologists, ear, nose, and throat doctors (ENT's) and other trained health providers can determine whether a hearing problem is due to the nerve or conduction of sound.

Nerve related hearing loss is permanent and can get progressively more severe with time. Conductive hearing loss, in most cases, is temporary and reversible.

Q. My child has had numerous ear infections. Will he have permanent hearing loss because of them?

No. We'll talk about this more in Chapter 16, Common Infections, but here is the basic idea:

Your ear is made up of three parts: the external ear (what you can see and the ear canal), the middle ear (the ear drum and the space behind it), and the inner ear (which resides in the skull bone and contains the hearing and balance organs). See the picture below.

Middle ear infections occur when bacteria or viruses infect the area behind the ear drum. Instead of air, which is supposed to be there, fluid fills the area behind the ear drum, blocking the transmission of sound (that is, a "conductive" hearing loss). The Eustachian tubes (the body part that helps your ears pop on airplanes) help to drain that fluid.

Kids who are prone to ear infections have trouble clearing the fluid (sometimes for a couple of months). They continue to have a conductive hearing loss as long as the fluid stays there. Once the fluid clears, their hearing returns to normal.

Although it is temporary, it is problematic for toddlers who get ear infections frequently while they are trying to learn language skills. Kids with language delays due to frequent ear infections do catch up to their peers. But if your child is getting ear infections month after month, this is one good reason to visit an ear, nose, and throat specialist.

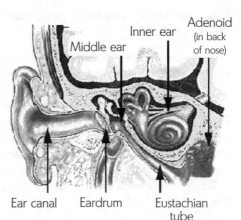

Middle ear · Inner ear · Adenoid (in back of nose) · Ear canal · Eardrum · Eustachian tube

Q. My child failed her hearing test at preschool. Should I worry?

Probably not. Most of the time, it is due to fluid in the ears (see conductive hearing loss above). Your doctor can examine your daughter's ears to see if there is fluid. On rare occasion, we find other things in the ear that prevent sound waves from being transmitted—like hard chunks of earwax, beads, toys, and pebbles from the playground.

If your doctor does not identify a problem, a referral can be made to an audiologist or an ear, nose, and throat specialist for further testing.

Q. My child is deaf in both ears. Is there any treatment for her?

Yes. Cochlear implants can make a huge impact for a congenitally deaf child. These electronic devices that are placed in the bone behind the ear by a specialized surgeon. It is FDA approved for kids as young as one year of age.

While members of the deaf community find this treatment controversial, it is something you should at least investigate so you can make your own decision.

Vision Disorders

Q. My husband and I have really bad vision. Should our toddler get his vision tested?

Testing little kids for refractive errors (visual acuity problems requiring glasses) is pretty tricky. Ophthalmologists are able to do limited testing in toddlers if there is truly a concern. In most pediatric practices, we will try to perform testing at age four.

Q. Our child was born prematurely. Should she get her vision tested?

Yes. Kids who are born before 31 weeks gestation or under three pounds are at risk of having **RETINOPATHY OF PREMATURITY (ROP)**. Babies are tested while they are in the neonatal intensive care unit and need to be followed up periodically once they are at home. Of the kids diagnosed with ROP, 90% will improve without intervention. However, children with more severe disease can have vision impairment or even blindness if they are not treated. Treatment involves laser surgery or cryotherapy, a procedure that applies extreme cold to destroy diseased tissue.[32]

For other eye problems, like lazy eyes, check out Chapter 17, Common Diseases.

Sensory Processing Disorder

Q. My child was being tested for some motor delays and his therapist thinks he has sensory processing disorder. What's that?

Sensory Processing Disorder (SPD) refers to a constellation of symptoms identified by Dr. A. Jean Ayres, a pioneering occupational therapist. Ayres found children with this disorder have problems processing inputs from their five senses. Some kids are over-sensitive to normal stimuli, while others are under-sensitive. Here are some red flags that might indicate Sensory Processing Disorder. A child may have some or all of these traits:[34]

- ◆ Does not like being touched.
- ◆ Touches everyone, constantly needs body to be touched.
- ◆ Trouble with balance.
- ◆ Loves spinning, twirling without getting dizzy.
- ◆ Sights and sounds are over-stimulating.
- ◆ Child fails to interpret visual cues like facial expressions.
- ◆ Food texture aversions.
- ◆ Eating non-edible items.

Because Sensory Processing Disorder has not been formally recognized by the medical world, your pediatrician may give you a strange look if you ask about this subject. Other physicians feel that sensory processing issues are just one manifestation of another diagnosis (like Pervasive Developmental Disorder or autism) and not a diagnosis unto itself.

Here's our take: we believe the dispute over semantics is just a lack of coordination between different disciplines (doctors don't always see eye to

CHALLENGES

SENSORY PROCESSING DISORDER: A PARENT'S EXPERIENCE

As parents of a child with Sensory Processing Disorder (SPD), we can attest to the problems in diagnosing and treating this disorder. Yes, we realized our son showed several of the classic symptoms of SPD, including sensitivity to loud sounds, failure to interpret visual cues, food texture aversions and dislike of being touched. But it took a caring kindergarten teacher to point us in the right direction.

Unfortunately, both our son's preschool and doctor missed the clues. And that's one of the frustrating parts of SPD—since this is an evolving field of medical research, not every preschool teacher or doctor is trained in deciphering the clues.

As we will discuss on the next page, some pediatricians view occupational therapy (OT) with skepticism. Our son's doctor was one of them, but that didn't stop us. And in our case, we saw impressive progress in our son after six months of occupational therapy. In fact, today he exhibits few of the behaviors he had in kindergarten. He's still a picky eater, but that's another story.

So, what did therapy do for our son? It helped him come to terms with the world. He can tolerate loud sounds like car alarms much better today. When another child is crying and getting on his nerves, he knows to leave the room. He can interpret visual cues much better, making social interactions less stressful. And touch is no longer an issue at all.

What did therapy do for us? We learned ways to help our son calm down when he becomes over-stimulated. For example, we spin him on a swing set or using brushing techniques. We even make "kid sandwiches" with a couple beanbag chairs—oddly, this is soothing to kids with SPD.

As with other kids with SPD, our son was also diagnosed with other learning disabilities. Our occupational therapist referred us to a speech and language therapist to help out with other issues.

So, if you suspect your child has SPD, here is our advice:

◆ Seek help early. If your child is exhibiting signs of SPD or other disabilities, the earlier you can seek help, the better. Most school districts offer early testing and intervention for preschool children as well as referrals to private therapists.

◆ Read the *Out of Sync Child*, a great book on this subject (see info on the next page).

◆ Discuss concerns with your doctor . . . but realize some might not recognize this problem. Get a referral to a specialist or therapist.

Bottom line: There is help out there. If you suspect your child suffers from Sensory Processing Disorder it's often up to you as the parent to seek that help.

eye with therapists). *Bottom line: your child doesn't need a diagnosis code to need help.*

So, how is Sensory Processing Disorder treated? Anecdotally, parents report success in treating SPD with a mix of both occupational and speech/language therapy. Unfortunately, there is little scientific data to back up whether these approaches work, as research into this disorder is still in its infancy. Therapy can be very expensive, unfortunately (often, $60 to $80 per hour) and few insurance plans cover it.

An excellent book on this subject is *The Out of Sync Child: Recognizing and Coping with Sensory Processing Disorder* by Carol Stock Kranowitz. We highly recommend it.

Motor Disorders

ORAL MOTOR DISORDER: FEEDING AVERSIONS

Feeding problems can develop in infancy, while others show up in the toddler years. Regardless of when problems start, it is often hard to separate what might be a true medical problem (such as poor oral motor skills) versus behavioral causes for feeding problems (control issues, etc).

Some feeding aversions are caused by **oral motor delay**—kids have a problem controlling the muscles of their mouth. Eating requires the ability to suck, chew, bite, and move food around the mouth with the tongue. If there is an oral motor problem, a child may avoid eating foods with certain textures. He may also have trouble controlling his secretions (for example, drooling beyond 18 months of age).

On the other hand, behavioral reasons may be the cause of other feeding problems. Infants who have had acid reflux (see **GERD**) may be fearful of eating because they remember that eating hurts. This fear may persist long after the acid reflux is gone. Infants who are force-fed may learn to hate eating, too. And then there are the toddlers who view mealtime as a battlefield. They may dig in their heels in the name of independence.

There can also be an overlap of reasons. Kids with other developmental disorders may have feeding issues. Children with sensory processing disorder (see sensory disorders above) may dislike the way certain textures feel in their mouths.

Helpful Hints: Feeding aversion advice

◆   *Play it cool:* Don't force your child to eat.

◆   *Keep offering:* Even if your child has refused a certain type of food, keep trying.

◆ *Get tested:* Kids with feeding aversions or oral motor delays can have trouble gaining weight (see **FAILURE TO THRIVE**) Occupational therapists and speech-language therapists can help. Some medical communities even have "feeding teams" which provide a collaborative approach from different health professionals.

FINE MOTOR DELAYS AND DISORDERS

Q. My child has trouble using his hands. What could the problem be?

Some children have poor muscle control, others have difficulty with the mental process of writing. Here are some red flags: if your two year old is unable to maneuver a spoon or hold a crayon, or if your five year old cannot write his name, it's worth investigating. Occupational therapists are the experts in this department.

Here are two specific fine motor disorders:[33]

♦ **Finger Agnosia** refers to trouble finding fingers in space while writing. Writing is a major task for these kids. They have a tight finger grip on the pencil and take extremely long to write things out. Finger agnosia can be associated with other neurological abnormalities.

♦ **Dyspraxia** refers to difficulty writing letters due to either trouble visualizing the letters in space or lacking a "motor plan" on how to write the letters. Some kids have trouble processing visual information and transcribing it onto paper, others have trouble listening and writing simultaneously.

Q. Our child developed a hand preference when he was a year of age. Is this a sign of a problem?

Although it is rare, yes, it can be a clue to a problem. Kids should use both hands interchangeably until at least 18 months of age. Why is this a concern? If a kid uses just one hand, there may be something wrong with the non-dominant hand.

Some neurological problems create hand weakness. One cause, **ERB'S PALSY,** is a weakness of the arm caused by damage of the nerves that control the arm. Most often, this is due to birth trauma and resolves with physical therapy (and occasionally surgery). One very rare cause is a stroke or **CEREBRAL VASCULAR ACCIDENT (CVA)**. A fetus can sustain a stroke while in the womb or a premature infant may have one as a complication. Just like an adult who has a stroke, children can have motor deficits as a result of the brain injury.

RED FLAGS:
Fine motor disorders

Here are the red flags to look for when it comes to fine motor disorders:[34]

Prolonged newborn reflexes (beyond six months of age)
Prolonged fisting of hands (beyond three months of age)
Disuse of one entire limb or side of body
Lack of pincer grasp at one year of age

GROSS MOTOR DELAYS AND DISORDERS

Q. My child is behind on all his motor milestones. Could he have Cerebral Palsy?

Cerebral Palsy (CP), by definition, is a non-progressive muscle and movement disorder (that is, it neither improves nor worsens over time). It is caused by complications surrounding pregnancy, infections, trauma, or environmental toxins. While 50% of kids with CP have normal intelligence, a significant number are intellectually disabled. The bottom line: all CP kids will be behind in their gross motor milestones, although some children will have decreased muscle tone while others do not.

If your child has severe motor delays, he should be evaluated by a neurologist to test for cerebral palsy.

Q. Our son has gross motor delays. Will he ever be able to play sports?

Although it depends on the cause of the delay, many kids are able to participate in sports. And you should encourage your child to do so because it provides motivation to work on those motor skills.

If your child has motor planning problems or difficulty with eye-hand coordination, you may want to try karate, gymnastics, or swimming to start. Leave basketball or soccer for later.

Language/Communication Disorders

EXPRESSIVE LANGUAGE DELAY

Some kids will have an *isolated* delay in speaking words. That does NOT mean your child is autistic.

While it is true that boys speak later than girls, we are talking just a month or two. If your child misses this milestone by more than two months, then contact your doctor.

FYI: it is true that second and third children will talk later. And kids hearing two languages in bilingual households may speak a little later, too.

APRAXIA

Q. My son has delayed language and his speech therapist thinks it is apraxia. Should I be worried?

Speaking involves the movement of multiple muscles in the lips, tongue, jaw and palate—if you think about it, this is a rather complex process. When a motor disorder prevents a child from forming words, that's called apraxia. Of course, adults may also develop apraxia after a stroke causes a brain injury. Kids who have "developmental apraxia" are born that way . . . and more boys have it than girls. These kids understand language (receptive language) but have trouble with getting words out (expressive language). Here are the red flags to watch out for with apraxia:

RED FLAGS: Apraxia
Incorrect rhythms and inflections in speech.
Several attempts at saying the same word.
Difficulty saying longer words.

If your speech-language pathologist has identified this as a problem, he/she will have a specific strategy to treat it. In more severe cases, kids need fairly intensive therapy.[35]

STUTTERING

Q. My child suddenly started stuttering. Is this normal?

We discuss this topic in Chapter 3, Milestones.

AUDITORY PROCESSING DISORDER (APD)

Q. My four year old is having trouble in preschool. His teacher says he doesn't follow instructions and looks like he doesn't understand her. His hearing is normal. What could the problem be?

If it's more than just having a teenager attitude at age four, you may want to test for auditory processing disorder. What's that? The simplest explanation: kids with APD misinterpret language that they hear. Most of the time, this disorder is detected once a child enters school. Here's what to look out for:

RED FLAGS: Auditory Processing Disorder
Difficulty paying attention to verbal instructions.
Difficulty remembering verbal instructions.
Problems following multi-step directions.
Poor listening skills.
Normal hearing.

Helpful Hints: Advice for parents of APD kids
One of the challenges with this diagnosis is that it can occur in association with other disorders like autism spectrum disorder, attention deficit disorder, and dyslexia. It makes it harder to tease out what the problem is.

Kids suspected of having this diagnosis should have a hearing test done right off the bat. If hearing is normal, speech-language pathologists and audiologists may work together to provide a treatment plan.

There are some things that can be done in a classroom setting to help a child with APD. Teachers can wear a microphone and the child can wear a headset to minimize distracting noises. It's also helpful to place the child in the front of the classroom.[36]

Here's some sage advice from a parent of a child with Auditory Processing Disorder:

◆ *Ask your child to repeat directions back to you.* That way you know they heard and processed what you just said.

◆ *Insist on eye contact.* When talking with a child with APD, you both need to maintain eye contact.

◆ *Minimize time in loud/noisy environs.* Lunchrooms can be a problem, as are any chaotic noisy places.

◆ *Emphasize VISUAL learning.* Kids with APD often compensate by having strong VISUAL learning skills—processing info they see in WRITTEN form. Simple directions and written notes work well.

Genetic, Chromosomal, and Metabolic Diseases associated with developmental delays

Q. What medical problems can cause developmental disorders?

There are many medical diseases that have developmental delays associated with them. This list is not comprehensive, but should give you an idea of what your physician or group of specialists will be ruling out in an evaluation.

Fragile X Syndrome

This is a defect of a specific location on the X chromosome. Eighty percent of boys who inherit the Fragile X gene will have characteristics of the syndrome. Girls can have the syndrome, but it is much less common. Diagnosis can be made by doing chromosome testing.

Here are some clues to making this diagnosis:

◆ Poor muscle tone (hypotonia).
◆ Delayed language skills.
◆ Hyperactivity.
◆ Features of pervasive developmental disorder (hand flapping, poor eye contact).
◆ Lower IQ.
◆ Subtle characteristic facial features (narrow face, large ears).

Down Syndrome

This is a disorder caused by extra genetic material (chromosome 21) that is only present in people with this syndrome. It causes a variety of changes in physical and brain development. Kids with Down Syndrome have classic facial and body features and varying degrees of intellectual disability.

Down Syndrome is usually diagnosed by physical exam and confirmed by chromosome testing.

Neurofibromatosis (NF)

A genetic disorder (gene defect) that causes tumors of the tissue covering nerves. Most babies are symptom-free at birth although some are born with three or more *café au lait spots* (light brown, flat marks). As a child grows, he develops numerous (more than five) spots and freckles in the armpit and groin. NF is associated with learning disabilities and developmental delays. When a child is being assessed for these problems, NF should be ruled out. Neurofibromatosis is diagnosed primarily by a physical exam.

Inborn Errors of Metabolism

These disorders are also known as metabolic storage diseases. They are a group of diseases that all cause an inability to break down certain food products. As a result, byproducts of metabolism accumulate. In some of these disorders, that accumulation goes to body parts (liver, heart, brain, kidney, eye) causing permanent damage or even death. The more common storage diseases are tested for on the state newborn metabolic screening tests (PKU, galactosemia). Some of the less common disorders can be tested on supplemental newborn screens.

For some disorders, modifying the diet of the affected person prevents irreversible (or further) damage. So, when a child is diagnosed with loss of developmental milestones, autism, or intellectual disability these disorders should be considered. Diagnosis is made by laboratory testing of blood and urine. Some tests must be performed in very specialized laboratories.

Assessments

Q. I have discussed my concerns with my child's doctor and he agrees with me. Now what do I do?

Once you and your child's doctor have identified a concern or problem with your child's development, it is likely that you will be referred to another medical provider(s). Depending on what the problem is, you may meet one or several people.

If you and your doctor have global concerns with your child's development, an expanded assessment is in order. Depending on where you live, you may see some variability in the referral process. If you live in a small town, you may want to consider seeking evaluation in a larger community with more medical services and implement a treatment plan at home.

Based on my own experiences working at the Children's Hospital Boston Developmental Assessment Program, I admit a personal bias. I believe that it is worth the time (and often, money) to get a complete assessment with a "multidisciplinary team." This means that an entire group of professionals will thoughtfully evaluate your child from various perspectives. This group consists of a developmental pediatrician, occupational therapist, physical therapist, speech/language pathologist and a social worker.

In your community, you may find some professionals who are involved only in the assessment phase. Some providers do both the assessment and implementation of a treatment plan. Length and frequency of therapy depends on the diagnosis and the progress the child makes. Some children need intensive therapy with more than one therapist until they make significant progress. Don't expect big changes quickly. Most progress is sure and steady. If you are seeing a plateau, it's time to reassess and modify a strategy.

Here are the people you may meet:

1 DEVELOPMENTAL/BEHAVIORAL PEDIATRICIANS are physicians who have additional training beyond general pediatrics in the assessment and treatment of children with developmental or behavioral disorders. Most of the time, you find these folks at an academic medical center working with a multidisciplinary team. In general, they do a thorough evaluation to determine a diagnosis (and sometimes a cause) of a child's delays. Based on their findings, referrals are made to appropriate providers for treatment.

2 NEUROLOGISTS are physicians who specialize in disorders of the nervous system (brain, spinal cord, and nerves). Pediatric neurologists have specific training in disorders unique to kids. Some neurologists focus on kids with developmental disorders. Your pediatrician may refer your child to a neurologist to perform neuropsychological testing (see more about this below).[37]

3 **OCCUPATIONAL THERAPISTS** (OT's) are healthcare professionals who help with development or rehabilitation of daily living activities. For kids, these activities include feeding oneself, writing/coloring, and playing. Specifically they work on improving eye-hand coordination, fine (small) muscle coordination, and strength (grip). Children with fine motor and oral motor delays may benefit from occupational therapy.

Occupational therapists have also become involved in therapy for kids with sensory processing disorder (see more on this topic earlier in this chapter). This therapy tries to reduce negative responses to noises, motion, touch, and movement (sensory stimuli).

4 **PHYSICAL THERAPISTS** (PT's) are healthcare professionals who focus their work on large muscle groups. They help children with posture, muscle strength, coordination, and range of motion exercises. Kids who have gross motor delays or muscle/bone/joint injuries may benefit from physical therapy.

5 **SPEECH-LANGUAGE PATHOLOGISTS** are healthcare professionals who help children with a variety of communication disorders. They evaluate the underlying problem and then create a therapy plan. Kids with receptive language disorders (trouble understanding/processing language) and those with expressive language disorders (delay in producing words, articulation, stuttering) may all benefit by speech therapy.

Q. The medical team assessing my child wants to do neuropsychological testing on her. What is that?

That is a fancy term to describe a standardized battery of tests. It depends on the particular test, but in general, they objectively look at a child's cognitive strengths and weaknesses compared to children her age. The testing may also uncover subtle indicators of neurological disorders.

Where to get help

Q. My child has been diagnosed with a developmental disorder. What services should he receive?

This depends on the diagnosis and the age of the child. The medical providers who have performed the assessment should give you recommendations for a treatment plan, and may also be the ones implementing that plan.

One program you should be aware of is *Early Childhood Intervention (ECI)*. ECI is a government-subsidized program, which offers multidisciplinary services to all children who have developmental disorders from birth to age three years. The program is available to all families, regardless of ability to pay. If a child has health insurance, ECI bills insurance companies (and charges co-payments). You can find your local program in the phonebook. *Easter Seals* also has a national program based on ability to pay. You can contact them at easter-seals.org or at 800-221-6827.

Once your child turns three, the public school system provides services to developmentally disabled kids. Federal law requires states to provide free and appropriate public education for kids ages three to five years who are at risk for developmental delay or are disabled. However, states have individual discretion to define who is "at risk."

Q. My child has so many specialists, I'm afraid that they don't talk to each other.

It can be a real challenge to coordinate care for a child who has special needs. Theoretically, your child's primary care doctor (pediatrician, family practitioner) should be receiving periodic notes from therapists and other doctors regarding your child's progress.

But things can get out of control if there are too many cooks in the kitchen. Well child visits with your pediatrician are a good opportunity to review the therapies your child is receiving, but these visits may occur only once a year if your child is over the age of two. It is a good idea to schedule a consultation with your pediatrician periodically if you are uncertain what direction to take next.

Most parents will become experts in their child's disorder and create a medical dossier of their own to keep track of evaluations and treatments. We definitely encourage you to do so.

Alternative therapies

Q. We have gone the traditional route to help our child, but we have seen little progress. We are now looking at alternative therapies. What do you think?

We know that most parents want to research all the available therapies for their child. And you should be as informed as you possibly can be. Thanks to the Internet, any parent can research both conventional and alternative therapies 24/7.

However, there is a dark side to the 'net's treasure trove of "medical" info . . . some "alternative" therapies can be harmful, very expensive or both.

Thanks to the web, hucksters and snake oil salesman can pitch their dubious cures to parents with little oversight. Our message: don't be lured into thinking a miracle cure exists for some disorder because some yahoo in New Zealand has designed a fancy web site to sell his Cure-O-Rama. Go to *reliable* resources online for info, such as those referenced earlier in this chapter. We'll also have expanded online references in Appendix E, References.

Now that you've learned all about your toddler's development, it's time to move on to those every day topics that challenge all parents. From picky eaters to sleep walkers, toddlers can throw you a curve ball when you least expect it. But first let's talk about that milestone you've all been waiting for: potty training.

Toddler 411

section two

The Potty, Sleep & Feeding

TOILET TRAINING
Chapter 7

"Always go to the bathroom when you have a chance."
~ King George V

A frightening fact: the average child goes through 7400 diapers by the time they potty train.

So, it might be around Diaper Change Number 7289 that you'll be wondering: hey, is there a day when I won't have to do this? When will my toddler actually use the toilet? Will this be before college?

Welcome to the Land of Potty Training. We'll give you our patented Toddler 411 Five Step Program to flawless potty training . . . as well as advice on potty seats, training pants and more. Finally, we'll look at the Dark Side of Potty Training: When Things Go Wrong.

Come along now and join us in the Diaper-Free World.

Toilet Training 411

Q. When is the right time to toilet train?

First of all, let's go over what "toilet trained" means. Simply put, a child senses the need to pee and poop and performs these functions—without any prompting—on a toilet. If you are taking your child to the bathroom every couple of hours and she is successful, *you* are toilet trained but she is not. **Toilet training takes one day—you just have to pick the right day!**

Being toilet trained is a developmental milestone. Your child will be ready when she is ready! Here are the two criteria to be successful:

1. Your child must be clued into the *urge* to go, not clued in that she has already gone.
2. Your child must want to be clean.

There are no other incentives to get a kid to toilet train. No matter how many M&M's you give her, it will not happen without the desire to be clean. And boys usually care less than girls do about being clean—which is why girls almost always train earlier than boys. Until the day arrives, keep using those diapers!

DR B'S OPINION

"Don't waste any- one's time toilet training when your child isn't ready. Toilet training hap- pens in a day. You just have to pick the right day!"

So how do you know which day is the right day? Is your child hiding behind the couch, disappearing into his room, or waiting until nap or bed time to poop? Is your child coming to you and asking for a diaper change? These are very positive signs that your child may be ready. On the other hand, if your child poops right in the middle of your living room, and then contin- ues to play with his trains, he is not ready.

If it seems like the right day, (and we would pick a weekend day; long hol- iday weekends are even better!), put your child in training pants (cotton under- wear with a few extra layers) and see what happens. If she has ten accidents, you picked the wrong day. Go back to diapers and try again another time. If she has a couple of accidents and is upset about it, you are on your way!

We do not recommend training a child for weeks or months on end. Your child will sense she has failed with all those accidents and you will have an awful lot of cleaning up to do. Just pick another day down the road when your child seems more ready.

Here's some science to back up our approach: Kids who began "early" toilet training spent more time training than their peers and they didn't get out of diapers any earlier![1]

So when do kids toilet train on average? Most toddlers will hit this mile- stone around age three. According to a study by the Medical College of Wisconsin, researchers found that the average age for potting training was 35 months for girls and 39 months for boys. Yep—do the math—that is nearly three years of age for girls and a bit over three for boys.

New Parent 411: When is this a problem?
Toilet training is not considered "delayed" until a child is FOUR years old.[2]

Q. Which happens first—poop or pee training?

It really depends on the kid. They can both happen simultaneously. But children who struggle with potty training usually accomplish peeing before pooping on the potty.

Helpful Hint: Toilet etiquette
Here are a few practical tips regarding your child and the bath- room experience.

◆ *The right amount of toilet paper is four squares.* Let your

POTTY

THE ZEN OF TOILET TRAINING: THE 5 KEY STEPS

Take notes. There will be a pop quiz on this Friday.

Step 1: The Pep Talk
◆ Avoid peer pressure. Toilet training is not a race.
◆ Toilet training is not a reflection of your child's IQ or your parenting skills.
◆ Relax. This is just another milestone. It only becomes special if your anxiety makes it so.
◆ It happens when *your child is ready*—not when you are ready.

Step 2: The Signs
◆ *Physically*: Your child can sense and control the urge to eliminate. It's also helpful if he can remove his pants by himself.
◆ *Cognitively*: Your child understands the connection between using the toilet and staying clean.
◆ *Emotionally*: Your child wants to be clean and wants to be like you.

Step 3: The Warm Up
◆ Demonstrate. Let your child watch you use the potty. Same sex role models work best.
◆ Talk about it. Don't be shy about using potty words. When your child is clearly pooping in your kitchen say, "You are pooping."
◆ Read books to your child. Our favorite is *Everyone Poops* by Taro Gami.
◆ Pick a weekend to begin this experience. You will want the time to devote to it.

Step 4: D—Day
◆ Put your child in training pants and tell him to go to the bathroom when his body tells him he needs to pee or poop. Tell him the goal is to keep his underwear clean and dry today, but it's okay if he has an accident.
◆ Take your child to the potty the first thing in the morning, before and after naps, every two hours if he does not go on his own, after meals, and before bedtime. If your child is ready, he will catch on and go on his own.
◆ If there is a regular time your child poops, take him to the bathroom then.
◆ Have your child sit on the potty for five minutes after each meal. The bowels are stimulated to empty after a meal. Have a special basket of toys and books that are only looked at while in the bathroom.
◆ Keep your child company in the bathroom if he likes. If your child prefers privacy, make sure the bathroom is a safe place for him.
◆ Praise success. Sitting on the toilet should be praised even if there is no result!
◆ If your child has numerous accidents, you picked the wrong day. Go back to diapers.

Step 5: False starts
◆ Relax—if your child isn't ready, take a deep breath and move on.
◆ If every other word out of your child's mouth is "no", avoid making toilet training a control issue. Your child will have accidents just to win the battle.
◆ You may have several false starts. Don't worry. Your child won't get on the school bus in diapers.

toilet training

child count them.

◆ *Girls need to wipe front to back.*
◆ *Boys need to learn that their penis should not be used as a water gun.*
◆ *Always wash hands.*

Q. What is infant potty training? Should we let our child go diaper-less?

Some folks believe babies give subtle clues that they need to eliminate as early as infancy and just need their parents to respond to those cues. Proponents of "infant potty training" claim that babies can consciously empty their bladder and bowels from birth. Hence, babies can be potty trained at under a year of age.

Well, color us a bit skeptical on this. Most experts say that babies under a year of age do NOT have these skills.

We'll let you decide—if you want more info on this approach, a good web site to check out is DiaperFreeBaby.org. This site has tips, advice and local support groups for parents who want to learn more about "elimination communication."

Q. My 18 month old seems interested in using the potty. Is it too early to toilet train?

No. Remember toilet training is a developmental milestone. Some kids are early-achievers.

However, remember that to be officially toilet-trained, your child needs to be aware of the urge to go and needs to have the desire to be clean. If you are having to take your child to the bathroom every two hours or your child would have accidents in her undies otherwise, you are the one that is technically toilet trained—not her. In baseball terms, that's a long run for a short slide. Why bother? Just wait until she can do it all by herself.

Q. Should I teach my son to sit or stand up to pee?

We vote for sitting. Toilet training for boys is probably easier if he squats like a puppy. He can pee like a big dog when his aim gets better! It depends on your son's motor skills when he starts to toilet train. Aiming requires good hand-eye coordination!

When you are ready for shooting practice, you may want to throw Cheerios into the toilet to give your son something to aim at.

Q. Should we use "pull up" diapers now?

This is personal opinion, but we think they are a waste of money. The so-called advantage is that your child will be able to take his diaper off whenever he needs to go to the bathroom. Reality check: the only incentive for a child to use the toilet instead of a diaper is the desire to be clean. Disposable training pants (yes, even those new Huggies Pull-Ups Training Pants) are almost as absorbent as regular diapers, so why should your child bother to stop playing and go to the bathroom?

Bottom line on disposable training pants: they will give your child the

POTTY

freedom to take off his diaper when and wherever he feels like it . . . but will not motivate your child to potty train. Our advice is to skip the disposables and buy cotton training pants (see below).

Insider Tip: Pull-ups at night?

There is also no advantage to having your toddler wear "Pull-Up" diapers at night when there is no way in heck he is going to wake up and take himself to the bathroom in the middle of the night. Just stick with diapers.

New Parent 411: Training pants

Training pants are basically cotton underwear with a few extra layers in the center portion. You can buy them at any baby store, Wal-Mart, or Target. They are reusable and washable. If your child has an accident, he will feel it, but it won't leave a puddle all over your kitchen floor.

Q. Should I use a potty chair or a toilet seat insert?

It's really your call. A potty chair sits on the floor and is easier for smaller toddlers to use. Toilet seat inserts are made to reduce the opening size of the toilet for your little one's hiney.

In our *Baby Bargains* book, we came down on the side of toilet inserts (versus the potty chair). Why do we like the inserts so much? First, they are easier to clean. Most kid potties have a separate container you have to clean out. With inserts, your child can flush the toilet herself and save you the clean up. Second, inspiration. When kids get to use the "big potty" just like mom and dad they are often more motivated to give up diapers. Third, transitioning. It will be so much quicker and easier to transition to the adult seat when your child is already familiar with the toilet. Finally, portability. You can easily pack along a seat insert on trips to Grandma's without having to take a whole floor potty.

The only other purchase to consider when using an insert is a step stool. These are necessary so your toddler can climb up on the toilet, as well as to give them a place to push off from when pooping.

When would a seat insert not work? Smaller toddlers may find inserts hard to use if their feet can't reach a step stool. In that case, consider a traditional floor potty. And if you have a boy, a toilet insert may be a little challenging when you are teaching him to pee standing up.

Toilet tantrums

Q. My child seems to be afraid of pooping on the potty. What do I do?

Children have some very irrational fears of sitting on the toilet to poop. Some are afraid they will get sucked into the potty and flushed down the drain. Others view poop as a part of their body and do not want to give it up. Know where your child's mind is developmentally—fantasy and reality are one in the same. See Chapter 3, Milestones for more information.

POTTY

? ?

If your child is afraid to poop on the potty, here is a four-week plan to gradually overcome any fear:

◆ *Week One:* Tell your child it is okay to poop in his diaper, but that he needs to do his business in the bathroom (not under the dining room table).

◆ *Week Two:* Tell your child to sit on the potty with his diaper on to poop.

◆ *Week Three:* Cut a hole in the diapers. Let your child wear the diaper on the potty. The poop goes through the hole into the potty.

◆ *Week Four:* No more diaper; use underwear or cotton-training pants!

Q. My 3 year old has been wearing panties for a few months now, but she still has poop accidents in them three or four times a week. What should I do?

Just because your child is wearing underwear doesn't mean she is toilet trained. If you are the one taking her to the bathroom every couple of hours, and she would otherwise have an accident…YOU are the one who is potty trained.

If she happily poops in her undies and continues playing as if nothing happened, then she needs to go back to diapers until SHE is ready to toilet train. Remember the two required developmental milestones: 1) sensing the need to eliminate and 2) wanting to be clean.

Your daughter has no desire to be clean, so she could care less about soiling her underwear. Put her back in diapers for the time being. When she seems bothered by sitting in poop, you can try to train her over a weekend. It may seem like a step backwards, but it will save a lot of frustration and clean up!

Q. My child was toilet trained and now is having accidents again. Help!

This is often a sign of stress. Any change, good or bad, in a child's life can be stressful. A new baby in the house, a move, a new childcare center, or even a vacation can set things off. If there is an obvious stressor in your child's life, expect that it may take a few weeks to get back on track.

If there is no stressor, and your child is suddenly wetting him/herself again, you should check in with your pediatrician. You will want to make sure your child doesn't have diabetes, a bladder infection, or vaginitis. And believe it or not, constipation is often the cause of leaking poop or skid marks on the underwear.

If your child has no medical reason for this new behavior, and doesn't snap out of it, it's time to remind your child what to do when he has the urge to pee or poop. Tell your child that he is responsible for his body. And discuss the natural consequences for the behavior. Example: if you cannot stay dry/clean, you will have to help clean yourself up. Never punish your child for having an accident, however.

Q. My child is toilet trained at school, but has accidents at home. What is wrong?

POTTY

If your child is capable of staying dry at school, cut him no slack for his attitude at home. Why do home accidents happen when a toddler is toilet-trained at school? One answer: the attention he gets at home with an accident. Any attention—good or bad—is still attention. Home accidents can also be caused by toddlers who are so absorbed by an activity, they forget they need to go!

It's time for boot camp. Tell your child he is now responsible for himself at home. You will remind him every couple of hours that it is time to use the bathroom. If he has an accident, he needs to clean up. Have clean underwear where he can reach them. If he poops, you can assist him, but be very low key about it.

You may also want to try using a sticker chart, with a reward for each time he successfully uses the bathroom at home.

Feedback from the Real World

Take yourself out of the loop, and have your child wear an alarm watch to remind him when he needs to go to the bathroom. The alarm can be set to go off every hour or two. (See information about Absent Minded Professors below).

Q. My son is three and he is still not toilet trained. His daycare will not let him advance to the older classroom until he can do it. Help!

This is one of our pet peeves. Daycare should NOT force toddlers to toilet train before they are ready. Unfortunately, some centers have those guidelines because the older classrooms have fewer teachers (and hence, not enough free hands to change diapers all day).

Remember: toilet training is a developmental milestone. If a child isn't ready, don't push it. And don't let your daycare center or preschool dictate this change.

There is nothing wrong with your child. He just needs a little more time to figure it out. Until then, he can be the big fish in the younger classroom.

Feedback from the Real World

Our son was three and a half before he was ready to toilet train. My husband and I had a bet going whether he would first learn to read or poop on the potty. As he sat on the potty one night before his bath, we got out a new toilet paper roll from the package. He said to us, "What's CH—arm—in?" He accomplished both milestones in the same week.

Take home message: The age your child toilet trains has nothing to do with his intelligence!

Q. My child is scared to death of auto-flush toilets. Will we ever be able to use a public restroom?

This is quite common, and yes, it can be

DR B'S OPINION

"Never punish a child for having poop or pee accidents. He can learn natural consequences, though—if he has an accident, he can help clean it up."

toilet training

overcome. You can stand in front of the sensor so it doesn't flush while your child is sitting on the seat.

Or, you can play a counting game with your child to see how long it takes for the flush to happen.

Q. We have tried numerous times to toilet train our child and we are still struggling. He is four years old now. What is the problem?

When it comes to late-potty trainers, we divide these kids into four groups. Here is our advice for each:

1. **The Absent-Minded Professor:** This child gets so engrossed in his activity that he ignores the urge to poop/pee. Solution: set a timer or let your child wear a watch that alarms on the hour. When the alarm goes off, he needs to stop his activity to use the bathroom.

2. **The Withholder:** This child had a bad experience with constipation and never wants to poop again. It will take some time to have non-painful experiences (and to clean out all the backed-up poop) to get on track. Solution: read our Poop Group section in Chapter 13, The Other End for tips.

3. **The Control Freak:** This toddler wants to do anything—as long as it is NOT what *you* want him to do! If he realizes that toilet training is important to you, he will dig in his heels and avoid success. This also applies to toddlers who have a new sibling in the house. Solution: play it cool. Pretend you don't care. Let your child control his pee and poop instead of controlling you. He can be reminded to use the potty by his body or by a timer, not by you. (Nagging is adult whining). Remove the diaper safety net and make him wear underwear. Praise success. Resist the urge to scold him for accidents.

4. **The Toilet Monster.** Some children have very vivid imaginations. Your child may have some really scary ideas about the toilet and his body's elimination products. He may or may not be able to articulate them. Solution: demystify the process. Explain that body garbage needs to come out and the urges your child feels are the body garbage asking to leave.

Feedback from the Real World

If you are going to use "incentives" to encourage your child to successfully toilet train, make sure *you* retain the ownership of them. Once you *give* that Thomas train to your son for his one potty success, he no longer is motivated by it. It's much more valuable to lend that toy to him for 30 minutes each time he poops. It will save you a lot of money, too!

Bottom line: even though kids may be dry during the day, it is normal not to be dry at night until age seven. (We can hear you gasping right now.) Don't take away the safety net of a diaper at night until your child has been consistently dry in the morning for a month. For more about this, see Chapter 13, The Other End.

Up next: sleep. Let's discuss moving a toddler out of a crib and into a big kid bed. Plus we'll go over naps, sleepwalking, early risers and more.

SLEEP
Chapter 8

*"Hyper-exhaustion
sounds like an oxymoron
unless you are two."*
~ Haiku Mama, by Kari Anne Roy

Now that your child has passed his first birthday, everyone in the house should be getting decent sleep.

If you just laughed out loud at that last sentence, well, we're here to help. This chapter will discuss sleep problems, along with what's normal when it comes to sleep, naps, night owls and early birds. Plus, we'll talk about moving your toddler from a crib to a big kid bed, a major transition for everyone in the family!

As the parent of a newborn, getting your baby to sleep through the night was the Holy Grail. Hopefully, this is a distant memory for you. If you are still dreaming of having a good night's sleep, we've got some solutions. And even if your child sleeps 12 hours a night, things come up to spoil that wonderful routine. We can help with that, too.

To know how to address sleep problems, you have to understand the science of sleep. So, let's first review the basics about toddlers and sleep.

Normal Sleep Patterns

In case you haven't read our first book *Baby 411*, let's take a quick second to review the types of sleep, sleep cycles and how much sleep your child needs. Newborns spend about 70% of their day asleep. Adults spend about 25% of their day asleep. Kids gradually reduce the length of time they sleep and organize their sleep cycles more like adults once they start sleeping through the night.

◆ **Type of sleep:** There are two types of sleep: REM sleep (Rapid Eye Movement) and Non-REM sleep.

Type	Brain activity	Timing
REM	Active (dreams)	Second half of night, am nap
Non-REM	Quiet	First half of night, pm nap

Sleepwalking and night terrors usually happen during non-REM sleep. We'll talk more about this later in the chapter. Newborns spend up to 80% of their sleep in REM. Adults spend about 25% of their sleep in REM.

◆ **Sleep cycles:** Humans go through a series of sleep cycles throughout an evening's rest. Adults tend to bunch all the non-REM cycles first, and then go through the REM stage. Babies do more flip-flopping. Each sleep cycle has a beginning and an end, where a person goes from light sleep to deep to light again, before entering the next cycle. Humans recheck their environments and body comfort at that time. At the end of each cycle, a *partial wakening* occurs. Kids wimper, cry or talk during a partial wakening (sometimes my husband does this as well).

◆ **Length of cycles:** The average sleep cycle for a child or adult is about 90 minutes.

Reality Check

Your child rechecks his environment every time he has a partial wakening. So it's important to be consistent about where he falls asleep and limiting objects (pacifiers, etc.) he falls asleep with.

Q. How much sleep do kids need?

You may be surprised—that's because many children do not get as much sleep as they should. Here is a ballpark guideline for the amount of sleep a child should get (including time spent napping):

1-3 years old: 12-13 hours
3 years old: 11-12 hours
4-5 years old: 11 hours

You may argue that your child gets less sleep than that and does perfectly fine. While that may be true, she'll be even happier and more interested in playing and learning if her mind is more rested. We cannot guarantee that your child will be tantrum-free if she gets more sleep . . . but she might be less edgy.

Here's the key point: sleep is GOOD for your child. It improves your child's memory, academic performance and adjustment to school.[1] Sleep may even boost your child's immune system.[2] Another study says enough sleep may

TODDLERS & THE LATE, LATE SHOW

True story: while at the movies the other night, we saw a strange sight—parents with toddlers in tow. Nope, this wasn't a matinee. This was an EIGHT O'CLOCK movie during the middle of the week. Yes, it was well after 10:30pm by the time the movie let out.

We realize babysitters can sometimes be hard to come by (we were fortunate that night to have one), but come on folks! And you wonder why your toddler is so cranky and sleepy?

This seems to be a trend, based on our unscientific survey of the our local mall at mid-week . . . dozens of families with tots going out to dinner, shopping and so on well into the evening hours.

What ever happened to a 7 or 8 pm bedtime for preschoolers? Apparently, we aren't the only ones to notice this. A recent hospital study by found that children under age five got only 8.7 hours of sleep at night and 9.5 hours total with daytime naps.[4] As you read on the previous page, the actual number of sleep hours recommended for children under age five: 11 to 13.

The take-home message: your toddler NEEDS that sleep . . . more than you need to hit the mall, dinner or a late-night movie! Ok, we'll stop the preaching now.

even prevent obesity. Kids who are tired are less interested in exercising and more interested in snacking.[3] If your child isn't sleeping as much as he should, hopefully these reasons will motivate you to do something about it.

DR B'S OPINION

"Next time you are struggling to get your toddler in bed, remember how important sleep is to your child's growth and development."

Q. We have a family bed. Is there any problem with this?

You can have a happy, well-adjusted child no matter where he sleeps. If this arrangement works well for everyone, stick with it. We'd suggest, however, that you move your kid out before he graduates college.

Q. How long are naps supposed to be?

Naps can be as short as 30 minutes or as long as three hours. If your toddler is still taking two naps a day, he probably has one short nap in the morning and a longer stretch in the afternoon.

Once your toddler moves to one nap a day, it will most likely last from one to three hours. As your child gets older, that power nap will get shorter.

Many parents wonder how they can encourage their child to have a longer naptime. Believe it or not, the answer is to put the child down *earlier* for his nap. If you start naptime *before* your child is rubbing her eyes and acting cranky, she might fall asleep earlier and sleep longer. Once she is showing you the signs of being tired, she is already overtired.

Q. What is a typical nap and bedtime schedule for a toddler and a preschooler?

Here's a breakdown to give you a rough idea of what you can expect. We know that all two year olds do not wake up and go to sleep at the same time. Use this as a general rule of thumb.

15 month old's schedule: a total of 13 hours a day of sleep:

6:30 am	Wake up
10:00-11:00 am	Morning nap
1:30-3:30 pm	Afternoon nap
7:30 pm	Bedtime

Two year old's schedule: a total of 13 hours a day of sleep:

7:00 am	Wake up
1:00-3:00 pm	Nap
8:00 pm	Bedtime

Four year old's schedule: with a total of 11 hours a day of sleep:

7:00 am	Wake up
8:00 pm	Bedtime

Q. When will my toddler drop down to one nap a day?

Most one year olds will take two naps a day—one in the morning, and one in the afternoon. Somewhere around 12–21 months of age, your toddler will cut out one of those naps. When your toddler plays in his crib instead of napping, you will know it is time to make the change. You may find your child will successfully take two naps on some days and one on others. And you will be hesitant to stop offering naptime. That's fine—hold onto it as long as you can! Consider naptime to be your toddler's downtime. He can do what he wants. But when your child is consistently playing instead of sleeping, it's time to move on.

Here is another classic scenario: Your toddler plays for an hour during the second "nap" and then he falls asleep in the late afternoon. If you let him, he sleeps for hours and then has trouble falling asleep at bedtime. This is also a sign that you need to drop the second nap. That second nap is really part of his nighttime sleep.

How do you make the transition from two naps to one nap? Keep your toddler up longer and put him down for a midday nap instead of mid-morning. And give up the second nap. Your toddler will be tired and cranky for the first few weeks, so you may need to make bedtime a little earlier to accommodate for it.

Q. My toddler only gets one nap at daycare even though he likes taking two naps at home. He is exhausted when he gets home from daycare. Any suggestions for what to do?

It's frustrating to have to follow group dynamics at daycare. A toddler up to 21 months may still need two naps a day. Not everyone drops a nap when they turn one. But childcare centers usually change the schedules when kids enter the toddler room. (It's due to teacher-student ratios and ease of scheduling).

So what happens to the kid who needs that second nap? Either he combines those two naps into one really big one or he goes home exhausted. In your situation, your child will do best if you aim for an earlier bedtime so he can catch up on sleep. We know you want to spend time with him when you get home from work, but he really wants to spend time horizontally with his eyes closed. That may mean a 6 pm bedtime.

Unless your work schedule or your childcare is flexible, the earlier bedtime is really the only option you've got.

Q. When will my child stop napping altogether?

Yes, all good things must come to an end. Wouldn't it be nice to take a nap everyday as an adult? Kids don't realize how good they have it!

Virtually all two year olds take one nap a day, usually for a couple hours. About 90% of three year olds take a one to three-hour nap. But by age four, the naps really drop off. Only 35% of four year olds still take a nap, from 30 to 90 minutes a day. And less than 20% of five year olds will continue to take naps (not on a daily basis).[5]

Real-life story: my son was three years and one month old when our daughter was born. During my pregnancy, I had visions of getting both kids to take a nap simultaneously (so I could catch one, too). Fat chance. My son gave up his nap on his third birthday, four weeks before my daughter was born! He had to be one of the 10% who didn't nap at age three. This is one reason why I only have two children.

Reality Check: Tips on dropping naps

Here are some tips for dropping from two naps to one, or dropping naptime altogether:

◆ *Dropping the morning nap:* when your toddler skips the morning snooze, start the afternoon nap a little earlier (aim for noon–1 pm to begin naptime). She will probably be cranky, so it will be obvious when it is time for her to take a nap! As her body adjusts to the new sleep routine, naptime may start later than 1 pm.

◆ *Late afternoon nap:* if your child plays for a while in bed and then drifts off to sleep, do not let him sleep past 5 pm. Start the afternoon nap earlier or wake your child up if he tries to snooze past 5 pm. Otherwise, he may not be ready to go to bed before 9 pm (which is too late for most toddlers).

◆ *Dropping naptime:* if your child is playing in his crib/bed instead of sleeping five out of seven days a week, it's time to drop the nap completely. Make bedtime earlier if he is cranky.

◆ *Continue quiet time or relaxation hour:* even though your child is no longer napping, she may still need some down time in the afternoon (and you might, too). Establish a regular routine for activities that fill the naptime void—maybe that becomes reading hour or independent playtime.

Moving from the crib to a big-kid bed

Q. When should we move our toddler into a big-kid bed?

There is really no rush to relocate unless you have a new baby who needs the crib. And besides, some kids enjoy their cribs until they are three years old . . . so why be in such a hurry?

Even with a new baby, we'd argue this isn't enough reason to bump your toddler out right now. Most toddlers really like being in their cribs—it's their home. And from your end, the crib is a safe place to sleep. You know where your toddler is at night. Once he graduates to a bed, he could end up wandering around your house if you don't have a good way to contain him. This becomes even more mission-critical if you also have a newborn in the house. Do you want a newborn up all night *and* a toddler up, too?

If you are expecting again, you still have plenty of time before your baby needs the crib. Chances are, your newborn will use a bassinet or cradle for the first couple of months.

One obvious sign your toddler is ready to move out of her crib: she starts climbing out. We'll discuss this shortly.

So, at what age do most kids move out of the crib to a big kid bed? While we don't have firm stats on this, judging from the feedback from readers on our message board, the magic age seems to be about 20 months. For many kids, that's the time "crib jumping" becomes an Olympic sport in the nursery. On average, we estimate most kids make the transition out of the crib to big kid bed between 20 months and three years of age.

Once again, let's stress that you do NOT have to move your child out of the crib at 20 months . . . if she is happy and not climbing out of her crib, let her stay!

Q. We have a two bedroom home, a toddler, and a baby on the way. We don't want the baby to disrupt the toddler's sleep. Where should everyone sleep?

First of all, the newborn will probably be in your room for a little while—in a bassinet or co-sleeper for the first couple of months. If you want to keep the baby nearby even longer, you could buy a room divider that would visually separate your bed from the "nursery" area. You can continue this scenario until the baby is sleeping through the night without night feedings.

At that point, move both kids in the same room, and put the younger child to bed first. That requires some cooperation from your toddler—but by then, he should be old enough to follow your directions and keep quiet when he goes to bed.

Reality Check: Free range toddlers

Just because your toddler has graduated from his crib, it doesn't mean he has all-night access to your entire house. He is free to roam around his *room* (which needs to be completely safe). But make his room his "crib" by putting up a safety handle on his bedroom door or installing safety gates in the doorway.

SLEEP

Q. I read in another book that you can use a crib tent to stop crib jumpers. Is that safe?

Ages 1-3

Yes, it is, in our opinion. Products like Tots In Mind's Crib Tent ($54, web: totsinmind.com; see image at right) serve two purposes: they keep a wandering toddler in his crib and they keep out family pets (yes, we're talking about you, Tinkerbell).

If you are not ready for your toddler to make the big kid bed transition, a crib tent is a reasonable short-term solution as long as it is installed correctly.

Of course, you can choose the opposite course to deal with crib jumpers: remove the crib's side rail so the child can climb out safely. That might be a way to buy yourself a bit of time before you need to buy the big kid bed. (Some cribs have a toddler rail that accomplishes the same result.) This is an acceptable alternative, but you'll want to consider closing the bedroom door or putting a gate up to keep your toddler in her room.

Q. How do we move a toddler into a big-kid bed?

Ages 2-3

Here are six tips for making this transition, as reprinted from our other book *Baby Bargains* (see back of this book for details).

Easing the transition to the big bed: Our six tips

Every child reacts differently when it comes time to graduate to a big kid bed. Our second child was excited to move out of the crib, wanting to sleep in a big boy bed just like his older brother. First-born kids, however, might resist, as they don't want to give up "their" crib to a newborn baby sister or brother. Here are our six tips to making this transition easier:

1 **MATTRESS ON THE FLOOR TRICK.** Going to a big bed can be scary. Ease the transition by first putting the twin mattress on the floor next to the bed and letting Junior sleep there for the first week or so. This also allays fears that your child might fall out of the toddler or twin bed in the first few days. Eventually, transition the mattress onto the bed frame. Another advantage to this tip: you can do the mattress on the floor trick BEFORE you buy the actual twin bed frame, which will give you some more time to shop.

2 **PUT THE NEW BED IN THE SAME POSITION AS THE CRIB.** That way the child's perspective of the room (nightlight, door) is the same and will be comforting.

3 **LEAVE THE CRIB SET UP IN THE ROOM FOR A FEW DAYS.** This can make the transition less jarring, as they see the crib still in the room. Of course, it's no big deal if the child goes back to the crib for a few days after trying out a big bed.

4 USE THE SAME FAVORITE CRIB BLANKET. It may be tempting to chuck the crib bedding for twin bedding, but using the same crib blanket can be helpful during the transition. And don't forget the all-important "lovey." Telling your child that his or her lovey is excited to sleep in the new bed can be encouraging too.

5 HAVE A BIG BED PARTY. This is an exciting time; celebrate the move from crib to bed with an informal party with friends and family (we always love an excuse for cake and ice cream anyway).

6 INVOLVE YOUR CHILD IN SHOPPING FOR A NEW BED. Build excitement for the transition by taking your child with you shopping. He might be more excited about this change if he can choose his new bed. Of course, you can always limit choices by having your child choose between two or three options if you think this will be too overwhelming.

DR B'S OPINION

"Don't expect a toddler to reach a milestone just because another baby is on the way. You can't toilet train him or make him sleep in a big kid bed just because you are ready!"

Q. What about safety side rails? Do we need them?

Ages 2-4

As readers of our other book *Baby Bargains* know, we aren't big fans of safety side rails.

We've been troubled by the number the injuries (and deaths) attributed to this so-called "safety product." Designed to keep a toddler from falling out of a bed, portable bed rails have caused 18 deaths and 40 "near miss" incidents in a recent sixteen-year period (Consumer Product Safety Commission statistics, 1990 to 2006). During the same time, there have been several recalls for defective bed rails that also caused death and injury.

Most of the cases of death and injury were caused when a child became entrapped in an area between the mattress on the bed and the attached bed rail, according to the CPSC.

But isn't it dangerous to put a two or three year old in a bed without a rail? No, it isn't. While the CPSC noted 47 deaths involving young children who fell out of beds from 1990 to 2000, the vast majority (38) were to children *under a year old* and most children died when they fell into or onto an object (a bucket, for example). Any parent who puts a child under one year of age in a twin bed (instead of a crib) should have their parenting license revoked.

Bottom line: cases of children who fall off a twin bed and die "due to blunt force trauma are rare," says the CPSC.

The CPSC has been so concerned with portable bed rail safety they voted to toughen the safety standards for this category in 2003 and again in 2005. Hence most new bed rails sold today are designed to stay snug against the mattress (preventing the gap that proved so dangerous in the past). But . . . there are an untold number of old, unsafe bed rails sold at garage sales, on Craigslist and so on.

The bottom line: we don't recommend safety side rails for toddler beds.

SLEEP

Instead of using rails, consider these tips:

◆ *If you are worried about your child falling out of a twin bed, put the mattress on the floor until he gets used to sleeping in it.*

◆ *Never put a young child to sleep on an adult bed.*

◆ *Avoid putting your child's bed or mattress up against a wall.* Entrapment could occur between a mattress and wall.

◆ *Never put objects (buckets, toys, etc) next to a bed that a child might hit if she rolled off the mattress.*

Q. We need to squeeze two kids into one bedroom, so bunk beds sound like a solution. But our oldest is four and all the bunk beds have warnings saying the child on the upper bunk should be at least six years old. Is it safe to put a kid under age six in the upper bunk?

No. Those rules are there for a reason! Younger kids are prone to rolling off a bed during sleep and obviously, an upper bunk would be dangerous. Even if you have a "big" four year old, it would not be safe to have them sleep in that upper bunk—size is not the issue, rather neurological development is what counts here. It isn't until a child reaches six years of age that he can consistently avoid rolling out of bed.

Also: be careful with captain's beds (those large beds with storage underneath). While fine for older kids (six or older), these beds can be a hazard for toddlers. Why? The huge distance between the mattress and floor makes it that much further for a toddler to fall.

Q. When is it okay to let our child use a pillow or blanket?

Now. The greatest risk of Sudden Infant Death Syndrome (SIDS) is when babies are under one year of age (90% of SIDS deaths occur in the first six months of life). A small travel pillow and a light blanket are fine to use with a toddler.

Reality check: Most toddlers will rotate 180 degrees in bed and rarely sleep under sheets and a blanket. Sleeper pajamas are a more practical option for toddlers to keep warm. Once kids are around four years old, they will actually stay put.

Q. Are comfort objects okay to have in the crib? What about toys?

It's fine to give your toddler a small stuffed animal when he's alone in a crib. Just make sure the eyes and nose are not removable (a choking hazard). Toys are also okay as long as they are safe to play with unsupervised. Board books are a nice choice . . . unless your child uses them as a teething toy. Both books and a stuffed animal may give your toddler something to do when he wakes up . . . so he doesn't immediately call for you!

Q. Our twins have slept in different cribs, but the same room since they were born. Should we move them to separate rooms?

Ages 1-4

If your kids do not wake each other up (or keep each other up), it's fine for them to share a room. If one child is a boy and the other is a girl, it's probably wise to separate them by about five years of age.

Q. My child is an early riser. Any way we can change that?

Ages 1-4

Everyone has his own body time clock. Some people are early risers and some are night owls. It's hard to change that clock. But you can tinker with it.

If your child likes to start her day at 5 am, that's fine—but she can start without you. Toddlers are capable of independent play. Just be reasonable about what you ask of your child. You can let her play in her crib or her room until it is time for you to wake up. You can gradually increase the time allotted for independent play.

For example, if your child wakes up at 5 am, start by giving her 30 minutes before you arrive on the scene. Add ten minutes to that playtime every few days, with your ultimate goal being 6 am. We know, even 6 am on a Sunday morning sounds like cruel and unusual punishment. You can pay her back when she's a teenager and you drag her out of bed on weekends.

Another strategy: try putting her down a little earlier for bedtime. Counter-intuitive, we know, but some kids will sleep longer if they are not overtired when they go to bed at night. This strategy will not work with a toddler if he is already getting a good night's sleep, however.

One more idea: cut out naptime. Kids need a certain number of hours of sleep in a 24-hour cycle. Daytime sleep reduces the number of hours of sleep a child needs at night. If you have a three year old who is transitioning out of his nap anyway, try giving up the nap completely and see what happens.

Reality Check

Getting your early riser to stay in bed or in his room until 6 am can be a real trick when your kid cannot read a clock yet. Some parents tell their child to stay in bed until the sun comes up.

While that strategy may work during some months of the year, it won't work during daylight savings time or if you live in Alaska.

Here's a great tip from Dr. Jodi Mindell, one of our favorite sleep experts—use a lamp timer. Set up a timer to turn on a lamp in your child's room at 6 am (or the wake-up time of your choosing). If your child awakens and the light is off, he knows he needs to go back to sleep. If the light is on, he knows it is time to start his day.

Q. My child is a night owl. Any way we can change that?

Ages 1-4

Just like the early riser, you cannot change someone's internal time clock. But do not stay up to watch the late-late show with him either.

Your child may do better with a 9 pm bedtime instead of 8 pm.

The problem arises when you need to get him up for daycare or preschool and he wants to sleep in. He may be tired and slow to get going in the morning. . . then get his second wind after dinner.

Again, give your child the opportunity to engage in independent play, if he cannot fall asleep. Let him look at books for a while or play quietly, until he is tired.

If you have a two-and-a half or three-year old who takes a late afternoon nap, eliminate naptime. It may help him to fall asleep earlier.

Disrupted Sleep Patterns

Q. My child talks in his sleep. Is this normal?

Yes, and it might give you an idea about what he is thinking! Kids and adults may talk in their sleep during a partial wakening period between sleep cycles. It's nothing to worry about.

Q. My child is a sleepwalker. Help!

Sleepwalking occurs during non-REM sleep . . . and the person has no recall of what happened during the walk. Sleepwalking can be common among preschoolers and school aged kids.

The best thing to do is to keep your child safe. Safety gates may be the best solution.

Q. Is it normal for a preschooler to have nightmares?

Yes. Nightmares (and dreams) occur during REM sleep, in the second half of the night. Kids will wake up anxious, but are consolable by their parents. And they may remember the nightmare the next day. Kids start having true nightmares around age three.

Some kids will use "Mommy I had a nightmare" as a strategy to get some extra snuggles at night. We've got tips on how to manage this in the section below. If your child is truly having nightmares on a regular basis, you should figure out what is happening during the daytime that is setting off nightmares.

Q. My child wakes up around midnight every night and seems possessed. What is going on?

These are called **NIGHT TERRORS**. They occur during the first third to first half of the night during non-REM sleep. The classic story: a child goes to bed and "wakes up" about three or four hours later in a panic. The child is not consoled by his parents' presence and may act like he doesn't even know them. These episodes may happen every night at the same predictable time.

Night terrors happen to kids over eighteen months of age. What triggers a night terror? Stress and over-tiredness are two likely causes. Oddly, kids with night terrors don't remember the event the next morning (but

SLEEP

? ?

NEW PARENT 411: NIGHT TERRORS VS. NIGHTMARES

Here are the differences between night terrors and nightmares:[5]

	Night Terrors	Nightmares
Age of onset	Older than 18 mo.	3-6 years old
Sleep state	non-REM	REM
Sleep period	First third of night	Last half of night
Consolable?	No	Yes
Easily returns to sleep	Yes	No
Recall of event	No	Yes

parents sure do).

Here's a solution to stop night terrors: set your alarm clock and wake your child up 15 to 30 minutes before his usual night terror happens. This will cause him to have a partial wakening, bypass the end of the cycle when the night terror occurs, and move on to the next sleep cycle. If you are seeing night terrors with some regularity, it's time to address the underlying reasons. Be sure that your child is getting enough sleep (by going to bed earlier and napping if necessary). Or figure out what is the real problem is—there's probably some other anxiety or stress that's happening.

Q. My child snores louder than my husband. Is this normal?

No. It may be kind of cute, but it may also be a sign of **SLEEP DISORDERED BREATHING** or **OBSTRUCTIVE SLEEP APNEA (OSA)**. These kids have enlarged tonsils and/or adenoids that obstruct their breathing at night. Whether a child actually stops breathing momentarily (apnea) or not, both disorders create a horrible night's sleep. Kids awaken several times a night to catch their breath. Children do not recall these night wakenings . . . but their bodies do. The disrupted sleep leads to poor behavior (sometimes misdiagnosed as attention deficit disorder) and poor performance in school as a result of sheer exhaustion.

Besides snoring, here are some other red flags for these problems: restless sleeping, bed sheets that look like a tornado blew through, and major drool marks on the pillow (due to the child breathing with his mouth open all night).

If you think your child has OSA, you can tape record the sounds and let your doctor listen to them. Then, a referral to an ear, nose, and throat specialist is made to discuss surgical therapy.

Bad habits and how to undo them

Disclaimer: The suggestions we offer below may involve some crying. Some parents feel very uncomfortable with the idea of letting their child cry. You are not the first parent to say, "It just doesn't feel right to hear my child cry." There is a specific pitch that a child emits that is uniquely bothersome to only its parent. We know. We are parents, too.

Crying is a form of protesting. It is not cruel and unusual punishment to set healthy limits on your child's behavior when you are doing it in your child's best interest. There will be MANY situations in your life as a parent where you set a limit to protect your child's well being ... but your child protests. When she has words, she will tell you she doesn't like your rules or will throw out the dreaded, "I hate you." Remember this. Believe it or not, the protest will be shorter than you think. Kids are resilient and adaptable. Set up a new "normal routine" and your kid will move on. You just have to be strong enough to live through the protest for a few days. *You are not doing your child a favor by depriving her of sleep in the name of keeping the peace.*

DR B'S OPINION

"View healthy sleep routines in the same way you view discipline. You are helping your child do the right thing for his body. Would you buy your child candy every time you are at the grocery store checkout line because you don't want to hear him to protest?"

We (Dr. Brown, that is) have spent more fifteen years doing sleep consultations with exhausted parents and children and have the experience to comment on what generally works and what doesn't. We also admit that there is no one-size-fits-all solution to every sleep problem.

If you choose to throw our advice out the window, that's fine. And if you have a method that works that you want to share with other tired parents, let us know. We love reader feedback.

Reality Check
Chronic sleep disruption and nightly bed jumping takes a toll on marital relationships. Poor sleep routines impact everyone.

Helpful Hint: Understanding why your toddler does not want to go to bed.
At the end of a busy day, you would think your child would be thrilled to crawl under the covers and get a little shut-eye. Nope. While there are a few kids who listen to their body cues, many don't want to go to sleep. Why? While toddlers are in their room, they envision the adults having fun elsewhere. Think about what you do once you put your child in bed:

You turn on the TV to watch the news (boring).
Your child thinks: They are watching Dora without me!

You pack your lunch to take to work the next day (boring).
Your child thinks: They are eating ice cream sundaes without me!

You get undressed and ready for bed (boring).
Your child thinks: They are getting ready for a party without me!

You get the picture. If your child hears you "partying" in your living areas, while he is in solitary confinement, it's no wonder that he will come up with a million reasons to avoid sleeping. He has no idea how boring it is to be a grown-up.

Q. My toddler STILL isn't sleeping through the night. What is the problem?

Well, there may be a variety of reasons. We will walk you through most of the common ones in this section. But they basically boil down to these problems:

Lack of/or poor sleep routines.
Poor sleep associations.
Lack of self-soothing skills.
Trained night feeding.

So, let's take a look at this in-depth:

The Top 10 Mistakes parents make with sleep routines

1 **LACK OF ROUTINE!** Kids are creatures of habit. If your child's schedule is erratic, his sleep will also be erratic.

2 **NAPS ARE SACRED.** If toddlers skip naps, or take them on the run (in the car or stroller), they are more tired and punchy at night when they need to wind down.

3 **SLEEP CRUTCHES.** If your child still relies on something like a pacifier, a bottle, or a parent to fall asleep, he will expect that sleep crutch when he stirs at the end of each sleep cycle...every 90 minutes!

4 **TRAINED NIGHT FEEDING.** Your toddler does not need to eat at 3 am. Unlike newborns that need nighttime feedings, your toddler can make it all the way to breakfast without a midnight snack. Don't let him snow you into feeding him. He's not really hungry . . . he's just been trained by a parent to expect food in the middle of a night!

5 **LACK OF SELF-SOOTHING SKILLS.** Your toddler is perfectly capable of falling asleep on his own (and has been since he was six months old). Cut the umbilical cord and give him a chance to figure it out.

6 **LATE TO BED.** Here's a classic blunder for working parents: you feel guilty about not seeing your toddler all day . . . so you keep him up at night. Bad idea—you aren't doing your child any favors. Let your toddler get the sleep he needs.

7 **INCONSISTENT MESSAGES.** Bedtime is 8 pm every night—except when your toddler wants to watch a movie. Or, when grandma comes over. Again, this is a mistake, sending inconsistent messages about what is

? ?

SLEEP

acceptable. And your toddler will quickly realize what she can get away with to change that bedtime.

8 **RESETTING NORMAL.** Teething, illness, and travel are just a few of the situations that conspire to ruin perfectly good sleep patterns. Remind your child what his normal sleep routine was, otherwise he will accept the new disrupted pattern as normal.

9 **UNNECESSARY INTERVENTIONS.** Both kids and adults have partial wakenings between one sleep cycle and the next. Your child may talk or cry out. That is not your cue to rescue him. If you intervene every time your child makes a peep, he will rely on you to get him back to sleep (See Mistake #3).

10 **GUILT.** It's a fact of life: your child will push your parental guilt buttons. Parents fear that their child will hate them if they . . . don't let her stay up . . . don't give her a pacifier . . . don't let her have a late-night snack, and so on. But remember this bottom line: if your child is getting good sleep, she will be happy to see you in the morning—and you will be happier to see her. Lose the guilt.

Q. I'm worried that if my child cries out in the middle of the night, he might be sick or injured. I can't ignore it.

If your child is usually a good sleeper and suddenly cries out in the night, you should check it out. If your child cries out EVERY night, it is quite unlikely to be a medical problem (and very likely to be a disrupted sleep pattern). Many families have asked me to examine their child to deem him officially "disease and teething free" before they address poor sleep habits. See your doctor if you'd like this reassurance.

There is a classic dilemma here: if your child cries out and you walk into the room to make sure he is OK, you might interrupt his sleep cycle. Yet, you feel guilty if you DON'T check on them. One possible solution for the child who cries out every night: video monitors. That way you can look at a screen to see if everything is all right . . . or if your child has gotten his leg stuck between the crib rails! That happened to our son once—talk about parent guilt. He was born in the pre-video monitor generation. (We discuss video monitor models in our other book, *Baby Bargains*).

5 REASONS PARENTS CAN'T LISTEN TO THEIR CHILD CRY

1. *You feel like you are helpless and not doing anything for your child.* Not true.
2. *You are a working parent and feel guilty.* Don't.
3. *You think you will scar your child for life.* You won't.
4. *You think you are an inadequate parent if you can't get your child to settle down.* You aren't.
5. *You think something must be wrong with your child.* Probably not.

Q. We still use a bottle to get our toddler to sleep. Is that okay? We also have middle of the night feedings.

Let's put this in bold italics—*your child's ability to sleep is independent of how full his belly is!* Sleep and full tummy have not been related since your child was about four months old (or maybe six months old if you had a preemie). Don't get suckered into this one. Although it is a sweet, loving experience to hold your toddler and feed him a bottle like you did when he was a baby, he's not a baby anymore!

If that isn't a good enough argument, here is a health related one: he has teeth now. If you must give your toddler a bottle before bedtime, you need to be brushing his teeth afterwards. Otherwise, the milk sugar will get left on his teeth overnight and might lead to cavities.

You can still do the loving, cuddly stuff before bedtime . . . just take the bottle out of the equation. And if you miss having a baby in the house, you can always have another one.

If you feed your toddler in the middle of the night, he is a trained night feeder. It's kind of like working the night shift. If you eat lunch at 3 am, your body is used to being hungry at that hour. If you stop eating at that hour, your body adjusts and eats more during the day. Adjust your toddler's hunger clock and stop offering food at night. If you feel strongly about offering your child a drink when he wakes up in the middle of the night, give him water. That way, there is no cavity risk.

As a side note, my husband thought someone should create a water bottle to hang on our son's crib (like in a gerbil's cage) so he could get his own water in the middle of the night. If you see this at your local baby store someday, you'll know who has the patent.

We'll talk more about kicking the bottle habit in the nutrition section of this book, but the Cliff's note version is here: Stop offering a bottle at one year of age. Your toddler is capable of drinking from a cup or a cup with a straw. And he doesn't need constant access to a baby bottle at night to fall back asleep. You don't need to suck on a bottle to fall back to sleep—and neither does your child.

Q. We took our 18 month old's pacifier away last week and she refuses to take a nap now. We are miserable! Should I give her the pacifier back?

No! Don't go backwards. She doesn't need the binky any-more. Follow through with a consistent nap routine and sched-ule. Your daughter can play, protest, or nap for an hour. If she doesn't take a nap, just make bedtime a little earlier. Eventually, she will adjust and return to napping. You'll be glad you stuck with it.

Q. Our child falls asleep in front of the TV and then we turn it off. Are we setting up bad habits?

YES, for several reasons. First of all, where is your child sleep-ing? Is the TV in his room? We discussed television use in Chapter 5, Play & Preschool, but here's the lowdown when it comes to TV and sleep.

We do not recommend having a TV in your child's room because it reduces your ability to monitor what and how much your child is watching.

If your child is falling asleep on the couch or in your room and then you move him to his bed, you are setting up a sleep association that will not be the same when he stirs after each sleep cycle. If he wakes up someplace different than where he fell asleep, he is likely to be disoriented, upset, and have trouble falling back asleep (not what he wants or what you want).

If your child associates falling asleep with watching TV, he will rely on this crutch to fall back asleep when he awakens (potentially every 90 minutes). Will he be turning the TV back on, or will you? Ultimately, it leads to poor sleep.

Q. Our preschooler comes into our room almost nightly and tells us she had a bad dream. Should we believe her? What should we do?

Your child is probably using the "bad dream" strategy from the "Toddler Handbook on How to Drive Your Parents Nuts" because it worked the last time she tried it. However, you won't know which time she really had a bad dream . . . and which time she is using the tactic to get another snuggle out of you. It's like the boy who cried wolf. No one believed him when the wolf finally showed up.

Since you won't know if it is the real deal or not, respond consistently every time. Quietly take her back to her room without arguing. She can tell you about the dream on the walk. Give her a hug and a kiss and say goodnight. Don't do anything different than you normally do (that is, if you don't normally sleep together, don't start now). It's that change in behavior that encourages her to use this tactic.

And remember, you can prevent having a free range toddler by installing a safety door handle or gate in the doorway. She may still call out for you in the middle of the night, though. Check out the tips at the end of this chapter on how to ease your child's mind.

If she is truly anxious or stressed and this is occurring on a regular basis, call your doctor.

Helpful Hint: Monsters, Inc.

Does your toddler think monsters lurk in her closet? Does a certain TV character freak her out? Yes, there really is nothing scarier than a clown. Especially in the dark.

For toddlers, imaginations are vivid and the line between reality and fantasy is fuzzy. Santa Claus and the Tooth Fairy are the real deal. And some things that are meant to be kid-friendly can be very frightening. (It always makes me sad to see a toddler crying when Mickey Mouse approaches at Disneyworld). Books, movies, and routine daily activities can turn into some very scary fears—especially when the lights are turned off. An obvious suggestion: preview movies or programs *before* letting your child see them. Most of the time, you know what will freak your child out.

Let your toddler know it is okay to be afraid of things. Telling her that monsters aren't real is not satisfactory. She'll continue to believe, but stop telling you about it because she knows you won't listen to her. And give her the power to overcome these fears. She can decide to leave the light on, or the closet door open. Monster spray and teddy bears with super-powers are also ways for her to be in control.

Real world tip: Install a dimmer switch in your child's room. That way you (or your child) can create just the right lighting to avoid scary shadows.

Q. We just got back from a trip and now our child's sleep routines are completely messed up. What can we do to get back on track?

As you've discovered after a trip, kids will adapt to a "new nor-mal" routine which may not be optimal—later bedtimes, extra rocking, and middle of the night soothing sessions and so on. Solution: you need to give your child a refresher course in his *regular* sleep routine.

Getting back on track just takes a couple of nights of returning to your regular plan. That may mean starting your routine EARLIER (wind down, etc.) to get back to the normal bedtime hour. It may also mean inten-tionally ignoring your toddler's requests for the third tuck-in you did back at Disneyworld.

Will there be crying and protesting? Probably. Is your child fine? Yes. Remember, it just takes a night or two to go back to "normal."

Q. We moved our son to a big boy bed and now he ends up in our bed every night. Help!

The key issue here is safety: when your baby was in a crib, you knew that was a safe zone. Now your toddler is in a big kid bed . . . and that means he can roam around the house at will. Again, our advice is to turn your child's room into his "crib." That is, put up a safety gate (or two, if your toddler is a climber) or keep the door closed. The basic rule: your child is to stay in his room while you are sleeping. Again, this is less about him sneaking into your bed and more about his general safety in the house.

If you decide not to go the safety-gate route, what happens if your child sneaks into your room at night? If this is becoming a regular event, quietly take him back to his room. Keep things low key. Do not argue. You can snuggle briefly or hug, but do not rock him to sleep. Remember, devi-ation from your normal routine is what reinforces him to come back the next night.

Feedback from the Real World

If your toddler can scale a safety gate quicker than you can say, "Time for bed," vertically install two gates, one on top of the other. That way your toddler can see out and call for you, but he cannot get out of his room. We recommend keeping the gates up until you can trust your child to be unsupervised around the house at 2 am (usu-ally four or five years of age).

SLEEP

Q. We have had a family bed. Now we would like our child to sleep in his own room. How do we go about accomplishing this?

Yep, that's a tough one. You will need to devise a plan and stick to it. Be consistent. You can accomplish this either gradually (over several months) or rapidly (in a few nights), depending on your own comfort level. Your child needs to learn how to a) fall asleep on his own, b) sleep in his own room and, c) not expect you to be there every time he wakes up in the middle of the night. As kids get older, they get less flexible. So, there is likely to be prolonged protesting!

DR B'S OPINION

"If you are a family bed person, that's great. If you are not a family bed person, don't become one when your toddler starts having sleep issues."

sleep

Motivate him to sleep in his own room. You may want to have a sticker chart for nighttime behaviors. Your child gets a sticker for going to bed without protesting. He also gets a sticker for staying there all night.

You can use safety gates in the doorway, close the door, or be a hallway monitor and sit outside his room until he falls asleep if you feel more comfortable. If he tries to make a break, quietly escort him back to his room.

Q. Our toddler never had a problem going to bed. Now he protests every night. Why is this happening? What do we do?

As toddlers and preschoolers lie in bed, their imaginations start to run wild. What are mom and dad doing while I am cooped up in here? Why can't I stay up and play longer? What's that shadow on the wall—is it a monster? Who will protect me—I'm up here all alone?!

You get the idea. The mind is a powerful thing. You need to help your child learn how to relax and not let her brain get carried away. You can also convince her she's not missing out on any fun by keeping quiet yourself after bedtime.

Here are some tips for how to ease your child's mind:

- ◆ **Transition time**. Do quieter activities to slow their motors down as bedtime approaches. Everyone needs time to wind down.
- ◆ **Reminders**. Tell your child that you will read X number of stories, then it is time for bed.
- ◆ **Stick to the plan**. If your child pleads for one more story and gets it, he will demand it every night.
- ◆ **Empower your child**. Your child lives in a fantasy world (see Chapter 4, Is This Normal? for more on this). Let his bunny or favorite object have super powers that will protect him from monsters. Or, spray your child's room with monster spray before bedtime (a nice air freshener will do—he can't read the label yet).
- ◆ **One last-request token**. Once you say goodnight, your child can have a token to cash in for one last request. This may be one more hug, a drink of water . . . you know the drill. But then, that

is it for the night. Bottom line: this gives kids a sense of control. Make it clear you will not be coming back after that and stick to it. A recent study on this token approach showed that kids who got one last request faired better than the group that didn't. They quieted in half the time (25 minutes versus 43 minutes) and stayed in their rooms 93% of the time vs. 44% of the time![7]

Establish a routine you want to keep…just like when he was a baby. Say good night and let your child fall asleep on his own. Follow through. If you wait in his room until he falls asleep or go back in, that's creating a routine YOU don't want. And remember, you are in charge.

Your toddler will follow, even though he may put up a little protest at first. If he chooses not to sleep for a while, so be it. You cannot force him to sleep. When he is exhausted, he will fall asleep. He may be tired for a few days, but if you follow through, so will he.

Q. My child has a screaming fit every night at bedtime. I go in to calm him down and it's two hours before he eventually falls asleep. Help!

Admitting you have a problem is the first step. Next, realize that the longer this agony goes on, the less sleep your child gets. This is a vicious cycle . . . the more tired he is, the harder it will be for him to wind down the next night.

So, take a step back and look at the big picture. What you are doing now is not working and your child is screaming at you. Try something new. Remember: it's not cruel and unusual punishment to take charge of your child's sleep habits. And it won't take months to turn things around if you don't back down—it's a matter of days. But if you cave, your child's behavior will only be reinforced and he will persist with twice the determination. Our advice:

- ◆ *Start the bedtime routine earlier.* If the screamfest lasts for two hours, start winding down at 5 pm so that the 7 pm bedtime happens at 7 pm, not 9 pm or later.
- ◆ *Empower your child with a comfort object* and use our one last-request token tip.
- ◆ *Stick to your plan.*
- ◆ *Say goodnight and mean it.* Do not go back in.
- ◆ *If your child is out of a crib, make the room safe.* Your child may tear up his room. He may try to escape. Or he may decide to play for a while once he realizes you are not coming back in. He is allowed to do any of these things. He may end up sleeping on the floor by the door. That's fine, too.

DR B'S OPINION

"Decide on your middle-of-the-night strategies during daylight hours. It's hard to think rationally at 2 am. Otherwise, you will just resort to the quickest way to get back to sleep."

SLEEP

Q. My 3 year old wears a pull-up at night. Once we put her in bed and say goodnight, she calls for us numerous times to take her to the bathroom. Should we respond every time she calls?

Nope. This is another classic bedtime stall tactic from the toddler playbook. Your daughter knows that you support her desire to use the potty, thus she is using it as ammunition to get your attention and avoid going to bed.

Set up the plan with her and stick to it. Once she is in bed for the night, you are not going to escort her to the bathroom. Assuming she is out of a crib and has access to the bathroom or a potty chair in her bedroom, she can do her business all by herself (and you will praise her for being so independent!). And if her pull-up is wet in the morning, that's okay too.

Q. Our toddler eats the crib rail. Should we be concerned?

If your child is demonstrating termite-like behavior, a possible solution is the Gummi Crib Rail ($15, KidKusion.com) to protect your child from splinters. Alternatively, you can just take the mattress out of the crib and let your child have free reign of his room. But then you'd have to worry about him eating the bookshelves!

Old Wives Tale
Nightlights cause near-sightedness. False.

Now that you've become the Master of Your Toddler's Sleep Domain, let's talk about that your child's growth. What's normal? What isn't? That's what is up next!

GROWTH
Chapter 9

"My mother's menu consisted of two choices: Take it or leave it."
~ Buddy Hackett

WHAT'S IN THIS CHAPTER

◆ **GROWTH CHARTS**

◆ **HOW TALL WILL YOUR TODDLER BE?**

◆ **OBESITY & BMI**

◆ **EATING OUT SMART**

◆ **8 RISK FACTORS FOR OBESITY**

Remember when your baby was little and you'd get a babysitter for the occasional date night with your spouse? When you checked on her in her crib, she looked like she'd already grown in the short time you were gone!

Good news: your toddler will finally slow down a bit in the growth department. She may wear out her clothes before she outgrows them! In fact, parents are so used to watching their infants grow out of their clothes almost overnight, that they become concerned when that stops happening with their toddler.

So let's discuss what those growth charts really mean and how to predict your child's adult height. And we will talk about that trendy little number—the body mass index or BMI.

Finally, you've heard about it and vowed your child won't join the statistics, but obesity—even among kids—is rampant. As a parent, you have a unique opportunity to stop the obesity epidemic by teaching your child about nutrition and lifestyles that are good for all of you. Now is the time to instill the habits that lead to health and well-being. And maybe, you can get something out of this too! Being an example for your kids is part of the job description when you hired on as Mom or Dad. It is probably the hardest part of the job as well. But if you want your kid to be healthy, now is the time to step up to the plate (so to speak) and teach them the skills they need to make healthy lifestyle decisions.

Q. What do those growth charts at the doctor's office really mean?

Growth charts are a good way to track how your child's body is growing. At every well-child visit with your doctor, your child's height and weight are checked—head size is also measured, but only until your child turns two. Weight is usually checked at sick visits, too, as it is used to assess severity of an illness (for example, dehydration) and to determine dosages of medications.

So what does your pediatrician do with your toddler's growth chart? The percentiles on the charts compare your child to other children the same age and gender in America. For example, a boy in the 75th percentile for height is taller than 75% of boys his age. (See Appendix E, References, for boys' and girls' growth charts). And check out Toddler411.com for a link to the World Health Organization's newest growth charts that reflect more of a global view of child growth patterns.

The key issue: is your child's growth consistent? A toddler will establish his or her general growth trends and stick with them by the time they reach age two. Babies who are born extremely large or small are not necessarily destined to remain that size on the growth charts. However, seeing kids fall off or rise above the charts raises a red flag . . . further investigation by your doc is needed.

What does it mean if the height and weight percentiles are significantly different? Check out our discussion on the body mass index later in this chapter.

Q. How much weight can I expect my child to gain from age one to two years? Two to three years? Three to four years?

Here are some general guidelines. Babies double their birth weight by four to five months of age. They triple their birth weight by one year, and quadruple their birth weight by two years of age. After age two, kids gain about four pounds a year until they hit puberty.

Let's take an average seven-pound newborn, for example.[1]

Age	Weight
Birth	7 lbs
5 months	14 lbs
1 year old	21 lbs
2 years old	28 lbs
3 years old	32 lbs
4 years old	36 lbs

Q. My toddler has dropped off the growth charts for his weight. What is wrong with him?

This is known as **FAILURE TO THRIVE**. Kids whose weight percentiles start off fine, then plateau or fall below the 3rd percentile need to be evaluated. The causes are various and include: poor feeding routines, feeding aversion due to a prior issue (like gastroesophageal reflux disease—**GERD**), malabsorption of food from intestinal problems, kidney disease, metabolic disease, hypothyroidism, and anemia.

An extensive medical evaluation is usually performed, unless a cause is found easily. Most of the time, there is no medical reason for this problem. The solution? A higher-calorie diet. While that's easy for us to say, it's much more challenging to implement if you have a picky eater. For tips on how to accomplish this goal, see Chapter 11, Food Tricks & Treats for details.

Q. How tall will my toddler be?

Height-wise, a good rule of thumb is 10-4-3-3-2. Babies grow ten inches in their first year of life, four inches the second year, three inches per year for ages three and four, then two inches per year until they reach puberty.

Here is how that measures up, for an average 20 inch newborn:[2]

Age	Height
Birth	20 inches
1 year old	30 inches
2 years old	34 inches
3 years old	37 inches
4 years old	40 inches

Q. Can you predict how tall my child will be?

For Boys: Add five inches to Mom's height and average that number with Dad's height.

For Girls: Subtract five inches from Dad's height and average that number with Mom's height.

This number is your child's growth potential. Of course, some people exceed their potential and others never reach it.

Your child's height at age two is the first (and usually most) accurate prediction of adult height. Kids have established their growth curves by then, so you can look at the child's percentile at age two and compare that with the same percentile for an 18 year old. See Appendix E, References for the growth charts. Bingo, there is your child's approximate height as an adult. Another option: multiply your two-year-old's height by two—kids are about half their adult height at 24 months old.

PREEMIES & CATCH-UP GROWTH

Babies born prematurely grow faster than those born on time. Most preemies catch up on the growth charts by two years of age. Your child's measurements can be plotted on the full-term baby and child growth chart both by chronological age (determined by birth date) and by adjusted age (determined by due date).

The head catches up the fastest, followed by weight, then height.[3]

GROWTH

? ?

Q. Why do you measure my child's head size?

Your child's brain grows at a tremendous rate–particularly in the first two years of life. Measuring the head proves this is happening. The soft spot on top of a baby's head (anterior fontanelle) is an opening between the skull bones that makes room for the brain to grow. The spot normally closes between nine and 18 months of age. If the soft spot closes prematurely, the brain may not have growing room (see **CRANIOSYNOSTOSIS**).

Some kids have huge heads (see **MACROCEPHALY**) and other toddlers have tiny heads (see **MICROCEPHALY**). This is usually hereditary–frequently you can look at the parents and figure out whose head the child inherited! But if the head size is enlarging too quickly or not enough, it's something your doctor will want to check out.

FYI: the height and weight percentiles are frequently not in sync with the head percentile. And that's fine.

The average newborn head size is 35 centimeters. It grows 12 centimeters in the first year of life, but only another ten centimeters for the rest of a child's life.

Q. My one year old still has a flat head. What should I do? Does he need a helmet?

Many babies will have a flat spot on the back of their head because they spend so much time on their backs. If your child still has a pronounced flat area by the time she is one year of age, you should discuss it with your doctor. What about helmets? They are not typically used for toddlers; this option is more appropriate for infants under a year of age who have severe deformities.

Q. When does the soft spot (fontanelle) close? Why does my doc check this?

As we mentioned above, the soft spot (anterior fontanelle) closes between nine and 18 months of age, providing for rapid growth of your baby's brain. The soft spot has another useful purpose, however. It's also kind of like an oil gauge—letting your doc know how much fluid/pressure is inside the skull.

Before it closes, pediatricians use that spot to assess for dehydration, infection (meningitis), and extra pressure in the skull (brain tumors, hydrocephalus). If the fontanelle is sunken, it can be a sign of dehydration. If the fontanelle is bulging, it can be a sign of extra pressure or fluid.

Hence, you'll find that the first thing many pediatricians do is touch your child's head during an exam.

Q. My toddler has a Buddha belly. Is this normal?

Most of the time, yes. Toddlers will position their center of gravity with their bellies protruding outwards. They also stand fairly bowlegged. As they get their sea legs, their posture improves and the belly gets pulled inward.

Rarely, this is a sign of a medical problem. Here are some red flags:

◆ Belly is full and protruding while standing or lying down
◆ Belly feels tense and hard, or a mass is felt

These red flags may indicate a solid tumor or celiac disease—check it out ASAP with your doctor.

Overeating, Obesity, and the Body Mass Index

Q. My toddler eats as much as I do. Should I worry?

Yes. There is an obesity epidemic going on in our country (and in other developed countries too). In 1970, only 5% of toddlers were overweight. Today, 12% of American two to five year olds are obese (and 17% of six to 19 year olds are obese). Obese toddlers become obese adults. A recent study showed that kids who gain weight the most rapidly in the first two years of life have NINE times the risk of being obese adults.[4]

Why are toddlers obese? It goes back to that nature vs. nurture question. Are some children destined to be overweight because their genetic material code makes them that way? Or, are parents and society giving kids the wrong messages about eating? A loaded question, we know.

We're going to hedge here on the nature issue. Even if a child is predisposed to obesity, there is nothing science can do right now to alter these genetics. Experts wonder, though, if obese parents increase the risk of childhood obesity partially because of the family's eating habits. The point is, at least there is something we can do about nurturing healthy food habits.[5]

DR B'S OPINION

"Healthy lifestyles begin in infancy. It's much easier to create good habits than break bad ones."

FAST FOOD OUTLETS VS. FRUITS & VEGGIES

Do the number of fast food outlets near your home have an effect on the number of fat kids in your neighborhood? Activists on this issue have postulated that for years, but a recent study casts doubt on that theory.

In a 2005 study by the Rand Corporation that appeared in the journal Public Health, researchers did NOT find a link between children's weight gain and the mix of grocery stores, fast-food outlets and restaurants near their homes.[6]

Interestingly, researchers on the study DID find a link between obesity and the relative prices of fruits and vegetables in their communities. After studying the weight gain of 6918 kids in 59 metro areas, the study found that "kids who live in areas where fruits and vegetables are expensive are more likely to gain excess amounts of weight than kids in areas where those foods are relatively cheaper."[7]

You should not only be watching *what* your child is eating, but also *how much*. Offer appropriate child sized servings (more on this below) and do not serve "family-style" where second helpings are easily accessible at the kitchen table.

Q. Our pediatrician checks our child's body mass index. What is it and what does it mean?

The body mass index is the standard way to assess obesity risk and is better than just comparing height to weight percentiles. The BMI measurement can objectively identify kids and adults who are at risk for complications of obesity that include diabetes and heart disease. The formula has been used for children age two and up, but the World Health Organization now encourages checking this number starting at birth. The ranges of normal vary for gender and age (up to age 20) because the BMI varies as kids grow. Adults have standardized norms because we have stopped growing.

Here is how we do the calculation:

$$\frac{\text{Weight in lbs.}}{(\text{height in inches}) \times (\text{height in inches})} \times 703 = \text{BMI}$$

Now, take this number and plot it on the BMI chart in Appendix E, References. We'll make an analogy to a stoplight here. If your child is in the green, keep up the good work. If he is in the yellow, be more careful about diet and exercise. If he is in the red, STOP what you are doing and make some serious changes in lifestyle habits:

Childhood BMI Norms
Green light:	BMI less than 85th percentile	Keep going
Yellow light:	BMI 85th to 95th percentile	Watch it
Red light:	BMI over 95th percentile	Stop!

If you want to find out your own body mass index, take the number based on the calculation above and compare to these norms:

Adult BMI Norms
Healthy BMI	18–25
Overweight BMI	25–30
Obese BMI	Over 30

If you hate doing math, go to KeepKidsHealthy.com (click on "useful tools" and then "BMI calculator"). For more info on the body mass indices for both children and adults, check out the Centers for Disease Control's web site (cdc.gov–search for BMI calculator). Or, check out our web site Toddler411.com for a link to the World Health Organization's Body Mass Index chart and growth charts.

Reality Check: Metabolic Syndrome
Metabolic syndrome describes the health-related consequences of obesity. Diabetes, high blood pressure, and high cholesterol all result from obesity and are more likely to occur

in kids whose BMI's are high in early childhood.

A whopping 30% of overweight American teens have metabolic syndrome. It affects boys more than girls, and is more common in African Americans, Mexican Americans, and Native Americans.

How are kids tested for metabolic syndrome? First, doctors look at a kid's waist circumference, measured around the level of the belly button. If the waist circumference is over the 90th percentile (we have a link on Toddler411.com to a web site with a chart on this) and your child has *two of the three* following problems, he or she has metabolic syndrome:

- ◆ Elevated blood pressure (over 90th percentile for age, gender, height).
- ◆ A fasting blood sugar level GREATER than 100 mg/dL or any blood sugar at or above 200 mg/dL.
- ◆ A fasting level of: triglycerides greater than 100 mg/dL; HDL cholesterol less than 40 mg/dL in boys; or HDL cholesterol less than 50 mg/dL in girls.

Children who have metabolic syndrome already are at greater risk of having it as adults[8] . . . and can end up with heart disease at an early age. We don't say this to scare you—but you should realize how serious this is for your child and make a change.

Feedback from the Real World:
Eating out smart.

Who is to blame for the obesity epidemic in children? Fast food outlets? Soda companies? Food makers who emblazon cartoon characters on junk food? What about parents?

No matter how easy it is to cast blame for obese kids on some evil, dark force in the marketplace, we parents must also take our share of the blame. . . especially for poor food choices and the volume of food consumed when eating out. We know that people will eat more food if they are presented with large serving sizes.[9] We also know that kids consume an extra 187 calories on a day when they have eaten fast food (versus a home-cooked meal).[10]

Of course, all families still find themselves eating out from time to time. So if you do eat out, try to make it a healthier experience. Here are some tips:

- ◆ Pick milk or water as a beverage, if you have that option.
- ◆ Visit the salad bar (try the low fat dressing options too).
- ◆ Select a place that offers fresh fruit and vegetables as a side dish.
- ◆ Avoid all-you-can-eat buffets (sorry, Vegas fans).
- ◆ Select grilled, baked, or poached items instead of fried ones.
- ◆ Eat fish occasionally—not the fried stuff or ones smothered in a butter or cream sauce.
- ◆ Look for heart healthy icons on menus.
- ◆ Don't SUPER-size anything.
- ◆ Try Japanese or Vietnamese food. It's lower in fat.
- ◆ Share an adult meal with your child. At restaurants that have huge portions (yes, we're talking about you, Cheesecake Factory), consider ordering ONE adult meal and splitting it.
- ◆ Pick a restaurant with HEALTHY kids menu choices. Example: Wendy's now offers deli sandwiches; Red Lobster offers grilled

mahi and Chili's now offers a choice of side including black beans, steamed broccoli and corn on the cob (as an alternative to ubiquitous French fries.) Hint: go ONLINE to look at restaurant kid menus. Nearly all chains today have web sites with their kids' menus online . . . take a second to surf your way to healthier choices.

Reality Check: **Taking the time to cook**

We know the drill. Both parents work outside the home. You rush out of work at the end of the day. You rush to pick your little one up from childcare. And you rush home to eat dinner. Trying to get a home cooked meal on the table with a toddler who is begging for your attention can be a real challenge. It's a "Calgon, Take Me Away" moment.

Guess what? We live this life too. And we manage to eat a fairly healthy diet with food that has been prepared in our home on a nightly basis. Here's how we make it work:

◆ **Plan ahead.** Make menus for the week and shop for all those items on the weekend. If you are missing a key ingredient, you are less likely to run out and buy it and more likely to just eat out.

◆ **Prepare ahead.** Prepare casseroles, lasagna, etc. on weekends so they are ready to cook or re-heat on workdays.

◆ **Crockpots rule.** Stews, meats, and soups are extremely easy to simmer all day.

◆ **Make extra.** You can make several meals in one cooking session and freeze servings separately for another time.

◆ **Pick up healthy convenience foods.** Salads in a bag, pre-sliced fruits and vegetables, frozen veggies. And many health food markets like Whole Foods and Wild Oats now offer healthy prepared foods that can be reheated quickly at home. Yes, this can be more expensive than cooking yourself, so you'll want to use this as a safety net occasionally, not frequently.

The typical American eats 30% of his meals outside the home. If we can lower that number, we'll be one step closer to stopping the obesity epidemic.

Q. Do kids naturally overeat?

Good question. It's a difficult one to answer.

In general, infants will eat what they need to. And if they occasionally overindulge, they just throw it back up.

However, as children get older, some of them adopt unhealthy eating behaviors. One interesting study theorized that some children eat when they aren't hungry because they have trouble delaying gratification. In other words, if the food is sitting in front of them, they cannot resist the temptation to eat it. And they may learn these behaviors from their parents. In this particular study, children at age four who ate food simply because it was there had a higher rate of being overweight at 11 years of age.[11]

Here are a couple of questions to consider:

◆ Who is making the food available 24/7?
◆ Who is buying the high calorie, low nutrient food choices?

It's hard to teach a child to be patient and to delay gratification, but it's certainly an important life skill for many issues a child will face (not just with food). Something to think about!

Q. Are there any factors that put a child at risk for obesity?

Yes. A British study identified the top risk factors in kids under age three that predict obesity later in life:[12]

1. Children with an obese parent or parents.
2. Children with a body mass index at or above 95% at age three.
3. Children who watch more than eight hours of TV per week at age three.
4. Babies who start out small and have "catch up growth" in the first two years of life.
5. Children whose weight at both eight and 18 months is over the 75th percentile.
6. Babies who have excessive weight gain in the first year of life.
7. Low birth weight.
8. Sleep duration less than 10 1/2 hours at age three.

A recent American study boiled it down to three key lifestyle issues that DOUBLE a preschooler's risk for being obese. Here they are:

1. Eating family dinner together less than five times a week.
2. Sleeping less than 10.5 hours a night.
3. Watching more than two hours of television a day.

Q. Are there things I should do now to help my child grow up healthy?

Yes! And you should start right now! Offer a healthy diet and don't let your child become a couch potato! A recent study showed that sedentary lifestyles start as early as age three.[13]

However, the beauty of children is that they are relatively malleable. The die has not been cast yet. It is much easier to teach a child how to live a healthy lifestyle than to try to change an adult's poor lifestyle habits.

DO offer your child a healthy diet (he can choose whether or not to eat it—more on this later).
DON'T force your child to eat . . . or to "clean his plate."

DO offer appropriate child-sized servings of food.
DON'T offer food every time your child is whiny (for a toddler, that could be 20 times a day).

DO prepare most of your family's meals in the home and eat together.
DON'T let your child graze while he is playing.

DO have healthy snacks. It may be your child's main source of nutrition for a while. (Tips for healthy snacks are coming up in the next two chapters.)
DON'T serve family style. Plate your child's food for her rather than putting it out for self service.

? ?

DO be a good role model. Eat your veggies!
DON'T be sedentary. Your child is watching you.

DO encourage an active lifestyle. Keep your child moving.
DON'T put a TV in your child's room.

DO limit media use. The American Academy of Pediatrics recommends no media use for kids under age two years and less than two hours a day of all media (TV, computers, videos) for kids over the age of two.
DON'T let your kid stay up too late. Establish healthy sleep routines.

Now that you have the low-down on your toddler's growth, let's move on to that tricky sequel: what your toddler eats (or doesn't eat).

NUTRITION
Chapter 10

"I do not like broccoli. And I haven't liked it since I was a little kid and my mother made me eat it. And I'm the President and I'm not going to eat any more broccoli."
~ George H.W. Bush

WHAT'S IN THIS CHAPTER

◆ HOW MANY CALORIES DOES A TODDLER NEED?

◆ TYPICAL SERVING SIZES

◆ THE NEW FOOD PYRAMID

◆ TOP 3 MOST IMPORTANT NUTRIENTS

◆ LIQUIDS: FORMULA, MILK, JUICE

◆ ORGANIC FOOD: WORTH THE PRICE?

◆ WEANING

◆ DOES YOUR TODDLER NEED A SUPPLEMENT?

◆ FLUORIDE

And now, the chapter you've been waiting for . . . food. Here is the nitty gritty on what your child is *supposed* to be eating.

A word of caution—no one else's kid follows these rules either. (We've devoted Chapter 11 to tackling this battle). But we know you want to have some idea of what direction you should be heading, so we'll give that our best shot. You'll learn about caloric needs, serving sizes, and recommended daily intake of various nutrients.

Remember that one-size-fits-all food pyramid we all grew up with (and had to memorize in science class)? No more! Now we have a much better and more rational approach to health put out by the USDA. This time, the pyramid is individualized to age and daily exercise levels.

Plus we'll discuss whether your child needs to take a multivitamin, whether sippy cups are a good idea and more.

Q. How many calories does a child need a day?

First of all, let's explain what calories actually are. Calories are a measure of energy. Protein and carbohydrates both contain four calories per gram of food. Fat contains nine calories per gram of food. Think of calories as body fuel.

How much "energy" does it take to fuel a child? The answer depends on the child's age, gender, activity and stress levels (one example: an illness can impact how many calories your child needs per day).

NUTRITION

??

A CONVERSION CHEAT SHEET

For the mathematically challenged (that is, us writers) and for those who have forgotten the metric system, here is a refresher course for what you need to know to survive this chapter. *Note: cc (cubic centimeter) or ml (milliliter) are ways of measuring fluid volumes.*

1 cc	=	1 ml
5 cc or 5 ml	=	1 teaspoon
15 cc or 15 ml	=	1 tablespoon
3 teaspoons	=	1 tablespoon

There are 30 cc per ounce, or 2 tablespoons per ounce (oz).
There are 16 ounces (oz) in 1 pound (lb).
There are 2.2 pounds in 1 kilogram (kg).

Yes, there is a magic number. And we'll tell you how to calculate this . . . but don't get carried away. If you obsess over this figure, you will drive yourself, your spouse, your child, and your doctor crazy.

The average estimated energy requirements (EER) for a one to three-year-old are about 82 calories per kilogram of body weight in 24 hours. In English, that's how many calories your child needs every day to grow. But even if you convert your child's weight to kilograms and multiply by 82, it's not that simple. Kids who were born prematurely will have higher calorie needs to achieve catch up growth. And kids who are more physically active, or are recovering from an illness will also have greater calorie (energy) needs.

So here is your math quiz for today:

Convert your child's weight into kilograms by dividing the weight in pounds by 2.2.

Multiply the weight in kilograms by 82.

That number is your child's recommended daily caloric intake.[1]

Here is an example, but remember these are just ballpark figures:

Age	Weight (lbs)	Weight (kgs)	Calories per day	Range (cals/day)*
Birth	7 lbs	3.2 kg	368	350–700
1 year	21 lbs	9.5 kg	1000	700–1200
2 years	28 lbs	12.7 kg	1044	1000–1500
3 years	32 lbs	14.5 kg	1192	1000–1600
4 years	36 lbs	16.4 kg	1341	1100–1800

*The calorie *range* is based on a child's activity level. A sedentary child needs fewer daily calories than an active child. Hence, a four-year old who eats 1800 calories a day and plays videogames for exercise is overeating.

Q. How many times a day should my toddler be eating?

In general, young children will eat three meals and two snacks a day. Often, kids will eat more at snack time than at mealtime. One mom recently told me that her child ate her best meals

NUTRITION

while sitting in the shopping cart at the grocery store. Take home message: offer good food options when your child is interested in eating!

Q. What is a typical serving size for a 1-2 year old?

We will answer this question with a big disclaimer: the government does not provide a food pyramid for kids under the age of two. Here's the basic idea, though. *Toddlers eat about ONE-QUARTER of an adult serving size.* Here's another way to visualize average serving sizes for toddlers:[2]

One serving of meat	=	4 marbles
One serving of chopped fruits/veggies	=	3 dominoes
One serving of cooked pasta/rice	=	a ping pong ball
One serving of cheese	=	2 dice
One serving of juice	=	a shot glass

Knowing this, you should feel better when you watch your toddler eating like a bird!

Q. What is a typical serving size for a 3-4 year old?

Here are serving sizes recommended by the US Dept of Agriculture Center for Nutrition Policy and Promotion (2000). We've compared the portions to real world sizes to give you a better visual on what this really means.[3]

One serving: Grains   *Visual size: 1/2 Tennis Ball*
- ◆ 1 slice of bread
- ◆ 1/2 cup cooked rice or pasta
- ◆ 1/2 cup cooked cereal
- ◆ 1 oz ready to eat cereal

One serving: Fruit   *Visual size: 2 golf balls*
- ◆ 1 piece of fruit/melon wedge
- ◆ 6 oz juice
- ◆ 1/2 cup canned fruit
- ◆ 1/4 cup dried fruit

One serving: Vegetables   *Visual size: 2 golf balls*
- ◆ 1/2 cup chopped or raw vegetable
- ◆ 1 cup raw leafy vegetable

One serving: Milk   *Visual size of cheese: 9 volt battery*
- ◆ 1 cup milk
- ◆ 1 cup yogurt (kid yogurts are 1/2 cup FYI)
- ◆ 2 oz of cheese

One serving: Meat   *Visual size: A deck of cards*
- ◆ 2–3 oz cooked lean meat, poultry, fish
- ◆ 1/2 cup cooked dry beans = 1oz meat
- ◆ 1 egg = 1oz meat
- ◆ 2 Tbsp. peanut butter = 1oz meat

Q. How many servings a day of each food group should my child eat?

The famous "Food Pyramid" is designed for kids ages two and up. We've included this information because we think it's important to know the specific recommendations. But don't get too hung up on achieving these goals on a daily basis. It's more realistic (and less stressful) to look at your child's food intake over a week.

Here is the official, revised Food Pyramid, created by the US Dept. of Agriculture. You can access it by going to mypyramid.gov.

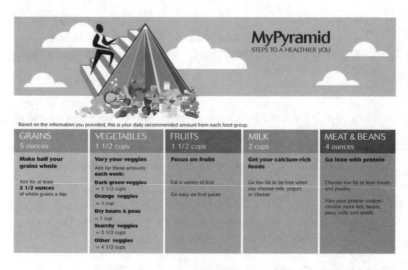

Based on the information you provided, this is your daily recommended amount from each food group.

GRAINS 5 ounces	VEGETABLES 1 1/2 cups	FRUITS 1 1/2 cups	MILK 2 cups	MEAT & BEANS 4 ounces
Make half your grains whole	**Vary your veggies** Aim for these amounts each week:	**Focus on fruits**	**Get your calcium-rich foods**	**Go lean with protein**
Aim for at least **2 1/2 ounces** of whole grains a day	**Dark green veggies** = 1 1/2 cups **Orange veggies** = 1 cup **Dry beans & peas** = 1 cup **Starchy veggies** = 2 1/2 cups **Other veggies** = 4 1/2 cups	Eat a variety of fruit Go easy on fruit juices	Go low-fat or fat-free when you choose milk, yogurt, or cheese	Choose low-fat or lean meats and poultry Vary your protein routine- choose more fish, beans, peas, nuts, and seeds

If you go to the website, you can individualize you and your child's daily food requirements by inputting the age and activity level of the person. The chart above is for your average three year old.

One cool part of the MyPyramid site: you can print out a meal-tracking worksheet. And you can find out what your child should eat over a WEEK rather than just on a daily basis. Again, we think this makes more sense when you are talking about toddler diets.

Q. Are there any nutrients that toddlers eat too little of?

Yes. Calcium, iron, and fiber. Let's take a look at these important nutrients:

CALCIUM. Kids need different amounts of calcium as they grow up:

◆ Kids from age one to two need 500 milligrams per day (mg/day).
◆ Kids ages three to eight need 800 mg/day.
◆ Kids ages nine to 18 need a whopping 1300 mg/day!

If your child has a milk intolerance or allergy, there are other ways to get that calcium. Calcium-fortified orange juice has the same amount of calcium ounce-for-ounce as milk. Other calcium rich foods include: broccoli, green leafy vegetables, rhubarb, and tofu. Yes, we are parents too—we realize it is nearly impossible to get kids to eat green leafy vegetables, especially in the serving sizes needed to get much calcium.

If you want to give your child a vitamin supplement containing calcium, choose one that includes Vitamin D too—it helps the body better absorb the calcium.

Here are some examples of the calcium content in foods:[4]

Calcium content of foods, in mg per serving (approximate); 1c = 1 cup

100mg	150 mg	200mg	250mg
15 brazil nuts	1 c ice cream	1 c beet green	1 c almonds
6 broccoli stalks	1 c oysters	1 oz cheddar	1 oz Swiss cheese
2 c farina	1 c rhubarb	1 oz muenster	1 oz parmesan
1 c cooked kale	1 c spinach*	3 oz sardines	1 c milk (300mg)
1T blackstrap molasses	1 oz mozzarella	4 oz yogurt	1/2 c ricotta
3T light molasses	1 oz feta cheese		
1 c cooked navy beans	1/2 c collards		
3 1/2 oz tofu	3 oz canned salmon		
3.5 oz sunflower seeds			
5T maple syrup			
1 c cottage cheese			

*Spinach contains a fair amount of calcium but our intestines do not absorb it very well. The same is true of whole bran cereals that claim to be a good source of calcium.

BOTTOM LINE

A recent study examined the current calcium recommendations and adult bone health. It determined that one of the most important factors influencing bone health was exercise. So, it's not just milk that builds healthy bones![5]

2 **IRON.** Iron is needed to carry oxygen on your red blood cells throughout your body. Babies are born with an iron bank, thanks to Mom. Once that supply is depleted, they need to replenish it through their diets, like the rest of us. Iron deficiency causes **ANEMIA**, which leads to fatigue, poor weight gain, and poor intellectual functioning. If you are concerned about your child's iron levels, ask your doctor for a simple blood test (see Appendix C, Lab Work & Tests for details on testing).

The iron requirement for kids fluctuates based on age. Although infants under a year of age need 10 mg of iron a day, toddlers aged one to two years need only seven mg of iron a day. The amount of iron increases again as kids get older: children aged three to eight years need 10 mg of iron every day.[6]

Beef may come to mind when you think of iron-rich foods, but there are many types of foods that contain iron, including cereals that are iron-fortified. One important point: "Heme" sources of iron (that is, meats) are more easily absorbed by our bodies than "non-heme" iron sources (that is, grains, legumes, nuts, vegetables). And note: Vitamin C-rich foods help the body absorb iron . . . BUT calcium rich foods interfere with iron absorption.

We've noted in bold print the foods with the highest iron content.

Iron content of foods (approximate)[7]

Food	Serving size	Amount of Iron in mg
Breads and Grains		
Bagel, plain, toasted	1	2.8
Bread, whole wheat	1	1.3
English muffin, toasted	1	1.5
Chex mix	2/3 c	6.9
Fruits		
Dried Apricots	10	1.6
Avocado, California	1 medium	2.0
Dried figs	10	4.1
Dried peaches, halves	10	5.2
Dried prunes	10	2.0
Raisins	2/3 c	2.0
Cereals		
40% Bran flakes, Post	**2/3 c**	**8.1**
100% Bran	1/2 c	3.4
All-Bran, Kelloggs	1/2 c	4.5
Cheerios, General Mills	**1 c**	**8.1**
Grape Nuts, Post	**1/2 c**	**8.1**
Wheaties, General Mills	**1 c**	**8.1**
Total, General Mills	**3/4 c**	**18**
Cream of Wheat, instant	**3/4 c**	**9.0**
Corn grits	1 c	1.5
Meats/Seafood		
Lean ground beef	1 oz	1.3
Beef liver	1 oz	2.5
Pork loin	1 oz	1.2
Chicken breast	1 oz	0.3
Turkey, dark meat	1 oz	0.7
Clams	**9**	**23.7**
Nuts and Seeds		
Cashews	1 oz	1.7
Mixed nuts w/peanuts	1 c	5.0
Pistachios	**1 c**	**8.7**
Sesame seeds	1 T	1.3
Sesame butter/tahini	1 T	1.3
Sunflower seeds	1 oz	1.4
Legumes and Veggies		
Beet greens	1 c	2.7
Garbanzo beans	1 c	3.2
Great Northern beans	1 c	4.1
Kidney beans	1 c	3.1
Pinto beans	1 c	4.4
Baked potato w/skin	1	2.5
Tofu	**1/2 c**	**13.2**

NUTRITION

3 FIBER. Fiber keeps us regular guys and gals. It also can reduce the risk of colon cancer, high cholesterol, and heart disease. The typical American diet—for kids and adults—is much lower in fiber than what is recommended. So, make it a little family project to increase everyone's fiber intake.

The fiber requirement for children is easily calculated by age in years + 5 = number of fiber grams/day. For example, a three year old needs eight grams (3+5) of fiber per day. FYI: adults max out at 25-30 grams of fiber per day.

Fiber will be your friend when your child starts toilet training. We'll explain that further in Chapter 13, The Other End. Whole grain breads and cereals, legumes, and green leafy vegetables are great sources of fiber. If your kid loves kale, that's great. If not, pick a high fiber cereal and make it into trail mix for a snack. Another clever trick is to add a teaspoon or two a day of *Benefiber,* a natural fiber supplement, to basically anything your child eats. He will never know it is in there (one warning: we have had anecdotal reports of clogged sippy cups thanks to Benefiber).

Here is the top list of fun fiber foods. We've noted in bold print the highest fiber foods (or the ones that pack the biggest fiber punch).

Product	Serving Size	Fiber grams/serving
Bread/Grains		
Whole wheat Bread	1 slice	2 grams
White Bread	1 slice	0
Pepperidge Farm		
HeartyWheat Crackers	3 crackers	1 gram
El Galindo Wheat Tortillas	**1 tortilla**	**9 grams**
Hodgson Mill		
Whole-wheat pasta	2 oz	6 grams
Brown Rice	1/4 cup	0.9 grams
Cereal		
Baby Rice	1/4 cup	0
Baby Oatmeal	1/4 cup	1 gram
Baby Mixed	1/4 cup	0
Cheerios	1/2 cup	1.5 grams
Quaker Oat Bran	1/2 cup	2.4 grams
Quaker Oatmeal Squares	1/2 cup	2.5 grams
Kellogg's Nutragrain bars	1 bar	1 gram
Fiber One Cereal Bar	**1 bar**	**9 grams**
Wheat germ	**1 Tbsp**	**1 gram**

(I like wheat germ because you can sneak it into food and your child might not even notice)

Fruit (raw) Note: The peel is often the part of the fruit that contains the fiber. Since most kids hate the peels, the fiber ends up in the garbage and not in your child.

Apple (with peel)	1/2 medium	1.8 grams
Apricots	1/4 cup	0.8 grams
Banana	1 whole	2.7 grams

Product	Serving Size	Fiber grams/serving
Blackberries	1/4 cup	1.8 grams
Dried Cranberries	1/4 cup	1.5 grams
Grapefruit	1/4	1 gram
Grapes	1/2 cup	0.5 grams
Orange	1/2	1.5 grams
Pear (with peel)	1/2	2.1 grams
Prunes	**1/4 cup**	**3.5 grams**
Raisins	1/4 cup	2 grams
Raspberries	1/4 cup	2 grams
Strawberries	1/4 cup	0.8 grams
Watermelon	1/2 slice	0.5 gram

Vegetables (Usually unpopular with children, however.)

Broccoli	1/4 cup	1.4 grams
Corn	1/4 cup	1 grams
Green beans	1/4 cup	0.7 grams
Green peas	1/4 cup	2.2 grams
Lima beans	1/4 cup	3 grams
Pinto beans	**1/4 cup**	**3.7 grams**
Refried Beans	**1/4 cup**	**3 grams**
Squash (baked)	1/4 cup	2 grams

Here are some of our favorite, kid-friendly fiber foods:

◆ Bean dip, bean soup, bean and cheese burrito
◆ Cracklin' Oat Bran cereal
◆ Oat bran muffins
◆ Pureed prunes mixed in yogurt
◆ Wheat germ mixed into anything
◆ Cranberry sauce—2 grams per 1/4 cup
◆ Garbanzo beans (hummus dip)—3 grams per 1/4 cup
◆ Creamed corn—2.5 grams per 1/4 cup
◆ Sunbutter (sunflower seed butter) —2 grams per Tbsp.

Q. Do I need to keep giving my toddler the baby cereal?

No. The beauty of *all* cereals (baby and adult) is that they are fortified with iron. And toddlers need a lot of iron to help them grow at the pace they do. But your toddler can eat regular Cheerios and still get that iron. (One bonus: adult cereals tend to be priced LOWER than special baby cereals).

If your child routinely eats rolled oats or other unprocessed grains, then you need to find another dietary source of iron (see above for details).

Q. When should we stop feeding baby food? That's the only way our toddler will eat vegetables.

Go with whatever works. Yes, baby food is expensive—and it would be nice to get your toddler to eat the food you pre-pare. But we realize that isn't always possible with a toddler. Any way you can get your child to eat vegetables is acceptable at this stage of the game.

? ?

NUTRITION

If your toddler hits age three and still will only eat baby food, it is time to check with your doctor.

BOTTOM LINE: The big picture

If you want to see a detailed list of your child's nutritional needs, milligram for milligram, check out the Institute of Medicine's website (iom.edu, click on Child's Health). They have a nifty PDF file on this topic—we have posted it on our website (Toddler411.com, click on Bonus Material).

Here is the big picture:[8]

Nutrient	Age 1-3	Age 4-8 years
Fat	30-40%	25-35%
Carbohydrate	45-65%	45-65%
Protein	5-20%	10-30%

Liquids

Q. My one year old is drinking formula. When do we make the switch to regular milk? How do we do it?

The American Academy of Pediatrics recommends making the switch at one year of age. Think of formula as an Ensure drink—it's loaded with tons of nutrients. But now your toddler is eating solid food and doesn't need to get his entire nutrition from what he drinks.

The recommendation for children ages 12 to 24 months is to drink 16 oz a day of WHOLE or 2% milk. Why whole milk? Toddlers need that fat for brain development. **Once kids turn two, they need to drink skim or 1% like the rest of us.** (Yes, that's what grown ups should be drinking—otherwise that fat will be clogging your arteries).

The decision of whether to use whole or 2% rests with you and your child's doctor. Who might need 2% milk? Kids ages 12 to 23 months who get enough fat in their diets and have obese family members or who already show in their growth charts that their weight is exceeding their height.[9]

How do you make the switch? Well, you finish out the formula you've got and buy a gallon of whole milk. With most kids, you do NOT have to mix milk half and half with formula or warm it up, etc. Of course, there are always those finicky toddlers who might require such tricks . . . but most don't.

Don't be too worried if your child refuses to drink milk. Kids can eat their dairy instead of drinking it. Yogurt and cheese are both loaded with calcium. The one advantage of milk over other dairy products is that it is fortified with Vitamin D. Only select brands of yogurt are Vitamin D fortified and cheese is not fortified at all. Your child needs a daily source of Vitamin D in his diet or he will need to take a vitamin supplement (see the section on vitamins later in this chapter).

What if your child doesn't like ANY dairy products? Or your family is on a vegan diet? Check the list of calcium-rich foods earlier in this chapter for non-diary suggestions. You can also choose to give your child a multivitamin that contains both calcium and Vitamin D. Just remember, the rec-

NUTRITION

? ?

ommendation is 500 mg of calcium a day for kids ages one to two years. From three to eight years old, kids need 800 mg of calcium. Children one to four years of age need 400 IU of Vitamin D a day. FYI: There is 100 IU of Vitamin D in each eight oz. cup of milk.

Again, here are some helpful stats:

Food	Calcium content
Milk, 8 oz (1 cup)	300 mg
Yogurt, 4 oz (kid size)	200 mg
Orange Juice, fortified, 8 oz	300 mg

Q. I've seen toddler formulas at the store. What do you think of them?

Frankly, we think these "toddler formulas" are an expensive gimmick—basically, a waste of money. No, most toddlers do NOT need toddler formula, which is similar to those meal-replacement drinks for adults. Remember: the goal is to have your child EAT their calories, not drink them. So unless your child is struggling to gain weight, don't bother.

Reality Check

Every parent worries that their child can't possibly grow on the food he is eating. Despite those concerns, most toddlers eat what they need to thrive. Avoid the temptation to give your child a nutritional supplement like a toddler formula or Pediasure to provide nutrients. Your child will end up drinking his calories and eating even less!

FYI: Got questions about hormones and antibiotics in milk? Does it pay to buy organic food? Pop over to Chapter 18, Environment & Your Toddler for the skinny on these hot topics.

Q. We'd prefer to give our child an alternative to cow's milk. How do the other options compare?

Whole cow's milk is the preferred dairy beverage because it contains almost half of its calories from fat, half of your child's daily calcium requirement, and 25% of your child's Vitamin D needs per cup. Other products have trouble measuring up to that. If you select an alternative beverage, just be sure your child gets his fat, calcium, and Vitamin D needs met elsewhere in his diet. Here's a look at different milks:

8 OZ SERVING	WHOLE*	SKIM**	SOY	RICE	GOAT	ALMOND	COCONUT	LACTAID
Calories	150	80	100	130	100	60	360	80
Calories from FAT	70	0	35	20	23	23	324	0
Total fat	8 g	0	4	2	2.5	2.5	36	0
Sodium	115 mg	125	96	90	115	150	40	125
Carbohydrate	11 g	12	8	28	11	8	4	113
Cholesterol	35 mg	0	0	0	10	0	0	5

NUTRITION

8 OZ SERVING	WHOLE*	SKIM**	SOY	RICE	GOAT	ALMOND	COCONUT	LACTAID
Protein	8 g	9	7	1	8	1	4	8
Vitamin A	yes	yes	yes	yes	yes	yes	no	yes
Vitamin C	yes	yes	no	no	no	no	no	no
Vitamin D	yes	yes	yes	yes	yes	yes	no	yes
Calcium	50%	50%	60%	<10%	50%	30%	no	100%
Other*			iron	B12				

* Whole milk has 3.5% fat. **Skim milk has .1% fat. ***Other nutrients.

Reality Check:
Does soy milk cause ADD or cancer or early puberty?
Soy milk has received some bad press lately. Because soy milk contains phytoestrogens (the plant version of estrogen), there is some concern it can interfere with reproductive or immune functions. Soy milk also contains manganese, which in extremely high doses can cause developmental problems in rats.[10]

Now, we didn't mention these news items to scare you. The fact is: these are just theories at this point . . . this isn't any scientific proof of soy milk being dangerous for either adults or kids. In fact, the National Institute of Health says this is not a concern. And until there is more data, don't lose sleep over having a gallon of soy milk in your fridge.

Q. I'm considering offering my child unpasteurized or "raw" milk. Is there any health risk I should worry about?

The risk outweighs the benefits for raw milk, in our opinion (and the opinions of other health experts).

Advocates of fresh-from-the-farm products say that raw milk contains nutrients that are killed off by the pasteurization process. Yes . . . but, pasteurization also kills off some pretty serious germs that you really don't want your child exposed to (like E coli 0157, which can cause food poisoning and life-threatening kidney failure).

To get similar benefits to raw milk without the risks, we suggest yogurt or kefir, both of which contain pro-digestive agents (a.k.a. probiotics).

Q. My toddler refuses to drink milk. Any ideas?

Don't sweat it—he can get his fat and calcium needs met in other ways. However, getting Vitamin D from other food sources can be a real challenge (see discussion in the vitamin section later in this chapter).

For starters, he can eat his dairy instead of drinking it. Try whole milk yogurt, cottage cheese, cheese cubes or slices, or smoothies made of whole milk yogurt. And while we don't recommend it on a regular basis...ice cream does contain calcium!

Some parents add a flavoring (yes, we are referring to chocolate) to the milk to encourage their child to drink it. Although it's not something we recommend, we know you may be tempted to do it anyway. If you choose this route, we suggest using a more nutritious choice like a teaspoon of Carnation Instant Breakfast powder or Ovaltine powder.

NUTRITION

? ?

We also have a whole list of non—dairy sources of calcium in a previous section of this chapter.

As for fat, kids under age two still need it for their rapidly growing brains. Although "healthy fat" sounds like an oxymoron, here are some reasonable choices: avocados, eggs, olive oil, nuts, and peanuts.

Q. My toddler drinks a lot of milk. Could this be a problem?

Yes. If your toddler is still chugging down 30 to 40 oz a day, he probably is not eating much in the way of other foods. Remember, milk is not his main source of nutrition anymore. *Kids ages one to three only need 16 oz of milk per day.*

So what can a parent of a milk-a-holic do? It's called limit-setting. After your toddler has reached his milk limit, offer water for the rest of the day. If he really enjoys his milk right before bedtime, ration the volumes so he can have that last nightcap.

FYI: weaning off the baby bottle goes a long way to fixing this problem. There is less chugging when a toddler is drinking from a cup.

Q. When should we stop using a bottle?

Now. If you have a child over one year of age, she has other ways to get fluid into her mouth. Trust us, if your child is thirsty, she will drink from a cup. The only exception to this rule is a child who has trouble controlling her mouth muscles (see oral motor delays in Chapter 6, Challenges)

Here is why you should kick the bottle habit:

◆ *Bottles encourage chugging fluid.* Your toddler does not need to do this anymore. And a preschooler definitely should NOT be drinking from a bottle!

◆ *Bottles encourage oral gratification.* You want your toddler to move on from this phase. The more she continues to explore her world with her mouth, the more germs she will acquire!

◆ *Bottles at bedtime (a popular sleep crutch) encourage both tooth decay (cavities) and ear infections.* Both are painful for your child and expensive for you.

RED FLAG: Sippy cups: friend or foe?

We know you love sippy cups. They don't spill and your toddler can walk around with them. However, not everyone is a fan of the sippy cup. Case in point: dentists. Since sippy cups bring fluid directly to the back of the top front teeth, they can promote tooth decay if the fluid your child is drinking has any sugar in it (yes, that means milk or juice).

If your child has not mastered a cup yet, try a cup with a straw as an alternative. If you must use a sippy cup, just use it for water.

Feedback from the Real World

One of our readers, Amy Clayman, who is both a mom and a speech pathologist (kidspeaktherapy.com) had this to share regarding sippy cups:

"An infant 'suckles' (protrudes her tongue to get liquid) when feeding from the bottle or breast. When a toddler (at or over one year of age) drinks from a straw or open cup, he draws his tongue *back* for a more mature sucking pattern.

Sippy cups, by their very design, require a ton of pressure (using mouth muscles) in order to get the liquid out. (Have you ever tried to drink out of one? It's nearly impossible.)

Therefore, the child resorts to a more immature "suckle" with tongue protruded. While not directly causing speech-articulation problems, if the child has some weakness in that area, it doesn't help. I urge all of my clients receiving speech therapy to cease sippy cup use immediately.

As an alternative, I love the First Years Take and Toss straw cups. There is no valve. Simply a plastic cup, lid and straw. They are about $2.99 for four at any Wal-Mart store. Now, if you shake them, they indeed will spill, but if they just fall over, no liquid will escape."

Q. I'm still nursing. Do I need to offer whole milk too?

Human milk is a fine source of fat and calcium for your child. In fact, a recent study showed that the fat content of breast milk increases with the length of time a woman nurses.[11]

Some older children continue to nurse for comfort, or get easily distracted and nurse for just a few minutes at a stretch. Since you cannot determine serving sizes if you are doing direct breastfeeding alone, just keep an eye on your child's growth chart. If she is gaining weight appropriately, you're doing just fine. If she isn't, you may need to supplement nursing with cow's milk or an alternative dairy product.

Q. I'm still nursing. When should I wean?

Nursing is a team effort. We feel you should nurse as long as both members of the team want to continue. Women in some cultures will nurse one child until the next one comes along, or even nurse a toddler and an infant simultaneously. However, if you have made it this far and have decided to wean—you get a gold star! You are allowed to say that you want your body back to yourself. Your child is also allowed to decide when to stop—and you should respect that decision, too.

Here are some tips on how to do it:

◆ *Weaning happens gradually.* If you stop abruptly, your body will be unhappy with you.

◆ *You can drop one feeding every few days, saving the most comforting one for last.* That is usually the last one of the night or the first one in the morning.

◆ *Once you stop nursing, you may feel full or even leak milk for a week or so.*

◆ *Wear your old bra*, even though it is a little binding.

◆ *If you feel like you are going to explode,* pump or manually express just enough milk to get comfortable.

◆ *Taking pseudoephedrine* (brand name: Sudafed) *during the day, diphenhydramine* (brand name: Benadryl) *at night*, and/or drinking three cups a day of sage tea may help with any discomfort.

NUTRITION

Q. How much juice should my child drink in a day?

The American Academy of Pediatrics says no more than SIX ounces a day. Make sure it is 100% juice and actually contains vitamins (check the package—apple juice, for instance, should be fortified with Vitamin C).

Here's how some juices compare, head to head:

V-8 V-FUSION ($)
◆ 100% juice (carrot, various fruits)
◆ 120 calories per 8 oz serving
◆ 45% Vitamin A and 100% Vitamin C requirements for an adult

LAKEWOOD ORGANIC ORANGE CARROT JUICE ($$$)
◆ 100% juice (organic carrots, oranges)
◆ 100 calories per 8 oz serving
◆ 300% Vitamin A and 100% Vitamin C requirements for an adult, plus other vitamins and nutrients

R.W. KNUDSEN ORGANIC APPLE JUICE ($$$)
◆ 100% juice (apple)
◆ 120 calories per 8 oz serving
◆ 6% Vitamin C requirements for an adult

STORE BRAND ORANGE JUICE ($)
◆ 100% juice (orange)
◆ 110 calories per 8 oz serving
◆ 120% Vitamin C requirements for an adult

$ = more affordable; $$$ = most expensive

Reality Check

Drinking one can of soda per day increases your risk of obesity by 60%. A 12 oz. can of soda contains 150 calories and ten teaspoons of sugar. Fruit flavored drinks are no better. They are loaded with sugar with little or no nutritional benefit. And kids who are juice-a-holics may graduate to soda.

If you are packing a lunch for preschool, give your child bottled water, milk, or 100% fruit/vegetable juice.

Q. How much water should my child drink in a day?

The Institute of Medicine recommends *four cups* of water a day for a one to three year old, and *five cups* a day for four year olds.[12] Yep, that is the size of a Big Gulp.

Ok, let's talk some reality here. Few toddlers ever drink that much water. BUT . . . that doesn't mean water isn't important. In fact, your child should drink water INSTEAD of juice of other sweetened beverages (hint: when you go out to eat, consider water as a beverage).

Of course, if your toddler actually drinks the recommended daily intake of water, do send us a note so we can send you a special award certificate!

NUTRITION

Vitamins and Nutritional Supplements

Q. My toddler eats nothing. Should I give him a multi-vitamin?

Nope.

Unless your child has a medical problem like anemia or failure to thrive, he does not need to take a multivitamin. We know that you worry about your picky eater, but they don't require any supplements. That's the official word from the American Academy of Pediatrics.

If your child has specific deficiencies (diagnosed after a visit your pediatrician), supplements may be recommended.

Reality Check

Lynn Goldman, R.D., a pediatric nutritionist, gave us her thoughts on multivitamins. She pointed out that many nutritionists recommend multivitamins for kids . . . more for the parent's benefit than the child! It doesn't hurt to have a kid take a multivitamin—and easing parent anxiety reduces the power struggles over food. But we suggest you aim for a healthier diet instead!

Q. My pediatrician recommends that my child take a Vitamin D supplement. We live in California. Don't you think he gets enough Vitamin D from the sun?

Nope.

You are correct that humans use sunshine as a catalyst to make Vitamin D in their bodies. And being a Texan, I used to think that I would have plenty of Vitamin D from living in the sunbelt. Wrong. When was tested, I was so deficient that my Vitamin D level didn't even register on the charts! I'm taking a supplement now.

It's a Catch 22. We know the sun can damage our skin and lead to skin cancer...so we lather our children up with sunblock. However, that interferes with the sun's job of aiding in the body's Vitamin D production.

Why do we all need Vitamin D? Well, it's critical for healthy bones because it helps the body absorb calcium and phosphorous. However, there are additional health benefits like protection against certain cancers, autoimmune diseases, and high blood pressure.

The American Academy of Pediatrics recommends that all kids get 400 IU of Vitamin D per day. But since the recommended intake of milk for a one to three-year old is two cups a day, your child will only get *half* of his daily needs met (there is 100 IU of Vitamin D in each eight oz. serving of milk). And there are very few other food sources of Vitamin D (a few yogurts are fortified with Vitamin D, and cod liver oil is about the only other option—yuck!).

Bottom line: most kids from ages one to three need a Vitamin D supplement. And once your child turns three: he also needs a Vitamin D supplement if he isn't drinking at least a quart (32 oz) of skim or low-fat milk a day.

Helpful Hint:
Calcium and Vitamin D supplements for kids
Looking for a calcium supplement? Flintstones Plus multivitamin

with "bone building support" contains 200 mg of calcium and 400 IU of Vitamin D per tablet. Those are intended for kids ages four and up. See Appendix A, Medications, for details.

Q. Can my child eat a protein/energy bar?

Our mantra (borrowed from Benjamin Franklin): everything in moderation. Protein bars are packed with vitamins—like 200% of an adult's Vitamin C and E requirement—for example. If you want to let your child take a bite out of your Balance bar, that's fine . . . but we don't suggest you buy these items for your child or let him eat an entire bar. Besides being packed with vitamins, energy bars are also loaded with sugar. A chocolate chip Cliff bar has 21 grams of sugar.

Q. My child is anemic. What type of iron supplement should he be on?

We will talk about the specific iron supplements on the market in Appendix A, Medications. What you need to know is that multivitamins have lower concentrations of iron to provide a "maintenance" dose. If your child is anemic, he needs "replacement" doses of iron found in specific supplements.

Also: consider boosting the iron in your child's diet. See our section on foods that are good sources of iron earlier in this chapter.

Q. I've heard about Juice Plus capsules. Are these safe? Does my child need it?

Well, it's certainly one way to get your kids to eat kale! According to the Juice Plus website (juiceplus.com), one little capsule contains the "nutrimental essence" of 17 different fruits, vegetables and grains.

We'll give this company bonus points for backing up its claims with clinical research. While we think supplements like Juice Plus are safe, it's probably better in the long run to teach your child to eat fruits and vegetables than taking a little pill.

Q. I've heard DHA (fish oil) supplements are good for kids' brains. Does my child need it?

Maybe our grandparents did know something when they shoved cod liver oil down our parents' throats!

Let's talk for a moment about what these oils are in the first place. Docosahexaenoic acid (DHA) is an Omega-3 fatty acid used in our bodies to make nerve tissue, hormones, and cell membranes. Foods that contain DHA naturally are fatty fish, like salmon, trout, mackerel, sardines, and tuna. DHA is also found in organ meats (liver, etc.), and human breast milk.

There's another fatty acid called Alpha-Linolenic acid (ALA) that you should know about, too. Foods that contain ALA are flaxseed oil, soybean oil, canola oil, and walnuts. Although DHA and ALA are related compounds, their health benefits are not the same. The body simply uses ALA to convert it into other fatty acids—so there isn't much health benefit to consuming ALA. Eating ALA-rich mayo on your sandwich is not going to make much difference. And if a label just says, "rich in Omega-3", it's probably ALA that's in there.

We know that these fish oils promote brain and vision development in infancy. But do older kids really need them in their diets? And if there are health benefits, how much do kids need?

Let's look at each issue. The health benefits of DHA have been studied to treat everything from acne to PMS. The most compelling studies show protection against heart disease and high cholesterol. And humans aren't the only ones on the DHA bandwagon. My dog even takes it for his arthritis. (He's not keen on the flavor of it, by the way. I mention this because your child may not be, either.)

Currently, the jury is out about adding fish oil supplements to a child's diet. Your child can get a fair amount in his diet if he eats fatty fish a couple of times a week. Other foods that are fortified with DHA are really only adding micro-amounts of the fatty acid (see chart below). Fish oil tablets are available for kids, but your child (like my dog) may not like the taste or the aftertaste. The good news: Fish oil tablets do NOT contain mercury in any significant amount. (We discuss the problem with fish and mercury in Chapter 18, The Environment and Your Toddler).

But here's another complication: we don't even know WHAT the recommended daily allowance of fish oil is for kids! For adults, the American Heart Association recommends that adults eat two servings of fatty fish per week. And adults who already have heart disease should get 1000mg of DHA per day.

Here is a list of foods that contain DHA, both naturally or fortified:[13]

3-oz. serving	Omega-3 content (EPA & DHA, in mg)
Salmon, Atlantic	1825 mg
Herring, Atlantic	1700
Salmon, pink, canned	1400
Whitefish	1400
Swordfish **	695
Tuna, bluefin *	1300
Mackerel, Atlantic	1000
Trout, rainbow	1000
Bluefish	800
Sardines, oil-canned	800
Mussels, blue	700
Tuna, water-canned, white *	700
Fish sticks	680
Bass, freshwater *	600
Shark (fried) **	600
Smart Balance Omega Plus Buttery Spread (1 Tbsp)	160
Land O Lakes Omega 3 eggs (1 egg)	150
Breyers Smart DHA Yogurt (6 oz)	30
Horizon Organic DHA Milk (1 cup)	30
Silk Plus DHA Soy Milk (1 cup)	30

* May be high in mercury; see earlier in chapter for precautions.
** Contains the most mercury. We do NOT recommend kids eat these fish.

? ?

NUTRITION

Q. Does my child need a fluoride supplement?

This is a more difficult question than you might think. The answer: it depends on how much fluoride is in the water your child drinks at home, preschool, or childcare. Check with your local water department to see if fluoride occurs naturally in your community's water or is added. For an in-depth discussion of fluoride, pop over to Chapter 12, Hygiene.

As you know, fluoride is a mineral that prevents tooth decay. If your family drinks tap water AND your community's water supply contains adequate amounts of fluoride (0.7ppm–1.2ppm) your child should get enough fluoride by drinking a glass of water a day.

However, if your family drinks bottled water, reverse osmosis filtered water, or well water, and doesn't drink water any place but home, your child will need a fluoride supplement. We'll give you details on fluoride supplements in Chapter 12, Hygiene.

Was that confusing or what? Here is the recap for which children need a fluoride supplement:

◆ Your child only drinks well water.
◆ Your child only drinks tap water that does not contain recommended fluoride levels.
◆ Your child only drinks bottled water that does not contain fluoride.

Okay, now that you know WHAT your toddler should be eating, let's get real. Few toddlers really eat this stuff. How do you sneak fruits and veggies into a toddler's diet? In the next chapter, we'll explore all the tricks and treats parents use to get a toddler to eat something other than goldfish crackers!

FOOD TRICKS & TREATS

Chapter 11

"That spaghetti squash does not resemble pasta or fool a two-year-old."
~ *Haiku Mama, by Kari Anne Roy*

And now, for our next trick, we will need a volunteer!

For this part of the show, we will actually make a toddler eat . . . *something healthy!* Yes, we know this has been attempted many times before; but no one in the Western Hemisphere has actually succeeded.

Sure, the term "balanced diet" to a toddler may mean sprinkling bacon bits over her macaroni and cheese. But seriously folks, your kid does need to eat SOMETHING . . . and it is your responsibility to make sure that something is worthwhile.

So let us arm you with a series of tricks, treats and light weaponry as you do battle with your toddler to develop healthy dietary habits. First, let's review the three GOLDEN RULES of getting a toddler to eat:

Rule #1: Be a good role model. If you expect your child to eat well, you need to eat well.

Rule #2: Play it cool. If your child realizes how important it is for you to win the food battle, he will dig his heels in with even more persistence.

Rule #3: Read this chapter. You'll learn how to avoid the dessert incentive trap, how to introduce new foods and the secrets of toddler food prep . . . along with handy advice, ideas and more.

FOOD

? ?

Helpful Hint: Understanding the Toddler Diet

Having trouble understanding the Toddler Diet? Here is a primer:

◆ Eat one good meal a day.

◆ Decide you are hungry every three days.

◆ Eat most of your calories during snack time.

If we all ate like toddlers, we wouldn't need South Beach.

The Real Toddler Food Pyramid

Remember that nifty food pyramid in the last chapter? Nicely balanced with all sorts of healthy food? Okay, let's take a look at the typical toddler food pyramid:

Yep, right where the fruits and veggies should be are those Goldfish crackers; and the Macaroni & Cheese and Cheerios have muscled out other healthy stuff. So how do you change this? Let's discuss.

Q. Every meal with my toddler is a battle. Is this normal?

The typical toddler eats as much as one meal a day or as little as once every three days. Isn't it amazing they grow on air? Every child goes through this stage and every parent worries that her child will be malnourished. Don't be too concerned. Believe it or not, most kids get their nutritional needs met despite their quirky diets. If you are really worried, check your child's weight periodically (like once a month or so) to be sure he is gaining appropriately. Remember that toddlers and preschoolers gain weight much more slowly than infants. Check out Chapter 9, Growth regarding expected weight gain.

Our advice? Don't get into a battle over food. We've been there, too. Staring our toddler down with a single pea on the high chair tray saying, "EAT IT!" Guess what? We failed too. This approach fails every time. We state our mantra for toddlers: You can't make them eat, sleep, or poop on the potty. It's got to be *their* idea.

Here are some typical toddlers and practical advice on how to get them to eat.

FOOD

1 **ELSIE.** Is your child more of a grazer than an eater? Does she wander around the house, returning to the kitchen or coffee table to nibble here and there? Is she more content with snacks than with mealtime with the family?

While eating five small meals a day is fine—grazing all day is not. Here are a few tips:

- ◆ Don't let your toddler walk around all day with a juice or milk cup. If you want her to have constant access to a liquid, offer water.
- ◆ Don't let your toddler graze while watching a video or TV program. She's more likely to overeat.
- ◆ Set some limits for formal mealtime. That's likely the time of day you are together as a family. Once your toddler loses interest in food, she is excused from the table for the evening.
- ◆ Make sure snacks are nutritious—that will be where the majority of her food intake will come from. View snacks as small meals, not just something to tide your toddler over.

2 **SAM I AM.** Every toddler has a bit of this behavior in him. A toddler will only eat a limited variety of foods—and it is only on his terms. He may love eating a turkey sandwich (cut in a particular way, and the crust removed, etc.) every day for a month and then wake up one morning and simply refuse it.

Then, it's back to the drawing board for you to figure out what your toddler is willing to eat. Be patient. And keep offering new foods in a non-confrontational way. Eventually Sam I Am will try green eggs and ham.

Here are a few pointers:

- ◆ Be sure he is not filling up on snacks.
- ◆ Don't load up on milk. Toddlers only need 16 oz a day.
- ◆ Get your child to help in food preparation.
- ◆ Grow a fruit/vegetable garden with your child.

If your child is more involved with the preparation of food, he might be more interested in eating it.

3 **JOHN BELUSHI.** There's more food thrown on the floor and used as finger paint than ingested.

Kids are messy, but that is part of the food experience. They will usually eat what they need to. When the food starts flying, that's your child's way of saying he is done with the nutritional part of the meal!

Here are some tips:

- ◆ Food throwing is your cue to proclaim that mealtime is over. Take him out of the high chair and let him go play somewhere else. He will quickly learn that when he throws his food, he is excused from the table.
- ◆ Remind your child at the beginning of the meal that he will be excused if food is thrown.
- ◆ Offer only a bite or two on the plate. That reduces the temptation to shoot free throws.
- ◆ Avoid spaghetti sauce for a while. It's really hard to get off the walls.
- ◆ Get a dog or borrow one. It makes for easy cleanup.

RED FLAGS

Occasionally, quirky food behaviors can be a clue to an underlying problem. Here is when to check in with your doctor. If your toddler is:

◆ Refusing to eat and not gaining weight.
◆ Unable to self feed by 15 months.
◆ Unable or refuses textured foods by 15-18 months old

There is a prescription appetite stimulant medication that can make a child hungrier. However, it's reserved for children who are failing to thrive and lack an underlying medical reason.

Reality Check: The Dessert Incentive Plan

Yes, we have all turned into our own parents at some point and tried to bargain with our toddlers. *If you eat your veggies, you can have dessert.* It always backfires, folks.

True story: one recent study looked at children's attitudes about trying a new food (mild sweet peppers). One group of kids was offered incentives to try the food (stickers). In another group, no incentives were given, but the peppers were offered numerous times. Guess who ate the peppers? *The group without the stickers.* Bottom line: tricks and gimmicks don't work.[1]

Q. My child wants to feed herself but she can't hold utensils yet. Help!

Ages 1-2

It's frustrating to be a toddler. You want to do feed yourself but lack the skills.

Here are some ways to let your toddler feel in control, yet still eat a decent amount of food:

◆ **Dipping.** Give your child an edible utensil like a cracker, sliver of bread, or cheese stick. She can dip it into foods that otherwise require a spoon to eat like yogurt, avocado dip, bean dip, hummus, or apple sauce.
◆ **Two spoons.** Give your child one spoon for her to use, while you shovel the food in with yours.
◆ **Get a dog.** The take home message here is: don't worry about the mess. Your child's tray may look like a finger painting project after the meal is over. Allow her to eat like a cavewoman until she masters the fork and spoon. And yes, dogs are really good at cleaning up.

Reality Check: High Chair Hijinks

Ages 1-3

In another attempt for independence, you may find your toddler trying to escape his high chair. Of course, there is no federal law that requires toddlers to sit in a high chair at meal-time. So here's a solution.

Consider bringing a kid-friendly picnic table and chair set into your kitchen. That will give your toddler the autonomy to leave

DR B'S OPINION

"Your child will eat what he needs to, when he needs to. Your child will not go hungry."

when he wants to. Just remember to set up the ground rules first—once he leaves the table, his food will be cleared. This will discourage the temptation to graze.

Q. My one year old prefers to nurse instead of eating meals. Is this okay?

While it is perfectly fine to continue nursing beyond the first year of life, your child does need other nutrients beyond breast milk. And kids who want to drink instead of eat can have real difficulty gaining weight. So, no, it is not okay.

Change your mindset. You probably let him nurse on demand 24/7 because you are worried he isn't eating and isn't gaining weight—but that's exactly why he isn't eating. Limit nursing sessions to three times a day. No snacking or comfort nursing or night nursing. Then, offer him a variety of foods without any pressure—if he knows you want him to eat, he will just dig his heels in and refuse. He's a toddler, remember! Offer high calorie, nutritious foods like avocados, eggs, meat, whole milk yogurt, plus high-iron foods like meats and fortified grains.

Q. My child only eats beige food. Any ideas?

Beige food is usually the preferred food group for toddlers. It includes bread, cereal, French fries, and chicken nuggets. Yes, this too shall pass. But while you are waiting, here are some ideas for healthy foods that are the right color: whole grain pasta, brown rice, yogurt, hummus, tofu, bananas, pears, white bean spread, chicken salad, egg salad, cauliflower, almond butter, carrot/banana bread and pumpkin butter.

Q. Can my child survive on chicken nuggets and Cheerios?

We know you think your child will never live to see kindergarten with her diet. But they all do. And most of the time, they eat what they need to. That's why most kids do NOT need to take multivitamins or supplements, as we discussed earlier.

A recent study in Finland looked at 500 picky preschoolers and found their diets were not that different from kids described as good eaters. The picky eaters ate a little less fiber and calcium. The biggest difference was *when* the picky eaters ate most of their calories: at snack time. So, take advantage of those rare moments when your child actually feels like eating something and make it nutritious.[2]

Unfortunately, many parents fall into the trap of offering "kid food" to their children while the parents eat more interesting selections. They do this because they want to avoid battles, yet still have their kids eat something. However, this may not be a good idea in the long run. Some studies show that kids with broader palates are less likely to be obese later in life. Frankly, it's troubling that

DR B'S OPINION

"Most toddlers eat what they need . . . and that food will meet their dietary requirements. If you resort to offering 'kid food' in the name of keeping the peace, your child's waistline may pay for it later."

food tricks & treats

the most commonly consumed vegetable by toddlers ages 15–24 months is (no surprise) French fries![3]

Here's our advice. Don't get into a food fight, and, don't give up. Offer foods prepared the way you would eat them—including herbs and spices. Put three different foods on your child's plate. One item can be a food you know your child will like. He may have one serving of that food—no seconds. The other two items should be food that you are eating. If your child is hungry, he will eat. If not, he can eat at the next meal. Most children do not go on a hunger strike for long. Don't force your child to eat.

If you do resort to "kid food," attempt to make it healthy. Bake your own chicken nuggets (try breading chicken chunks with cornflakes) or make mac 'n cheese with whole grain pasta. Grilled cheese sandwiches can be made with whole wheat bread and low fat cheddar instead of Wonderbread and American cheese. And so on.

Q. How many times should I introduce a new food to a picky eater?

The answer may surprise you. According to a book on picky eaters (*Finicky Eaters: What To Do When Kids Won't Eat*, Ernsperger & Stegen-Hansen, Future Horizons, $15), parents need to try a new food at least TEN TIMES before giving up! Yep, you read that right—*ten times*. The authors note that many parents fail at this because they give up after three to five tries. (A recent study by Gerber, the baby food giant, also backed up this assertion).

One suggestion to crack the picky eater puzzle: try food chaining. Does your child like French fries? Try sweet potato fries. Then, graduate to sweet potatoes. Does your toddler like chicken nuggets? Then, try baked chicken nuggets. Finally, introduce small bits of meat that aren't breaded.

Stealth sauce is another tactic—cover up a new food in a familiar sauce (ketchup is the all-purpose example, but you could also try a mild cheese or BBQ sauce.)

Helpful Hints: Do's and Don'ts
Do's: Ways to inspire your child to enjoy food
   ◆ Help with food prep.
   ◆ Grow a garden.
◆ Select food at grocery store together.

Don'ts: What NOT to do
   ◆ Become a short order cook.
   ◆ Allow your child to eat only kid food.
   ◆ Chase your child around the house with a spoon.
   ◆ Allow your child to graze at the kitchen table.
   ◆ Force your child to eat something.

Feedback from the Real World
Offer food in courses, as if you were at a fine dining establishment. Our kids are much more likely to eat their salad if it arrives before the spaghetti does. So we do the same at our own kitchen table. Hunger has a way of making food much more appealing!

Kid friendly food preparation

Insider Secrets:
Sneaky ways to get your kids to eat veggies

Sometimes, what your child doesn't know can really help him! In our house (the Fields), we have the ultimate picky eater. Our son doesn't like sauce on his pizza or pasta. He only eats breaded chicken, his favorite meats are pepperoni and bacon. He loves bread, but doesn't like the texture of whole grain breads. And so on. How do we handle it? We buy "flavored" pasta, like spinach noodles, for example. But we've also found pasta made with beets, peppers, carrots and more. A veritable smorgasbord. (Of course, we don't tell our child he is eating spinach pasta . . . like most things in life, it's all in the marketing).

We hide pumpkin in pancakes and call them orange pancakes—they're quite popular at Halloween. We also make pumpkin soup, zucchini bread and carrot cake. And we never give up. We continue to give Ben a couple bites of the other foods we're serving in the hopes that someday, he'll try it. We were excited when he decided he liked scrambled eggs. That didn't happen until he was eight years old. So, now we occasionally have breakfast for dinner.

The point? Be creative. Don't give in. And remember, when they're hungry enough, they'll eat just about anything you put in front of them.

Here are some more ideas for foods kids like but may not realize are good for them.

We are proud to say that we came up with this original list in 2006 when our first edition of *Toddler 411* went to print. That preceded both *The Sneaky Chef* and *Deceptively Delicious* cookbooks by over a year. We won't sue anyone for stealing our ideas, because moms have been resorting to stealth tactics in the kitchen for eternity!

We will also comment that, although we like both of those books, we do not encourage you to make spinach-laden brownies. We say this for two reasons: A. They taste bad. B. Brownies out in the real world do not have spinach in them . . . and we don't want you to encourage your child to eat brownies on a regular basis.

- Pumpkin butter: (1 Tbsp = 30% of Vitamin A requirement for an adult)
- Pumpkin soup
- Carrot soup
- Carrot/banana bread: (1 slice= 50% Vit. A requirement for an adult)
- Carrot/zucchini bread
- Veggie lasagna
- Avocado dip
- Scrambled eggs mixed with pureed carrots
- Sweet potato pancakes
- Spinach quiche
- Spinach laden spaghetti sauce
- Carrot/Orange juice
- Lentil soup
- Vegetable and meat stew

FOOD

? ?

- Shredded carrot/cream cheese tortilla roll up
- Any veggie with ranch dressing dip
- Edamame
- Grilled veggie skewers
- Lettuce wraps (shredded chicken rolled up in lettuce)
- Cabbage wraps (ground beef rolled up in cabbage leaf)

Our personal faves
- *Kozlowski Farms Pumpkin Butter.* It's sold at retail grocery stores and found in the jelly section. It's a reasonable alternative to jelly and it's "jam" packed with Vitamin A. Just one tablespoon is half your child's daily requirement.

- *Bruce's Sweet Potato Pancake Mix.* We dare you to try this one with your beige food-loving toddler. Not only do they taste great, but they sneak in Vitamin A, calcium, and iron.

- *Vruit.* (web: americansoy.com) comes in juice boxes and is a blend of fruit and vegetable juices. It is 100% juice with Vitamin A and C.

Feedback from the Real World:
Daycare menus
Some childcare centers are more concerned about your child's nutritional intake than others. Most toddler and preschool age programs serve a meal or at least a snack—as opposed to infant programs where the parent supplies breast milk or formula.

You should feel empowered to speak up if you don't like the menu selections. You are paying a lot of money for your child to be there. When choosing among daycare programs, the nutritional content of snacks or meals should be an important criterion.

Q. Any tips for nutritious snacks?

How about 31? (Yes, we are all about value here at *Toddler 411*).

Apple slices and cheese chunks
Apple slices with peanut butter
Orange slices
Bean and cheese nachos/ quesadillas
Carrots, broccoli and ranch dressing
Pineapple spears and graham crackers
Bran muffins and apple slices
Whole wheat mini-bagel pizzas
Hummus and pita
Celery and cream cheese
Celery and peanut butter
Raisins, cream cheese, wheat thins
Corn bread and applesauce
String cheese

Scrambled eggs and wheat crackers
Edamame
Macaroni and cheese
Yogurt smoothies
Half a boiled egg and yogurt
Pumpkin butter on wheat bread
French toast fingers and apple sauce
Pear wedges
Whole wheat or spinach tortillas, cream cheese, and shredded carrots
Banana and cheerio skewers
Half bagel, cream cheese
Avocado dip and whole wheat tortillas
Chicken salad on wheat bread
Egg salad on wheat bread
Nut or seed butter on toast
Fresh fruit or dried fruit, granola, and yogurt
Chilled fruit soup
Vegetable soup (carrot, pumpkin)

Reality Check: Fresh, frozen, or canned?

Do you think fresh produce is the healthiest? If you buy it from your local farmer's market, that may be true. However, most of the produce you buy at the grocery store may have been in transit for a week or two before it gets to you. Some nutrients can be lost in that time period.

In contrast, frozen and canned produce is processed immediately after being harvested, retaining most of the nutrients. The bad news: canned and processed produce may include added salt or sugar. Read labels to make sure you aren't getting an unhealthy dose of sugar or salt in canned produce.

Q. We eat fairly spicy food. Is it okay for our toddler to eat it?

Yes, in fact we encourage you to feed your child food that is prepared the way *you* like. Kids who are more likely to eat a variety of flavors are less likely to become obese later in life.

And it saves you a lot of prep time in the kitchen when everyone is eating the same thing! Start with milder spices and work your way up.

A couple of tips: use WHITE pepper instead of black pepper. It is milder and invisible, yet still adds a little flavor. Ground spices and herbs (for example, cumin powder seasoning for taco meat) are easier to sneak by a toddler than leaves or seeds (basil, rosemary).

Reality Check: Hold the salt

Yes, our bodies need some salt for bodily functions. The recommendation is 2300 mg of salt a day (in real world terms, that's about one teaspoon) for people ages two and up. Most American diets have 50% more than that. And too much salt can lead to high blood pressure and heart disease. Processed and pre-prepared foods are notoriously high in salt. So that's another good reason to prepare food in your home. Select alternative herbs and seasonings when you do!

Feedback from the Real World:
Eating out healthy—real parent advice

Veteran moms and dads devise all sorts of creative ways to keep it healthy when eating out with their toddler. Here is some of the advice from readers of our last book, *Baby 411*:

◆ *Fruit, not fries*. Finally, the chain restaurants like Wendy's and McDonald's are now offering mandarin oranges and apple slices INSTEAD of the standard-issue fries. Sarah R. of Victor, NY always asks for a fries substitute: "Even if the kids menu doesn't have substitutes for fries, I always ask for veggies instead—especially if they are elsewhere on the menu. Most servers are willing to do this, especially if you stress you only need a child-sized portion of the veggie of the day."

◆ *Go local.* Paige L. of Charlottesville finds locally owned restaurants are healthier than some chains. "I've found that our local neighborhood restaurants offer much more diverse children's menus than the chains, and will readily agree to downsize portions of regular meals, or even whip something up that isn't on the menu."

◆ *Order off menu*. Heather L. of Austin, TX notes that Chipotle restaurants will let you order off the menu for kids. "Even though it isn't on the menu, Chipotle will make a cheese quesadilla (small or large) for the kids at a low price."

◆ *Bring your own.* Yes, it takes a bit more effort, but consider taking a small container of fruit along to restaurants that don't serve it. We've often discretely packed a jelly sandwich for our picky eater. Sometimes that overcomes the veto factor (where your toddler refuses to go to XYZ restaurant that mom and dad likes because there is nothing on the menu for him).

◆ *Split adult meals "family style."* Some restaurants have such huge portions that it makes sense to split an adult meal with a child. Example: the Cheesecake Factory. We split three meals for a family of four. Daniella L of Gilbert, Arizona agrees, noting the cost savings: "We found our two kids can share an adult meal for the same price as two kids meals." The Olive Garden and Chili's are good examples of restaurants where this works.

◆ *Avoid the cold shoulder from non-kid friendly places*. Let's get real: not all restaurants like kids (hint: no kids menu, snotty waiters with the evil eye, etc). While it might seem obvious to avoid such places, we're still amazed to see parents trying to shoe-horn a toddler into a place that clearly doesn't care for their business.

◆ *Go ethnic.* Many ethnic restaurants offer healthy options. Example: sushi. No, toddlers may not be big on raw fish, but the gyoza (dumplings) and edamame (steamed soy beans) are healthy and entertaining.

◆ ***Deli sandwich instead of burgers***. Kudos for Wendy's for finally offering kids' size deli sandwiches. "With a side of mandarin
oranges and white milk, it's practically what I'd offer at home,"
remarked one mom. We also applaud regional chains like Cosi
that offer baby carrots on the side instead of chips.

Special diets/considerations

Ages 1-2

Q. **My toddler still only eats pureed foods. Is
this a problem?**

We all have our issues. For toddlers, it can be the texture of
food. Why? Kids may not take the time to chew up food . . . or
they don't have the ability to chew it up . . . or others are simply bothered
by funky textures.

While it's okay for your toddler to eat pureed foods indefinitely, you
should probably check in with your doctor if he is 18 months old and still
not willing or able to eat textured food. See more about this in Chapter 6,
Challenges.

Q. **My toddler has fallen off the growth chart and I can't
get him to eat anything. Any ideas?**

This is called **FAILURE TO THRIVE**. We talk about the medical evaluation
of this problem in Chapter 9, Growth. But if your child does not have a
medical cause for it, you will need to balance the need for him to eat with
his need to be in charge.

In cases of failure to thrive, parents will do anything to get their child to
eat. Some of my own patients' families have resorted to turning the TV on
during mealtime or reading books to their child during a feeding. Some
parents even chase their child around the house all day with a spoon. If it's
that bad, you need professional help (ask your pediatrician for a referral).

Your goal in this situation: make what he *does* eat count as far as calories go. This is the only time we recommend eight ounces a day of a toddler formula, Pediasure, or Carnation Instant Breakfast as a nutritional supplement. The cheapest option is to buy the Carnation powder and add it
to whole milk. It's also a good idea to give a daily multivitamin with iron to
a child with failure to thrive.

Here are some other healthy high fat choices:

◆ Scrambled eggs   ◆ Egg salad
◆ Whole milk yogurt   ◆ Cheese
◆ Almond butter*   ◆ Peanut butter*
◆ Avocados   ◆ Meats
◆ Sunflower seed butter— 100 calories per Tbsp.
◆ Flaxseed oil disguised in apple sauce

*Yes, some of these foods are on the Top Ten list of food allergies. And
yes, it is okay to offer them to your toddler. If your child has other food
allergies or severe eczema, chat with her doctor first.

food tricks & treats

How Ovaltine, Pediasure, and Carnation measure up

8 oz serving	Pediasure	Carnation (+ whole milk)	Ovaltine (+whole milk)
Calories	237 calories	280 calories	230 calories
Fat	11.8 grams	8 g (from milk)	8 g (from milk)
Price	$$$	$$	$$

All products contain vitamin and mineral supplements.

Q. How will I know if my toddler has a food allergy?

Parents with food allergies are much more likely to have children with a food allergy. The risk is about 20% for these kids, compared to the general population whose risk is about 6%. And kids who have asthma are more at risk for serious allergic reactions to food.

Food allergies are definitely on the rise. There's a "hygiene hypothesis" that speculates that our immune systems today have less work to do fighting germs, so they start paying attention to more minor exposures like food allergens.

So what does a food allergy look like? Here is what you're looking for after feeding your child: an impressive rash (not just a dot or two), profuse vomiting, abdominal pain, or horrible diarrhea.

The allergic response occurs within minutes or, at most, four hours after an exposure. A chemical in the body called **HISTAMINE** is released in massive quantities with an allergic reaction. Histamine can cause a tingling or itchy mouth, mouth or lip swelling, shortness of breath, and dramatic diarrhea. You may also see hives (raised borders of red plaques or lesions that look like mosquito bites with red circles around them). See our website Toddler411.com (click on Bonus Material) for a picture.

The extreme scenario is called an **ANAPHYLACTIC REACTION**. This is when loss of consciousness and airway swelling occurs—obviously, this is a life-threatening situation!

Some kids with chronic **ECZEMA** may have food allergies as a cause. If your child has moderately severe eczema, it's a good idea to get tested for food allergies. We'll talk more about this in Chapter 16, Common Diseases.

Feedback from the Real World

If your child ends up having a life threatening food allergy, be sure to have an Epi-pen on hand at home, while traveling and at preschool or daycare. Epi-pen is a prescription rescue medication (epinephrine) in injectable form (i.e. a shot). The prescription will come with a practice pen so people can learn how to use it. Everyone who is supervising your child should know how to use the Epi-pen. And be sure to have one available that is not expired. Their shelf life is one year.

Having an antihistamine like diphenhydramine or cetirizine (brand names: Benadryl or Zyrtec) is also a good idea to keep around the house, daycare and in your purse. For mild reactions like hives, antihistamines can treat your child quickly and effectively. See Appendix A, Medications.

? ?

FOOD

Q. What is food intolerance?

This term refers to an adverse reaction to a food or food product, not an allergic reaction. It means your digestive system is unhappy with you, but your immune system is not bothered a bit.

Allergic reactions produce histamine. Food intolerances do not. If a person has an intolerance to a food, he might have stomach cramps or bloating. For example, an adult with lactose intolerance feels bloated when he drinks milk, but doesn't get hives. He'll probably avoid dairy in the future, but he'll never have a life-threatening reaction if he is exposed to it.

Food Allergy Factoids:[4]
- 2.5% of newborns have a cow's milk allergy. 80% outgrow it by age five.
- 1.5% of children are allergic to eggs.
- 1.5% of children are allergic to peanuts, but only 20% of those kids outgrow it.
- Most food allergies occur in the first three years of life and affect 6% of all kids.
- Only 4% of adults have a food allergy, and of those, 50% are allergic to either peanuts or tree nuts.

Q. Any foods that my toddler should still stay away from?

Ages 1-3

In short, no. But before delving into that answer, here is a list of the top six most allergenic foods for kids:

The Top 6 food allergies in kids:
- Milk
- Egg
- Peanuts
- Wheat
- Soy
- Tree nuts (walnuts, cashews, almonds, etc)

Bubbling under the Top 6 are:
- Shellfish
- Citrus fruits
- Cocoa/Chocolate*
- Corn*
- Fish
- Berries*
- Tomatoes*

*These foods are less likely to cause true allergic reactions.

CELIAC DISEASE: WHAT IS IT?

Celiac disease is an immune response to gluten (a form of protein) found in cereal grains like wheat, barley and oats. This response causes injury to the intestinal lining. The result: chronic diarrhea, failure to thrive, vomiting, and bloating, to name a few symptoms. It's a genetic disorder, so more than one family member may have this problem.

Although celiac disease is rare, it does occur in kids and often takes a while to get diagnosed. Ask your doctor about celiac disease if your child really has a Buddha belly all the time, has frequent bouts of diarrhea for no good reason, or isn't gaining weight. See more on this disease in Chapter 17, Common Diseases.

food tricks & treats

The Top 4 food allergies in adults:
◆ Peanut   ◆ Treenuts
◆ Fish   ◆ Shellfish

If you have no family history of allergies, the American Academy of Pediatrics says your child can have any of the high allergy foods after six months of age. However, if you have a strong family history of food allergies, or your child has horrible eczema, it's probably best to ask your child's doc before testing the waters.

The truth is leading food allergy researchers believe we've had it all wrong. Perhaps early exposure to highly allergenic foods, like peanuts, can actually *prevent* food allergies. While we have all heard debates about avoiding peanuts during pregnancy, breastfeeding, and infancy, none of these interventions have made one bit of difference in lowering the number of peanut allergic kids in Western countries. In fact, the rates of peanut allergic children in the U.S. and U.K. have DOUBLED in the past ten years.

New Parent 411:
What are cross reactions?
Some people who are allergic to one particular food may be allergic to another food or seasonal pollen. Why? Some foods and plants originate from the same plant family. Other sensitivities are due to cross contamination (for example, when kiwi pickers wear latex gloves while picking). Here are some examples:

Allergy To:	Risk of Reaction to at least one:	Risk:[9]
Legume (peanut)	Other legumes (peas, lentils, beans)	5%
Tree nut (walnut)	Other tree nut (brazil, cashew, hazelnut)	37%
Fish (salmon)	Other fish (swordfish, sole)	50%
Shellfish (shrimp)	Other shellfish (crab, lobster)	75%
Grain (wheat)	Other grains (barley, rye)	20%
Cow's milk	Beef	10%
Cow's milk	Goat's milk	92%
Pollen (birch, ragweed)	Fruit/veg (apple, peach, honeydew)	55%
Peach	Other tree fruit (apple, plum, cherry, pear)	55%
Cantaloupe	Other fruit (watermelon, banana, avocado)	92%
Latex	Fruits (kiwi, banana, avocado, papaya)	35%
Kiwi, Banana, Avocado	Latex	11%
Mango	Poison Ivy	N/A
Cashews	Pistachios and mango	N/A
Hazelnuts	Kiwi	N/A

N/A: Risk rate is not available.

Reality Check: Peanut allergy on the rise
If you think you're hearing about more and more kids who have peanut allergies, it isn't your imagination. There has been a two-fold rise in the number of folks diagnosed with peanut allergies in a recent five-year period.[7] Why? One reason may be how peanuts are processed. In the US, peanuts are roasted (most other countries eat boiled

peanuts). For some reason, boiled peanuts don't seem to spur the same allergenic response as roasted nuts. And Americans eat many more peanuts (in peanut butter, etc) per capita than other countries. So it's not a big surprise that peanut allergies in the US are on the upswing . . . countries that eat larger amounts of fish, for example, have more fish-allergic people.[8]

Feedback from the Real World:
Hidden sources of dangerous foods

If your child has a food allergy, educate yourself and your family on how to avoid the food and what to do in an emergency.

A great resource for parents is Food Allergy Network (foodallergy.org; 800-929-4040). The web site offers recommendations for hidden sources of allergenic foods, cookbooks, and reliable links to medical websites.

Here are some take-home messages:

◆ *Be a label reader.* Food ingredients can be deceptive. For instance, products containing milk may be listed as: casein, sodium caseinate, whey, or lactoglobulin. Good news: U.S law now requires manufactured foods to list major food allergens in plain English! Bad news: more and more foods now bear labels that say they were "processed on equipment that also manufactures XYZ" or "may contain traces of XYZ." Families with tree nut allergic children, for example, may not be able to find a brand of sandwich bread anymore that guarantees it is completely nut-free. This is no doubt unnerving for the child and frustrating for the parent. We applaud companies who are willing to make changes in their production process to guarantee food allergy safety (and yes, you tend to find those manufacturers at natural food stores and pay twice the price, unfortunately).

◆ *Beware of deli slicers.* They are often contaminated with dairy. The same slicer may be used for both cheese and lunchmeat.

◆ *Beware of Chinese food.* Egg rolls may be sealed with peanut butter.

◆ *Beware of ice cream and gelato shops.* There are two issues here: scoops that are not cleaned between customers, and ice cream shops that "mix-in" toppings into ice cream on a slab—the slab may contaminated with trace amounts of nuts and other allergens. Our advice: ask for a clean scoop. And avoid mix-in toppings.

Q. How are food allergies tested?

There are four basic ways to test for a food allergy. Unfortunately, this is not a perfect science, however.

1 **ELIMINATION DIET.** Eliminate the food from the diet for three to six weeks. Then watch for improvement in the symptoms (that is, eczema, diarrhea, etc). This is a trial and error method, but it often works.

2 **CAP-RAST TESTING.** Blood tests detect an elevation of the body's IgE antibodies (an allergic response to a chemical). CAP-RAST tests rule in a food allergy if the test is positive—but a negative test does not rule

food tricks & treats

one out. That's because not all food allergies cause an elevation in IgE levels. And IgE levels aren't detected if a child is allergic to a particular *way* the food allergen is processed or cooked. The newer CAP-RAST tests have been shown to be 95% predictive in food allergies for milk, eggs, peanuts, and fish. Soybean and wheat tests are only about 73% predictive.

Sometimes, results are given in class scores, from zero to five—the higher numbers suggesting the greater likelihood of an allergic reaction if a child is exposed to that food. But the actual results are reported in kU/L. And the higher numbers predict the higher chance of an allergic response. So a child can have an annual CAP RAST blood test to see if their allergic response lessens before offering the food in question.

For example: a child with a peanut allergy whose CAP RAST is 15 kU/L has a 90% chance of having a significant allergic reaction if he eats peanuts. If his level drops to less than 0.7 kU/L, his chances of reacting are about 40%. Allergists use this information to determine who is a good candidate to offer a food challenge (see below).[10]

3 **SKIN TESTING.** Skin prick tests detect a true allergic response to a food. If skin testing shows an allergic response, CAP-RAST testing can be done for confirmation. In general, skin testing is more accurate in (and more tolerated by) school-aged kids. But even if a child has a positive skin test, he may not have a significant response if he eats that particular food. Unfortunately, this test also has some degree of inaccuracy.

4 **FOOD CHALLENGE.** When a person is known to be allergic to a certain food, periodic (typically, annual) CAP-RAST testing may show a decrease in allergy response levels. A child can try a certain food again in a controlled medical setting (not your kitchen table) to see if he is still allergic to a particular food. This is the only 100% accurate way to test for a food allergy.

Feedback from the Real World:
Food allergies and nutrition—call in an expert

I had an 18-month-old patient whose weight percentiles were dropping. His parents were vegans. He was allergic to milk, soy, and eggs and had terrible eczema. With a child so highly allergic, I wasn't about to suggest tree nuts or peanuts. And because of the family's diet, meat was not an option for fat. I was out of ideas and referred them to a nutritionist. These folks can be a tremendous resource for families struggling with complicated food issues.

A personal fave: Sunbutter

Here is a terrific option for kids with peanut allergies—Sunbutter. This product has the consistency of peanut butter, but is made of sunflower seeds. No, it is not a low-fat food choice, but Sunbutter contains no transfats. For more information, check out sunbutter.com.

Q. My toddler had a milk allergy as a baby. When is it safe to try milk products again?

The good news is that most kids outgrow their food allergies, in fact half of them do it by age one. The foods that tend to be lifelong problems are seafood, peanuts, and tree nuts.[11]

When can you reintroduce your child to milk? It depends. If your child had a bad reaction (hives, lip swelling), your doctor may want to do a CAP-RAST test (see above) and re-challenge your child to milk in a controlled medical setting (that is, a doctor's office).

If your child had a milder reaction in the past, your doctor may suggest starting with dairy products first (yogurt, cheese) and then trying whole milk, if your child does not appear to have a problem.

Don't be too disappointed if the first attempt flops. You can stick with milk alternatives and try again another time.

Q. Is it okay for my toddler to eat honey now?

Yes. As you might remember reading in our *Baby 411* book, kids under one year of age are advised not to eat honey. Why? Botulism spores in honey can cause illness in the immature digestive systems of infants. Once kids have been out in the world for a year, however, their guts are full of "good" bacteria that can break down the botulism found in honey. So honey is safe for kids over one year of age.

Q. Is it okay for my toddler to have artificial sweeteners?

Yes, but we might argue, why would a toddler need to consume artificial sweeteners?

Don't get us wrong, we do NOT recommend routinely giving your child non-nutritious foods loaded with sugar, like candy and soda. But there's no reason to choose artificial sweeteners—aspartame, saccharin, Nutrasweet, and Splenda—over natural sugar for healthy children.

Why? Many of the products that contain artificial sweeteners are things you should avoid or limit in your child's diet anyway (processed foods, diet soda, etc).

Artificial sweeteners appear to be safe when eaten in moderation. For instance, the acceptable daily allowance for aspartame is equal to four diet sodas a day. So a sip of your soft drink won't hurt. Just don't feed your toddler four diet drinks!

Q. So, are there any other foods we should still avoid?

Yes. Foods that are choking hazards are probably better to be avoided in kids under age three. Here is that list:

- Hot dogs (unless cut lengthwise into quarters).
- Whole nuts/peanuts (see discussion earlier).
- Raw carrots.   ◆ Raisins.
- Hard candy.   ◆ Fruits with seeds.
- Grapes (unless cut into quarters).

food tricks & treats

FOOD

? ?

Q. Is it safe for my toddler to eat raw fish? He really likes eating sushi with us.

Aren't you lucky—your child has expensive tastes!

Toddlers and adults take the same risks every time they eat raw fish. There are some very unpleasant infections that can be passed to humans. These include: parasites, bacterial food poisoning, and Hepatitis A. Many of these infections can be avoided by proper food handling and preparation. That's not to scare you away from your favorite sushi palace, but merely to warn you.

If your family enjoys eating sushi, here are some tips to eat it safely:[12]

- ◆ Eat at a reputable establishment.
- ◆ Make sure the sushi temperature is cold.
- ◆ Get freshly made sushi (not the pre-prepared stuff in a display case)
- ◆ Pick more cooked items (eel, shrimp, crab, egg) and vegetarian items (avocado) for the kids
- ◆ Get vaccinated for Hepatitis A (See Chapter 15, Vaccines).

Q. As vegans, how do we mix our diet with our toddler's nutritional needs?

While most adults can get their nutritional needs met with a vegan diet, it's a bit more challenging for a growing child. Toddlers need calories, especially those from fat, for their brain development. Some reasonable vegan options for this fat include: oils, nuts, nut butters, avocados, olives, and dates.

For families who maintain purely vegan diets, kids may need a vitamin supplement to get their daily requirements of iron, calcium, Vitamin B 12, Vitamin D, and zinc. Lacto-ovo vegetarians usually can achieve nutritional needs for a growing child without too much difficulty.[13]

Q. We have a strong family history of high cholesterol. Do I need to worry about my child's fat intake?

There's high cholesterol, and then there is HIGH cholesterol. If a child's parent has a cholesterol of 240 or more, and/or has had a heart attack before age 55, the child's fasting lipid levels should be tested once he turns two years of age (and periodically after that).[14] If your family history is that significant, your whole family should be keeping a close eye on the amount of fat in your diets. We'll discuss more about cholesterol and kids in Chapter 16, Common Diseases.

The next section of this book is what we call Toddler HealthWatch—we'll discuss hygiene, vaccines, sickness and first aid. So let's start off in the next chapter with the spa treatment: taking care of a toddler's skin, hair, teeth and more.

Toddler 411

Part Two

Toddler HealthWatch

Hygiene, Vaccines, Diseases,
Infections, First Aid

HYGIENE

Chapter 12

Sweater, *n. garment worn by child when its mother is feeling chilly.*
~ Ambrose Bierce

WHAT'S IN THIS CHAPTER

As veteran parents of toddlers, we realize just about nothing can shock you now when it comes to bodily fluids. Yet, even with the elite-level membership you've earned on the Pee & Poop Express Train, there are still new curves your toddler will throw at you when it comes to hygiene.

That's what this chapter is for . . . we'll launch into new territory (like when your daughter announces she wants to wipe herself) and cover such issues as skin care, dental care and more. Finally, we'll cover thumb-sucking and how to kick the pacifier habit (yes, your child needs to give that up before prom). So, off we go!

Skin and Hair

Q. We are still dealing with diaper rash. Any tips?

Some kids have more sensitive skin than others. Until your child is toilet trained, you may need to use a cream to create a barrier between the skin and the poop/pee. I suggest using petroleum jelly (Vaseline) or zinc oxide (Balmex, Desitin) at every diaper change if your child has 100,000 frequent flyer diaper rash miles.

For severe rashes, try Dr Smith's Diaper ointment, Triple Paste, or Boudreaux's Butt Paste (wish I had come up with that name!). Another tip—if you have any leftover lanolin cream from early breastfeeding troubles, use it.

Diaper rashes that just won't go away may be due to a yeast infection (the equivalent of jock itch). Check out a picture of a diaper yeast infection on our website at Toddler411.com (click on bonus material). If it is yeast, you can try using clotrimazole cream (brand name: Lotrimin AF) twice daily for a week. It is available over-the-counter.

Q. My child is out of diapers, but we still use pull-ups at night. His diaper rash looks worse than when he was an infant. Help!

Pull-ups may be convenient for an older child who is learning to toilet train, but they are inherently less absorbent than regular diapers. So, there is more moisture coming in contact with your child's little hiney.

If your child is not dry at night anyway, just put a diaper on him or use "Goodnights" (the equivalent of Depends for kids).

Reality Check
If your child soaks through a diaper or pull-up at night, try double diapering or putting a plastic diaper cover over the diaper.

Q. How often do I need to bathe my toddler?

There's no science here. Once every few days is probably fine. Because a toddler gets dirtier than an infant, you might want to bathe her more often now.

Helpful Hints: When your toddler hates baths
◆ Try a shower instead.
◆ Bribery: bath books, Tub Tints (colored bath soap), bath crayons, new toys
◆Take a bath or shower together (yes, we'd suggest discontinuing this practice with an opposite sex child once he/she is four years old for obvious reasons).

Q. Do I still need to use baby shampoo and soap?

It depends. If your child has sensitive skin or eczema, it's wise to use hypoallergenic, perfume/dye-free products. For everyone else, you can use what the rest of the family uses. The advantage of kid shampoo is that it stings less if it accidentally gets into the eyes.

Q. Is bubble bath okay to use now?

No. We do NOT recommend using bubble bath, especially for girls. The soap can be irritating to their genitals and make it painful to pee (see below). Bubble bath also dries out the skin, making an eczema problem that much worse.

Q. Do I need to use a special laundry detergent for my toddler's clothes?

HYGIENE

Again, it depends. For kids with skin issues (eczema, etc), the entire family's laundry should be washed with a perfume/dye free laundry detergent or soap. For all other families, normal laundry detergents are just fine.

Q. Any hygiene tips for kids with eczema?

The key is to keep the skin moist. This means applying moisturizing cream several times a day, especially right after bathing. Special care needs to be taken when choosing household soap, shampoo, laundry detergent and more (see below for more discussion). Here are some pointers from eczema expert, Sally Joo Bailey, M.D., Assistant Professor of Pediatrics/ Pediatric Allergy, Weill-Cornell New York Presbyterian Hospital . . . along with our own experiences and observations from being a parent of a child with extreme eczema:

1 **ALL SOAPS ARE NOT CREATED EQUAL.** Avoid bubble baths, anti-bacterial soaps, oils, perfumes, dyes . . . basically, any skin-care product with those ingredients. Try Dove bar soap (not the liquid), Aveeno, or Cal-Ben's Seafoam liquid soap (available online or at natural food stores). Cetaphil is another great mild soap.

2 **MOISTURIZE.** According to Dr. Bailey, "Hydration is very important in breaking the itch-scratch cycle which allows the skin to heal." Apply a thick moisturizing cream (cream is more effective than lotion) as many times a day as you can (reality check: we realize you are dealing with a squirming toddler here, but do your best). Make it a bonding time by doing some massage if you like. Our recommendations: Vaseline Creamy Formula, Eucerin, Lubriderm, Aveeno or Cerave. One thing to avoid: "natural" moisturizing creams that contain food ingredients. About 25% of these products contain peanut oil, almond oil or citrus extracts, which can cause flare-ups of eczema and potentially sensitize kids to later food allergies.

3 **AVOID DETERGENTS.** Think about what detergents do—they break things down. So, it makes sense that detergents might break down skin that is already very sensitive. Some kids with eczema improve when their homes go detergent–free, switching to soap alternatives. We realize this is a huge commitment to avoid dishwashing and laundry detergent, not to mention personal hygiene products. Another challenge: finding soap alternatives can be challenging, as most stores don't stock them. Our advice: check out your local natural foods store or go online. Companies that sell soap alternatives to detergent include Cal-Ben (CalBenPureSoap. com) and Soap-Flakes.com.

4 **WATCH FOR TRIGGERS.** About one-third of kids with mild to moderate eczema have a food allergy as a trigger. Up to 60% of kids with severe eczema have a food allergy. See if you can detect a correlation between an eczema flare-up and a particular food at home. If not, ask your doctor to do a blood test to detect food allergies (see CAP RAST testing in Chapter 11, Food Tricks and Treats). Dr. Bailey's advice: "90% of the food triggers are either milk, egg, soy, wheat, or peanut...in cases where the history is consistent with a food allergy but the tests are 'falsely negative' (this

happens), we would place the patient on a trial diet restriction." Another possible trigger: seasonal allergies.

5 **ASK FOR HELP.** Your doctor will have a few tricks up her sleeve to treat eczema. Dermatologists and allergists are also good resources if you cannot get it under control.

BOTTOM LINE

With eczema, you will win the battle but you won't win the war. Eczema is an allergic condition of the skin. The best you can do is minimize the flare-ups. The good news: most kids outgrow eczema. More on this topic in Chapter 17, Common Diseases.

Q. My toddler still has cradle cap. Is this normal?

Yes, but don't worry—he still has several years before the dating scene starts! Some kids will even have cradle cap well into their school years.

Cradle cap looks like yellow, greasy scales in the scalp. If you try to pull the scales off, you often will take a clump of hair with them. Cradle cap (see **SEBORRHEA**) is caused by hormonal changes and occasionally yeast. It is similar to dandruff, and can be treated the same way. Anti-dandruff shampoos like Head and Shoulders or Selsun Blue work well if used two or three times a week. You can also massage vegetable oil or margarine into the areas prior to shampooing. After rinsing, use a fine comb to lift off the scales.

Reality Check

Cradle cap may bother you, but it won't bother your toddler until you pick at it.

Q. What is the recommendation on sunblock?

Everyone, but especially children, should wear sunblock. The lifetime risk of skin cancer is about one in 75 and sunburns early in life are what carry the highest risk for future cancer. There are two different types of ultraviolet rays from the sun that can cause skin damage: UVA causes the skin to tan; UVB causes a burn. But both can cause skin cancer. Here are some practical tips to consider:

1. **Use at least SPF 30**. Sunblock products currently label their sunburn protection factor (SPF) based on their ability to protect the skin from UVB rays that cause sunburn. Look for SPF 30 or higher for the best protection. The FDA is revising its regulations and someday you will also see products listing their UVA ray protection with one to four stars (from least protection to greatest) so you can make a more informed decision of what to buy. We recommend four stars for UVA protection.
2. **Reapply frequently**. If your child is sweating or swimming, reapply sunblock afterwards. It's also a good idea to put on more sunblock every couple of hours if you are spending the day outside (even if the sunblock says it lasts eight hours).
3. **Avoid peak sun times**. If you can stay in the shade or indoors between 10am and 4pm, you will avoid the strongest rays.

4. **Wear a hat and sunglasses**. It's hard to convince a toddler to wear either of these, but if you can, do it.
5. **Apply sunblock on cloudy days.** Sure it looks safe to go outside without sunblock when it is cloudy, but that is deceptive. The sun's harmful UV rays still get through—so wear that sunblock.

Reality Check

Even if you have darkly pigmented skin, you still need to wear sunblock. The rule of thumb—if you have skin, you need to protect it.

Q. What is the recommendation on insect repellent?

We've all heard about West Nile Virus (WNV), an infection that is spread by mosquito bites. Although the odds of getting bitten by a mosquito that is a carrier for WNV is pretty rare, it's still scary.

The safest way to avoid getting bitten is to stay indoors at dawn and dusk, when mosquitoes are out in full force. It's also a good idea for your child to wear light colored clothing, long sleeves, and long pants when he is outside. But sometimes that can be very impractical—like when it tops 100 degrees on an August evening.

So, insect repellent is really the way to go. The Centers for Disease Control has approved two chemicals as effective insect repellents: DEET and Picaridin. Oil of Eucalyptus, while effective, is not recommended for kids under three.

Many parents are leery of using chemicals on their child's skin and prefer to use natural products, like citronella. That's understandable, but let's look at the science. A recent study showed that citronella repels mosquitoes for about 9.6 minutes, while 23% DEET works for five *hours*.[1]

That doesn't mean DEET is risk free. The chemical can be absorbed through the skin, and in high amounts, can cause dizziness. However, there are ways to use DEET safely. The American Academy of Pediatrics says products containing even up to 30% DEET are safe for kids. Here are some do's and don'ts:[2]

◆ *DON'T* apply DEET to open wounds or near the mouth or eyes.
◆ *DON'T* apply DEET under clothing—just to exposed skin areas.
◆ *DON'T* apply DEET more than once a day.
◆ *DON'T* use a product that combines sunblock and insect repellent. Sunblock should be reapplied and DEET should not.
◆ *DO* use 10% DEET if you are outside for a couple of hours. Do use 30% DEET if you will be outside for up to five hours.
◆ *DO* wash the DEET off after coming inside.

What about Picaridin? This chemical repellent is odorless and appears safe for humans of all ages. The Environmental Protection Agency considers Picaridin to be essentially non-toxic and non-carcinogenic . . . and there are no significant health concerns with it. It may not be as strong as DEET, but Picaridin works pretty well in most situations. The Centers for Disease Control recommends Picaridin products (Cutter Advanced or Off Clean Feel) as an alternative to DEET repellents.

Another bonus about Picaridin: you can reapply it every three to four hours and it does not have to be washed off.

Ear piercing

Q. When is the right time to pierce my child's ears?

Ear piercing is a safe procedure for infants and young children. Obviously it is a personal choice whether you want to have your child's ears pierced before she (or he) decides on their own. Here are the medical issues to consider:

◆ *Infection.* Inserting a needle through the ear carries a small risk of infection. A localized skin infection, called **CELLULITIS**, can cause redness, swelling, drainage of pus, and potentially a fever.

◆ *Allergy.* Some people are allergic or sensitive to the metal in the posts or backing. To avoid this problem, use either a surgical steel or 14K gold product.

◆ *Scar formation.* Some people have poor wound healing where a thickened scar develops at the site of the skin injury. If anyone in your family has this problem (called **KELOIDS**), you may want to have the ears pierced before age 11 to reduce the risk of scarring.

◆ *Cosmetic result.* Kids are moving targets. Be sure your child can sit still through the procedure or you may get undesirable results!

The Boy Parts

Q. My son is not circumcised. When should I start pulling back the foreskin to clean it?

Don't pull it back until it loosens up on its own.

With an intact penis, the foreskin naturally attaches to the shaft of the penis with tight tissue called adhesions. (Note: this is a different situation than when circumcised boys develop adhesions—which are not normal). Most of the time, the adhesions loosen up by five years of age. Some boys may have adhesions into their teen years and this is still okay (but check it out with your doctor).

Occasionally, the foreskin remains tight and hard to pull back (see **PHIMOSIS**). The foreskin can also get pulled back and unable to be manually brought back down (see **PARAPHIMOSIS**).

Here are some ways to avoid a problem:

DR B'S OPINION

"I have cared for more than one little boy who got his penis stuck in his fly. Ouch! I'd suggest using pants with elastic waistlines until you are confident in your son's fine motor skills!"

◆ *DON'T* forcefully pull the foreskin back to clean the penis.
◆ *DON'T* worry about the dead skin (smegma) that collects under the foreskin. It will come out on its own.
◆ *DO* clean under the foreskin once or twice a week once the foreskin pulls back on its own. Remember to push the foreskin back down after pulling it up to clean it.

? ?

HYGIENE

Once your son is a teenager, he should clean under the foreskin daily.

BOTTOM LINE

If your son has a red, swollen penis or dribbles instead of peeing in a steady stream, call your doctor.

Q. My son is not circumcised. The skin of the penis is red and swollen. What do I do?

Start with a nice warm bath.

The foreskin may get stuck in a pulled back position. It then swells up, making it difficult to bring back down. The warm water may reduce the swelling and allow the skin to return to its normal position. If this doesn't work, check in with your doctor

Q. My son is circumcised, and I can't see the head. What's wrong with it?

This is the dreaded "Hidden Penis." And no, it is not a new reality TV series on Fox.

Boys who have a nice little fat roll below their bellies often have a penis that looks like it has gotten sucked inside their bodies. Not to worry, it hasn't actually disappeared and it is fully functional.

The problem is purely cosmetic. If the penis is perpetually sitting in this position, the skin on the shaft of the penis will stick to the head (see **PENILE ADHESION**). The circumcised penis now looks like it is no longer circumcised.

The adhesions may loosen up on their own (usually around age two).

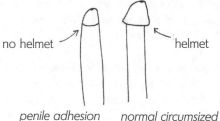

no helmet

helmet

penile adhesion   normal circumsized penis

Otherwise, the adhesions can be pulled back manually (docs hate doing this), loosened by applying prescription steroid cream, or surgically cut (by a urologist). Check with your doctor to decide on the best management plan.

The Girl Parts

Q. My daughter is toilet trained. She wants to wipe herself. Should I let her?

Ages 2-4

It's okay to let her wipe herself, but we suggest supervising the experience. Make sure she wipes front to back. Give her a goal of using four squares of toilet paper—otherwise, she may use the entire roll on one outing. (Come to think of it, this is good advice no matter what gender your toddler!) A smart move: use kid wipes which are disposable equivalents of diaper wipes (one brand is Candoo Flushable Toilet Wipes by Pampers). Because these wipes are moist and have soap on them, the clean up is better than your average toilet paper.

Hygiene

? ?

Reality Check

My daughter was toilet trained at two and a half. By age three, she demanded independence and wanted to go into public restroom stalls without me. She was fairly good at wiping herself, so I obliged.

Just like my own mom used to do, I would say, "Remember to put paper down on the seat." (Although sitting on a public potty doesn't spread AIDS or other cooties, I am still grossed out by it!)

She would always reply, "I did, Mommy."

A year later, I peeped through the gap between the door and the wall while she was using the restroom and saw her little bottom on the exposed seat. I was horrified! When I expressed my unhappiness, she cried and admitted—"Mommy, I can never get the toilet paper to stay on the seat!"

Lesson learned: Don't trust a three year old.

Q. My daughter complains that it hurts when she pees. Does she have a bladder infection?

Ages 2-4

Probably not, but it's a good idea to check it out. Most of the time, little girls get irritated in their genital areas from poor hygiene (see **VAGINITIS**). Typically, it happens to girls who are toilet trained and do most of their own wiping. It also happens when girls use bubble bath or run around in wet bathing suits for prolonged periods of time.

The skin of the genital area is red and swollen. Most of the time, there is no discharge coming from the vagina. Because the skin is irritated, it stings every time that urine touches it. So, technically, it hurts AFTER the girl pees, not during the pee. But little girls have trouble expressing that in words.

Vaginitis causes a variety of symptoms that may seem like a bladder infection. The skin irritation leads to a vicious cycle:

◆ **Frequency.** Because it hurts, girls will not fully eliminate when they pee. So, they urinate in small amounts very frequently.

◆ **Constant urge.** Because they don't completely eliminate, they have a constant urge to pee because their bladder is always full of urine.

◆ **Accidents.** They start having accidents because their bladders are full and they are afraid to pee.

So, if your daughter is not running a fever, the first thing to do is look at her genital area. If it is red and swollen, try these things to alleviate the discomfort:

1. *Bathe her in warm water, without soap.* Avoid bubble bath.
2. *If she is toilet trained, let her sleep without panties.* Air drying helps.
3. *Use Vaseline or diaper rash cream* on the area for a few days to provide a barrier for the skin.
4. *Use kid wipes* (see above) to let her clean herself after pooping and peeing.
5. *Try Tucks medicated pads* (they contain witch hazel) to wipe the area. These are very soothing.

If the skin is not red or if your daughter has a fever, call your doctor and plan on getting a urine specimen.

Insider Tip
Most people don't know this, but Strep infections (of Strep throat fame) can also cause skin infections around the vagina or anus. See the doctor if your daughter has a really red vaginal area for no good reason—especially if she has fever or a sore throat.

Dental Care

Q. I am getting tired of teething. How many baby teeth are there?

There are twenty baby teeth in all. Twelve of those are incisors and canines (the front teeth). Four are the one-year molars, and four are the two-year molars. After the first two bottom teeth come in, the rest erupt in random order. Molars may arrive before many of the other teeth show up.

Contrary to their names, the one-year molars may not erupt until age two and the two-year molars may erupt as late as age three. The good news: by age three, your child should be done with teething. You can then look forward to the drama of them falling out (this starts around kindergarten).

See the graphic below for when baby teeth come in.[3]

Q. My child's molars are coming in. What can I do to help with teething?

Molars hurt much more than the front teeth when they erupt. Think about it. There are four prongs (called mammelons) for each molar to break through the gums. And because of sheer size, it takes longer for them to break through (sometimes a couple of months).

Don't be fooled into thinking your one year old has an ear infection just because he is pulling on his ears. Check the back of his mouth to see if the gum is swollen or purple (from bruising as the molar breaks through) *before* you book an appointment to see your doctor. It will probably save you a co-payment. Kids have trouble localizing pain and those molars are in the back of the jaw line, near the ears. Even your two or

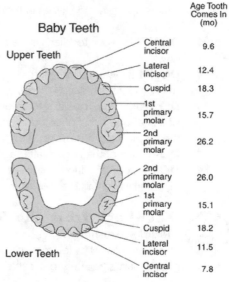

Baby Teeth

	Age Tooth Comes In (mo)
Upper Teeth	
Central incisor	9.6
Lateral incisor	12.4
Cuspid	18.3
1st primary molar	15.7
2nd primary molar	26.2
2nd primary molar	26.0
1st primary molar	15.1
Cuspid	18.2
Lateral incisor	11.5
Lower Teeth Central incisor	7.8

three year old may have trouble telling you that his erupting molars are bothering him.

What to do about the pain? The most effective pain relievers are acetaminophen (Tylenol) and ibuprofen (Motrin). Both medications provide at least four hours of relief. If your child is having trouble falling asleep due to gum pain, it's okay to use one dose at bedtime for several days. Try other techniques during the day such as these:

◆ *Cold things feel good.* Offer popsicles or smoothies.
◆ *Cold massage.* Apply cold water on a washcloth to the area
◆ *Teething gel.* I'm not a big fan of this product because overuse can be problematic, but it provides temporary relief (for about 30 minutes). But remember, more does not equal better.

Q. How should I clean my child's teeth?

Once kids have teeth, you need to clean them. Otherwise, they will get cavities just like you do.

Clean them at least twice daily using a toothbrush, washcloth, or rubber cleaning tool applied to your finger.

Fluoride toothpaste is not recommended until your child is old enough to spit it out (usually around age three or four). We suggest using just water on the toothbrush because the mechanism of brushing is the key to preventing plaque buildup. The fluoride-free "kid" toothpastes are very sweet and encourage kids to suck on the toothbrush once it is in their mouth—making it even more of a challenge for you to get in their mouth and clean. Another reason not to use kid's toothpaste: they are too darn expensive.

Don't forget to floss. And yes, you should be flossing too.

Reality Check: **Ways to prevent paying for your dentist's early retirement**
If you've been to a dentist lately, you know that a simple cavity can cost hundreds of dollars to fill. And since few folks have dental insurance, this cost can be a major hit to the wallet of parents with toddlers. So how do you avoid paying for your dentist's new Lexus? Here are some simple tips to avoid cavities in toddlers:

◆ **DON'T** let your toddler walk around with a bottle of juice all day.
◆ **DON'T** let your toddler go to bed with a bottle of milk (no, that won't make them sleep longer!).
◆ **DO** brush your toddler's teeth at least in the morning and at bedtime—and don't offer a drink of anything besides water after the evening tooth-brushing.
◆ **DO** get rid of the pacifier after age one.
◆ **DO** check on the fluoride content of your community water supply (see later in this chapter for more info).

Feedback from the Real World:
Toddler Brushing Tips
Here are some tips for coercing your toddler into good dental hygiene habits, courtesy of Heather Fagin, DDS, MS.

- ◆ *Give one toothbrush to your child,* while you brush with another one.
- ◆ *Try a spin brush.* These are battery powered brushes that vibrate and make noise. Spin brushes sell for about $5 at the grocery store and they are worth it!
- ◆ *Try tooth-brushing in the bathtub* while they are playing with something else (obviously, you don't use a battery-powered toothbrush in the tub!).
- ◆ *Play a song* and tell your little one to brush until the song is over.
- ◆ *For those who love gadgets,* DrFresh.com makes a Firefly Flashing toothbrush ($2 at drugstore.com) which flashes red for 60 seconds to encourage longer brushing.

Again, some of our best tips on tooth brushing come from our readers. Here are some great ideas:

"Keep your plan of attack fresh on this one, but develop good habits along the way. Currently, we let our toddler do the first few minutes of 'brushing.' After that, it's our turn, and he knows that we're going to count to ten (practicing our numbers!) while we brush, so he has a gauge on how long to expect us to be in his mouth. We've gotten fun character toothbrushes and let him choose which toothbrush to use as well as which toothpaste. We let him brush *our* teeth, let him walk around with the toothbrush 'brushing' while we're brushing our own teeth, and the like, depending on what the day required. The latest victory was with the purchase of a character battery-powered toothbrush that our son chose for himself at the store. He's excited to use this toothbrush, and always asks to brush with it while I'm brushing with my own battery-powered toothbrush."
– *Heather S., Cincinnati, OH*

"My son LOVES Elmo and I got him an electric Elmo toothbrush. The toothbrush comes with a stand and as long as he can hold the stand that has Elmo on it he will let me brush his teeth. This is a recent accomplishment, he fought for a few weeks until I bought the toothbrush."
–*Ilana B., Los Angeles, CA*

Q. When should we go to the dentist for the first time?

Age 1 Now. The American Academy of Pediatrics and American Dental Association recommend that your child visit the dentist for the first time after her first birthday. This is particularly important if your child is at increased risk of cavities. This includes kids:

- ◆ whose mothers who have cavities.
- ◆ who have special medical needs.
- ◆ are formula/milk bottle or breastfeeding throughout the night.
- ◆ who have visible plaque buildup on their teeth.

The first dental visit is brief and intended to make your child feel comfortable visiting the dentist. The dentist will do an assessment and perhaps an abbreviated cleaning session. Don't worry: x-rays are reserved for subsequent visits.

Some family dentists feel comfortable seeing little patients and some do not. Ask your pediatrician for his/her recommendation for a pediatric dentist (pediodontist) in your community if your own dentist is uncomfortable with toddlers.

Reality Check

Cavities are contagious. The bacteria that cause cavities can be transmitted from parent to child. So, often if a parent has had cavities, their kids may be at risk as well. A few ways to prevent the spread of your mouth bacteria are:

◆ **DON'T** share a toothbrush with your child.
◆ **DON'T** lick off a dirty pacifier then put it into your child's mouth.
◆ **DON'T** pre-chew food and then feed it to your child (yes, some folks do this).

Q. My child's baby teeth are crooked. Should I start saving money for the orthodontist?

Not necessarily. The baby, or primary teeth erupt in interesting places. When the rest of the teeth come in, they tend to shift around. Once the entire twenty teeth erupt, your dentist will have a better idea of what to expect of the adult, or secondary teeth. And x-rays help make the call. But if the baby teeth are crowded, the adult teeth are also likely to have a tight fit. In that case, you can start a savings plan for your friendly orthodontist now.

Q. My child is two and she is still drooling. Is this normal?

It can be.

Some toddlers continue to drool because they do not have good oral-motor skills (that is, the muscles of their mouths and tongues are relatively weak). These same kids have difficulty with textured foods. Usually, they figure out how to manage their mouth muscles given some time, but if it is bothering you, an occupational therapist can help.

Other kids drool because their mouths are perpetually open. These children are known as "chronic mouth breathers." You should check with your doctor to see if your child has a chronic sinus infection, enlarged adenoids (lumpy clusters of spongy tonsil-like tissue that sit in the back of the nose above the roof of the mouth) or enlarged tonsils, all of which cause mouth breathing. (See Chapter 17, Common Diseases for more information.)

Q. My child has a gap between his two front teeth. Will he look like David Letterman when he grows up?

In some people, a piece of muscle called a "frenum" attaches lower between the front two teeth (**DIASTEMA**). If that tissue remains intact and the adult/secondary teeth erupt, your child will have a permanent gap. Some of the time, toddlers break the tissue during a fall into a coffee table in their living room. But if the tissue doesn't break on its own, your dentist (or oral surgeon or ear/nose/throat doc) can clip it before those permanent teeth erupt.

Q. My toddler still uses a pacifier/sucks his thumb. Is this going to affect his permanent teeth?

It depends on how long he does it. A recent study showed that children who used a pacifier or sucked their thumbs beyond the first year of life had a higher chance of having a cross bite later.

Dentists contend that neither habit will lead to permanent problems if the habit is stopped before the permanent teeth erupt (around age five or six). However, I can usually tell who is the thumbsucker/pacifier addict by the roof of her mouth. There is a higher arch and the top front teeth protrude.

DR B'S OPINION

"I admit it: I can't stand seeing a toddler with a pacifier. I'd rather see that child learn how to soothe himself without a plug being put into his mouth!"

Helpful Hints:
Tips on kicking the thumb-sucking habit

Ages 2-4

If the orthodontist bills aren't enough to encourage breaking these habits, maybe germs will motivate you. Think about where that thumb has been before it goes into your child's mouth!

While some parents have contemplated surgical removal of the thumb, we don't recommend it. Here are some less painful methods:

- *Only allow thumbsucking in the child's bedroom.* If he needs to do it, he can be excused from the family setting to go to his room. This should significantly reduce the amount of thumbsucking.
- *Make the thumb less tasty* with a product like Mavala Stop or Orally No Bite ($4 to $7, both in drugstores or online at sites like Folica.com). These harmless liquids are applied like nail polish and have an unpleasant taste.
- *Try a finger splint* (about $5 in drugstores or online).

KICKING THE PACIFIER HABIT: 5 TIPS

You will be amazed by how quickly even the most pacifier-addicted child can give it up. But you have to give it a try to find out. Here are a few tricks to lose the pacifier:

- *Just stop, cold turkey.* Find a new comfort object like a doll or blanket.
- *Cut a hole in the pacifier* so the sucking action is no longer works.
- *Give the pacifiers away to another baby.* Let your child participate in the hand-off.
- *Wean off by only offering it at bedtime.*
- *Parents Magazine* had an interesting suggestion: go with your toddler to *Build-A-Bear Workshop* (buildabear.com) and have the pacifier sewn inside a bear![4]

HYGIENE

? ?

◆ *Offer a stress ball* or another comfort object that the child can hold in his hands.

◆ *Talk to your dentist* about a dental appliance to discourage the thumb from entering the mouth. It's a temporary device attached to the teeth that prevents the thumb from being there. This is usually reserved for older kids who risk permanent tooth damage. Obviously, this is a last resort and quite expensive.

Q. Does my child need a fluoride supplement?

(Yes, we did discuss this topic earlier in Chapter 10, Nutrition, but here is an expanded version). Fluoride is a mineral that prevents cavities. Kids need daily fluoride intake from six months until 16 years of age to reduce cavities in primary (baby) and secondary (adult) teeth. The natural fluoride content in community water supplies varies significantly. The fluoride level should be 0.7 to 1.2 parts per million (ppm). If the natural amount of fluoride in a community's water supply is less than 0.7ppm, some (but not all) cities decide to then ADD fluoride. However, adding fluoride to the water supply is expensive and fairly challenging to manage, so you may be unpleasantly surprised to discover that your community may not treat your water. Being an urban dweller, I was stunned to learn my community's water is not treated with fluoride.

So which toddlers need a fluoride supplement? Your child should have a supplement if:

◆ Your home has well water and your child does not drink fluoridated water elsewhere (that is childcare, school, bottled water).

◆ Your home water supply contains less than the recommended daily intake either due to low natural fluoride levels or you use a reverse osmosis filtration system, and your child does not drink any fluoridated water elsewhere. See chart below for recommendations.

If your child falls into one of these categories, the American Academy of Pediatrics and the American Dental Association recommend the following doses of daily fluoride. You need to ask your doctor for a prescription or consider buying fluoride added bottled water (sold at major grocery store chains).

How much extra fluoride does your child need?

	Amount of fluoride in your community's water supply (in parts per million- ppm)		
Age	*less than 0.3 ppm*	*0.3-0.6 ppm*	*greater than 0.6 ppm*
0-6 months	None	None	None
6 months-3 yrs	0.25 mg	None	None
3-6 years	0.5 mg	0.25mg	None
6-16 years	1 mg	0.5 mg	None

Reality Check

Fluoride containing toothpaste has about 1 mg of fluoride per ribbon. Kids tend to eat toothpaste instead of spitting it out. For this reason, it is suggested NOT to use toothpaste until your child can spit (around age three). It's also a good idea to limit it to a pea-sized ration.

New Parent 411 : Bottled water with fluoride

Most bottled water (except for distilled) contains some fluoride. However, the bottlers do not have to list the amount of fluoride on their labels. If your child is getting less than the daily recommended fluoride, you may want to consider buying fluoride-added water instead of getting a prescription fluoride supplement. Dannon (dannon.com) makes "Fluoride to Go," water with fluoride added—each 8.5 oz bottle contains 0.25 mg of fluoride (the daily requirement for a six month to three year old). It costs about 60 cents per bottle. Other bottled water makers are adding fluoride as well—Nestle's Poland Spring, Deer Park and Ozarka brands now contain added fluoride.

Also: some bottled water has enough natural fluoride content that bottlers don't have to add it. Arrowhead bottled water is an example with 1.2 milligrams per liter. Remember, the optimal range of fluoride is 0.7 to 1.2 milligrams of fluoride per liter.

Q. Is fluoride safe? I've heard it can cause bone cancer.

There have been debates about fluoride ever since communities began adding it to their water supplies sixty years ago. An article in the *Wall Street Journal* questioned its safety based on unpublished data linking fluoride ingestion and a rare form of bone cancer.[5] However, looking at published studies, fluoride appears to be safe as well as effective in preventing cavities.[6]

A 2006 report by the National Research Council confirmed this, but cautioned against excessively high fluoride levels (above four parts per million). About 200,000 folks live in communities with water that has a high concentration of naturally occurring fluoride. This seems to be a problem in cities in South Carolina, Texas, Oklahoma and Virginia, as well as less populated areas of Idaho, New Mexico and Colorado. In these communities, ten percent of kids developed severe enamel fluorosis, a permanent discoloring of the teeth and enamel loss.

Bottom line: a moderate amount of fluoride in drinking water (most communities have less than two part per million) is safe and beneficial in preventing tooth decay.

In the next chapter, let's talk about stuff that most folks don't want to talk about: what if your toddler becomes constipated? Which poops are worrisome? What are the signs of a bladder infection? We'll answer this and more when we visit The Other End (cue dark music intro).

THE OTHER END
Chapter 13

"Welcome to Uranus. Please don't make fun of our name."
~ Adventures of Super Diaper Baby

So, you might ask, why devote an entire chapter to pee and poop? First, we know you have questions. Besides, we noticed no other parenting book covers this subject in depth.

Readers of our first book Baby 411 know where we are going here. But in case you just joined us, let's put a warning label on this chapter: it is not for the faint of heart, or those with weak stomachs. We are going to have a graphic discussion about poop (as well as gas, burps, pee, and vomit).

For example, how can you cure a toddler's constipation? We have detailed advice and tips on this subject. Plus we'll also cover the warning signs for bladder infections, which poops are most worrisome and what to do if your child takes a ride on the Vomit Comet.

Before we get too far, we want to make sure everyone is on the same page. Everyone seems to have cute little words to describe these terms, so we want to be certain that there is no confusion.

◆ **Stool.** Stool is the trash from digested food. The stomach and intestines breakdown the food to get the nutrients, then get rid of the leftovers through the anus. Stool contains bacteria (germs) because germs that live in our intestines help us digest food. It makes sense that some will exit with the garbage. Other terms to describe stool include: poop, poo, feces, caca, Number 2, bowel movement....for this book, we will use the term poop.

◆ **Urine.** Urine is the trash from your bloodstream. The kidneys filter (clean) the blood and get rid of the leftovers through the urethra (the hole in the penis or the hole above the vagina). Urine is germ-free. Popular terms for urine include: pee, pee-pee, wee-wee, whiz…for this book, we will use the term pee.

◆ **Gas.** This is air inside the intestines that is the by-product of food transit. Other terms include: toot, fart… we will just stick with gas.

◆ **Burps.** This is air that gets swallowed. It then returns back up the esophagus.

◆ **Hiccups.** This is caused by a muscle spasm of the diaphragm (the muscle that divides the chest and abdomen). There is nothing wrong with you if you have the hiccups.

Poop

Q. How often should my child be pooping?

As kids eat more solid food, they poop less. Here are some guidelines for what is normal:[1]

Age	Number of poops/week
6-12 months	5-28
1-3 years	4-21
Over 3 years	3-14

Of course, some kids are overachievers and some are underachievers. If your child only poops once or twice a week, but it is soft and easily passed, your child is not constipated and does not have a problem. *By definition, constipation is not how often you poop, but what it looks like when it comes out.*

On the other hand, if your child poops four times a day, but passes little marble poops, he probably is constipated and is not completely eliminating each time he goes.

Q. What should toddler poop look like?

Your child's poop should look like yours now. It should be soft and formed. You may find pieces of undigested food in it, and that is okay.

It should no longer look like that watery, seedy stuff that she had as a baby.

Q. My child just had a BLUE poop. Should I worry?

Nope. It is just the blue food coloring (natural or artificial) in what your child has eaten. Blue yogurt and blue juice drinks are often the culprits.

By the way, beets cause a dramatic red hue in both the poop and pee. The antibiotic, Omnicef (cefdinir), also can occasionally cause brick-red poop.

None of these poops should be a cause for alarm. See the next question below for more info on worrisome poops.

Q. I found blood in my child's poop. Should I worry?

Most of the time, this is not due to a serious problem, but you should get it checked out. Here are some questions to determine whether or not this is serious . . . and what to do about.

1. Is the blood mixed with diarrhea or mucous? *Call Dr. immediately.*
2. Does your child have fever, vomiting, or a stomachache? *Call Dr. immediately.*
3. Do you find the blood in a diaper? On a wipe? *Call during office hours.*
4. Is your child constipated? If it looks like he is giving birth when he is pooping, he is probably constipated. The poop may look like a large ball, marbles, or deer pellets. *Call during office hours.*
5. Do you find blood frequently? *Call during office hours.*

Constipation is the number one reason for blood found in the diaper or on the wipe. If your child is constipated, he may strain and push forcefully to get a poop out. He can tear some skin around the anus during this process. That tear or crack is called an **ANAL FISSURE**. The broken-down skin will bleed initially, and, with subsequent poops, until it heals. If you examine your child's anus, you may be able to see the crack. If you feel uncomfortable examining your child's anus or do not see anything unusual, let your pediatrician take a look. (Pleasant, I know. That's why they pay us pediatricians the big bucks.)

If you fix the constipation problem, the skin will have a better chance to heal. We'll discuss how to fix that next. Applying petroleum jelly (Vaseline) to the skin also helps it heal.

Other concerns for chronic blood in the poop include food allergy, polyps, and hemorrhoids. Chronic blood in the poop definitely warrants a doctor's visit.

We will talk about poop emergencies that present with blood in the poop in Chapter 19, First Aid. These symptoms include: diarrhea, mucousy poop, fever, vomiting, or stomachache with the blood. Problems include: **FOOD POISONING, HEMOLYTIC UREMIC SYNDROME, INTUSSUSCEPTION, MECKEL'S DIVERTICULUM.**

Q. My child is constipated. Any tips?

There are basically three reasons why kids get constipated:

1. Not enough fiber.
2. Not enough fluid.
3. Withholding (otherwise known as the Poopie Dance).

FIBER. As we discuss in Chapter 10, Nutrition, kids ages two and up need a certain amount of fiber per day (you can calculate this by adding your child's age plus five to get the grams of fiber per day).

So, a two year old needs seven grams of fiber a day, and so on. (There are no specific fiber guidelines for kiddos ages one to two. You'll just have to figure out what the right amount is for your individual child to stay regular.) Check the fun fiber food list (again, in Chapter 10) and see how much

the other end

fiber your child gets on a daily basis. If your child is like most kids, he probably does not get enough in his daily diet. It's not that difficult to opt for high-fiber foods. We suggest this become a family affair because a) your child watches you as his role model and b) because you probably don't get enough fiber in your diet either!

Here is an example of how making small dietary changes makes a big difference:[2]

Meal Plan A	Fiber Content	Meal Plan B	Fiber Content
1 cup cornflakes	1.0 grams	Instant oatmeal	3.0 grams
1/2 sandwich (white)	0.5 g	1/2 sandwich (wheat)	2.1 g
1/2 cup orange juice	0.3 g	1/2 c. mandarin orange	2.1 g
flour tortilla	1.0 g	corn tortilla	2.4 g
2 choc. cookies	0.1 g	2 fig bars	0.6 g
TOTAL Fiber (grams)	**2.9**	**TOTAL Fiber (grams)**	**10.2**

2 **FLUID.** Fluid helps move things along in the intestines. Some kids' intestines will remove a lot of fluid from their digested food, resulting in a hard poop. Other kids don't drink enough to meet their daily needs. Either way, a child may end up with constipation. If your child is constipated, increase his fluid intake. Drinking more water is always a good idea. Pear juice and prune juice are other fluid options. They are both full of sorbitol (sugar), an ingredient that keeps the poop soft by pulling fluid into it. (Prune juice also has fiber in it—an added bonus).

3 **WITHHOLDING.** Some kids will have a painful poop and never want to poop again! They become very fearful of every bowel movement. When they feel the urge to poop, they try to hold it in instead of letting it come out. They dance around the room, cross their legs, and even grunt. While it may look like they are pooping, in reality, they are trying to hold it in. The scientific term for this is "The Poopie Dance."

Unfortunately, this is a vicious cycle and a self-fulfilling prophecy. The child is afraid to poop so he holds it in. By holding onto the poop (known as withholding), more water is pulled out of the poop while it sits in the intestines. The poop becomes harder the longer it sits and waits to come out. So, the poop, indeed, hurts to come out…thus, validating the fear that the child has about pain and poop in the first place! If your child is a withholder, you'll need some help from your doctor to stop the vicious cycle. You also need to know that there is no overnight solution. It takes a long time to get this backed up and a long time to get cleaned out and start fresh. But read the section below for info on how docs treat constipation medically.

Special Section: Our 3 Step Program to Solve Constipation

In my practice, I schedule consultations known as "Poop Group." The name originates from a Boston Children's Hospital's program where I learned all these tricks! Poop Group is a series of office visits with the parent(s), child, and myself where we gradually make medical and behavioral interventions to solve the poop problem. I am going to walk you through one of my typical consultations.

Point #1: It takes a long time to get backed up with poop, so it takes a long time to get rid of it all. Don't expect miracles overnight. If your child tends to get constipated, you need to make permanent changes in your child's diet and schedule to keep things regular. That is, don't stop offering high fiber foods once the immediate crisis is over. And make sure your child takes the time to sit on the potty—both at home and at school.

Point #2: The child has to be committed to fixing the problem. Your child is scared to death every time he thinks he needs to poop. We need to eliminate that fear by making the poop soft and pain free. Then your child will be more willing to let it come out like it is supposed to. I like using sticker charts to praise a child's successes and remind him of how well he is doing. It motivates the child to succeed.

Before You Start: Rule Out Medical Causes First

Most of the time, constipation is NOT due to a medical problem, but rather a behavioral one. However, it's important to rule out the diseases that cause constipation. The diseases are very rare. These problems can be diagnosed by a thorough discussion, physical exam, and an x-ray.

HIRSCHPRUNG'S DISEASE is a genetic disorder (present since birth) due to lack of nerves in the last part of the intestines. Children with this problem have trouble moving their poop out because they lack the nerve input to instruct the body to do it. Most children are diagnosed soon after birth because they cannot pass their first poop (meconium). But some kids have limited ability to poop despite the disease, delaying the diagnosis.

INTESTINAL OBSTRUCTION is a mechanical blockage that interferes with the body's ability to move poop.

HYPOTHYROIDISM is an endocrine disorder where the thyroid gland does not produce enough thyroid hormone. This hormone controls the pace of your body's metabolism, kind of like an accelerator. When the pace is too slow, the result is constipation (as well as weight gain, lethargy, and coarse hair).

MEDICATION like iron supplements (not just a multivitamin) can also be a cause of constipation.

MILK INTOLERANCE sounds like an old wives' tale, but there may be some merit to it. Occasionally the switch from breast milk or formula over to cow's milk may set off constipation. If there is clearly a connection in the timing, a dietary change may solve the problem.

Step 1: The Cleanout

Assuming there is not a medical cause for constipation, the first step is to clean out all the old poop that has been sitting there since last Christmas (okay, I am exaggerating but some kids have been backed up for a while). I usually get a plain abdominal x-ray to see just how FOS (Full of Stool) he is.

Ideally, it is best to do a cleanout from above (oral medications) rather than from below (suppositories or enemas). What I mean by this is, your child will be less freaked out if you are not putting suppositories or enemas into his anus. He is already focused on that body part—don't make it any worse.

The length of the cleanout depends on how much poop there is. A typical cleanout takes one or two weeks. The goal is to have one or two soft poops a day. A popular over-the-counter product is called Miralax (see chart

THE OTHER END

? ?

below). It is a tasteless powder laxative that can be mixed with any liquid beverage, although I would choose something other than juice since that combo can create a lot of gas. The poop will definitely come out (whether they want it to or not) and most kids do not complain of cramping.

Another alternative is to use a stimulant laxative and a stool softener at the same time. Those medications are a little trickier to convince a child to take and may cause more cramps. I would discuss the options with your doctor before trying a home version of this process.

Here are the common products used for constipation:

Laxatives: Type of medication used to move poop through the intestines more quickly. There are three types of laxatives: osmotic, stimulants and enemas/suppositories:

MEDICATION	DOSAGE	INFO
1. Sorbitol	1/2 - 1 Tbsp twice daily for 20 lbs 1-2 Tbsp twice daily for 40 lbs	Natural sugar found in pear and prune juice
2. Magnesium (milk of Magnesia)	1 tsp twice daily for 20 lbs 2 tsp twice daily for 40 lbs	Overdose can cause electrolyte problems
3. Polyethylene Glycol (Miralax)	8 grams (1 1/2 tsp) daily for 20 lbs 17 grams (1 Tbsp) daily for 40 lbs	Can cause gas when mixed with fruit juice
4. Lactulose (Cephulac) *RX only*	1 1/2 tsp once daily	Made from sugar. Cautioned for diabetics, galactosemics

2. Stimulant: these products increase the intestine motility.

MEDICATION	DOSAGE	INFO
1. Senna (Senokot)	1/2-1 tsp a day for age 2-6 years	Can cause stomach upset
2. Bisacodyl (Dulcolax)	1 tablet a day for > age 2 years	Do not give with milk, antacid

3. Enemas/Suppositories: These products stimulate rapid poop elimination by working directly on the rectum. Chronic use is not recommended.

MEDICATION	DOSAGE	INFO
1. Bisacodyl Suppositories (Dulcolax, Fleet)	1/2 suppository inserted into anus once daily	
2. Glycerin Suppository/enema (Fleet Babylax)	2-5 ml as enema once daily or 1 infant suppository once daily	

? ?

THE OTHER END

Stool softeners: Type of medication that lubricates the poop, making it easier to pass. Options include:

◆ *Mineral oil.* Available over the counter, mineral oil can be used for kids over three years of age who do not have any neurological problems (i.e. choking and getting mineral oil into the lungs can be harmful). The mineral oil will come out with the poop and have an orange, liquidy look to it. Do not be alarmed. You can just cut back on the dosage. Mineral oil is well, an oil. So, as you can imagine, kids do not like to drink it straight. I would suggest refrigerating it and serving it mixed with either chocolate syrup or yogurt. Starting dose is 1 tsp. twice a day. You can decrease the dose once the poop slides out easily.

◆ *Docusate sodium* (Colace) syrup does not require a prescription, but it can be hard to find. Because docusate syrup is sold by the pint, you may need to ask the pharmacist if he stocks it behind the pharmacy counter. Starting dose is half a teaspoon twice daily for a 20 lb. child, and one teaspoon twice daily for a 40 lb. child.

Step 2: The Maintenance Plan

Once your child's poop evacuation plan is completed, you can start fresh to prevent the poop from backing up again. Your child may need to be on a mild laxative for several weeks (or even a couple of months) to prevent a recurrence. And she may need to stay on a stool softener for longer than that. The goal is to have your toddler forget that it hurts to poop.

Your doctor will have to walk you through this step to determine the length of time the child needs to stay on medication. Don't worry: your toddler will not become addicted to laxatives and forget how to poop on his own—but, it is important to keep in touch with your doctor because we obviously want medication to be a short-term solution. Behavior modification is the long-term solution.

Another key element of the maintenance plan is to improve your child's diet. That may also mean improving your diet as well. *Don't expect your kid to eat whole grain cereal and green vegetables if you don't.* Look at the fun fiber food list in Chapter 10, Nutrition for some hints.

If your dietary intervention is failing, we have a word for you: BENE-FIBER. This is a natural fiber supplement that comes in powder or pill form. Each tablespoon has 1 gram of fiber in it. You can sprinkle it in a drink or on food and your child will not even notice it is there. You'll find it at any drug store or Target. Fiber One products are also very effective and tasty.

Step 3: Toilet Training

Don't even think about toilet training a child while he is constipated and withholding. Once he has forgotten all this drama surrounding poops, he will be much more likely to toilet train.

Have your child sit on the toilet for five minutes after each meal. This is the most likely time people need to poop. The body naturally starts moving out the old poop to make room for the new food that needs to be digested.

Have a special basket of toys or books that are only played with in the bathroom to encourage your child to sit there. You can also use a sticker chart to praise toilet sitting. If your child actually poops, he gets an extra sticker.

For more details on toilet training itself, read Chapter 7, Toilet Training.

Congratulations! You have graduated from Poop Group.

Parent 411: **The Poopie Dance. Should your child attend a WA meeting? (Withholders' Anonymous)**
Here are the classic signs of a withholder:

◆ Leg crossing like a laughing pregnant woman.
◆ Tiptoeing around like a ballerina.
◆ Squatting like a football lineman.
◆ Grunting and turning red like a weight lifter.
◆ Standing stiffly.

If you ask your child if he needs to poop, he will deny it vehemently. Although it may look like he is trying to poop, he is actually trying his best to keep it in. Get help.

Red Flags for worrisome poops
These poops all deserve a phone call to your doctor.
◆ **Streaks of blood.** As mentioned already, it is probably due to an anal fissure (tear in the anus) if you find a streak on a hard/firm poop. It should be checked out, though.
◆ **Streaks of blood/mucous.** This is more concerning for infections, particularly if poop is loose or diarrhea. Be prepared for a homework assignment—you'll need to collect a fresh specimen for your doctor to culture. See more about this in Appendix C, Lab Work & Tests.
◆ **Clay (white) colored poop.** The term for this is **ACHOLIC STOOL**. This can happen with a stomach virus. If your child's skin looks yellow and his poop is white, this is a concern—contact your doctor.
◆ **Meconium redux.** Black, tarry poop can be a sign of bleeding in the upper part of the intestinal tract. The blood looks black instead of red because it has been partially digested. It can indicate irritation and inflammation of the intestines. Your doctor will do a test to check for blood in the poop. Non-serious reasons for black (but non-tarry) poop are iron supplements and Pepto-Bismol use.
◆ **Grape Jelly poop.** The doctor term for this is "currant jelly" stool. This is a medical emergency. It is a sign of **INTUSSUSCEPTION** where the bowels have kinked. Severe cramping accompanies this unusual looking poop. FYI: the peak incidence of this problem is between six and eighteen months of age.
◆ **Bulky, REALLY stinky, greasy, floating poops.** This may be a sign of difficulty in absorbing/digesting food (see **MALABSORPTION**).

Q. My child poops all the time! Is there something wrong with him?

Probably not, but it is a good idea to check in with your doctor to be sure. A pediatrician should make sure there is not a chronic infection (like a parasite) by checking a stool culture. And if your child has bloating, cramps, weight loss, or really foul-smelling poops, he should be checked for a rare disorder called **CELIAC DISEASE**. More on this in Chapter 17, Common Diseases. Food allergies and lactose intolerance are also problems that can cause frequent poops. Look for more info on lactose intolerance in the "gas" section later in this chapter.

The most common "diagnosis" for your toddler's diarrhea is actually called, drumroll please, **TODDLER'S DIARRHEA**. This happens to kids aged one to four and is usually due to too much juice intake. Juice is full of sugar . . . and that pulls water into the poop (which is why it is used to treat kids who are constipated!). Hence, juice-swilling toddlers poop more often—and the poop is looser. The best solution: decrease the juice, increase the fat and fiber, and offer yogurt daily to boost the good bacteria that helps digest food. For a list of Fun Fiber Foods, see the chart in the Nutrition section (Chapter 10, Nutrition).[3]

Q. My child has wet poop marks in his underwear. It's brown and watery, not solid. Does he have diarrhea?

It's not diarrhea, and, believe it or not, it is due to constipation. This is going to gross you out, but that watery poop is overflow that is trying to escape around the concrete mass of old poop that is blocking the exit. Your child needs a serious cleanout (see above for details on constipation).

However, if your child just has a bit of formed poop or a small mark in his underwear, he probably just needs more help wiping himself.

Pee

Q. How often should my child urinate (pee)?

A ballpark figure is three to eleven times a day for a three year old. By age four, most kids pee five to six times a day.[4] Too little pee or too much pee deserves a call to your doctor. If your child is urinating less than three times a day, you need to be sure he is not dehydrated. If your child is peeing constantly, see below.

Q. My child is peeing much more often than in the past. Should I call the doctor?

Yes. If your child is urinating constantly, you need to rule out **DIABETES, BLADDER INFECTION, VAGINITIS/URETHRITIS**, or a kidney problem. It's helpful to look at accompanying symptoms to determine what the problem is—like excessive drinking, weight loss, fever, pain with urinating, or redness around penis or vagina. Those are the questions your doctor will ask.

Q. My daughter complains that it hurts when she pees. Does she have a bladder infection?

Maybe, maybe not. *Pain while peeing is a big red flag for a bladder infection.* However, lots of girls have pain AFTER they pee and then complain about it. The pain after the pee is due to red, irritated skin in the private parts (i.e. vagina, urethra). When the acidic urine touches raw skin, it stings! The doctor term for this is **VAGINITIS**. Vaginitis is broken down, swollen skin due to poor hygiene. (Yes, we discussed this in the last chapter, but let's take a second to review our tips on this).

Girls who are freshly toilet-trained and in charge of doing their own wiping (usually at preschool or daycare) can develop vaginitis.

If your daughter does not have a fever BUT does have raw skin, start by using the hygiene tips below and see if the pain resolves. If the redness persists, it's time to check in with the doctor.

Here are some tips to *treat* vaginitis:
- ◆ Use diaper rash cream or petroleum jelly (Vaseline) several times a day to protect skin while it heals.
- ◆ Air dry as much as possible. Use a blow dryer on a cool setting to dry the genital area.
- ◆ Use Tucks medicated pads to wipe. The witch hazel is soothing.

Here are some helpful hygiene tips to *prevent* vaginitis:
- ◆ Skip the sleeper pajamas. Let your daughter wear a nightgown and even go undie free at night if she is no longer urinating at night. It helps to air her private parts out.
- ◆ Wear cotton underwear and avoid tights. This helps air things out.
- ◆ No bubble baths. Perfumed soaps irritate the vaginal area.
- ◆ Get out of wet swimsuits. Don't let your daughter sit in a wet swimsuit all day.
- ◆ Use kid wipes. Let your daughter wipe with disposable soap cloths (code word for diaper wipes you can flush). She will do a better job with these.
- ◆ Remind her about front to back wiping.[5]

Red Flag for bladder infections:
If your daughter has fever, unusual looking urine (cloudy or brown), and has normal looking skin, see your doctor.

Q. What are the signs of a bladder infection (UTI)?

Here are the classic signs: pain while peeing, frequent urination, new wetting accidents (if toilet trained), foul smelling or cloudy pee, and a fever (but not always). These signs always deserve a trip to the doctor.

And if a child under age three has a fever without an obvious source, he/she should have a urinalysis (see Appendix C, Lab Work & Tests) to check for a bladder infection.

Of course, there is a real-world complication here: some toddlers may not be verbal enough to communicate a problem (pain, fever, etc). Some kids may have pain while peeing, but not tell their parents.

Girls are much more likely to get bladder infections than boys, simply because of their anatomy. Girls have a very short tube (urethra) that connects the bladder to the outside world. That makes it much easier for bacteria to make a pilgrimage up to the bladder and infect it.

The urethral opening sits just above the vagina—and just below this is the anus. Remember that poop has bacteria in it and urine is sterile. If the poop ends up in the nooks and crannies around the urethra, the bacteria can climb right in. That's why girls in diapers (or those who wipe incorrectly) can get bladder infections. *About three to five percent of all girls get bladder infections.*

Boys rarely get bladder infections because the urethral tube is much longer from the bladder to the opening (the urethra tube is inside the penis and the opening is at the tip). It is much harder for those bugs to travel that far. But boys who are uncircumcised have ten times higher the risk of bladder infections than their circumcised peers. The overall risk of bladder infections in boys is about 1 in 100.

Q. My child had a bladder infection. The doctor wants to do special tests. Is this really necessary?

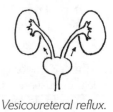

Yes. There is a rare abnormality of the urinary system that causes urine to flow backwards into the kidneys called **VESICOURETERAL REFLUX (VUR;** see right). If untreated, the reflux is a set-up for recurrent infections that can scar the kidneys permanently (this leads to kidney failure and high blood pressure). Although most bladder infections occur due to poor hygiene and bad luck, about 30-45% of all children who have a bladder infection will have this abnormality.

Normal urine flow.

Vesicoureteral reflux.

There are five grades of VUR, ranging from Grades 1 (least severe) to Grades 4 and 5 (most severe). Kids with the most serious VUR are at the greatest risk of kidney infection and permanent damage. The good news: most children with VUR outgrow this disorder by age seven—even 70% of kids with Grade 3 VUR will outgrow it.

However, those with Grade 4 or 5 are the least likely to outgrow VUR and may need surgery to correct the problem. Why surgery? Because of the potential for permanent kidney damage, pediatricians have always been cautious about little ones who have bladder infections.

In the past, *any* child with his or her first bladder infection *before reaching puberty* would have been tested for VUR. That testing involved an ultrasound of the kidneys (easy and relatively cheap) and either a Voiding Cystourethrogram "VCUG" or a radionuclude DMSA scan (more involved and expensive). See Appendix C, Labs and Tests for details on these studies. If the child was diagnosed with VUR, she was prescribed a low-dose antibiotic to take at bedtime to prevent future infections. This antibiotic was taken every night until she outgrew her VUR (discovered by repeating these fun imaging studies annually.)

Recently, this evaluation and preventative antibiotic treatment for kids with VUR has come under fire. Evidence shows that kids with severe VUR will likely be sicker, and have their first urinary tract infection before being potty trained.

We should be able to identify these high-risk children without screening everyone. And except for the most severe VUR (Grades 3,4,5), preventative nightly antibiotics only lead to bladder infections that are resistant to that antibiotic. However, the lack of research studies on this issue makes doctors hesitant about changing how VUR is treated.

Here's the take-home message: any *boy of any age* or any *girl under*

THE OTHER END

? ?

age two who has a bladder infection needs to be tested for this abnormality. Other children at high-risk for having VUR include those with: more than one bladder infection, bladder infection with bloodstream infection, poor urine stream, bladder infection with unusual bacteria, abnormal urinary tract on prenatal ultrasound, or continued symptoms after being on antibiotics over three days.[6]

VUR also has a hereditary factor. Siblings of affected children may need to be screened as well. Three to five percent of all girls and one percent of boys will get a bladder infection before puberty. Forty percent of these children have VUR.

Bottom line: your doctor may want to screen your child for VUR, even if she doesn't fall into the high-risk category. That is still the standard of care and there is no harm in following the precautionary principle.[7]

Here are the current recommendations for who should get tested for VUR:

◆ All kids under age five who have a fever with a bladder infection.
◆ All girls under age three with their first bladder infection.
◆ All boys (any age) with their first bladder infection.
◆ Kids of any age with more than one bladder infection.
◆ Kids whose infections do not clear up quickly.[8]

There is ongoing discussion in medical literature regarding the appropriate evaluation for VUR, so stay tuned for updates as they happen on our website, Toddler411.com.

Reality Check
There is a 60% chance of a child having VUR if a parent has the disorder. There is a 30% chance of having VUR if a brother or sister has the disorder.[9]

Red Flags: Worrisome pee that your doc should see
Here is the kind of pee that needs to be checked out:

◆ **Red**: May be due to blood in pee, but also caused by medications, foods, and muscle breakdown (myoglobinuria, hemoglobinuria). Check for infection, kidney, muscle, or red blood cell problem.
◆ **Coke colored**: Blood in pee looks like Coca-cola. Check for kidney infection or malfunction.
◆ **Mucous:** Check for infection.
◆ **Foul smell**: Check for infection, metabolic problem.
◆ **Lack of**: Check for dehydration.
◆ **Too frequent**: Check for infection, skin irritation (vaginitis, urethritis), diabetes.
◆ **Painful**: Check for infection, skin irritation.
◆ **Poor stream**: Check for **URETHRAL MEATAL STENOSIS** in boys or **LABIAL ADHESION** in girls.

Reality Check: Red pee
There are many reasons that a child's pee is red, and most of them are not serious. Food coloring and dyes derived from

blackberries and beets cause red urine. Many medications also cause red pee including ibuprofen and rifampin.

Q. When is it normal to be dry at night?

85% of kids are dry at night by age five. 90% are dry by age seven.[10] So, although you may be concerned that your pre-schooler still wears diapers at night, he is not alone! Remember: just because your toddler is toilet trained (dry) during the day . . . that doesn't mean she will be dry all night. It can take several months to achieve both milestones.

The most common reason kids can't stay dry at night is because they have teeny bladders. Yes, this is a real phenomenon. The average three year old's bladder can only hold five ounces of pee! (Yes, there is a formula for this: bladder capacity in ounces = age in years plus two).

By comparison, an adult's bladder can hold 12 to 16 ounces.[11] And some kids have even smaller bladder capacity than the norm. Other kids simply do not wake up when the urge to pee arises. Parents always describe these kids as deep sleepers.

If your child still isn't dry at night, the best thing to do right now is to limit fluid intake after dinner and avoid products that contain caffeine. And do not punish your child for having accidents. Just put him in a diaper and let time solve the problem.

Q. So when does bedwetting at night become a problem?

Bedwetting becomes a disorder (called **NOCTURNAL ENURESIS**) when child is seven years old and still wetting the bed. Boys are more likely to have trouble. And there is usually someone else in the family who had the same problem (but no one ever talks about it at family gatherings).

For now it is nothing to be alarmed about.

Spit up, regurgitation and vomit

Q. My child just had his first birthday and he is still spitting up. I thought we would be done with this by now. Will I ever have clean clothes again?

Fifty to 70% of all babies spit up, peaking at around four months of age. Spitting up drops off sharply as babies grow older—only 5% of ten to 12 month olds still spit up.

One cause of late spitting up: acid reflux. Officially called GER or Gastroesophageal Reflux, acid reflux becomes a problem when it interferes with weight gain, desire to eat, or causes breathing difficulties. When it is a problem, it is labeled **GASTROESOPHAGEAL REFLUX DISEASE (GERD)**. Your child should be evaluated and treated for GERD if he is not gaining weight, refusing to eat, or chronically coughing or wheezing. See Appendix A, Medications for treatment of GERD.

What if your toddler doesn't have any of those symptoms? It's a bummer, we know, but there isn't a medical solution . . . keep wearing your old t-shirts and know he will eventually outgrow this problem.[12]

For more info on GERD, check out the North American Society of Pediatric Gastroenterology, Hepatology and Nutrition at naspghan.org or the University of Missouri pediatric gastroenterology group at marci-kids.com

Helpful Hints: Acid reflux and wheezing

Some children with acid reflux have a chronic cough and wheezing symptoms. This happens because the food/liquid comes up and irritates the airway. So even if your child is not spitting up large volumes or avoiding eating, he may be suffering other health complications from persistent reflux.

Doctors are usually pretty aggressive about treatment if a child is wheezing due to acid reflux. See Appendix A, Medications for details on treating GERD and wheezing.

Insider Tip

Some babies with acid reflux grow up to be children and adults with acid reflux. Older children may complain that their stomach is upset or that they feel like they are going to throw up when they have reflux symptoms. Other kids may just avoid eating because it hurts. The clues can be different and subtle. The good news is that once your child can talk to you, it may be easier to figure out which foods trigger symptoms and then you can keep them out of your child's diet.

Q. My child throws up every time we give him whole milk. Is he allergic?

Maybe. If a previously breastfed child suddenly starts vomiting when he drinks cow's milk, that's a red flag for milk protein allergy. You can try soy milk and see if the vomiting stops. If the vomiting persists, you should check in with your doctor. For more information on food allergies, see Chapter 11.

Q. My child chronically throws up only in the morning. Should he see the doctor?

Yes. Morning vomiting can be a sign of a serous problem: increased pressure inside the skull. This can be caused by abnormal fluid collection or a mass (**HYDROCEPHALUS, BRAIN TUMOR**). If your child's soft spot (fontanelle) is still open, it will bulge due to the added pressure. Morning headaches accompany the morning vomiting with these disorders, but it is often hard for a young child to verbalize that his head hurts. Bottom line: see your doctor ASAP.

Q. What should I let my child drink while he is vomiting?

Nothing. When your child is actively vomiting, give him nothing to eat or drink unless you want to see it come right back out.

Wait until it has been at least an hour since the last vomit to test the waters. If your child is willing to drink Pedialyte (it tastes like salt water), go for it. If he refuses, try flat ginger ale, Gatorade, or apple juice. Give one teaspoon every five minutes. Do not let your child drink as much as he would like to. He will be very thirsty, but eight ounces at once on an unsettled stomach will be an idea you later regret. If the fluid stays down for a couple of hours, then you can increase the volume he drinks. Once your child keeps down the clear fluid, he can move onto milk, if he prefers. If your child fails to keep down clear fluids, you should check in with your doctor.

Red Flags: Worrisome Vomiting
All of these scenarios deserve a phone call to your doctor.

◆ **Vomiting Bile.** Bile is a fluorescent green/yellow color that can indicate a blockage in the intestines. It is especially worrisome if associated with stomachache, a bloated looking tummy, or fever (see **ACUTE ABDOMEN**).

◆ **Vomiting blood or "coffee grounds."** If the blood looks fresh, it is probably coming from someplace near the mouth (for example a bloody nose—see **EPISTAXIS**). Blood that has been partially digested by the stomach looks like coffee grounds when it is thrown up. This can be caused by bleeding in the esophagus or the stomach (see **ESOPHAGITIS, ULCER**).

◆ **Vomiting repeatedly over six hours.** Excessive vomiting can be caused by stomach viruses (see **GASTROENTERITIS**), food poisoning (see **BACTERIAL ENTERITIS**), or an intestinal blockage (see **ACUTE ABDOMEN**). Most of the time, it is a stomach virus. But you should check in with your doctor if the vomiting occurs for more than six hours. Dehydration can become a problem as well.

◆ **Vomiting associated with fever and irritability.** This is worrisome for **MENINGITIS**. This triad of symptoms should always be evaluated. Little kids can't say to you, "my head really hurts, my neck is stiff, and the light is bothering my eyes."

◆ **Morning vomiting.** As discussed above, this can be a sign of a brain tumor or extra fluid collection in the skull (see **BRAIN TUMOR, HYDROCEPHALUS**).

Gas

Q. My child passes a lot of gas. Should I be worried? It's embarrassing.

Ah, the force is strong in this one. Embarrassing, yes. Worrisome, probably not.

The average person passes half a liter of gas every day, in ten to twenty little bursts (I'm glad I wasn't the researcher doing this study!)[13] The smell is affected by food or medications (such as antibiotics). The quantity is also affected by certain food products, like fiber and sorbitol.[14]

However, if your child has significant discomfort or bloating associated with the gas, he might have **LACTOSE INTOLERANCE**. Folks with lactose intolerance have a problem digesting the natural *sugar* found in cow's milk.

? ?

THE OTHER END

Children are rarely born with lactose intolerance; instead, certain populations (Asians, African Americans, Native Americans, Hispanics) are predisposed to it later in life—usually starting around age five.[15]

Some people will also develop temporary lactose intolerance after experiencing a stomach virus. You can try switching to lactose-free milk or give your child a lactase supplement (a digestive enzyme) when he eats a dairy product. Lactase tablets (such as Lactaid) are available over the counter.

Reality Check: Gas products

Truthfully, there is no magic bullet to relieve gas. There are a few products that are worth trying, though. Simethicone (Little Tummies, Mylicon), Gripe Water, and Beano are safe to use and may help provide some relief. See Appendix B, Alternative Medicine for details.

Next up: routine doctor visits. How do you minimize the waiting time at your doc's office? And what check-ups does a toddler need?

You & Your Doc

Chapter 14

"Never go to a doctor whose office plants have died."
~ Erma Bombeck

WHAT'S IN THIS CHAPTER

◆ EASING DOCTOR FEARS

◆ WELL-CHILD VISIT SCHEDULE

◆ AVOIDING THE WAIT

◆ EMERGENCIES

Yes, by now, you and your pediatrician are well-acquainted. After racking up frequent visits during your baby's first year, you probably have the office number memorized. And hopefully, at this point, you have a trusting and comfortable relationship with your baby's doc.

There is good news to report: you will be visiting your doctor LESS now that your baby is a toddler. There are fewer well-child visits (we'll discuss this in detail later in the chapter) . . . so your doctor trips will be dependent upon how often your child gets sick.

No matter how well things are going doctor-wise, we're sure a few visits have been frustrating—like sitting for 45 minutes in the waiting room with a bored/hungry/crying child. In this chapter, we'll give you some tips on how to avoid such frustration.

First, however, let's share some advice on making a toddler more comfortable at the doctor's office. Unlike babies, toddlers can see that doctor visit coming! Next, we will go over the normal well-child visit schedule and provide some insider tips on how to avoid those dreaded long stays in the waiting room.

Q. My child panics every time we visit the doctor. Any tips to help with this?

Ages 1-2 Many kids in the 12-24 month age group are afraid of visiting the doctor. And sometimes, this

YOUR DOC

? ?

fear continues even longer than that. Feel better knowing your kid is not the only one being dragged in kicking and screaming. Developmentally, it is normal. Toddlers are afraid of strangers (especially those poking at them with cold, black instruments) and are all about control. So, when confronted with a situation where a stranger is talking to them, touching them, and not allowing them to be in charge, you can understand why toddlers revolt.

The well-child visits at 15 and 18 months are usually hit or miss. It just depends on what kind of mood the kid is in that day! Some days, it is easier to have the visit without the toddler, as you might guess.

The good news: your doctor expects your child to be skittish and has lots of tricks up his/her sleeve on how to work with a toddler.

Insider Secrets:
Doctor Tricks to Ease Toddler Anxiety
Here are some time-honored tricks pediatricians use to make the toddler well-check go smoothly:

1 **TALK TO THE PARENT FIRST.** I always chat with parents before speaking to the child. Kids decide whether or not a stranger passes muster depending on how their parents respond to that person.

2 **CHANGE THE SCENERY.** If the toddler is afraid of the exam room, I examine her someplace else. I will let toddlers in my private office and have them play on the floor or sit on the couch. Hallways are also a good location to distract patients while I am examining them.

3 **GO TO THEIR TURF.** I usually examine a toddler while he is sitting on a parent's lap. This is a safety zone. Kids feel less threatened there than being up on an exam table by themselves. I also occasionally follow a child as he explores the exam room. Heck, I'll even get on the floor if I have to. (It's nice that I can still do this and get back up).

4 **GIVE CHOICES.** Toddlers are all about control. So, I let them control part of the exam. For example, I will ask, "Which ear do you want me to look at first?"

5 **PREP TIME.** If a toddler or older child is particularly anxious about a doctor's visit, here's one good idea: buy pretend doctor equipment and practice at home. Let the child examine a parent or doll and let mom or dad examine the child. There are also several good books and videos which can prepare a child for what to expect.

6 **BRING A DOLL.** I am happy to examine a favorite doll or stuffed animal before I examine a patient (most pediatricians I know indulge in this practice). Bring one along to the visit.

7 **TAKE THE COAT OFF.** Contrary to popular belief, it's not the white coat that is the problem. Kids know who we are with or without the coat. But for an extremely anxious child, I will try anything to help calm the storm.

YOUR DOC

8 **BRIBERY**. I may offer a toy, a tongue depressor, or cup as a peace offering. Convincing a child that I am a friend buys a few more seconds of cooperation.

Q. Does my child still need well checks?

Yes.

The American Academy of Pediatrics recommends well child visits (or "health maintenance visits") at the following ages: 15 months, 18 months, two years, two-and-a-half years (see below), three years, four years, and five years old. And we continue to see your child annually until they graduate from high school! These visits assure your doctor that your child is growing and developing normally. Plus your doc can give you a heads up for issues that will arise during the time period between well checks. It also gives you a chance to address concerns and questions you may have. And yes, some of those visits also include shots (more on this next).

FYI: the two-and-a-half year well check is a new recommendation from the American Academy of Pediatrics as of 2008. It's particularly important because it gives your doctor another chance to track your child's development. But insurance plans may not cover the cost of this visit and as such, many doctors have not yet implemented this health visit into their schedules. But if you have any concerns about your child, you can always schedule this visit as a developmental consultation.

Q. Does my child need any more shots?

Yep. Sorry about that. The list of the standard immunization series is found in Chapter 15, Vaccines. We also discuss what shots are needed below.

Q. Is there a standard well child visit schedule?

Here is the table of well child visits for the next few years and a list of standard procedures at these visits.

Age of Visit	Screening Tests	Immunizations*
12 months	Hematocrit, Lead screen	MMR, Prevnar, Hepatitis A
15 months		DTaP, HIB, Varicella
18 months	Lead screen, Autism screen	Hepatitis A
2 years	Dental referral, Body Mass Index (BMI), Lead screen, Cholesterol risk assessment, Autism screen	Prevnar 13 Booster**
3 years	Blood pressure, BMI Lead screen	Prevnar 13 Booster**
4-5 years	Hearing, vision, Hematocrit, Blood pressure, BMI, Cholesterol risk assessment, TB screening, Lead screen	DTaP, MMR, IPV Varicella booster Prevnar 13 Booster**

See to Chapter 15, Vaccines for more info on these vaccines.
**Ask your doctor if your toddler needs this booster shot.*

you & your doc

Screening Tests

- **Blood Pressure.** The American Academy of Pediatrics recommends annual blood pressure screening, starting at three years of age. This simple test can give clues to underlying heart defects, kidney problems, and high blood pressure. (**HYPERTENSION**).

- **Body Mass Index (BMI).** This calculation is based on body weight in relation to height and identifies children (and adults) who are overweight or at risk for it. The BMI is checked annually, starting at two years of age.

- **Body Measurements**. Height and weight is measured at each well child visit and plotted on a growth chart based on the age and gender of the child. Head circumference is measured at each visit until age two or three.

- **Hearing Screen.** Your child should have a formal hearing screen (the one where you raise your hand when you hear the beep) before starting school. Hearing tests may be repeated annually through school screening programs, at the well child visit or if concerns arise.

- **Hematocrit.** A blood count is routinely checked at 9–12 months of age and again as needed to assess for iron deficiency anemia.[1]

- **Immunizations.** See Chapter 15, Vaccines for details.

- **TB screening**. All children used to be tested for exposure to **TUBERCULOSIS (TB)**, a bacteria that causes chronic lung infection. A simple skin test called a PPD (purified protein derivative) confirms exposure. Most schools no longer require a TB test prior to entry. So, testing is only done now if a child is exposed to someone with TB or has a chronic cough. Screening questions to assess potential exposure may be asked at each well child visit.

- **Vision Screen.** A formal vision test (the chart with the E's or cute pictures) is performed at age four or five and may be repeated annually through school screening programs, at well child visits or as needed.

- **Urinalysis.** As of 2008, the American Academy of Pediatrics no longer recommends doing routine testing of urine. Urine samples only need to be tested if there is a concern for infection, diabetes, or kidney function.[4]

- **Lead Screen.** All children are screened for lead exposure at nine months, 12 months old and 18 months. Children are also screened annually from age two to six with a series of questions on lead—this is to assess to see if future testing is necessary.[2] If you have any other concerns about potential lead exposure, your child can have a blood lead level tested at any time.

YOUR DOC

BEHIND THE SCENES: WHO IS THE AAP?

The American Academy of Pediatrics (AAP) is an organization representing over 60,000 pediatricians practicing in the United States. One of the AAP's key goals: child health advocacy. The AAP has various committees consisting of the top experts in their fields who make recommendations and policy statements. These guidelines are usually considered the standard of care for managing childhood disease and preventative health.

Pediatricians apply for membership to this organization after passing a standardized board exam. Such docs are designated with the letters "FAAP" or Fellow of the AAP. Fellows take a recertification exam every seven years to remain board certified.

To access policy statements, information on a variety of health related topics, or even find a pediatrician in your community who is a member of the AAP, go to aap.org.

Q. How do I know if my toddler has been exposed to lead?

Here are the questions that screen for possible lead exposure, courtesy of the American Academy of Pediatrics: If you can answer "yes" to any of the following questions (especially numbers one, two or three) your child may need to be screened for lead.[3]

1. Does your child live in or regularly visit a house that was built before 1950, including a home child care center or the home of a relative?
2. Does your child live in or regularly visit a house built before 1978 that has been remodeled in the last 6 months? Are there any plans to remodel?
3. Does your child have a brother, sister, housemate, or playmate who is being treated for lead poisoning?
4. Does your child live with an adult whose job or hobby involves exposure to lead?
5. Does your child live near an active lead smelter, battery-recycling plant, or other industry likely to release lead into the environment?
6. Does your child live within a block of a major highway or busy street?
7. Has your child ever been given home remedies such as azarcon, greta, or pay looah?
8. Has your child ever lived outside the United States?
9. Does your family use pottery or ceramics for cooking, eating, or drinking?
10. Have you seen your child eat paint chips?
11. Have you seen your child eat soil or dirt?
12. Have you been told your child has low iron?

Q. What kind of appointment do I schedule if my child is ill?

You schedule a "sick visit." These appointments are focused on the problem at hand. There is usually less time designated for this type of appointment as opposed to, say, a well child visit or a consultation (see below).

Q. What kind of appointment do I schedule if I have several/chronic issues I want to discuss?

If your child has a problem that has been going on for a while (like two months of constipation) or you have a laundry list of questions, it's a good idea to schedule a consultation with your doctor. These office visits are usually strategically placed at the end of office hours to allow a more relaxed and lengthy evaluation.

Insider Secrets:
Tricks to Avoiding "The Wait" At Your Doc's Office

Okay, when is the best time to show up at the doctor's office? When no one else is there. Yes, we did discuss this in the *Baby 411* book, but it bears repeating—how do you avoid the crowds at your pediatrician? Here are the slowest times (and the best times to schedule a visit):

♦ Schedule well checks in September or May (if it fits with the time your child is due to be seen).
♦ Schedule the first appointment of the morning or the first appointment of the afternoon. It's the least likely time your doctor will be running late.
♦ Schedule any appointment on Tuesday, Wednesday or Thursday.

Like a beach vacation at spring break, there are several times when your doctor's office will be most busy:

BEHIND THE SCENES: WHY IS MY DOCTOR SO LATE?

Do you ever wonder why your doctor is late? I'll let you in on the secrets behind the waiting room door. Let's look at a typical morning at my practice:

♦ "Dr. Brown, your 8:00am well child appointment is stuck in traffic, can you see them at 8:20am?" (Answer—"Yes.") That patient actually arrives at 8:25am and is brought to an exam room at 8:30am.
♦ My 8:15am well-child appointment is brought back to a room at 8:35am because they had new insurance that needed to be verified first (this takes my business office about 20 minutes on the phone).
♦ My 8:30am sick child with the flu also has asthma and needs a breathing treatment. I need to go back and examine him a second time after my nurse administers a treatment.
♦ "Dr. Brown, your 8:45am sick visit has a sister who is sick, too. Do you have time to see her?" (Answer—"Yes," . . . but now I am double booked at 8:45am.)

So, at 8:35am, I have five patients in four exam rooms that all need to be seen. By 9:00am, I'm already 20 minutes behind and will need to play catch up. It's about this time I'm dreaming of sitting on a

YOUR DOC

◆ **Cold and flu season**. More kids are sick. That's basically October until April.

◆ **Summer vacation.** Well checks for school aged kids are most popular when kids are out of school. And kids who go to summer camp need physicals and health forms to be filled out before participating.

◆ **National holidays**. Parents don't miss work and kids don't miss school. So, these are extremely popular days to visit the doctor if the office is open (and many are).

◆ **Fridays and Mondays.** Docs are always busy on these days, no matter what time of year. This is especially true if your doctor's office doesn't have weekend hours. There is a mad dash to get in before spending the weekend with a sick child . . . and a mad dash to get in on Monday if parents have spent the weekend with a sick child.

Bottom line, if you want to avoid sitting in the waiting room, don't schedule a well-child visit on a Friday afternoon in the middle of January.

Helpful Hints: Doctor office etiquette
Here are some tips for making friends with the office staff:

◆ Bring your insurance card to every visit.
◆ If it is your first visit, show up 30 minutes early to fill out paperwork and have your insurance verified.
◆ If you have changed insurance, show up at least ten minutes early for your appointment to have it verified.

you & your doc

(PER POPULAR DEMAND, AN ENCORE FROM BABY 411)

beach somewhere with a drink adorned with a cute umbrella.

All hope is not lost. Some sick visits are simple and will take less time than the appointment slot (that is, rashes, ear infection rechecks). Some days, there are only sick kids that are "sicker than billed" and parents that need extra hand-holding. I will be behind all morning.

Reality check: doctors are notoriously behind schedule because we try to address the needs of each patient, no matter how long it takes. It helps if we can anticipate what those needs are. If you want to discuss your child's school problems during an appointment for a sore throat, tell the appointments person. Otherwise, it's likely your doctor will ask you to schedule another appointment so there is more time to talk.

For more tips on when is the best time to schedule your child's check ups, see the tips earlier in this chapter. Finally, another point to remember: some doctors now have amazing office hours. A few are even open until 9pm each night and on Saturdays and Sundays! What a concept. Yes, these are typically larger practices in bigger cities, but they do exist. And if a practice has longer "operating hours" and more doctors, odds are the waits will be less. Again, the key is to shop around and see what is available in your community.

◆ Let the staff person making the appointment know the true nature of your visit—even if it is embarrassing or confidential. You and your doctor will appreciate having an extended period of time to discuss a sensitive or chronic problem (see previous discussion on consultations).

◆ Schedule an appointment for each child you want to be seen. If all parents actually did this, there would be less waiting in the waiting room.

◆ If you are running late, call the office. Most doctors' offices can modify their schedules if they know ahead of time.

Parent 411: The Doc's Crew (& Their Training)

Here is the usual crew that you will get to know:

◆ **Medical provider:** This is the politically correct term for the person directly responsible for your child's medical care. This may be a pediatrician or a family practice doctor. That person's training includes either medical school (M.D.) or osteopathic school (D.O.). After medical training, the provider has specialty training in children's health exclusively (pediatrics) or a combination of child and adult health (family practice). Regardless of background, providers will have at least seven years of training beyond college before they have their own office.

◆ **Midlevel provider:** This term refers to nurse practitioners (N.P.) or physician assistants (P.A.) who do many of the routine sick and well-child visits. They evaluate and treat patients under the supervision of your doctor. Nurse practitioners have at least two years of training beyond a bachelor's degree in nursing (B.S.N.). Physician assistant training is a two-year program after college—P.A.'s also often have previous healthcare experience. Midlevel providers are a popular addition to busy pediatric offices.

◆ **Nursing staff.** This staff has a variety of degrees. The head nurse may be a registered nurse (R.N.) or a licensed vocational nurse (L.V.N.). Many pediatric offices also utilize medical assistants who are trained to administer shots and perform screening tests.

Q. What are my options for nights and weekends if my child gets sick?

The instruction manual for children clearly states that they are only allowed to get sick when their doctor's office is closed. So, it's a good idea to find out where your doctor suggests you take your child in the event that he/she is not available (and yes, it will happen to you).

The most convenient place to go—the emergency room at a nearby hospital—may not be the best option. Why? Most community hospitals do not staff their emergency rooms with pediatric specialists. For stitches or broken bones, it probably doesn't matter if you head to any ER. But for some pediatric emergencies, your child may get better care when there is a pediatric specialist in the house. The best advice: ask this question of your doctor

YOUR DOC

BEFORE there is an emergency.

It's also a good idea to call your doctor's office *before* you go running anywhere to be sure that your not wasting your time or money (emergency rooms and minor emergency centers charge higher co-payments for their services). What may seem like an emergency to you may, in reality, be less serious—that is, it can be taken care of with an office visit the next day.

Q. What is the best way to contact my doctor's office?

Pick up the phone. Although doctors are trying to live in the 21st century, most practices still do not use email as a method of communicating with patients' families. One reason: medical privacy issues limit what can be discussed via email. HIPAA is the acronym for the U.S. policy that protects medical information. But to make it even more confusing, the law is subject to interpretation by individual medical offices.

A smart move: Ask your doctor's office what the options are for getting questions answered or appointments made. You may be surprised to find out that your office utilizes modern technology or offers an interactive website.

Q. I am thinking about switching doctors. Any advice?

For whatever reason, you may not make a love connection with your doctor (or the office). You may not see eye to eye with a doc's parenting philosophy. Or you find yourself enduring unbelievably long waits before appointments. Maybe you just don't feel like the doctor meets your needs. That's okay. Don't feel guilty—chances are, your doctor may feel like you aren't a good fit for the practice either.

I'm not suggesting that you doctor shop on a regular basis, but I do think you should have a medical home where you feel comfortable. If you are having second thoughts, first try out a different doctor in the practice for a sick visit and see how it goes. If your doc practices alone, see if you can arrange a consultation or meeting with another practice in town. Some offices offer this as a free service, while others charge for it. It's a little different than the typical free prenatal consults you remember from your pregnancy.

If you decide to leave the entire practice, don't forget to get copies of your child's medical records. That allows your new doc to pick up where the old one left off. There may be a fee for the records to be released.

One major reason for toddler doctor visits: vaccinations. We'll cover this subject in-depth next.

VACCINES
Chapter 15

"Health is not valued till sickness comes."
~ Dr. Thomas Fuller

Shots are for more than just newborns. As you read in the last chapter, there are still several more scheduled vaccinations ahead for your toddler.

It's hard to imagine something as successful as childhood vaccinations would be controversial . . . but here we are.

Google "vaccine" (better yet, don't) and you'll be bombarded with all sorts of anti-vaccine propaganda, as activists push fear over science in an attempt to stop kids from getting shots.

Ask a grandparent about this and they will give you a quizzical look. That's because they have *lived* through actual outbreaks of deadly diseases that once killed their friends and neighbors, but now are assigned to the dustbin of history, thanks to vaccines.

Speaking with my own mother about "polio season" was enough to convince me that we live in a truly fortunate generation. She recalls the summer that she could not go to the community swimming pool or the movies because her parents feared she would catch polio. And she remembers standing in line for *hours* to get her polio vaccine when it was first introduced. I think the last time I stood in line for that long was for *Avatar* in 3D. It's a different world today in many ways, and we have vaccines to thank for it.

Ironically, vaccines are in many ways victims of their own success. Shots have been so powerful in stopping disease that we now wonder if we need them at all. Of course, that all changes when a new disease rears its head (think H1N1 flu). Then folks *demand* vaccines to protect their family!

So, let's put it in black and white: we ARE pro-vaccine and darn proud of it. This position comes from being in the trenches of the pediatric war against disease. I have watched a child die after losing the fight against chicken pox and cared for more than one baby gasping for each breath with whooping cough.

Seeing such things makes you realize one truth about kids and germs: we must *respect* infectious diseases. They are powerful, adaptable, and sometimes lethal. And the best protection is immunization.

Do you wonder why virtually every doctor is adamant about vaccinating his/her patients? It's not some dark conspiracy between the government and big pharmaceutical companies. Nor are doctors raking in the cash from vaccines (I would have become a plastic surgeon if I wanted to get rich).

No, here is the shocking truth: *doctors want to vaccinate our patients because it is our job to protect them.* And every doctor has his own story to tell about caring for a patient with a vaccine-preventable disease. It is heartbreaking to feel helpless while our patient suffers.

DR B'S OPINION

"I consider my patients to be my own children. I would not sleep at night if I knew they were not protected. If a parent chooses not to vaccinate their child, it is their responsibility . . . and risk. But it is not one I will share with them."

But we also understand where parents are coming from because, well, we are parents too. We want to protect our children in the best way we can. So we encourage parents to investigate the safety of vaccines before signing off on those shots—but check out the FACTS and SCIENCE in this debate, not fear and innuendo.

So, let's look at the Top 10 questions parents have about vaccines. Then we'll discuss the shots your toddler will get. And finally, let's tackle the most controversial vaccine issues. But first, here's a bit of history to understand the vaccine story.

A bit of history

So what exactly are vaccines? Simply put, vaccines are shots filled with dead or inactivated disease components that stimulate the body's immune response in order to prevent *future* infection. Smallpox was the first disease to be treated with vaccines—and here's how it happened.

Smallpox was a deadly virus that used to wipe out entire civilizations. The Turks tried to immunize for it as early as the ninth century. In the 1700's, an English country doctor named Edward Jenner made a brilliant discovery: milkmaids who had been exposed to *cowpox* (a common disease in cattle at the time) did not get infected with smallpox. He proposed that injecting humans with cowpox virus (which was usually not deadly) would make them immune to smallpox. His research paper in 1798, entitled "Vaccination," changed public health forever. By the way, he coined the phrase vaccination after the hybrid cowpox virus' scientific name—vaccinia. (Just in case you ever get on Jeopardy.)

Well, vaccination worked. People were inoculated with a small amount of cowpox virus on their arms. It caused a local infection at that site (hence the scar that thirty-somethings and above bear). And true to Dr. Jenner's hypothesis, it provided protection against smallpox disease. In 1977, the last known case of smallpox occurred in Somalia. In 1980, the World Health Organization declared the world free of smallpox, thanks to global vaccination efforts.

Smallpox vaccine was crude and occasionally deadly. It was a live vaccine that actually caused one disease to protect from another one. So, it is no surprise that anti-vaccine groups emerged by the 1830's. Of course, in those days, you could be jailed for refusing to vaccinate, much less leading a campaign against vaccines. Now, you'd get a guest shot on Oprah or Larry King.

But this first immunization led the way to creating newer (and much safer) vaccines that are remarkably effective in preventing diseases and epidemics our grandparents and parents can still remember.

Reality Check: The decision to vaccinate YOUR child impacts ALL children.

As a parent, you'll face many personal choices in raising your child. Perhaps you'll decide to spend extra on organic milk or other foods. Or make the decision that your toddler shouldn't watch TV. Some parenting decisions happen in a bubble. It is your choice and affects only your family. Do whatever makes you happy.

However, deciding whether or not to vaccinate your child is NOT such a decision. That's because your decision will have an impact not just on your child but on everyone else's.

It's like stopping your car at a stop sign. Sure, you don't HAVE to stop . . . and running the sign puts your family at risk. But you also risk the lives of other drivers, bicyclists and pedestrians.

And that's why we are so passionate about vaccines. We don't want to see *any* child—yours or anyone else's—harmed by devastating diseases that can be prevented.

Vaccines do not work as well if a large number of folks opt out of the system. Vaccines are not 100% effective in any one individual. It is the *collective* immunity of the population (known as **herd immunity**) that keeps a germ from reaching epidemic proportions. You may think that if everyone else's kid is protected then your child doesn't need to be. But . . . germs don't think that way. They just look for a new person to infect. And the more people who opt out, the more vulnerable the entire population is (particularly its youngest members).

The good news is that, despite all the media reports you might hear, very few parents actually choose to opt out of vaccines. While the number of parents who've not vaccinated their kids has risen slightly in recent years, these folks (thankfully) represent a very small minority.

The Top 10 vaccine questions

Here are the top questions that parents typically ask. For *Baby 411* veterans, use this as a refresher course or skip to the next section. There, we

vaccines

will go over specific vaccine questions and the schedule for toddlers.

1 **WHAT ARE VACCINES?** Vaccines are given to a person to protect him from disease. Vaccines prevent viral and bacterial infections that can cause serious illness and death.

2 **HOW DO VACCINES WORK?** Your immune system is your body's defense against foreign invaders (viruses, bacteria, parasites). Vaccines prepare your body to recognize and kill these invaders without getting infected. A vaccine revs up your immune system to make antibodies (smart bombs with memory) for the signature of a particular germ. So, if the body sees the real germ, it already knows how to fight it.

There are three types of vaccinations: inactivated, live attenuated, and inactivated bacterial toxins:

◆ *Inactivated vaccines* do not contain any living germs. An immune response forms against either a dead germ, part of the germ (recombinant DNA), or a protein or sugar marker that sits on the outer layer of the germ (its signature). These vaccines are safe to give to immune-compromised people. The only downside is that several doses are needed to provide full, lifelong protection against disease. Some of these vaccines include: *Flu, Hepatitis A and B, HIB, Pertussis (whooping cough), Inactivated Polio, Prevnar.*

◆ *Live attenuated vaccines* are weak forms of the germs that cause infection. An immune response occurs just as if your body had the infection. So, one or two doses of vaccine give you lifelong protection. These vaccines are not given to immune-compromised people because it can make them sick. Examples include: *MMR, Oral Polio, Smallpox, Varicella (chickenpox), Rotavirus.*

◆ *Toxoids* (inactivated bacterial toxins) are vaccines that create a defense against a toxin (poison) made by bacteria germs. Examples include: *Diphtheria, Tetanus.*

3 **WHICH DISEASES ARE PREVENTED BY VACCINES?** You probably haven't heard of most of the diseases that are prevented by vaccines—that's because vaccines have done their job! Grandparents, however, know them well. We have a list of the recommended vaccination series following this section and explanations of the diseases. Some vaccine-preventable diseases are viruses which are difficult to treat once a person becomes infected—that's why vaccines are so important!

4 **HOW ARE VACCINES TESTED TO ENSURE SAFETY?** Vaccines are researched extensively for an average of 15 years before being approved for use. Once safety is proven, the vaccine is tested in several thousand volunteers to check for rare adverse effects. Unfortunately, nothing in this world is 100% foolproof, including vaccine science. But the research trials that occur before licensing are very rigid. If you think there are a lot of vaccines on the market, imagine how many never made it. And just in case you are wondering, each new vaccine must be tested with other existing vaccines to ensure safety and effectiveness when given in combination.

The Food and Drug Administration (FDA) governs this process. The FDA is the watchdog for any medication that is sold over the counter or by prescription. If you are a conspiracy theorist, you may be skeptical of putting your trust in them. But look at the big picture: the standards for medication and vaccine safety are extremely strict. Using today's rules, aspirin probably would never be approved!

5 WHY IS MY CHILD GETTING MORE SHOTS THAN I DID? There has been a tremendous effort to create more vaccines because they are so effective in preventing serious infections. Many of the vaccine-preventable diseases are viruses. There are very few "anti-viral" medications, so once you have a viral infection, there is not much to do about it (for example, Hepatitis B). And consider vaccines like Prevnar that protect your child against bacterial diseases such as meningitis. These diseases are very serious since they are resistant to many antibiotics. Instead of thinking, wow, there are too many shots, look at it this way. Thank goodness there are so many ways to prevent deadly diseases!

6 CAN MY CHILD'S BODY HANDLE SEVERAL SHOTS AT ONCE? Yes—and it is also okay to get shots when he is sick. Your child can handle these shots better than you! Your child is exposed to thousands of germs on a daily basis (even if he is not in daycare). Exposing your child to five or eight different germs in the form of vaccines is a spit in the bucket. And young kids have a better immune response to vaccines than older children and adults.

Kids develop a good response to various vaccines simultaneously. This is studied before a vaccine is licensed. Even if your child got 11 shots at the same time, he would need to use only about 0.1% of his immune system to respond.[1]

The goal is to protect your child as quickly as possible from diseases that are very dangerous to young children.

And even though the number of shots has gone up, the actual load on the immune system has gone down. That's because today's vaccines are "smarter" and better engineered than the shots from a few decades ago.

Case in point: whooping cough. Before 1991, the whooping cough vaccine had 3000 different germ particles (antigens). Today's whooping cough shot has just three to five particles—just as effective, but much better designed to be easy on your immune system.

Before 1996, the polio vaccine was "live"—this carried a small risk of actually getting polio. Today's polio vaccine is dead (inactivated) . . . and carries NO chance of getting the disease.

So, here's the irony: *your* parents took much greater risk when getting vaccinated back in the 50's, 60's and 70's. Today, even though we have many more vaccines, the risk is much lower.

Our children are really getting smarter, safer vaccines today and better protection than we ever got as kids.

Bottom line: *Vaccines do not weaken the immune system, they boost it.*

VACCINES

7 CAN'T YOU GIVE JUST ONE BIG SHOT THAT HAS ALL THE VACCINES IN IT?

We wish we could. Everyone hates shots—those who give them and those who get them. Scientists are working on it. There are some combination vaccines that your child may have already received such as Pentacel, which covers more than one vaccine in a shot. But as of this writing, there is just not a single shot that will protect your child against all diseases.

FYI: It is true that some vaccinations require a booster dose to keep antibody levels high or improve immunity. That's one reason why toddlers still need some shots.

8 AM I REQUIRED TO VACCINATE MY CHILD?

No. However, choosing not to vaccinate means exposing your child to a potentially serious infection. And it puts your community at risk as well.

Vaccination is required in all fifty states for school entry, but each state has their own requirement for particular vaccines. Some require special vaccinations for daycare and preschool entry. All fifty states allow vaccine exemptions for medical reasons and 48 states allow vaccine exemption for religious reasons. Some states also allow vaccine exemption for philosophical reasons. You can find out what your state's requirements are by going to your state health department's website.

DR B'S OPINION
ALTERNATIVE VACCINE SCHEDULES

The Centers for Disease Control publishes a recommended vaccine schedule for all children in the US—this schedule wasn't created from thin air . . . doctors, scientists and researchers work together to decide the best (and safest) time to give shots. The goal: protect as many babies as soon as possible from deadly disease. The youngest children are the most likely to suffer serious complications from these diseases.

Now, one of the popular myths about autism is that somehow kids are getting "too many shots, too soon." Despite the scientific evidence that shows vaccines do NOT cause autism, some parents think that if they space out their kids' vaccines in an "alternative schedule" this is somehow safer. It's not. In fact, it puts the most vulnerable at risk.

Dr. Bob Sears is the most vocal proponent of alternative vaccination schedules. Through his website and books, he proposes that families use his own homemade vaccination schedule. So who is Dr. Bob, anyway? He is a pediatrician in private practice—not an infectious disease expert or vaccinologist. Hence, he is making up this vaccine schedule all by himself. There's no science behind it.

Don't take our word for this, however. Here is Dr. Bob in his own words about his schedule: "My schedule doesn't have any research behind it. No one has ever studied a big group of kids using my schedule to determine if it's safe or if it has any benefits."[2]

As a doc and a parent, I'd much rather follow a schedule that has been extensively researched for both safety and effectiveness by multiple people who are truly experts in the field of vaccines.

9 **ISN'T NATURAL IMMUNITY FROM THE DISEASE BETTER THAN GETTING VAC-CINATED?** No. Vaccine-preventable diseases are not minor illnesses. For instance, would you rather have your child get meningitis and potentially die . . . or get the vaccine? Getting chickenpox or any other disease the "natural way" can have serious consequences with no real benefit.

10 **WHAT ARE THE SIDE EFFECTS FROM VACCINATION?** Up to 80% of the time, kids may have a mild local response to a vaccine. That means

---

REASONS NOT TO VACCINATE

There are very specific medical reasons to discontinue or hold off on certain vaccinations:

1. *An immune-compromised patient or family member.*
2. *Had disease (for example, if you've had chicken pox, you don't need the vaccine).*
3. *Encephalitis or degenerative brain disorder.*
4. *Allergy to vaccine or an additive in vaccine.*

If your child has a food allergy to eggs or gelatin (Jell-O), or an allergy to antibiotics (such as Neomycin, Streptomycin, Polymyxin B), notify your doctor before any vaccinations are given. Several vaccines are grown in chick embryo cells and therefore contain a small amount of egg protein: flu vaccine (Flushield, Fluzone, Fluvirin), MMR, rabies (RabAvert), and yellow fever vaccine (YF-VAX). The MMR, Fluzone, Varivax, and yellow fever vaccines also include gelatin.

Rabies, MMR, Chickenpox and Polio vaccines include several different kinds of antibiotics to prevent contamination of the vaccine itself. Check with your doctor if your child is allergic to any antibiotics.[3]

If your child has a food allergy to eggs, it is recommended that your child be observed for allergic reaction for 90 minutes after receiving the MMR vaccine at one year of age.[4] The flu vaccine USED to be off limits for an egg-allergic person.[5] Not anymore. Allergists now believe many people can safely get it even if they have an egg allergy. If your child has an egg allergy, ask for a referral to an allergist for a skin test. Your child may have outgrown his food allergy, or he may tolerate the vaccine in graduated doses even if he is still allergic.

If your child has taken oral steroids for at least 14 days, he is considered temporarily immune-compromised and should not get any live attenuated vaccines.

To review: it is OK to get shots if: your child has a minor illness. Or a mild fever. Or if your child is taking antibiotics. Or if your child was born prematurely.

Real world tip: tell your doctor or nurse if your child has:
◆ any food or medication allergies.
◆ any serious vaccine reactions in the past.
◆ seizures, neurological problems.
◆ cancer, leukemia, HIV, or otherwise weakened immune system.
◆ taken oral steroids in the past three months.
◆ received blood transfusions, or immune globulins.
◆ been vaccinated for anything else in the past four weeks.[6]

you might see redness or a lump at the site of the injection. Occasionally, a child will have fever, body aches, or a headache. Here's an overview of possible side effects:

Inactivated vaccines cause an immediate immune response. The body reacts as if it was truly being invaded by the disease. The result, typically, is a fever within 24 hours of vaccination. Kids sometimes feel like they are coming down with a cold or flu (body aches, pains). Some children prefer to sleep through the experience; others choose to tell you how they feel! All of these symptoms resolve within 24 hours of vaccination.

Live attenuated vaccines (MMR, Varicella) cause a delayed immune response. This occurs one to four *weeks* after the vaccination is given. Long after the doctor's visit, your child may wake up one morning and have a fever. This may be accompanied by a rash that looks like measles (pimples) or chickenpox (clear, fluid filled blisters). The rash can sometimes be dramatic. Both the fever and the rash tell you that your child is forming an immune response to the vaccination. Kids are not contagious and most are

---

LESSONS LEARNED: SAN DIEGO 2008 OUTBREAK

Yes, vaccine-preventable diseases are real. While we've done a good job eliminating such diseases from the U.S. and Canada, many are just a short plane ride away. And that's the rub: Americans love to travel. And kids bring home germs like souvenirs.

Case in point: San Diego, January 2008. A seven-year-old boy who was unvaccinated by parent choice took a trip to Switzerland . . . and came home with measles. By the time he was diagnosed a week later, he had already infected his two unvaccinated siblings, four unvaccinated (again, by parent choice) friends in school . . . and four kids who were sitting with him in a doctor's waiting room.

This child's school had a very high number (about 10%) of children who were unvaccinated by parent choice (California permits parents to file "personal exemptions" to avoid vaccinations). Hence, this school was ripe for a measles epidemic . . . and that germ was only a flight away.

We feel sorry for the kids that got sick—their parents relied on the rest of us to vaccinate OUR kids to protect theirs. It's not the kids' fault they got measles—it was the parents'.

What's most appalling are the innocent victims—those helpless kids sitting in the doctor's waiting room who got the measles. Three of the four children were *babies* under a year of age—they were too young to be vaccinated for measles. Families with kids too young to be vaccinated do rely on their community's vaccination rates to protect their kids—and their community failed them. One of those babies was hospitalized for two days. Imagine the anguish (and expense) these families endured, all because another family foolishly opted out of vaccinating their child.

And San Diego isn't alone. There were 131 cases of measles in 2008. Fortunately, there were no deaths.

The bottom line: vaccination doesn't just protect your child—it protects your entire community.[7]

VACCINES

not bothered by the rash. You don't need to call your doctor. This reaction is expected.

Redness at the injection site is common. In particular, the fifth booster dose of the DTaP (at age four to six years) can cause a huge area of redness. This happens because our bodies already recognize these germs pretty well. Doctors get many phone calls on this reaction.

A firm lump may develop at the injection site if some of the fat in the arm/leg gets nicked as the needle goes into the muscle. This is called **FAT NECROSIS**. It usually goes away within six to eight weeks. It doesn't hurt.

DR B'S OPINION

"Never promise your child that he does not need any shots. Then you can be pleasantly surprised if your visit is shot-free."

Parent 411: Adverse Reactions

Adverse reactions are the worst possible side effects from vaccines. This is the equivalent of an allergic reaction to a medication—and fortunately, they are all quite rare. Adverse reactions include:

1. Death.
2. Encephalitis.
3. Fever related seizure (convulsions).

There is about a one in 1.5 million risk of having an anaphylactic reaction from vaccines. Most of these can be avoided by asking about food and medication allergies, and previous reactions to vaccinations.

Both the CDC and FDA keep close tabs on adverse reactions to vaccines via a Vaccine Adverse Event Reporting System (VAERS). Both doctors and patient families may submit a VAERS form if any adverse reaction occurs. You can contact VAERS by phone at 800-822-7967 or at vaers.hhs.gov.

Keep in mind that medical illness reports do not prove an association of a particular illness with a particular vaccination. The job of both the CDC and FDA is to review each report that occurs and see if there is a pattern of subsequent illness after vaccination.

Yes, vaccines have some risks associated with them, but remember that the risk of adverse reaction is *significantly* lower than the risk of leaving your child unprotected.

In 1986, recognizing that there are rare, serious reactions that occur as a result of vaccinating children, the U.S. Department of Health and Human Services created the Vaccine Injury Compensation Program (VICP). This program tries to determine whether adverse reactions from vaccines cause injuries or death. VICP then provides the victim with compensation.

We agree that an adverse reaction only has to happen to one child for it to be heartbreaking. But if we look at the big picture, we can point to the *millions* of children who might have experienced illness, disfigurement and death if diseases like smallpox or polio were not controlled by vaccinations.

Red Flags

Call your doctor if your child does any of the following after a vaccination:

vaccines

VACCINES

? ?

◆ Inconsolable crying over three hours.
◆ Fever over 105 degrees.
◆ Seizure activity.
◆ Extreme lethargy.

Reality Check: **Your child's shot series may vary a bit from your neighbor's child.**

There are four governing panels of experts in infectious diseases that make recommendations for vaccinations. These smart folks include: American Academy of Pediatrics (AAP), American Academy of Family Physicians (AAFP), Advisory Committee on Immunization Practices (ACIP), and the Centers for Disease Control (CDC). Because there are several groups involved in this effort, there is some variability in vaccination schedule recommendations. You will see a bar on the vaccination chart (see page 278) that shows the recommended period of time when kids should get each shot. Therefore, don't be surprised if your neighbor's child is on a slightly different schedule then your own.

Helpful hint: **Keep a medical passport**

It's a good idea to have a medical passport for your child. This should include an immunization record, growth chart, list of medical problems, list of surgeries, drug allergies, and name and dosage of any medications that are used regularly (such as asthma medicine).

Q. Does my toddler need any more shots?

Yes, sorry about that. Your child will complete his initial immunization series between 12 and 18 months, depending on what schedule your doctor follows. Then his next booster shots will be at his four to six year well check before kindergarten.

Your doctor should remind you at each well child visit when you need to return. But in general, your child will need a well child visit at 12, 15, 18, and 24 months, and then annually after that. And assume there will probably be shots at each of those visits until age two.

Q. Are some shots optional?

The flu vaccine is optional (except for a mandate in New Jersey), but is recommended for all children six months and up. The dreaded H1N1 or "swine flu" strain is included in the current seasonal flu vaccine.

For the rest of the vaccination series, the answer varies state to state. It also depends on the frequency of disease in particular counties within a state. We have provided a table of the most recent requirements in the U.S. on our web site Toddler411.com (click on "Bonus Material"). For instance, Hepatitis A vaccine is required in some states, but optional in others unless a particular county has twenty cases of Hepatitis A per 100,000 population.

Vaccination Schedule

On page 278 is the schedule for vaccinations. For details on these specific vaccines, see the following section. Cool tool: if you want to know what shots your child needs, use the CDC's free Immunization Scheduler. Go to our web page (Toddler411.com) for the link and just type in your child's birth date!

As a quick summary, the diseases your child will be vaccinated for after one year of age are listed below. We explain these diseases in the next section.

- ◆ Hepatitis B booster dose (if series is not completed by 12 months old)
- ◆ Diphtheria, Tetanus, and Whooping cough (Pertussis) booster doses
- ◆ HIB (Haemophilus influenzae B) booster dose
- ◆ Polio booster dose(s)
- ◆ Measles, Mumps, and Rubella–primary and booster dose
- ◆ Chickenpox (Varicella)–primary and booster dose
- ◆ Pneumococcal (strep or "Prevnar") booster dose
- ◆ Hepatitis A–primary and booster dose
- ◆ Flu (influenza) annually

Disease And Vaccine Specifics

Enough of the alphabet soup, here is a breakdown of the vaccines and the diseases they are designed to stop. Check our website at Toddler411.com for a visual library of these diseases (click on "Bonus Material").

Here's a run-down of the vaccines and diseases . . . but first, let's look at the CDC's recommended immunization schedule.

Diphtheria, Tetanus, Pertussis: The diseases

◆ **Diphtheria**: This is a *bacteria* that causes a serious throat infection. It invades the tonsils, kills the tissue, and creates a thick pus lining that can block off the airway. Diphtheria also produces a toxin that enters the blood and injures the heart, kidneys, and nerves. It is spread by respiratory droplets (coughs and sneezes). There is a 10% mortality rate from infection, even today. Before the vaccine, 200,000 Americans had this disease every year–and 20,000 died.

◆ **Tetanus**: This is a *bacteria* that causes wound infections. It is not contagious person to person. Tetanus bacteria produce spores that are found in the soil and dust around the world. These are resilient little germs, so we will never eliminate them. Tetanus spores can enter open wounds (especially puncture wounds, animal bites, and umbilical cord stumps) and create a toxin that attacks nerves. The affected nerves cause muscles to spasm (tetany). These spasms prevent breathing and swallowing (lockjaw). There is a 30% mortality rate from infection.

◆ **Pertussis (Whooping Cough):** This *bacteria* causes irritation and inflammation of the throat. The resulting swelling prevents mucous from being coughed up and creates a blocked airway, particularly for those with the smallest airways (infants). Pertussis infection initially looks like the common cold. Over time, infected people have coughing fits or spasms. As a per-

Continued on page 279

VACCINES

??

Recommended Immunization Schedule for Persons Aged 0 Through 6 Years—United States • 2010

For those who fall behind or start late, see the catch-up schedule

Vaccine ▼ Age ▲	Birth	1 month	2 months	4 months	6 months	12 months	15 months	18 months	19–23 months	2–3 years	4–6 years
Hepatitis B[1]	HepB	HepB			HepB						
Rotavirus[2]			RV	RV	RV[2]						
Diphtheria, Tetanus, Pertussis[3]			DTaP	DTaP	DTaP	see footnote[3]	DTaP				DTaP
Haemophilus influenzae type b[4]			Hib	Hib	Hib[4]	Hib					
Pneumococcal[5]			PCV	PCV	PCV	PCV				PPSV	
Inactivated Poliovirus[6]			IPV	IPV		IPV					IPV
Influenza[7]					Influenza (Yearly)						
Measles, Mumps, Rubella[8]						MMR			see footnote[8]		MMR
Varicella[9]						Varicella			see footnote[9]		Varicella
Hepatitis A[10]						HepA (2 doses)				HepA Series	
Meningococcal[11]										MCV	MCV

Range of recommended ages for all children except certain high-risk groups

Range of recommended ages for certain high-risk groups

son tries to get a breath in, he makes a characteristic "whoop." Infants, who have smaller airways, are unable to breathe at all. Instead of whooping, they stop breathing and their faces turn red or purple. Children often throw up during a coughing fit. What makes Pertussis so dangerous is that the infection is spread by respiratory droplets. Prior to vaccine development, there were 200,000 cases a year in the U.S. There were 10,000 deaths annually, mostly in infants.

Whooping cough is still around and is on the rise. There were over 25,000 cases in 2005. Although there were 10,000 cases reported in 2008, the number of unreported cases is probably much higher.

If you want to know what whooping cough sounds like, check out this website: vaccineinformation.org/video/pertussis.asp

Here are some things you should know:

1. Whooping cough epidemics occur about every three to four years.
2. Immunity to whooping cough wanes in teens and adults despite vaccination. Now that a vaccine is available for these age groups, it's time to roll up your sleeve and get a shot, too!
3. Many cases of whooping cough are undiagnosed and untreated in older people. Have you ever had a cough that just "hung on" for several weeks? You may have had whooping cough and not known it.
4. Dropping immunization rates allow the disease to spread quickly through a community. It's no surprise that communities with high anti-vaccine sentiment (Boulder, Colorado, for example) have also seen serious outbreaks of whooping cough.

DTaP: The vaccine

This combination vaccine, around since the 1940's, protects against **D**iphtheria, **T**etanus, and **P**ertussis (whooping cough).

An older version of this vaccine (DTP) was called a "whole cell" vaccine because it was derived from a whole dead whooping cough germ. This vaccine was effective, but caused a significant number of high fevers and convulsions. A newer formulation is an "acellular" vaccine known as DTaP. The immune response is formed to a piece of the bacteria (its signature) rather than the whole cell. This safer vaccine came out in 1991 and there are many fewer side effects.

DTaP is given in a series of doses, five total. The fourth and fifth booster doses are more likely to cause a fever or redness at the injection site because our bodies recognize it and have an immune response ready to go. After the fifth dose of DTaP, boosters are given every ten years—yes, that means YOU need to get it! Our immunity to whooping cough wanes over time, leaving adults as the ones spreading the disease! Here are shot details for toddlers and older kids:

◆ The fourth dose of DTaP is given at 15 to 18 months of age.
◆ The fifth dose of DTaP is given at four to six years of age.
◆ Teens (age 11 and up) and adults should get a whooping cough booster shot as well.

VACCINES

Polio: The Disease

Polio is a *virus* that attacks the spinal cord and brain. It has particular affinity for the nerves that control leg muscles and the diaphragm muscle (that helps you breathe). As a result, polio can paralyze its victims . . . or leave them dependent on a machine to breathe. Prior to modern-day ventilators, people survived the illness by living in iron lung machines until they could recover enough strength to breathe. The virus spreads through the stool of infected people. This was a common summertime epidemic, and whole households would get the infection. Before the vaccine, there were 20,000 cases of paralysis per year in the U.S. *Since 1979, there have been no cases of naturally occurring polio infection in the U.S.*

So why keep vaccinating if there is not any polio? Because the infection is an airplane flight away! Polio infections occur in 30 countries around the world. There has been an extraordinary effort to eradicate the disease, like smallpox. Yet, as of this writing, polio is still a threat.

Polio: The Vaccine

In the U.S., we give the inactivated form of the vaccine as a shot. The vaccine that was given from 1963 to 1996 was a live vaccine called OPV (a drink) that carried a small risk of acquiring vaccine-associated polio disease. In 1997, doctors switched to an all-inactivated (IPV) vaccination series. IPV—which is a four dose series—does not cause polio disease.

- ◆ The third dose of IPV may be given from 6 to 18 months old.
- ◆ The fourth dose of IPV is given at four to six years of age.

Haemophilus Influenzae B (HIB): The disease

This is a *bacteria* that causes a potentially fatal throat swelling (**EPIGLOTTITIS**) and infection of the brain lining (**MENINGITIS**). Despite the similar-sounding name, HIB has no relationship to influenza (flu)—yes, we realize that is confusing. HIB is spread by respiratory droplets (sneezing, coughing). Prior to vaccine development, there were 20,000 cases of HIB infection annually in the U.S. and 500 deaths. Most infections occurred in children less than five years of age. Survivors of meningitis may be permanently deaf, blind, or intellectually impaired.

Haemophilus Influenzae B (HIB): The vaccine

The development of the HIB vaccine is a true success story of modern-day medicine. The vaccine was licensed in 1985. By 1992, HIB infections were virtually eliminated (less than 200 cases per year).

The HIB vaccine can be given either individually or in a combination product. Examples of such combo vaccines include Pentacel (which combines DTaP, Inactivated Polio, and HIB) or Trihibit (which combines DTaP and HIB). Children form a good immunity with any of these products.

- ◆ The final dose of HIB vaccine is given from 12 to 15 months old.
- ◆ The current HIB vaccine products require four doses to complete the vaccination series.

Measles, Mumps, Rubella: The diseases

◆ **Measles:** This is a *virus* that infects the entire body. Infected people start out with cold symptoms and pink eye. It causes a dramatic head to toe rash, then spreads to other organ systems including the intestines (diarrhea), lungs (pneumonia), and brain (encephalitis). The highest rate of these complications is in children under age five. The virus is highly contagious and is spread through respiratory droplets. Before the measles vaccine, the disease was as common as chickenpox, affecting an amazing four MILLION people per year is the U.S. . . . and killing 500.

Scary, but true, measles outbreaks can still hit close to home. In 2004, 12 children adopted from China had measles infections when they landed on U.S. soil. In 2008, 131 cases of measles occurred in nine states. Ninety percent of those infected were unvaccinated—and one in five of those folks ended up in the hospital, including very young children.

◆ **Mumps**: This is a *virus* that attacks the salivary glands. Mumps infect the glands located along the jaw line and cause a marked swelling. It also infects other body parts that swell up, including the testicles, ovaries, and brain. Mumps attack the brain (meningitis) about 15% of the time. It can cause deafness and intellectual impairment in survivors. Like measles, mumps is spread through respiratory droplets. Before the mumps vaccine was developed, there were 200,000 cases per year. After the vaccine, in recent years, there were fewer than 600 cases a year in the U.S. However, 2010 was a banner year for the mumps virus, which mounted a comeback tour. As of this writing, there were over 2000 cases reported in New York, New Jersey, and the surrounding New England area. Just a reminder that these diseases still exist!

◆ **Rubella** (German measles): This is a highly contagious *virus* that causes mild infection in children, but fatal or disabling infection in unborn fetuses. Rubella spreads through respiratory droplets and causes a runny nose, swollen glands, and a rash in children. If a pregnant woman gets rubella, the fetus can die in the womb (miscarriage) or be born with severe intellectual impairment, deafness, or blindness (called congenital rubella syndrome). An epidemic in 1964 (prior to the rubella vaccine) affected 20,000 babies. The good news: the CDC took rubella off the U.S. disease "threat list" in 2005 because only nine cases were reported in the previous year. However, we need to continue vaccinating since this disease is not eliminated worldwide.

Measles, Mumps, Rubella: The vaccine

The vaccines for measles, mumps and rubella are given together as the MMR vaccine. This combination vaccine has been used since 1975. Prior to that, the vaccinations for each disease were given separately.

So, here's a controversial question making the rounds of playgroups: does MMR cause autism?

One small study of only eight patients in 1998 led a British research group to conclude that the combination MMR vaccine might cause autism. But in March 2004, after questions were raised about the study, ten of the 13 researchers of the study withdrew their claim of having found a possible connection between MMR and autism.[8] *The Lancet* (the medical journal that originally published the paper) ultimately retracted the entire paper in 2010.

VACCINES

? ?

Numerous major studies since 1998 also soundly refute this alleged link. The most prominent: the Institute of Medicine's 2004 report clearly dispelled any link between MMR and autism.[9]

Perhaps the most compelling argument that the MMR vaccine does NOT cause autism is Japan—in 1993, that country stopped using the combination MMR vaccine. Instead, Japanese children were given three separate shots for these diseases. Despite this change, autism rates in Japan continued to rise.[10]

The hysteria surrounding the MMR vaccine and the false 1998 report did have one serious consequence in England: a sharp rise in measles, mumps and rubella after parents stopped giving their kids the vaccine. In 2004, only 80% of children in the U.K. were vaccinated against MMR. And look at the rise in cases of mumps:

1995: 1936 cases of mumps
2003: 4265 cases
2004: 15,503 cases

And remember, autism rates are rising in the U.K. as well. So, now they've got both autism AND vaccine-preventable diseases. It's a lose-lose battle—and the casualties are kids.

Here's the bottom line: as a doctor who sees a large volume of kids, I have never seen a perfectly normally developing kid walk into my office, get his MMR vaccine . . . and come back next week with autism. It doesn't happen.

Q. Should my child get MMR as three separate shots?

Given the past concern over MMR, some parents wonder if their child should get the MMR vaccinations separately. Well, this option is no longer on the table. The MMR vaccine manufacturer no longer makes individual vaccines. But even if this was an option, it's not something we would recommend. In short there is no additional risk when the vaccines are given in combination. Because the MMR is a live-attenuated vaccine, your child may develop a rash that looks like measles (red pimples) and/or a fever one to four weeks after being vaccinated.

◆ The first dose of MMR vaccine is given at 12 to 15 months.
◆ The booster dose of MMR vaccine is given at four to six years.

Reality Check

One of the criteria used to make a diagnosis of autism is a language delay—and kids under one year of age do not speak much. An autistic child is more easily identified when he lacks communication skills as a toddler. This is about the same time that the MMR vaccination is given. That's why MMR looks like a villain . . . even though kids are probably showing signs of autism long before they get this shot. Again, there is no credible scientific proof that the MMR vaccine causes autism. It is a coincidence of timing.

VACCINES

Hepatitis A: The disease

This is a virus that attacks the liver, causing jaundice, diarrhea, vomiting, and dehydration. It is spread through infected poop, contaminated water and food. Hepatitis A spreads rapidly in childcare centers due to all the kids in diapers. Fortunately, children infected with Hepatitis A have a relatively minor illness. Some children don't even have symptoms. Adults, however, get very sick. There are over 150,000 reported cases per year in the U.S., but many more go unreported. And about one in five people are hospitalized with the infection.

You may think of Hepatitis A as an exotic disease that only happens if you travel to Belize or eat oysters. The truth is, it is as near as your next taco salad. The last major outbreak of Hepatitis A was linked to contaminated green onions at a Mexican restaurant in Pittsburgh. (As a Texan, one might argue that's what you get for eating Mexican food in Pittsburgh.) There were over 400 cases of Hepatitis A and five deaths.

Hepatitis A: The vaccine

As of October 2005, the Hepatitis A vaccine is recommended for all children between ages one and two years.[11] Vaccinating toddlers protects them, and prevents the spread of disease to others. An example of this vaccine's effectiveness: since Israel began its universal toddler vaccination against Hepatitis A in 2000, they have seen a 98.5% reduction in the disease rate.[12]

- ◆ First dose of Hepatitis A vaccine is given at 12 months.
- ◆ Booster dose of Hepatitis A vaccine is given six to 18 months after the first dose.
- ◆ Any child can get the Hepatitis A vaccine series after one year of age.

Hepatitis B: The disease

This is another *virus* that attacks the liver. There are various types of hepatitis, so don't get lost here. Hepatitis B is spread through blood and body fluid contact (saliva, vaginal discharge, and semen). It is extremely contagious (and usually more serious than Hepatitis A). It is spread primarily by sexual contact but don't think of this disease as one that only happens to IV drug users or people with multiple sex partners. *Thirty percent of people who get Hepatitis B have neither of these risk factors.* About 30,000 children were infected annually before the introduction of the Hepatitis B vaccination.

The infection causes skin to turn yellow because the liver is unable to metabolize bilirubin as it should. It causes stomach upset and lack of appetite. Some people with Hepatitis B recover quickly, while others die. Still others have a chronic infection that goes on for twenty years until they die. And some people become carriers of the disease once they survive the infection.

Reality Check

There are *1 million* Hepatitis B carriers walking around the U.S. If this isn't enough to convince you to protect your child, Hepatitis B is also a known cause of liver cancer. And there is no *cure* for the infection—that's why the vaccine is so important.

Some anti-vaccine parents skip the Hepatitis B vaccine because they wrongly assume this disease is just sexually transmitted . . . and they don't think they need to worry about that now with their toddler. The truth is, Hepatitis B is more than a sexually transmitted disease. There is no way to predict when your child might be exposed. Like all other vaccinations, the point is to protect your child before an exposure occurs.

Hepatitis B: The vaccine

The vaccination series for Hepatitis B (three doses) may be completed before your child has his first birthday. Hepatitis B series may be given to any child who has not been vaccinated.

DR B'S OPINION

"If you still harbor doubts about vaccination, ask your pediatrician if she has vaccinated her own children. We would never do anything for your kids that we wouldn't do for our own."

Chickenpox (Varicella): The disease

Chickenpox is a *virus* familiar to most of us. Prior to the development of the chickenpox vaccine, 3.7 million people got chickenpox every year in the U.S. So most of you reading this book probably remember having this illness. What you may not remember is that chickenpox also led to 10,000 hospitalizations and 100 deaths annually.

The varicella virus spreads by respiratory droplets and by the fluid found in the skin lesions. It is incredibly contagious. The virus attacks the whole body via the bloodstream. Infected people feel tired and run a fever, then break out in classic clear fluid-filled blisters that arrive in clusters. The average number of skin lesions is 350. Does it make you feel itchy just thinking about it? People are contagious for seven days on average.

The virus itself can cause pneumonia and encephalitis. Even more problematic is that Strep bacteria have a field day with the open wounds when the blisters pop. These secondary infections can be deadly.

Varicella (Chickenpox): The vaccine

Varicella vaccine is a live-attenuated vaccine—it contains a weakened form of the germ that causes chickenpox. As a result, some children will get a rash that looks like chickenpox one to four weeks after being vaccinated. There is also a small chance of getting **SHINGLES** later in life. Shingles is an infection due to reactivation of the chickenpox virus.

The Centers for Disease Control currently recommends a two-dose series for the vaccine since 2006. This vaccine has been a part of the routine immunization series since 1995.

About one in five kids who get only ONE dose of vaccine may get a *mild* case of chickenpox when exposed to someone with the infection. Although those may not look like good odds to you, it's actually a win-win situation. Either a child is completely protected from the illness or protected enough to prevent a serious infection. But adding a booster dose should reduce the number of infections in kids who have been vaccinated.

Some parents are concerned that the vaccine may not provide lifetime protection. That's why docs now recommend the two-dose chickenpox vaccine series. The first dose is given at 12-15 months of age, and a booster dose is given at age 4-6 years old.

Other people worry that their child will get shingles due to the vaccine. As of this writing, the best evidence suggests you are more likely to get shingles if you have had chickenpox than if you have been vaccinated.[13]

◆ A single dose of varicella vaccine is given at 12–15 months of age; a booster dose is given at age 4-6 years old.

◆ Varicella vaccine may be given to anyone over one year of age who has not had chickenpox.

GETTING CHICKENPOX THE "NATURAL WAY"

Boulder, Colorado (the hometown of one of the co-authors of this book) has often been described as 20 square miles surrounded by reality. A good case in point: vaccinations. Basically, many Boulder parents have come up with all sorts of mental gymnastics to justify their decision not to vaccinate their kids.

Exhibit number one: we had a neighbor once who told us she intentionally didn't vaccinate her kids against chickenpox in hopes they'd get the disease the "natural way."

We realize this theory is somewhat in vogue among anti-vaccine advocates—somehow, getting the disease "naturally" is a better (read: organic) alternative to a vaccine, which is viewed as sinister.

In case you forgot what joy it was to have the chickenpox "naturally," let's review some of the fun here. First, you get an itchy rash and fever, not just for one day or two BUT an entire week or longer. Then, you spread the disease "naturally" to other siblings who get to enjoy the same experience.

If you are unlucky, you may suffer some serious complications from chickenpox . . . like pneumonia and encephalitis. There's no more natural fun than having your brain swell!

Yet another possible fun secondary infection is . . . flesh-eating bacteria! This "natural" bacteria loves the opened pustules of chickenpox. Sure, not every Strep bacterial infection that follows chickenpox is as deadly as the flesh-eating type, but that's worth the risk of getting chickenpox naturally, right?

Finally, let's consider the cost of chickenpox the natural way. Not only will you be shelling out for doctor visits and co-pays, you'll probably have to take several days off from work. Lost wages, used-up sick days, vacation time . . . all that is gone, with this "alternative" choice. Add in multiple kids and you can see those numbers grow exponentially.

So, think about the TOTAL cost of chickenpox infection versus the very small inconvenience of a chickenpox vaccine.

Strep Pneumoniae: The disease

This is a *bacteria* that is in the Strep family. Strep pneumoniae is NOT the bacteria that causes Strep throat. It's a distant cousin. This bacteria causes meningitis, pneumonia, blood infections (sepsis), sinus infections, and ear infections.

Respiratory droplets spread the bacteria. Once the bugs get in, they travel through the blood to the respiratory system (ears, sinuses, lungs) or the brain. Infected people run a high fever when the bacteria are in the bloodstream. Fortunately, many infections are treated before meningitis occurs. Prior to the Prevnar vaccine, there were over 500,000 cases of serious Strep pneumoniae infections a year in the U.S. and 10,000 to 40,000 deaths.[14] In babies, Strep pneumoniae is the #1 cause of bacterial meningitis. The highest risk groups for serious infection are young children and the elderly.

There are antibiotics to treat Strep pneumoniae, however, drug-resistant strains are emerging quickly. It's survival of the fittest for germs—and these germs are some of the smartest around. Twenty percent of Strep pneumoniae are drug-resistant. *Ten percent are resistant to three or more types of antibiotics.*

Daycare children are at higher risk for Strep pneumoniae infection, particularly the drug-resistant strains.

Prevnar or PCV 13 (Strep pneumoniae): The vaccine

This vaccine is recommended as part of the routine immunization schedule by the American Academy of Pediatrics as of 2000. The Prevnar vaccine protects against the top thirteen strains of Strep pneumoniae (there are 90 total) that cause serious infection.

Millions of children have been vaccinated and there has been an 87% decrease in serious Strep infections (meningitis, blood infection, pneumonia) since 2000.

◆ The fourth and final dose of the Prevnar booster is given at 12 to 15 months of age.*

◆ The Prevnar vaccine series can be given to any child under five years of age, but the number of doses in the series depends upon the age the series begins. Kids from age two to five years old who did not get the series in infancy should be vaccinated if they attend childcare or have chronic medical problems.

*Prior to 2010, the Prevnar vaccine protected against seven strains of Strep pneumoniae. The newer form of the vaccine adds protection for six more drug-resistant strains. If your child completed the "PCV 7" vaccine series and is under five years of age, he should get one additional booster shot of the PCV 13. If your child is under six years of age and has a chronic health condition, he also should get a PCV 13 booster shot.

Influenza (Flu): The disease

This is a virus that arrives every winter. It is an infection that attacks the respiratory tract. Worse than the common cold, flu causes higher fevers, body aches, headaches, and a crummy feeling in general. The runny nose and cough arrive later and last longer than the typical cold. Secondary bacterial infections (ear infections, sinus infections, pneumonia) occur more often with the flu than with other respiratory viruses.

In 2009-2010, 281 American children died from the new H1N1 flu strain. The take-home message: the flu can be deadly.[15]

Influenza (Flu): The vaccine

Although it's not required for school entry (except in New Jersey), it is a good idea for your child to get the flu vaccine. Here are the latest recommendations from the Centers for Disease Control:

The flu vaccine is *recommended* for people who are:

◆ Immune-compromised (weak immune systems).
◆ Suffering from chronic illness (asthma, heart disease, diabetes) in anyone six months old or older.
◆ Pregnant women during flu season (November-March).
◆ Children ages six months old to 18 years of age.

The flu vaccine is *encouraged* for:

◆ Household contacts and caretakers of any child aged birth to five years.
◆ Any person who wants to be vaccinated.

The flu vaccine is an inactivated vaccine—no, it will NOT give you the flu. It takes two weeks for the vaccine to provide immunity and then lasts for a year. Why does it only last one year? That's because the flu virus strain changes from season to season, requiring a new vaccine. And some years the vaccine is more effective than others, depending on which strain decides to show up.

One cautionary note: children with egg allergies should first consult their doctor about the flu vaccine, since it is made using chicken eggs. Allergists can test egg-allergic people to see if they can get a flu vaccine without having a significant allergic reaction.

Currently, there is only one flu vaccine shot that is "preservative free" and allowed for use in children as young as six months old. It's called Fluzone (Aventis Pasteur). The other flu vaccine shots contain a trace amount of thimerosal (0.025 milligrams per dose). The acceptable limit of exposure to thimerosal is over 12 times this dose (0.2-0.4mg). See the section "The Mercury Controversy" later in this chapter for more information on thimerosal.

There is another form of flu vaccine, given as a nose spray. It is a live-attenuated vaccine that is available for healthy children over two years of age. The nose spray vaccine is thimerosal preservative free. More tips:

◆ Flu vaccine is given annually starting in October.
◆ Children aged six months to nine years of age who have never received flu vaccine before should get a series of two doses given one month apart for better protection.

As of 2010, the seasonal flu vaccine will include the H1N1 flu strain. So there's no need to get an extra vaccine for that.

VACCINES

? ?

Q. My child is two. Which flu vaccine is better—the shot or the nose spray?

The flu nose spray, which is a live attenuated vaccine, provides comparable protection against the flu to the inactivated flu shot. There are a few more people who report body aches and cough after getting the nose spray than the shot. However, all things being equal, we'd suggest going for the nose spray if your child is at least two years old and your doctor has it available. It's usually easier to sell to your child than taking a shot!

FYI: The nose spray is NOT currently approved for use in children under age two or those who have asthma.

Q. Is there a vaccine for the stomach virus?

Yes. A vaccine for rotavirus (a horrible stomach virus) was approved by the FDA in February 2006.

Rotavirus comes to visit every winter. Doctors always know rotavirus has arrived in a community. The littlest patients come into the office with so much watery diarrhea that parents can't keep up with diaper changes. The vomiting part is pretty miserable, too. Because there is so much water lost in the poop, infants are at a high risk of becoming dehydrated. This infection causes 50,000 hospitalizations of young children in the United States every winter. There are also about 30 deaths per year in the U.S. from Rotavirus. Worldwide, rotavirus kills 440,000 kids every year. You can see why we've wanted a vaccine for this disease.

The vaccine is given to infants at two, four, and six months of age. It may be approved for older children in the future. Again, check our blog (Toddler411.com) for updates.

Q. Is there another bacterial meningitis vaccine for kids?

Yes. The Menactra vaccine, which protects against Neisseria meningitis, is routinely given to kids starting at 11 to 12 years of age or kids who are about to enter college. These are the children at greatest risk of getting this form of bacterial meningitis. The Advisory Committee on Immunization Practices recently recommended, however, that certain at-risk children from age two to ten should also be vaccinated to protect them. Children who have injury to or lack of spleen function, HIV, or certain immune deficiencies should get Menactra.

The Mercury Controversy

Q. I've heard there is mercury preservative in vaccines. Is this true?

Not anymore. It was removed from all required childhood vaccines by 2001. This deserves repeating: *YOUR child will not be getting vaccines that contain mercury (thimerosal) as a preservative.*

The only exception to the above statement is the flu vaccine, which is not a REQUIRED immunization (except in New Jersey). Yes, one version of the flu vaccine shot has thimerosal . . . but there is a thimerosal-free shot

(Fluzone) available as well as the thimerosal-free nasal spray, Flumist.

Despite the fact that vaccines are mercury preservative-free now, speculation persists about vaccines *previously* containing mercury and whether this caused autism. This speculation continues even after the Institute of Medicine published a conclusive report in 2004 failing to link vaccines and autism. (The IOM spent four years studying both the mercury issue and the MMR combo vaccine, publishing a series of eight reports on the subject.).

Because of ongoing concerns, we present to you . . . more than you ever wanted to know about thimerosal.

Q. I heard that I should still ask my doctor for thimerosal-free vaccines. Do I need to do this?

Since 2001, the entire childhood vaccine series went thimerosal (mercury) preservative-free. If your doctor has a 2001 vintage vaccine vial sitting on the shelf, he needs to re-stock. To give you some perspective, my practice buys our vaccine supply on a monthly basis.

Because the flu vaccine is recommended and not "routine," it comes in two versions for kids under two years of age: one with thimerosal preservative and one without. Flumist, the thimerosal-free nasal spray, is also an option for kids aged two and up. You can ask for the T-free version, but it may not be available in times of vaccine shortages.

There are four vaccines that use thimerosal in the production process and then extract it before the final product is bottled. As such, they must list that trace amounts of thimerosal (less than 0.003 mg) may exist. There is probably little or no thimerosal in the finished product, but the manufacturer must declare it. We have no concerns about these vaccines, but if you are completely freaked out about the thimerosal thing, there are other alternatives to these specific vaccines: the vaccine names are Tripedia (one brand of DTaP), Pediarix (one brand combo of DTaP/HepB/IPV), Trihibit (DTaP/HIB), and Engerix-B (one brand of Hep B). The FDA has a chart online that tracks thimerosal in vaccines (vaccinesafety.edu/thi-table.htm).

Reality Check

If the only option for flu vaccine is the mercury-containing one, don't sweat it. One 5.6oz can of tuna has about 0.115mg of mercury. A thimerosal-containing flu vaccine has about 0.025mg of mercury. The bottom line: there is five times more mercury in your tunafish sandwich.[16]

Q. Does thimerosal cause autism?

No. Here is the scientific evidence:

◆ The Institute of Medicine spent four years studying this issue. Their conclusion, issued in 2004: mercury preservatives in vaccines did NOT cause autism . . . and the Institute said it was time to move on to look at other possible causes. Several other leading medical organizations (both nationally and internationally) agree with this conclusion.

◆ Mercury preservative (thimerosal) was removed from vaccines in the U.S.

in 2001, but the rates of children being diagnosed with autism are still sky-rocketing. A survey of autism rates in California in 2008 confirms that mercury is out and autism rates are still going up.[17] If thimerosal was the cause of autism, and it was taken out NINE years ago, autism rates should be going down by now. That's because autism spectrum disorders are usually diagnosed by three years of age.

THIMEROSAL 411

Vaccines have preservatives and stabilizers to remain potent and uncontaminated over time. A popular preservative *used* to be a chemical called thimerosal, which contained trace amounts of *ethylmercury*. Thimerosal use began in the 1940's.

A quick chemistry lesson: Certain compounds have completely different properties even though they may be related. For instance, take the alcohol family. *Methanol* is anti-freeze; *ethanol* is a Bud Light. Keep this in mind when we discuss mercury.

We are all exposed to small amounts of mercury. The type of mercury that has raised health concerns is called *methylmercury*. High concentrations of methylmercury can be found in tuna, swordfish and shark from contaminated waters. The information known about mercury poisoning comes from unfortunate communities that have experienced it. There is a large amount of data from the Faroe Islands, near Iceland. The people there would eat whale blubber contaminated with toxic levels of methylmercury and polychlorinated biphenyls (PCBs). Children, especially those exposed as fetuses during their mother's pregnancy, seemed to have lower scores on memory, attention, and language tests than their unexposed peers. (They were *not* diagnosed with autism or Attention Deficit Disorder, however.)[18]

Chronic exposure to liquid mercury causes Mad Hatter's Disease, named for hat makers who used liquid mercury in the hat-making process and went crazy. The disease consists of psychiatric problems, insomnia, poor memory, sweating, tremors, and red palms. Chronic mercury poisoning also impairs kidney function—again, not autism or ADD. In contrast to methylmercury, ethylmercury is a preservative that pops up in everything from cosmetics to eyedrops, contact lens solutions to topical medications.

Because of the increased number of vaccinations that children get, the potential *cumulative* exposure to mercury became a concern in 1999.

There are three federal groups that set standards for acceptable daily mercury exposure (Environmental Protection Agency, Food and Drug Administration, Agency for Toxic Substances and Disease Registry). In 1999, the federal government calculated the cumulative exposure to mercury in kids through vaccines. They found the dose was higher than the acceptable level set by the EPA (the other groups' standards were not as strict). As a result, the Food and Drug Administration mandated the removal of thimerosal from the routine childhood immunization series. It took two years for the transition to occur (that transition is now complete).

Vaccines still contain other preservatives (more on this in the additives section on page 292).

BOTTOM LINE: Thimerosal will remain in the news, the legislature, and in the courts. But it does not remain in any of the *required* vaccines that YOUR child will get.

◆ Mercury preservatives were removed from vaccines in Denmark in 1992. Canada and the European Union have followed suit. Their autism diagnosis rates are still going up too.

◆ Mad Hatter's Disease (mercury poisoning) and autism are very different disorders, as in the box on the previous page (Thimerosal 411).

◆ A study of 100,000 kids in England compared those receiving mercury-containing vaccines to those who did not. The ones who had the mercury-free shots had HIGHER rates of autism.[19]

◆ A study in 2007 showed that children between seven and ten years of age who got those mercury containing vaccines (before 2001) had no significant differences in tests of attention and processing information.[20] Although the study did not look specifically at autism, it showed that mercury preservatives did not make much of an impact on brain functions in general. A follow up study that specifically looks at autism will be published after this book goes to print. We'll keep you posted.

Reality Check: Paging Dr. Jenny McCarthy

Actress Jenny McCarthy has become the self-proclaimed leader of the anti-vaccine movement, declaring that kids get "too many shots, too soon" . . . and that vaccines need to be "greener."

McCarthy's 15 minutes of vaccine fame is a result of her book, *Louder Than Words*, which recounts her struggle with her son's autism. Her frequent claim: her son was normal until he got his MMR shot . . . which caused his autism.

If you read McCarthy's book (which I have), I can't help but point out McCarthy's numerous medical inaccuracies. (McCarthy admits her knowledge on the issue is thanks to a degree from the University of Google.)

On page 56 of her book, McCarthy says: "Looking back, I can see that little signs presented themselves here and there, but as a loving mother who wanted to see only the good, I looked past most of the red flags along the way. My friends' babies had all cracked a smile way before Evan did…he was almost five months old…though Evan continued to hit all of his milestones, I can see things now that stuck out slightly. They were never that obvious to me until now."

So Jenny's child was missing milestones (like smiling) long before he got his MMR shot, which is given around 12 to 15 months of age. Yet the shot caused his autism. Right.

McCarthy also assails the mercury preservative thimerosal, which she says caused her son's autism. Yet here's an inconvenient truth: McCarthy's son was born in 2002. Thimerosal preservative was removed from childhood vaccines *the year before*, in 2001. Oops.

VACCINES & AUTISM

"We have pumped a lot of money into these studies (looking into a link between autism and vaccines), and when do you stop pouring money into a theory which has no evidence supporting it?"
Dr Eric Fombonne, autism researcher at McGill University in Canada.

None of this has stopped McCarthy's media machine, which has landed her guest shots on Good Morning America, Oprah and CNN's Larry King. Sadly, when a celebrity talks, people listen—and the resulting panic lingers for months in doctor's offices nationwide.

Let's come out and say it: McCarthy's misguided advocacy is jeopardizing the lives of children. Example: one family I care for has twins—one girl and one boy. At their one-year well checks, the mom chose to give the MMR vaccine to her daughter but refused for her son. Why? Because Jenny McCarthy told Oprah that in her opinion, boys are more likely to develop autism from vaccines. Now my patient is vulnerable to a deadly disease that is only a plane ride away.

The bottom line: I don't get my medical advice from former MTV stars; I urge you don't either![21]

Reality check: Pregnant Moms

Yes, it's true the flu vaccine given to pregnant women may contain trace amounts of thimerosal. Again, there is five times more mercury (and the toxic kind, no less) in your tunafish sandwich. There are thimerosal-free versions available and you can ask for them. But we'd still recommend getting the flu vaccine, even if it does have preservative in it. Pregnant women are at high risk of complications from the flu.

And contrary to what you may hear, the Rhogam injection given to pregnant moms who have a negative blood type is thimerosal free.

In case you are wondering, thimerosal is also present in mascara, eye drops, and numerous other products you probably have in your own home.

Q. Are there other additives in the vaccines?

Yes. And you should know about them

Vaccines contain the active ingredients that provide immunity. However, there are inactive ingredients that improve potency and prevent contamination. Here is a list of additives and why they are there.[22]

1. *Preservatives*—prevent vaccine contamination with germs (bacteria, fungus): 2-phenoxyethanol, phenol.
2. *Adjuvants*—improve potency/immune response: aluminum salts.
3. *Additives*—prevent vaccine deterioration and sticking to the side of the vial: gelatin, albumin, sucrose, lactose, MSG, glycine.
4. *Residuals*—remains of vaccine production process: formaldehyde, antibiotics (neomycin), egg protein, yeast protein.

Now, after reading the above list, you might be freaking out—aluminum salts? MSG? Formaldehyde? We should point out that only TRACE amounts of most of these additives are in vaccines. None have been proven harmful in animals or humans in these amounts.

VACCINES

Reality check: Green Vaccines

If vaccines contain ingredients like aluminum or formaldehyde, wouldn't it be better if vaccine makers got rid of these additives? Shouldn't vaccines be "greener"?

We agree that this sounds reasonable—but it doesn't mean that current vaccines are UNSAFE.

Here's the key point: additives like aluminum in vaccines are in EXTREMELY SMALL amounts (often, just a trace). We are all exposed to *significantly higher* levels of environmental toxins in our everyday activities.

Let's look at aluminum. Babies ingest 50 micrograms of aluminum per liter of breast milk per day . . . and 500 micrograms of aluminum per liter of formula per day. By contrast, the amount of aluminum in a vaccine is much smaller. Example: Prevnar has 125 micrograms, HIB has 225 mcg, Hep B has 250 mcg and so on. Hence, babies *drink* much more aluminum in breast milk or formula then they ever get from vaccines.

Do you wear antiperspirant? That's got aluminum in it too. And aluminum is found in most food, soil and water. So, to avoid aluminum exposure, you'd have to stop wearing antiperspirant—and basically leave the planet.

And aluminum poisoning does not cause symptoms of autism, either.[23] Trace amounts (far less than what your baby eats everyday) of aluminum improve the body's immune response to some vaccines. That's why it is in there.

Why is formaldehyde in vaccines? Well, small amounts sterilize the vaccine fluid so your child doesn't get something like the flesh-eating Strep bacteria when he gets his shots.

If you use paper towels or mascara, or have carpeting in your home, you've been exposed to formaldehyde. Obviously, exposure to large amounts of formaldehyde is not a good thing for anyone's health. But again the amount in vaccines is extremely small.[24]

The bottom line: vaccine additives are there for a reason—to make them safer and more effective.

Helpful Hint: Where to get more information

Where can you find *accurate* information on vaccines? Try these sites:

- *CDC's National Immunization Program* cdc.gov/nip (800) 232-2522
- *American Academy of Pediatrics* aap.org (800) 433-9016
- *Immunization Action Coalition* immunize.org
- *Vaccine Education Center, Children's Hospital (Phila.)* vaccine.chop.edu

There are also two excellent reference books written for parents:
Vaccinating Your Child: Questions and Answers for the Concerned Parent. Humiston, S., Atlanta: Peachtree, 2003.
Vaccines: What You Should Know. Offit, P., New York: MacMillan, 2003.

BOTTOM LINE

Vaccines have become the scapegoat for disorders that we simply don't have the answers to yet.

The take home message: many parents question vaccine safety, but very few choose to delay or skip vaccines entirely. Ask questions, but please get your child vaccinated.

Vaccines are effective in preventing disease . . . but that doesn't mean your toddler will never get sick, of course! Next up: common infections that can strike your child, from the benign (pink eye) to the serious (Strep, RSV and more).

COMMON INFECTIONS

Chapter 16

"For my birthday I got a humidifier and a de-humidifier... I put them in the same room and let them fight it out."
~ Steven Wright

Infections: coming to a toddler near you.

While all humans are at risk of infection, kids get the lion's share because they are born with a clean slate when it comes to their immune system. Toddlers build an immunologic memory "bank" as each new illness is "deposited." Okay, enough of the money metaphors.

We only cover diseases in this chapter that are caused by germs. Ailments that are not caused by infections are in the next chapter (Chapter 17, Common Diseases).

Before we go into the specific bugs that will bug your child (and occasionally, you), we'll give you a harmless lesson in microbiology (trust us, it won't hurt). This will magically transport you back to the days you spent in 7th grade science (pimples not included). Fun, we know!

If you read our first book *Baby 411*, some parts of this chapter will be a refresher course. But note: we cover infections here that are more common in the toddler and preschooler set (*Baby 411* focused on babies). Yes, some diseases overlap . . . but there are some new ones just for toddlers! To simplify things, we've divided infections by the part of the body they, well, infect.

So here we go:

Microbiology 411

Infections are caused by a variety of fun organisms. Let's divide these into four groups: viruses, bacteria, parasites, and fungi.

1 VIRUSES. By far, viruses are the most likely culprits in the infectious disease lottery. Most viruses blow through like a hurricane—as quickly as they arrive, they are gone. Viruses grow (replicate) for a few days, and then leave to infect someone else. The symptoms that we feel are the result of our immune response to the invasion.

Because viruses move so quickly through our bodies, there are very few medications targeted to fight viruses (called anti-virals). Anti-viral medications work by interfering with the replication of the virus, which generally happens in the first two to three days of illness.

Examples of viral infections include: *the common cold* and *influenza.* Some viruses lie dormant after the initial infection, then re-activate to torture us again. That's right, once these special viruses infect us, they live within us for the rest of our lives. Examples include: *Herpes* and *Varicella-zoster virus (chickenpox/shingles).*

2 BACTERIA. Bacterial infections are less common. Believe it or not, most bacteria live in harmony with us and are called *normal flora.* They live on our skin, in our mouths, nostrils, vagina, and intestines. Bacteria that cause infection move into our bodies when conditions are right, such as when you're already run down after fighting a virus. They find a nice spot to grow and fester. Yet because bacteria are such slow-movers, antibiotics can effectively kill these bugs. Examples of bacterial infections include: *Strep throat, impetigo, bladder infections.*

3 PARASITES. Parasites are organisms that use our bodies as an unsuspecting host. When people worry they have worms, this is what they are referring to. Examples of parasites include: *Giardia, amebiasis,* and *pinworms.* We should also mention mites in this group; they are tiny bugs that fit in somewhere between parasites and ticks. Mites who cause problems for us are *scabies* and *chiggers*.

4 FUNGI. Fungi are plant relatives (yeast, mold) that do not need light to survive. They prefer places where there is little competition (in other words, low bacteria levels). And some fungi thrive on humans whose immune systems are compromised. Examples of fungal infections include: *ringworm* (it's not really a worm) and *thrush.*

Putting It Together

Q. So how do doctors know what is causing an infection and how to treat it?

When a child has a fever, your doctor looks for signs of an infection. There are other causes for fever, but infection tops the list. The symptoms *in addition to* the fever are the clues to the diagnosis. Those symptoms include vomiting, diarrhea, cough, runny nose, decreased appetite, rash, crying with urination, etc.

It's this MIX of both symptoms and the results of a physical exam that help solve the puzzle. Lab work and x-rays may be useful in certain situations.

Viral infections usually do not require medication and are fought off effectively by the body's immune system. Bacteria, fungi, parasites, and mites respond to medication that eliminates the infection. The medication choice is often based upon the usual suspects for an illness. Depending on the location of the infection, cultures of the site (for example, throat, urine, blood, skin lesion) may identify the bug and the right medication to treat it.

Bacterial infections frequently arise secondary to a pre-existing viral illness. So red flags for a bacterial process include a child who is ill and suddenly gets worse instead of better (for example, new fever, new green snot, new irritability, new labored breathing).

And by the way, some infections like yeast or pinworms do not cause a fever. Those bugs are detected by the symptoms that they cause (characteristic rash, itchy hiney, etc).

Q. Can't we just do a test to make the diagnosis?

Sometimes yes, sometimes no.

We can easily test for bacterial infections in the urine (bladder infections), for example, by obtaining a urine specimen. Urine is normally sterile (bug free). So, finding bacteria and white blood cells (cells that fight infection) in the urine is a pretty good clue that there is an infection. We then put urine in a culture medium that bacteria really like. If the culture plate is covered with thousands of bacterial colonies a couple of days later, we confirm the diagnosis.

Other infections can be identified by rapid lab tests (assays) that detect an infection's signature or detect a person's specific antibody response to a current infection. Examples include rapid flu, Strep throat, and mononucleosis (mono) tests. For details on all those tests, see Appendix C, Lab Work & Tests.

But not every infection can be caught on a culture or picked up by a rapid assay. So, while we all wish there was a test to confirm every infection, doctors still rely on our clinical expertise for some bugs.

Q. Does a fever mean that my child is contagious?

Most likely, yes. Assume that your child is contagious if he has a fever.

We will go into more detail about fever (and myths surrounding it) in our special fever section in Chapter 19, First Aid. And we will give you a "green light" list for when your child's "quarantine" can be lifted for individual illnesses later in this chapter.

In a nutshell, the human body temperature is highest at night and lowest in the morning. If your child has a fever when he goes to bed at night, he should not be going to childcare or school in the morning even if he looks fever-free.

Q. Do I have to go running to the doctor every time my child has a fever?

Not necessarily. If you can tell *why* your child has a fever and you can manage the symptoms, you can give her some TLC and wait it out a few days. Your child is older now and it is easier to tell what is going on (plus you have probably had some practice at being Dr. Mom).

Here are the red flags for when you should see your doctor when your child has a fever:

Red Flags

◆ You cannot figure out why your child is running a fever.
◆ Fever lasts for more than three days in a row.
◆ New fever after being fever free for over 24 hours.
◆ Irritable or lethargic.
◆ Not urinating at least every eight hours.
◆ Blood/mucus in the poop.
◆ Blood in the urine.
◆ Sore throat *without* cough and runny nose.
◆ Pain with urination.
◆ Severe pain anywhere.
◆ Fever and a rash (see Rash section later in this chapter).
◆ Fever of 104 degrees or greater.

Dr. B's 3 Rules on Infections

Rule #1: If you are going to play the odds, it's usually a virus causing the infection.

Rule #2: If your child doesn't look too sick, he is probably isn't.

Rule #3: Most of the time, the child does not need a doctor's help to get better!

BOTTOM LINE

It is likely that your child will be diagnosed with a viral infection and will be sent home without antibiotics. However, it's better to be safe than sorry! Peace of mind is worth the co-payment.

Infection Control

Q. How do we prevent the spread of germs?

◆ Wash your hands frequently.
◆ Cover your coughs.
◆ Wash hands after using the bathroom.
◆ Avoid touching your eyes, nose, or mouth.
◆ Do not share drinks or food.
◆ Kiss at your own risk.
◆ Cook foods properly.
◆ Clean kitchen counters/cutting boards.

Q. Our family seems to be passing the same cold back and forth to each other. How do we stop it?

Although there are a few exceptions (such as head lice), once you have a particular strain of a germ, you are immune to it. So, you are not playing germ volleyball with just one cold virus. Your family has been attacked by two illnesses back to back.

However, this brings up an interesting topic—household infection control. People often ask me if I get sick from all the germs I am exposed to at work as a pediatrician. The answer is no. I wash my hands obsessively and do not touch my face.

THE SECRET LIVES OF GERMS: WHERE ARE THEY?

Viruses can be airborne or live on surfaces for a period of hours . . . or even days. Viruses and bacteria live on surfaces called fomites. Fomites include door handles, grocery carts, high chairs at restaurants, shared toys, etc. Here is a list of other germy locales:

◆ Sandboxes (pinworms).
◆ Swimming pools (molluscum contagiosum, intestinal germs).
◆ Area lakes, water parks (parasites, intestinal germs).
◆ Undercooked ground meat and eggs, raw seafood, unpasteurized juices (intestinal germs).
◆ Airplanes (respiratory viruses).

I only get sick when my daughter or son comes down with something. That's because I do the same things that every other parent does—I kiss my kids, I share drinks with them, and I do not wash my hands after I hold their hands!

If you want to keep the entire house from getting sick, be more aware of how germs are spread. Ask yourself if it's really worth it to eat your child's half-eaten, leftover chicken nugget.

Q. My child never got sick when he was a baby. Now that he is a toddler, he gets sick all the time. Is there something wrong with his immune system?

Probably not. Your toddler is just being exposed to the world of germs more than before. If your child has been in a group childcare setting since infancy, you are already an infectious disease specialist. But if your toddler has previously stayed at home and now has more out-of-home activities, he will get whatever comes down the pike. At some point in every human's life this will happen. If you keep your toddler at home for five years, he will just get his share of illness in kindergarten.

Here are some startling stats. Are you sitting down? *The average number of viral infections that a young child gets per year is EIGHT.* Each of those illnesses lasts seven to ten days, on average. And most of those illnesses occur between October and April. *That gives toddlers a grand total of 80 days of illness in a six-month period.* Yep, that's an illness about every other week.

Children with immune deficiencies have more than just frequent colds. They are prone to recurrent (and often, serious) bacterial infections like sinusitis, pneumonia, or skin abscesses. They may also have problems with anemia, growth, yeast infections, or eczema. So, just having lots of colds doesn't make your child immune deficient. It's those additional problems that indicate a possible red flag.

Q. When can my child return to daycare or playgroup?

All your questions are answered with the chart on the next page!

THE VIRUS MERRY GO-ROUND: WHEN & WHAT

Just like accountants, I look forward to reaching April 15th every year. Although viruses invade year round, the bulk of viral infections arrive between October and April.

Here are the seasonal patterns of some of the most kid-o-genic viruses:

◆ *Summer*: Coxsackievirus (hand/foot/mouth), Enteroviruses (stomach, skin, respiratory, eye).
◆ *Fall*: Parainfluenza (croup), Rhinovirus (common cold).
◆ *Winter*: Influenza (the flu), Rotavirus (stomach flu), RSV (bronchiolitis).
◆ *Spring*: Parainfluenza again, Varicella (chickenpox).

Although viruses are always around, they do seem to have a particular affinity for certain seasons. It seems to be a combination of atmospheric conditions and human behaviors that lead to the perfect conditions for a viral attack. Yes, viruses may attack in their off season, but not at epidemic levels. Doctors usually know what is going around in their communities because just about every patient they see has the same illness for a few weeks.

When can Johnny go back to childcare/playgroup?[1]

DISEASE	TREATMENT	RETURN TO CHILDCARE?
Common cold	None	When fever is gone.
Influenza	+/- Anti-viral Rx	When fever is gone.
Croup	+/- Steroid Rx	When fever is gone.
Hand-foot-mouth	None	When fever is gone.
Herpes stomatitis	None	When lesions are healed.
Conjunctivitis/Pink eye	None if viral infection	When eyes are clear.
Bacterial conjunctivitis	Antibiotic eye drops Rx	After 24 hrs. of treatment.
Stomach virus	None	When poop is formed.
Viral rashes	None	Depends on the infection.
Chickenpox	+/- Antiviral Rx	When all lesions crusted (1 wk).
Fifth disease	None	Not contagious once rash appears.
Impetigo	Antibiotic Rx	After 24 hours of treatment.
Food poisoning	Depends on the bug	When poop is formed.
Giardia	Anti-parasitic Rx	When poop is formed.
Ringworm	Anti-fungal Rx	After 24 hours of treatment.
Scabies	Body wash Rx	After 1 treatment.
Head lice	OTC shampoo	After 1 treatment.
Pinworms	Anti-parasitic Rx	After 1 treatment.

KEY—Rx: prescription medicine; OTC: over-the-counter medicine

Antibiotic Resistance

Q. **My doctor prescribed Amoxicillin. It never works. Can't we use a stronger antibiotic?**

This is a common question. There is a reason why doctors cling to that pink bubble gum antibiotic. Besides the fact that it is well tolerated and our patients like the taste, Amoxicillin is the infantryman of antibiotics. Why pull out the cannons when the foot soldier can do the job?

Ever since antibiotics were created in the 1940's, bacteria have been adapting to survive. It truly is survival of the fittest, germ-style. If bacteria see our stronger ammunition, we promote an evolution of stronger germs that are harder to kill. In short, using the big guns depletes our ammo. That is the concept of antibiotic resistance. *A person does not become antibiotic resistant, the bacteria does.*

The way to stop the downward spiral of antibiotic resistance is for docs to:

◆ Be cautious about prescribing antibiotics in the first place. Antibiotics do not treat a virus (and most of our illnesses are due to viruses).

◆ Use first-line antibiotics to start (example: Amoxicillin).

◆ Adopt a wait and see approach if a bacterial infection is questionable. Example: all green snot does not require an antibiotic.

◆ Follow ear infection treatment guidelines for kids over age two. More on this in the ear infection section later in this chapter.

That said, some children are more likely to get drug resistant bacterial infections than others. Drug resistant bugs love childcare settings, so a child who spends several hours a week there is more prone to pick up one of these bugs and bring them home. Tip offs for a drug-resistant bug include:

◆ Infection does not clear well with Amoxicillin.

◆ Infection recurs within four to six weeks of being on Amoxicillin.

Yes, doctors know that each "treatment failure" with Amoxicillin costs you more co-payments for office visits and at the pharmacy—not to mention the bribery involved to get your child to take another ten days of antibiotics. We know this treatment plan is unpopular for these very reasons. But the strategy works to outwit some very smart bacteria.

DR B'S OPINION

"As a pediatrician, I play the odds and use the least-potent antibiotic that will solve the problem. The 'big gun' antibiotics will only be effective if we limit their use to times when they are absolutely necessary!"

Parent 411: Amoxicillin

Amoxicillin works about 80% of the time to clear a middle ear infection. And even if your child is in daycare, that doesn't mean Amoxicillin will never work for her. For instance, Strep throat is almost always cured with Amoxicillin.

Disease Specifics, by body/organ system[2]

I. Eye Infections: Pink eye

Q. I think my child has pink eye. What is it and will I get it too?

Disease: Conjunctivitis (Pink eye)

Pink eye or **CONJUNCTIVITIS** is an irritation of the tissue surrounding the eyeball. As you might guess, conjunctivitis causes the eye to look red and irritated (especially the inner eye-lid). Conjunctivitis can be caused by infection (bacterial or viral), but it can also be caused by allergies or a chemical irritation. FYI: Infection-caused conjunctivitis is very contagious.

How can you tell the difference between infectious pink eye and just allergies? Viral pink eye usually causes watery eye discharge and a feeling like there is something gritty in the eye. Bacterial pink eye causes goopy eye discharge that keeps recollecting. Both viral and bacterial pink eye can make the eyes crusted over in the morning. By contrast, allergic conjunctivitis is itchy and usually accompanied by an itchy, watery nose as well.

True to infectious disease mantra #1, most pink eye infections are viral. However, the odds of it being bacterial are higher in kids *under* age two. And about 30% of those kids have an ear or sinus infection to go with it. Bacterial pink eye can be treated with antibiotic eye drops and/or an oral antibiotic if the ears or sinuses are infected too.

Most kids *over* age two have viral pink eye, which will not respond to antibiotic drops. Viral pink eye can go hand in hand with a sore throat virus. It takes one to two weeks to clear up on its own.

Disease: Conjunctivitis (Pink eye)
Symptoms? Watery or goopy eye discharge, red eye, itchy or gritty feeling. Sometimes fever, ear pain, nasal discharge, or sore throat too.
Diagnosis? Based on physical exam. A culture is rarely done.
Contagious? Very. Spread by cough and nose droplets, direct contact, and fomites. Use separate hand towels, wash hands often, and do not touch your eyes.
Treatment? Antibiotic orally or eye drops for bacterial pink eye. For viral pink eye, there's not much to do but wait it out.
Return to school? After 24 hours on antibiotic drops for bacterial pink eye, or after eye discharge subsides for viral pink eye.
Incubation? Two to 14 days before the next person gets it.

Q. My child has had a cold and now she has a red, swollen eyelid. Is there anything to worry about?

Disease: Preseptal cellulitis, orbital cellulitis

Yes. The red eyelid may just be a skin infection causing swelling of the eyelid (*preseptal cellulitis*). However, the combination of symptoms is concerning for something more serious—a sinus infection invading the eye socket (*orbital cellulitis*).

A sinus infection can extend into the area where the eye rests in the skull (orbit). It happens in stages, and the prognosis is obviously better if caught early. The first sign is redness and swelling of the eyelid. It then progresses to a bulging eye with limitation of eye movements (orbital cellulitis).

There are much less serious things that cause an eyelid to get swollen and red—like an allergic reaction to a bug bite. But your child should be seen if he has had a cold and now has fever, redness, swelling, or bulging of the eye.

Disease: Preseptal cellulitis, orbital cellulitis
Symptoms? See toddler411.com for a picture of this.

Preseptal cellulitis: Red and swollen eyelid, possibly fever, recent runny nose

Orbital cellulitis: Bulging of eye, pain with eye movements, limited eye movements, double vision, recent runny nose, possibly fever

Diagnosis? Physical exam, blood work, CT scan of sinuses and eyes
Contagious? No.
Treatment:

Preseptal cellulitis: Oral antibiotics, possibly IV antibiotics.

Orbital cellulitis: IV antibiotics, surgical drainage.

Return to school? When child is feeling better.

2. Ear, Nose, Throat and Upper Respiratory Infections

- ◆ *Middle ear infection (acute otitis media)*
- ◆ *Swimmer's ear (external otitis)*
- ◆ *Common cold*
- ◆ *Sinusitis*
- ◆ *Adenoiditis*
- ◆ *Pharyngitis: Strep, adeno, coxsackie, herpes, mono*
- ◆ *Cold sores*
- ◆ *Cervical adenitis*
- ◆ *Croup*

SPECIAL SECTION: Ear infections

Q. My child is prone to ear infections. What exactly are they anyway?

Disease: Acute Otitis Media (middle ear infection)

When you hear the term "ear infection," most folks are referring to a a middle ear infection (**ACUTE OTITIS MEDIA**). Let's explain some ear anatomy here to understand what is going on.

In simple terms, young children are prone to middle ear infections because their Eustachian tubes don't work well. Kids over age three and adults rarely get ear infections because their Eustachian tubes work much better.

The Eustachian tubes are the connection between the ears and the back of the nose. They equalize pressure changes in the ear and drain fluid created by infection or allergies. Newborns have round heads to pass through the birth canal and thus, their Eustachian tubes lie horizontally. As a baby grows, his facial structures elongate and the Eustachian tubes slant downwards. This happens around three years of age. As you might guess, a horizontal tube is ineffective at draining, while a tube that slants downwards is much more efficient.

When a young child gets a cold or upper respiratory infection, the virus causes the lining of the Eustachian tubes to swell, making the tubes even less functional. The tubes then collect fluid. Bacteria like to grow in that stagnant fluid. The body's immune response to the bacteria creates pus, and that is the definition of a middle ear infection.

Think of the infection like a zit or pimple. It has to drain before it gets better. It can either rupture the eardrum and drain (undesirable) or drain down the Eustachian tube (desirable). The use of antibiotics taken by mouth clears the pus and decreases the chance of the pimple bursting (**PERFORATED EARDRUM**).

Ear infections can form in a matter of hours. So you can visit a doctor for an upper respiratory infection one day, only to find yourself back at the office for an ear infection the same week. The doctor didn't MISS the ear infection; it just developed quickly after the first visit!

Disease: Acute Otitis Media (middle ear infection)

Symptoms? Ear pain, ear discharge (not wax), fever, irritability, vomiting, disrupted sleep.

Diagnosis? Based on physical exam.

Contagious? No.

Treatment? Antibiotics for kids under age two, wait and see approach for kids over age two. Pain medication. Consider PE tubes for a child with recurrent infections or poor response to antibiotics.

Return to school? When child feels better.

> **DR B'S OPINION**
>
> *"Just like a pimple, ear infections can pop up overnight. Ears can go from normal to bulging with pus in a matter of hours. That's why I only give a 24-hour guarantee on my ear exams when I see a patient in the office with a cold or flu."*

Old Wives Tales: Ear Infections

No, NONE of these old wives tales are true!

Cover your child's ears from the wind to prevent an ear infection.
Ceiling fans cause ear infections.
Immersing your child in bathtub water causes ear infections.
Putting olive oil, vodka, or candles in the ear eases the pain of an ear infection.

Your Child's Ear, in a nutshell

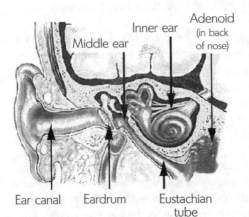

Adenoid (in back of nose)
Inner ear
Middle ear
Ear canal   Eardrum   Eustachian tube

Notes:

1. The ear is divided into three parts—the inner, middle, and outer areas.

2. The Eustachian tubes attach to the middle part of the ear.

3. The eardrum (tympanic membrane) is a piece of tissue that separates the middle and outer ear.

4. The eardrum protects the delicate middle ear bones and nerves.

Q. So what do you see in the ear with a middle ear infection?

A normal looking eardrum is gray and translucent. The bones that control hearing are visible behind it.

An infected eardrum has pus behind it and is swollen and red (remember the pimple analogy). This obscures the view of the middle ear.

If your child is prone to middle ear infections, it may be tempting to buy your own otoscope (a device that checks for ear infections). Don't waste your money. It's not just the scope, but the years of experience looking at eardrums that makes the diagnosis. The obvious bulging red eardrum is one you could easily spot. But not all middle ear infections look like that. Some are more subtle.

Q. If the eardrum pops, will my child have hearing loss?

No. Perforated eardrums usually heal like a piece of skin that has been cut. Back to the pimple analogy: the eardrum is under pressure with all the pus behind it. When the pimple pops, the pus can drain out. The perforation hole is usually small. The ear feels better if this happens, but the infection should be treated with antibiotics. And the eardrum usually heals without any long-term consequences.

Q. What's the difference between a middle ear infection and swimmer's ear?

Disease: Otitis Externa (Swimmer's Ear)

Swimmer's ear is actually a skin infection in the lining of the ear canal (**OTITIS EXTERNA**). It is caused by water that chronically collects in the ear canal or from skin irritation from being scratched (one reason the Q-tip box states "Do not use swab in ear canal" in bold print). Both situations allow bacteria to penetrate the skin and cause infection. Swimmer's ear causes extreme pain with touch or movement of the outer ear (the part you can see). There is redness, swelling, and sometimes debris in the canal, but the eardrum is normal.

Contrary to popular belief, your child will not get a swimmer's ear from lying in bath water. Bath water is fairly clean and very little collects in the outer ear canal. And now that you understand ear anatomy, you know that bath water will also not cause a middle ear infection in a child with an intact eardrum (a middle ear infection is on the other side of the eardrum).

Disease? Otitis Externa (Swimmer's Ear)
Symptoms? Pain with touch or movement of the outer ear, occasionally fever.
Diagnosis? Physical exam. A culture is rarely done.
Contagious? No. But more likely in a child who swims underwater or uses Q-tips.
Treatment? Antibiotic ear drops. Pain medication. No swimming until ear feels better.
Return to school? When child feels better.

Q. Is there a way to prevent middle ear infections?

While there are some risk factors you can control, others are out of your hands. Here are the top risk factors you can control:

1. **Common cold/flu**: Respiratory infections create the fluid in the Eustachian tubes. Teach your child good hand washing techniques and get him a flu shot every year.

2. **Daycare attendance**: Exposure to other children is a set up for those upper respiratory infections. And remember that drug resistant bacteria love childcare settings. Your child may not only be prone to ear infections, but these are more likely to be drug-resistant ones. If you have a child prone to ear infections, see if other childcare options are available. Prevnar vaccine protects against some of the most drug resistant strains of Strep that cause ear infections. Make sure your child is vaccinated.

3. **Second-hand smoke**: Smoke irritates the entire respiratory tract, from the nose to the lungs. Smoke irritates the Eustachian tubes, making them swollen and inefficient. Bottom line: don't smoke near a toddler.

4. **Pacifier use.** Research shows that constant sucking of a pacifier creates a backup of fluid in the throat and Eustachian tubes. If given an option of going pacifier free or having ear surgery, this should be an easy choice. Lose the binky!

5. **Bottle propping.** Here is one good reason to get rid of the bottle at one year of age. Drinking from a bottle while lying down allows fluid from the back of the throat to end up in the Eustachian tubes. The fluid is a set up for infection.

Parent 411: Ear infection fun facts!

◆ By the age of three, 75% of all children have had at least one ear infection.

◆ 50% of all antibiotics prescribed for kids under age four are for ear infections.

◆ The peak age of ear infections is six to 18 months.

◆ Four to five percent of kids from ages one to two have PE tubes inserted.

◆ 90% of ear infections are caused by bacteria. 10% are caused by viruses (RSV and Flu being the tops).[3]

Q. Why do we need to see the doctor again after an ear infection?

Once the acute infection is over, the pus behind the eardrum will liquefy (*serous otitis*), drain, and eventually dry up. That process takes a matter of weeks and sometimes months. There's really no way to accelerate that process (believe us, it has been studied for decades). About 40% of children will still have sterile fluid behind their eardrums one month after an acute ear infection. 10% still have fluid after three months.

The fluid sitting behind the eardrum interferes with normal eardrum function. The eardrum is supposed to resonate when a sound wave hits it. Yet it can only resonate if there is air on both sides of the drum. Thus, a child with residual fluid will have difficulty hearing normally while the fluid is present. While this is temporary (**CONDUCTIVE HEARING LOSS**), it is a concern because young children are in the midst of learning language skills.

INFECTIONS

BEHIND THE SCENES: PICKING THE RIGHT EAR MED

There are three top bacteria that cause ear infections: Strep pneumoniae (Prevnar vaccine fame), Moraxella, and H. influenzae non-typable. And there are basically four classes of antibiotics that kill all of these bugs.

Doctors usually choose high-dose Amoxicillin (if the child isn't allergic to Penicillin) as their first line choice because it works about 80% of the time. It is well tolerated . . . and it's cheap!

If it has been less than thirty days since a previous ear infection, a doctor may select a different class of medication because the bug is more likely to be one that is resistant (and has grown back once the antibiotics have stopped). And if pink eye is involved, there is a good chance that the bug is H. influenzae, which is resistant to Amoxicillin. More on this topic in Appendix A, Medications.

Our final treatment option is to use a broad-spectrum antibiotic (brand name, Rocephin) in the form of a shot. To give you an idea of how potent this drug is, doctors also use it to treat meningitis. Clearly, this is why docs reserve it as a last ditch effort!

The good news: studies show that children with language delays due to conductive hearing loss catch up to their peers by school age.

Doctors like to reexamine a child to be sure that both the infection and the fluid clear up. Antibiotic resistance runs rampant, so it is important to make sure that the infection has been treated. Chronic fluid accumulation for three months or more deserves a specialist's (ear-nose-throat doctor) evaluation.

Q. What will happen if we do not treat the infection with an antibiotic?

Not all middle ear infections require antibiotics to clear up. A small percentage of ear infections are viral, which will not respond anyway. And a certain percentage of bacterial infections will clear on their own without any complications.

However, untreated bacterial infections can cause three problems: hearing loss (from chronic fluid accumulation, chronic infections, and chronic eardrum perforation), *mastoiditis* (infection that invades the skull bone), and brain abscesses/meningitis. In the olden days before antibiotics, 80% of ear infections would resolve on their own. But the other 20% that were untreated led to these serious complications.[4]

Helpful Hints: Ear infection treatment guidelines

Due to the rise in antibiotic resistance, the American Academy of Pediatrics and the American Academy of Family Physicians revised their recommendations for treating ear infections in 2004. Here they are:

For ages six months to two years

◆ Acute middle ear infections need antibiotics.

◆ Questionable infections should wait for a couple of days. A doctor can recheck the patient or provide a prescription medication if symptoms do not improve.

For ages two years and up

◆ Severe pain or fever of 104 or greater with ear infection needs antibiotics.

◆ Mild pain or fever under 104 can wait a couple of days to see if symptoms improve without antibiotics.

Reality Check:
Can we fly when our child has an ear infection?

Yes. As you probably know, chewing gum or yawning helps your eardrum move and adjust to the pressurized air in the cabin. When a child has an acute ear infection, pus (instead of air) fills the middle ear space. There's no pain with the change in cabin pressure because the eardrum cannot move. In fact, the pressure change may make the eardrum pop to release the pus. That's okay.

It is more of a problem when an ear infection is starting to clear up. Then there is both air (normal) and fluid (not normal) in the middle ear. The eardrum attempts to accommodate to the pressure change and is only partially successful. This really hurts. A few tips to minimize that pain: use decongestant nose spray (example: Neosynephrine) before takeoff and let your child drink something during takeoff and landing.

Q. How many ear infections are too many?

We have recruited Mr. Dr. Brown (ENT extraordinaire) for this question. His philosophy is: "most kids outgrow the problem of ear infections by about three years of age. So, theoretically, we can all wait until your child turns three to decide if this is a problem. But there are some important considerations that compel doctors to take a more active approach." Here are some key questions:

1. **How many rounds of antibiotics are too many?** The downsides of antibiotics for your child include diarrhea and yeast infec-

---

TREATING THE PAIN OF EAR INFECTIONS

For the most part, we recommend using either acetaminophen (Tylenol, Tempra, etc) or ibuprofen (Motrin, Advil, etc) for pain associated with ear infections. They are both excellent pain relievers. Using a heating pad on a low setting may also be useful.

Some doctors like to use ear-numbing drops (brand name: Auralgan) for temporary pain relief. A recent study has shown some positive benefit when children are having severe pain.[5] The argument against using the drops is that if the eardrum ruptures, the drops end up in the middle ear, where they can cause problems. (It also makes it hard for us to examine the ear for infection if the drops are in there).

? ?

INFECTIONS

tions. The downsides for *you* include the cost of doctors' visits, missed work, and pharmacy co-payments.

2. **How old is the child?** If your child is only one year old, you will be dealing with these infections for a while. If your child is almost three, he may be outgrowing the problem. Chronic ear infections cause reversible conductive hearing loss, right at the time your child is acquiring language skills (see discussion above). The good news: kids with recurrent ear infections with PE tubes have the same long-term language skills at age six as those without tubes—that's comforting to know.[6] But what happens between ages two and six? Lots of frustration due to poor communication skills.

3. **How miserable is the child?** Ear infections hurt. Respect them. It interferes with sleep and mood of the child (and probably yours as well if your child is keeping you up at night). This key point tends to get overlooked by both parents and doctors.

Dr. B's Opinion:
When I call in an ENT

Here's my approach to making a referral to an Ear, Nose, and Throat specialist for recurrent ear infections. By the way, it is not my job to determine who needs surgery or not. It is my job to decide if my therapeutic treatment options have been exhausted and I need help managing the patient!

As you will see, some of the decision making process depends on the time of year. Ear infections occur mostly in cold and flu season since that is when there is usually fluid sitting in the Eustachian tubes. Kids who get middle ear infections in the off-season are just time bombs for the winter.

So, here's my take on when ear infections need to be referred to an ENT:

◆ Four infections in the peak (winter) season
◆ Three infections in the off peak (summer) season
◆ Three months of persistent residual fluid (serous otitis)
◆ Three back-to-back courses of antibiotics for the same ear infection.

Q. My doctor is recommending PE tubes for my child. What are they and how do they work?

Pressure equalization (PE) tubes are an alternative to antibiotics. The tubes are the length of a pencil point and the diameter of angel hair pasta (really small). Their presence in the eardrum allows the middle ear to drain properly and prevents the buildup of fluid. They significantly reduce the number of ear infections a child has, and make subsequent infections easier to treat. With PE tubes, topical antibiotic drops can be used instead of oral antibiotics.

How are PE tubes implanted? An ENT specialist makes a tiny hole in the eardrum, cleans out any fluid or pus, and inserts the tube. The tube normally falls out on its own after six to 18 months. And the eardrum heals beautifully 99% of the time.

This procedure can be done in a day surgery facility. It requires anesthesia, but *not* an IV, breathing tube, or ventilator. The whole procedure takes about five minutes and kids are back to running around later that day.

We know that contemplating any surgical procedure on your child is sure to freak you out. Your ENT doctor should be able to reassure you about any concerns that you may have. But here are the ones that come up most often:

- ◆ Anesthesia: The risk of anesthesia is no greater than the risk of all those antibiotics your child has been taking.
- ◆ Persistent eardrum perforation: Very rarely, the eardrum does not heal over when the tube falls out. It may require another procedure to repair it.

BOTTOM LINE ON PE TUBES: Most parents (and kids) view PE tubes as a life changing experience. Even the most anxious parents wonder why they waited so long to do it. As my husband says, "Once your patients see me, they don't need you anymore!" While I do love seeing my patients, I would much rather see them when they are well.

Q. What is the difference between the common cold and the flu?

The common cold is a viral infection caused by one of over a hundred rhinoviruses (rhino = nose). The virus enters our body through our nose and starts to reproduce, causing symptoms of fever and body aches when this happens. Runny nose, cough, and maybe a sore throat follow. The symptoms last ten to 14 days with day three or four being the worst.

Disease: The common cold.
Symptoms? Fever, runny nose, cough, body aches, maybe sore throat. Fever typically lasts two to three days, maybe four at the most.
Diagnosis? Based on physical exam.
Contagious? Yes, via hand-to-hand contact with snot, nasal/cough droplets in the air.
Treatment? Treat the symptoms.
Return to school? Two or three days, or fever free for 24 hours.
Incubation? Two to seven days until you get sick.

The flu is a specific upper respiratory infection caused by Influenza virus A or B. Each year the flu virus morphs into different strains, causing a widespread outbreak or epidemic. Because influenza is a more virulent bug than the common cold, it makes you feel much worse when you get it. There is a higher risk of complications from the flu as well, including dehydration and secondary bacterial infection (ear/sinus infections, pneumonia).

Disease: Influenza (the Flu)
Symptoms? High fever, body aches, and chills. Runny nose, cough, and sore throat come later. Often fever is over 102 and can last five to seven days. H1N1 strain sometimes begins with nausea and vomiting as the first symptoms.
Diagnosis? Based on physical exam. Blood work helpful. Rapid flu test available.
Contagious? You bet. Spread via respiratory droplets, fomites.
Treatment? Antivirals (Amantadine, Tamiflu, Relenza) may lessen the severity and duration of symptoms if started within 48 hours of symptoms. However, some flu strains are resistant to some antivirals so they don't

? ?

INFECTIONS

always work.

Return to school? When child is fever free for 24 hours.

Incubation? One to three days. Anyone over three months of age who is a household contact of someone with the flu can be treated preventatively with antivirals.

Reality Check:
H1N1 (a.k.a. "swine") flu—is it really a threat?

In short, yes. Should we panic? No.

We do need to respect infectious diseases for their ability to adapt to their foes and cause serious and potentially, fatal disease.

It's likely that H1N1 flu strain will stick around for some time. That's why it will be included in seasonal flu vaccine.

Q. How can I tell if my child has a sinus infection and not just a cold?

In the wintertime, your child may have more days with snot smeared on his face than not. By the way, no toddler likes to have it wiped. You will start to ponder whether your child has a cold that is lasting forever, or if he has a sinus infection that he is not telling you about.

So, how will you know if a cold is turning into a sinus infection? Here are some red flags:

◆ As we discussed above, you already know that each common cold will last ten to 14 days. If the symptoms are getting worse instead of better, that is one red flag.

◆ If your child's fever breaks after the first few days of illness, then spikes again after being fever free for over 24 hours, that's another red flag.

◆ Finally, if the nasal secretions have been clear for 14 days and then turn green, your toddler should be assessed for a sinus infection.

The difference between a cold and a sinus infection

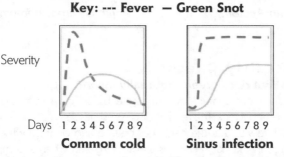

Key: --- Fever — Green Snot

Severity

Days 1 2 3 4 5 6 7 8 9   1 2 3 4 5 6 7 8 9
Common cold   **Sinus infection**

The common cold causes a short lived fever with several days of snot. A sinus infection causes prolonged fever and prolonged snot.

Disease: Sinusitis

Acute sinus infection (**ACUTE SINUSITIS**) is fairly easy to diagnose. Kids have a fever for more than four days straight, or new onset green snot after two weeks of clear nasal secretions.

Chronic sinus infections are much trickier to diagnose. Why? They fly under the radar, smoldering rather than flaring up. A child will probably not run a fever, but instead has discolored snot that comes and goes for over two weeks. A chronic nighttime cough may occur from postnasal drip, caused by infected sinuses.

A quick anatomy lesson: babies are born with only one pair of sinuses. The other three pair will develop by three years of age. So a young child under age three with recurrent or chronic sinusitis symptoms mostly probably has a chronically infected *adenoid*. (We will discuss adenoiditis later in this chapter).

Symptoms?
Acute sinusitis: New fever after being fever free for 24 hours, new onset green snot and fever after having a clear runny nose, fever more than four days straight with runny nose.
Chronic sinusitis: Discolored snot more than two weeks, nighttime cough, bad breath.
Contagious? No.
Diagnosis? Physical exam. Plain X-rays are not very helpful. On the other hand, CT scan of sinuses can be helpful when the diagnosis is in question. Blood work sometimes useful.
Treatment? Oral antibiotics. Prolonged treatment for chronic sinusitis (often three weeks of antibiotics).
Return to school? When child feels better.

Tonsils

Mouth Anatomy

— Adenoid

Tonsils

Mouth & Throat Anatomy

Reality Check:
What does green snot really mean?
When our immune system (white blood cells) fights against a virus or a bacteria, the result is discolored nasal secretions. The color change simply tells us that the battle has been going on for a while.

The change from clear secretions to yellow/green when accompanied by fever, headache, fussiness, or symptoms over two weeks is a red flag for a bacterial sinusitis or adenoiditis.

Can your child go to playgroup or childcare? Yep. Will the other moms look at you and be annoyed? Yep. Tell them to pick up a copy of this book.

So, here are two facts about green snot:

◆ Green snot does NOT always mean you or your child has a sinus infection.

◆ Green snot does NOT mean your child is contagious.

Dr. B's Blue Plate Special

There is a bacteria that likes to infect the eyes (pink eye), the ears, and the sinuses all at once. If there is green stuff coming out of every head orifice, this bug (Haemophilus influenzae non-typable) is probably around. All of the infected areas respond well to a second-line (that is, stronger) antibiotic.

Q. My child has a chronic runny nose. Is it a sinus infection?

As we discussed earlier in this chapter, young children have fewer sinuses (one pair) compared to adults (four pairs). As a result, kids suffer from fewer sinus infections . . . but when kids have symptoms similar to chronic sinusitis, the prime suspect is really their adenoid.

Just to recap, the adenoid is a piece of lymph tissue (like the tonsils) that sits behind the nose. (See the figure on the previous page depicting the sawed in half person to see where it is.) In Chapter 17, Common Diseases, we discuss adenoid enlargement as the cause of chronic mouth breathing, sleep disordered breathing, and chronic runny nose. Like the tonsils, the adenoid can get infected with the bacteria it is trying to kill. Because we cannot see the adenoid just by looking in the nose or the throat, it can be hard to tell if it is infected. But a chronically green runny nose that does not respond well to antibiotic therapy is a good clue that there is a festering infection in the adenoid (*adenoiditis*).

If this problem does not resolve on its own, it is time to visit an ENT specialist. An operation to remove the adenoid may be the solution. For details on adenoidectomy, see Chapter 17, Common Diseases.

Disease: Chronic adenoiditis.

Symptoms? Chronic runny nose, chronic green snot, mouth breathing, sleep disordered breathing, nighttime cough.

Diagnosis? Physical exam and history.

Contagious? No.

Treatment? Prolonged course of antibiotics, nasal steroids, possible adenoidectomy surgery.

Return to school? When child feels better.

Q. My child has a fever and has stopped eating. What does he have?

Here is an insider tip. If your child has a fever without any other obvious symptoms, look in his mouth!

Sore throats (*pharyngitis, tonsillitis, pharyngotonsillitis*) are a common cause of fever and frequently your child will not tell you his throat hurts. He may tell you indirectly by refusing to eat (but that's probably nothing new with a toddler!).

As usual, most infections that cause a sore throat are viruses. Yes, that means they will go away on their own. The only exception to this rule is oral herpes (more on this later). Kids under the age of two rarely get Strep throat

infections: throat

INFECTIONS

? ?

(a bacteria), but it happens occasionally. For this reason, a child with a red throat without runny nose/ cough symptoms should see his doctor. Here are the different bugs you should know about (see Toddler411.com for pics).

Group A Strep ("Strep throat")

Disease? Strep is a bacterial infection caused by one of the many strains of Streptococcus called Group A Strep. Just to confuse you, there are different strains that cause different infections. Strep throat usually hits school-aged kids, but preschoolers get it too (especially if they are around older children). It's very rare for an infant to get Strep throat.

Classically, kids with Strep throat will have a fever and a sore throat *without* cough/runny nose symptoms. The textbook photo of Strep pharyngitis is on our website at Toddler411.com. (see Bonus Material, then Visual Library). The most common Group A Strep symptoms are: tonsils that are red (usually with white pus on them), tiny red dots on the roof of the mouth, bad breath, and swollen/tender lymph nodes in the neck.

However, Strep can ALSO present with some other symptoms:

◆ Slight runny nose, prolonged fever, and lack of appetite.
◆ "Strawberry tongue"—raised dots on the tongue.
◆ Vaginal redness and irritation, redness around the anus.
◆ Headache, stomachache, with or without vomiting.
◆ Sandpapery red raised rash on the trunk (*scarlet fever*).

Don't panic if your child is diagnosed with scarlet fever! Before the days of antibiotics, it would mean that the infection might get more serious. But Group A Strep infections, even ones accompanied by the skin rash, can be easily treated with the first antibiotic ever created: Penicillin.

It's important that your child takes the entire course of antibiotics to clear a Strep infection. Untreated or partially treated Group A Strep infections can lead to infection in the heart, called *acute rheumatic fever.* That's not to scare you, but it's a reminder of the importance to take all the antibiotics that are prescribed. The good news: kids under age three are less likely than older children to have this complication.

Symptoms? Fever, decreased appetite, sore throat, swollen lymph nodes (glands) in the neck, headache, stomachache, vomiting, rash, vaginal or anal redness (see above).

Contagious? Person-to-person via respiratory droplets, saliva. Typical seasons: late fall, winter, spring (when school is in session).

Incubation? Two to five days.

Diagnosis? By physical exam, confirmation by rapid testing and/or throat culture.

Treatment? Antibiotics.

Return to School? After 24 hours of antibiotics, and feeling better.

Old Wives Tales

Dogs are carriers of Strep throat infections. FALSE.
The truth: You may not want to kiss your dog for other reasons, but Strep is not one of them.

Adenovirus

Disease? This is the classic sore throat virus. The back of the throat looks red, and may even have some pus on it. It may be accompanied by cough, runny nose, and fever like the common cold. One classic tip off for adenovirus: pink eye with a sore throat.

Symptoms? Sore throat, runny nose, pink eye, fever.

Contagious? Person-to-person contact, air, fomites.

Incubation? Two to 14 days.

Diagnosis? Based on physical exam.

Treatment? Time and pain medication. It takes about a week (but sometimes two weeks) to clear.

Return to school? Fever free, usually two to three days.

Coxsackievirus

Disease: This virus gets a special name for where it likes to hang out. It's called *hand-foot-and-mouth* (not Hoof and Mouth, the cow disease). It causes mouth sores (*herpangina, stomatitis*) usually found in the back of the throat *with or without skin* lesions on the hands, feet, extremities, and anus. (Technically, it should be called hand-foot-mouth-and-butt). Resembling ant bites, skin lesions can look like flat red dots or white pus filled dots.

Symptoms? Fever, sore throat, mouth sores, rash on hands/feet/anus.

Contagious? Spread person-to-person, via infected saliva and poop. Typical season: summer and early fall.

Incubation? Three to six days.

Diagnosis? Based on physical exam.

Treatment? Time—it clears up in about a week. Avoid citrus and salty foods as they will sting. A combo of a few drops of liquid diphenhydramine (Benadryl) mixed with a few drops of liquid Maalox provide temporary relief before mealtime.

Return to school? Fever free, or after two or three days.

Oral Herpes virus (HSV Type 1)

Disease: This is a mouth infection (*gingivostomatitis*) caused by Herpes Simplex Virus Type 1 (Most folks think of genital herpes when they hear the word herpes—but this is different). Herpes initial infection may be symptom-free . . . but not always. Kids with gingivostomatitis may have numerous ulcers in their mouths, including gums and tongue. The pain is so severe that they avoid swallowing, even saliva. Dehydration is common with young children who have this virus. Once a person is infected, the HSV-1 virus lies dormant for life and can re-activate as a cold sore.

Symptoms? Fever, often over 102 degrees for a week. Numerous mouth ulcers, gum swelling and bleeding.

Contagious? VERY, for about a week! Spread by direct contact with active cold sores or saliva during active infection.

Incubation? Two days to two weeks.

Diagnosis? Based on physical exam, confirmation by culture (rarely necessary).

infections: throat

INFECTIONS

? ?

Treatment? Oral antiviral medication if diagnosed within 48 hours of outbreak. Pain control with oral and topical pain medications. Hydration.
Return to school? For gingivostomatitis, child returns when ulcers disappear. For subsequent cold sores, children may attend school.

Reality Check: Cold Sores

Cold sores are those unsightly ulcers that show up on the lips of someone who has oral herpes. They occur during times of illness, stress, just before family portraits, and often, sun exposure. If you have a cold sore, do not kiss your family members. Herpes is one thing you don't want to share. While docs cannot make cold sores go away, they can be treated within 48 hours to shorten their duration.

Mononucleosis ("Mono")— EBV virus

Disease: You may know this virus as Mono or the Kissing Disease. And you may think only teenagers get it. But the EBV virus can infect just about anyone. In fact, some young children get mono and doctors just assume it is a run-of-the-mill sore throat virus. Not everyone who has a mono infection has chronic fatigue so often associated with this virus.
Symptoms? Sore throat, tonsils may be full of pus, swollen lymph nodes in the neck, enlarged spleen, fatigue, fever.
Contagious? Spread by close contact with infected saliva (kissing, sharing drinks/food).
Incubation? 30 to 50 days!
Diagnosis? Based on physical exam, confirmation by blood test
Treatment? For severe cases, oral steroids reduce tonsil swelling. Pain medication. No contact sports (rough-housing) until spleen size normalizes (about six weeks).
Return to school? Fever free and feeling better.

FYI: Once you have had an EBV infection, you have it for life. It's a member of the Herpes virus family and it hangs out with its host forever. But it does not mean you are contagious forever.

Insider Tip

Strep throat and Mono can have similarly disgusting red tonsils full of pus and swollen neck lymph nodes. If your child is presumptively treated for Strep throat with Amoxicillin, then develops a rash, it may not be an allergic reaction to the antibiotic. *Kids with mono may develop a rash when they are taking Amoxicillin.* Go back to the doctor and ask for a mono test!

Parent 411: How to examine your child's mouth

Whether it's for tooth brushing or examination, children are never thrilled to open their mouths. Examining your child's mouth may require two adults. Have one adult (the "holder") hold the child on his lap, keeping his hands restrained under the adult's arm. The adult's second hand is placed on the child's forehead to keep it in one place. The adult (the "examiner") can open the child's mouth with either a popsicle stick or the back of a baby spoon. Take a flashlight and look at the mouth and the back of the throat.

Hint: try this once before your child gets sick. That way you know what a normal mouth looks like!

Q. My child seems to get Strep throat all the time. Does he need his tonsils taken out?

Some kids are prone to Strep throat infections and it may be due to the anatomy of their tonsils. These tonsils have nooks and crannies that allow infectious bacteria to colonize.

In the pre-antibiotic era, anyone who got Strep throat once had his tonsils removed. That's because a Strep infection could lead to heart and kidney disease. But thanks to antibiotics, most folks can keep their tonsils, even if they get Strep every now and again.

So which kids should have their tonsils removed? There is no real answer. Doctors make recommendations based on how an individual child is affected by multiple infections (severity, missed school days, weight loss, drug allergies, etc). One general rule of thumb: kids with three Strep throat infections in one season (or five infections in a year) are candidates for possible tonsil removal.

We asked Dr. Michael Cunningham, professor of pediatric otolaryngology (ENT) at Massachusetts Eye and Ear Infirmary for his advice on this topic. Dr. Cunningham bases his decision on the severity of infections, not just the number.

Dr. B's Opinion: Are some kids strep carriers?
Yes, some people can chronically carry Strep bacteria in their tonsils. No, they aren't sick and do not constantly spread their germs. As a result, these kids do NOT need antibiotics to stop their "carrier" status.

Yet, some docs will treat Strep carriers with antibiotics in hopes of "curing" it . . . despite the lack of consensus in medical research on this topic.

The real problem with being a Strep carrier is that it's difficult to test for Strep infection when your test is always positive!

Reality Check: Three reasons why your child needs to take all his medicine for Strep throat.
Have you read the children's classic, The Velveteen Rabbit? Did you wonder why the little boy had to throw away all his toys when he had scarlet fever? The answer is: Strep is scary stuff. Before the days of antibiotics, people could get pretty sick (or die) with it. Thanks to a little mold that became the antibiotic Penicillin, we don't need to worry about Strep infections like we used to. But you need to respect this bacteria. Just because your child feels better after Dose #1 of his medicine, doesn't mean you can skip the rest of the doses. Here are some of the reasons:

◆ *Acute Rheumatic Fever:* Heart and heart valve inflammation, arthritis, rash, and odd body movements.
◆ *Glomerulonephritis*: Kidney inflammation that can cause acute kidney failure.
◆ *PANDAS*: Acute onset of body tics, obsessive-compulsive traits, and odd body movements.[7]

INFECTIONS

? ?

Recap of sore throats

Here are the most common sore throat bugs and their symptoms:

BUG	TYPE	SYMPTOMS
Strep	Bacteria	Pus on tonsils, swollen glands, sandpaper rash.
Adenovirus	Virus	Red throat, sometimes pink eye.
Coxsackievirus	Virus	Ulcers on back of throat, rash on hands/feet/anus.
Herpes virus	Virus	Ulcers in mouth, gums, tongue, bleeding gums.
Mono	Virus	Pus on tonsils, swollen glands.

Q. My child has a fever and a swollen, red area on his neck. What's wrong with him?

Looking in the throat is a good place to start. As mentioned earlier, there are sore throat infections associated with impressive swollen lymph nodes in the neck. However, sometimes the infection itself settles into the lymph node (*lymphadenitis*).

Disease: Lymphadenitis is caused by a virus, bacteria, or mycobacteria.
Symptoms? Warm, red, swollen, very tender lymph node—usually just on one side. Fever.
Contagious? Only if infection is still active elsewhere (like Strep throat).
Incubation? Depends on the cause of the illness.
Diagnosis? Based on physical exam, blood work, tuberculosis test, or culture after incision and drainage.
Treatment? Antibiotics. Possible surgical procedure to incise and drain it if an abscess develops.
Return to school? When child feels better.

Q. What is Kawasaki Disease?

Nope, it has nothing to do with motorcycles.

If your child has had a daily fever for over FOUR days, it's time to see the doctor. Why? Your doctor will be concerned about possible Kawasaki Disease (KD).

KD is a funky immune vasculitis (swollen blood vessels) disorder that if untreated, can lead to some pretty serious complications like heart attacks, heart blood vessel aneurysms, and heart failure. Although it is fairly rare, it occurs most often in children ages two to five years.

Here are the symptoms:

◆ High fever (usually at least 104) for five or more days straight.
◆ Single swollen lymph node in neck.
◆ Pink eye.
◆ Cracked red lips, strawberry tongue.
◆ Nonspecific body rash.
◆ Rash on hands/feet, often peeling.
◆ Edema (swelling) of hands/feet.
◆ Irritability (not just cranky).

Q. My child was up all night barking like a seal. What is it and what can I do about it?

Disease: Croup. This is a viral infection of the voice box area. Infants have the most problems because the smaller the child, the smaller the child's airway is. Infants are at highest risk of having a high-pitched squeal (**stridor**) that indicates significant airway swelling. Older children will bark with croup. Adults just get laryngitis.

Symptoms? Barky, seal-like cough predominantly at night, for about three nights. Stridor more than ten minutes without relief needs medical attention. Typically a fall or early winter illness.

Contagious? While coughing. Spread by direct contact, fomites, respiratory droplets.

Incubation? Two to six days.

Diagnosis? The bark and hoarse voice is the big clue. Rarely, an x-ray is done.

Treatment? Take your child into the bathroom and turn on the shower. The steam may relax the airway. Or go outside into the night air. Place a humidifier in the child's room. Steroids by mouth or injection help reduce the airway swelling. In emergencies, an epinephrine breathing treatment is needed. For severe cases, hospitalization is necessary.

Return to school? Usually after two or three days.

3. Lower Respiratory/Lung infections

◆ RSV
◆ Bronchitis/walking pneumonia
◆ Pneumonia

Let's take a quick look at your child's lungs:

Note on diagram: The respiratory tract is just one big tube. The nose, mouth, and throat lead into the trachea. The trachea branches off into two bronchi. The bronchi divide into smaller bronchioles. And the bronchioles dead end into small sacs called alveoli, where oxygen exchange occurs.

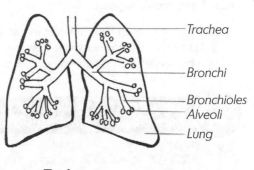

Trachea

Bronchi

Bronchioles
Alveoli

Lung

The Lungs

Q. My child is wheezing for the first time. The doctor says its RSV. What is that?

Disease: RSV stands for Respiratory Syncytial Virus. It is also known as **bronchiolitis** because it attacks the tiny bronchioles of the lungs and makes them swell (see diagram above). The airflow through those swollen bronchioles causes a wheezing noise. RSV is most serious in infants, especially those born prematurely. But not everyone wheezes with RSV. Older kids and adults may just have common cold symptoms. Of the kids who wheeze, 30% will go on to have asthma. *It's unknown* *whether the RSV causes asthma or kids who are already prone to asthma just so happen to wheeze with RSV.*

Symptoms? Fever, runny nose, happy wheezers (breathing faster than normal but not in distress). Symptoms can go on for several weeks—be prepared. RSV is a winter illness.

Contagious? Spread by contact, fomites, respiratory droplets.

Incubation? Two to eight days.

Diagnosis? Based on physical exam. Nasal swab test can confirm RSV infection.

Treatment? A small percentage of kids will respond to asthma medications. Some need oxygen, which requires hospitalization.

Return to school? Usually after three days and fever free.

Prevention? Kids under two years of age who were born prematurely (less than 32 weeks gestation) or who have chronic lung disease can receive monthly injections of RSV-antibody during the RSV season.

Helpful Hints: Take home tips on RSV

◆ RSV symptoms last for several weeks.

◆ Most kids are happy wheezers. See the doctor if your child looks like he is in respiratory distress (see Chapter 19, First Aid for details)

◆ About 30% of kids who have RSV will get an ear infection. See the doctor if your child runs a new fever after being fever free from the initial illness.

FYI: RSV is the most common virus that makes kids wheeze. But other viruses like influenza and parainfluenza can do it, too. So even if your child is wheezing and tests negative for RSV, he can still be wheezing from a virus.

Q. My child has been diagnosed with walking pneumonia. I am freaking out.

Disease: It's called walking pneumonia because, well, people walk around with it and do not know they have it. This is an infection caused by a bug called Mycoplasma pneumoniae. It usually infects school-aged

THE DIFFERENCE BETWEEN BRONCHITIS, BRONCHIOLITIS, AND PNEUMONIA

They are all infections in the lungs, but occur in different places. Take a look at the lung diagram at the beginning of this section. The bronchi are the big airways and the bronchioles are the little ones. Bronchitis causes a hacking, deep sounding cough. Bronchiolitis usually causes a wheeze. Viruses cause both bronchitis and bronchiolitis. The exceptions for non-viral causes of bronchitis are whooping cough and walking pneumonia (see above).

Pneumonia is the granddaddy of all lung infections. It refers to an infection (viral, bacterial, or fungal) in the actual lung tissue, not the tubes. A portion of the lung tissue gets inflamed and fills with fluid/pus. That part of the lung cannot work properly until it clears the fluid. The result: a wet productive cough and labored breathing.

kids and teens, but can infect little ones, especially if they have older siblings.

Symptoms? Sore throat, ear pain, dry hacking cough, or wet productive cough.

Contagious? Respiratory droplets, close contact.

Incubation? Two to three weeks.

Diagnosis? Physical exam, possible chest x-ray.

Treatment? It eventually goes away on its own, but antibiotics will treat pneumonia or an ear infection (usually kids under age eight).

Return to school? Usually not contagious by the time a patient is diagnosed. In other words, your child has probably infected everyone already.

Q. My child has difficulty breathing and a fever. Should I worry about pneumonia?

Yes. Pneumonia classically shows up with a rapid onset fever, chills, wet cough, and labored breathing after a person has already had a cold or flu infection. And yes, pneumonia is a serious infection. The good news: it is treatable.

Disease: Viruses (such as influenza and RSV), bacteria (such as Strep pneumoniae), and even some fungi can cause pneumonia. Despite all the possible causes, the usual suspects in a pneumonia infection are viruses.

Symptoms? Fever, wet/productive cough with discolored mucus, shaking chills, labored breathing ("air hungry;" see Chapter 19, First Aid for details), vomiting.

Contagious? Varies, depending on the bug or patient. For instance, immune-compromised people are at greatest risk of getting fungal pneumonia.

Incubation? Depends on the bug.

Diagnosis? By physical exam, confirmed by chest x-ray, blood work, culture of cough droplets (sputum), oxygen saturation test.

> ### DR B'S OPINION
>
> *"Having a child with pneumonia is a scary experience. However, most of the time, it is simply due to bad luck. You do not have to worry that you have a child with a weak immune system. I always hesitate to say the word 'pneumonia' because it sends parents into a tailspin. For some reason, bronchitis is much more acceptable."*

infections: lungs

Treatment? Even though viruses are the top players, doctors don't take chances with pneumonia and will treat with antibiotics. If infection is serious, hospitalization is necessary for IV antibiotics and oxygen support.

Return to school? When child is fever free and feels better.

Old Wives Tales
Going out in the cold leads to pneumonia. FALSE
Going outside with wet hair can cause pneumonia. FALSE
Truth: Having a cold may lead to pneumonia. But going out INTO the cold without a jacket or with wet hair, does NOT cause pneumonia.

4. Intestinal infections

- ◆ *Viral gastroenteritis*
- ◆ *Food poisoning*
- ◆ *Parasites*

Q. How do I know when it is just a stomach virus and not something more serious?

Good question. As you can probably tell by now, people can have slightly different manifestations of the same infection. With stomach viruses (or the stomach "flu"), symptoms may include fever, vomiting, stomachache, and diarrhea. A child may have all those symptoms and his parents may only get the diarrhea part. The red flags for what is *unlikely* to be a plain old stomach virus are found in Chapter 19, First Aid but include persistent vomiting without diarrhea, severe abdominal pain, and blood/mucous in the diarrhea.

Disease: There are many types of viruses that are collectively known as the "stomach virus." They are all treated the same way—with lots of fluids to prevent dehydration. The most notorious one is Rotavirus. It arrives every winter and almost all kids get infected with it by three years of age.
Symptoms? Fever, vomiting as first symptom followed by extremely watery diarrhea (often more than twenty times a day). Symptoms last one full week. There is so much water loss in the diarrhea, it is challenging to keep the fluid intake greater than output. Dehydration (see signs of dehydration in Chapter 19, First Aid) including lethargy and diminished urination.
Contagious? Oh yeah. It's spread through contact with infected poop and saliva. It spreads like wildfire through childcare and households.
Incubation? One to three days.
Diagnosis? Usually obvious by the number of diapers being changed. Rapid assay test for rotavirus is available.
Treatment? Lots of fluids (see Chapter 19, First Aid for rehydration tricks). Lactobacillus (probiotic) supplement, high fat diet. Probiotics.
Return to school? When the poop is solid again. That takes about a week.

Factoid: Although people refer to it as the stomach flu, this ailment is NOT caused by the influenza virus. So, your annual flu shot will not protect you from catching a stomach bug.

Q. How can I tell if my child has food poisoning? Is it treated any differently than a stomach virus?

Bacterial food poisoning and stomach viruses can look the same initially. Both infections often begin with vomiting. But the telltale difference is that food poisoning will cause blood/mucous in the diarrhea.

Is food poisoning treated any differently? Well, it depends on the bug that is causing the infection. Some bugs need to be treated to shorten the duration of the illness, but others actually get *worse* if they are treated with antibiotics. That's why doctors will usually wait to see what bug they are dealing with before treating it.

Disease: E. coli, Salmonella, Shigella, and other bacteria spread through contaminated food and infected people's mouths and poop.

? ?

INFECTIONS

Salmonella is the most common cause of food poisoning. E. coli Type 0157:H7 is less common but potentially much more serious because it can cause **HEMOLYTIC UREMIC SYNDROME** (anemia, low platelet count, and kidney failure).

Symptoms? Vomiting, diarrhea mixed with blood/mucous, fever, body-aches, abdominal pain.

Contagious? Spread by contaminated water/food (poultry, under-cooked eggs, alfalfa sprouts, unpasteurized milk/dairy products, under-cooked ground beef), breast milk, fomites (raw meat on countertop), direct contact with infected poop and saliva, pet iguanas, turtles.

Incubation? Six to 72 hours, but varies on the bug.

Diagnosis? Stool culture, blood/white blood cells in poop, occasionally blood test.

Treatment? Lots of fluids to prevent dehydration. Some bacterial infections will need antibiotics.

Return to school? When poop is solid again.

 Reality Check: I'll have my burger well done and don't touch that cow, honey.
E. coli 0157 comes from cow and deer poop. Ground meat can have bacterial contamination throughout, so the meat must be cooked thoroughly to kill all these bugs. Whole muscle cuts are only contaminated on the surface of the meat, which are always cooked well. After caring for a patient with hemolytic uremic syndrome, I will never again eat a cow that can moo back at me.

In 2005, there was an outbreak of E.coli infections linked to kids who went to a petting zoo. The animals enjoyed rolling around in cow manure before being penned up. *Make sure your kids wash their hands well after visiting a petting zoo.*

Q. How can you tell if a child has worms?

Parasites can also cause diarrhea. The symptoms are different than a stomach virus or food poisoning though. Kids with parasitic infections tend to have chronic intermittent diarrhea, gas, bloating, and lack of appetite. If your child has diarrhea going on for more than two weeks, he deserves to be tested for worms!

Disease: The top parasites are Giardia and Cryptosporidium. The peak incidence is in the late summer and early fall (no surprise, since it spreads through swimming pools, lakes, rivers, etc.). Cryptosporidium is a popular cause of traveler's diarrhea.

Symptoms? Chronic, intermittent foul-smelling diarrhea, loss of appetite, bloating, gas, weight loss, fatigue, nausea.

Contagious? Spread via contaminated drinking and recreational water (including swimming pools, hot tubs, area lakes), food, and direct contact with infected poop. Outbreaks in childcare facilities are a huge problem.

Incubation? One to four weeks.

Diagnosis? Stool culture, Giardia assay test on poop.

Treatment? Anti-parasitic medication. Lactose-free diet for one month after treatment. Probiotics.

Return to school? When poop is solid again.[8]

infections: stomach

INFECTIONS

? ?

5. Bone/joint infections

♦ *Osteomyelitis*
♦ *Septic Arthritis*

Q. My child has a fever and is limping. Should I take him to the doctor?

Yes. The combination of new onset limping with a fever is a red flag. There are several diagnoses here that can be serious and need prompt evaluation. We will cover the infectious causes in this chapter but you will find more info on limping in both Chapter 17, Common Diseases and Chapter 19, First Aid.

Disease? Bacterial infections (usually Staph or Strep) can infect a joint (*septic arthritis*) or a bone (*osteomyelitis*). Osteomyelitis is usually caused by bacteria circulating in the bloodstream and settling into a long bone (legs usually) that has had recent minor trauma. Septic arthritis has three possible causes: direct skin trauma overlying the joint (which allows bacteria to enter), bacteria in the blood, or extension of osteomyelitis into the joint space.[9]

Symptoms? A limp, or avoidance of motion of affected bone or joint. Several days of worsening bone or joint pain, warmth, swelling, redness at joint, fever.

Contagious? No.

Diagnosis? Imaging studies, blood work/culture, joint fluid culture, occasionally bone biopsy. The diagnosis can be tricky sometimes.

Treatment? Hospitalization and then home IV antibiotics for four to six weeks.

6. Skin infections/Rashes

♦ *MRSA*
♦ *Cellulitis*
♦ *Impetigo*
♦ *Head Lice*
♦ *Slapped Cheek (Fifth Disease)*
♦ *Roseola*
♦ *Varicella (Chickenpox)*
♦ *Scabies*
♦ *Pinworms*
♦ *Tinea Capitis (Ringworm of the scalp)*
♦ *Tinea Corporis (Ringworm)*
♦ *Verrucae (Warts)*
♦ *Molluscum Contagiosum (Mini-warts)*

Q. My child has an insect bite that looks infected. How can I tell if it is?

Here is how you tell the difference between a skin infection and an allergic reaction. A skin infection (**CELLULITIS**) is warm and tender to the touch.

INFECTIONS

An allergic reaction is swollen, red, and sometimes itchy.

But it's probably not an insect bite. There is a nasty little bacteria out there called **MRSA** (Methicillin-Resistant Staph Aureus). MRSA causes skin infections that look like spider bites, boils, or red, tender areas. They can be a real problem to treat as the bug is resistant to several antibiotics. But there are two or three antibiotic choices that are very effective. See Toddler411.com (click on Bonus Material) for a picture.

Disease: MRSA is a type of Staph infection that likes the skin (but can also infect other body parts). It resides in harmony in some people's noses and on their skin. But a break in the skin allows the MRSA to get under it and cause infection. MRSA can set up shop with the entire family, requiring everyone to get treated to eradicate them as carriers.

Symptoms? Red, swollen, tender skin area or pus-filled wound. If the doctor lances it and it drains disgusting green pus, it's probably MRSA. And about 15% of MRSA abscesses will recur. If you've had one before and it comes back, you can assume it's MRSA again.

Contagious? By direct contact.

Incubation? About four to ten days, but it can vary quite a bit.

Diagnosis? Based on physical exam. Wound can be lanced and cultured to confirm diagnosis and figure out which antibiotic will kill it.

Treatment?

For infection: oral antibiotics with possible lancing and draining of the wound. Occasionally, IV antibiotics are needed.

For MRSA carriers: topical prescription antibiotic ointment is applied to nostrils for a week and regular bathing in chlorhexidine (brand name: Hibiclens) soap.

Return to school? MRSA is everywhere, so exclusion from childcare is not required. Covering the wound and good hand washing is a nice idea.

Reality Check: Flesh Eating Superbug Kills Athletes; More Deaths than AIDS

Okay, that wasn't exactly the headline in 2007 but it was close! When several high-school athletes in three states died from flesh-eating superbug infections (MRSA), the national media went into hyperdrive—reporters linked these cases and a CDC report that said more folks died of "hospital-acquired" MRSA infections than AIDS.

Of course, this led to a flurry of frantic phone calls and doctors' office visits any time a child had a pimple. And some schools brought in hazmat teams to disinfect locker rooms in a scenario reminiscent of the anthrax scare a few years ago.

Here's what you need to know: most people (who are NOT hospitalized) get MRSA skin infections that are NOT life-threatening.

You can reduce the chances of getting one of these infections by not picking open bug bites, scratching eczema, or picking your nose and then picking open your skin . . . all things little kids like to do! Religious hand-washing with plain old soap and water is also important. For athletes, it's important to shower after exercising and to use your own towels, razors, and athletic equipment.

If someone in your house already has an MRSA infection, make sure wounds are covered. And everyone can bathe with antiseptic soap

infections: skin

INFECTIONS

? ?

(chlorhexidine) to keep MRSA from spreading through the household.

We are glad the cable news networks succeeded in improving public awareness of MRSA. But we give the media a D- for not appreciating the difference between types of MRSA infections—and, as a result, scaring the heck out of everyone.

FYI: Not all skin infections (cellulitis) are caused by MRSA, but those are the most annoying ones to treat.

Q. What does impetigo look like? I know it is very contagious.

Disease: Impetigo is another skin infection caused by either Staph or Strep bacteria. These bugs normally live with you *on* the skin, but they get *under* the skin of an open wound (raw nostrils, bug bites, burns) and cause infection.

Symptoms? Impetigo looks red with a golden, crusty, weeping discharge over it.

Contagious? Spread by direct contact with wound.

Incubation? Seven to ten days.

Diagnosis? Based on physical exam. Wound culture can be done.

Treatment? Topical antibiotics, or oral antibiotics if severe.

Return to school? After 24 hours on medication.

Parent 411

Did you know that untreated Strep impetigo can sometimes cause kidney disease (*glomerulonephritis*)? We mention this not to scare you . . . but take impetigo seriously!

Q. Are there any other rashes that are related to certain infectious diseases?

Yes. Back by popular demand, it's our famous Rash-O-Rama chart from *Baby 411*! (It starts on page 328). If you go to our website at Toddler411. com (click on Bonus Material), you can see pictures of many of these rashes! The bottom line: many childhood rashes are caused by infections. However, many of them do not require any treatment to go away.

Doctors call the rashes caused by viruses *viral exanthems*. There are several classic viruses that are diagnosed by the unique rash they create. The two that we'll expand on are *roseola* and *parvovirus* (also known as Slapped Cheek or Erythema Infectiosum).

Roseola

Age 1

Disease: Roseola is caused by Herpes virus 6—if you are over age one, you've had this one! Because it is a herpes virus, it stays with us forever and we constantly shed it in our saliva and respiratory droplets. A mother's antibodies protect a baby until she is about a year old. When the immunity wanes, a child will get the infection.

Symptoms? Fever over 102 for about four days with no other symptoms. When the fever breaks, a rash appears. The rash can be subtle or dramatic. It's red, blotchy, not itchy, and flat with some raised areas on the chest, back, and arms. It goes away within hours to days.

Continued on page 330

IT'S TIME TO PLAY GERM JEOPARDY!

Alex, let's do the category "Things That Make You Itch."

◆ *For $400, the answer is, "There's a fungus among us."*
Alex, what is **Ringworm**?

Contrary to the name, ringworm is caused by a fungus and not a worm. But the shape of the skin lesion is ring-like. Look for raised red dots in a circle with an overlying scale. Ringworm on the skin can be treated with topical anti-fungal cream. Ringworm of the scalp requires medication by mouth. Kids can go to school once they get treated for a day.

◆ *For $800, the answer is, "These mite-y small creatures like to bug us."*
Alex, what is **Scabies**?

Scabies are caused by little mites that burrow into our skin and lay eggs. A female mite lays 200 eggs in eight weeks. When the eggs hatch, the babies burrow into our skin and start eating. This is the itchiest rash, ever! Even after treatment, people are itchy for weeks.

The mites prefer to live between fingers, elbow creases, armpits, belly buttons, and genitals. In kids under two, they like the neck, palms, and soles. You will see streaks (burrows) that are red and bleeding from the itching.

This one is fun for the whole family, so everyone should be treated with a prescription scabicide.

◆ *For $1200, the answer is, "I'm feeling louse-y today."*
Alex, what are **Head Lice**?

The human louse feeds on our hair. Lice travel from one head to the next by crawling, so it's helpful to them if people share combs, hair-brushes, and hats. Lice prefer Caucasian hair texture.

Adult lice are brown and visible to the naked eye, but they move quickly. Lice are more often diagnosed when the white nits (empty eggshells) are found. Nits stick firmly to the hair shaft close to the scalp. Kids with head lice usually have itchy scalps, especially behind the ears and back of the neck.

Over the counter shampoo treatments like Nix may or may not work. Lice are clever and increasingly resistant. See Appendix A, Medications for more treatment ideas.

Although many schools have no-nit policies, kids should be able to go to school once they have been treated.

◆ *For $1600, the answer is, "I have an itchy bottom."*
Alex, what are **Pinworms**?

Yes, you've hit the daily double on this one. If your child complains at night of an itchy hiney, pull out your flashlight and see if you find some little white pinworms coming out of his anus. The mommy worms come out at night to lay their eggs.

Pinworms spread when one worm-ridden child scratches his bottom and spreads the worm eggs elsewhere (such as a sandbox). The next child plays in the sandbox and then puts her hands into her mouth. It also spreads through households.

When one child is infected, household members can be treated with an anti-worm medication.

? ?

RASH-O-RAMA: COMMON RASHES SEEN WITH

Viral exanthems: (rashes caused by viruses)

	Rash looks like	Where?
Chickenpox	fluid filled blisters come up in crops	all over avg. 350 lesions
Shingles	fluid filled blisters	1 patch
Measles	red, raised pimply	face to body
German measles	red, raised	face to body
Roseola	FLAT red ovals/ lace	chest, arms, neck, +/- face
Parvovirus (Fifth disease)	"slapped cheeks" Flat, red, lacy on body	chest, arms, cheeks
Coxsackievirus (hand, foot, and mouth)	red dots or blisters	palms, soles, mouths +/- buttocks
Unilateral Latero-thoracic Exanthem	raised red bumps, scaly on top	one armpit
Pityriasis rosea	raised red streaks a little scaly	back, angled like a fir tree

Special viral rashes:

Herpetic Whitlow	blister, red around	thumb, finger
Molluscum Contagiosum	pinpoint blisters	anywhere

Bacterial infections:

Impetigo*	red, raised with weeping golden crust	anywhere
Scarlet fever* (usually over 2 yrs old)	red, sandpaper feel, rough raised dots	armpit, groin, neck, body
Meningitis*	petechiae (purple freckles)	spreads head to toe

Fungal infections:

Ringworm*	circle, red raised edge +/- overlying scale	anywhere
Yeast diaper rash*	raw meat red with surrounding pimples	diaper area

Tick borne illness:

Lyme Disease*	bullseye with bite in the center	bite site
Rocky Mountain Spotted Fever*	starts out flat, red then petechiae (purple freckles)	wrist, ankles palms, soles

Mites:

Scabies*	lines of red raised bumps (burrows) blisters in babies	head, neck, palms, soles, armpits, finger webs

Other:

Kawasaki Disease*	red cracked lips peeling skin on fingers flat/mildly raised red spots	lips, palms, soles of feet

Denotes an infection that needs treatment

INFECTIONS

INFECTIONS, HOW LONG THEY LAST AND MORE!

Duration	Other symptoms
1 week	fever, itchy
1 week	painful
1 week	fever, pink eye
3 days	swollen glands
1 day	high fever that breaks then rash appears
2-40 days	mildly itchy, joint pains
1 week	fever, sore throat with ulcers
4-6 weeks	mildly itchy
6 weeks	mildly itchy
1 week	very painful
1-2 years	
gets worse until treated	very itchy
3-4 days	sore throat, fever
hours	fever, irritability, light sensitivity
gets worse until treated	very itchy
gets worse until treated	itchy
enlarging diameter	fever, fatigue
1-6 days	fever, vomiting irritability light sensitivity
worse until treated	**ITCHIEST RASH EVER!**
Over five days	fever for more than 5 days pink eye swollen lymph nodes in neck

infections: skin

Contagious? The whole world is contagious.

Incubation? Ten days.

Diagnosis? An index of suspicion. A happy feverish one year old with no other symptoms is a clue. Diagnosis is confirmed when the fever breaks and the rash arrives.

Treatment? Fever relief.

Return to school? When the child feels well. The diagnosis is usually made after the rash appears and the child is fever free.

Parvovirus

Disease: This is a virus that occurs more in school aged children.

Symptoms? Often kids have no symptoms while they are contagious. Occasionally, there is a fever, bodyache, or headache. Ten days after the infection is gone, a rash shows up. The cheeks are bright red, as if someone slapped them . . . plus a lacy, flat red rash on the chest, arms, and legs. The rash can last several weeks.

Contagious? Spread by respiratory droplets, blood products. Child is contagious before the rash erupts, not after.

Incubation? Four to 21 days.

Diagnosis? Easy, once the rash has erupted. Antibody levels in blood can be checked.

Treatment? None.

Return to school? When child is fever free. The rash is not contagious.

Q. My child has lost a patch of hair. What is the problem?

Disease? It may be ringworm of the scalp *(tinea capitis)*. This fungus prefers African American hair texture.

Symptoms? Look for a patch of hair loss with overlying scale, or dots of hair loss with stubs of broken hair. Occasionally a big ugly pus pocket will form in the scalp too.

Contagious? By direct contact and infected combs, brushes, and hair accessories.

Incubation? Unknown.

Diagnosis? Based on physical exam. A confirmatory culture takes two to three weeks to grow.

Treatment? Oral anti-fungal medication for one month (or more). An anti-fungal shampoo (like Nizoral AD) is also a good idea.

Return to school? Once treatment begins.

Q. My child has warts. What should I do? Are warts contagious?

It's true, warts are contagious. They are spread by skin-to-skin contact, especially in areas where the skin may be broken. Warts are caused by a virus that lives for a couple of years. If left alone, they go away . . . eventually.

Most people are less patient than the virus' lifespan and want to do something to get rid of them. Here is one method: buy some duct tape. No kidding. A recent study showed that smothering the warts suppresses the growth of the virus that causes them. Apply a new piece of duct tape to the wart nightly and leave on for the day. It takes about six weeks.

Alternatively, you can try treating warts (especially ones on the feet) by doing a nightly routine recommended by one of our favorite dermatologists, Dr. Jason Reichenberg:

Soak the body part with the wart in warm water for 10–20 minutes, file down the dead skin with either a nail file or a PedEgg (it looks like a miniature cheese grater and you can buy it at Bed Bath and Beyond for about $10), apply an over-the-counter salicylic acid product (like Compound W or Duofilm), and cover it with a Band-Aid or duct tape. Your doctor can give you a prescription medication to add to the process to help speed things along. Repeat every night for four to six weeks.

Warts can also be frozen off by using liquid nitrogen in a doctor's office. This is not the most popular choice among kids because it really hurts.

And with any of these therapies, warts can return.

Bottom line: no wart remedy works well or quickly. Be patient.

Q. My child has mini-warts. What are they?

These are called *molluscum contagiosum* (see Toddler411.com for a picture) and they are also due to a virus. Yep, they are also contagious.

They are spread by skin-to-skin contact and scratching and picking. (Gee, I wonder why preschoolers get them all over their bodies!) Molluscum seem to spread easily in bathtub water and in swimming pools. If you have one child with this problem, do not bathe siblings together. About 40% of kids with molluscum have a brother or sister with molluscum. And kids with eczema have more trouble with molluscum because their tendency to itch/scratch enables the molluscum to spread.

Like warts, molluscum eventually goes away (about six months to up to four years). If they are driving you or your child crazy, there are a few ways to treat them:

◆ **Treat the itch**. Kids tend to scratch these lesions, which causes more lesions to crop up. You can give your child an antihistamine like diphenhydramine (Benadryl) or cetirizine (Zyrtec) to cut down on the itchiness. Some dermatologists also recommend using prescription steroid cream to relieve the temptation to scratch (but this isn't approved by the FDA).

◆ **Destroy them.** Dermatologists can kill the molluscum virus with a blistering solution, freeze them off, or pop them with a curette. For all of these treatments, the child must be squirm-free during the procedure (a challenge, we know). Some treatments are painful. And it may take several treatments to get rid of them.

◆ **Immune boost.** A prescription cream, called imiquimod (Aldara), can be applied three times a week (for several weeks). It sends the body's white blood cells to attack the molluscum. This has about a 50% success rate. For kids who have eczema and molluscum, an oral prescription medication called cimetidine (used for several months) can help boost the body's immune response to the molluscum.

◆ **Home remedies.** Some parents will try poking the molluscum open with paperclips or by repeatedly applying tape to open the lesions. In most cases, this doesn't work. Other home remedies include Vitamin A/lactic acid/salicylic acid/herbal solution skin treatments, which can be ordered online. These aren't terribly helpful either and may cause significant skin irritation.[10]

7. Urinary Tract infections

See Chapter 12, Hygiene for more info on urinary tract infections.

8. Other infections

- ◆ *Viral meningitis*
- ◆ *Bacterial meningitis*
- ◆ *Sepsis*
- ◆ *West Nile virus*

Q. What are the signs of meningitis?

Disease: Meningitis is an inflammation of the tissues that cover the brain. This can be caused by a virus, bacteria, or fungus. Viral meningitis occurs mostly in the summer and fall and usually resolves without any significant long-term consequences. Bacterial meningitis is a medical emergency, which even if treated immediately, may be devastating. Fortunately, vaccines protect against the top two bacteria that cause meningitis in young children (Strep pneumoniae, and H. Influenzae), and a third vaccine protects against bacterial meningitis (Neisseria) in older kids and teens.
Symptoms?
Viral: Rapid onset of fever, headache, neck stiffness, nausea, vomiting, light bothers eyes.
Bacterial: All of the above with or without irritability, lethargy, coma, seizures, petechiae (see rashes in Chapter 19, First Aid).
Contagious? Yes. It varies with the bug, but generally spread through direct contact or respiratory droplets, infected poop.
Incubation? Varies with the bug.
Diagnosis? Examination of spinal fluid, spinal fluid culture, blood work.
Treatment? Some anti-viral medications available, IV antibiotics, hospitalization.
Return to school? When child is fever free and feels better.

Dr B's At-Home Meningitis Test
If you are worried your child might have meningitis, try this maneuver at home. Have your child stand up. Ask him to lift his head up and look at the light. Then, ask him to look down at his toes. If he can move his head in both directions and is not bothered by the light, he probably does not have meningitis.

INFECTIONS

Parent 411: When someone in your child's school is diagnosed with meningitis

My office gets a flurry of phone calls every time a child in school is diagnosed with meningitis. Understandably, everyone wants to protect his own child from getting it. Here are the first two questions doctors will ask:

◆ Has the health department been notified? If the answer is yes, officials should be making recommendations for preventative measures.

◆ Does the child with meningitis have a definitive infection? If so, what is it? Most of the time, the diagnosis is viral meningitis and there is nothing to do but watch and wait.

Pediatricians can provide preventive treatment for meningitis only in these circumstances:

◆ Kids under age four who are exposed to a person with H. influenzae meningitis.

◆ Kids exposed to a person with Neisseria meningitis.

Q. My child has a high fever but no other symptoms. The doctor did a blood culture and treated him with antibiotics, just in case. Why are we doing this?

It's not out of fear of malpractice. Young children can have a bacterial infection in the bloodstream (*sepsis*) that initially causes a high fever with no localizing symptoms. One of the only ways doctors know this is going on is by looking at the white blood cell (WBC) count in the bloodstream. The normal range is about 4,000-10,000. If the white blood cell count is over 15,000, chances are greater that a bacteria is involved.

While viruses are the culprit of most illnesses, the odds an infection is BACTERIAL go up as the WBC count rises.

So here is a typical plan for a child under age three who looks sick, does not have any obvious source of infection, and has an elevated WBC count: get a blood culture to look for bacteria and give an antibiotic shot (as a precaution) until the culture is proven bug-free in 48 hours.

The most classic bacterial bloodstream infection is Strep pneumoniae. Now that a vaccine for this has been around for a while, this scenario is much less common.

Q. Is West Nile Virus really anything to worry about?

Well, you shouldn't obsess over this . . . but we would recommend using insect repellent.

Disease: West Nile Virus is a virus that causes encephalitis (brain inflammation) and meningitis, mostly in the summer and early fall.

Symptoms? Vary from none to severe. About 20% of infected people do not have symptoms. Others have fever, bodyache, arthritis, headache, eye pain, loss of appetite, rash, vomiting, diarrhea. Neurological symptoms occur more often in adults. As you've probably seen in the news, West Nile Virus has killed some victims and perma-

infections

nently disabled others. Most deaths have been in adults.

Contagious? Spread by mosquito bites, blood products, breast milk, organ transplants, and in newborns across the placenta.

Incubation? Five to 15 days.

Diagnosis? Spinal fluid, blood antibody test.

Treatment? Supportive care.[11]

Infections are just part of the fun of being a toddler—our discussion of how kids get sick continues with the next chapter on disease like allergies, diabetes, hearing problems and more.

COMMON DISEASES

Chapter 17

"The law of heredity is that all undesirable traits come from the other parent."
~ Anonymous

WHAT'S IN THIS CHAPTER

The magical mystery tour of toddler illness continues in this chapter . . . and now, diseases.

Here we will focus on the most common diseases that occur between ages one and four. These are illnesses NOT caused by infections (those bugs get their own chapter, Chapter 16). And these aren't common first aid situations or emergencies, which get their own special treatment in Chapter 19.

We know this is a big chapter, so check the index in case you can't find what you are looking for. Like the last chapter, we've divided this discussion by which part of the body these diseases impact.

Allergies

◆ *Allergic rhinitis (hay fever)*
◆ *Eczema/atopic dermatitis*
◆ *Food*
◆ *Insects*

Allergic disorders, in a nutshell, are a body's hypersensitivity after being exposed to certain foreign substances. These hypersensitivities may be limited to a certain body part or may result in a total body response. Examples of limited body response: **ECZEMA** (see Toddler411.com for a picture) is an allergic skin disorder and **ALLERGIC RHINITIS** ("hay fever") is an allergic nose disorder. An example of total body response: **ANAPHYLACTIC**

REACTION is a life-threatening reaction to a food allergy.

Kids who suffer from allergies may have a single or multiple problems. For example, some toddlers have a food allergy . . . but are not allergic to dogs. Other people may be unlucky enough to have eczema, allergic rhinitis, and asthma. Those with this unholy trinity get a special designation—it is called **ATOPY**.

As you might guess, allergic disorders may be hereditary. And identifying one allergy makes doctors more suspicious that you'll see additional allergic problems down the road. For instance, a baby who has eczema has a 30% chance of developing asthma or allergic rhinitis.[1]

Q. My spouse and I both have allergies. What are the odds that our child will also have this problem?

Fifty-fifty. For each parent who has allergies, a child has a 25% chance of developing allergies too. We are not only referring to that runny nose every time the pollen count rises, but asthma, eczema, and even some food allergies.

Allergic kids start off with eczema and food allergies as infants. Asthma is usually diagnosed after a year of age. Seasonal allergies show up even later.

Parent 411 : Allergies & Heredity

Hereditary patterns of allergies do not apply to drug allergies. So, even if you have an allergy to Penicillin, it is perfectly fine for your child to take this medication. As with any new medication, it's wise to watch for adverse reactions. But just because you're allergic to drug XYZ, that doesn't mean your child will be.

FYI: Allergies to latex (found in gloves and balloons) is an emerging problem. The next time you have a birthday party, choose mylar balloons instead!

Q. I think my child is allergic to everything! Is there a test for that?

Your child probably has **ATOPY** or atopic disease. While there are skin and blood tests (serum IgE levels, blood eosinophil levels; see Chapter 11, Food Tricks & Treats and below for details) to confirm it, the diagnosis of atopy can be made by simply adding up the child's symptoms.

Specific testing can be done to identify the most likely suspects that are triggering allergies.

Q. When can my child get allergy tested?

Before we talk about any testing, the question your pediatrician should ask herself is, "Will a test result change what I do to manage this patient?" If the answer is yes, the test is worthwhile. If the answer is no, why bother?

That said, your child can get allergy tested at any age, but certain tests are more helpful at certain ages for certain problems.

For food allergies and eczema, a CAP-RAST blood test can help detect certain food(s) that may be causing an allergic response. Testing can be done as early as six months of age. Blood tests are specific, meaning a positive result on the test is fairly accurate in detecting an allergy. However, CAP-RAST tests are less sensitive than skin testing (that means a negative

? ?

DISEASES

test does not rule out an allergy). Key point: the most accurate test of a food allergy is to do a food challenge. That is, give the child a small amount of the food in question and see what happens. (This should be done at the allergist's office or a hospital—not at home!)

Skin testing can be performed to further identify a food allergy as a child gets older (see below for specifics). This is important since some food allergies can be potentially fatal.

For seasonal and year round allergic rhinitis ("hay fever"), skin testing is the preferred way to detect allergies to certain pollens. In my experience, many allergists hold off on skin testing for this disorder until a child is at least four or five years of age. Why? For starters, most kids do not have seasonal allergies until this age. They are also not candidates for "allergy shots" even if the specific allergens are identified. So most kids get treated with medications and preventative measures to reduce exposures. They only get tested if these measures are not effective.

For insect bite/sting allergies, skin testing is very effective. And kids who have severe allergic reactions to certain bug bites/stings are candidates for allergy shots.

Here is a list of the common allergy tests available:

- ◆ **Skin prick test:** A small scratch is made in the skin and a drop of allergen is placed in it. People who are allergic will produce a chemical called histamine and form a local allergic response (a swollen, red area that looks like a mosquito bite) within about 15 minutes.

- ◆ **Intradermal test**: An allergen is injected just under the skin to detect an allergic response. This is more sensitive than the prick test.

- ◆ **CAP-RAST test:** Blood test detects an elevation of the body's IgE antibodies (an allergic chemical response) to certain allergens—particularly good for food allergy testing.

FYI: board-certified allergists consider IgE testing as the gold-standard of allergy tests. Alternative practitioners may use very non-specific (and not very accurate) IgG testing and discover 100 or more things that come up positive. We recommend steering clear of any lab that offers IgG testing.

Allergic rhinitis (a.k.a. Hay fever)

Q. My toddler has a constant runny nose. Does he have allergies?

Probably not. If you are betting in Vegas for the cause of a toddler's runny nose, viral infections win hands down. We'll give you the skinny on upper respiratory infections in the Chapter 16, Common Infections, but suffice it to say that toddlers will have about 60 to 80 days of runny noses a year due to viruses.

However, some children do have chronic runny noses for reasons besides infection. Allergic rhinitis is the $10 term for runny nose due to allergies. Chronic swelling of the adenoid tissue is another reason (see the Ear-Nose-Throat section of this chapter for details).

Allergies to certain particles in the air can irritate the nose (and lungs) of some children. Year round allergies are called *perennial allergies*. Allergies to particles that show up at certain times of year are termed *seasonal allergies*.

diseases: allergies

Here's how we divide these up:

◆ *Perennial allergies*: Year-round allergies caused by something a child is exposed to on a daily basis. This is usually something inside your house. The most common causes are dust mites, cockroaches, and animal dander. Molds are found both inside and outside the house all-year round. See the end of this chapter for more info on controlling household allergens.

◆ *Seasonal allergies*: These are allergies caused by something in the air during certain times of the year. These include weeds, trees, grasses, and molds. You may be able to figure out the trigger based on the time of year that symptoms reoccur. Most allergic kids develop seasonal allergies over time. The peak age for seasonal allergies is school age and young adulthood. (Again, we emphasize that a two-year old is less likely than an eight-year old to have seasonal allergies as the cause of his runny nose.)

So how do you tell the difference between an allergic runny nose and the common cold? Here's a table to compare symptoms:

	COMMON COLD	**ALLERGIES**
Snot	thick, clear, white or discolored	watery, clear
Cough	dry or wet	dry
Eyes	no problem	can be itchy, watery
Nose	snotty	itchy
Throat	sore	scratchy
Fever	some or none	none

To summarize, a kid with allergies tends to have itchy and watery nose and eyes. And contrary to the term "hay *fever*," people with allergies do not run a fever. Worn down and achy, yes, but fever, no. If your child is running a fever with a snotty nose, you can assume it is an infection and not just allergies.

How can doctors tell if a child has allergies? Here are some classic clues:

◆ The *Allergic salute* is a horizontal line along the nose due to a child constantly pushing the tip of his nose upwards to wipe the snot.

◆ *Allergic shiners* are dark, puffy circles under the eyes due to chronically irritated and swollen blood vessels.

◆ *Cobblestoning*, a bumpy appearance to the back of the throat, is from chronic postnasal drip.

Occasionally, the nostrils will have a bluish, boggy appearance but this is not as common as the other findings.

FYI: Hay fever refers to ragweed allergy in the fall. Cedar fever refers to juniper allergy in the winter. If you want to know what pollen is going around your town, check out the National Allergy Bureau's website at Aaaai.org.

Helpful Hints

1. Perennial and seasonal allergies can be a trigger for asthma. It's wise to see an allergist if your child's asthma is not under good control.

2. Allergies may be a set up for a sinus infection. If your child's chronically clear snot is now green, or he has a fever or headache, see your doctor.

Eczema

We first discussed eczema in Chapter 12, Hygiene; here is a more in-depth look at this issue.

Q. What is eczema?

Eczema or "atopic dermatitis" refers to chronically irritated skin thanks to allergies. It varies in severity by the extent of the irritation and the percentage of skin that is affected. The skin looks red, with overlying scaling, crusting, and sometimes even weeping (see Toddler411.com, Bonus Material for a picture). The rash appears in different places depending on the age of the child. Younger kids tend to get it on their elbows, knees, and face. Older kids get it in their elbow and knee creases. Because eczema is an allergic disorder, doctors can't make it just go away. Fortunately, about 70% of kids outgrow it. The chances are lower if your child develops eczema outside of infancy.

As we discuss in Chapter 12, Hygiene, eczema flares up with dry skin. Perfumes, dyes, and detergents can worsen symptoms. And sometimes, food allergies can be the culprit.

Q. How is eczema treated?

Moisturize, moisturize, moisturize. Lube your child up as much as possible on a daily basis (especially right after bathing). It's best to use a thick, greasy, perfume and dye-free cream as opposed to lotions. Our favorites: Eucerin, Cetaphil, Cerave, Aquaphor, or Vaseline Creamy Formula.

Besides keeping your child's skin as moist as possible and avoiding triggers, a daily dose of "good germs" may also help. The bacteria found naturally in yogurt (lactobacillus) has been found to reduce the severity in some kids with eczema. But kids need a larger dose of germs than what is found in yogurt for it to be effective. You can give your child lactobacillus or "probiotics" as a dietary supplement. See Appendix A, Medications, for details.[2]

The gold standard of treatment is steroid cream/ointment. We know the word *steroid* scares the heck out of people, but topical steroids are very effective anti-inflammatory medications that reduce skin irritation. Long-term use (for months or years) with high potency products can cause unwanted side effects (we'll discuss this in Appendix A, Medications).

That's why it is best to use the *lowest* potency possible for the *shortest* length of time. Doctors may use higher strength products to get eczema under control and then taper down quickly. Ointments work best, followed by creams and lotions. High potency steroids should not be used on the face. And always use the product as prescribed. More is not better.

The alternative to steroids is a class of products called immunoregulators, an alternative to steroids. They are sold under the names Elidel and Protopic. Both of these drug creams are approved by the FDA for use in kids over the age of two. It appears that they are a safe alternative for

diseases: allergies

DISEASES

? ?

eczema treatment if steroids are not working or not desired. And these products are particularly good for the face—where higher potency steroid products can thin the skin.

One side note on immunoregulators: the FDA requires a "black box" warning on their labels as these drugs might be linked to an increased risk of skin cancer and lymphoma. However, most data is reassuring about these drugs.

The newest addition to the eczema regimen: prescription essential fatty acid creams that replenish the skin's top layer. Brand names are Mimyx and Atopiclair (see Appendix A for details). Epiceram is another new prescription skin barrier emulsion cream.

Like other allergic disorders, eczema is itchy. Try to keep your child from scratching or picking. It's a good idea to keep your child's nails short. Some children may also benefit from a sedating antihistamine at bedtime to keep them from scratching when you aren't looking.

Parent 4 1 1: Eczema & Skin Infections
Kids whose skin is irritated by eczema may be prone to bacterial and viral skin infections. Contact your doctor if you see drainage, weeping, or pustules. Sometimes antibiotics will be needed to get an eczema flare-up under control. A rare and unpleasant complication of eczema is *Eczema Herpeticum*, where a herpes infection can invade a site of eczema.

Food allergy

Q. My child has a food allergy. Will he outgrow it?

It depends on the food and the age your child developed the allergy. (See Chapter 11, Food Tricks & Treats for more info on food allergies).

The most common food allergies in childhood are ones that kids ultimately outgrow. Milk, soy, wheat, and egg allergies are usually identified in the first three years of life and are outgrown by five years of age. That's the good news.

The top food allergies in adulthood are peanuts, tree nuts, seafood, and shellfish. So, if your child is allergic to one of these players, it is less likely he will outgrow the problem.

If your child has a known food allergy, he can be tested annually with a blood test called CAP-RAST (see Chapter 11, Food Tricks & Treats for details) to see if his allergic response is waning. Recent research suggests that this is particularly true for tree nut allergies.[3] If test results look reassuring, he can have a food challenge in a medical setting to see if he has truly outgrown his food allergy.

Insect Allergy

Q. My child had an allergic reaction to a bee sting. How worried should I be about future bee stings?

Allergic reactions to bug bites or stings can range from a mild local irritation to a full blown **ANAPHYLACTIC REACTION**. Fortunately, most kids get some redness, itching, and swelling around the area that goes away on its own. So if your child had a minor reaction, you don't have to worry too much. Just have an antihistamine on hand in your medicine cabinet.

If your child experiences hives, severe swelling of the area, tongue swelling, dizziness, or difficulty breathing with an insect bite/sting, he needs immediate medical attention. You'll need an Epi-Pen in your medicine cabinet in case of future stings. (For more on Epi-Pens, see Appendix A, Medications). An appointment with an allergist for testing, education, and treatment is also in order.

Allergy "shots" (official term: immunotherapy) are a very effective way to desensitize a person who is severely allergic to bees, hornets, yellow jackets, wasps, and fire ants. However, it is very labor intensive—it may take up to five years of frequent injections to work. But it is worth it if the alternative is a life-threatening reaction to an insect sting. And most kids do not outgrow severe insect allergies.[4]

Reality Check: History repeats itself
According to Dr. Edward Peters, board certified allergist, immunologist, and pulmonologist, history repeats itself when it comes to allergic reactions. So if your child gets hives from a bee sting the first time, he probably will get hives (and not an anaphylactic reaction) the next time.

Blood

♦ *Anemia*
♦ *Lead exposure*
♦ *Sickle cell disease*

Q. What is anemia?

Let's start with a lesson about red blood cells first. Red blood cells carry oxygen to our body tissues and remove carbon dioxide. Hemoglobin is the name of the protein that performs this function in each red blood cell. And the building block of hemoglobin is iron.

Anemia basically means that there are not enough red blood cells circulating in the bloodstream. The causes of anemia are either excessive destruction or inadequate production of red blood cells. The top cause of childhood anemia is iron deficiency. Kids who are severely anemic are pale and fatigue easily. But anemia sometimes presents with odd symptoms like breath-holding or poor school performance.

Examples of excessive destruction of red blood cells include:
♦ More blood being lost than made (example: menstruating women)
♦ Abnormal red blood cells are made and then destroyed (for example, sickle cell disease)

Examples of inadequate production of red blood cells include:
♦ Poor nutritional intake of key ingredients (iron, B12, folate)
♦ Bone marrow production slows (for example, bone marrow suppression by a virus)
♦ Lead poisoning (the lead competes for the iron's binding site on the cell)

DISEASES

? ?

Q. My child has iron deficiency anemia. What do I need to do about it?

Improve your child's iron intake. In short: feed your child a diet high in iron (see Chapter 10, Nutrition for tips) and give her an iron supplement.

Although iron supplements are available over the counter, make sure you ask your doctor or pharmacist for the correct product. There is a difference between the maintenance dose of iron found in your typical multivitamin and a therapeutic dose needed for someone with iron deficiency. See Appendix A, Medications for details.

Once your child has been on Popeye's diet and iron supplements for three months, your doctor can re-check her blood count.

Helpful Hints: Iron Supplements

Iron supplements taste bad. The brand name products taste a little better, like Icar and Feostat brands. Some tips:

◆ You can mix the medicine in juice. Just make sure your child drinks all of it. Vitamin C helps the iron get absorbed into the bloodstream, so orange juice is a good mix-in.

◆ DO NOT MIX WITH MILK. The calcium in milk competes with iron and blocks absorption.

◆ Iron can cause a temporary gray/brown stain on the teeth. Use baking soda on a toothbrush to remove it.

◆ Iron can make poop look black. Don't worry—that's not blood.

Q. We live in an old house. I am worried about lead exposure. How do I get my child tested?

Since lead exposure qualifies as an environmental health hazard, we've got detailed info on this over in Chapter 18, The Environment and Your Toddler. But what you need to know in this chapter is that lead exposure can cause anemia. So if your child is diagnosed with anemia and it's possible that your child has had a significant exposure to lead, be sure to ask your doctor to have a blood lead level drawn.

Q. My child has sickle cell disease. What should I worry about?

Sickle cell disease is caused by abnormal protein (hemoglobin) in red blood cells. This protein causes the red blood cell shape to be deformed. Instead of an oval shaped cell, these cells look like half moons (like the "sickle" on the old Soviet Union flag).

Sickle cells die more quickly, have trouble carrying oxygen, and clog up blood vessels. This blood vessel clogging kills the tissues that the blood vessel supplies (muscle, bones, spleen, lung, kidney, intestine).

The consequences in early childhood are the following:

1. **Chronic Anemia.** This is a lifelong problem. Folate supplements are given to promote red blood cell formation.
2. **Non-functional spleen.** The spleen filters red blood cells and white blood cells (infection fighters). Because the spleen is a filter,

it gets clogged up by the sickle cells and stops working. Without the spleen, children are prone to infection (particularly with Strep pneumoniae and H. influenzae bacteria). These kids need Prevnar 13 vaccine, flu vaccine, and the Pneumonia (pneumococcal) vaccine to protect them from serious infections. Kids under age five need a daily dose of the antibiotic Penicillin to prevent infections.

3. **Failure to thrive.** Because of a chronic lack of oxygen to the tissues, these children are shorter and smaller than their peers.

4. **Pain crises.** Children and adults experience severe pain in the arms, legs, chest, and abdomen. This is the most common symptom in children over two years of age.

If your child has sickle cell disease, he should be seen regularly by his doctor. Any signs of infection or pain need to be addressed promptly.

Bones & Joints

- ◆ Nursemaid's elbow
- ◆ Intoeing
- ◆ Flat foot
- ◆ Toewalking

- ◆ Bowlegged
- ◆ Knockneed
- ◆ Arthritis/ JRA

Q. My daughter pulled away from me while I was holding her hand and now she won't use her arm. Is it broken?

Nope. It's a dislocated elbow, also known as **NURSEMAID'S ELBOW.** We'll discuss how docs fix this in Chapter 19, First Aid.

Q. My toddler is pigeon-toed. My doctor says not to worry, but my mother-in-law says to get corrective shoes. What should I do?

This is called **INTOEING** and the right answer is to wait it out. Corrective shoes were all the rage about 30 or 40 years ago. However, we have since learned that (most of the time) this is not a permanent problem . . . it will improve on its own, without any intervention.

When does intoeing become a concern? If your child turns five years of age and still turns his feet in or stumbles frequently, get evaluated by a bone specialist. If your child has pain, limping, or swelling—none of these things are found with plain old intoeing—then you need to see your doctor.[5]

Q. My child has flat feet. Does he need special shoe inserts?

Probably not. Yes, some toddlers lack a natural arch in the bones of the feet. Some flat feet are flexible (the arch is seen when standing on tip-toe) and some are rigid (always flat). Rigid flat feet may become painful in young adulthood. But placing an orthotic (shoe insert) into a toddler's shoes is not going to change the outcome. The American Academy of Pediatrics feels orthotics are not necessary for kids with flat feet.

Flat feet only need to be checked out by a doctor if a child is com-

DISEASES

? ?

plaining of pain or has difficulty walking. Otherwise, just buy shoes that have arch supports.

Q. My daughter always walks on her tip-toes. Should I worry?

No. Toddlers toe-walk because their Achilles tendon (which attaches the calf muscle to the heel bone) is short and tight. Ultimately, kids outgrow it.

When to check it out: if she cannot plant her whole foot on the ground or if it continues beyond two years of age, then consult with your pediatrician.

Note: Some children with autism spectrum disorders will toe-walk, but those kids have other symptoms accompanying the toe-walking. If toe-walking is the only issue going on with your child, it probably isn't due to autism.

Q. My toddler is bow-legged. Will he always walk like this?

No, it is a center of gravity thing. When toddlers first start walking, they bend their knees to support their body weight. Hence, you see the cowboy gait. As kids get older, they often go the opposite direction and look knock-kneed (see below). If your child is still significantly bow-legged by age two, he probably should have some x-rays done to look at the bones.

When to call your doctor: if one leg looks misshapen or both legs look severely deformed.

Q. My preschooler is knock-kneed. Is this a problem?

Nope. Preschoolers often appear knock-kneed and may continue to have this gait until age seven. When to check it out: if there is a severe deformity, asymmetry of the legs, or pain.

Q. My child complains of joint pain. Does he have arthritis?

By definition, arthritis is inflammation of a joint or joints ("arth" means joint, "itis" means inflammation). And inflammation causes *swelling*, *pain*, and sometimes *warmth* in the joint area. In most cases of kiddie joint pain, though, there is pain without swelling or warmth. That's called **ARTHRALGA** ("algia" is Latin for pain)—pain in the joint, but no inflammation. As you might guess, arthralgia is less serious than arthritis. (My husband chides me for taking Latin in high school, but it actually has come in handy. And the toga parties were pretty fun. But I digress.) Let's take a look at both problems:

Juvenile Arthritis (JRA or JIA) has several subtypes based on the number of joints involved and other accompanying symptoms. Some children will complain of pain, and others may limp. And there is one type of JRA where recurrent spiking fevers and an intermittent rash occur long before there is any joint pain. This type of arthritis can be tricky to diagnose in children. When to check it out: persistent complaints of pain in the hips/knees/ankles/wrists/elbows, joint swelling, finger swelling, limping, or unexplained fever. Physical examination, lab work, and imaging studies help identify the problem.

Arthralgia is more common and has many causes. Fortunately, most of the time the cause is not serious. Infections like parvovirus (also known as slapped cheek) cause joint pain for weeks after the illness—see Chapter 16, Common Infections for more on this. And **TRANSIENT SYNOVITIS** (inflamed

BEHIND THE SCENES: GROWING PAINS

Growing pains are really a misnomer. The child's growth has nothing to do with it. Leg pains (muscle cramps/aches) that occur in the evening or overnight, in both lower legs, without joint swelling may be due to flat feet, hypermobility syndrome (flexible joints) or rarely, restless leg syndrome (rls).

Traditionally, doctors have recommended dietary interventions to treat leg cramps. Although it is never a bad idea to give potassium, iron, and calcium-rich foods, these nutritious foods may not relieve the symptoms of all sufferers. Some kids find relief by doing calf and foot stretches before bedtime and wearing shoes with good arch support It's wise to check in with your doctor to figure out what is going on if the nightly pain is becoming a pain for everyone. And here are the red flags that should always be checked out:

- only one leg is consistently painful
- pain occurs in the joints, not the muscles
- pain interferes with activities of daily living
- pain is associated with swelling or redness
- pain occurs during the day and night
- fever

synovium—tissue that lines the joint space) is a benign condition that causes hip pain and a limp that goes away in a few days. More serious causes include bacterial infection, cancer, leukemia, and **Legg-Calve-Perthes Disease** (lack of blood flow to the bone). When to check it out: persistent pain, severe pain, RED and swollen joint, fever, or a limp. We'll talk more about limping in Chapter 19, First Aid.

FYI: Back pain is a rare complaint for the one to four year old age group. So if your toddler is complaining, it should be checked out.

Brain & Nerves

- *Seizures*
- *Headaches*

Q. My child had a seizure with a fever. Do I need to worry about brain damage?

You don't need to worry about brain damage, but you do need to be prepared for this to happen more than once.

Kids from six months to five years of age are prone to having a **Febrile Seizure** or convulsion as a fever is spiking. About 30% of kids who have a febrile seizure will have more than one. Yes, the first time is terrifying. It gets a little less scary after that. To reduce the likelihood of a febrile seizure in children prone to them, give fever medicine around the clock to keep the temperature from rising sharply. Children who seize on a regular basis may be candidates to have seizure control medicine in the house (diazepam rec-

DISEASES

? ?

tal gel). However, most febrile seizures are so short that the seizure stops before you have time to get the medicine out of your first aid kit.

With a first time febrile seizure, children should be evaluated thoroughly by a pediatrician. Once this diagnosis is made, evaluation and treatment focuses on the cause of the fever. Febrile seizures do not cause brain damage. However, there is a small risk of having a seizure disorder (*Epilepsy*) later in life.

Q. My child had a seizure without a fever. Will he have this problem his whole life?

It's hard to predict whether this is a one-time event or a recurrent disorder called epilepsy. If there is a particular reason for the seizure—like infection or trauma, then odds are good that it will only happen once. But if no cause is found, there is a 24% chance of having another seizure within a year.[6]

By definition, a seizure is a result of brain nerves that are firing off abnormally. It can last a few seconds or several minutes. And the result can vary from momentary lip smacking to complete body jerking. Epilepsy is the term used for recurrent seizures.

For a first time event, some doctors prefer to observe a child for further problems. Others will order an EEG (Electroencephalogram) and brain imaging (MRI) to confirm the diagnosis of a seizure and rule out other causes such as brain trauma or tumors. Additional testing may be done if there are other medical issues with the patient. Treatment with anticonvulsant medication is typically started only after more than one seizure occurs.

Q. My child complains of headaches occasionally. Should I get it checked out?

As a general rule, headaches should always be checked out—especially in toddler and preschool aged children since it is a rare complaint.

Young children have difficulty localizing pain, so a "headache" may actually mean ear pain, throat pain, or tooth pain. Common causes of headache in this age group include: infection (ear, throat, sinus), trauma, cavities, or even tooth grinding.

A rare cause of headaches is increased intracranial pressure (ICP). Translation: too much pressure inside the skull due to a tumor, head injury, or clogged cerebral spinal fluid. Kids with increased ICP will wake up at night or the early morning with a headache, vomit occasionally, have a rapidly increasing head circumference (with a bulging soft spot if still open), have worsening headache with coughing, and may develop problems moving their eyes symmetrically.

We know every parent's first concern with headaches is the fear of a brain tumor. While rare, it is certainly one thing we all want to rule out. A physical examination, looking especially at the eyes and nervous system assesses for this concern. But if there is any uncertainty, imaging studies can be ordered.

Although children can get migraines, it is uncommon in this age group. Preschoolers who develop migraines later in life may have motion sickness (like in the backseat of your car) or "abdominal migraines."

Parent 411: Scary Headaches
Another scary headache is one associated with fever, neck stiffness, and light sensitivity. This is not your "occasional" headache. It's

meningitis until proven otherwise. Get your child to a hospital immediately.

Cancer

◆ *Leukemia*   ◆ *Solid tumors*

Q. I know I am a nervous parent, but how will I know if my child has leukemia?

In leukemia, the body produces abnormal blood cells that interfere with the bone marrow's ability to produce normal blood cells (white, red, and platelets). Because the body lacks these necessary cells, there are tell-tale symptoms.

The typical symptoms include: unexplained fever, fatigue, paleness of the skin, excessive bruising or bleeding, **petechiae** (see Chapter 19, First Aid for details and Toddler411.com for a picture), swollen glands, and joint pain. A complete blood count will detect the abnormalities in the red, white, and platelet counts.

Leukemia is not a problem you can miss. You might not know what is wrong with your child, but your toddler would look ill and your instincts would tell you to seek medical attention.

Acute leukemia (ALL) occurs most commonly in the two to three year old age group and the incidence is about 2.8 in 100,000 in the U.S.[7] The good news: leukemia has a high cure rate. Some forms of ALL have an 80% five-year survival rate.[8]

Q. What other cancers do children get? And what should I be looking out for?

In general, worrisome symptoms that should always be evaluated include: weight loss, lack of appetite, unexplained fever, fatigue, excessive bruising or bleeding, bone pain, limp, back pain, and masses.

Here is the list of the most common pediatric malignancies and what to be on the look out for:

MALIGNANCY	SIGNS/SYMPTOMS
Leukemia	Limp, bruising, petechiae, bone pain, fatigue
Lymphoma	Night sweats, intense itching, back pain, respiratory problems, vomiting blood
Wilm's tumor	Abdominal fullness/mass felt, blood in urine
Neuroblastoma	Vomiting, diarrhea, limp, bruising around eyes, respiratory problems, dancing eyes and feet (opsoclonus-myoclonus), dropping eyelid and constricted pupil, head/neck/chest/or abdominal mass
Brain tumor	Irritability, headache, vomiting, seizure, eye movement asymmetry, vision changes, eye bulging, shaky gait
Testicular tumor	Abdominal pain, mass/swelling in scrotum
Bone tumor	Limp, back pain, bone pain, fracture
Histiocytosis	Excessive urination, excessive drinking, ear drainage, unusual skin lesions, swollen glands, paleness, fatigue, back pain, bone pain
Retinoblastoma	Irregular pupils, "white" reflex instead of red reflex (similar to the red eye you see in a photo)[9]

???

WHAT'S THAT LUMP?

After going over the list of cancers, you will probably examine every lump or bump your child develops. Relax—most lumps are normal. Here is how to tell what is normal and what isn't.

Lymph nodes are generally found in the front of the neck, back of the neck, armpits, and groin. Their function is to respond to areas of the body that have inflammation or infection. And their location determines the region of the body where they work. Lymph nodes are lined up like a string of pearls and are quite small. But when they go to work, they swell to several times their normal size. The official term for swollen lymph nodes is reactive.

For instance, a simple bug bite can make a group of lymph nodes "react"—and it usually takes six to eight weeks for those reactive nodes to return to their normal size, so don't be too alarmed. Reactive nodes are rubbery and move about under your fingertips. Sometimes these nodes are tender to the touch.

Here are the worrisome lumps: firm, hard masses that are stuck and do not move under your fingertips. Rapidly growing lumps also need to be checked out.

FYI: Lymph nodes can themselves get infected in the process of fighting infection. This is called lymphadenitis and is discussed in Chapter 16, Common Infections.

Endocrine

- ◆ Diabetes
- ◆ Poor growth
- ◆ Cholesterol

Q. Diabetes runs in my family. When should my child be tested for it?

Your child can be tested at any time. But let's discuss what diabetes is first.

Diabetes mellitus is a chronic disease where the body fails to break down sugars. There are two types (Type 1 and Type 2). They are divided by the cause of the disorder and the treatment. Although both can be inherited diseases, Type 2 tends to run in families more often.

Here is a brief explanation of the malfunction:

Since a person with diabetes doesn't break down sugar properly, the sugar ends up in vast quantities in the bloodstream. The body tries to eliminate the sugar by filtering it through the kidneys and into the urine. The sugar pulls excessive amounts of water with it into the urine. The result?

- ◆ Elevated blood sugar level.
- ◆ Excessive urination (with sugar found in the urine).
- ◆ Excessive thirst to keep up with fluid loss in the urine.
- ◆ Weight loss (from poor metabolism and fluid losses).

Type 1 Diabetes is an autoimmune disease—that means the cells in the pancreas that make insulin get killed off by a person's own body. Insulin is the chemical in our body that controls blood levels of sugar.

There are some genetic defects associated with Type 1 diabetes, so it can be passed on to offspring. Treatment is life-long with insulin injections and dietary modifications. Onset of Type 1 diabetes is usually around school age (six to seven years old). It is rare to be diagnosed with diabetes when you are still in diapers.

Type 2 Diabetes is caused by the body's impaired response to insulin—this impairment is related to obesity. Type 2 Diabetes used to be an adult disease. Unfortunately, there is a virtual epidemic today of Type 2 Diabetes in pre-teens and teens. Children at risk are obese (defined as a Body Mass Index greater than 85%—see Chapter 9, Growth for details on the BMI) but this type of Diabetes can also be inherited. Treatment includes dietary modifications and oral medications. FYI: There is a higher risk of developing this disorder among African-Americans, Hispanics, and Native Americans.[10]

Children who are newly diagnosed with diabetes (especially kids under age five) may have additional symptoms caused by ***Diabetic Ketoacidosis***. They are quite ill with weight loss, dehydration, lethargy, deep breathing, and fruity breath.[11] Older kids have excessive thirst, urination, and weight loss.

The diagnosis is confirmed by having a fasting blood sugar of 126 mg/dl or more or a random blood sugar of 200 mg/dl or more. There is not a routine schedule for your child to be tested for diabetes when he is not showing any symptoms, but it is easily done at any time during a regular office visit.

For more information, check out this web site: diabetes.org.

Reality Check

Does your child have a constantly dirty looking neck? Have you scrubbed it raw and yet the brown area still remains? It might be something called ***Acanthosis Nigricans***. This discoloration can be associated with early insulin resistance (the precursor to Type 2 Diabetes). If you see this skin condition, your doctor should assess your child's blood sugar, insulin level, and urine.

Q. My child seems awfully short for his age. Would he benefit from hormone shots?

There are many reasons a toddler is short. Most short kids are short thanks to their parents. Others may be short because of a constitutional growth delay—where a child is just a late bloomer who gets his growth spurt later than his peers.

However, there is a subset of short children who actually have medical problems causing their height issues. Doctors become concerned for growth hormone deficiency, hypothyroidism, or other endocrine abnormalities in a child whose height curve starts to plateau without any good reason. Lab work, x-rays to determine "bone age," and even chromosome testing may be part of an evaluation.

If a child is really short or has growth hormone deficiency, he may be a candidate for hormone shots. However, the shots are expensive, labor intensive, and not without side effects.

Eyes

- ◆ Esotropia
- ◆ Color blind
- ◆ Refractive Errors
- ◆ Blocked tear ducts

Q. I think my child has a lazy eye. When should I get it checked out?

Now. Both eyes should be moving together. If you notice a difference in the eye movements, get a referral to an ophthalmologist. Eye doctors like to assess for *esotropia* (eye turning in) or *exotropia* (eye turning out) as soon as possible.

Frequently a child does not have a true lazy eye, but has a wide nasal bridge that gives the appearance of a lazy eye (**PSEUDOSTRABISMUS**). No treatment is required for this.

For a true lazy eye, patching the strong eye is the first line of treatment. Applying a paper patch, optical patch with glasses, or medication drops to blur the vision of the stronger eye forces the weaker eye to work harder. Surgery is also a treatment option if patching fails.

Q. My spouse and I both wear glasses. When should my child's vision be tested?

Your doctor will check your child's eyes at every visit, but formal vision screening is not performed until your child can cooperate (usually around age three or four). The recommendation from the American Academy of Pediatrics is to do formal screening as soon as it is feasible with the patient.

But if your child was born prematurely, has other medical problems, or has a family history of eye problems, she can visit a pediatric ophthalmologist to have an assessment that does not require her ability to read lines on a chart.

Q. My two year old cannot discriminate colors. Is he color blind?

Okay, this is really a trick question. Parents frequently panic when they hang out with precocious two year olds and then wonder why their own child doesn't know his colors yet. (Remember our discussion in Chapter 3, Milestones about how kids achieve milestones at different times.) Although some kids master color recognition by age two, doctors don't expect them to discriminate four colors until they are five years old.

If your five year old cannot discriminate colors, then there may be a problem. The most common color-blindness form is red-green, but yellow-blue, and complete color blindness also exist. Because this is a genetic disorder found on the X chromosome, males are affected more commonly than females. Your doctor can test your child in the office for this disorder.

Q. My one year old still gets blocked tear ducts. Shouldn't he be over this by now?

Yes. Blocked tear ducts are usually limited to infancy. As the child grows,

Age 1 the tear ducts expand and stop clogging. 90% of blocked tear ducts will clear up by six months of life. If your child continues to have blocked tear ducts by his first birthday, there is little chance he'll outgrow it . . . and you'll need to see an eye doctor.[12] The duct can be probed to open it up. This is a minor surgical procedure.

Ear, Nose & Throat

We have recruited Mark Brown, M.D. FACS, Ear, Nose, and Throat Surgeon extraordinaire to help us shed light on these topics. A former ENT professor at Johns Hopkins Hospital, and now in private practice, he is a terrific source of information. And since he is married to one of the authors, his price was right.

◆ *Tonsil/adenoid hypertrophy*   ◆ *Aphthous ulcers*
◆ *Geographic tongue*   ◆ *Hearing problems*
◆ *Mucoceles*

Q. My child never breathes through her nose. Why?

There probably is an obstruction somewhere. First, doctors check the nostrils and inside the nose. If all is clear, then the problem is likely with the *adenoid*, which sits behind the nose. (See illustration below).

The adenoid is a piece of lymph tissue (like a tonsil) that sits where the nose meets the throat (not a visible area). It can be chronically enlarged and that interferes with the passage of air from the nose into the throat. Kids adapt to this by keeping their mouths open to breathe. Most of these children snore and/or drool all over their pillows. They have perpetual runny noses, and often, ear and sinus infections.

Although an ENT doctor can easily visualize the adenoid with a mirror or fiberoptic scope in an older child or adult, toddlers are not cooperative enough to allow these exams in an office setting! An option for toddlers: a plain x-ray of the neck can show the adenoid enlargement (**ADENOID HYPERTROPHY**).

Treatment of this problem requires removal of the adenoid, called an adenoidectomy. It is a relatively straightforward procedure with a quick recovery. Kids have their operation and go home later that day. They are back to themselves again within a few days, and they can breathe through their noses.

diseases: ENT

Tonsils

Mouth Anatomy

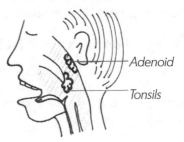

Adenoid

Tonsils

Mouth & Throat Anatomy

DISEASES

Parent 411 Adenoids—just one!

Contrary to popular belief (and use of the term "Adenoids") there is only one adenoid. And once it is removed, there are no more left. Surgeons don't leave some behind for a rainy day and it does not grow back.

Q. My child snores louder than my husband. Should we check this out?

Yes. Here are the questions the ENT doctor will ask you:

◆ Is your child napping more often than he should be?
◆ Is he restless at night? Do the sheets look like a tornado has passed through?
◆ Is he hard to arouse in the morning?
◆ Is he grumpy, hyper, or punchy all the time?
◆ Does he have loud breath sounds followed by a pause when he is sleeping?
◆ Does he chronically breathe through his mouth?

Your child may have **SLEEP-DISORDERED BREATHING**. Some children snore so loudly that they cannot sleep through it. Others have true sleep apnea where they actually stop breathing and must awaken to catch their next breath. Either way, both problems result in a chronically tired child.

If your child has sleep-disordered breathing and huge tonsils, the solution is to remove the tonsils and the adenoid. If your child's tonsils are normal sized, the solution is removal of the adenoid alone.

Adenoidectomy (adenoid removal) or adenotonsillectomy (adenoid and tonsil removal) are both short procedures. As we discussed above, the adenoidectomy is a simple operation where children usually go home later that day. After adenotonsillectomy, children may stay overnight in the hospital if they have sleep-disordered breathing.

A word about tonsillectomies: The procedure is not difficult, but the recovery can be. This is especially true with a young child under age three who is less likely to cooperate with post-operative directions (such as drinking enough fluids). An ENT usually quotes a two-week recovery for this procedure for toddlers. Kids feel better after a few days then suddenly hit the wall, feel crummy again, and do not want to drink. Dehydration makes matters worse. Some end up getting IV fluid in an ER if they refuse to drink enough. It's always good to be prepared for the worst so you can be pleasantly surprised if your experience is not this bad!

Q. My child has a weird looking tongue. Should I worry?

No. Does it look like a map of the world? It is called a geographic tongue. It's just a variation in the tissue lining the tongue. There is no medical problem associated with it, although it may be more common in children with allergies.

Red Flag

If your child has a tongue that looks like a strawberry—red with raised dots on it—see your doctor. It can be a sign of Strep throat!

Q. My child has a lump on the inside of his lip that will not go away. What is it?

This is called a *mucocele*, a cyst that varies in size, but never goes away on its own. They usually arise after a person bites his lip accidentally and blocks a minor salivary gland. Treatment is surgical removal.

Q. My toddler gets canker sores. What can I do about it?

The $10 medical term for canker sores is ***aphthous ulcers***. Unlike cold sores, aphthous ulcers are not caused by a virus as far as we know. They tend to show up after a person bites his cheek or tongue accidentally, or when a person is ill or stressed. And no matter what you do, they last about a week.

Believe it or not, a combination of liquid Benadryl and Maalox (a few drops of each) will coat the ulcer and provide about thirty minutes of relief. That gives your child enough time to eat a meal. It is also a good idea to avoid salty or citrus foods while one has a canker sore (they sting!).

Q. My child is having trouble hearing. He has had several ear infections. What should I do?

We cover the subject of ear infections in-depth in Chapter 6, Challenges and Chapter 16, Common Infections. Check those chapters for details.

Genitals

Girls:

- ◆ *Labial adhesion*
- ◆ *Breast tissue*

Boys:

- ◆ *Penile adhesion*
- ◆ *Uncircumcised penis*
- ◆ *Hernias*
- ◆ *Retractile testes*

Girls

Q. The skin of my daughter's genitals is sticking together. My doctor said not to worry about it. . . but I'm worried.

Your doctor is right: don't worry. This is a common problem called **LABIAL ADHESIONS**. The labia and vaginal areas stay lubricated and open when estrogen is being produced. Young women produce estrogen when they start menstruating. So pre-pubertal girls are prone to the labia getting stuck together until they go through puberty.

The only time this becomes a medical issue is when the labia are so fused together that the urethral opening is blocked too (that's where urine comes out). See the graphic on the next page to understand what we are talking about.

Labial adhesions are treated by using a prescription estrogen cream twice daily on the area that is stuck together for a couple of weeks. Then, applying petroleum jelly (Vaseline) on a daily basis after that keeps the area moist and open. Very rarely, a surgical procedure is necessary to open the area.

diseases: genitals

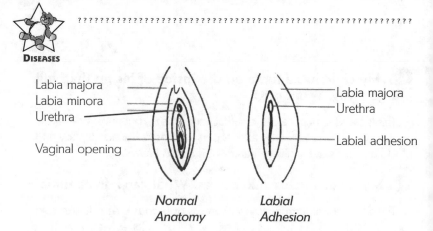

Labia majora
Labia minora
Urethra

Vaginal opening

Labia majora
Urethra

Labial adhesion

*Normal
Anatomy*

*Labial
Adhesion*

Q. My toddler has breasts! Is she going through early puberty?

It's probably not puberty, but rather a brief estrogen spike. As discussed above, little girls do not start making estrogen until they go through puberty. But occasionally, there may be a small elevation in the estrogen hormone level of a little girl that will cause some breast tissue to grow. This is temporary! As long as there are no other signs of puberty (armpit/pubic hair, vaginal discharge) and the breast tissue shrinks back down, it is nothing to worry about.

Your doctor will probably watch your child over the next three to six months to make sure this issue goes away. A simple hand x-ray can determine your child's "bone age" to be sure she is not growing faster than normal. She can also have blood hormone levels checked if there is any uncertainty.

Q. My daughter's genitals are always red and irritated. What should I do?

This is called vaginitis. If your daughter is toilet trained, it is probably caused by poor wiping technique. See Chapter 12, Hygiene for solutions.

Boys

Q. My son is circumcised, but he doesn't look circumcised anymore. What should I do?

This is called the hidden or concealed penis. See Chapter 12, Hygiene for some helpful tips.

Q. There is a bulge in my son's groin area. Could he have a hernia?

Yes. Any time you see a bulge where there shouldn't be one, it's time to call your doctor. Boys, especially those born prematurely, have an increased risk of having an **INGUINAL HERNIA.** These are usually diagnosed in the first year of life, but occasionally occur later.

A hernia is a bulging out of tissue or organ due to a muscle wall weakness. The risk of all hernias is that the organ that is bulging out will get stuck in that position and blood supply to the organ will be cut off.

? ?

DISEASES

Q. I can't see both of my son's testicles. Should I worry?

No, no need to worry. The testicle is most likely playing hide and seek with you. Take a look at your son when he is in the bathtub and see if it re-appears. It is called a *Retractile Testes*.

The testes are temperature-sensitive organs as their job is to keep the sperm at a constant temperature (like wine in a wine cellar). When a boy is cold, the testes rise upwards to keep warm. When a boy is hot, the testes slide down to keep from overheating. So, when your son is in a nice warm bathtub, you should be able to see both testes sitting in the scrotum.

Toddler boys who have a testes that never descends into the scrotum (**UNDESCENDED TESTES**) should have it brought down surgically as it is unlikely that it will come down and function normally after six months of age.[13]

Red Flag
If your son complains of pain in his testes, or his testes have a red or blue appearance, this warrants an emergency call to your doctor. The testes can get twisted and lose their blood supply (*Testicular Torsion*).

Heart

- ◆ Innocent murmurs
- ◆ Pathological murmurs
- ◆ Hypertension
- ◆ High cholesterol

Q. My doctor detected a heart murmur at my three-year old's well check. He said it is "innocent" and there's no need to worry . . . but I'm worried.

The words "heart murmur" will send chills up any parent's spine, but there is a big difference between an *innocent* murmur and a *pathologic* one.

Innocent murmurs are caused by the turbulence of blood flow through a valve or vessel in the cardiovascular system. These sounds come and go and have a typical location where they are heard. About 80% of children will have an innocent murmur at some point in their lives, but the peak is around age three or four.[14] Most pediatricians can easily spot innocent murmurs.

If the murmur seems more than "innocent," a referral can be made to a pediatric cardiologist for further assessment. An echocardiogram (ultrasound of the heart) can also be performed if there is any uncertainty of the diagnosis.

Q. My child has a heart defect. What special precautions do I need to take?

Your child's doctor and cardiologist can advise you on any exercise limitations. For **VENTRICULAR SEPTAL DEFECTS (VSD)**, the most common heart defect, your child can run around as much as he wants to!

FYI: Kids with certain congenital heart defects need a preventative dose of antibiotics prior to dental or surgical procedures involving the upper respiratory tract. The antibiotics keep bacteria from floating around in the bloodstream and infecting an at-risk heart (*infectious endocarditis*).

Note: these recommendations were updated in 2008. The following people need preventative antibiotics one hour before a procedure if they have:

1. Artificial heart valves.
2. Prior history of infectious endocarditis.
3. Heart transplant that has developed valve problems.
4. Specific heart defects present from birth, which are:

◆ Unrepaired or incompletely repaired cyanotic heart defects, including shunts and conduits.
◆ Completely repaired congenital heart defect with artificial material or device, during the first six months after the procedure.
◆ Repaired congenital heart defect with residual defect at the site or next to the site of an artificial patch or device.

Q. High blood pressure runs in our family. When does our child need to be checked for it?

The American Academy of Pediatrics recommends annual blood pressure screening beginning at age three. If high blood pressure is diagnosed in a young child, an extensive evaluation is done. Docs look for kidney disease, endocrine disease, a tumor, or a heart defect. Obesity and high blood pressure also go hand in hand. So as we have seen a rise in childhood obesity, we've also seen more kids with high blood pressure.

In kids, it is more likely that high blood pressure is caused by a completely different medical problem. In adults, the high blood pressure *itself* is the problem.

Q. High cholesterol runs in our family. When does our child need to be checked for it?

Children can have a blood cholesterol/lipid panel performed at any age, but it is generally done after the age of two for children who are at high risk of cholesterol-related health complications. It is up for debate whether all children should be screened for high cholesterol, risk factors or not. The American Academy of Pediatrics recommends cholesterol screening for the following children:

◆ Kids who have a parent or grandparent diagnosed with heart disease (coronary artery disease) at or under 55 years of age.
◆ Kids who have a parent or grandparent with a documented heart attack, heart related chest pain (angina), vascular disease, or sudden cardiac death at or under 55 years of age.
◆ Kids who have a parent with an elevated blood cholesterol level of 240 mg/dl or higher.
◆ Kids who are diagnosed with obesity.

Children under the age of two need a higher amount of fat in their diets due to their growth and brain development needs. But after age two, kids need to eat a low fat diet like everyone else—especially if there is a family history of cholesterol problems.

If your child has elevated cholesterol levels, he will be monitored closely and will need a strict diet regimen. Doctors typically hold off on medications for high cholesterol until children are over age ten.

Intestines/Stomach

◆ Chronic abdominal pain ◆ Umbilical hernia
◆ H pylori ◆ Celiac disease
◆ GERD

Q. My child frequently complains that his tummy hurts. What is the problem?

This is on the Top 10 list of most common kid complaints. Kids somehow believe that the belly button is the root of all evil. (If you ask a child where it hurts, he will almost always point there–you can try this one at home!)

And what tops the list for *recurrent abdominal pain*? Constipation. If your child is out of diapers, you may not be looking at his poop quite so frequently anymore. Take a look and see what is going on. If it looks like marbles, deer pellets, or clogs the toilet with the sheer mass, it is constipation.

If the diagnosis is not so clear cut, keep a diary of the following info before seeing your doctor:

1. How often is the pain occurring?
2. When is the pain happening? Before meals? After meals? Awakening from sleep?
3. Does the pain happen only on weekdays? (Some kids use this trick to avoid school.)
4. How long does the pain last? Does it keep your child from playing?
5. Where does it hurt? (If your child actually points somewhere OTHER than the belly button, it can be very helpful.)
6. Does anything make the pain worse?
7. Does anything make the pain feel better?
8. How often does your child poop?
9. What does the poop look like?
10. Does your child have bloating or excessive gas?
11. Does your child vomit, spit up, or feel food/liquid in the back of her throat?
12. Any other symptoms? Weight loss, lack of appetite, fever, back pain?

Most of the time, the cause of recurrent or chronic abdominal pain is not serious. The answers to the questions above give doctors some direction for how they evaluate the situation. Physical examination, blood tests, stool (poop) tests, and imaging studies are also useful. Just a warning here: your doctor may go on an extensive (and expensive) fishing expedition and may still not determine a medical cause for the stomach pain. This evaluation can rule out serious and/or treatable medical problems. If no cause is found, the pain is still real but may fit into the "psychological" category. As you can guess, this is the most challenging to solve.

Reality Check: Ulcers can be contagious

When I was in medical school in 1988, a professor told us he was convinced that ulcers were caused by an intestinal infection. Yeah, right, we all thought. Everyone knows that ulcers are caused by stress.

Whoops. We were all wrong and he was right. As it turns out, a bacterial infection called Helicobacter pylori is the top cause of peptic ulcers (ulcers in the stomach) and a frequent cause of duodenal ulcers (ulcers in the small intestine). Treatment with a combination of antacids and antibiotics will treat the disease. If treated with antacids alone, the ulcer may return after therapy.

If you or your doctor think your child has an ulcer, there are non-invasive ways to test for this infection by obtaining a blood, poop, or a breath test.

Q. I have a toddler and we are still dealing with acid reflux. I thought she would outgrow this by now.

Spit up happens. As some of our *Baby 411* veterans may know, acid reflux disease (**GASTROESOPHAGEAL REFLUX DISEASE/GERD**) is a problem that peaks at about four months of life and then progressively resolves on its own. Although most children outgrow this by one year of age, some continue to have problems into toddlerhood and beyond. However, toddlers' symptoms may change. Infants tend to spit up, act cranky, and arch their backs. On the other hand, toddlers and preschoolers avoid eating or eat excessively slowly, and complain of tummy aches. Older kids complain of heartburn. And some children have other complications, like asthma flare-ups.[15] Acid reflux treatment depends on the severity of the symptoms. Kids who have respiratory problems or poor weight gain should be treated until the GERD improves. There are several medications available for GERD. See Appendix A, Medications for details.

Q. My toddler still has an umbilical hernia. Does he need surgery?

If your child is under two years of age, try some baby Pilates instead.

Umbilical hernias are caused by bowel protruding between the abdominal wall muscles. As the muscles get tighter with age, most umbilical hernias resolve on their own. Your child strengthens those muscles as he goes from a lying to sitting position—hence the suggestion for Pilates.

If your child turns two and still has an umbilical hernia, it is unlikely he will outgrow the hernia . . .and it is time for surgery. This procedure will sew the weak muscles together to keep the bowel in place.

Q. My child gets bloated and has loose poops frequently. Should I check this out?

Yes. As we mentioned in Chapter 13, The Other End, while the likely diagnosis is **TODDLER'S DIARRHEA** or a lactose intolerance, it is also possible that your child has **CELIAC DISEASE.** People with celiac disease form an immune response to the protein gluten, causing injury to the intestinal lining. Gluten is found in grains like wheat, barley, and oats. Chronic injury to the gut results in chronic diarrhea, bloating, vomiting, and poor weight gain.

Children can be tested for this disorder by a blood test. Biopsies of the inflamed intestinal lining confirm the diagnosis. Celiac disease is hereditary;

so more than one family member may have this problem.

Virtually all people with celiac disease have one or two specific genetic defects. And if celiac disease runs in your family, you may want to consider finding out if you or your child has the gene or genes for it. There are labs in the U.S. (University of Chicago is one) that can test your child's DNA.

The upside of doing this test: you know if your child is at risk for developing celiac disease. The downside: even if your child does carry the gene, he may never have the disease—hence, the test may create unnecessary anxiety! Fact: less than 40% of folks who carry the gene for celiac disease will actually get the disease. Getting a DNA test will neither prevent the disease, nor necessitate a change in your child's diet. What it will do is encourage you to watch closely for early warning signs.

Reality Check: **Testing for future illnesses**
What if you could test your entire genetic code and determine what fate had in store for you? That creepy question is the fodder for science fiction movies (like *Gattaca* from 1997). The reality: it might freak you out . . . and it might make you uninsurable. Perhaps ignorance is bliss.

Kidneys

♦ *Glomerulonephritis*
♦ *Nephrotic syndrome*
♦ *VUR*

Q. My child's urine looks like Coke. Is this a problem?

Yes. When you see tea or Coke-colored urine, doctors worry about a kidney disease called ***glomerulonephritis***. There are many causes of this disorder, one of the classic ones being a Strep infection (see Chapter 16, Common Infections for more info). Without getting too technical here, the kidney filtration system gets inflamed and starts to malfunction. The urine looks brown due to broken down red blood cells.

There are other problems that cause blood in the urine, like infection, trauma, or kidney stones. But the blood usually looks like blood or is pinkish in color. Any of these colored urine needs to be evaluated by your child's doctor.

For more on worrisome pee, check out Chapter 13, The Other End.

Q. My child's eyelids look puffy. What's up with that?

It could be due to a different kidney disorder, called ***nephrotic syndrome***. If you get nephritis and nephrotic confused here, join the club.

Nephrotic syndrome is another problem with the kidney filtration system. It gets leaky and allows protein to pass through into the urine. The blood protein level drops as the protein is spilled into the urine and the body retains water as a result—hence the puffy eyes. Other body parts start to retain water too. Look at your child's legs. Are they swollen? If you press on them, can you see your fingerprint? Is your child's belly swollen or distended?

While other problems like heart failure or liver failure can cause fluid retention (***edema***), children usually look much sicker with these disorders.

DISEASES

? ?

Diagnosis of nephrotic syndrome can be made with a urine and blood test. If your child looks puffy, get it checked out.

Q. My daughter had a bladder infection and was found to have reflux in the urinary system. When will she outgrow this?

See Chapter 13, The Other End for details on this condition.

Lungs

◆ *Asthma*

Q. What is asthma?

Asthma is an abnormal immunologic/allergic response in the lungs to infections, allergies, weather, exercise, and emotions. The response creates swelling, muscle tightening, obstruction, destruction, and mucus production in the big and little airways of the lungs. The result? Narrowed airways with turbulent air passage.

An asthma flare up makes a person "air hungry." Narrowed airways interfere with the lung's job of air exchange (getting clean air in and dirty air out). The classic wheezing noise comes from air traveling through a narrowed passageway. The body tries to get more air in by breathing faster and pulling the rib muscles in with each breath (called ***retractions***).

Increased respiratory rate and retractions are clues that a child is working to breathe. An older child may have trouble saying a complete sentence without catching his breath. They may also be able to describe a sense of tightness and difficulty getting a good breath.

Asthma attacks occur periodically, depending on what seems to be a child's trigger. Some people only have symptoms during allergy season. Others have more than one trigger . . . and more frequent asthma attacks.

Q. What are the symptoms of asthma?

Asthma can range in severity. Some children cough excessively or have a chronic nighttime cough. Others wheeze dramatically and have difficulty

IS THERE AN ASTHMA/MELATONIN CONNECTION?

One of the curious things about asthma is that symptoms tend to be worse at night. Researchers are looking at melatonin levels as a possible reason. (Melatonin is a hormone that helps regulate our sleep/wake cycles). People with nocturnal asthma seem to have higher levels of melatonin than non-asthmatics and asthmatics that do not have nighttime symptoms.[16]

We will have more to come on this evolving medical breakthrough at Toddler411.com. But for now, we do not recommend having your child use melatonin as a sleep aid if he suffers from nighttime asthma attacks!

catching their breaths.

A doctor may point out to you that your toddler has "reactive airways" or is diagnosed with "bronchitis" frequently. Ultimately, these episodes may be signs of asthma.

Q. So how is asthma diagnosed?

Asthma is a diagnosis made by physical examination. Think of it as three strikes. The first time a child wheezes is bad luck. The second time, it's really bad luck. The third time, it's a trend. So, if your child is found to be wheezing on three separate occasions and responds to asthma medication, he is diagnosed with asthma.

Of course, there are other causes for wheezing that do NOT involve asthma. RSV infection is the top culprit for non-asthmatic wheezing. We talk more about this in Chapter 16, Common Infections. Kids can also inhale a piece of food (peanuts and un-popped popcorn are classic) that gets lodged into a tiny airway in the lung. That's why when a wheezing child does not respond to asthma medication, doctors look for another cause (perhaps that stuck peanut). Chest x-rays are helpful to rule *out* other diagnoses, but do not rule *in* asthma. Asthma is one of those diseases that require docs use that trusty, yet simple stethoscope.

> **DR B'S OPINION**
>
> *"Being diagnosed with asthma does not mean your child should be labeled as "sickly" or weak. Kids with asthma can and should still partici-pate in exercise and sports. And many children out-grow their tenden-cy to wheeze."*

A phenomenon called **cough-variant asthma** can make the diagnosis somewhat tricky. Kids with this disorder cough incessantly instead of wheeze. A child may have nighttime symptoms or symptoms after exercising.

Asthma is categorized by the frequency of symptoms. These categories were created to standardize the treatment guidelines put forth by the National Asthma Education and Prevention Program. The table below lists the revised 2007 guidelines for management of children under five years of age. We will explain what these treatments are in the next section of this chapter. Your pediatrician should be able to develop an asthma manage-ment plan based on these guidelines. However, the National Heart, Lung, and Blood Institute suggests consultation with an asthma specialist if your child has moderate or severe persistent symptoms.

SEVERITY	SYMPTOMS DAY/NIGHT	RX TO MAINTAIN CONTROL
Intermittent	2 or less days/week Uses rescue meds < 2 days/week	No daily medications Use rescue meds as needed
Mild Persistent	>2 days/week but not daily 1-2 nights/month Uses rescue meds >2 days/week	Low-dose inhaled steroid 2nd choice: Singulair or Cromolyn

diseases: lungs

SEVERITY	SYMPTOMS DAY/NIGHT	Rx TO MAINTAIN CONTROL
Moderate *Persistent*	Daily symptoms 3-4 nights/month Uses rescue meds daily	Medium-dose inhaled steroid
Severe *Persistent*	Continual symptoms >1 night/week Uses rescue meds several times a day	Four Steps (see below)

Steps with severe persistent asthma:

1. Medium-dose inhaled steroid or
2. Step 1 plus long-acting rescue or Singulair
3. High dose inhaled steroid plus long-acting rescue or Singulair
4. Step 3 plus oral steroids[17]

Q. How is asthma treated?

There are two approaches to the treatment of asthma: rescue and prevention.

1 **FOR IMMEDIATE RESCUE:** A bronchodilator (albuterol or levoalbuterol) acts very quickly to relax the airways. This can be administered orally (the least effective way), inhaled via an inhaler device, or inhaled through a nebulizer machine (a souped-up vaporizer). The medication not only opens up the lungs, but also elevates the heart rate. Kids feel like they have had a Starbuck's double shot espresso—so be prepared.

If your child has asthma, he should have a rescue medication with him wherever he goes. Obviously, an inhaler is the most convenient to carry around. But younger children have difficulty mastering the technique to inhale the medicine. Nebulizer machines are available by prescription at medical supply companies and many pharmacies. (Insurance companies cover the cost of these machines because they know the machine costs a whole lot less than an ER visit or hospitalization for asthma!).

If your child has an asthma flare up, you can give him the rescue medicine without running to your doctor's office or nearest ER. If he does not respond and continues to have labored breathing, then you need to seek medical attention.

The medication can be administered for prolonged periods in a medical setting because a child is monitored. At home, it should only be administered every four hours. If your child needs it more frequently than that, call your doctor.

The medication can be discontinued once a flare up is over. Your child no longer needs rescue medication when he doesn't need rescuing!

2 **FOR PREVENTION:** Kids who wheeze more than twice a week or more than one night per month benefit from medication to keep their asthma in check.

The gold standard for asthma prevention is steroids. Inhaled steroids, either via an inhaler or nebulizer, go directly to the lungs to stabilize and restore them to normal function. The goal with preventative therapy is to avoid needing rescue therapy! These medications reduce the number of flare-ups, the severity of flare-ups and improve lung function.

If the asthma is under good control, flare-ups will be minimized. If your child is in an asthma category (see chart above) that requires daily treatment, he will need to be followed more closely by his doctor. A treatment plan should be reassessed periodically to gradually reduce medications. Asthma (like eczema) therapy is a step up/step down approach. Step up the medications when your child's symptoms are not well controlled. Step down when all is well. According to the 2007 guidelines, kids under age five should have asthma symptoms well controlled for *at least three months* before stepping down therapy.

There are other classes of medications that can be used in conjunction with inhaled steroids to keep asthma under control. They can also be useful in step-down therapy to wean off steroids. These include leukotriene receptor antagonists (brand name Singulair) and mast cell stabilizing agents (brand name Cromolyn).

For children over four years of age with moderate or severe persistent asthma, there is a steroid/long acting rescue combination product (brand name Advair) that works well and is easy to administer. See Appendix A, Medications for more information!

Parent 411

Dr. Allan Frank, a pediatric pulmonologist, suggests using a valved aerochamber or spacer device attached to an inhaler for all patients with asthma (see picture at right). It ensures the medication gets in! Ask your doctor for a prescription.

Q. Why does my child need medication if he is not having symptoms?

One thing we know about asthma is that it can cause irreversible damage to the lungs. Airways may be destroyed (called remodeling) during flare-ups.

People with moderate or severe childhood asthma are at the greatest risk of having reduced lung function in adulthood.[18] Another consideration: chronic obstructed airways decrease the amount of oxygen getting to the body on a daily basis. In light of this, a child who has frequent asthma flare-ups is treated aggressively to prevent permanent lung damage.

If a child only has an occasional flare-up, he does not need to be on daily preventative medication.

Q. What can we do to prevent flare-ups?

There are a variety of triggers for kids who have asthma. Some triggers can be avoided, others cannot. Here is a list:

ALLERGIES. Seasonal allergies are unavoidable, unless you can travel away from your home during the peak time of year that seems to trigger your child's symptoms. It's wise to monitor pollen counts and keep the windows closed during peak allergy times.

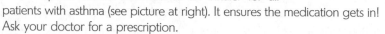

DISEASES

? ?

Perennial (all year round) allergies are something you can try to minimize. If your asthmatic child is allergic to cats or dogs, find your furry friend a new home. We are dog-lovers and completely understand that your pet is a family member. However, it's your child's health we are talking about here. You can also reduce your child's exposure to dust mites, cockroaches, and molds. See the helpful hints on the next page for some tips.

2 **INFECTIONS**. It's impossible to prevent all respiratory infections, but getting the flu vaccine for your child and all family members is a good start. Teaching your child good handwashing technique also helps limit infections.

3 **EXERCISE**. If your child's symptoms flare up with exercise, give him his asthma medication before he starts running around. We realize that is a bit difficult with a preschooler who is running around non-stop. This technique works better for a child who has a gym class or regularly plays a sport.

Parent 411

If your child continues to have asthma as he gets older, you can monitor his asthma by having a peak flow meter. This is a handheld device that objectively assesses your child's lung function. No, this gadget doesn't work well for preschoolers (who might not get the technique right), but it is an option for older children.

Q. Will my child outgrow asthma?

The odds are pretty good. Unfortunately, no one can predict if and when your child will outgrow asthma. As a general rule, kids who are diagnosed with asthma before the age of five are more likely to outgrow it. Kids who are diagnosed when they are older have worse odds.[19]

Q. I've heard that asthma can be set off by allergies. Is this true?

Yes. There are five common triggers for asthma: common colds/respiratory infections, allergies, change in weather, exercise, and emotional upset. Odors like cigarette smoke, perfume, and frying fish can also set off an attack. Figuring out what triggers your child's symptoms goes a long way to preventing an attack. Of course, some risk factors are out of your control, but others can be minimized.

The National Institute of Allergy and Infectious Diseases found that the number one environmental trigger of asthma in inner-city homes was cockroaches. People are allergic to cockroach saliva and droppings. Cockroach allergen levels are the greatest in high-rise apartment buildings in northeastern states.

Dust mites are another common household allergen that can trigger asthma symptoms. Mites are tiny bugs that love to eat human skin flakes. Mite droppings trigger allergic reactions. Their favorite areas are bedding, drapes, carpeting, upholstery, and, sorry to say this but... stuffed animals. Because they thrive in humid, temperate climates, they are more prevalent in the southern and northwestern U.S.

Molds (both indoors and outdoors), cat and dog allergens, and cigarette smoke are also asthma triggers.[20]

Helpful Hints:
How to keep household allergens under control

◆ Only eat in the kitchen and dining room.
◆ Keep non-refrigerated foods in airtight containers.
◆ Take the garbage out every day.
◆ Clean countertops regularly.
◆ Repair leaky faucets.
◆ Damp-mop hardwood floors.
◆ Dust regularly with a damp cloth.
◆ Vacuum carpeting regularly (or remove it).
◆ Use dust-proof mattress covers and pillow covers (zippered, "allergy-impermeable").
◆ Wash bed sheets, blankets, and covers weekly in hot water.
◆ Limit the number of dust collectors (stuffed animals, trophies, etc) in your child's room. Better yet—buy washable stuffed dolls and wash them weekly.
◆ Try to lower the humidity in your home to less than 50%. (You can test levels with a hygrometer available at hardware stores.)
◆ Don't smoke!
◆ Go pet-free if your child is allergic to pets. If that is not possible, keep your pet outdoors or at least out of your child's room.[21]

Food For Thought: Kids whose mothers smoked during their first year of life have twice the risk of developing asthma than their friends whose moms don't smoke.[22]

Skin

◆ Poison ivy
◆ Hemangiomas
◆ Café au lait spots
◆ Moles

◆ Paronychia
◆ Ingrown toenail

Q. I think my child has poison ivy. Will I get it too?

Not to worry, *poison ivy is not contagious*. It is an allergic skin response to the plant oil found on poison ivy, oak, and sumac. (See Toddler411.com for a picture). A person (usually unknowingly) brushes up against the plant, and then proceeds to touch other areas of the body and spread the plant oil elsewhere. About one to four days later, a streaky raised red rash appears where the plant oil touched the skin. This is a localized allergic reaction. Although other spots may appear several days later, it is all part of the allergic response.

The only time poison ivy passes from one family member to the next is if a child (or family pet) has plant oil on his skin/fur/clothing and then gives another family member a big hug! Once the child or pet has taken a bath, the plant oil is no longer a concern. You can treat the symptoms by using over the counter 1% hydrocortisone cream on the rash, and an antihistamine by mouth (such as diphenhydramine or cetirizine– brand names Benadryl or Zyrtec). If your child develops significant swelling–particularly around the eyes and genitals–call your child's doctor.

Q. My child has a hemangioma. The doctor told me it will go away eventually, but when?

Hemangiomas are vascular birthmarks that have a finite lifespan (see toddler411.com for a picture). They usually shrink or disappear between two to ten years of age. A good rule of thumb is that hemangiomas regress by 10% each year. So 50% will disappear by age five and 90% are gone by age nine. If the color starts to change from bright red to a dullish purple or grey, you are heading in the right direction. If the hemangioma is prone to irritation due to its location, or is not resolving, talk to your doctor about potential treatment options.[23]

Q. My child has more birthmarks showing up. Should I get it checked out?

Yes. Multiple "new" birthmarks should be checked out. There is a rare disorder called **NEUROFIBROMATOSIS** (NF) that causes flat light brown marks (*café au lait spots*) (see Toddler411.com for a picture) to appear on the body. Freckling in the armpits and groin areas are another sign of NF.

Q. We have a family history of skin cancer. What should I be looking for with my child's moles?

The general rule is to follow the ABCD's.

◆ A is for Asymmetry: Round or oval moles are normal.
◆ B is for Border: Borders should be sharp and well defined.
◆ C is for Color: Color should be uniform.
◆ D is for Diameter: Diameter should not get any bigger.

So, if a mole is speckled, has irregular borders or is getting bigger, get it checked out!

Q. My child gets ingrown toenails. What should we do about them?

Infants and young children have funky toenails. They are soft and edges may get stuck under the skin. If the skin around it gets red and tender, the nail needs to be lifted up to relieve the pressure. If there is discharge, pus, or fever, you need to check in with the doctor.

As a general rule, cut the nails straight across (not curved). If the nail is stuck, try lifting it up with your own fingernail after your child takes a bath. The skin will be more pliable.

As you read above, many of the diseases in this chapter are treatable. But is the environment the culprit in some of these problems? We'll examine this hot topic next.

THE ENVIRONMENT & YOUR TODDLER

Chapter 18

Government warning: According to the surgeon general, reading this chapter may cause 1) paranoia 2) an impaired ability to walk into Whole Foods without muttering to yourself 3) and other health problems.

"Baby pools cause learning disabilities."
"Cell phones cause brain tumors."
"Twinkies cause attention deficit disorder."

Nope, those aren't headlines out of the *Star* . . . but actual statements of "fact" you can find online, on the 24/7 cable news shows and other media.

Today, any activist with a rudimentary knowledge of HTML and flash animation can create an online portal to scare the daylights out of parents. Add to that dubious studies from places like the New Zealand Community College For Pediatric Medicine . . . plus the ever-hungry beast that is 24 hour cable news . . . and you've got trouble, sir.

So, how is a parent to figure out what hazards to avoid? Fasten your seatbelts, we're going to head right into the thick of environmental controversies swirling around the 'net and playgroups.

While it might be easy to dismiss some environmental scares as just that, there are serious issues here . . . certain diseases like autism, ADHD, asthma and some cancers *are* on the rise.[1] Why? Is it something in the water—literally—that is causing this?

It is human nature to want to blame something . . . anything . . . for these problems. One potential cause in vogue is the

? ?

ENVIRONMENT

environment, which truly may be partially responsible for some ailments. But pinning the ENTIRE blame for an illness on an environmental cause is often too simplistic. There are too many other factors (scientific speak: confounding variables) at work here. Yes, you can find a study online to back up any viewpoint, no matter how thin the logic—but that doesn't change the essential truth that science has a long way to go in PROVING conclusive links for these threats.

So it is with that caveat that we begin our grand tour of the environment and your toddler's health. One more caution: this chapter will likely be quite frustrating. Here is a typical way the discussion will go:

Q. Do Hostess Ho-Ho's cause low SAT scores?
A. We don't know, but scientists are working on it.

We jest, but as you'll see, this is how most of this chapter will go. The fact is scientific research into these questions is at best incomplete and at worst, missing altogether. In other cases, researchers are looking into these questions . . . they'll have the answer in about 15 years. The take home-message is: these issues are evolving, so watch our social media (blog/twitter/facebook—see Toddler411.com for links) for the latest updates.

So why cover this subject at all, if the science is lacking? First, we know you are concerned and have questions. Second, it is true that as society advances, the more enviro hazards we are exposed to. And the youngest members are the ones most at risk: babies and young children are the most susceptible to these hazards because of their developing bodies, their faster breathing rate, and their closer proximity to the ground. Some exposures happen before your child is even born. A disturbing study by the Environmental Working Group detected over 200 toxic chemicals in the umbilical cord blood they tested.[2]

But short of taking the next express train to Mars, we can't escape the environment. It's important to learn about environmental exposures and limit them where we can. But we will never be able to eliminate the risks entirely.

Use this chapter to think twice about your habits and lifestyle. You may be able to avoid or limit certain risks easily. But . . . and this is a big but . . . don't panic when a new study from Finland hits CNN. Changing your life based on a single news story is going to make you crazy.

So, let's take a look at what's out there.

Q. Why are children vulnerable to environmental toxins?

As we discussed in the introduction to this chapter, children's bodies make them particularly sensitive to environmental exposures.

- ◆ **Breathing**: Kids breathe at a faster rate than adults and, therefore, they take in more air. They also breathe lower to the ground, where chemical matter settles.
- ◆ **Fluid intake:** When you compare ounces to pounds, children drink the adult equivalent of 1.75 gallons of fluid per day.[3]
- ◆ **Food intake:** Kids eat three times more food (given their body weight) than adults.[4]
- ◆ **Oral exploration:** This is a nice way to say that kids stick stuff in their mouths! They are at risk for coming in contact with toxins and ingesting them (example: lead in the soil).
- ◆ **Surface area:** Children have twice the skin surface area per

pound as adults do. This allows more chemicals to be absorbed.

- ◆ *Location, location, location:* Kids spend many more hours on the floor, grass, carpeting, wood decking, and playground equipment than adults. This exposes them to more chemicals and pesticides.

- ◆ *Developing bodies:* Kids are exquisitely sensitive because they are affected as their bodies are growing. An exposure at a critical period of development may interfere with how a certain organ develops.

- ◆ *Lifetime burden:* Kids today not only have an increased amount of environmental exposure, but also a longer lifespan. That means there is more opportunity for negative effects to surface.

Reality Check
- ◆ Childhood leukemia, brain tumors, and non-Hodgkin's lymphoma rates have been rising since 1974.[5]
- ◆ Childhood asthma rates have doubled from 3.6% in 1980 to 7.5% in 1995. Five million American kids have asthma today.[6]
- ◆ 3% of developmental disabilities are due to known toxins (cigarette smoke, chemicals, etc.). [7]

Q. Where are environmental hazards lurking?

Well, they are everywhere. Scary thought, we know. Harmful agents are in the air we breathe, the water we drink, the food we eat, and the surfaces we touch. Do you just want to give up and say, to heck with this, we're all going to die of something? Yep, we feel that way too. But take a look at this list below. Many of these items can be avoided:

- ◆ *In air:* radon, carbon monoxide, second hand smoke, radio frequency/electromagnetic fields, industrial chemicals.
- ◆ *In water:* lead, mercury, industrial chemicals.
- ◆ *In food:* additives, antibiotics, hormones, arsenic, mercury, PCB's.
- ◆ *Surface contact:* phthalates, lead, arsenic, flame retardant.

Q. What exactly are these hazards and what can they do to you?

These hazards are both natural and synthetic. Some have known harmful properties, which we list below. Unfortunately, this is just the tip of the iceberg—scientists don't really know about every potential problem. Again, our goal is not to scare the dickens out of you . . . but knowledge is power. Here's the list:

- ◆ *Carcinogens:* These are known cancer-causing agents. (Example: arsenic, tobacco).
- ◆ *Mutagens:* These agents increase the rate of change ("mutation") in genetic material. It can lead to defective cells and cancer. (Example: ionizing radiation).
- ◆ *Teratogens:* These agents alter a fetus during development in the womb. Abnormalities are present at birth. (Example: alcohol).
- ◆ *Neurotoxins:* These agents damage or interfere with nerve/brain function. (Example: lead).

SMOG 411

Smog is an air pollutant formed by the atmosphere, ozone and volatile organic compounds (VOC's). It's a combination of motor vehicle exhaust, power plants, chemical plants, and refineries. No surprise, these pollutants are suspected of causing health problems. Concerns include asthma flare-ups, neurological impairment, and possible cancer.

◆ *Endocrine disruptors:* These agents mimic the body's natural chemical messengers (hormones) and can potentially interfere with body responses in the reproductive system and thyroid gland. (Example: phytoestrogen).

◆ *Irritants, allergens*: These agents cause allergic response in the airway and/or skin. (Example: volatile organic compounds or VOC's).

Toxins

Here's an overview of the four types of toxins:

Industrial Chemicals
Toxins: PCB (polychlorinated biphenyls), dioxin, solvents
Source: Industrial waste
Exposure: Prenatal, breast milk, seafood, air
Health risk: Lower IQ, lower developmental scores, endocrine disruptor

Pesticides
Toxins: organophospate, organochlorine, pyrethroids, carbamates, boric acid, CCA (copper chromium arsenate), DEET (N,N-diethyl-m-toluamide)
Source: Pesticides, insecticides
Exposure: Food, household exposure, water, air
Health risk: Nausea, vomiting, muscle weakness, allergic reaction, neurotoxin, carcinogen, endocrine disruptor

Metals
Toxins: arsenic, cadmium, lead, manganese, mercury
Source: Contaminated water from industrial waste
Exposure: Food, water, blinds, treated wood, imported pottery, lead pipes
Health risk: Anemia, learning/kidney problems, lower IQ, carcinogen

Volatile Organic Compounds (VOC)
Toxins: benzene, xylene, styrene, formaldehyde, aliphatic and aromatic hydrocarbons
Source: Household products, air pollution
Exposure: Rug/oven cleaners, paints, lacquers, paint strippers, dry cleaning
Health risk: Nasal congestion, eye irritation, headache, nausea, vomiting, possible carcinogen[8]

ENVIRONMENT

WHAT'S AN ACCEPTABLE LEVEL OF EXPOSURE?

So there is bad stuff in the air, water and soil. As a society, how do we determine what is an "acceptable level" of exposure? It's a guessing game where the target may be moving. As scientists learn about environmental toxins, the threshold for an acceptable level of environmental exposure tends to go down. For instance, the acceptable blood lead exposure level in 1972 was 40 mcg/dl (micrograms per deciliter). Today, we know that any lead exposure is unacceptable as it may cause subtle, but permanent health effects.[9]

Food

Should you buy an organic peach for $4 a pound? Or is the conventionally-grown peach just fine for $1.60?

As natural food stores expand around the country, parents nationwide are facing this dilemma: is organic worth the extra bucks? Is organic really safer than conventionally grown foods, or is it just hype?

As most Whole Foods shoppers know, to be labeled organic, food must be produced without most conventional pesticides, chemical fertilizers, or biotechnology-bred plants. But this does not mean they are 100% pesticide free. Let's put that into bold caps: ***ORGANIC DOES NOT MEAN A FOOD IS FREE OF ALL PESTICIDES.*** Yes, organic farmers use "natural" pesticides like pyrethrum (which in on the EPA's list of probable carcinogens) and Rotenone, which causes Parkinson's Disease in lab rats.

Concern about environmental toxins is driving much of the growth of organic food . . . and we know that kids today are exposed to more of this than past generations.

That said, there are no official guidelines from groups like the American Academy of Pediatrics to eat organic. And there is no scientific data that links, say, lunchmeat to specific diseases like leukemia. Yet we can certainly understand why many parents want to limit their kids exposure to toxins found in conventional foods, even if they are just erring on the side of safety.

Yes, organic foods are really expensive. Here is just a small sampling:

Gallon of organic milk: $5.99	Gallon of store brand milk: $3.99
Organic apples/lb: $2.49	Conventional apples/lb: $1.99
Organic raspberries (pint): $5.99	Conventional raspberries: $2.50

We could go on with this and compare an entire shopping cart of organics versus your average store brand foods, but you get the idea. (One promising trend: lower-cost organic "store brands" now showing up in some grocery stores—these cost 10% to 15% less than organic name brands. Look for the "O" brand at Safeway, Nature's Best at Albertson's—heck even Wal-Mart now sells organic food under its Member's Mark label).

Is it worth it? There is no clear answer on this. But there are some important considerations to ponder when you look at the sheer volume of environmental toxins today's children are exposed to. Even before they reach the world, fetuses are exposed in the womb.

environment

Because the jury is still out on the question of whether organic is really "safer" then conventional foods, we might make the argument that it is wise to limit the number of exposures to chemicals and pesticides *as much as possible*. And where do you have the most control over this? At the grocery store.

Bottom line: we should know what we are eating, even if organic foods aren't perfect or pesticide-free.[10]

As a consumer, you'll have to make trade-offs between price and perceived "risk" of conventional foods. You may decide some items are worth the extra expense and some are not.

So, let's take a look at common foods . . . and what concerns you should consider when weighing whether to buy organic or conventional.

Fruits and Vegetables

Top concern: Pesticides.

As you know, pesticides are used in farms to improve the quantity and quality of produce. Although there is no proven association in humans, high levels of pesticide exposure in lab animals can cause cancer. One more scary thought: kids may be more sensitive to pesticides than adults. Washing produce thoroughly before eating is a good idea, although some pesticide residue will still be present. Some produce contains higher amounts of pesticide than others—see the chart below for examples.

Top 12 foods with the highest concentration of pesticides:

1. Peaches	7. Red raspberries
2. Strawberries	8. Imported grapes
3. Apples	9. Spinach
4. Nectarines	10. Celery
5. Pears	11. Potatoes
6. Cherries	12. Sweet bell peppers

Least contaminated foods:[12] Asparagus, avocados, bananas, broccoli, cauliflower, sweet corn, kiwi, mangos, onions, papaya, pineapples, sweet peas.

Use these lists in the supermarket aisle to decide if the premium for organic is worth it. If money is tight, we'd suggest buying conventional versions of fruits like bananas and avocados (since they are the least contaminated). Spend your organic food money on items like peaches and strawberries.

Meat

Top concern: Antibiotics, nitrite preservatives.

Antibiotics are given to healthy animals in their feed to prevent disease and improve growth. In fact, at least 40% of antibiotics used in the U.S. are used in animals destined to become our next meal. Antibiotics used in the food industry are indirectly a problem for humans because they allow drug resistant bacteria to evolve.[13] If you want to eat antibiotic-free meat, buy meat labeled "USDA Organic."

Sodium nitrite is a preservative used in processed lunchmeat and hot dogs to prevent botulism. There was a report of a potential increased risk of cancer linked to hot dogs in the 1990's, but the data is not there to prove a "link" (pardon the pun) at this point. Is it okay for your child to eat a hot dog occasionally? Sure. But don't make it a staple in his diet for a variety of reasons![14]

Milk and Dairy products

Top concern: Bovine Growth hormone (rBGH)

Conventional milk contains "bovine growth hormone" (BGH). It's given to lactating cows to improve their milk production . . . and we've heard the charges by some environmentalists that BGH causes early puberty in kids. But let's look at the facts: the latest scientific research on BGH does NOT support this theory. In fact, both the American Academy of Pediatrics and the Centers for Disease Control think that conventional milk is fine.

Now, that said, we DO know that kids today are exposed to more environmental toxins than any previous generation. So, limiting that exposure in any way we can is never a bad idea. It is possible that future research may shed more light on any concerns with BGH.

Buying organic milk comes down to personal choice. If it were the same price as conventional, we'd say go organic. But at $5+ a gallon, organic milk costs considerably more than conventional milk. And considering how much milk kids will drink in a year, that adds up to real bucks. Bottom line: if you can afford it, go organic. If not, drink conventional milk . . . and don't feel guilty for making that choice.

One cheaper option: "Conventional" Borden milk is not technically "organic," but it is BGH-free.

FYI: Some organic milk brands are fortified with DHA/Omega 3 oils. However, the amount is minimal compared to eating one serving of salmon.

Fish

Top concern: Mercury.

Yes, fish can absorb ***methylmercury*** from coal-fired power plant waste that ends up in nearby rivers, lakes, and oceans. Unfortunately, cooking fish does not remove the mercury. And excessive mercury intake during brain development of a fetus or young child can lead to language, attention, and memory problems. Mercury intoxication of fetuses while in the womb can also cause blindness, deafness, and seizures.

The FDA advises pregnant women, breastfeeding women, and children to avoid eating ANY shark, swordfish, mackerel, and tilefish. So should you avoid all fish? No. Fish is considered a healthy food choice in general, so you should include it in your toddler's diet. BUT you should be aware of which types of fish should be avoided because of high levels of mercury.

In general, saltwater fish are "safer" than freshwater. Low mercury fish choices include shrimp, salmon, pollock, and frozen fish sticks. And grocery store fish is probably safer than those beauties that your husband caught on his fishing trip. Since there are fewer regulations on sport fish, these are likely to contain more mercury and PCB's (industrial waste).

Here are guidelines for which fish to avoid:

HIGHEST MERCURY LEVELS: AVOID

Grouper
Marlin
Tilefish
Shark

Mackerel
Orange roughy
Swordfish

HIGH MERCURY LEVELS: STEER CLEAR*

Bass
Croaker
Lobster (American/Maine)
Tuna (fresh bluefin and ahi)

Bluefish
Halibut
Tuna (canned, white albacore)
Sea trout

MEDIUM MERCURY: LIMIT INTAKE**

Carp
Crab (blue and snow)
Mahi Mahi
Perch (seawater)
Snapper
Tuna (fresh Pacific albacore)

Cod
Herring
Monkfish
Skate
Tuna (canned, chunk light)

LOW MERCURY: OK TO HAVE 12 OZ PER WEEK

Anchovies
Calamari (squid)
Caviar (farmed)
Crab (king)
Flounder
Hake
Lobster (spiny/rock)
Perch (ocean)
Salmon
Scallops
Shrimp
Sturgeon (farmed)
Trout (freshwater)

Butterfish
Catfish
Clams
Crawfish/Crayfish
Haddock
Herring
Oysters
Pollock
Sardines
Shad
Sole
Tilapia
Whitefish

*Steer clear means no more than one serving every one to two months.
**For kids under 30 lbs, no more than one six-ounce serving every two weeks. For kids over 30 lbs, no more than three six-ounce servings per month.

To sum up:

◆ The FDA has issued an advisory for pregnant or breastfeeding women, and children to avoid eating ANY shark, swordfish, mackerel, and tilefish. These predator fish eat many smaller fish and concentrate the mercury in their bodies.

◆ The Environmental Protection Agency suggests eating six ounces or less of local fish if your community's fishing advisories are unknown.[15]

Canned light tuna contains less mercury than white albacore tuna and tuna steaks. So, if you really love tuna fish, you have some options. There are also a couple of certified low-mercury tuna fish products: Carvalho Fisheries and King of the Sea. Look for their labels next time you are at the grocery store.

FYI: The EPA's acceptable mercury threshold is 0.1 mcg per kilogram body weight per day.

BOTTOM LINE

At this point, we cannot prove that chemically laden foods cause cancer, or any other malady. We also cannot prove eating organic foods will protect you from getting certain diseases. We'll keep you posted on this evolving discussion via our website.

Food Additives

Q. Does food coloring cause ADD?

Scientists have looked into the possibility that a link exists between food coloring and attention problems. Called the "Feingold Hypothesis," this theory gathered dust for several years as researchers failed to prove such a link. The focus of this research was on whether food colorings FD Yellow #5 and #6 caused attention problems. In 2007, researchers published an article in the journal, Lancet, resurrecting this theory. Kids who drank beverages with red or yellow dye, or sodium benzoate (a common preservative) had more hyperactive behavior than their peers. (Kids who drank sugary drinks had no change in their behavior, by the way).

While you shouldn't change your life on the basis of one study, we think limiting processed foods (which usually contain food coloring and preservatives) isn't a bad idea anyway. And while you may have fond memories of Twinkies as a kid, they really aren't that great. We've done a recent taste test for this book, just to make sure!

Q. Can my child have artificial sweeteners?

According to the National Cancer Institute, artificial sweeteners like Splenda, Nutrasweet, and Equal have no increased risk of cancer. Saccharin, however, has been linked to bladder cancer in animal studies.

Does that mean your toddler can drink Diet Coke? Yes, one occasional Diet Coke will not hurt her. But that doesn't mean your toddler should become a diet soda addict. And truthfully, you shouldn't need to worry about artificial versus natural sugar if your child eats a balanced diet. Bottom line: no need to lose sleep over this one.

Q. Is it okay to grill food?

It's okay to BBQ . . . in moderation. (We know those are fighting words in Dr. B's home state of Texas, where BBQ is a religon.)

Here's the deal. Cooking foods quickly at high temperatures—whether it be grilling, frying, or broiling—produce HCA's (heterocyclic amines). HCA's are on the National Institute of Health's "reasonably anticipated to be carcinogens" list.[16]

Certain foods produce more HCA's than others. Chicken is at the top of the HCA list and hamburgers are at the bottom.

environment

Additionally, fat drippings on the grill emit PAH's (polycyclic aromatic hydrocarbons). These are also on the carcinogen hit parade. Charred meat has more PAH's as well.

Bottom line: Grill in moderation, limit the fat drippings, and scrape off any charring.

Water

Q. Is it okay to drink tap water?

Yes. Bottled water is probably not any safer, and certainly more expensive. The regulations for tap and bottled water are exactly the same. However, it's a good idea to run the tap water for a couple of minutes when you start using it for the day. It reduces the amount of lead running through your pipes. (Even if you live in a newer home, some large cities still have 100% lead piping that connects water mains to your home.)

Some people feel better about their tap water if they use a water purification system. Faucet mounted filters that are ANSI or NSF approved will filter out greater than 95% of the lead, chlorine, asbestos, sediment, and benzene from the water.

One bit of practical advice if you own a water purification system: change your filters regularly or you will be harboring a veritable playground for bacteria.

Helpful Hint: Water purifiers and fluoride
Water softeners do not affect the fluoride in your tap water. But there is some concern that your water filter might. Systems that use reverse osmosis or distillation techniques may lower the fluoride content by over 80%.[17]

Household

Q. Can I reheat food in a Styrofoam container?

Styrofoam is a product made out of polystyrene and benzene, both of which are carcinogens. Environmentalists argue that these products are leeched out into our food and drinks—particularly when they are heated. Scientists, however, have not jumped onto this bandwagon.

Regardless, we've all experienced one too many microwave explosions after re-heating our leftovers in styrofoam. We'd err on the side of caution: microwave food on a plate to be safe—and clean.

Q. Can I use plastic wrap in the microwave?

You can, but use a napkin instead if it's handy.

Plastic wrap uses *phthalates,* plasticizers that make plastic soft and durable. Phthalates are classified as weak estrogens and androgen-blocking chemicals (endocrine disruptors), as well as animal carcinogens. Like many environmental exposures, there's a lot of controversy about phthalates, but no scientific consensus that they are dangerous.

Unfortunately, phthalates are everywhere. Even if you don't microwave food with plastic wrap, the food may already be contaminated by the plastic packaging it came in. To really bring home the point that phthalates are ubiquitous, a recent study showed phthalates are even in baby shampoo and diaper rash creams! And phthalates can be both ingested and absorbed through the skin. Studies show babies eliminated the breakdown products of phthalates in their urine after these products were used on their hair or skin.[17]

Now, we're not telling you this to scare you—there is no need to throw out the baby shampoo. We're simply trying to point out that it's exceedingly difficult to avoid some of these things, even if you want to. The take-home message: reduce exposure phthalates if you can. But don't panic over baby shampoo.

DON'T TRY THIS AT HOME

Here's a true story. A mom once arrived at her son's 18-month old well-check armed with a list of "lab" results. It was a scary report: her child showed high levels of several environmental toxins.

"Where did you have this testing done?" I inquired. The mom said she bought a home toxin test ($65) at a local health food store and sent off her child's hair specimen to a private laboratory. No surprise: the test was positive for mercury, lead, and cadmium exposure. The mother was in tears, feeling guilty for exposing her child to toxic chemicals.

Feeling sorry for this mom, and being intellectually curious, I decided to investigate. I got a test kit of my own. It states on the package "this product has not been evaluated by the Food and Drug Administration" and is "not intended to diagnose, cure, mitigate, treat, or prevent diseases." Perhaps they should add on the label, "But it will scare the heck out of you."

Just to test whether this kit is accurate, we submitted a sample of hair from our dog, Shadow. No, Shadow doesn't eat any fish . . . nor is her backyard a former industrial waste site. Lo and behold, she has excessive toxic metals in her system too! (Okay, now we regret feeding Shadow that Mighty Dog "Kibbles & Cadmium" brand dog food).

Specifically, our dog had high levels of aluminum, arsenic, cadmium, nickel and tin. Now that is one toxic cockapoo! It is also noteworthy that our dog's mercury levels were low, despite the fact that dog vaccines contain that dreaded thimerosal preservative.

We suppose we should applaud this company for finding a way to make a living by scaring parents. But here's a key point: using a store-bought HAIR test to determine toxins is bogus. Hair sampling for mercury exposure is only used in *research* settings, not in clinical practice. Instead, doctors would use a blood test to determine accurate mercury levels. FYI: The average amount of mercury in a person's hair is 1 ppm (parts per million).[18]

And let's be real: there is only so much you can do in this world to protect your child. Limit environmental exposures where you can, and don't obsess about the rest. As for my dog's toxic cadmium levels, maybe that explains why she tries to catch invisible bugs.

environment

Q. Are plastic toys okay?

Yes and no. Many plastic toys contain phthalates. However, there is good news: since February 2009, both the U.S. and Canada require toys and products that are intended for use in the mouth (baby bottles, pacifiers, teething toys) to be phthalate-free. But as we all know, kids don't read directions that come with toys and may decide that the rubber ducky bath toy makes a good teether. That bath toy may contain phthalates because it is not a "teething toy."[19] Bottom line: do your best to keep soft plastic toys that are not intended as teethers out of your child's mouth. Yes, we realize that is tall order, but give it your best shot!

Key point: toys manufactured prior to February 2009 were NOT recalled. So, don't buy second-hand toys or those in resale shops if you want to avoid phthalates.

Q. Are plastic bottles and sippy cups toxic?

Plastic baby bottles and sippy cups have made headlines in the past few years, after a series of health reports raised questions about their safety. The concern is Bisphenol A (BPA), a chemical found in polycarbonate bottles and sippy cups, as well as the lining of formula cans.

Perhaps the most damning report on BPA came from a federal panel in 2007—this panel (part of the National Institutes of Health/National Toxicology Program) reviewed dozens of BPA studies and came to this conclusion: there is "some concern that exposure to BPA causes neural and behavioral effects" in infants.

This report set off a chain reaction of events: Canada has proposed banning BPA products and retailers in the U.S like Wal-Mart and Babies R Us have gone BPA-free. In 2010, several states including Vermont and Minnesota passed BPA bans.

We have an expanded discussion of BPA in our *Baby 411* book, but here is our basic recommendation: avoid polycarbonate bottles and cups. Instead, consider these alternatives:

◆ *Use no spill cups made of opaque plastic.* These cups (made of polyethylene or polypropylene) do not contain BPA. (Note polycarbonate-containing bottles have a #7 on their recycling label). Also consider cups made of metal (Thermos has an entire line of such cups). Glass is another option. As for the ubiquitous sippy cup: we aren't big fans (for reasons discussed earlier in this book). Instead, we urge your toddler to learn how to drink from a cup or straw. But what do you use when you are on the go? Consider a metal straw bottle like the Foogo by Thermos ($15)—this BPA-free insulated bottle is leak proof, yet has a straw instead of sippy spout.

◆ *Consider a BPA-free plastic bottle.* Born Free makes a BPA-free clear plastic bottle (Newbornfree.com) sold at Whole Foods for $10. Although, we'll remind you that a toddler has no business drinking from a baby bottle!

◆ *Avoid store-bought food in metal or plastic containers.* BPA lines the inside of many baby formula cans—at press time, only Baby's Only Organic formula had BPA-free cans. BPA is also found in the liner of metal liquid food containers.

A good blog with a detailed guide to BPA-free products is Z Recommends (zrecs.blogspot.com).

Q. Help! We've got bugs! Can we bomb our house with pesticides?

If you have to use pesticides, it's probably wiser to set traps or treat the outside of the house than to use an insecticide spray or "bomb" technique indoors. The insecticide residue can collect on upholstery, rugs, and stuffed animals.

Another bit of advice: only treat for pests when there is a problem. Skip scheduled or routine pesticide applications.

Q. Can we fill our baby pool from our garden hose?

Although the water in the baby pool is intended for swimming, toddlers tend to drink it too. (It's particularly gross when they've already peed in it.) But the real concern here is that garden hoses may contain lead. How? When garden hoses are manufactured, lead is used to stabilize the hose material (which is made of polyvinyl chloride). If the water in the hose has been standing for a while, the lead concentration may be even higher.

No, you don't have to go out and replace all your garden hoses. But if you do buy a new hose, get one that is labeled "safe for drinking." And whether you are using a new or an old garden hose, let the water run for a minute before filling up the baby pool.[20]

Q. Is it okay to let my child play on playground equipment? I heard it contains arsenic.

Arsenic, a poison better known for its appearance in mystery novels, was used as a preservative to treat wood prior to 2003. And you guessed it: much of this wood ended up in playgrounds, picnic tables and decks.

The EPA banned the use of arsenic (technically, it was chromated copper arsenate) in such wood in 2003 out of concern for kids who were exposed to it when they put wood chips or contaminated hands in their mouths. Today, pressure-treated lumber is treated with a new chemical called ACQ, which the government thinks is safe. (We're sure we'll find out ACQ causes abnormally high rates of cheerleading in teenage girls in 2012, but we digress).

So, all new playground equipment built after 2003 is safe. But what about older equipment? Unless your child is a beaver and munches through a dozen two by fours during a playground visit, we don't see much of a threat. That said, it would be wise to have your child wash his hands after playing on any old wooden decking or play equipment![21]

Q. Does carpet cleaner cause Kawasaki Disease? I heard John Travolta's child had this problem.

Yes, John Travolta and his family made this disease a household name. In case you missed the headlines, the Travoltas claim their son developed Kawasaki Disease after their carpets were cleaned.

As we discussed in Chapter 16, Common Infections, Kawasaki Disease (KD) is an immune disorder that causes vasculitis (swollen blood vessels). If untreated, KD can lead to some pretty serious complications like heart attacks, heart blood vessel aneurysms, and heart failure. Although it is fairly rare, it occurs most often in children ages two to five years. At this point, doctors know more about how to treat KD than what causes it.

Although researchers have investigated the carpet cleaner link, it does not appear to be the cause of KD. Experts think Kawasaki Disease may be set off by an abnormal response to infection. The problem is that no one has figured out which bug is at fault.

While the evidence strongly suggests an infectious agent at work here, scientists don't completely rule out an environmental trigger. Other possible risk factors for KD: humidifiers and living near a body of standing water.

Bottom line: Although carpet cleaners may not cause Kawasaki Disease, it's probably smart to keep your kids from playing on the carpeting until the cleaner has completely dried.[22]

Parent 411

Want to know what's in your common household cleaning products? Check out the National Library of Medicine's website at hpd.nlm.nih.gov

Q. Should I install a carbon monoxide detector?

Yes.

Carbon monoxide is an odorless, colorless, and tasteless toxic gas that is produced by a variety of products including motor vehicle exhaust, poorly ventilated gas space heaters, gas appliances (stoves, dryers, water heaters), woodstoves and fireplaces, leaking chimneys, and tobacco smoke. Intoxication can have variable health effects ranging from lethargy to, in severe cases, death.

The most practical thing to do to prevent carbon monoxide poisoning is to use fuel-burning appliances properly and to inspect them annually. Buying a carbon monoxide detector is just an additional level of protection. If you choose to purchase a detector, look for one with UL certification on the label and know that they are not nearly as reliable as smoke detectors. But having a carbon monoxide detector is worth the extra $40 to $50.[23]

Q. Should I have my home tested for radon?

Yes.

Radon is an odorless, colorless, tasteless radioactive gas formed from the decay of naturally occurring uranium in the world's rocks, soil, and water. Radon gets into homes via cracked foundations, granite walls, and porous cinderblocks. Exposure is usually more of a problem in homes with basements.

Because radon exposure is a known cause of cancer, you should get your home tested. For more info, check out the Environmental Protection Agency's website at epa.gov/radon or call their Radon Hotline at 800-767-7236.[24]

Q. I heard that formaldehyde levels in some nursery furniture can be dangerous. What should we look for?

The concern here is medium density fiberboard (MDF), which is an engineered wood product made of wood fibers that are glued together under high pressure and temperature. Because of its low cost, MDF is increasingly found in nursery furniture, especially dressers. Some crib makers use MDF support boards under the mattress.

The problem with MDF is the glue, which can outgas formaldehyde, which in high concentration can cause breathing difficulties, headaches and other health problems. When added to other sources of formaldehyde found in a home, levels of this chemical can cause unhealthy indoor air quality.

As of this writing, Congress was considering a bill to set limits on formaldehyde in furniture. In the meantime, consider these tips to avoid over exposure to formaldehyde:

◆ Skip the MDF. Yep, not buying any furniture with MDF for your baby's nursery is a key way to avoid this problem! Of course, solid wood furniture is more expensive than MDF, so there is an obvious trade-off (our other book Baby Bargains reviews and rates furniture makers, including discussion of which companies use solid wood versus MDF).

◆ Ventilate. Keep the nursery well ventilated. And air out any new furniture that contains engineered wood products like MDF outside until any smell is gone.

◆ Use an air conditioner and dehumidifier. The higher the temperature and humidity in a room, the more formaldehyde will offgas. Control the temperature and humidity to limit emissions.

Q. I'm worried that my child might have been exposed to lead. What do I do?

Lead exposure can impact IQ, attention, and behavior, so it's wise to check it out.

Kids who live in homes (or regularly visit homes) built before 1950 are at greatest risk of lead exposure in the pipes, paint, and soil surrounding the home. Children who live in homes built before 1978 that have been renovated within the past six months are also at risk.

Doctors usually screen for lead exposure at nine to 12 months of age and may repeat annually until six years of age. In urban communities with older homes, all children should have a blood test to detect lead exposure. In low risk areas, doctors screen for lead with a risk factor question list. If there is a possible exposure, a blood test is done. But you can always ask for your doctor to order the test if you have concerns.

As we have discussed, there is no safe or acceptable blood lead level. Even low levels of exposure may lead to subtle, but permanent health effects. If your child does have an elevated blood lead level, the source of lead needs to be identified and removed. Then blood levels can be checked periodically after that to make sure they are going down. Only extremely high levels require medical therapy to remove the lead.

For more information, go to the Environmental Protection Agency's website at www.epa.gov/lead/ or call the National Lead Information Center (NLIC) at 800-424-5323. For information on toys that were recalled due to lead, check out the US Consumer Product Safety Commission at cpsc.gov.

While the EPA recommends consumers turn to professionals to have their homes tested for lead, there are several home tests available at your local hardware store. Unfortunately, the accuracy of these tests is somewhat suspect.[25]

Other Environmental Hazards

Q. Do cell phones cause brain tumors?

Research on extremely low frequency magnetic fields (ELF) and radio frequencies (RF) has led the International Agency for Research on Cancer to identify them as a "possible human carcinogen." These common exposures occur everyday in our home and community in the form of power lines, baby monitors, cordless phones, Wi-Fi, and, yes, cell phones. The World Health Organization plans further research to see if there is a link to childhood leukemia and brain tumors.[26] A study from Sweden raised concerns that there may be a long time (latency period) between cell phone use and its potential health risks to see an obvious link at this time.[27] Then another Scandinavian study claimed there was nothing to worry about.[28] Confusing, no?

Bottom line: toddlers should probably limit the time they spend on a cell phone. But at this point, there is no scientific consensus that cell phones cause brain tumors or leukemia. If you want to be really cautious, let them text message Grandma instead. Or check out the Environmental Working Group's assessment on when it is time to upgrade your phone: ewg.org/cellphoneradiation/Get-A-Safer-Phone

Factoid: The rate of childhood leukemia is four per 100,000 in the developed world and 2.5 per 100,000 in developing countries.[29]

Q. Is it safe to let my toddler to use a computer?

Yes. Many household products emit magnetic field energy at low levels that are not strong enough to break down or alter DNA (genetic material) or body tissue. Computers are actually one of the lowest emitters. Hair dryers and electric razors are at the top.

Of course, while it is safe to let a toddler use a computer, you don't want them spending hours in front a screen watching streaming cartoons. Limit computer use like you would any media.

Q. Is it ok to live near power lines?

The short answer: yes.

The long answer: living near a power line only gives you a visual aid to remind you of your exposure to electromagnetic fields. But families who don't see their power lines can have the same or even higher amount of exposure to electromagnetic fields, thanks to household electronics.

Researchers are currently looking at a potential link between electromagnetic field exposure and childhood cancer.[30] However, for now, most researchers do NOT think living near power lines is dangerous.

Q. Does black mold cause illness?

For starters, mold is everywhere. It's inside and outside your house, whether you have water damage or not.

Most people are not bothered by mold exposure. Others have allergy symptoms like runny noses, eye irritation, coughing, and wheezing. Allergies are serious, but that doesn't mean you need to evacuate your house when it rains.

In particular, stachybotrys ("black mold") is a mold that produces a mycotoxin. There have been reports that mycotoxin from black mold causes bleeding in the lungs (acute pulmonary hemorrhage) of young infants. However, this relationship has not been proven. So does mold cause illness? This question led the insurance industry to limit policy-coverage for mold in water-damaged homes to avoid huge settlements. Yet, scientists don't have all the answers here.

We all saw the pictures of water-logged homes in New Orleans after Hurricane Katrina. Now that was mold on steroids . . . and clearly more dangerous than that spot of mold under your kitchen sink.

If you find mold in your house (on the baseboards, under the sink, etc), it usually means the house is damp. Check for water leaks and then clean up with a bleach/water solution. For bigger areas, you may need professional help.[31] For more info on mold control and cleanup, check out the Centers for Disease control at cdc.gov/health/mold.html or call 800-433-4318.

Q. What can I do to reduce my child's environmental exposure?

Here are some common sense ideas to limit exposure:

Food:
◆ Buy fresh produce in season.
◆ Buy local or domestically grown produce.
◆ Consider buying organic produce, especially the Top 12 (Dirty Dozen) list discussed earlier in this chapter.
◆ Wash produce well and if possible, peel it.
◆ Microwave with a napkin cover to reduce splatter. Avoid plastic wrap or Styrofoam touching the food.
◆ Limit fish intake, particularly those on the high mercury list.
◆ Consider buying organic milk.
◆ Barbeque in moderation. Limit fat drippings and charring.

Water:
◆ Tap water is fine, just run the water for two minutes the first thing in the morning.
◆ If there is any concern, get your tap water tested for lead.
◆ Test well water before use.
◆ Consider getting a water purification system.

Air:
◆ Don't smoke. If you must, do it outside your home and change clothes once you get indoors.
◆ Avoid second hand smoke.
◆ Consider staying inside on ozone alert days.
◆ Don't live downwind from a lead smeltering plant.

ENVIRONMENT

Home:

♦ Minimize pesticide use. Use traps or outdoor treatments instead of indoor sprays or bombing. Keep your kids and pets off the grass for 24 hours after treatment.

♦ Wash insect repellent off your child after coming indoors.

♦ Use adequate ventilation when renovating, painting, putting down new carpeting, etc.

♦ Check for lead exposure in homes built before 1950 or built before 1978 and renovated in the past six months.

♦ Fix any water damage or leaks.

♦ Inspect your chimney and stove every year.

♦ Consider a carbon monoxide detector, especially if you have a wood-burning stove or fireplace. Check for UL certification on the package.

♦ Get your home tested for radon, especially if you have a basement.

♦ For wooden decks and playground equipment built prior to 2003, be sure your child does not eat the wood and washes hands after playing.

♦ Use adequate ventilation when using craft supplies (toluene, paint fumes).

Reality Check

"The environment can be hazardous to your child's health. The burden is on parents to ask questions, take precautions, and call on decision-makers to reduce these risks." Lisa Doggett, MD, Physicians for Social Responsibility.

Helpful Hint: Where to get more info
♦ hyosemite.epa.gov/ochp/ochpweb.nsf
♦ cpsc.gov

Was that a bit scary or what? Now that we've cataloged all the ways the environment can potentially make you sick, let's talk about real-life toddler scrapes and boo-boos. Our next chapter deals with all those little emergencies (both big and small) you may find yourself in with a toddler.

FIRST AID

Chapter 19

"To avoid delay, please have all your symptoms ready."
~ Notice in an English doctor's waiting room.

WHAT'S IN THIS CHAPTER

◆ **WHAT IS A MEDICAL EMERGENCY?**

◆ **TOP 10 TODDLER MEDICAL EMERGENCIES**

◆ **ALLERGIC REACTIONS**

◆ **BREATHING PROBLEMS**

◆ **FEVER**

◆ **VOMITING**

◆ **RASHES, BURNS, STINGS**

◆ **SEIZURES**

◆ **IS IT BROKEN?**

◆ **POISONINGS & SWALLOWED OBJECTS**

Medical problems are always a little scarier when it's 3am and your pediatrician's office is closed. This is the chapter that will carry you through those wee small hours until the office opens. The information will help you determine which problems are emergencies and which ones aren't. But if you're worried, the right answer to any emergency is to call the after-hours line and/or go to the nearest hospital.

Being "on call" is part of every doctor's job description. We know kids get sick after business hours and on weekends. You need us to be around. So we don't mind answering your questions. (If we start to mind, it's time for us to retire!)

Some doctors' offices will handle their own phone calls after business hours. Others will utilize a nurse call center. Either way, there is a decent chance that you will be talking to a medical provider who does not know you or your child. That said, here are a few suggestions to make the most of your phone encounter:

◆ **DO** volunteer information about your child's past medical history and drug allergies.
◆ **DON'T** expect the doctor on call to have your child's medical chart available.
◆ **DO** call if there is an emergency.
◆ **DON'T** call after business hours if you need to book an appointment, get non-emergency med-

FIRST AID

? ?

ication refills, or want to know the best diaper rash cream.

◆ *DO* keep your cell phone on once you've paged the doctor.
◆ *DON'T* call an old friend while you are waiting for the doctor to call you back.
◆ *DO* have a pharmacy number handy in case you need a prescription to be called in.
◆ *DON'T* use caller ID to call the doctor back. Besides it being just plain creepy, the person on call is taking calls in the order they were received via voicemail or pager. If you have follow up questions or concerns, use the appropriate answering service number to page the doctor again.

Q. How do I decide what is a medical emergency?

If you are worried that your child's life is in danger, call 911. Otherwise, call your doctor's emergency line. We've listed some medical emergencies below to help you decide. We'll also walk you through specific situations later in the chapter.

Call 911 if your child has:
◆ Extreme difficulty breathing, or is not breathing.
◆ Altered mental status (unarousable, unresponsive, confused, lethargic, or irritable).
◆ A seizure.
◆ A fever with stiff neck, severe headache, and light sensitivity.
◆ Uncontrollable bleeding.
◆ A head injury with altered mental status (confusion, lethargy, unresponsive, or combative), vomiting, trouble walking, headache.
◆ Blue, purple, or gray lips or skin.

PARENT 411: THE HOME FIRST AID KIT

Here are some items you should always have on hand:

Band-Aids
Sterile non-stick dressing and tape
Butterfly bandages or thin adhesive strips
Ace wrap
Roll of gauze dressing
Thermometer (more on which type is best later in this chapter)
Petroleum jelly
Acetaminophen (Tylenol, Tempra)
Ibuprofen (Motrin, Advil)
Antibiotic ointment
Diphenhydramine (Benadryl)
Saline nose drops
1% hydrocortisone cream
List of emergency phone numbers including poison control (800-222-1222), doctor, and dentist

◆ Severe pain or is inconsolable.
◆ Vomiting blood (not just a streak).

Go to the nearest emergency room if your child has:
◆ A cut/laceration that may need stitches.
◆ Not been urinating at least three times a day with an illness.
◆ Fever and looks very ill.
◆ A large amount of bloody poop.
◆ Petechiae rash that is spreading quickly. (See box later in this chapter for more details, and Toddler411.com for a picture.)[1]

Parent 411: How to take vital signs

Vital signs are an objective way to determine how one's life systems are working (brain, heart, lungs, and blood vessels). They include the heart rate or "pulse," respiratory rate (breaths per minute), temperature, and blood pressure. You can help your medical provider tremendously if you can assess these and give that info to the doctor. The only thing you cannot do at home is the blood pressure.

Note: When a person runs a fever, it revs up all the vital signs. Parents worry that their child's heart feels like a hummingbird's when he has a fever. That is normal.

1. **Temperature:** Have a thermometer and know how to use it. We'll talk details on which thermometer to buy and how to interpret readings in the fever section.

2. **Pulse:** Feel your child's pulse in the inner part of the elbow, the groin, the neck, or on the wrist just above the thumb. Count the number of pulsations for 15 seconds and multiply by four. This gives you the beats per minute. The average heart rates are:
   Age one to three years: 90–150
   Age four to five years: 65–135
   Adults: 60–100

3. **Respiratory Rate:** Watch your child's chest as it moves in and out. Count one breath for each time he breathes in for 30 seconds and multiply by two. This gives you the number of breaths per minute. The average respiratory rates are:
   Age one to three years: 22–30
   Age four to six years: 20–24
   Adults: 12–16

Q. I am so afraid I will miss something serious with my child. What should I be looking for?

After working with families over fifteen years, I can tell you that parents don't miss serious medical problems. They may not know what the diagnosis is, but they know something is wrong with their child. Think about it. You spend most of your waking hours with your child. You watch them eat, play, bathe, and sleep. You will notice if something is awry. Trust yourself. Then, read the rest of this chapter.

first aid

Insider Tips

◆ Have your child near you when you speak to a medical provider over the phone. You may be asked to describe what you see (like a rash, or breathing pattern).

◆ Read the "what the medical provider will ask you" sections so you are ready to respond.

Parent 411: Top symptoms parents need to notice

Here are the top three symptoms you as a parent need to pay attention to:

◆ **Labored breathing**
DON'T worry if you feel a "rattling in the chest."
DO worry about the ribs being pulled in with each breath and an above normal respiratory rate.

◆ **Abdominal pain**
DON'T worry about appendicitis every time your child has a tummy ache.
DO worry when your child is so uncomfortable he cannot jump up and down.

◆ **Fever**
DON'T worry about the number itself.
DO worry if your child is confused/unarousable or is irritable/inconsolable.

Dr. B's Top Tips for Emergencies:
It may not be as be as bad as you think!

1. Appendicitis. If your child can jump up and down, he probably doesn't have appendicitis.

2. Meningitis. If your child can look up at the ceiling and down at his feet without neck pain, he probably doesn't have meningitis.

3. Labored breathing. Look at your child's chest. If his chest is not pulling in with each breath, and the respiratory rate is not elevated, he probably does not have labored breathing.

Insider Secrets
Top tips to having a pleasant ER experience

After speaking with your medical provider, you may need to take your child to an emergency department ("ER") at your local hospital. But even if your doctor calls ahead, don't expect them to roll out the red carpet. (And you thought the wait in the doctor's office was bad...)

Emergencies are handled by the severity of the situation, not the time you checked in. And the waiting room may look deceptively quiet. We won't bore you with what could be going on in the back.

So here are some suggestions to make your ER experience a little more tolerable:

1. **Pretend you are camping out for concert tickets.** Bring a bag of food, diapers, toys, iPod/iPad, pillow, etc. You may be there for a while.
2. **Ask the triage nurse if it is okay for your child to eat or drink.** A full tummy may delay getting an imaging study done or worse, surgery.
3. **Bring an extra adult with you, if you can.** Avoid bringing extra children, however. It's bad enough having to entertain one child for an extended period of time.
4. **Ask for copies of lab and x-ray results for your doctor.** If possible, have the ER doctor contact your practice's on-call doctor directly.
5. **Ask questions and write everything down.** Having a sick child is very stressful. It's easy to get flustered and forget the details.

Top 10 Toddler Medical Emergencies

We wish we could cover every medical problem you may encounter in this chapter, but we wanted to write a book that weighed less than your child. We've hit the highlights here with the scariest and the most common emergencies you may have to deal with. We'll help you handle some of these things at home, and troubleshoot situations that need immediate care.

We have categorized the information based on the urgency for medical attention. In doctor lingo, it's called "triaging." If you are an *E.R.* or *Grey's Anatomy* groupie, you know what we are talking about. Yet every problem is unique. If you have concerns, call your doctor.

- ◆ **911:** Denotes symptoms that are medical emergencies.
- ◆ **Priority 1:** Needs immediate treatment—NOW.
- ◆ **Priority 2:** Needs appointment the next day.
- ◆ **Priority 3:** Watch and wait. Needs appointment if there is no improvement or worsening of symptoms.

#1 Allergic reactions

Allergic reactions are an abnormal response to something the body comes in contact with. The body responds with a chemical chain reaction that releases a chemical called histamine. Allergic reactions can range in severity from a mild, localized skin irritation to life-threatening shock. The allergic response begins within minutes to hours of exposure (most within an hour). The reaction can involve several body systems like the skin, respiratory tract (mouth, throat, lungs), gastrointestinal tract (stomach and bowels), cardiovascular system (heart and blood vessels), and nervous system (brain and nerves). The most serious reactions can involve all these body systems (**ANAPHYLACTIC REACTION**).

FYI: it may take several exposures to the same thing before a reaction occurs. For example, your child may have an allergic reaction to an antibiotic he has had before. Or, he may react several days after starting the meds.

FIRST AID

? ?

Allergic reactions that cause labored breathing require immediate rescue with epinephrine (Epi-Pen) and stabilization with injectable/oral steroids and antihistamines. Beware: children with asthma are more likely than others to have serious breathing problems with allergic reactions.

In general, rashes due to an allergic reaction are not emergency issues and can be evaluated when your doctor's office is open. The exception: blisters and/or mouth sores need immediate medical attention for a severe reaction (**STEVENS-JOHNSON SYNDROME**).

Diphenhydramine (Benadryl), cetirizine (Zyrtec), and other antihistamines can make allergic rashes less red and itchy, until the dose wears off. Because histamine levels stay elevated for several days in an allergic response, the rash may come and go for quite a while. Here are three typical toddler rashes associated with allergies:

◆ Hives (*urticaria*): Look like mosquito bites with flat red circles surrounding them or large flat red areas with raised edges that come and go. (Commonly seen with drug allergy).

◆ **ECZEMA**: Red plaques with a scaly rough appearance, often on elbows and knees but can occur elsewhere. (Commonly seen with food allergy).

◆ *Contact dermatitis*: Patches or streaks of red pimples or blisters in very localized areas. (Commonly seen with poison ivy). See Chapter 17, Common Diseases for more info on poison ivy.

(See our web site, Toddler411.com, Bonus Material—Rash-O-Rama for pictures of these rashes. Quite a bit of fun at 3am.)

Common diagnoses: Eczema, hives (urticaria), poison ivy (contact dermatitis)
Uncommon diagnoses: Anaphylactic reaction, Stevens-Johnson Syndrome

What to do:
◆ If your child has had previous allergic reactions, you should have an Epi-Pen at home (a emergency rescue medication given in shot form). If he has any problems breathing, call 911 and use that Epi-Pen immediately.

◆ If your child has hives or contact dermatitis, give a dose of an antihistamine (over the counter or prescription—both work. See Appendix A, Medication for dosing information).

◆ If you are sure it is a contact rash (for example poison ivy) or eczema, try applying 1% hydrocortisone cream to the area. If you're not sure, get it checked out first.

◆ Try to think of anything your child has been exposed to (food, medications).

◆ Discontinue any medications until your child sees a medical provider.

◆ Take a picture of it (just in case the rash disappears before your child's appointment).

Take home tips:
◆ If your child has more than a small, localized rash with an allergic reaction to food, medication, or insect bites/stings, you should have an Epi-Pen available wherever your child goes (and know how to use it). See Appendix A, Medications for details on Epi-Pens.

◆ Consider having your child wear a medic-alert bracelet if he has a severe allergy.
◆ See an allergist for testing and treatment options.

What the medical provider will ask you about ALLERGIC REACTIONS:
◆ Is your child having any trouble breathing?
◆ Is he anxious, drooling, having lip swelling, or a tickling in his throat?
◆ Is your child dizzy or fainting?
◆ Is your child vomiting, having diarrhea, or complaining of a stomachache?
◆ What does the rash look like? Where is it on the body?
◆ When did you first see the rash?
◆ Is the rash itchy?
◆ Are there any blisters or mouth sores?
◆ Is your child currently taking any medication?
◆ Has your child been exposed to any new foods, bee stings, insect bites, skin care products, jewelry, or plants?

911: Call an ambulance
◆ Shortness of breath, wheezing, drooling.
◆ Lip swelling, tickling in the throat.
◆ Dizziness, fainting, or unconsciousness.

Priority 1: Needs medical attention now
◆ Vomiting, diarrhea, or stomachache with allergic reaction.
◆ Blistering rash with erosive lesions in the mouth, eyes, or genitals.

Priority 2: Needs an appointment the next day
◆ Hives (**urticaria**) but no breathing problems.
◆ Poison Ivy or a localized itchy rash (**contact dermatitis**) that is not improving with over the counter steroid cream.

Priority 3: Wait and see
◆ Eczema.
◆ Poison ivy (contact dermatitis).

Q. If my child got hives from an allergic reaction, what are the odds he will have a worse reaction next time?

As we discussed in Chapter 17, Common Diseases, our allergist friend Dr. Ed Peters, says that history tends to repeat itself when it comes to allergic reactions. So a child who gets hives without labored breathing after eating peanuts will probably not have an anaphylactic reaction the next time he is exposed to peanuts.

That's not a free ticket to the Land of PB &J, but hopefully will make you worry less if a preschool classmate accidentally eats peanut butter ten feet away from your child. The severity of response is also influenced by the extent of the exposure. Example: it's a bad idea for a peanut-allergic child to eat an entire jar of peanut butter.

And remember, young children outgrow most food allergies.

FIRST AID

? ?

#2 Bruising and Bleeding (Nosebleeds, Blood in vomit, Blood in poop)

Bruising:

Kids get bruises all the time. Have you ever watched a toddler run around? Bruising on the skins, knees, and forehead are par for the course. So what's *abnormal*? Bruising in areas that are less susceptible to toddler wear and tear, like the chest and back, can be a red flag. A little rash called **petechiae** (pe-TEEK-E-eye) can also be a serious symptom. (See more in the box below).

Excessive bruising, petechiae, and bleeding can indicate a problem with platelets (the blood cells that clot blood) or a problem with blood clotting.

Bleeding:

Bleeding in the nose, vomit, or poop usually has nothing to do with a platelet problem or a bleeding disorder (although excessive bleeding anywhere can be a clue). It may indicate a different problem entirely:

1. Nosebleeds. Nosebleeds are usually caused by self-induced digital trauma (a nice way to say that a kid is picking his nose!). In rare cases, there is an abnormal piece of tissue that is prone to bleeding.

2. Blood in vomit. If a person vomits bright red blood, the source is somewhere near the mouth. It may be from blood that has been swallowed from a nosebleed or from a tear in the esophagus lining due to forceful vomiting. By contrast, blood that is coming from the stomach is partially digested and looks like coffee grounds. In this case, doctors worry about accidental ingestions (see poisoning at the end of this chapter) that irritate the gastrointestinal tract and other serious problems.

3. Blood in poop. Blood in the poop always needs to be checked out. (Bring a fresh specimen when you visit the doctor!) If the blood looks red, it is coming from some place near the anus. Poop that looks like meconium (black tarry poop—you remember this from those newborn days) is due to blood that has been digested in the intestines.

If your child looks like he is giving birth every time he poops and the poop clogs the toilet, there's no real mystery why there is blood on the toilet tissue. Look for a tear or crack in the anus (called an **ANAL FISSURE**). A bad diaper rash will also cause blood on the diaper wipe.

Diarrhea with streaks of blood and mucus, is a concern for food poisoning or a bacterial infection.

Poop that looks like grape jelly is a concern for a problem called **INTUSSUSCEPTION**. The bowel telescopes on itself and creates an intestinal blockage. Symptoms include abdominal pain (pulling up of the legs), irritability, and grape jelly poop.

Persistent bloody diarrhea is a concern for a chronic condition called **INFLAMMATORY BOWEL DISEASE** (also called **CROHN'S DISEASE/ULCERATIVE COLITIS**).

Common diagnoses:

Excessive bleeding/bruising: trauma.

Petechiae: forceful coughing, vomiting, straining, Strep throat, viral infection.

Nosebleed: nose picking.

Blood in vomit: nosebleed, forceful vomiting.

Blood in poop: constipation leading to anal tear/fissure, bad diaper rash.

Uncommon diagnoses:

Excessive bleeding/bruising: Bleeding disorder (hemophilia, von Willebrand's disease), leukemia, idiopathic thrombocytopenic purpura (ITP), Henoch-Schonlein Purpura (HSP).

Petechiae: leukemia, meningitis, Rocky Mountain Spotted Fever.

Nosebleed: bleeding disorder.

Blood in vomit: gastritis, toxic ingestion.

Blood in poop: food poisoning, intussusception, inflammatory bowel disease.

What to do:

◆ **To control bleeding:** Apply moderate pressure over the area for five minutes.

◆ **For a nosebleed:** Lean your child's head *forward*, not backwards. Pinch the nostrils together for five minutes. If this doesn't work, you can spray some medicated decongestant nose drops into the nostrils (Little Noses or Children's Afrin are two name brands). This causes the blood vessels to shrink and stop bleeding.

◆ **For constipation/anal fissures**: Treat the constipation and you will solve the problem. (see Chapter 13, The Other End for tips). Apply petroleum jelly to the anus several times a day so the skin can heal.

PETECHIAE: THE RASH YOU DON'T WANT TO SEE

Petechiae are flat, purplish dots that almost look like freckles. When you push down on them, they remain there (unlike other rashes that fade to skin color when pushed). Petechiae are caused by broken blood vessels and/or low platelet count. They occur for the following reasons:

◆ **Pressure:** Straining while pooping, giving birth, coughing, or forceful vomiting, breaks tiny blood vessels in the head and neck area.

◆ **Infection:** Due to Strep throat, meningitis, Rocky Mountain Spotted Fever.

◆ **Low platelet count:** Due to viral infections, autoimmune problems, leukemia.

If a child has a perfectly good excuse for petechiae, (like forceful coughing) you are in good shape. Otherwise, your child needs to be seen immediately.

first aid: bleeding

FIRST AID

? ?

Take home tip:

◆ Cefdinir (brand name Omnicef) is an antibiotic notorious for causing bright red to brick colored poop. It's not blood!

What the medical provider will ask you about BRUISING or BLEEDING:

Where are the bruises?

Are there any other rashes on the body? Any petechiae?

Does your child bleed excessively?

Are you able to control the bleeding?

Does anyone in your family have bleeding problems?

Has your child been unusually tired or running a fever with no explanation?

Does your child have fever, irritability, and light sensitivity?

Is your child faint or unconscious?

What the medical provider will ask you about NOSEBLEEDS:

◆ How long has the nose been bleeding?

◆ Are you able to control the bleeding?

◆ Did your child have an injury to his nose?

◆ Does your child pick his nose? Does he have allergies or a cold?

What the medical provider will ask you about VOMITING BLOOD:

◆ Have you been suctioning your child's nose with a bulb syringe?

◆ Has your child had a recent nosebleed?

◆ Has your child been vomiting forcefully?

◆ What does the vomit look like? Is it all blood or streaks of blood? Does it look like coffee grounds? Is there mucus too?

What the medical provider will ask you about BLOOD IN THE POOP:

◆ What are you seeing? Streaks of blood mixed in poop? Solid poop with blood on the diaper wipe or tissue? Explosive bloody diarrhea? Is there mucous too? Does it look like grape jelly?

◆ Is there a diaper rash?

◆ Has anyone in the house had diarrhea?

◆ Does your child look sick or well? Any fever?

◆ Is your child's belly full and tense?

◆ Is your child interested in eating? Is he throwing up?

◆ Has your child been taking antibiotics recently?

911: Call an ambulance

◆ Unable to control bleeding.

◆ Petechiae with fever, irritability/headache, and light sensitivity.

◆ Faint or unconscious child.

Priority 1: Needs medical attention now

◆ Petechiae with fever.

◆ Petechiae and bruising, regardless of body temperature.

◆ Bruising and lethargy.

◆ Excessive bruising, not just shins and knees.

◆ Nosebleed that does not stop after 10–20 minutes of applying pressure and nose spray.

♦ No obvious reason for blood in the vomit.
♦ Vomit that looks like coffee grounds.
♦ Vomiting straight blood.
♦ Bloody diarrhea.
♦ Grape jelly poop.

Priority 2: Needs appointment the next day

♦ Bruising with no other symptoms.
♦ Recurrent nosebleeds.
♦ Blood streaked solid poop, or blood found on diaper wipe/tissue and child looks well.

Priority 3: Wait and see

♦ Constipation and tear seen in anus.
♦ Diaper rash with raw skin.
♦ A nose-picker who has nosebleeds.

#3 Breathing problems (labored breathing, wheezing, choking, cough)

As discussed in an earlier chapter, the respiratory tract is one big tube from the nose down to the lungs. Air goes in and out of this tube with each breath. The *upper* respiratory tract includes the nose, sinuses, throat, and voice box (larynx). The *lower* respiratory tract refers to the tube as it branches off into smaller tubes in the lungs, plus the lung tissue itself.

Upper respiratory tract emergencies include choking and severe croup. With croup, kids will have a hoarse voice. If your child sounds like Darth Vader, you will know he has croup. But the hallmark of respiratory distress with croup is a high-pitched squeal noise called **STRIDOR**. Stridor indicates that the airway is really swollen and immediate medical attention is necessary. With choking, it's worrisome if a person cannot make any noise.

Lower respiratory tract emergencies include wheezing and pneumonia. Parents often hear or feel a "rattling in the chest" and worry that their child has pneumonia. Most of the time, that rattling is due to air going through a snotty nose (called transmitted upper airway noise). Since the respiratory tract is all just one tube, the sounds from above can be heard and felt below. It's kind of like flushing your toilet upstairs and hearing the water in the kitchen downstairs.

As a doctor, I can tell when a child has labored breathing without using my stethoscope. I just look at the child's chest. A child who is working to breathe is air hungry. He will use the accessory muscles of the chest to pull in more air with each breath. The result? The rib muscles and skin above/below the breastbone pull in with each breath (called **RETRACTIONS**). The child's nostrils may also be flaring (*nasal flaring*). And there may be a grunting noise at the end of each breath. An air hungry child breathes rapidly and shallowly, so his respiratory rate will be elevated too. (See the guide to vital signs earlier in this chapter). An older child will have trouble speaking in full sentences. No surprise here: a child who has labored breathing needs immediate medical attention.

Coughing is a protective mechanism to keep nasal secretions from collecting in the lungs. Coughs are usually worse at night because the snot in the nose is dripping down the back of the throat when a child is lying down. Coughs coming from the lungs are usually associated with other symptoms (labored breathing, wheezing). So coughing is not typically a medical emergency. Bothersome, yes. Emergency, no. The symptoms in addition to the cough are what concern us (for example: stridor, wheezing, shortness of breath, elevated respiratory rate).

What to do:

For choking:
- Do nothing if your child is alert and making noises (crying, gagging, coughing). He is trying to clear his airway.
- If your child is in distress and NOT making any noise, try to get the item out of his mouth with your fingers (but only if you can see it). Do not blindly sweep your finger in the mouth as it may push the object further into the airway.
- If your child becomes unconscious, call 911, and then try to dislodge the object doing the Heimlich maneuver. (Get behind the child. Make a fist and hold it with your other hand and place your hands just under the ribcage. Quickly thrust your hands upwards, several times in a row).

For croup:
- Run a humidifier in your child's room.
- If your child is making a high-pitched squeal noise (stridor), take him into the bathroom and turn on the shower. Try this for five to ten minutes.
- If the stridor persists, put a coat on and go out into the cold night air.
- If you live in a warm climate, open the freezer and let your child breathe in the cold air.
- If the shower trick and cold air trick both fail, head to the ER.

For wheezing:
- If your child has wheezed before and you have rescue medication (albuterol) at home, use it.
- Administer treatments (nebulizer/inhaler) as frequently as every four hours at home. If your child needs treatments more often than that, he needs to be seen by a medical provider.

For coughing:
- Run a humidifier in the child's room to loosen up the mucus and relax the airway.
- Use saline nose drops liberally, especially before meals and bedtime.
- Resort to decongestant nose spray if your child is unable to sleep. Use for a few nights only.

Take home tips:
- One cough doctors do worry about is whooping cough. Coughing episodes followed by gasping (with or without a "whoop" noise) need to be checked out.
- Remember: coughs that are worse at night are usually coming from nasal congestion. Using saline nose drops and decongestants may reduce the cough.

◆ *Cough medicines do not work.* Several studies have shown there is no significant reduction in the cough (or improvement in everyone's sleep) when a child is taking cough medication.

What the medical provider will ask you about LABORED BREATHING:

◆ How long has your child had trouble breathing?
◆ Could he have swallowed something?
◆ Does he have a fever?
◆ Is he barking like a seal? Any high-pitched squeals?
◆ What does your child's chest look like? How fast is he breathing?
◆ Has your child ever wheezed before? Has he ever stayed overnight in the hospital for it?

What the medical provider will ask you about COUGHING:

◆ Is he having coughing spasms? Is he gasping? Is he vomiting or turning red with the cough?
◆ Is it wet or dry? Are you able to see what is coming up?
◆ Is it worse at night or in the daytime?
◆ Is he able to catch his breath?
◆ Does the cough seem to be getting better or worse?

911: Call an ambulance
◆ Choking and unable to speak
◆ Not breathing
◆ Unconscious

Priority 1: Needs medical attention now

◆ Signs of air hunger (elevated respiratory rate, retractions, grunting, nasal flaring).
◆ Stridor (see explanation above).
◆ Child with asthma with a flare up.
◆ Repeated coughing spasms, followed by reddening of the face, maybe a "whoop," or vomiting.
◆ Fever over 105° with cough.

Priority 2: Needs an appointment the next day

◆ Barking like a seal but no squeal.
◆ Coughing more than two weeks.
◆ Cough is getting worse.

Priority 3: Wait and see

◆ Rattling in the chest.
◆ Cough less than two weeks.
◆ Intermittent wheezing noises without labored breathing.

CHOKING HAZARDS: WHAT TO AVOID

Every year, 10,000 kids under the age of 14 choke on something and end up in the emergency room. Seventy-five percent of those children are under three years of age. And sadly, some of those kids die. Want to know what the deadliest choking hazard is? Hot dogs. Other food choking hazards include grapes, peanuts, hard carrots, and hard candies.

first aid: breathing

#4 Fever: SPECIAL SECTION a.k.a How to chill when your toddler has a fever!

Fever is the top reason parents call their pediatrician. And fevers usually occur at night (which is why we get those calls after office hours!) Because fever phobia is a common diagnosis of parenthood, we are going to devote a few pages to this topic to help ease your mind.

Fever is a misunderstood symptom. It is the body's response to infection or inflammation. It's not dangerous—it's helpful. Contrary to popular belief, fever does not *cause* anything bad to happen to you. Let's repeat that—*fever is not bad*. It does not cause brain damage, death, or the release of evil humors. Fever does occasionally cause benign seizures (convulsions), but this only occurs in children who are prone to them between the ages of six months to five years of age (see **febrile seizure** in Chapter 17, Common Diseases). Okay, we know the words "benign seizure" sounds like an oxymoron, but trust us, it is—at least in this case.

Did you know that our body temperature is not 98.6° every moment of the day? It varies based on the body's hormone levels (circadian rhythm). Our body is the coolest in the morning (as low as 97.6°) and the hottest (as high as 100°) at night. *The true definition of a fever is a body temperature of 100.4° or higher taken rectally.*

Here's another eye-opener: *your child will not self-destruct if you leave the fever alone!* The body temperature only rises to a certain point (around 106°) when it is responding to an infection. Because fever does make you feel crummy, it's okay to use a fever-reducing medicine. But know that fever reducing medicines like acetaminophen or ibuprofen will only bring the body temperature down a couple of degrees. (That's why they are called fever *reducers* and not fever *eliminators*). You don't have to throw your child into a cool bath or sponge him down. While this will make him complain loudly and shiver, it will not bring his body temperature down much.

Fever is really just a clue that something is brewing within your child. So, quit worrying about the fever and start searching for why he has one! Fever is often the first sign of infection. Over the next few hours, look for symptoms like vomiting, diarrhea, runny nose, cough, decreased appetite (look for a sore throat), or a rash. If you cannot figure out the cause of the fever, it's time to get professional help.

Finally, you should know *that fever usually lasts three to four days with the average viral infection.* The degree of fever is the highest in the first days of the illness and diminishes with time. Red flags that should be checked out include a rising fever curve, a fever that persists more than four days, or a new fever after being fever free for more than 24 hours.

Common diagnoses: Viral infection (cold, flu, stomach virus), bacterial infection (Strep throat, ear infection).

Uncommon diagnoses: Kawasaki disease, rheumatoid arthritis, leukemia, serious infections.

DR B'S OPINION

"Fever is not the problem, it's the clue. Your mission: figure out what is causing the fever!"

Old Wives Tales: Fever

◆ *Fever causes brain damage.* False. Even children who are prone to febrile seizures do not sustain brain damage.

◆ *Feed a fever, starve a cold.* False. Your child needs fluids, regardless of what illness he has.

◆ *Put your child in a tepid bath if he has a fever.* False. This is not an effective way to bring the body temperature down. It is an effective way to torture your child.

◆ *Don't give your child a bath if he has a fever.* False. Then you will have a stinky, sick child.

◆ *Don't give milk if your child has a fever.* False. This one's not even worth explaining.

◆ *Teething causes fever.* False. Don't chalk it up to teething. Your child can be teething AND have an infection.

Q. At what body temperature do I start to worry?

We know you will worry if your child is over 102°. The doctor's comfort zone is much higher than that. Once your child is older than three months of age, doctors will hang our hats on things other than the number. As a pediatrician, I am much more concerned about a child who looks like a wet noodle with a fever of 101° than one who is topping 104° and running around my exam room. I am also more concerned about a child who does not have an obvious source of infection.

DR B'S OPINION

"If a child doesn't look that sick, he probably isn't."

Dr. B's opinion: When I worry about a fever

◆ I worry about feverish kids who are either inconsolable or unresponsive.

◆ I worry when I cannot find an obvious source of infection.

◆ I want to see a child who has had a fever more than four days straight. I worry about more serious viral infections, bacterial infections, and things other than infection that cause a fever.

◆ I want to see a child whose fever has broken for over 24 hours and spikes a new fever (a secondary bacterial infection is the concern here).

◆ I want to see a child whose fever curve is progressively rising during the illness. Like above, this is a concern for a secondary bacterial infection.

Q. Should I worry that the fever reducer did not bring the temperature down?

First of all, check the dose of the medication you are giving. Dosing is based on your child's weight. If you are still giving your toddler the same dose she got as a baby, you are probably under-dosing her. Give the appropriate dose (see our dosing chart below) and then see what happens.

Next, remember that these medications are fever *reducers* and not *eliminators*. At best, they will bring the body temperature down by a couple of degrees. If your child's fever was shooting up as you administered the medicine, it will look as if the medicine did nothing. In reality, it kept the fever from rising even more.

Q. What's the best way to take a toddler's temperature?

In an older child, the demeanor of the child is more important than what the thermometer reads. It's not going to change your doctor's management approach if a child is 101.4° or if he is 102.3°. As a pediatrician, I base my medical decisions on whether my patient "has fever" or "does not have fever." I am more likely to order studies (labs, x-rays) if a child's temperature is over 104°, but that's only if the diagnosis is not obvious.

That said, what's the most effective way to take a toddler's temperature? *Rectal thermometers are the most accurate way to take anyone's temperature*. Getting your toddler to accept this method, however, may be a challenge. Thermometer makers recognized this reality and have flooded the market with all sorts of new gadgets (ear thermometers, pacifier thermometers, temporal artery scanners, plastic skin stickers, etc).

Here is the bottom line: once your child is cooperative, use a cheap digital oral thermometer under the tongue. As an alternative, it is acceptable to use that oral thermometer in the armpit as well.

What about ear thermometers? These are notorious for giving false readings. I'm not a fan because ear thermometers can give falsely elevated results, causing parents to panic.

Whatever thermometer and method of temperature taking you use, report what you actually read on the thermometer. Don't add a degree or subtract three-quarters of a decimal point. Doctors are just trying to get a ballpark figure when it comes to older kids with fevers!

Top 10 tips for fever reducing medications

1. **Fever reducers will reduce fevers, not eliminate them.** Don't expect miracles.
2. **Never give your child aspirin.** Aspirin can cause Reye's Syndrome, destroying the liver and possibly causing death.
3. **Always follow the dosing instructions** on the package for acetaminophen and ibuprofen and use the dropper or cup that comes with the bottle. Key point to remember: the *infant drops* are a different concentration than the *children's syrup*.
4. **Alternating acetaminophen and ibuprofen is not usually recommended.**
5. **If your child is dehydrated, it's wise to use acetaminophen instead of ibuprofen.** Ibuprofen is metabolized through the kidneys, which are already working overtime with dehydration.
6. **Avoid combination fever and cold products.** It limits your ability to re-dose the fever medication and is a set up for potential overdosing.
7. **Use a syringe or medicine cup** (not a silverware spoon) to dose teaspoons.
8. **Suppositories** (medicine bullets inserted in the anus) are unpleasant, but they are one way to get fever reducing medicine in if your child is vomiting or refusing to take medicine.

9. **Acetaminophen is the generic name for Tylenol,** Feverall, Tempra. Ibuprofen is the generic name for Motrin or Advil. Acetaminophen is dosed every four hours, Ibuprofen is dosed every six hours.

10. **Make sure you have dosed the medicine based on your child's CURRENT weight.** It won't make a dent in your child's fever if you are under-dosing him.

Dosing chart
Acetaminophen:

CHILD'S WEIGHT IN LBS.	18-23 LBS	24-35 LBS	36-47 LBS
Dose in milligrams (mg)	120 mg	160 mg	240 mg
Infant drops (80mg per 0.8 ml)	0.8 +0.4ml	0.8 + 0.8ml	–
Children's syrup (160mg per tsp)	3/4 tsp	1 tsp	1 1/2 tsp
Suppository (80 mg)	1 1/2 supp	2 supp	–
Suppository (120 mg)	1 supp	1 1/3 supp	2 supp

Ibuprofen:

CHILD'S WEIGHT IN LBS.	18-23 LBS	24-35 LBS	36-47 LBS
Dose in milligrams (mg)	75 mg	100 mg	150 mg
Infant drops (50 mg per 1.25 ml)	1.25 + 0.625ml	1.25 + 1.25ml	–
Children's syrup (100mg per tsp)	3/4 tsp	1 tsp	1 1/2 tsp

What to do:
◆ If your child feels hot, take his temperature.
◆ Give appropriate dose (based on weight) of fever reducing medicine if your child seems miserable.
◆ Start looking for other symptoms of infection.

Take home tips:
◆ Fever is not a disease. It is a symptom.
◆ Your child will not self-destruct if he has a fever.
◆ Sponge bathing or tepid baths make your child angry, not cooler.
◆ The most important thing is how your child looks with a fever. If he is smiling and playing with his toys, he is probably not that ill.

What the medical provider will ask you about FEVER:
◆ How old is your child?
◆ Have you given any fever reducing medicine?
◆ What other new symptoms are you seeing?
◆ Is anyone else in the household sick?

first aid: fever

- How many days has the fever been going on?
- Any recent illnesses prior to the fever?
- Any rashes?
- How does your child look? Unarousable? Irritable and inconsolable? Will he play or talk to you?
- Does he perk up after taking fever-reducing medicine?

911: Call an ambulance
- Fever and unarousable.
- Fever and inconsolable.
- Fever with headache, light sensitivity, neck stiffness.
- Fever with spreading petechiae rash.
- Fever with a seizure (if it is the first time).

Priority 1: Needs medical attention now
- Fever and lethargy.
- Fever and very cranky mood.
- Fever with a limp or limb pain.
- Fever of 104° or above with no obvious source of infection.
- Fever with labored breathing.
- Fever with petechiae rash.

Priority 2: Needs an appointment the next day
- Fever lasting more than three days straight.
- Fever under 104° with no obvious source of infection.
- New fever, after being fever free for more than 24 hours.
- Rising fever curve over a period of days.
- Fever with a rash that is not petechiae.

Priority 3: Wait and see
- Fever less than three days duration, with an obvious infection (cold, stomach virus, etc).

#5 Vomiting, Diarrhea, and Dehydration

Vomiting is the forceful elimination of food and fluid that is in the stomach. As you might guess, the stomach can only hold a fixed amount of stuff (that's a medical term). So, if a child vomits repeatedly, he will eventually have dry heaves (vomiting with nothing coming out). If a child vomits bile (fluorescent green/yellow fluid), this is from the small intestine and may signal an intestinal blockage. Serious (and uncommon) diagnoses include **INTUSSUSCEPTION** and **APPENDICITIS**.

Yes, repeated vomiting can cause dehydration. If your child is vomiting more than 18 hours straight, he will not be able to take in adequate fluid. However, this rarely happens with most garden-variety stomach viruses, since vomiting usually stops within 12 hours and kids are drinking again. Diarrhea carries a GREATER risk for dehydration, especially if it accompanies the vomiting. FYI: dehydration usually occurs later in the course of the illness.

Not all vomiting is from an upset stomach. Young children have very active gag reflexes. Forceful coughing can cause vomiting (*post-tussive emesis*). So, a child may vomit when he has a respiratory infection like a cold. Headaches can also be accompanied by vomiting. This category includes ear infections, head injury, brain tumors, and meningitis. That's why vomiting without a really good reason (that is, without diarrhea) needs to be checked out.

On the other end, diarrhea is loose (and usually frequent) poop. Most of the time, it is a sign of a stomach virus (**VIRAL GASTROENTERITIS**). And most of the time, it is not a "24-hour bug." You'll be lucky if it only lasts a day. Stomach viruses usually begin with vomiting in the first several hours of the illness, and are followed by *five to seven days* of watery diarrhea. Because so much water is lost in that diarrhea, doctors and parents need to aggressively push fluid intake to prevent dehydration.

Food poisoning (**BACTERIAL ENTERITIS**) is a concern when there are streaks of blood or mucus in the diarrhea. The good news: bacterial infections only account for 10% of all intestinal infections. So, once again, odds are that you are dealing with a stomach virus when your child has diarrhea.

Chronic diarrhea (going on for more than two weeks) is a separate topic. For details on that, see Chapter 17, Common Diseases.

How do you know your child is dehydrated? Some of the easiest and most objective measurements are the child's weight and the number of times he has urinated (peed) each day. Here's a rule of thumb: if your child pees at least three times a day, he is getting enough fluid to counteract the loss from diarrhea and vomiting (and hence, is not dehydrated).

Common diagnoses:
> ***Vomiting and diarrhea:*** Stomach virus, food intolerance
> ***Vomiting only:*** forceful coughing, ear infection, kidney infection

Uncommon diagnoses:
> ***Vomiting and diarrhea:*** Food poisoning (bacterial gastroenteritis), parasitic infection, intussusception
> ***Vomiting only:*** intussusception, appendicitis, head injury, meningitis, brain tumor, metabolic disorder

What to do:

Vomiting:
- ◆ Do not give your child anything to eat or drink while he is actively vomiting. Parents are so afraid their child will get dehydrated, they offer fluids immediately—don't. It will only come right back at you.
- ◆ If it has been at least one hour since your child has vomited, try a few sips of a rehydration drink (such as Pedialyte). Offer small volumes frequently—like a teaspoon every five minutes. Do not let him drink as much as he wants. He will be thirsty and want to chug it. Again, it will only come right back at you.
- ◆ If the rehydration plan results in vomiting, call your doctor.
- ◆ If the frequent sips stay down, you can increase to a couple of ounces per attempt.
- ◆ If your child has been vomit-free for four hours, resume regular fluids (yes, milk is okay).
- ◆ If regular fluids stay down, resume a normal diet.
- ◆ Make sure your child is peeing at least every eight hours. If not, check in with your doc.

Diarrhea:

◆ The BRAT diet is out. In the olden days (prior to 2000), the pervasive wisdom was to give a child Bananas, Rice, Applesauce, and Toast (BRAT) to reduce the volume of diarrhea. Doctors now know that restrictive diets interfere with a child's ability to catch up when his nutritional stores have been depleted by illness.[2] So go back to your child's normal diet.

◆ Let your child eat what he wants (well, you know what we mean).

◆ Offer foods that are high in fat (avocados, meats, eggs, nuts, fish) as the fat helps to bulk up the poop. Fiber helps for the same reason.

◆ Offer yogurt every day. It's a source of good bacteria (lactobacillus) that helps the body digest food. Or add the powder of one lactobacillus/probiotics capsule to any other food your child is willing to eat. These are the same good germs found in yogurt but available in capsule form. Some studies show a 50% reduction in diarrhea with probiotics.

◆ Dairy products are fine. Your child will have diarrhea no matter what he is eating! Dairy products only become an issue if you are dealing with chronic diarrhea over two weeks. Review the section in Chapter 17, Common Diseases for info.

◆ Anti-diarrheal medication needs your doctor's blessing. The party line used to be that young children should not receive any of these medications (there were previous concerns about safety and a lack of effectiveness). However, more recent studies suggest that salicylate-based products (for example, Pepto-Bismol) are probably safe and somewhat beneficial. BUT . . . ask your doc before using these.[3]

Take home tips:

◆ Persistent vomiting without an obvious cause needs to be checked out.

◆ Pedialyte, Ricelyte, and Rehydralyte are brand names for rehydration drinks that are perfectly formulated with water, salt, and sugar. Unfortunately, kids over a year of age often refuse them because they tastes like salt water. You can try Pedialyte frozen popsicles or add a splash of juice for flavoring. Flat ginger ale, 7-Up, Gatorade, or clear chicken broth will do if you have no other options. We have a recipe to make your own rehydration drink in Appendix B, Alternative Medicine under "vomiting and diarrhea."

◆ Put a tissue in the front part of the diaper to see if your child is making urine (pee). It should be yellow because the urine will be concentrated.

Parent 411: How to tell if your child is dehydrated
1. Urine output. When our body needs fluid, less water is released as urine. If your child pees at least three times every 24 hours, he is NOT severely dehydrated.

2. Weight loss. If a child has lost 10% of his body weight, he is severely dehydrated. This is an emergency.

3. Sunken fontanelle. Some children under 18 months of age have an open fontanelle (soft spot on top of the head). That's their oil gauge equivalent. If the tank is low, the soft spot is sunken. Doctors can't use that trick once the spot closes.

4. **Skin turgor.** You know what your skin looks like if you have been in the bathtub too long. We call this the Phyllis Diller look. Skin is nice and doughy if it has water in it. It's pruney if you are dehydrated.

5. **Dry lips and mouth.** A dehydrated person stops making saliva.

6. **Capillary refill.** Press down gently on your fingernail. See how the pink color turns white? When you release the pressure, the pink color should return in two seconds. In severe dehydration, that refill will take more than two seconds because the blood supply is sluggish.

7. **Lethargy.** If your child is confused or looks like a wet noodle, he may be dehydrated.

What the medical provider will ask you about VOMITING:
- How old is your child?
- How long has he been vomiting?
- What does the vomit look like? Any bile? Any coffee grounds?
- Does he have a fever?
- Does he have diarrhea?
- Is anyone in the house sick? Does he spend time around other children?
- Does his stomach hurt? Is he doubled over or kicking his legs?
- Does his head hurt? Does the light bother his eyes? Is his neck stiff?
- How often is he urinating (peeing)? Does it hurt to pee?
- Any recent head injuries?
- Is he coughing and then vomiting, or just vomiting out of the blue?

What the medical provider will ask you about DIARRHEA:
- How old is your child?
- How long has the diarrhea been going on?
- Has there been vomiting or fever?
- What does the diarrhea look like? Watery? Bloody? Mucus or blood-streaked? Grape jelly?
- How often is your child peeing (urinating)?

What the medical provider will ask you about DEHYDRATION:
- How often is your child peeing (urinating)?
- How much does your child usually weigh? What does he weigh now?
- Is your child responsive and talking to you?

 ### 9 1 1 : Call an ambulance
- Unarousable or extremely confused.

Priority 1: Needs medical attention now
- Vomiting over 12 hours straight.
- Vomiting blood or coffee grounds.
- Vomiting with a head injury.
- Vomiting bile.

- Vomiting with headache, fever, light sensitivity, neck stiffness.
- Vomiting with a significant stomachache.
- Dehydrated. Not peeing at least three times a day.
- Grape jelly diarrhea.
- Blood or mucus in the diarrhea.
- Lethargy.

Priority 2: Needs an appointment the next day

- Persistent vomiting without an obvious cause.
- Vomiting only in the mornings.
- Diarrhea for over a week.
- Fever more than three days with the illness.

Priority 3: Wait and see

- Isolated episode of vomiting in a well appearing child.
- Watery diarrhea for less than one week, with frequent peeing (urination).

#6 Skin (rashes, burns, cuts, bites, and stings)

Trying to diagnose a rash over the phone is always fun. At best, docs try to determine whether the rash fits into a worrisome or non-worrisome category. Worrisome rashes need prompt attention. Non-worrisome rashes can wait until the office opens the next day.

You probably have your own division for rashes: contagious or not contagious. Rashes can be caused by infections, allergies, inflammation, and blood cell abnormalities. Check out our rash-o-rama visual library of rashes at Toddler411.com and follow along with the text in Chapter 16, Common Infections.

The only rashes that are true emergencies are petechiae and allergic reactions on the skin accompanied by difficulty breathing. Petechiae are covered in the bleeding and bruising section of this chapter.

As for burns, any type of burn (stove, spilled coffee, sun) damages the top layer of skin. As you probably have heard, burns are categorized by degrees:

- ***First degree burn.*** This causes redness.
- ***Second degree burn.*** Burns that go deeper than that cause a blister to form.
- ***Third degree burn.*** This is much more serious, where the burn extends deeper into tissue, causing extensive destruction. These burns may look white or charred and cause numbness.

The skin is the body's protection against foreign invaders like infection. So a burn leaves the skin susceptible. That's why second degree burns, or worse, need to be seen by a medical provider. Doctors clean away any dead skin that interferes with healing and can lead to infection. Your doc will also assess the damage and look for infection.

When it comes to cuts, we can't wait until the office opens to decide whether or not stitches (sutures) are needed. Stitches need to be placed within 12 hours of the injury or else there is a greater risk of wound infection. See below for how to make the call on whether a cut needs stitches.

Bites are another frequent injury with toddlers. Getting bitten by a neighbor's dog, a playmate, or a pet gerbil are all set ups for potential skin infection. While you may worry about rabies or tetanus, the more common infection is from the usual bacteria that live in the biter's mouth. Human bites tend to be the dirtiest, but fortunately most toddlers don't bite hard enough to break the skin. Cat bites (usually puncture wounds) frequently get infected since they are the hardest to clean. Whether your child is bit by another child or a cat, however, both bites deserve preventative antibiotics. Stitches are not usually required as it increases the risk of infection. Any bites that break skin should be seen by a medical provider to clean the wound well and assess for infection.

Insect *bites* are itchy, but not an emergency. Some children get a local allergic reaction to a bite that may cause swelling and redness of the area. The difference between an allergic response and infection is that infected skin is very tender to the touch.

Insect *stings* may hurt and also cause an itchy allergic response. Some children have severe allergic reactions to insect stings. See the allergic reaction section in this chapter for details.

Common diagnoses:
For rashes: viruses (***viral exanthems***), bacteria (Strep, MRSA, cellulitis, impetigo), scabies, fungus (ringworm), contact irritation (poison ivy), eczema, molluscum contagiosum, allergic reaction
Uncommon diagnoses:
For rashes: Kawasaki disease, rheumatoid arthritis, idiopathic thrombocytopenic purpura (**ITP**), Henoch-Schonlein Purpura (**HSP**)

Helpful Hints: Does it need stitches?
1. What happened? If the injury is from a human or cat bite, it is usually not stitched as this increases the risk of infection.
2. How long ago did the injury happen? Wounds over 12 hours old should not be sutured.
3. **Where is the cut/laceration?** Location of the wound is a deciding factor because of cosmetic issues (for example, the face) and potential nerve damage (such as the hands).
4. **How deep is it?** If you can see fat, it needs stitches. That's usually deeper than one-quarter of an inch.
5. **If it is on the face, does it cross the lip/skin line or the eyebrow line?** These cuts need stitches for a better cosmetic result.
6. **Is the bleeding under control?** If not, it needs stitches.

Stitches 411: Top tips about stitches
◆ **Brows and liplines**. Cuts to the eyebrows and lip lines always need stitches for the best cosmetic result.
◆ **Mouth and lips.** Cuts on the lip, tongue, or gums rarely need stitches.
◆ **Watch for infection.** Redness, tenderness, drainage, and fever are all signs of wound infection that need to be evaluated by a doc.
◆ **Got your shots?** Your child should be more up to date on his

first aid: skin

tetanus shots than you. Tetanus is given at two, four, six, and 15–18 months. A booster is given at four to six years of age.

◆ **Keep it clean.** It is okay for stitches to get wet. Keep the wound clean.

◆ **Take it out.** Stitch removal depends on the location. For instance, face stitches are removed in four days. But palm-of-the-hand stitches take 14 days. Follow the directions of the person who puts them in. Delayed suture removal impairs the cosmetic result. It also hurts more!

◆ **Hand me the Elmer's.** Dermabond and Indermal are types of skin glue which can be used in place of stitches. It is fairly easily applied and dissolves on its own. Its use is limited to areas where there is not much tension (for example, you can't use skin glue over a joint).

◆ **Staples anyone?** Staples are easier to put in, but more painful to take out. They are useful in non-cosmetic areas like the scalp.

What to do:

For Hives:

◆ See section on Allergies in this chapter.

For burns:

◆ Apply cool water or a cool pack to the area.
◆ If it blisters, do not pop it.
◆ Apply antibiotic ointment and cover it with a non-stick dressing. If you have prescription antibiotic salve (brand name Silvadene) in the house from a prior episode, use it.

For minor cuts/lacerations:

◆ Control bleeding by applying moderate pressure over the wound for about ten minutes.
◆ Clean area well with plain old soap and water. It's not what you use, but how you use it. Flush the wound several times. For puncture wounds, try irrigating it with a Water-Pik if you've got one.
◆ Apply antibiotic ointment and cover the wound with a clean, non-stick dressing for two or three days. This prevents infection and improves cosmetic results.
◆ Look for redness, draining pus, increasing tenderness, and fever over the next few days.

For bites—human, animal, insect:

◆ Apply moderate pressure for ten minutes to control bleeding.
◆ Clean wound well with soap and water. If possible, flush or irrigate the wound several times.
◆ Apply antibiotic ointment and cover the wound with a clean, non-stick dressing.
◆ Human bites (that break the skin) and cat bites should be seen by a medical provider.
◆ If the bite was from another family's pet, find out if the animal's rabies shot is up to date. If not, contact your local health department.

◆ If the bite was from a wild animal that may be a rabies carrier (see below), seek immediate medical attention.

◆ If the bite was from an unknown, sick looking domestic animal, try to keep the animal contained and contact your local health department. Seek medical attention for your child.

For Insect Stings:

◆ If you see a stinger in the skin, scrape it off with your fingernail or a dull blade. Do not squeeze or pull it out with a tweezers (that injects more venom into the skin).

◆ Apply a cold compress to the area.

◆ Give a dose of such as diphenhydramine (Benadryl) to reduce the allergic response.

◆ Get immediate medical attention if your child has any trouble breathing.[4]

Helpful Hint:
Which animals carry rabies?

◆ These are the top rabies carriers: bats, coyotes, foxes, raccoons, and skunks.

◆ These animals you do NOT have to worry about: chipmunks, gerbils, gophers, guinea pigs, hamsters, mice, moles, prairie dogs, rabbits, rats, and squirrels.[5]

Take home tips:

1. It's a good idea to keep an oral antihistamine like diphenhydramine (Benadryl), antibiotic ointment, and 1% hydrocortisone cream in your medicine cabinet.

2. One year olds may develop a raised, red pimply rash in response to the MMR vaccine (about one to four weeks after being vaccinated).

3. One year olds can get *roseola.* (see Chapter 16, Common Infections for details). You'll see a red blotchy rash after three days of having a feverish child. Unfortunately, you won't know it's roseola until the rash shows up!

4. Drug resistant Staph infections (*MRSA*) may look like a bug bite or spider bite to you, when they are really bacterial skin infections. If the skin area is red and *tender,* instead of itchy, get it checked out. For more on MRSA, see Chapter 16, Common Infections.

What the medical provider will ask you about RASHES:

◆ How old is your child?
◆ How long has the rash been there?
◆ Where on the body did the rash start? Is it spreading? Where?
◆ Is there a fever?
◆ Is it itchy? Really really itchy?
◆ Does anyone else in the house have a rash?
◆ What color is the rash?
◆ Is it scaly?
◆ How big are the spots?
◆ When you press on the rash, does the color turn white? Or does it remain discolored?

◆ Is your child taking any medications? Any new foods?
◆ Have you used any new skin care products?

What the medical provider will ask you about BURNS:
◆ What happened?
◆ How long ago did it happen?
◆ What body parts got burned?
◆ Is the area red? Blistering?

What the medical provider will ask you about CUTS/LACERATIONS:
◆ What happened?
◆ How long ago did it happen?
◆ Are you able to control the bleeding?
◆ Where is the cut?
◆ How deep is the cut? Can you see fat? Bone?
◆ Is there a foreign object in the wound? Are you able to remove it?

What the medical provider will ask you about BITES:
◆ What happened?
◆ For animal bites: Did the child tease or provoke the animal or did the bite just happen?
◆ For animal bites: What kind of animal bit him? Do you know this animal? Are his shots up to date? Did he look ill?
◆ Are you able to control the bleeding?
◆ For insect bites: Is your child having labored breathing?

What the medical provider will ask you about INSECT STINGS:
◆ What happened?
◆ Do you still see a stinger in the skin?
◆ What does the skin look like?
◆ Is your child having any trouble breathing?

911: Call an ambulance
◆ Hives with difficulty breathing.
◆ Petechiae with fever, headache, light sensitivity, neck stiffness.
◆ Extensive burns to the entire body.
◆ Uncontrollable, extensive bleeding.
◆ Labored breathing after an insect bite or sting.

Priority 1: Needs medical attention now
◆ Extensive burns to a single body area.
◆ Burned area looks infected (red, weeping pus, fever).
◆ Cut/laceration that may need stitches.
◆ Cut/laceration that looks infected (red, weeping pus, fever).
◆ Cut/laceration that is bleeding after ten minutes of applying pressure.
◆ Cut/laceration in a cosmetically undesirable location.
◆ Skin injury and immunizations are not current.
◆ Animal bite by an animal who is a rabies carrier, whose vaccine status is unknown, or who looks sick.
◆ Cat bites or human bites that break the skin.
◆ Severe animal bite.

FIRST AID

Priority 2: Needs an appointment the next day

◆ Non-petechiae rash associated with a fever.
◆ Scaly rash without fever.
◆ Itchy or painful rash.
◆ Rash that is not going away after being treated by a medical provider.
◆ Second degree burns (blisters).
◆ Burns on the hands or genitals.
◆ Superficial cuts that may be infected.
◆ Animal bites that may be infected.

Priority 3: Wait and see

◆ Diaper rash.
◆ One year old with a raised red rash one to four weeks after his MMR vaccine.
◆ One year old who develops a blotchy red rash after a fever.
◆ First degree burns.
◆ Superficial cuts, scrapes, insect bites/stings, or animal bites.

#7 Pain (headache, stomachache, chest, back)

We'll cover the top aches and pains in this section. FYI: younger kids have more trouble localizing their pain and expressing it verbally. As your child gets older, it will be easier for him to tell you what hurts.

Abdominal pain (stomachache) is divided into acute (a new event) or chronic (ongoing for a couple of weeks). We'll address acute abdominal pain here. See Chapter 17, Common Diseases for advice on chronic abdominal pain.

Tummy aches are a top toddler complaint. Most of the time, the cause is constipation (see Chapter 13, The Other End, for how to deal with that one). A constipated child has a tummy ache but does *not* have vomiting, fever, or a screaming fit when you touch his belly. Insider tip: always try a trip to the bathroom before heading to the ER. Other common causes include gas and heartburn (**GASTROESOPHAGEAL REFLUX**). Also note that all abdominal pain is not coming from the intestinal tract. Strep throat can cause a tummy ache.

More serious causes of abdominal pain are those that require a procedure or surgery to fix. This list includes **APPENDICITIS, INCARCERATED HERNIA, INTESTINAL OBSTRUCTION** and **INTUSSUSCEPTION** (a piece of bowel is kinked, blocked, or infected). With any of these situations, there is considerable pain and kids look progressively sicker. Symptoms include: swollen/tender belly, lack of interest in eating, persistent vomiting (with or without diarrhea), pulling up of the legs, and grape jelly poop. What are the clues of appendicitis? A child with appendicitis will not want to jump up and down because it hurts.

Toddlers rarely complain of headaches, so if yours does, it should not be ignored. Little kids don't get tension headaches or migraines. Some kids will complain of headaches with an ear infection, sinus infection, or Strep throat.

Headaches to worry about are caused by **MENINGITIS** (see Chapter 16, Common Infections) and brain tumors. With meningitis, the headache is

first aid: pain

FIRST AID

? ?

severe and incapacitating. It is associated with fever, vomiting, neck stiffness, light sensitivity, and petechiae (see section on bleeding and bruises earlier in this chapter). This is not something you will miss. With brain tumors, there are additional symptoms besides a headache. Kids will complain of morning headaches, in particular, and may vomit only in the morning. They may have new onset neurological abnormalities, including lazy eye.

Chest pain is almost never due to a heart problem. If Grandpa complains of chest pain, go to the nearest ER. In children, chest pain is most often due to muscle pain between the ribs from coughing forcefully or a lung infection/wheezing. Rarely, an older child will describe heartburn (**GASTROESOPHAGEAL REFLUX**) as chest pain too. Bottom line: do get your child's chest pain checked out. But don't worry the pain is caused by a heart condition.

Back pain is another rare complaint of toddlers. If you are a baby boomer and have a backache every morning, that's allowed. If you are a just a babe, it's not. Usually, a child has pulled or strained a muscle in the back that causes discomfort. More serious causes include tumors and slipped discs. For these reasons, doctors often get imaging studies on a child who complains of back pain.

Common diagnoses:
> *Abdominal pain:* Gas, constipation, early viral gastroenteritis (stomach virus), gastroesophageal reflux, Strep throat.
> *Headache:* ear infection, sinus infection, Strep throat.
> *Chest pain:* muscle pain, lung infection, wheezing.
> *Back pain:* musculoskeletal injury.

Uncommon diagnoses:
> *Abdominal pain:* Appendicitis, intestinal obstruction, intussusception, incarcerated hernia.
> *Headache:* meningitis, brain tumor
> *Chest pain:* cardiac angina, cracked rib, pericarditis
> *Back pain:* bone tumors, abdominal tumors, leukemia, *spondylolysis* (spine defect)

Parent 411: What is appendicitis anyway?

Appendicitis is an inflammation of (you guessed it) the appendix, a tiny, nonfunctioning piece of tissue attached to the large intestine. Typically, you can the find the appendix in the lower right side of the abdomen (see graphic). However, its location can vary a bit, making the pain and symptoms of an appendicitis vary as well. Why does the appendix swell up? There are a variety of reasons including infection and inflammation. But once it starts, it only gets worse. The appendix eventually gets so swollen that it can burst, spewing bacteria all over the abdomen.

Here is the classic story for appendicitis: nonspecific tummy ache in the belly button area, followed by vomiting and maybe a little fever. Next, there is severe pain on the lower right side of the belly. All cases of appendicitis are not this classic, but the symptoms do not just go away. Things only get worse if the appendix bursts. Then there might be high fever, really tense and painful tummy, and shortness of breath. A child with appendicitis will also refuse to jump up and down.

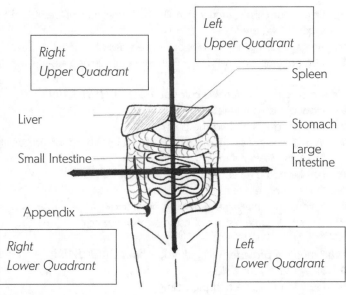

What to do:

For abdominal pain:

- ◆ Take your toilet-trained child to the bathroom and see if he needs to poop.
- ◆ Put your child in a warm bathtub or place a heating pad on his tummy.

For headache, chest pain, or back pain:

- ◆ Give acetaminophen or ibuprofen.

What the medical provider will ask you about HEADACHES:

- ◆ How old is your child?
- ◆ How long has he had the pain?
- ◆ When is the pain happening? All day long, or only certain times?
- ◆ Where is he complaining of pain?
- ◆ Is he consolable?
- ◆ Is he confused or unresponsive?
- ◆ Does he have a fever?
- ◆ Any neck stiffness, light sensitivity, vomiting, or rash?

What the medical provider will ask you about ABDOMINAL PAIN:

- ◆ How old is your child?
- ◆ How long has he had the pain?
- ◆ Where is he complaining of pain? Is it moving?
- ◆ Is the pain getting worse?
- ◆ Does anything make the pain worse or better?
- ◆ Is he consolable?
- ◆ Is he interested in eating?
- ◆ Does your child have a fever?
- ◆ Is your child vomiting? What does the vomit look like?
- ◆ Does your child have diarrhea? Is it watery, bloody, mucousy, or look like grape jelly?

◆ Does your child's tummy look like he is pregnant? Does it hurt to touch it? Where?

◆ Are you seeing any bulges or swollen areas?

◆ Can he jump up and down without complaining of pain?

What the medical provider will ask you about CHEST PAIN:

◆ How old is your child?

◆ How long has he had the pain?

◆ When is the pain happening? At rest? With coughing? With breathing? After a meal?

◆ Has he had a recent respiratory infection?

◆ Does he have a fever?

◆ Is your child having any trouble breathing?

◆ Does he have a history of asthma or wheezing?

What the medical provider will ask you about BACK PAIN:

◆ How old is your child?

◆ How long has he had the pain?

◆ Where is he complaining that it hurts? Does it shoot down the legs?

◆ When does he complain about it?

◆ Does anything make the pain worse or better?

◆ Is he consolable?

◆ Does he have a fever?

◆ Is he interested in eating? Is he losing weight?

911: Call an ambulance

◆ Headache with fever, vomiting, neck stiffness, light sensitivity, and/or petechiae rash.

◆ Inconsolable.

◆ Unarousable.

◆ Severe chest pain with labored breathing.

Priority 1: Needs medical attention now

◆ Abdominal pain and fever without diarrhea.

◆ Projectile vomiting and abdominal pain.

◆ Abdominal pain and grape jelly poop.

◆ Abdominal pain and tense, distended belly.

◆ Abdominal pain for over two hours straight.

◆ Headache with fever.

◆ Headache with confusion or irritability.

◆ Chest pain with fever.

◆ Chest pain with labored breathing.

◆ Back pain with fever.

◆ Back pain with pain shooting down the legs.

Priority 2: Needs an appointment the next day

◆ Abdominal pain with constipation.

◆ Mild headache with no other symptoms.

◆ Mild chest pain with no labored breathing.

◆ Mild back pain with no other symptoms.

FIRST AID

Priority 3: Wait and see
◆ Abdominal pain resolves after pooping.
◆ Headache, chest pain, or back pain resolves after pain medication.

#8 Neurological Emergencies (seizures)

A seizure is involuntary muscle (motor) activity caused by an electrical brainwave that has fired incorrectly. The most common seizures are those caused by a fever that is rising quickly (*febrile seizure*). See Chapter 17, Common Diseases for details.

Common diagnoses: Febrile seizures (convulsions)
Uncommon diagnoses: Head trauma, meningitis, poisoning/ingestion, metabolic disorder, seizure disorder.

What to do:
◆ Call 911.
◆ Put your child on a safe surface—like a carpeted floor.
◆ Make sure he can breathe.
◆ Do NOT put anything in his mouth to hold his tongue.
◆ Start CPR (mouth to mouth resuscitation) if your child looks blue.

Take home tips:
◆ Don't panic. (Easy for us to say, we know).
◆ Once the seizures stops, your child will be tired and confused for an hour or two.

What the medical provider will ask you about SEIZURES:
◆ Have you called 911? Have they arrived? Has your child stopped seizing?
◆ How long did the seizure last? What did it look like?
◆ Has your child ever had a seizure before?
◆ Does your child have any other medical problems?
◆ How old is your child?
◆ Does he have a fever?
◆ Was anyone in the family prone to febrile seizures as a child?
◆ Has your child had any recent head trauma?
◆ Could your child have gotten into any chemicals, medications, or poisons?

 911: Call an ambulance
◆ First time seizure.
◆ Seizure activity that continues more than five minutes.

Priority 1: Needs medical attention now
◆ Known history of febrile seizures, with another episode.
◆ Known seizure disorder.

Priority 2: Needs appointment the next day
◆ Known seizure disorder and needs a medication adjustment.

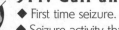

first aid: seizures

Priority 3: Wait and see

◆ Known seizure disorder with recurrent seizures whose medications are being adjusted.

#9 Is it broken? And other traumatic injuries (head, neck, eye, ear, back, nose, mouth, teeth, fingers, toes, arms, legs)

Even if you watch your child like a hawk, she will manage to injure some body part. Hopefully, it will happen on your spouse's watch so you will have someone to blame!

We will cover the common injuries by individual body part in this section. Skin trauma is covered in a separate section of this chapter.

The overriding question we will ask here is, "What happened?" *How* the injury happened is the most reliable factor in determining the severity. No, docs aren't trying to assign blame here, but to figure out what is going on.

Common diagnoses: subconjunctival hemorrhage, corneal abrasion, dislocated elbow (nursemaid's elbow), fractures, minor head injury (bruising under the skin), soft tissue injury (sprains, strains, bruises), subungual hematoma
Uncommon diagnoses: skull fracture, concussion, subdural hematoma (bleeding inside the skull), hyphema, septal hematoma, torn ligaments

Parent 411: Car Seat safety

Sadly, motor vehicle accidents are still the number one cause of injury and death to small children. Every year, about 250,000 kids are injured (and 1500 are killed) in auto accidents. As readers of our other books know, we are big proponents of child passenger safety.

While the current recommendation is to place a child in a rear-facing car seat until he is one year of age and 20 lbs., many experts advise keeping children rear-facing for as long as possible. We agree. Most children under TWO can safely remain rear-facing in convertible car seats that have a weight limit of 35 pounds. Bottom line: the rear facing position better supports a young child's head and neck in the event of an accident.

Another key point: keep your child in a *harnessed* seat as long as possible. Several models on the market today work up to 65 pounds (example: Graco Nautilus) or 80 pounds (example: Britax Frontier).

After your child outgrows a harnessed seat, go for a belt-positioning booster (the two models mentioned above convert to such seats). When a child is over 4'9" and can sit with his or her back straight against the back seat cushion (with knees bent over the seat's edge), then he or she can go with just the auto's safety belt.

This topic is much more detailed than we have space to discuss here. Please see our *Baby Bargains* book for reviews of car seats, advice on finding the best seat and more.

The details, by body part:

Head injury

In your toddler's rush to get to his destination, he trips and bonks his head on the coffee table. Most head injuries are minor, like this one. However, these often result in a big bruise under the skin. (The unofficial term for this is a goose egg.) It looks much worse than it is. It will go down in size and change into a rainbow of colors over a few weeks. You would be in the poor house if you headed to the ER every time your toddler got a goose egg.

So what are the red flags for a serious injury? Docs worry about a child who has fallen greater than his own height. Double that worry if he falls onto a harder surface than say, carpeting. If a child loses consciousness, vomits repeatedly, or seems confused after the event, it may be a bruise or bleeding in the brain (*concussion, subdural hematoma*). Seizures, blurred vision, dizziness, irritability, or amnesia also warrant a medical evaluation.[6]

Old Wives Tale

If you don't see a bruise on the outside of the head, there must be one on the inside. FALSE. While it is true that you don't have to have a goose egg to have sustained a serious head injury, docs are much more concerned with HOW an injury happened than the size of a goose egg!

Neck and back injury

Any injury to the neck or back should be treated as an emergency. Your child should be immobilized and transported to a medical facility by trained personnel. DO NOT MOVE YOUR CHILD because it can cause permanent nerve damage.

Eye injury

Because the eye is a delicate and critical organ, any injury is treated as an emergency. Fortunately, most eye injuries are not serious. Minor bleeding on the surface of the eye is called a *subconjunctival hemorrhage*. Although it looks like your child belongs in a horror movie, it isn't dangerous. Bleeding inside the eye (*hyphema*) is much more serious because it can lead to blindness. Kids can also get painful scratches on the eye surface (*corneal abrasions*) that need treatment.

Ear injury

Kids manage to injure both the outer and inner parts of the ear. If your child bruises the outer ear, it needs medical attention. The blood collection from the bruise can injure and kill the ear cartilage, resulting in a permanent deformity (*cauliflower ear*).

If your child sticks something inside his ear and makes it bleed, it should also be checked out. Another red flag: head injuries with bleeding from the ear, or bruising behind the ear.

Nose injury

Here is a reliable rule: If it bleeds, it is probably broken. Don't get too alarmed. Not all broken noses look like Owen Wilson's. If the nose is not crooked, it will look the same as it did before it got broken. But if your child's nose is markedly bent, it needs to be evaluated. Medical specialists (ENT, or plastic surgeons) will either set a severely broken nose immediately, or they will wait a few days to see what the nose looks like once the swelling goes down. The most serious emergency is a *septal hematoma*, where blood collects on the inside of the nose. A child who cannot breathe through one or both nos-

? ?

FIRST AID

trils after injuring his nose needs to be checked immediately by a doctor.

Head injuries that result in bleeding from the nose also need medical attention. These can be signs of a more serious injury.

Mouth injury

There is always a lot of bleeding! That doesn't mean it is serious. Most mouth injuries do not need stitches and heal very quickly.

Tooth injury

For toddlers and preschoolers, we've only got baby (primary) teeth to deal with. You can skip putting the baby tooth in milk to save it; they do not need to be re-implanted if they get knocked out.

If a baby tooth is injured, take a look and make sure the whole thing is there. Injured baby teeth that are dangling by a thread should be removed as soon as possible because they are a choking hazard.

If the tooth gets knocked out, clean the area with water and see the dentist when you can. The dentist will take x-rays to make sure that all of the tooth came out and that there is no damage to the permanent tooth. Occasionally, a baby tooth will get pushed back into its socket (***dental intrusion***) and it is a waiting game to see when it resurfaces.

A small chip in the tooth is not an emergency. The dentist can smooth it down later, if necessary. A big break in the tooth is an emergency—a front tooth may need to be removed; a back tooth may need a rescue attempt.

Dental injuries can become infected. Bubbles or blisters over the tooth, or really bad breath need to be checked out immediately.

Other tooth injuries can be managed when your dentist's office is open. Dentists need to evaluate injured teeth that are painful, or sensitive to heat, cold, or touch. (Kids usually don't verbalize this.) It's a red flag if your child stops eating or avoids biting hard foods.

FYI: Injured teeth can also get discolored. That means that the nerve of the tooth is dying. The tooth needs treatment to be salvaged, or it may fall out on its own.

 Insider Tip
It's a good idea to schedule that first dentist appointment *before* your toddler injures a tooth. Once you have a dental "home," find out what their emergency coverage is on nights and weekends.

Bone injury

Most injuries to the arms and legs are not serious. Muscles get pulled, or the muscle-to-bone or bone-to-bone attachments (tendons and ligaments) get strained or sprained. These are called "soft tissue injuries." While there are some serious soft tissue injuries, these are pretty rare in kids under age five.

Plain x-rays can identify bone injuries ("fracture" is medical lingo for a broken bone). However, x-rays are not good at identifying soft tissue injuries. A more sophisticated and more expensive imaging study (MRI) is the gold standard for that.

But not every injury needs an x-ray or an MRI.

Here's how docs figure out who needs an imaging study. First, let's consider the mechanism of injury and its severity. For instance, a child who puts her hand out to break her fall may have broken her wrist. A child who twists his ankle is less likely to have a fracture than one who has fallen while running. And a child whose arm gets jerked or pulled (usually in protest) who then won't move or use her arm probably has a dislocated elbow (**NURSEMAID'S ELBOW**)—not a broken bone.

When a doctor examines a child, he will look for signs of a fracture: swelling, tenderness, deformity of the limb, and crepitus (a crackling noise that's kind of hard to describe). He'll also check the function of the muscles, nerves, and blood vessels by moving the injured area, touching to check for sensation, and checking for pulses and blood flow.

BOTTOM LINE

We consulted Dr. Michael Andreo, an orthopedic surgeon, for his advice on this topic. "A growing child's bones are more susceptible to fracture at the growth area than the ligaments are to sprains. Any child whose injury develops swelling, especially around a joint should get an x-ray."

Because it comes up relatively often, we've devoted a special section below on how doctors evaluate limping.

LIMPING 411

Like everything else, most limps are not serious. A toddler trips or bumps into a piece of furniture and then starts limping for a day. But if you don't witness the traumatic event, it can be pretty concerning to both the parent and the child's doctor! Docs are most concerned about limps associated with a fever and those that do not resolve quickly.

There is a laundry list of reasons for why kids suddenly limp, and some can be quite serious. Once you read through this, you will understand why your doctor takes limping (without a good trauma story) very seriously. Here are the usual suspects that we need to rule out with a limp:

Non-Worrisome, Do Nothing
- minor trauma
- **TRANSIENT SYNOVITIS** (inflamed joint tissues; see Chapter 17, Common Diseases for details).
- Myositis (muscle soreness after a viral illness)

Not Serious But Needs Treatment
- splinter/foreign object in the foot
- ingrown toenail
- broken bone (often called a **TODDLER'S FRACTURE**)
- osteoid osteoma (benign bone tumor)

Serious category
- *osteomyelitis* (bone infection)
- *septic arthritis* (joint infection)
- **LEUKEMIA**
- arthritis
- developmental dysplasia of the hip
- *Legg-Calve-Perthes* (breakdown of hip bone due to lack of blood flow)
- bone cancer (Ewing's sarcoma, osteogenic sarcoma)

first aid: injuries

? ?

FIRST AID

Fingers and toes

Finger and toe injuries that result in bruising or swelling deserve an x-ray. But most minor injuries like jammed fingers and stubbed toes usually do not create bruising or swelling. It's reassuring if a child can wiggle his toes or straighten his injured finger.

A blood clot (*subungual hematoma*) may form beneath the nail after a finger/toe injury. If it is really painful, it may need to be lanced to reduce the pressure.

Q. I was walking with my child and holding her hand. She pulled away from me and now she will not use her arm. Is it broken?

Nope. The elbow joint can get pulled out of its socket (subluxated) with a rapid jerking motion. It's called a **NURSEMAID'S ELBOW**, in honor of nannies who would drag reluctant toddlers behind them. (Picture the nannies who ran screaming from the Banks house before Mary Poppins arrived).

A medical professional can fix the elbow with a simple maneuver (it takes me about two seconds). If a child does this on a regular basis, ask your doctor to teach you how to perform this maneuver (a fun parlor trick at parties). Your child will start using her arm within about ten minutes.

How do you avoid a Nursemaid's elbow? Don't pull your child up by her arms or jerk her arms when she resists motion! And kids who are frequent flyers to Nursemaid's Elbow Land should avoid the monkey bars! FYI: up to 40% of kids have a nursemaid's elbow more than once in their lives.[7]

Q. I accidentally slammed the car door on my child's fingers. Do we need to get an x-ray?

This is a frequent question here at Pediatrician HQ. First, don't feel too guilty. Every other parent reading this book has been in your shoes!

Once the hysteria subsides, take a look at your child's hand. If there is significant bruising or swelling, it needs an x-ray. If you can distract your child and he begins using his hand and fingers again, it is probably fine.

Parent 411: Casting call

If there is a break (fracture), your child may need a cast. Some bone specialists prefer to place casts a few days after an injury when the swelling is down. A temporary splint cast can be used to keep the bone immobilized and comfortable until then. More significant injuries may need a procedure to realign bones. Often, this can be done in the specialists' office. Occasionally, an operation is needed.

Casts and splints are used to immobilize fractures while they heal. After the cast is applied, it is common to have some pain, but it should subside over time. According to Dr. Andreo (our orthopedist expert for this book), any worsening of pain or loss of sensation or muscle strength within a cast should alert parents to potentially serious complications (skin breakdown, *compartment syndrome*) and your doctor should be contacted immediately.

Both casts and splints are made of plaster or fiberglass. Plaster is used more for splints, but it loses strength if it gets wet. Fiberglass, on the other hand, is waterproof.

Regardless of material, you should ask your doctor how to care for the cast. Even if your child has a waterproof cast, the moisture within the cast can irritate and breakdown the skin. Note: Never put anything into the cast as it may disrupt the padding, increase pressure on the skin, and lead to skin breakdown.

◆ How long does the cast stay on? That depends on the type of fracture.

◆ Can I bathe my child? Yes. Cast covers are sold at pharmacies, but plastic wraps (like Glad Press 'N' Seal) are usually more effective.

What to do:
For minor head injuries:

◆ Put a bag of frozen vegetables on the goose egg, if your child lets you.

◆ Let your child go to bed. It's usually naptime or bedtime when these events happen. Monitor your child every few hours by watching his breathing and gently touching him to see if he stirs. Vomiting or seizure activity happens whether a child is awake or asleep.

◆ Watch for signs of concussion for the next couple of days (vomiting, irritability from headache, confusion, lethargy).

For eye injuries:

◆ Place a temporary gauze or paper patch over the injured eye, if your child cooperates.

For nose injuries:

◆ See the section on bleeding and bruising in this chapter.

For lip, mouth, and tooth injuries:

◆ Offer something cold to eat like a popsicle or ice cream. It numbs the area and slows down the bleeding.

◆ Rinse the mouth with water.

For minor injuries (sprains and strains):

◆ Give acetaminophen or ibuprofen for pain and swelling.

◆ Use the acronym, "RICE" to treat a sprain: Rest, Ice, Compression, and Elevation.

◆ **R**est: Avoid exercise or strenuous activity with the injured limb for several days.

◆ **I**ce: Apply a bag of frozen vegetables, boo-boo bear, or whatever your child will tolerate for short intervals every hour for the first day after the injury.

◆ **C**ompression: Put an Ace wrap snugly around an injured joint.

◆ **E**levation: Keep the injured body part above the level of the heart, if possible. Example: prop an injured ankle on a pillow while the child sleeps.

For immobilizing an injured limb:

◆ Use a scarf or large towel and wrap it around the shoulder to keep an arm in place. Pinning the end of a long shirt sleeve to the shirt also works.

◆ Use a piece of cardboard and an Ace wrap to form a makeshift splint for an arm or leg.

For immobilizing a finger or toe:

◆ It's called "Buddy Taping." Tape the injured finger or toe to its neighboring finger or toe. It will support and stabilize the injured one.

Parent 411:
Who needs a CAT scan?

When there is concern that a head injury may have resulted in bleeding within the skull, a CT (computer tomography) scan is the best way to check it out. Kids with these symptoms may need a CT scan:

◆ Loss of consciousness for over one minute.
◆ Trauma from a knife or bullet.
◆ Abnormal neurological exam (weakness, abnormal reflexes, etc).
◆ Vomiting.
◆ Seizures.
◆ Bulging soft spot in a child under 18 months old.
◆ Clear fluid draining from the nose.
◆ Depressed skull fracture (i.e. a break in the skull is detected on a plain x-ray).

Take home tip:

◆ **Growth plates.** Kids have areas in their bones called growth plates. It's the area at the end of each bone that gives it growing room. The plates fuse when a child goes through puberty. So, a normal x-ray of a child's bone shows a gap along the growth plate line. Occasionally, a fracture might be missed if it is right in the growth plate. That's why pediatricians like to send patients to a specialist if a child is still complaining a week after an injury.

What the medical provider will ask you about TRAUMA/ACCIDENTAL INJURIES:

◆ What happened?
◆ Are you able to control the bleeding?
◆ If your child fell down: What height did he fall from? What surface did he fall onto? Did he put his hand out to break his fall?
◆ With a head injury: Did he lose consciousness? Did he cry immediately? Did he vomit? Is there blood/fluid coming from his nose or his ears? Are his pupils equal in size? Does he have blurred vision (if he is old enough to tell you)?
◆ What is he complaining of now?
◆ Is he alert and responsive?
◆ Is your child able to move an injured limb without crying?
◆ Is your child limping or unable to bear weight on his leg? Did you witness a traumatic injury? Does he have a fever?
◆ Is there any bruising or swelling of the injured area?
◆ Is there any numbness of the injured area? (See if your child can feel you touching the injured area).
◆ Are there obvious broken bones sticking out of the skin?
◆ For a face/mouth injury: Are there any cuts crossing the eyebrow line or where the lip meets the skin?
◆ For a tooth injury: Is the tooth loose, relocated, or knocked out?

Are you able to find it? Does the tooth hurt? Is it sensitive to heat, cold, or touch?

◆ For a finger/toe injury: Can your child move the finger/toe fully? Is there a collection of blood under the nail? Is the fingernail injured?

911: Needs an ambulance
◆ Uncontrollable bleeding.
◆ Unconscious or unarousable after traumatic injury.
◆ Irritable and inconsolable after traumatic injury.
◆ Labored breathing after traumatic injury.
◆ Seizure after a head injury.
◆ Neck and back injuries. (Do not try to move your child. Wait for EMS.)

Priority 1: Needs medical attention now
◆ Child falls a distance greater than his own height.
◆ Child falls onto hardwood floors, tile, or concrete and hits his head.
◆ Child loses consciousness (blacks out) after a head injury.
◆ Child vomits more than once after a head injury.
◆ Child acts odd or confused after a head injury.
◆ Bruising behind the ear or bleeding from the ear after head injury.
◆ Clear fluid or blood draining from the nose after a head injury.
◆ Bulging soft spot (if it is still open) after a head injury.
◆ Any eye injury.
◆ A significant nosebleed after a nose injury.
◆ Inability to breathe through one or both nostrils after an injury.
◆ Nose is obviously crooked after an injury.
◆ Ear injury and there is bruising of the outer part of the ear.
◆ Cut through the tongue that goes through the full thickness.
◆ Cut that crosses the eyebrow line or where the lip meets the skin.
◆ Tooth injury where the tooth is dangling by a thread, severely displaced, or broken.
◆ Tooth injury where there is a bubble or blister above the tooth.
◆ Bone is exposed.
◆ Unable to move a limb without crying.
◆ Limping or refusing to bear weight.
◆ Impressive bruising or swelling after an injury.
◆ Increased pain or decreased sensation/muscle strength with a limb in a cast.
◆ Fingernail injury where the bed (base) of nail is affected.
◆ New fever (especially with increased pain) after recent trauma.

Priority 2: Needs an appointment the next day
◆ Child falls a distance less than his height, onto a padded surface, with no loss of consciousness.
◆ Nose injury without bleeding or obvious fracture.
◆ Child has a bone injury but is consolable and moving his limbs.
◆ Child had a minor injury a week ago and is still complaining of pain.
◆ Jammed finger. No bruising or swelling. Able to straighten finger.
◆ Painful blood blister under the finger or toenail.

FIRST AID

? ?

◆ Injured tooth is slightly loose, chipped, missing (pushed upwards), or brown. Or tooth is painful, sensitive to touch, heat, or cold (child stops eating or avoids biting hard foods). Appointment with dentist is preferred with these tooth injuries.

Priority 3: Wait and see

◆ Child has a minor head injury resulting in a large bruise on the head, no loss of consciousness, no vomiting, and is acting normally.

◆ Child with a minor injury who is able to walk, play, and sleep without difficulty.

#10 Poisonings/Ingestions/Swallowed objects

If your child accidentally swallows a poisonous substance or medication, call poison control immediately (**1-800-222-1222**). They are a wealth of information on any product a curious child might ingest. They will tell you whether the product can do potential harm to the body or not. And they know the antidotes.

Occasionally, a parent will not know that a child has swallowed something they shouldn't have. The only clue is that their child is acting odd. Other clues include: mouth burns, drooling, rapid or shallow breathing, vomiting without fever, seizures, extreme lethargy, or body/breath odor.

In the past, pediatricians recommended that parents have a bottle of ipecac on hand in case they needed to induce vomiting for a harmful ingestion. This has changed: using ipecac at home is no longer recommended. Why? Some chemicals can burn the esophagus if you make them come back up once they have already entered the stomach. If necessary, ipecac can be administered at an emergency room.

What to do:

◆ Make sure your child can breathe comfortably.
◆ Call Poison Control for management instructions.

Take home tips:

1. If poison control directs you to an emergency room, be sure to take the poison/chemical/medication with you if you have it. It helps determine the ingredients and the amount that was swallowed.
2. See below for the most dangerous household products to keep out of your child's reach.

Parent 411: **Dangerous household products**
Here's a list of common household items that should be placed out of your child's reach. Note: kids learn how to scale cabinets and climb on countertops as they get older. Make sure you have cabinet locks that your kids cannot open!

Chemicals:

◆ Cleaning products.
◆ Paint thinner.

 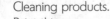

♦ Dishwashing detergent.
♦ Gasoline.

Medications:

♦ Mom's prenatal vitamin or iron supplements.
♦ Visiting grandparents who leave medication on the countertop (especially heart and blood pressure medications).

Plants:

♦ *Christmas favorites:* poinsettias, mistletoe, holly.
♦ *Flower garden plants:* autumn crocus, azaleas, bleeding heart, chrysanthemum, daffodil, elephant ear, four-o'clocks, foxglove, hyacinth, hydrangea, iris, jasmine, jonquil, lantana, lily of the alley, morning glory, narcissus, snow on the mountain.
♦ *House plants:* bird of paradise, castor bean, dieffenbachia, English ivy, holly, Jerusalem cherry, Mother-in-law, oleander, philodendron, rhododendron, rosary pea.
♦ *Trees and shrubs:* black locust, boxwood, chokecherry, elderberry, English yew, ground ivy, horse chestnut/buckeye, juniper, laurels, oak tree, water hemlock, wisteria, yew.
♦ *Vegetable garden plants:* asparagus, sprouts and green parts of potato, rhubarb leaves, green parts of tomato.
♦ *Wild plants:* belladonna, bittersweet, buttercups, Indian hemp, Jack-in-the-pulpit, jimson weed, larkspur, monkshood, mushrooms (some), nightshade, poison hemlock/ivy/oak/sumac, tobacco, skunk cabbage.[8]

Hygiene products:

♦ Mouthwash.
♦ Nail polish remover.
♦ Rubbing alcohol.
♦ Hair dye.
♦ Food and wine.
♦ Liquor.
♦ Pottery from foreign countries (contain lead).

What the doctor will ask you about POISONING:

♦ What happened?
♦ How much did the child ingest?
♦ Do you have the bottle or container the product came in?
♦ Is your child having trouble breathing?

9 1 1 : Call an ambulance

♦ Labored breathing.
♦ Completely disoriented or unarousable.
♦ Seizure.

Priority 1: Needs medical attention now

Poison Control instructs you to go to the nearest ER.

Foreign Bodies: We're not talking about David Beckham

Young children have a keen interest in their body holes—noses, ears, and mouths particularly. Besides exploring these cavities with their fingers, they like to put things into these places. Objects that do not belong there are

FIRST AID

? ?

called "foreign bodies."

Some doctors have a Wall of Fame for the things they have removed from children's orifices. Some of my personal favorites include pebbles, insects (dead and alive), beads, toys, coins, and popcorn kernels (see the box below).

Although it sounds funny, foreign bodies can be quite serious. Objects placed in the nose can get inhaled into the throat/lungs and obstruct the airway. The same goes for objects that are swallowed. Foreign bodies in the ears are not emergencies because they cannot move in the ear canal (the eardrum prevents the object from floating into dangerous territory).

THE POPCORN-ECTOMY

Here's a funny yet true story from a friend of ours, Jon Caldara and his daughter's "popcorn-ectomy."[9] Enjoy.

We all know it is dangerous, still we don't ban it. Madness.

But this time it was different. This time it was my little girl being carried into the operating room. During the ordeal, the doctors at the hospital told me horror story after horror story of children brought into surgery in the same condition.

My poor wife was there to witness the ugliness. She and my 3-year-old daughter made popcorn. And then it happened.

"Mom, there's popcorn in my ear."

"No, silly, there's no popcorn in your ear."

"Yes, there is," she giggled. "I put it there."

Sure enough, there it was, an un-popped kernel wedged into her ear like a ground hog. The girl was very proud. Who wouldn't be?

The next several hours were filled with the expected shaking, poking and whacking of a little 3-year-old. You know, the kind of stuff that you just know some social worker is gonna see. No luck. That kernel was wedged in like a dollar bill in Jack Benny's wallet.

After my suggestion of taking a hair dryer to her ear to see if we could get it to pop was soundly rejected by both mother and child, they were off to the doctor.

After attempts at the medical version of shaking, poking and whacking a 3-year-old failed, it was off to the operating room for a popcornectomy. The area's top popcorn experts convened. We had the world's leading popcornologist flown in from Vienna. His suggestion was to put her head close to a microwave oven and see if we could get it to pop. After that was rejected by mother and child, they put her under anesthesia to get her to stop wiggling and pulled the kernel out of her ear with ease.

As my daughter was sleeping it off, without worrying a bit about how she was going to come up with the cash for the hospital co-payment, the docs told me about the galaxy of fun things they've yanked out of kids' orifices. Kids' ears have played host to a smorgasbord of foods, toys, beads and bugs — yes, bugs. After yanking items out of one ear canal, the doc now regularly checks the other ear. Yep, if it felt

Primary care doctors may be able to remove foreign bodies from the ear or nose. Swallowed objects may need to be retrieved by a specialist if there is concern for it being stuck in the throat or lungs. Fortunately, most swallowed foreign bodies go into the stomach and intestines…and eventually end up in the poop. If your child has swallowed something and is having trouble breathing or is drooling, call 911. If not, offer him some bread and milk to wash it down.

The following objects if swallowed always need to be checked out by a doctor: quarters (or anything bigger than that), button batteries, and sharp objects.

good ramming something in one ear, it should feel good in the other.

The nose, however, offers many more opportunities. Cheese is a good thing to put up there. Start with a soft brie and work your way up to havarti.

The doc's favorite was a girl whose breath was so bad she was becoming a leper at school. After a quick examination he extracted a huge hunk of moldy foam rubber from her nose. "Oh, yeah," she said, "we went to Build-a-Bear," an overpriced store where kids can stuff their own teddy bears.

Having two toddlers doubles the fun for us. The 19-month-old boy is a Kamikaze.

But the thing I miss most of all is sleep. They won't let us sleep. I see all the liberals trying to protect the CIA's terrorist detainees from "torture" techniques, including sleep deprivation. Forget protesting the government. Picket my kids. Sleep deprivation is against the Geneva Convention. Where the hell is John McCain when you need him?

Here's how bad it is. Recently I faced the fear of all men—the midlife colonoscopy. My colon played host to a garden hose and a camera crew. But for the procedure they gave me anesthesia, sweet anesthesia. I slept for hours. My first real nap in years. Sleep so sound my kids couldn't wake me. Sleep so sweet I was sodomized by a medical team, and I didn't even care.

I am in such need of sleep, I have scheduled a colonoscopy every week since then.

Watching my daughter peacefully sleep off the anesthesia, I begged and bribed the doctors and nurses let me take a gas tank or some anesthesia or, hell, even a bottle of chloroform home. Anything. If not for my use, something to knock out my two kids at the same time.

I will eventually get my revenge. We saved the popcorn kernel. When I get old and am wearing my own diapers and my daughter is taking care of me, I plan on ramming the exact same kernel into my ear canal. Medicare will be broke by then. She'll have to pay to get it yanked out.

In the meantime, she is happy playing with the stuffed giraffe the good folks at the hospital gave her. She named it "Popcorn."

first aid

Reality Check
Swallowed pennies, nickels, and dimes usually pass through the intestines and end up in poop.

BOTTOM LINE
When in doubt, call your doctor.

Whew! You made it. Welcome to the end of the Toddler HealthWatch section of *Toddler 411*. But we aren't quite done with the book yet. In the next section, we'll give you a series of additional resources for more info on medications, alternative meds and lab tests. Plus we'll have a glossary of really big Latin words, references for more reading and some entertaining footnotes.

Toddler 411

Part Three

Reference Library

*Medications, Alternative Meds,
Lab Work & Tests, Glossary,
References, Footnotes*

MEDICATIONS
Appendix A

Here's a look at the most common medications used by children.[1] Obviously, with the huge universe of possible medications, this chapter is by no means comprehensive. Instead, we focus on the most popular and widely used meds in children. We will cover both over-the-counter products and prescription medications. Let's begin with some general questions regarding administering medicine to your child. FYI: If you are looking for info on which medications are safe during breastfeeding, check out our *Baby 411* book. We have an in-depth section on that topic there.

Q. If my child throws up right after I give him medicine, do I re-dose the medicine or wait until the next dose is due?

If your child throws up less than 20 minutes after administering medicine, give the dose again. It didn't have time to get through the stomach and be absorbed into the blood stream.

Q. Is a generic medication as good as a brand name?

For the most part, yes.

When a pharmaceutical company develops a medication, the company obtains a patent for it, which lasts for 17 years. Because it takes several years of research before a medication is approved for use, a medication may be on the mar-

MEDICATIONS

? ?

ket for an average of eight years before the patent runs out. Once the patent runs out, any pharmaceutical company can make their own product, which is the exact duplicate of the original brand.

The potency is the same, but sometimes the taste is not. And the cost is definitely not the same. Generic medications are often much cheaper than the brand name.

When you review our medication lists below, look for the asterisk (*) beside the name to find out if a generic product is available.

Q. If my doctor prescribes an expensive antibiotic, can I ask for a generic brand at the pharmacy?

The good news is that almost all antibiotics for children are now generic. There's only one major exception: cefixime (Suprax). This antibiotic is particularly good at treating bladder infections. And in the case of drug resistant bacteria, this may be the only antibiotic that will do the trick.

Helpful Hint

If you are paying out-of-pocket for prescription medications, speak up! Don't be shy about inquiring about the cost of the medication. Your doctor may have free samples available in the office. Or she will be able to prescribe a less-expensive generic drug if available.

Q. How do I get my child to take her medicine?

Here are a few tricks to getting all the medicine down:

1. Give small amounts over several minutes, instead of the whole dose at once.
2. It is okay to mix certain medications in with milk or juice—but check with your pharmacist for the particulars. The only problem with this plan is that your child has to drink the whole thing. Be sure to mix the medicine in a small volume of fluid (less than an ounce).
3. Some pharmacies offer a service called Flavor Rx (flavorx.com or 1-800-884-5771). For a relatively small fee (often worth it), a choice of 25 different flavorings is available—these can be added to your child's prescription to make it more palatable.
4. Taking a prescription medicine is not optional. It may take two parents to administer medicine to one strong-willed child.

Reality Check

Just a spoonful of sugar makes the medicine go down. Here are some tips from Edward Bell, Pharm.D., BCPS.

1. White grape juice or chocolate syrup masks a medicine's after taste.
2. Graham crackers get rid of the leftover drug particles in the mouth.
3. Strawberry jam mixed with a crushed chewable tablet disguises the flavor.

Q. Is it okay to use a medicine if it is past the expiration date?

No.

For the most part, medications start to lose their potency after the listed expiration date. So the medication may be less effective (for example, Albuterol for an asthma attack).

Q. The prescription medicine was supposed to be given for ten days. We ran out of it after eight days. What happened?

Most of the time, this happens when a "teaspoon" dose is administered with an actual teaspoon from your kitchen. Your silverware spoon may hold anywhere from 4-8 ml of fluid. A "real" teaspoon is 5ml. Buy a medicine syringe that lists both cc/mls and teaspoons on it.

Q. I have some leftover antibiotic from a prescription. Can I save it and use it for another time?

No.

First of all, you should never have leftover antibiotics. Your doctor wanted your child to have a specific length of therapy for that medication. If your child stops taking an antibiotic "because he feels better," you run the risk of the bacteria growing back. This is particularly true of Group A Strep (of Strep throat fame). Yes, people often forget to give all of the doses of antibiotic—we're human. But try to finish a prescription as it was prescribed.

Second of all, antibiotics that are in liquid form will only stay potent for about two weeks. They come as a powder from the manufacturer and the pharmacist mixes it with water when he fills the prescription order. If you have any medicine leftover—toss it.

Q. Are all medications administered to children of all ages?

No.

Many medications are FDA approved for certain age groups. Despite this, pediatricians traditionally feel comfortable using some products "off-label" for children. The government has gone back and forth with requiring drug companies to test medications in children. Because of this inconsistency, there are fewer products officially approved for kids than there probably should be. Thankfully, current regulations require pharmaceutical companies to include children in medication studies.

There are some products, however, that are never safe to use in children. For example, tetracycline is okay for adults but can cause permanent tooth staining in children.

Q. How do I know if there is a problem taking more than one medicine at a time?

The official term is "drug interactions".

Your doctor or pharmacist can answer this question. Don't assume that your doctor knows all the medications your child is taking. If your child received a prescription from another doctor/specialist, it might not be recorded in your child's chart.

Reality Check

Tell your doctor if your child is taking any herbal remedies. There can be overlap in effects of herbal and over-the-counter products. For instance, a medical student made national news for taking ephedra (an herbal decongestant) and Sudafed (a traditional decongestant) at the same time. He ended up in the ER with a heart rhythm disturbance. It pays to ask.

Q. Can you use acetaminophen (Tylenol) and an antibiotic at the same time?

It is okay to use a fever reducer, cough/cold medicine, and an antibiotic simultaneously.

Q. How do I read a doctor's prescription?

It's written in medical abbreviations, so here's how to read it. You'll need this for the medication tables later in this appendix.

How often to take a medicine
QD or QDay: once daily
BID: twice daily
TID: three times daily (preferably every eight hours)
QID: four times daily (preferably every six hours)
QHS: once daily, at bedtime
PRN: as needed

How medicine is given
po: taken by mouth
pr: insert in rectum
ou: put into each eye
au: put into each ear

How medicine is dosed
1 cc (cubic centimeter): 1ml (milliliter)
tsp: teaspoon (1 tsp is 5 cc or 5ml)
T.: tablespoon (1 T. is 3 tsp or 15cc or 15 ml)
tab: tablet
gtt: drop

Q. How do I know which medications require a prescription?

We've included some handy tables later in this chapter with information on common medicines used for treating kids. In the tables, you'll note the following symbols.

- ◆ **Rx**: Denotes that a product is available with a doctor's prescription only. If nothing is designated, assume the product in question is prescription-only.
- ◆ **OTC**: Denotes that a product is available Over The Counter (that is, without a prescription).

MEDICATIONS

Q. How do I know if a medication is safe for me to take while I am pregnant or breastfeeding?

We cover this topic in our first book, *Baby 411* with an in-depth look at which medications are safe for breastfeeding moms to take.

Medication Index

1. Allergies
2. Dental/Mouth
    - ◆ fluoride
    - ◆ teething products
3. Ear Problems
4. Eye Problems
5. Fever and Pain
6. Gastrointestinal
    - ◆ antacids/ gastroesophageal reflux
    - ◆ constipation
    - ◆ diarrhea
    - ◆ gas
    - ◆ vomiting
    - ◆ rehydration solutions
7. Infections
    - ◆ antibiotics (for bacterial infections)
    - ◆ antifungals (for fungal infections)
    - ◆ antihelminthics (for pinworms)
    - ◆ amebicides (for Giardia infection)
    - ◆ antivirals (for viral infections)
8. Nutrition
    - ◆ iron supplements
    - ◆ vitamins
9. Respiratory
    - ◆ asthma
    - ◆ cough and cold preparations
10. Skin
    - ◆ antibiotic creams
    - ◆ antifungal creams
    - ◆ scabies/ head lice medications
    - ◆ steroids
    - ◆ anti-inflammatory (immunomodulators)
    - ◆ diaper rash creams

medications

KEY FOR MEDICATIONS LISTS BELOW

RX: *Available by prescription only*
OTC: *Available over the counter (without prescription)*
(*): Available as generic option
Dose: For definitions of QD, BID, TID, see previous page.

Medications

1. Allergy Medicines

These medications are used for allergic reactions, itching, and nasal congestion. For skin allergy products, see skin section (10).

Antihistamines have been around for decades. They are classified by their "generation." The first generation products are very effective but also have more side effects (drowsiness, dry mouth). An example is Benadryl. Second and third generation products do not cause nearly as much sedation and can be dosed once every 24 hours. Examples include Zyrtec and Claritin.

Nasal steroid sprays are very effective in preventing itchy and congested noses due to allergies. However, they need to be taken on a daily basis since their job is to prevent symptoms. Using them only "as needed" is not nearly as effective.

Eye drops can be used to alleviate itchy eyes due to seasonal allergies.

Leukotriene antagonists are another category of medications used to treat both allergy and asthma symptoms. These medications can also be used preventatively to reduce swelling and mucous production in the nasal passages.

ANTIHISTAMINES

GENERIC	BRAND	DOSE	RX?	AGE LIMIT
Brompheniramine/ Phenylephrine	Dimetapp**	QID	OTC	over 2 years
Cetirizine	Zyrtec*	QD	OTC	over 6 months
Clemastine	Tavist*	BID	Rx	over 6 months
Chlorpheniramine	Chlor-Trimeton*	QID	OTC	over 2 years
Desloratadine	Clarinex	QD	Rx	over 6 months
Diphenhydramine	Benadryl*	QID	OTC	Infants ok
Fexofenadine	Allegra*	BID	Rx	over 6 years
Hydroxyzine	Atarax*	QID	Rx	Infants ok
Loratadine	Claritin, Alavert*	QD	OTC	over 2 years

Side effects: Drowsiness, dry mouth, headache, paradoxical excitability
Serious adverse effects: tremors, convulsions
**Note: Any product that contains the decongestant pseudoephedrine is held behind the pharmacist's counter and sold in limited quantities. The reason? This product can be used to make illegal drugs.

NASAL STEROIDS (NOSE SPRAY)

GENERIC	BRAND	DOSE	RX?	AGE LIMIT
Budesonide	Rhinocort	QD	Rx	Over 6 years
Fluticasone	Flonase*	QD	Rx	Over 4 years
	Veramyst	QD	Rx	Over 2 years
Mometasone	Nasonex	QD	Rx	Over 2 years
Triamcinolone	Nasacort	QD	Rx	Over 2 years

Side effects: nasal irritation, nosebleeds, yeast infection in nose/throat/mouth
Serious adverse effects: Only a small fraction of nasal medication gets absorbed into the blood stream. However, patients taking more than one

type of steroid medication (steroid nasal spray, steroid inhaler, steroid skin cream, oral steroid) should be counseled about chronic combined steroid usage and potential long-term side effects.

ALLERGY EYE DROPS

GENERIC	BRAND	DOSE	RX?	AGE LIMIT
Azelastine	Optivar	BID	Rx	Over 3 years
Epinastine	Elestat	BID	Rx	Over 3 years
Ketotifen	Zaditor	BID	OTC	Over 3 years
Olopatadine	Pataday	QD	Rx	Over 3 years

Side effects: burning, stinging, dry eyes, headache, temporary blurred vision

LEUKOTRIENE ANTAGONIST

Montelukast (Singulair) is a medication used to *prevent* both allergy and asthma symptoms. It is FDA approved for children over six months of age. For optimal response, the medication should be administered at bedtime each night.

Singulair made news in 2008 when the FDA reported patient complaints of depressed mood while taking this medication. Our take: this is still an effective and useful medication to prevent allergy and asthma symptoms. However, be on the lookout for any change in your child's behavior.

Side effects: headache, sore throat, possible depression, suicidal thoughts

ORAL (SYSTEMIC) STEROIDS

This is the most potent form of prescription steroid medication. It is used for severe asthma, eczema, croup, and allergic reactions. Oral steroids effectively reduce the allergy and inflammation symptoms. However, they also have the greatest potential for causing adrenal gland suppression and diminished growth velocity in children. That's why we reserve prescribing steroids by mouth for limited situations.

EPINEPHRINE (EPI-PEN)

Epinephrine is an immediate rescue medication for life-threatening allergic reactions. It relaxes the muscles in the bronchial tree of the lungs to keep the airways open. The medication provides temporary relief until emergency medical care is available. Children with a history of anaphylactic reactions (or the potential to have them) should carry injectable epinephrine (Epi-Pen) at all times. As we talked about in Chapter 18, First Aid, everyone in your child's life should know how to give an epinephrine shot. The prescription will come with a tester pen so both you and your child can practice. The mechanism is the same as clicking the end of a pen (hence the name). Another tip: ask your allergist if they have any expired Epi-Pens—you can practice using it on an orange to get a feel for the real thing.

Epi-Pen is the brand name for the most well-known injectable on the market, so docs often use this name to generically describe injectable epinephrine. But there is a competitor brand, called Twinject, which contains the same active ingredient.

FYI: Epinephrine pens need to be kept from light and heat to remain potent. Don't keep it in your glove compartment.

medications

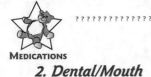
2. Dental/Mouth

FLUORIDE SUPPLEMENTS

As we have discussed in Chapter 12, Hygiene some children need fluoride supplements. See page 238 for a chart from the American Academy of Pediatrics and American Dental Association on recommended doses of fluoride.

Fluoride supplements include: Luride*, Fluoritab, Pediaflor*, Poly-Vi-Flor*, Tri-Vi-Flor*. These are all available by prescription only and dosed once daily. *Possible side effects:* Overuse of fluoride can cause white spots on the teeth (fluorosis). This occurs in daily doses of greater than 2 mg of fluoride per day.

Helpful Hint

Give fluoride drops on an empty stomach. Milk prevents the absorption of the medication.

TEETHING

Teething medications are topical numbing products. They are rubbed on the gums to provide temporary relief of gum pain due to tooth eruption. They are dosed four times daily. Their active ingredient is Benzocaine. The brand names are: Baby Anbesol, Baby Numz-it, Baby Oragel, and Zilactin Baby.

3. Ear Medication

ANTIBIOTIC EAR DROPS

For swimmer's ear (otitis externa) or for children who have ear infections with PE tubes, antibiotic eardrops are used. Below are the most popular antibiotic eardrops. Note: most products also contain a steroid. The steroid reduces the inflammation and swelling of the ear canal so the antibiotic can work more effectively.

GENERIC	BRAND	DOSE	RX
Acetic Acid	Vosol*	QID	yes
Acetic Acid + Hydrocortisone	Vosol-HC*	QID	yes
Chloroxylenol +Pramoxine + Hydrocortisone	Zoto-HC	QID	yes
Ciprofloxacin + Dexamethasone	Ciprodex	BID	yes
Ciprofloxacin + Hydrocortisone	Cipro HC	BID	yes
Ofloxacin	Floxin Otic*	BID	yes
Polymyxin B + Neomycin + + steroid	Cortisporin* Pediotic	TID	yes

Side effects: Irritation of the ear canal such as itching and stinging.

SWIMMER'S EAR PREVENTION DROPS

These drops dry up any left over water in the ear canal after swimming. Drops are placed in the ears immediately after swimming. These are used primarily for older kids, not infants.

You can make your own concoction: 2 drops of rubbing alcohol and 2 drops of vinegar per ear.

Brand names: Auro-Dri, Swim Ear. Both products are OTC. Active ingredient: rubbing alcohol.

EAR PAIN DROPS

These are topical numbing medications, in the same mindset as using teething gels for gum pain. They have a modest effect in providing temporary relief of pain in the ear canal. (Remember that middle ear infections occur behind the eardrum.)

Numbing drops are absolutely not intended for use if a child has PE tubes (see Chapter 16, Common Infections for more details) or has ruptured the eardrum with infection.

Brand names: Americaine and Auralgan*. Active ingredient: Benzocaine and antipyrine
Dosing: 2-3 drops to affected ear, QID
Rx only.

EAR WAX DROPS

These drops help loosen or dissolve earwax. Earwax rarely is a problem unless it is hard and stuck in the canal (impacted). If the earwax is impacted, earwax drops loosen up and break down the earwax.

Brand names: Auro, Debrox, and Murine eardrops. OTC Active ingredient: carbamide peroxide.
Dosing: 3 drops per ear, TID, for 3 days

Colace, a stool softener, also works nicely to soften up earwax. It's available OTC.

Helpful Hints

◆ Rub the eardrop bottle in your hands for a minute or two before administering the drops. Warm drops in the ear are less bothersome than cold ones.

◆ If a child has a perforated eardrum or PE tubes, many types of ear drops should NOT be used (exception: approved antibiotic drops). Check with your doctor.

Reality Check

ENT specialists frequently use antibiotic eye drops for the ears. If you get a prescription filled for your child's ear infection and it turns out to be eye drops, don't think we have lost our minds. One caveat here: It's okay to use *eye drops* for the ears, but you cannot use ear drops for the eyes!

4. Eye Problems

ANTIBIOTIC EYE DROPS/OINTMENT

These are used primarily for conjunctivitis (pink eye) and corneal abrasions.

GENERIC	FAMILY	BRAND	DOSE	RX ONLY?
Azithromycin	Erythromycin	Azasite	QD	yes
Ciprofloxacin	Quinolone	Ciloxan*	BID/QID	yes
Erythromycin	Erythromycin	(many)*	BID/QID	yes
Gatifloxacin	Quinolone	Zymar	QID	yes
Gentamicin	Aminoglycoside	(many)*	QID	yes
Levofloxin	Quinolone	Quixin	QID	yes
Moxifloxacin	Quinolone	Vigamox	TID	yes
Ofloxacin	Quinolone	Ocuflox*	BID/QID	yes
Tobramycin	Aminoglycoside	Tobrex*	QID	yes

Side effects: Burning, itching, local irritation

5. Fever And Pain Medications

See Chapter 19, First Aid for dosing information on these products.

6. Gastrointestinal Problems

ANTACIDS/GASTROESOPHAGEAL REFLUX

GENERIC	BRAND NAME	DOSE	RX?	AGE LIMIT
Aluminum Hydroxide	Gaviscon*	QID	OTC	ask Dr.
Calcium Carbonate	Mylanta,Tums*	TID/QID	OTC	None
Lansoprazole	Prevacid*	QD	OTC	ask Dr.
Metoclopramide	Reglan*	QID	Rx	None
Nizatidine	Axid*	BID	Rx	Over 6 mos
Omeprazole	Prilosec* Zegerid	QD/BID	Rx	over 2 yr
Ranitidine	Zantac*	BID/QID	Rx	None

Notes: This is one of those categories where some medications do not have FDA approval for use in young children, but are used routinely by pediatricians and pediatric gastroenterologists.

Several of these products are available in generic and over-the-counter pills or capsules (e.g. Axid, Prilosec, Zantac). The liquid versions are prescription only. Kids who can swallow a pill and weigh enough can use over the counter antacids.

Side effects:

◆ *Aluminum hydroxide and calcium carbonate both can cause constipation and decrease absorption of other medications.*

- *Most common side effects with Lansoprazole, Nizatidine,, Omeprazole, and Ranitidine are headache and stomach upset.*
- *Metoclopramide (Reglan) can cause sedation, headaches, and diarrhea.*

Helpful Hint
It is more effective to give these medications 30 minutes before a meal if possible.

CONSTIPATION

GENERIC	BRAND NAME	DOSE	Rx?	AGE LIMIT
Docusate	Colace*	QD/QID	OTC	over 1 year
Glycerin	(suppository*)	1 dose	OTC	None
Guar gum	Benefiber	QD	OTC	over 6 mos.
Lactulose	Duphalac, Chronulac*	QD	Rx	Ask Dr.
Malt soup	Maltsupex	BID	OTC	over 1 month
Mineral oil	Kondremul	QD/ TID	OTC	over 5 years
Polyethylene glycol	Miralax*	QD	OTC	Ask Dr.
Senna	Senokot*	QD	OTC	over 1 mo

Side effects: diarrhea, bloating, gas, body salt (electrolyte) disturbances with excessive or prolonged use.

DIARRHEA

GENERIC	BRAND NAME	DOSE	Rx?	AGE LIMIT
Acidophilus	Lactinex*	QD	OTC	None
Bismuth subsalicylate	Pepto-Bismol*	up to 6x day	OTC	Over 2 mos.
Loperamide	Imodium AD*	QID	OTC	over 2 yrs

Side effects: Pepto-Bismol has a common side effect of causing a temporary blackened tongue and black poop. Because it contains an ingredient similar to aspirin, do NOT use when a child has chickenpox or an influenza-like illness (there is a risk of Reye's syndrome).

GAS

GENERIC	BRAND NAME	DOSE	Rx?	AGE LIMIT
Ginger-Fennel	Gripe Water	QID	OTC	None
Simethicone	Mylicon, Phazyme*	up to 12x day	OTC	None

VOMITING

GENERIC	BRAND	DOSE	Rx?	AGE LIMIT
Dimenhydrinate	Dramamine*	QID	OTC	over 2 yrs
Diphenhydramine	Benadryl*	QID	OTC	over 6 mos.
Ondansetron	Zofran*	TID	Rx	Over 1 mo

GENERIC	BRAND	DOSE	Rx?	AGE LIMIT
Phosphorated-Carbohydrate	Emetrol*	QID	OTC	None
Promethazine	Phenergan*	QID	Rx	over 2 yrs

Helpful Hint

Home remedy: The equivalent of Emetrol is to give 1-2 tea-spoons of heavy fruit syrup (fruit cocktail juice) every 20-30 minutes. This occasionally works to relieve nausea.

REHYDRATION SOLUTIONS

These products are the Gatorade equivalent for kids. They are designed to replace water, body salts, and sugar lost when a child has vomiting and diarrhea. They are most helpful in the early phase of a stomach virus when a child is just starting to take fluids after actively vomiting. Doctors prefer rehydration solutions instead of plain water, juice, milk, or soda for young children. Once a child is keeping down this clear fluid, we usually suggest that your child resume his regular fluid intake. All products are available over the counter. See Chapter 19, First Aid for more information on using this product. See Appendix B, Alternative Medicine for a recipe you can make at home.

Brand names: Enfalyte, Gerber Pediatric Electrolyte, Kao-electrolyte, Pedialyte.*

7. Infections

ANTIBIOTICS (BACTERIAL INFECTIONS)

This list contains the most popular choices of antibiotics (taken by mouth). There are basically four classes of medications approved for pediatric use. There are more classes available to adults. Take special note of the class or family each medicine belongs to. If a person develops an allergic reaction to a medication, ANY antibiotic that belongs to that class is to be avoided.

In this chart, we note what these medications are typically used for (usage): Ear and sinus infections (1), Pneumonia (2), Skin infections (3), Bladder infections-UTI (4), Strep throat (5). Note: all products are available by prescription only.

GENERIC NAME	BRAND NAME	FORM	DOSE	USAGE
PENICILLIN FAMILY				
Amoxicillin	Amoxil, Polymox, Trimox, Wymox*	Liq/Chew	BID	1,2,4,5
Amoxicillin+ Clavulanate	Augmentin* Augmentin ES-600*	Liq/Chew	BID	1,2,3,4,5
(Clavulanate kills resistant bacteria strains)				
Penicillin V-K	Pen VeeK, V-cillinK*	Liquid	BID-QID	5

? ?

MEDICATIONS

GENERIC NAME	BRAND NAME	FORM	DOSE	USAGE
CEPHALOSPORINS				
Cefaclor	Ceclor*	Liquid	BID	1,2,5
Cefadroxil	Duricef*, Ultracef	Liquid	BID	3, 5
Cefdinir	Omnicef*	Liquid	QD/BID	1,2,3,5
Cefpodoxime	Vantin*	Liquid	QD/BID	1,2
Cefprozil	Cefzil*	Liquid	BID	1,2,3,4,5
Ceftibuten	Cedax	Liquid	QD	1,2,5
Ceftriaxone	Rocephin*	injection	QD	1,2,3,4,5
Cefuroxime	Ceftin*, Suprax	Liquid	BID/QD	1,2,3,5
Cephalexin	Keflex*	Liquid	TID/QID	3,5
MACROLIDES				
Azithromycin	Zithromax*	Liquid	QD	1,2,3,5
Clarithromycin	Biaxin*	Liquid	BID	1,2,3,5
Erythromycin	E.E.S., Eryped*	Liq/chew	BID/QID	2,3,5
Erythromycin + Sulfisoxazole	Pediazole*	Liquid	TID	1,2
SULFONAMIDES (SULFA)				
Sulfisoxazole	Gantrisin	Liquid	QD	1,4
		Used as preventative therapy only		
Sulfamethoxazole + Trimethoprim	Bactrim, Septra* Sulfatrim, TMP-SMX	Liquid	BID	1,4

Side effects:

The most common side effects include:

1. *Diarrhea.* The antibiotic kills the bacteria causing infection, but also some normal bacterial "flora" that helps us digest food in our intestines. Lack of bacterial flora can cause malabsorption (i.e. upset stomach). ANY antibiotic can cause this problem.

2. *Yeast Infections.* Again, the antibiotic kills both bad bacteria and certain bacterial flora that live in our mouths and on our skin. Lack of normal bacteria predisposes a person to yeast infections in the mouth (thrush) and in the genital area (yeast diaper rash).

Allergic reactions:

A true allergic reaction to these medications includes hives, lip swelling, or difficulty breathing. About 25% of patients who are allergic to the Penicillin family will also be allergic to the Cephalosporin family.

Rare adverse reactions:

1. Stevens-Johnson syndrome (severe allergic reaction)
2. C. difficile colitis (secondary bacterial infection in intestines)

ANTIFUNGALS

GENERIC	BRAND	DOSE	USAGE	AGE LIMIT	RX
Fluconazole	Diflucan*	QD x 2 wks	Thrush	None	Rx
Griseofulvin*	Grifulvin	QD x 1mo.	Ringworm of scalp	None	Rx
Terbinafine	Lamisil	QD x 6 wks	Ringworm of scalp	Over 4 yrs	OTC

Side effects: nausea, headache, rash, stomach upset
Griseofulvin can cause skin sensitivity to sunlight. Used with caution in patients with Penicillin allergy.

Helpful Hint
Griseofulvin is absorbed better when taken with something rich in fat (milk, ice cream...)

ANTIHELMINTHICS (FOR PINWORM INFECTIONS)

GENERIC	BRAND	DOSE	AGE LIMIT	RX
Mebendazole	Vermox*	2 doses, 2 weeks apart	over 2 years	Rx
Pyrantel	Pin-X	2 doses, 2 weeks apart	over 2 years	OTC

Side effects: stomach upset, headache

AMEBICIDES (FOR GIARDIA INFECTION)

GENERIC	BRAND	DOSE	AGE LIMIT	RX
Metronidazole	Flagyl*	TID	None	Rx
Nitazoxanide	Alinia	BID	Over 1yr	Rx

Side effects: nausea, diarrhea, hives, metallic taste, dizziness

ANTIVIRALS

GENERIC	BRAND	DOSE	USED FOR	AGE LIMIT	RX
Acyclovir	Zovirax*	4-5x daily	Varicella Oral herpes, Zoster	None	Rx
Amantadine	Symmetrel*	BID	Influenza A	over 1 yr	Rx
Oseltamivir	Tamiflu	BID (Dosed QD for prevention)	Influenza	over 1 yr over 1 yr	Rx
Zanamivir	Relenza	BID	Influenza	over 5 yrs	Rx

Side effects: stomach upset, insomnia, headache
Adverse reactions: kidney failure with acyclovir—patient needs to be well hydrated

BOTTOM LINE
Because antiviral medications work by preventing replication of the virus, the medication must be started within 48 hours of when the illness began. Otherwise, it will have no effect on the course of the illness.

8. Nutrition

VITAMINS

The American Academy of Pediatrics does not recommend routine multivitamin supplements for children (even if they are picky eaters and hate
vegetables). The AAP does, however, advise children ages one to four to
have at least 400 IU of Vitamin D everyday . . . and that is a nearly impossible feat (unless your toddler drinks a quart of milk a day!).

The top-selling kids multivitamins (Bugs Bunny Complete, Centrum Kids
Complete, Flintstones Complete) contain Vitamin A, B1, B2, B3, B6, B12, C,
D, E, plus calcium (about 100mg per tab), iron (18 mg iron per tab), folic
acid, copper, iodine, magnesium, phosphorous, and zinc.

None of these products are approved for children under two years of
age. Kids aged two and three can have half a tablet a day. Kids age four
and up can have one tablet a day.

Poly-vi-sol with iron is the only brand-name multivitamins approved for
children under age two. It contains 10 mg of iron and 400 IU of Vitamin
D per dropperful (1ml). D-vi-sol is solely a Vitamin D supplement which has
400 IU of Vitamin D per dropperful (1ml). If you have an extremely defiant
toddler who needs a Vitamin D supplement, there are super-concentrated
products like Baby D drops that have a daily dose of Vitamin D in just one
drop (not a dropperful).

IRON SUPPLEMENTS

Multivitamins often contain iron (see list above). Remember, one to two-
year-olds only need 7 mg of iron a day and three to eight-year-olds need
10 mg of iron a day. (See Chapter 10, Nutrition for details). If a child has
iron deficiency anemia, he needs daily nutritional iron requirements PLUS
an additional amount to fill back up his depleted iron stores. The only way
to get the higher dose of iron is to use the specific products listed below.

IRON REPLACEMENT THERAPY

Brand Names: Fer-In-Sol*, Feosol*, Icar, Niferex
Dose:
1. Iron replacement drops contain 15mg iron per 0.6 ml.
2. Depending on the brand, iron replacement syrups contain 44mg
   of iron or 60mg iron per 1 teaspoon.
3. For mild to moderate iron deficiency anemia, dosing is 3 mg of
   elemental iron per kg body weight per day. Ask your doctor or
   pharmacist to calculate it for you.

Rx: These drugs are OTC, but can be confusing. Ask the pharmacist to help
you select the correct product.

Side effects: constipation, black looking poop, nausea, stomachache, temporary teeth staining

Helpful Hints
◆ You can avoid staining the teeth by shooting the medicine in
the back of the throat. If the teeth do become stained, use baking soda on a toothbrush to remove the stains.

MEDICATIONS

? ?

◆ Vitamin C improves the absorption of iron. Calcium interferes with the absorption of iron. So if you are offering a drink with the iron medicine, offer juice—not milk.

◆ If you give the iron AFTER a meal, there is less stomach upset.

9. Respiratory Problems

ASTHMA

Asthma medications are divided into rescue medications and preventative/long term control medications. The rescue medicines are used as needed (with a certain interval between doses). A child is placed on preventative medicine if he:

1. needs rescue medicine more than twice a week
2. has his activity affected by asthma flare-ups
3. has problems at night more than twice a month

The idea is to get the asthma under control, then cut back on the amount of medications needed to minimize flare ups.

For information on asthma and home nebulizers, see the Chapter 17, Common Diseases.

A brief note about environmentally friendly-inhalers: In the past, asthma inhalers emitted CFC's (chlorofluorocarbons) into the atmosphere. All of these inhalers were phased out in 2008 and replaced with a new environmentally-friendly chemical (hydrofluoroalkane or HFA). We point this out not only so you know these meds are "greener" but also because HFA inhalers are more costly! Be prepared for sticker shock.

Other things you need to know about HFA inhalers:

◆ They have a lower volume "puff" than the CFC inhalers.

◆ They need to be cleaned (with water) once a week because they can clog.

◆ They taste different.

RESCUE MEDICINES

GENERIC	BRAND	DOSE	RX	AGE LIMIT
Albuterol Syrup or Nebulizer or Inhaler	Proventil, Ventolin Accuneb*	Syrup TID Neb Q4 hrs Inhaler Q4 hrs	Rx Rx	None.
Levalbuterol Nebulizer or Inhaler	Xopenex	TID	Rx	Over 6 yrs, ask dr.
Salmeterol	Serevent Advair (see preventative table below)	Diskus BID	Rx	Over 4 yrs.

This class of medication is called a Beta agonist. There can be effects on the body similar to caffeine. More side effects are seen with the dose given orally (syrup) than with the doses that are inhaled (nebulizer machine, inhaler). Levalbuterol is a newer product that seems to have fewer side effects than the older albuterol product. Because of this, it is often used off-label in infants and young children.

Side effects: Increased heart rate, palpitations, nervousness, insomnia, nausea, headache. Both Serevent and Advair, which contain a long acting rescue medicine (beta-adrenergic agonist), have a "black box" warning by the FDA for possible increased asthma related deaths in children over 12 years of age.

PREVENTATIVE/LONG TERM CONTROL MEDICINES

GENERIC	BRAND	DOSE	RX	AGE LIMIT
Mast cell stabilizer				
Cromolyn	Intal*	Nebulizer TID	Rx	None
Inhaled corticosteroid				
Budesonide	Pulmicort*	Nebulizer BID	Rx	over 1yr/ask Dr.
		Inhaler BID	Rx	over 6 yrs
Fluticasone	FloventHFA	Inhaler/Diskus BID	Rx	over 4 yrs
Leukotriene antagonist				
Montelukast	Singulair	Chew tab QHS Oral granules	Rx	over 6 mos
Long acting beta agonist				
Salmeterol	Serevent	Diskus BID	Rx	over 4 yrs
Combination steroid and beta agonist product				
Fluticasone + Salmeterol	Advair	Inhaler/Diskus BID	Rx	over 4yrs

Side effects:

Mast cell stabilizer: bad taste, cough, nasal congestion, wheezing.

Inhaled corticosteroid: sore throat, nosebleeds, cough, thrush (see below for more information).

Leukotriene antagonist: stomach upset, headache, dizziness, depressed mood.

Helpful Hint

◆ *In the past, there were no inhaled steroid options for children under four years of age.* We would use oral steroids (Prednisone) to get a severe flare up under control. We now have Pulmicort respules (a grainy substance dissolved in liquid), which can be administered in a nebulizer machine suited to handle it (look for the machine to state "Pari-LC Plus").

Note: If your child used to respond well to a nebulizer and no longer does, your nebulizer cup may have worn out. And if you are not using a "Pari LC Plus" cup for nebulized steroids, your child may be only getting a fraction of his medication. Pari-LC Plus seems to have a longer lifespan.

◆ *Always rinse your child's mouth after he has taken an inhaled steroid.* It reduces the incidence of thrush.

◆ *Steroid medications are always used cautiously.* Steroids given by mouth (liquid/pill) are more likely to cause systemic side effects if given for a long time (more than one to two weeks). Inhaled steroids (nebulizer or inhaler) have significantly fewer side effects because only a small amount is absorbed into the bloodstream. As with any medication, the risks of taking these medications are weighed against the potential benefit of therapy for the disease.

Risks of long-term steroid use:
1. Mood change
2. Stomach upset
3. Intestinal bleeding
4. Impaired body's stress responses (HPA axis suppression: hypo-thalamic-pituitary-adrenal)
5. Bone demineralization (*Osteopenia*)
6. Weight gain, hair growth (*Cushingoid features*)
7. Cataracts
8. Growth suppression. There is data which shows some evidence of decreased height curves while a pre-pubertal child is taking steroids chronically. However, children with chronic problems with asthma also have poor growth. Studies have not concluded whether or not these children have "catch up growth" when steroids are discontinued.[2]

Reality Check: **Too many steriods?**
Children with multiple allergy issues (for example, eczema, seasonal allergies, and asthma) may be simultaneously prescribed steroid creams, steroid nose sprays, inhaled steroids, and occasionally steroids by mouth. With the exception of oral steroids, other steroid preparations act locally (on the skin, nose, lungs) and are not significantly absorbed into the bloodstream. However, high-dose steroid creams and mid- or high-potency *inhaled* steroids should be used for the shortest time possible and then tapered down. It's also a good idea to let your pediatrician know all the steroid medications your child is using, as some may be prescribed by other specialists.

Cough And Cold Medicines

In 2007, the FDA recommended that children under the age of two should NOT use over-the-counter cough and cold medications. Manufacturers voluntarily complied with the FDA and took products aimed at babies and toddlers off the shelves. The FDA also advised that these products are only known to be safe for children six years of age and up.

Why did the FDA decide to do this after all these years? The risk of the medications outweighed the benefit. There were reports of four accidental deaths when parents inappropriately used more than one cough and cold remedy, leading to fatal overdoses.

Let's face it: these products aren't easy to use—ingredients are often listed in medical-ese. The problem: if a child got one medicine for a runny nose and another for cough and cold symptoms, he could be getting an overdose of a decongestant contained in both products.

Another issue: the right dosage for toddlers. Many parents buy products intended for older kids and then guess-timate the dose for their younger

? ?

MEDICATIONS

child. That's another recipe for an overdose. Finally, the ingredients in all these medications were tested in adults—not children—before their approval. So even doctors are left guessing what to dose a baby or toddler.

The bottom line: no cough and cold medication will ever cure an illness. And most products aren't even terribly effective in treating symptoms.

As parents, we know how it feels to have a sick child on our hands. We'll do anything to make them feel a little better. But time and lots of TLC are probably the best medicine of all.

Dr B's Opinion: Cough & cold meds

I've never really liked cough and cold medications (over the counter or prescription). They don't work very well, and sometimes have unpleasant side effects like irritability and insomnia. I'd rather have a snotty, sleeping child than a snotty, awake one!

If you decide to use cough and cold medications for your older child (older than age 6), here's the advice from the FDA:

1. Check the active ingredients in the DRUG FACTS section of the label.
2. Be very careful if you are giving more than one OTC cough and cold med to a child. Make sure you are not using two medicines that contain the same or similar active ingredients.
3. Follow the directions on the package for the amount and frequency of dosing.
4. Only use the measuring syringe or cup that comes with the medication or one made especially to dose medication.[3]

DECONGESTANT

These medications reduce or relieve congestion in the nose. They can be taken by mouth (absorbed into bloodstream) or sprayed into the nose.

Oral decongestants: Pseudoephedrine, phenylephrine, ephedrine.
Side effects: Insomnia, restlessness, dizziness, high blood pressure, heart rhythm disturbances.

Nasal spray: Oxymetazoline (Afrin), Phenylephrine (Neosynephrine)
Side effects: stinging, burning, nosebleed, rebound nasal congestion with prolonged use (greater than 4 days)

Nasal spray: Saline
Side effects: None! Saline is salt water. It is effective in loosening mucus and can be used as often as needed.

Note: remember that any pseudoephedrine-containing product is only available behind the pharmacist's counter. You'll have to ask for it and sign a consent form.

ANTIHISTAMINE

These medications combat the effect of histamine in the body. Histamine is released as an allergy response and causes nasal congestion. Antihistamines are frequently found in cough and cold medicines because they are sedating, improve the cough suppressant effect, and dry up a runny nose.

Common ingredients: brompheniramine, chlorpheniramine, diphenhydramine, (promethazine- Rx only), carbinoxamine

Side effects: sedation, dry mouth, blurred vision, stomach upset, paradoxical excitement in infants

EXPECTORANT

These medications make thick mucous looser. By doing this, the mucous in the bronchial tubes (lungs) can be coughed up more easily. These medications do not suppress the cough.

Common ingredients: guaifenesin

Side effects: sedation, stomach upset, headache

COUGH SUPPRESSANT

These medications are supposed to reduce the brain's "cough center" activity. Cough suppressants products are not recommended when someone has pneumonia. And some might argue that they should never be recommended. The American College of Chest Physicians, based on clinical evidence, determined that cough medicines do not work![4]

Common ingredients: Dextromethorphan, codeine (Rx only), carbetapentane

Side effects: drug interactions with psychiatric medications.

10. Skin (Dermatologic) Products

Here are seven points to remember about skin medications:

1. Antibiotic creams are used for wound care and minor bacterial infections (impetigo, mild cellulitis).
2. Antifungal creams are used for fungus infections (ringworm, yeast infection, jock itch, athlete's foot) on the skin.
3. Scabicides and pediculocides are used for scabies and head lice.
4. Steroids are used for contact irritations (bug bites, poison ivy, local allergic reactions), seborrhea, cradle cap, eczema. Steroids are divided into classes by their potency. Doctors try to use the lowest potency if possible. The higher the potency, the more risk of side effects (high potency products can get absorbed into the bloodstream).
5. Anti-inflammatories are FDA approved for kids over age 2 with eczema.
6. As noted in Chapter 17, Common Diseases, eczema products in the immunoregulator category (Elidel, Protopic) have a black box warning for potential of future malignancy. They are approved by the FDA for use as second line treatment of eczema in children over the age of two.
7. Diaper rash creams form a barrier between the irritated skin and recurrent insults caused by pee and poop.

MEDICATIONS

ANTIBIOTIC CREAM

GENERIC	BRAND	Rx
Bacitracin, Polymyxin B	Polysporin*	OTC
Used for minor cuts, scrapes, irritations		
Mupirocin	Bactroban*, Centany	Rx
Used for impetigo and cellulitis		
Neomycin,Polymixin, Bacitracin	Neosporin*	OTC
Used for minor cuts, scrapes, irritations, and superficial burns		
Retapamulin	Altabax	Rx
Silver Sulfadiazine	Silvadene*	Rx
Antibiotic salve used for second-degree burns		

Side effects: Burning, stinging, itching.

ANTIFUNGAL CREAM

Uses:
1. Yeast diaper rash (monilial dermatitis)
2. Ringworm of skin (tinea corporis)
3. Athlete's foot (tinea pedis)
4. Jock itch (tinea cruris)

GENERIC	BRAND	USED FOR	AGE LIMIT	Rx
Clotrimazole 1%	Lotrimin AF*	1, 2, 3, 4	None	OTC
Ketoconazole 2%	Nizoral*	1,2,3,4	Over 2 yrs	Rx
Miconazole	Micatin*	1, 2, 3, 4		OTC
	Vusion	1	Over 1 mo	Rx
Nystatin	Mycostatin, Nilstat*	1	None	Rx
Econazole	Spectazole*	1,2,3,4	None	Rx

Reality Check

Ringworm of the scalp (called tinea capitis) requires an antifungal medication by mouth for four to eight weeks. The fungus gets imbedded in the hair follicles and will not respond to an antifungal cream.

SCABICIDES AND PEDICULOCIDES

GENERIC	BRAND	DOSE	USED FOR	AGE LIMIT	Rx
Acetic acid	Klout	No limit	Head lice	None	OTC
Benzyl Alcohol	Ulesfia	1-2 doses	Head lice	Over 6 mos	Rx
Lindane1%**	Lindane	1 dose	Head lice, scabies	Over 1 yr	Rx
Malathion	Ovide	2 doses, 1 week apart	Head lice	Over 6 yrs	Rx
Permethrin 1%	NIX*	1-2 doses, 1 week apart	Head lice	None	OTC

‽?????‽???

GENERIC	BRAND	DOSE	USED FOR	AGE LIMIT	RX
Permethrin 5%	Elimite*, Acticin	1-2 doses 1 week apart	Head lice scabies	None	Rx
Pyrethrum***	A-200 Pyrinyl RID, Pronto	2 doses, 1 week apart	Head Lice	None	OTC

** Medication has significant side effects/potential for seizures. Other medications are better alternatives.

*** Medication is derived from the chrysanthemum flower. Avoid use with a ragweed allergy.

Side effects: burning, itching, redness, rash

Helpful Hints: Head Lice

1. Use OTC products as directed. I know you are grossed out, but don't overdose the medicine.
2. Don't use more than one medicine at a time.
3. Use the nit combs religiously every three days.
4. Wash clothing and bed linens in hot water and dry on the hot cycle.
5. Soak combs and hairbrushes in rubbing alcohol for one hour.

Reality Check

◆ When head lice enters your home, treat any family member who has an itchy scalp.

◆ When scabies enters your home, treat *all* family members, regardless of whether they have symptoms or not.

STEROIDS

◆ Low potency: can be used for longer periods (months) of time without side effects, okay to use on the face

◆ Mid potency: okay to use for short periods (weeks) of time without side effects, use with doctor's recommendation on the face

◆ High potency: okay to use for limited period (days) of time without side effects, do not use on the face

Note: None of these steroid creams are FDA approved for use under age two years. But they are used by medical providers who feel that they are safe and efficacious.

GENERIC	BRAND	POTENCY	DOSE	RX/OTC
Hydrocortisone 0.5%	Cortaid, etc*	Low	BID	OTC
Hydrocortisone 1%	Cortaid, etc*	Low	BID	OTC
Hydrocortisone 2.5%	Hytone*	Low	BID	Rx
Triamcinolone 0.025%	Aristocort, Kenalog*	Low	BID	Rx
Desonide 0.05%	Desowen*	Mid	BID	Rx
Hydrocortisone valerate	Westcort*	Mid	BID	Rx

???

GENERIC	BRAND	POTENCY	DOSE	Rx/OTC
Hydrocortisone butyrate	Locoid*	Mid	BID	Rx
Mometosone furoate	Elocon*	Mid	QD	Rx
Triamcinolone 0.1%	Aristocort, Kenalog*	Mid	BID	Rx
Betamethasone	Diprolene*	High	BID	Rx
Diflorasone diacetate	Psorcon*	High	BID	Rx
Fluocinonide	Lidex*	High	BID	Rx
Triamcinolone 0.5%	Aristocort, Kenalog*	High	BID	Rx

Side effects: skin irritation, decreased pigmentation, thinning of skin
Rare adverse reactions:
HPA axis (adrenal gland suppression)—only with high potency steroids

ANTI-INFLAMMATORY CREAM

GENERIC	BRAND	DOSE	Rx/OTC
Pimecrolimus	Elidel	BID	Rx
Tacrolimus −03%, 0.1%	Protopic	BID	Rx

Side effects: burning, redness, itching
Rare adverse reactions: worsens warts, herpes, and chicken pox infections

ESSENTIAL FATTY ACID CREAMS

These are eczema medications that repair the skin's top layer and reduce inflammation/itching. Brand names include Mimyx and Atopiclair, both are Rx only.

Side effects: burning, redness, itching.
Rare adverse reactions: Atopiclair is derived from the shea nut, so allergic reactions are possible.

EMOLLIENT CREAM

Another popular prescription non-steroid cream used for eczema is Epiceram. It is intended to protect the skin by providing a barrier.

DIAPER RASH CREAMS

The idea behind all of the products listed below is to provide a barrier between the skin and moisture (pee and poop). When applying these creams and ointments, it is key to apply liberally and frequently.

Dr. B's opinion: I prefer creams to powders. When powder is applied, there is a risk that the child will inhale the powder.

MEDICATIONS

? ?

DIAPER RASH CREAMS

NAME	Rx/OTC?
A+D ointment	OTC
Boudreaux's Butt Paste	OTC
Dr. Smith's Diaper Ointment	OTC
Miconazole (brand name: Vusion)	Rx
	Used for diaper rash due to yeast.
Silvadene	Rx
	Used for diaper rash that looks like a burn.
Triple Paste	OTC
Vaseline	OTC
Zinc Oxide (brands: Desitin, Balmex)	OTC

BOTTOM LINE

Many pediatricians have a secret recipe of salves and barrier creams that pharmacies will make especially for them. If none of these over the counter products are working, it's time to visit your pediatrician for some help.

ALTERNATIVE MEDICINES & THERAPIES

Appendix B

This appendix is devoted to the healing arts that fit under the category of Integrative Medicine. What the heck does that mean? Read on.

"Western medicine" is what most M.D.'s in the United States learn in medical school and practice once they hang their shingle. Western medicine applies the scientific method (therapies are based on rigorous scientific studies that look at benefits and risks) and uses evidence-based (code phrase for "show us it works") data to formulate standard guidelines for patient care.

But there are other complementary and alternative treatments that are based on different guiding principles. And many of these treatments lack strong (or any) scientific data to prove safety and benefit. Some of these are home remedies, some are hands-on treatments as opposed to medications, and some are based on ancient healing arts passed on through generations. That doesn't mean that these treatments are all bunk. It simply means it's hard for an M.D. to embrace them when they aren't tested or verified in a scientific way.

Based on increasing popularity for alternative remedies, the National Institute of Health created the National Center for Complementary and Alternative Medicine (CAM) in 1999. This center provides just what we docs want to see: proof that these remedies work and are safe.

Integrative Medicine is the new buzz phrase to describe, "mainstream medical therapies and CAM therapies for which there is some high-quality scientific evidence of safety and effectiveness," according to the National Institute of Health. The only therapies we will include in this appendix are those that cut the mustard, so to speak.

Traditional medical schools are adding integrative medicine coursework to their curricula so that new doctors at least have working knowledge of these therapies. We realize there are a variety of healing arts and all have their benefits for particular medical issues. We also know that parents may seek out these therapies, perhaps for natural or non-pharmacologic alternatives. Or they may seek alternatives because their child has a chronic medical problem that is not improving with standard, traditional therapy.

Finally, a brief precaution on herbs: the FDA considers these to be FOOD, not medicine. As a result, the dietary supplement industry is not regulated like the pharmaceutical industry. For example, kumquats are not tested to see if they cause strokes and neither is Gingko biloba.[1] That's why you will find the following list to be much smaller than the aisle at your natural foods store.

ALT MEDS

Top Six Natural Therapies

DR B'S OPINION

"If you decide to try a complementary therapy, please let your child's doctor know. Just like other medications, there can be significant drug interactions between the products."

Aloe Vera gel
Uses: Thermal skin injury (sunburn, frostbite, minor burns). Apply gel three or four times daily.
Scientific Data: Good evidence that it promotes wound healing.
Precautions: Allergic sensitivity to aloe plant.[2]

Calendula
(calendula officinalis)
Uses: Minor burns, sunburn. Apply three to four times daily.
Scientific Data: Some evidence that it promotes wound healing and has antiseptic properties.
Precautions: Allergic reactions can occur, and can cause eye irritation. Not recommended for use in the eye.[3]

Chamomile
(anthemis nobilis)
Uses: Mild sedation for sleep problems, minor skin injuries (acne, diaper rash, eczema). Tea can be given up to three times a day. Cream can be applied as needed.
Scientific Data: Some evidence of sedation, stress reduction, improved wound healing.
Precautions: Allergic reactions in people with allergies to ragweed, daisies, chrysanthemums.[4]

Ginger
(Zingiber officinale)
Uses: Nausea, motion sickness. For ages two to three: 25 mg of ginger root powder dosed four times a day. For ages three to six: 50–75 mg of ginger root powder dosed four times a day. Alternatively, you can prepare ginger root tea by taking 1 cup water, one-quarter tsp grated ginger root, plus a little lemon juice and honey. FYI: You can also buy ginger containing ginger-ale soda at some grocery stores.[5]
Scientific Data: Some evidence for use in motion sickness, pregnancy. No studies done in children.
Precautions: Ginger may alter blood clotting. Discontinue use two weeks prior to surgery or dental procedures.[6]

Probiotics
Uses: Diarrhea due to antibiotics, viral gastroenteritis, eczema. Use the powder of one capsule (or one powder packet) one to three times daily.
Scientific Data: Good evidence in shortening the duration of diarrhea due to antibiotic use and stomach virus. Emerging data on controlling eczema.
Precautions: Not for use in people with milk allergy or lactose intolerance.[7]
For more info, see box on probiotics and prebiotics on the next page
.

Peppermint
(Mentha piperita)
Uses: decongestant, cough, irritable bowel syndrome, headaches, itching. For itching, add a cup of peppermint tea to bathwater. Drink one cup of

ALT MEDS

PROBIOTICS & PREBIOTICS

Probiotics and prebiotics are thriving at natural food and conventional stores alike, thanks to potential health benefits for the gut.

What are PRObiotics? "Good" germs (bacteria or yeast) that help the body digest food. They are found naturally in yogurt, kefir, kombucha tea, and sauerkraut (we know there are tons of toddlers out there eating sauerkraut). You can also find them in nutritional supplements.

What are PREbiotics? Complex starches or polysaccharides in food that help the gut grow those good bacteria. This is what creates a sustained, healthy gut environment. They are found naturally in whole grains, honey, garlic, onions, bananas, leeks, and artichokes. Other food and beverage products are fortified with them.[8]

So, does your child need these "functional foods" or supplements? We know that PRObiotics, such as Lactobacillus acidophilus, lactobacillus GG, and Saccharomyces sp. are all safe and effective in preventing antibiotic-associated diarrhea and reducing diarrhea from a stomach virus in kids as young as one month of age.[9]

But do kids need probiotics on a daily basis? Right now, the answer is probably not. We know that probiotics only work while a person is taking them and the only clear benefit is when someone is actually sick. And there are some rare, but potential risks. Because they are germs, yes, some people with weakened immune systems can potentially get bloodstream infections.

But how about prebiotics? Sure, why not? These are the building blocks that help the gut make a nice nesting ground for those good germs to grow. So serve up another helping of whole grains and bananas (or leeks and artichokes if your toddler is so inclined!).

peppermint tea for stomach cramps or indigestion. Menthol chest rubs are okay to use in children over age two.
Scientific Data: Data shows that peppermint actually INCREASES nasal congestion but people subjectively report that they can breathe better.
Precautions: Heartburn. Allergic reactions. Not for use in someone with gallstones, liver disease, or who is taking calcium channel blocking medications.[10]

BOTTOM LINE

Just because it's natural doesn't mean it's safe. Get educated about these products before using them (beyond just asking the clerk at the natural foods store). For more information on natural remedies, check out *The Holistic Pediatrician*, by Kathi J. Kemper, M.D. (see References, Appendix G). She is a well-respected pediatrician who has done a great deal of research on complementary and alternative therapies. Check out her website at longwoodherbal.org.

Home Remedies

Not every ailment requires a trip to the pharmacy. Here is a list of household items and remedies that often provide symptomatic relief for various problems.

Abdominal pain/gas/colic. Give your child a bath. The warm water is soothing. Playing in the bathtub is also a nice distraction technique.

Bruises. Pull out a bag of frozen vegetables and place on the site.

Common Cold (URI). Make your own saline (salt water) nose drops. Take 1/2 teaspoon of salt and add to 8 oz. of water. Use as much as needed.

Chicken soup. Every culture has their own recipe, and for good reason. The high salt and water content is good for hydrating a child with a fever.

Honey. A study looked at the effects of offering a teaspoon of honey before bedtime. Parents subjectively reported that their child coughed less the night they gave honey compared to the night before. There were a few problems with this study. Flaw #1: There are probably fewer symptoms each night of an illness as it progresses anyway. Flaw #2: No one was objectively measuring how much the child was actually coughing. Flaw #3: This study was funded by the National Honey Board. Hmmm. Color us skeptical. But we don't have a problem with you taking out the honey the next time your child has a cold—as long as he is over one year old.[11]

Pull out the humidifier. This moistens the air your child breathes, and loosens the mucus in his nose.

Cradle cap. Massage olive oil or margarine into the scalp. Then lift off the plaques.

Croup. Take your child into the bathroom. Close the door. Turn on the shower for ten to 15 minutes. The warm mist will help relax the airway.

If this technique doesn't work, walk outside with your child. The cold night air will often shrink up the swollen airway. It also changes the scenery for your child, which has a therapeutic effect too. If you live in a warm climate, try opening your freezer and letting your toddler breathe in the air.

Diaper rash. Good old petroleum jelly (Vaseline) works well. It provides a barrier between the skin and moisture. Other possibilities:

Leave your baby open to air (diaper-less) in a safe place inside or outside your house.

Use a blow dryer on the lowest setting to dry your child's bottom.

Some doctors recommend applying liquid antacids (milk of magnesia, kaopectate) to the diaper rash. It might be worth a try.

Vomiting and Diarrhea. Make your own Pedialyte solution. Here is the recipe: 4 cups of water, 1/2 tsp of salt, 2 Tbsp. of sugar, 1/2 tsp of instant Jell-O powder for flavor.

Ear infections. Use a heating pad on low setting up to the ear. To prevent swimmer's ear, you can make your own "Swim-ear" drops. The alcohol will dry up the water left in the ear canal. The vinegar changes the pH of the ear canal so bugs won't want to grow there. Here's the recipe: 2 drops rubbing alcohol, 2 drops of vinegar.

Eczema. Keeping the skin moist is the key. The best moisturizer (although not very practical) is good old petroleum jelly. Lube your child up head to toe.

Eye stye. Place a warm tea bag over the eyelid. It is soothing and reduces the swelling.

Lice. Put mayonnaise on your child's hair at bedtime. Cover with a shower cap. Rinse off in the morning. There seems to be limited success in smothering the lice with this technique. Another popular alternative: tea tree oil. Over-the-counter shampoo products like Lice Ice use tea tree oil as their active ingredient.

Sore throat. Make a milkshake or smoothie. Cold drinks feel good and are a nice way to get fluid in. This idea makes me very popular with my patients.

Warts. Try duct tape. There is scientific proof that smothering the warts suppresses the growth of the virus that causes them. Apply a new piece of duct tape to the wart nightly and leave on for the day. It takes about six weeks.

LAB WORK & TESTS
Appendix C

When You Want a Test

Parents should feel comfortable requesting additional testing on their child. If you have concerns, speak up! If you're worried that your child might have leukemia, don't expect the doctor to read your mind (especially if you bring your child in with complaints of a common cold). Your doctor should not laugh at you—he should respect your concerns and address them. Just know that doctors are less excited about doing tests when they are certain that it's a cold . . and not Ebola virus.

And be reasonable about your requests. We wish there was a hand held body scanner like the doc on Star Trek had. But at this point, there is no one "test" that will detect every disease (like a total body CT scan or a comprehensive blood test panel). In the past, doctors would perform annual blood metabolic panels on adults like a fishing expedition for abnormalities. This is out of vogue for adults and has never been standard practice for children.

But if you ask, your doctor should be willing to do a specific test that would help to diagnose or rule out the concern you have.

When The Doctor Wants a Test

Pediatricians are trained to see specific patterns for diseases. Docs don't always need a lab test or imaging study to figure out what is going on with a patient.

But here are a few reasons that an evaluation beyond physical examination is reasonable.

30 Reasons to order a test
1. When there is something about the child's illness history or examination that may indicate a bacterial infection.
2. When there is a concern that an infection is bacterial and cultures are needed to know what bug the patient has (so it can be treated appropriately).
3. When a child has a fever with no obvious source.
4. When your doctor thinks your child has a broken bone.
5. When a child is vomiting bile or has intractable vomiting.
6. When a child has blood in his poop.

7. When a child has pain during urination.
8. When a child's head size is enlarging across percentiles (in other words, the head is growing much faster than the rest of the body).
9. When a child's head size is *not* enlarging.
10. When a child is failing to thrive (not gaining weight).
11. When a child wheezes for the first time and it doesn't sound like RSV or bronchiolitis.
12. When an abnormality is found during a regular exam (such as distended abdomen, swollen testes).
13. When a child is drinking or urinating excessively.
14. When a child has excessive bruising.
15. When a child has petechiae.
16. When a child has a persistent fever (five days or more).
17. When a child is disoriented.
18. When a child has a seizure for the first time.
19. When a child appears dehydrated and the doctor needs to decide how dehydrated he is (that is, does he need to be admitted to the hospital and get IV fluids?).
20. When a child bleeds excessively—with cuts or nosebleeds.
21. When your doctor thinks a child has pneumonia and wants to confirm it.
22. When a parent is worried.
23. When a child is limping.
24. When a child has recurrent bacterial infections (not just ear infections) such as pneumonia, sinus infections, skin infections.
25. When a child has chronic or severe problems with wheezing.
26. Anytime a child is jaundiced (outside the first few weeks of life).
27. When a child has a heart murmur that does not sound like an innocent heart murmur.
28. When a child has an irregular heartbeat.
29. When a child has a bladder or kidney infection.
30. When a child has swallowed a non-food object.

Here are the most common tests docs order and what they mean.

Imaging Studies

Ultrasound

The beauty of ultrasonography is that no radiation is used. The technology involves use of sonar waves and computer imaging. Doppler flow studies in addition to ultrasound pictures are helpful in looking at blood flow. Ultrasound pictures can be limited, however. Gas and fat obstructs the view.

Abdominal. Looks at the anatomy of the liver, gallbladder, spleen. Not as good at looking at intestines. Detects intussusception, gallstones, masses.

Head. Looks for bleeding or extra fluid inside the skull. Wand is placed on top of the anterior fontanelle (soft spot) to see inside. Not used once fontanelle has closed. Detects hemorrhage, hydrocephalus.

Heart (echocardiogram with Doppler). Looks at the anatomy of the heart and the great blood vessels coming off the heart. Detects heart defects.

Kidney (renal). Looks at the anatomy of the kidneys. Detects evidence of enlargement, fluid collection (hydronephrosis), and infection.

Pelvic. Looks at anatomy of the ovaries, uterus, bladder. Detects ovarian cysts, masses. Also detects location of testes if not descended into the scrotum.

Spine. Looks for spina bifida, an abnormal formation of the spine.

Testicular, with Doppler flow. Looks at the anatomy of the testes. Detects a twisted testes and can assess blood flow to the testes. Also detects some hernias.

Plain x-rays

X-rays use diffraction of low doses of high-speed electrons (radiation) to project an image. Solid or fluid filled objects appear white and air appears clear. As a general rule, plain x-rays are better at detecting bone problems, and less helpful at assessing problems with "soft tissues."

Abdomen. Looks at the anatomy of the intestines, liver, spleen. Detects intestinal obstructions, malrotations, constipation. Can detect some foreign bodies (swallowed objects that are metal).

Chest. Looks at the anatomy of the heart, lungs, ribs. Detects fluid (blood, pus) in lungs, masses in lungs, enlargement of the heart, rib fractures, foreign inhaled objects.

Extremities. Looks at the bones of the arms and legs. Detects fractures (broken bones), fluid or swelling occasionally. Less helpful in detecting problems with muscles, tendons, and joints.

Neck. Looks at the anatomy of the throat (epiglottis, tonsils, adenoid, trachea). Detects swelling of these areas, location of some swallowed objects.

Skull. Looks at the anatomy of the skull bones. Detects craniosynostosis, fractures.

Sinus. Looks at the anatomy of the sinus cavities of the face. Detects *acute* sinus infections by identifying an air/fluid level. Not helpful in detecting chronic sinus infections.

Spine. Looks at the anatomy of the vertebrae from the neck to the buttocks. Detects fractures, slipped discs, scoliosis.

CT/MRI with or without contrast

Computerized Tomography (CT) uses x-ray technology (radiation) to look at cross sectional slices of the body in a two-dimensional picture. Magnetic Resonance Imaging (MRI) uses a magnetic field to detect the body's electromagnetic transmissions. MRI's produce narrow slices of the

lab work & tests

body without radiation.

As a general rule, these studies are better at detecting abnormalities with soft body tissues and less helpful with bone problems. The decision to perform a CT versus an MRI is based on the particular problem that is being assessed.

Abdomen. Looks at the anatomy of the liver, spleen, pancreas, gallbladder, intestines, kidneys. Detects masses, tumors, abscesses—including appendicitis, fluid collections, trauma.

Chest. Looks at the anatomy of the lungs and heart. Detects masses, tumors, fluid collections, congenital abnormalities, trauma.

Extremity. Looks at the anatomy of the arm or leg. Detects fractures, torn ligaments, masses, tumors, osteomyelitis (infection).

Head. Looks at the anatomy of the brain. Detects masses, tumors, obstruction of spinal fluid flow (hydrocephalus), evidence of stroke (cerebrovascular accident), evidence of trauma, bleeding.

Lymph node. Looks at the anatomy of a swollen lymph node. Detects pus (infection), masses, congenital cysts.

Pelvic. Looks at the anatomy of the ovaries, uterus, bladder. Detects masses, tumors, fluid collections.

Sinus. Looks at the anatomy of the sinus cavities. More helpful imaging study than plain x-rays. Detects obstruction to flow in the sinuses, chronic sinus infections, masses/polyps.

Special studies
Barium swallow/Upper GI. Looks at the anatomy of the upper gastrointestinal tract (esophagus, stomach, upper small intestine). Detects anatomic abnormalities, hiatal hernias, ulcerations, narrowings. Although gastroesophageal reflux may be seen (barium goes backwards), it doesn't tell you the severity of the reflux. It also does not rule out reflux as a diagnosis.

Bone scan. Nuclear medicine study uses a radio-isotope to be visualized on x-ray. Looks at the all of the bones of the body in one study. Hot and cold "spots" detect areas of inflammation.
Detects: infection, tumors, avascular necrosis, child abuse.

Voiding Cystourethrogram. Looks at the flow of urine from kidney to ureters to bladder to urethra. Detects vesicoureteral reflux in children prone to bladder infections.[1]

DMSA Scan: Nuclear medicine study that also uses radio-isotope to be visualized on x-ray. Looks at the kidneys as the material travels through them. *Detects scarring of the kidneys due to infection.*

Laboratory Tests

Blood tests

Amylase. This test looks at the level of an enzyme that the pancreas makes.
Detects: pancreatitis.

Basic Metabolic Panel. This is a battery of tests that includes *sodium, potassium, chloride, bicarbonate, blood urea nitrogen, creatinine, glucose.* This combination of tests assesses body fluid and salt (electrolyte) balance as well as kidney and adrenal function.
Detects: Dehydration, kidney dysfunction, diabetes, hypoglycemia, adrenal dysfunction

Bilirubin. This test assesses the level of this substance circulating in the bloodstream.
A total level is assessed as well as *direct* and *indirect* levels. These indicate the cause of the total elevation. Beyond the newborn period, any evidence of jaundice prompts a lab evaluation.
Detects: Hyperbilirubinemia, Hepatitis, Biliary Atresia, gallstones, hemolytic anemia

Blood culture. see below

Blood sugar (glucose). This test assesses the body's metabolism of sugar. A random level above 110 is concerning for diabetes. Levels less than 60 in children is concerning for hypoglycemia.
Detects in children: Diabetes, hypoglycemia

Blood type. This test determines what proteins sit on the surface of a patient's red blood cells. There are A and B proteins. The AB blood type means both A and B protein are present. The O blood type means there are no proteins present. Rh typing refers to the presence (+) or absence (-) of another type of protein that sits on the red blood cell surface. These tests are necessary when a blood transfusion is needed. In an emergency situation, however, everyone gets O negative blood.

Cholesterol level. See lipid panel

Complete Blood Count (CBC). This refers to a test that looks at the number of white blood cells, red blood cells, and platelets that are circulating in the bloodstream.

1. *White blood cell count (WBC).* These cells fight infection, but also rise with inflammation. An elevated count is concerning for a bacterial infection. A depressed count is due to decreased bone marrow production (where white blood cells are made)—usually caused by viral infections (e.g. influenza, mononucleosis).

lab work & tests

2. *White blood cell count differential.* Not only is the number of white blood cells counted, but the types of white blood cells are identified in a CBC. The types of cells also give your doctor clues as to the disease process going on.

◆ *Neutrophils (PMN's)*: Cells that fight bacteria. If more than 50% of the WBC's are this type, the likelihood of a bacterial infection is greater.

◆ *Lymphocytes*: Cells that fight viruses. If more than 50% of the WBC's are this type, the likelihood of viral infection is greater.

◆ *Eosinophils*: Cells that fight parasites. Also revved up by allergies. If more than 10-15% of these cells are present, it prompts an investigation. (When all three cell lines—white, red, platelet—are depressed, there is a concern for leukemia.)

3. *Hematocrit/Hemoglobin.* These measurements assess the amount of red blood cells in the circulation. Low levels detect anemia.

4. *Platelet count.* These cells help clot the blood. A low level detects a cause for bleeding problems. A low level can also suggest bone marrow suppression (where platelets are made) or an autoimmune disorder. Platelet counts can be elevated with infection or inflammation.

Detects: infection, inflammation, leukemia, anemia, bleeding disorder

Comprehensive Metabolic Panel. This is a large battery of tests that assesses adrenal, kidney, liver, gallbladder, fluid and electrolyte balance, and a measure of general nutrition. Many physicians pick a select number of these tests and not the whole panel. These tests include:
Albumin
Alkaline phospatase
Alanine Aminotransferase (ALT)
Aspartate Aminotransferase (AST)
Bicarbonate
Bilirubin
Blood Urea Nitrogen (BUN)
Calcium
Chloride
Creatinine
Glucose
Phosporous
Potassium
Sodium
Total Protein
Detects: Liver dysfunction, hepatitis, gallbladder dysfunction, kidney dysfunction, dehydration, diabetes, adrenal dysfunction, malnutrition.

C-Reactive Protein (CRP). This is a substance that circulates in the bloodstream when there is an inflammatory process going on. It is one of several "acute phase reactants" whose numbers change by at least 25% during inflammation. It is not specific for any one disease, but it is accurate. *Detects: inflammation, infection, trauma, tumor.* [2]

Chromosome analysis. This test assesses a patient's chromosomes, the part of each cell that contains genes. Blood, tissue, or an amniotic fluid sample can be tested.
Detects: Chromosomal abnormalities related to developmental delays/congenital defects; determines the sex of a baby born with ambiguous genitalia.

Coagulation studies. These tests detect an abnormality in the clotting "cascade" or chain of events that allow blood to clot. These tests include: Bleeding Time, Factor levels, Prothrombin time (PT), Partial thromboplastin time (PTT)
Detects: Bleeding disorders—such as Hemophilia, von Willebrand's disease

Electrolytes. See Basic Metabolic Panel.

Erythrocyte Sedimentation Rate (ESR). This test looks at how fast it takes for red blood cells to settle at the bottom of a test tube. It is a very nonspecific test, but an elevated level suggests further testing. It is a non-specific sign of inflammation. Like the CRP test, it is an acute phase reactant.
Detects: inflammation, infection, pregnancy, malignancy, anemia.

Liver function tests. This is a battery of tests that evaluates how the liver is working. It looks at products the liver is in charge of metabolizing and producing. Some tests look at the breakdown product of liver cells, but these products are also seen in muscle breakdown, so they are not specific in detecting liver disorders.
  Alanine Aminotransferase (ALT)
  Albumin
  Aspartate Aminotransferase (AST)
  Bilirubin
  Total protein
Detects: Hepatitis, liver failure, drug toxicity, heart attack.

Monospot/EBV titers. For monospot, see rapid assays below.

Epstein-Barr Virus (EBV) titers detect a person's immune response (antibodies) to an EBV infection (mononucleosis). Because different types of antibodies are formed through the course of infection, this test differentiates a recent infection and a prior one.
Detects: Acute mononucleosis, prior mononucleosis.

Lipid panel/ cholesterol. This battery of tests looks at how the body metabolizes fat. Poor fat metabolism is associated with coronary artery disease (heart disease) in later life. In children, a random (non-fasting) cholesterol level is often obtained for those at risk (family history, obesity). If that level is elevated, a full panel is done with the child fasting prior to the test.
  Cholesterol
  HDL
  LDL
  Triglyceride level
Detects: Hypercholesterolemia, hepatitis, metabolic disorders, bile duct obstruction, nephrotic syndrome, pancreatitis, hypothyroidism

Reticulocyte count. Reticulocytes are baby red blood cells. They circulate in the bloodstream while they mature. This test looks at the number of these present in the blood. A high level suggests good bone marrow production in response to anemia.
Detects: body's response to anemia

Thyroid function tests. This is a battery of tests that assesses the function of the thyroid gland. An indirect way of testing thyroid gland function is to look at a Thyroid Stimulating Hormone (TSH) level, a hormone produced by the pituitary gland. If the thyroid gland is not functioning well (hypothyroidism), the TSH level is elevated to stimulate the gland to work harder.

   T3 (triiodothyronine)level
   Thyroxine Binding Globulin
   T4 (thyroxine) level
   Free T3, Free T4 levels
   TSH
Detects: Hypothyroidism, Hyperthyroidism

Viral titers. There are a few viruses for which a patient's antibody response can be detected. These tests are useful to make a diagnosis or confirm immunity to a particular virus.

   CMV
   Hepatitis A, B, C
   HIV
   Parvovirus
   Rubella
   Syphilis
   Toxoplasmosis
   Varicella

Urine tests

Urinalysis. This is a test that looks at the components of urine and detects any abnormalities. Urine is normally a sterile fluid, thus should not contain any bacteria or white blood cells (which fight infection). Urine does not breakdown sugar or protein, so it should not contain any of those substances. Urine is produced in the kidneys, so some abnormalities will point to a kidney dysfunction.

   In children, obtaining a urine specimen can be challenging. A urine specimen needs to be clean to be able to make any decisions based on its findings. The preferred method of obtaining this specimen is to insert a small catheter in the urethra of a non-toilet trained child. If the reason for testing urine is not to look for infection, a collection bag may be placed over the urethra.

   Specific gravity
   pH
   Color, odor
   White Blood Cells
   Red Blood Cells
   Glucose
   Protein

Nitrite
Microscopic analysis for bacteria
Detects: Bladder infection, dehydration, kidney disease, diabetes, adrenal dysfunction, metabolic disorder, kidney stones

Skin tests

PPD. This is the preferred test for exposure to tuberculosis. PPD stands for purified protein derivative, which refers to a synthetic protein "signature" that belongs to the tuberculosis bacteria. If a person has had an exposure to tuberculosis, their antibodies will also respond to this skin test. A positive test requires further evaluation and testing.

Stool tests

Occult blood. This test detects blood in the stool. A small amount of stool (poop) is placed on a special developing card. When a processing fluid is added to the specimen, it turns blue in the presence of blood.
Detects: Gastrointestinal bleeding (e.g. food allergy, infection, ulcer, inflammatory bowel disease, polyp).

Spinal fluid (CSF) tests

Cerebrospinal fluid (CSF) is a liquid that bathes the brain and spinal cord. It transports important chemicals through the central nervous system. A specimen of this fluid helps diagnose viral and bacterial infection, tuberculosis, meningitis (infection of the tissues protecting the brain), brain infection, and obstruction of the spinal fluid collection system.

CSF is obtained by performing a lumbar puncture or "spinal tap." This sounds scary, but it is a similar concept to having an epidural placed in childbirth. A small needle is inserted between two vertebrae in the back. A small amount of fluid is collected, and then the needle is removed.

Doctors look at the pressure of the fluid, the appearance of the fluid (should be clear/watery), the sugar/protein levels, and if there are any cells in the fluid (white, red, bacteria).

A culture of the fluid is also done (see below).

Sweat test

A specimen of sweat is obtained by warming the skin on the arm or thigh and obtaining a small amount of sweat.
Detects: Cystic Fibrosis

Cultures

This group of tests takes a particular body fluid and incubates it (creates ideal growing conditions for bugs). If there is a germ in a specimen, there is a chance a culture may identify it. Germs that grow are very accurate for infection growing in the patient (except for contaminated/dirty specimens). But lack of growth in culture does not necessarily rule out an infection.

Most germs will grow out in a culture within three days. Fungus infections, however, may take up to one month to grow.

lab work & tests

Blood. Detects BACTERIAL infections.
Urine. Detects bacterial infections.
Spinal fluid. Detects primarily BACTERIAL infections, some VIRAL infections.
Stool. Detects BACTERIAL, PARASITE, AMOEBA infections.
Throat. Detects BACTERIAL infection.
Sputum. Detects BACTERIAL infection.
Abscess. Detects BACTERIAL infection.
Viral. Detects limited number of VIRAL infections (such as Herpes, Varicella, Chlamydia).
Fungal. Detects FUNGUS infections.

Rapid Antigen Assays

As a group, these tests identify responses that infections have to certain chemicals. You might think of them in a similar way to a home pregnancy test. A positive test accurately confirms infection. But a negative test does not rule *out* infection. These "assay kits" also look like a home pregnancy test. The earlier these tests are done in the course of an illness, the less accurate they are.

Strep. Throat swab specimen.
Monospot. Blood specimen.
Influenza. Nasal secretion specimen.
RSV. Nasal secretion specimen. Not routinely offered in pediatric offices. Used in a hospital setting to isolate and treat patients who have this infection.
Rotavirus. Stool specimen[3]

GLOSSARY
Appendix D

Abdominal tumors. There are some solid tumors that occur more frequently in children than adults. These include Wilm's tumor and neuroblastoma. Patients with these tumors may (not always) have enlarged, firm bellies with a mass that can be felt. Other symptoms include weight loss, lack of appetite, or unexplained fevers.

Acholic stool. Official term for a clay colored poop. In isolation, it may have no significance. But it can indicate a problem with the biliary system (liver, gall-bladder, pancreas) if it is associated with other symptoms—particularly jaundice (yellowing) of the skin. Diagnoses can include hepatitis infection and biliary atresia. If you see this, check in with your doctor.

Acquired sensorineural hearing loss, see Hearing loss, forms of.

Acute abdomen. Term that refers to an emergency requiring surgical intervention to alleviate an intestinal problem. Examples of these problems include: appendicitis, intussusception, and intestinal obstruction.

Acute otitis media. Infection in the middle ear space. This is primarily caused by bacteria. When the infection comes up quickly, it is called "acute." Symptoms include fever, cranky mood, and vomiting. Occasionally, children may also seem dizzy. Ear infections that smolder for a long period of time are called "chronic" and do not have the same symptoms.

Adenoid hypertrophy. Enlargement of the immune system tissue called the adenoid that sits behind the nose. The enlargement can interfere with air passage from the nose into the throat. It can lead to chronic snoring and sleep disordered breathing, as well as chronic infection that looks like a sinus infection.

Air hungry. The inability of a person to get enough oxygen in with each breath. The person then tries to get more air in with each breath by using chest wall muscles and increasing the number of breaths taken per minute. This is also known as **respiratory distress.**

Amblyopia. (Known as lazy eye). A reduction of vision in an eye that is not correctable with glasses. This problem can be caused by a weakness of an eye muscle (strabismus). It is important to detect this eye problem early (under age two or three years) so it can be treated.

? ?

GLOSSARY

Anal fissure. A crack in the anus opening usually due to passage of a hard poop. The crack causes discomfort and occasionally blood in the diaper or on a diaper wipe.

Anaphylactic reaction. An allergic response to exposure to a particular item (that is, medication, food). The response is extremely serious and life-threatening. These body responses include: difficulty breathing, heart failure, drop in blood pressure.

Anemia. A reduced amount of the product (hemoglobin) that carries oxygen on red blood cells. Because the body is less capable of getting oxygen, symptoms include tiredness, pale appearance, and quick fatigue.

Ankyloglossia (tongue tie). The tongue is attached to the base of the mouth too close to the tip. Not all babies with tongue tie need intervention. If it is so tight that it interferes with feeding or talking, the tissue band can be clipped. This is more likely to be a problem if the tip of the tongue is forked.

Anomaly. Fancy word for abnormality, usually malformed prior to birth (congenital anomaly).

Antibiotic induced colitis. Inflammation of the lower part of the intestine which, rarely, can be caused by antibiotics. Symptoms of colitis include blood and mucus in the poop, diarrhea, and cramping. If someone has been on an antibiotic just prior to the onset of these symptoms, a specimen of poop can be checked for this problem.

Apnea. Pause, or temporary absence in breathing. See *obstructive sleep apnea*.

Appendicitis. Inflammation of a small piece of the intestine called the appendix. The appendix is usually located in the lower RIGHT side of the belly, but this varies occasionally. When the appendix gets swollen, symptoms include: vomiting, diarrhea, fever, and abdominal pain that worsens over time. Appendicitis is more common in school-age children and young adults.

Asperger's Syndrome. A developmental disorder that is part of the Autism Spectrum Disorders. Children with Asperger's have more social and language skills than those more severely affected.

Associative Play. When a child engages in play with another child.

Asthma. The swelling of the big and little airways in the lungs. The swelling can occur due to allergic response. The episodes happen intermittently. Symptoms include: coughing and labored breathing (respiratory distress).

Atopy. A classic triad of allergic disorders: eczema, asthma, and seasonal allergies (termed "allergic rhinitis"). Not everyone is unlucky enough to have all three problems, but some people are.

Atresia. Means that something is completely absent or is significantly narrowed.

Auditory Processing Disorder. This refers to an alteration in the way the brain interprets information that is heard. It causes difficulty in learning and social interactions and can be associated with other behavioral or learning differences.

Autism. A developmental disorder that is characterized by poor or no language development, lack of normal social skills and repetitive self-soothing behaviors. The disorder likely has a genetic basis. There is a broad range of this disorder from mild to severely affected. Thus, **Autism Spectrum Disorder** is the term now used to describe the group of developmental disorders.

Autosomal dominant. A genetically inherited trait that requires only one parent to have an abnormal gene to pass it on to a child. If one parent carries an autosomal dominant gene, the chances are 50% that a child inherits the gene.

Autosomal recessive. A genetically inherited trait that requires both parents to have the gene to pass it on to a child. If both parents are carriers of the autosomal recessive gene, the chances are 25% that they will have an affected child. If both parents have the disease, chances are nearly 100% that they will have an affected child.

Bacterial gastroenteritis. See *gastroenteritis*.

BAER. Brainstem Audio Evoked Response. An objective hearing test that measures the electrical activity of the inner ear in response to sound. This is a universal screening test done on newborns. It is recommended by the American Academy of Pediatrics and about 93% of babies get tested currently. States vary on their legislation regarding testing. Some mandate that all babies are tested, some require insurance companies to cover the cost of testing, and some allow exemption from testing only if a parent objects.

Bladder infection. See *UTI*.

Blood in stool. A symptom that may be caused by a variety of reasons. Blood can be found in poop due to skin irritation (diaper rash), a crack or tear in the anus (see anal fissure), inflammation in the intestine (milk protein allergy), intestinal infection (see gastroenteritis), or intestinal obstruction (intussusception). As you can see, the problem may be a minor or serious one. It always should be checked out by your doctor.

Brain tumor. Abnormal mass of cells that grow in the brain tissue. Although not all tumors are malignant (fast growing, aggressive), even a benign tumor can be life threatening depending on the location that it arises. Symptoms in young children include morning headaches accompanied by vomiting, increasing head size, behavior changes, imbalance, seizures, and new onset eye abnormalities.

Branchial cleft cyst. An abnormality in fetal development of the throat that results in a cyst that occurs on the neck.

Breath-holding spell. An episode where a child holds his breath when upset or angry. Usually occurs after one year of age. The episode ultimately results in a child losing consciousness and regaining normal breathing. Rarely, these episodes are due to anemia—but worth checking out if the episodes occur frequently.

Bronchiolitis. Swelling in the tiny airways in the lungs (bronchioles). In children, this is caused primarily by a virus called RSV (respiratory syncytial virus). When the little airways are swollen, it can be difficult to exchange oxygen poor air with oxygen rich air. In severe cases, particularly infants under a year of age or those born prematurely, some children need medication to reduce the swelling (see bronchodilators in medication appendix) and supplemental oxygen.

Bronchitis. Swelling in the larger airways of the lungs (bronchi). In children, this swelling is usually caused by a virus or bacterial infection.

Cafe au lait spots. As the name implies, these are light brown (coffee with milk) colored birthmarks. They occur in babies of all races. Most of the time, there is no significance to these marks. When a child has more than five of these birthmarks, there may be an association with a disorder called **neurofibromatosis.**

Carotinemia. A benign yellow discoloration of the skin due to a large dietary intake of carotene containing foods (carrots, sweet potatoes). The whites of the eyes remain white, as opposed to what is seen with jaundice—**see jaundice**.

Celiac disease. A disorder of the intestines which causes poor digestion and absorption of foods. The underlying problem is due to an abnormal response to "gluten" containing foods (e.g. wheat, oat, rye grains). The classic symptoms of this disorder include foul smelling, chronic diarrhea and failure to thrive (lack of weight gain). Treatment is a lifelong gluten-free diet.

Cellulitis. A localized skin infection, caused by bacteria (most often Staph or Strep). A drug resistant bacteria (MRSA) is becoming a more common cause of infection. Cellulitis will be red, warm, and tender to the touch. There may or may not be fever. Treatment is antibiotics, and possible drainage of the pus.

Cerebral palsy. An abnormality of the brain center that controls muscle tone and movement. Cerebral palsy does not cause any abnormalities in IQ. However, there are children who have *both* mental retardation AND cerebral palsy.

Cerebrovascular Accident (CVA). The common term is "stroke" used to describe inadequate blood supply to the brain. Long-term neurological complications can include seizures, one-sided body weakness, and cognitive impairment.

Coarctation of the Aorta. A narrowing or kink in the great artery (aorta) that leaves the heart and supplies the body with oxygen rich blood. This is a defect that occurs during fetal development (prior to birth). If the abnormality is severe, it is diagnosed in newborns who have weakened/no pulse in the legs. If the abnormality is small, it may go undetected until later in life. It is repaired by surgery.

Conductive hearing loss. See Hearing Loss, forms of.

Congenital. This refers to an abnormality in the *formation* of a certain organ/body part that occurs in the development of an unborn fetus. These abnormalities may be due to either hereditary problems or environmental exposures during pregnancy. The lay term for these disorders is **birth defect.**

Congenital sensorineural hearing loss, see Hearing loss, forms of.

Congenital heart disease. A defect in the structural development of the heart or the great vessels that attach to the heart. Because heart development occurs in the first trimester of pregnancy, many congenital defects can be identified on a prenatal ultrasound. Some abnormalities will resolve on their own. Some require surgical repair. The disease incidence is 1:1000. The most common defects are the least serious ones. Remember, there is a difference between an innocent heart murmur (no defect) and a pathologic murmur (caused by congenital heart disease).

Congenital nevus. (Known as moles, birthmarks) A mark on the skin which is present at birth, or appears within the first year of life. The most concerning moles are ones larger than 10 to 20 cm (really big) that are present at birth. These have more potential risk of skin cancer and removal is usually advised.

Congestive heart failure. When the heart is unable to perform adequately, the blood flow accumulates in the lungs and liver. Symptoms of heart failure include shortness of breath and enlarged liver size. In children, symptoms include failure to thrive, sweating with feedings, shortness of breath, and excessive fatigue.

Conjunctivitis. An inflammation of the lining of the eyelid. Otherwise known as "pink eye." The inflammation can be caused by a virus, bacteria, allergies, or irritation. All types of conjunctivitis cause redness and some discomfort. Here are the major types of conjunctivitis:
Allergic. An allergic response usually due to sensitivity to something in the air (e.g. pollens). Usually causes watery, somewhat itchy eyes. Antihistamines treat the symptoms.
Bacterial. A bacterial infection in the eye (often accompanied by ear and sinus infection). Causes thick yellowish eye discharge and may even cause the eyes to be caked over or "matted." Antibiotic eye drops treat the infection.
Viral. A viral infection in the eye (that may be accompanied by a sore throat). Causes watery and very itchy eyes.
Irritation. Eyes become inflamed because of a chemical irritant (e.g. shampoo).

Constipation. The texture of poop is significantly hard, and is passed either in small pieces or in a very large mass of small pieces stuck together. Contrary to popular belief, constipation is NOT defined by the infrequency of poop (although this can contribute to the problem). There is no defined length of interval for which a person needs to poop—it can vary considerably. If the poop is soft when it comes out, your child is unlikely to be constipated.

Craniosynostosis. A baby's skull bones have gaps that allow for the brain's growth in the first one to two years of life. This abnormality is a premature closure of the gaps (sutures). We detect this problem by finding a closed fontanelle (soft spot) or lack of head growth. This requires surgery to repair.

Cystic Fibrosis (CF). This is a genetic disease that causes body glands to produce abnormal secretions. Lung, sinus, pancreas, intestine, and reproductive organ problems occur because of it. One in 20 Caucasians are carriers of this genetic abnormality. The disease incidence is 1:1600 for Caucasian babies (it is much less common in other races). Many women now receive genetic testing during pregnancy for CF, although it is not a routine screening test.

glossary

Diarrhea. Frequent passage of watery or very soft poop. See *toddler's diarrhea* also.

Down Syndrome. This is a chromosomal abnormality (extra genetic material on the 21st chromosome) that causes classic physical features, organ defects, and mental retardation. It occurs in 1 in 700 births.

Eczema. A skin disorder that causes redness and scaling. The underlying problem seems to be allergic in nature, and children with eczema have flare-ups with exposure to perfumed products and certain chemicals. Eczema can be associated with other allergic disorders such as asthma, seasonal allergies, and food allergies but it can also occur without any other problems.

Egocentric. The inability to see things from someone else's point of view. This is a child's view of the world from age two to about seven years.

Emesis. The technical term for vomit.

Encephalitis. Brain inflammation usually caused by a virus or a bacterial infection.

Epistaxis. The official term for a nosebleed. Most commonly due to digital trauma (nose picking). If bleeding is excessive or uncontrollable, medical evaluation and treatment is in order.

Erb's Palsy. An injury to the nerves that supply the arm. This occurs as a result of a difficult delivery requiring the baby's head to be pulled out forcefully. On examination, the arm will hang limp. The nerve injury usually heals in a year, but may require surgery or physical therapy.

Esophagitis. The inflammation of the upper part of the gastrointestinal system (esophagus).

Expressive language delays. A child whose ability to speak words is behind his peers. A child with this delay may have completely normal ability to understand and process language that he hears (see *receptive language*).

Failure to thrive. When a child falls below the 3rd percentile on the weight curve. When the problem is a chronic one, height and head size also drop on the growth curves. Failure to thrive prompts a thorough medical evaluation.

Fat necrosis. An occasional complication from vaccination injection. As a needle goes through the fat under the skin, it can injure it and create a firm lump. This lump may be present for several weeks after the injection is given. It is painless and not harmful.

Flaring (nostrils). When an infant or young child is having trouble breathing (respiratory distress), he will use any additional methods his body can to get in more air. Nostrils will flare with each breath to try to capture more air. Thus, this is a red flag for respiratory distress.

Flat angiomata. Official term for an "angel kiss" birthmark on the forehead or eyelids. These are flat, reddish colored marks that eventually fade. The color becomes more dramatic with crying or anger.

Fomites. Objects handled by a person with an infection that subsequently allows passage of the germs to someone else.

Fontanelle. A space between the bones of the skull that allows room for the baby's head to pass through the birth canal and room for the baby's brain to grow after birth. The main fontanelle is on top of the head (anterior) and is sometimes called the baby's "soft spot." There is a smaller fontanelle in the back of the head (posterior). The anterior fontanelle closes between nine to 18 months of age.

Food poisoning. See *gastroenteritis*.

Foreign body/object. Term used to describe an object that has no place being where it is in someone's body. Kids have a way of putting objects like small toys in their noses, ears, etc. as well as swallowing them.

Fragile X Syndrome. This is a chromosomal abnormality that occurs in 1 in 1000 male births and about 1 in 2000 female births. It is due to unstable genetic material on the X chromosome. It is a common form of genetically-inherited autism in males. Children with Fragile X syndrome have varying degrees of intellectual disability, attention deficit disorder, learning disabilities, communication problems, and classic facial features.

Frenulum. The tissue that connects the tongue to the base of the mouth. (see **ankyloglossia**).

Frenulectomy. The process of clipping the tissue at the tongue base to correct a "tongue tie" or ankyloglossia. This procedure can be performed in an office setting if the baby is less than a few weeks old. An older child may require frenulectomy if he is experiencing speech problems with a tight frenulum. Frenulectomy for an older child is performed as day surgery.

Gastroenteritis. An inflammation of the stomach and intestines caused by either a virus or bacteria. The inflammation can cause both vomiting and diarrhea. Viral gastroenteritis is commonly known as the "stomach flu" and tends to cause watery diarrhea. Bacterial gastroenteritis is commonly known as "food poisoning" and tends to cause diarrhea mixed with blood or mucus.

Gastroesophageal reflux (GERD, acid reflux). The backflow of food and liquids from the stomach into the esophagus (and often all the way to the mouth). This is a common problem for babies, but it can continue beyond the first year of life. The muscle that separates the esophagus and the stomach (lower esophageal sphincter) is relatively loose in infants, allowing food to travel down to the stomach (good) and back up to the esophagus (not good). Once food contents make it to the stomach, they are mixed with stomach acid. So, when this partially digested food goes backwards, the stomach acid can irritate the esophagus (i.e. acid reflux).

Gingivostomatitis. Inflammation and irritation of the gums and lining of the mouth caused by the Oral Herpes virus. The amount of inflammation is usually extensive and may lead to refusal to eat or drink anything.

Glaucoma. Increased pressure behind the eye. Children with hemangiomas near the eye need to be evaluated by an ophthalmologist because they are at risk for glaucoma.

Hearing loss. There are two different forms of hearing loss. One is due to a defect in the nerves that control hearing (sensorineural hearing loss). The other is due to interference in the soundwaves traveling to the eardrum and middle ear bones (conductive hearing loss).

Forms of hearing loss:

Congenital sensorineural hearing loss. Hearing nerves defective since birth. Usually detected by newborn hearing screen (BAER) prior to hospital discharge.

Acquired sensorineural hearing loss. Hearing nerve injury that occurs after birth due to trauma or infection.

Conductive hearing loss. Temporary hearing problem due to poor sound-wave transmission through the ear. Due to excessive earwax, foreign object in the ear, serious fluid behind the eardrum or middle ear infection.

Heart murmur. A noise heard in addition to the normal heart sounds audible with a stethoscope. The murmur can be due to normal heart function (termed innocent, benign, or transitional). Or it can be due to a structural defect of the heart or great blood vessels coming off of the heart (termed pathologic). The type of noise, location of the noise, and other abnormalities found on physical examination help determine the cause of the murmur. All murmurs do not require an echocardiogram and a cardiologist evaluation to determine the cause.

Hemangioma. See Strawberry Hemangioma.

Hemolytic Uremic Syndrome. (Also known as HUS). A group of medical problems caused by some food poisoning (E coli, Shigella) infections. The problems include severe anemia, low platelet count, and kidney failure. HUS typically occurs in children ages four months to four years of age.

Hemophilia. A genetically inherited blood clotting disorder. People with this disorder lack a chemical clotting "factor" that impairs the body's chain reaction to clot blood when bleeding occurs. In general, this is a disease of males and women are only carriers (i.e. not affected) because the gene for the disorder is on the "X" chromosome.

Henoch-Schonlein Purpura. (Also known as HSP) Inflammation of the blood vessels (vasculitis) after a viral illness. Symptoms include a dramatic rash of raised bruised areas on the legs. Joint pain, abdominal pain, and blood in the urine also occur. Although the disease sounds and looks serious, 90% of children recover completely without any treatment. Occurs mostly in children aged four to ten years.

Hernia. The term used to describe a bulging out of tissue or organ where it is not supposed to be. It occurs due to a weakness of a muscle wall. The most common types include:

Diaphragmatic hernia—abdominal organs protrude into chest
Femoral hernia—intestines protrude into thigh
Inguinal hernia—intestines protrude into groin
Umbilical hernia—intestines protrude into belly button

The risk of all hernias is that the organ that is bulging out will get stuck in that position and cut off the blood supply to it. Umbilical hernias rarely get stuck (incarcerate), thus rarely require any treatment.

Hip dysplasia. Also known as developmental dysplasia of the hip. This is an abnormality where the leg bone is out of its socket at the hip. It is easily treated with a brace if detected in the first few months of life. Babies who are **breech** have a slightly higher risk of having this disorder. Toddlers with a severe limp may be tested for this disorder.

Hirschprung's disease. A congenital abnormality where the nerves of the rectum (intestinal exit) don't form. As a result, newborns cannot poop (stool) without assistance. Children with severe constipation may have a partial defect and are also tested for this disorder. Treatment is surgical.

Histamine. A chemical compound the body produces in an allergic response. Histamine causes the characteristic "allergy symptoms" that people experience such as hives, itchy eyes, and congestion.

Hydrocephalus. An abnormally large collection of cerebrospinal fluid (CSF), the fluid that bathes the brain and spinal cord. This can be caused by excessive production, blockage of the collection pathway, or decreased absorption in the body. Symptoms include: bulging fontanelle (soft spot), headache, vomiting, enlarged head size, loss of developmental milestones, and abnormal neurologic exam.

Hypermobility Syndrome. Term used to describe excessively loose joints. Some people have a few loose, extra mobile joints—called "benign hypermobile joint syndrome." Others, whose joints are all loose, can have more serious diseases associated with it (Marfan Syndrome, Ehler-Danlos Syndrome). Hypermobile joints do not always cause symptoms, but some people will have joint or leg pain due to it.

Hypertension. The fancy word for high blood pressure. Although adults are most at risk for high blood pressure, children can rarely have this problem too. The underlying cause of high blood pressure for children needs to be investigated thoroughly, looking for heart or kidney abnormalities.

Hypospadias. A congenital abnormality where the urethra (tube that connects the bladder to the outside) opening is on the underside of the penis instead of in the middle. This requires surgical repair, usually after six months of age. Because the foreskin is used to perform the repair, these babies are not circumcised.

Hypothyroidism. A poorly functioning thyroid gland produces a suboptimal level of thyroid hormone. Thyroid hormone is an essential chemical needed for body metabolism. Babies with congenital hypothyroidism can become mentally retarded (cretins) if they are not treated. This is one of the screening tests performed in the state metabolic screen. The incidence of congenital hypothyroidism is one in 4000 newborns.

Idiopathic Thrombocytopenic Purpura (ITP). The destruction of platelets due to an autoimmune response in the body. Can occur after a viral illness. Because platelets are needed to clot blood, a low count causes bruising and *petechiae*. Some children need medication to help the body increase platelet production in the body, others bounce back on their own. The good news is that almost 90% of kids do beautifully and have no further problems after the one episode.

glossary

Imperforate Anus. A congenital abnormality where the anus (opening of the intestines to the outside) does not form completely. This abnormality is often associated with a combination of abnormalities called VATER syndrome. It is repaired surgically.

Inflammatory Bowel Disease (IBD). Chronic swelling of the intestinal lining that results in bloody diarrhea. Crohn's Disease and Ulcerative Colitis are types of IBD. It is rare for a child under age two years to be diagnosed with this disorder.

Inguinal hernia. (see **hernia**)

Inhaled steroid. Medication used to control chronic asthma symptoms. The medication is administered via a machine that aerosolizes it (nebulizer) or via a hand-held "inhaler." The inhaled method is preferable because most of the medication goes to the location it is intended to help (i.e. the lungs). Very little of the medicine gets absorbed into the bloodstream—this means there is less of the unwanted side effects and more therapeutic benefit.

Intestinal obstruction. This is a general term to describe the blockage of the intestine. The gastrointestinal tract is like a big pipe, and in these terms, obstruction is a clogged pipe. This can occur due to intussusception, volvulus, malrotation (congenital defect), and hernias. Because the area is blocked, blood flow to the intestines decreases and may cause death of that tissue. This is a surgical emergency or an "acute abdomen." Symptoms include distended belly, vomiting bile.

Intoeing. Term used to describe feet that turn in during walking or running. Caused by an inward turning of the feet (metatarsus adductus), bowing of the lower legs (tibial torsion), or inward turning of the thigh (femoral anteversion). Regardless of the reason, almost all of these problems resolve on their own without surgery, braces, or special shoes.

Intussusception. When a piece of intestine telescopes upon itself creating an intestinal obstruction. The most common time this occurs is between six and 18 months of age. Symptoms include intermittent abdominal pain with pulling up of the legs. Vomiting, and poop that looks like "currant jelly" also occur. This is an emergency. Diagnosis (and treatment) can be done with a special radiological study.

Jaundice. Yellowing of the skin and the whites of the eyes due to a collection of body garbage called bilirubin. The newborn period is a unique time in life that causes a "normal" jaundice. Outside of the newborn period, jaundice is NOT normal. It requires a thorough medical evaluation to look for the cause.

Kawasaki Disease. An illness that causes the body's blood vessels to swell (vasculitis). The cause is unknown. Occurs mostly in children under two years of age. Symptoms include: fever for five or more days straight, rash on the palms and soles, peeling skin on the fingertips, pink eye, bright red lips/tongue, swollen lymph nodes in the neck, general body rash, and irritable mood. The most severe complication is swelling of the arteries that supply the heart (coronary artery aneurysm). This disease is one of the reasons that doctors want to see a child who has had a fever for five consecutive days or more.

Keloids. This is an exaggerated response to wound healing which results in a thickened skin deformity. In people who are prone to this, any injury to the skin (cut, ear piercing) can cause a disfiguring scar. There are several treatment options, but none of them promises a lifelong cure.

Labial adhesion. A condition where the labia minora (smaller lips) of the vaginal opening get stuck together. This happens in little girls because they do not make estrogen hormone yet (pre-puberty). The amount of tissue that is stuck can vary. The problem is that the urethra (opening for the bladder) is located beneath the labia. If the lips are almost completely fused shut, estrogen cream (RX) is applied so that the urine can flow out more easily. Once the labia are unstuck, it is prudent to put Vaseline on the area at diaper changes to prevent them from re-sticking. All girls outgrow this condition once they hit puberty.

Leukemia. Abnormal production of body's blood cells which then leads to failure of the bone marrow to produce normal blood cells necessary for body functioning. Symptoms include: fever, fatigue, paleness of the skin, excessive bruising, *petechiae*, and joint pain.

Macrocephaly. Official term to describe a big head. Most of the time, a child's big head is due to his genes (i.e. someone else in the family has a big head). But if the head size percentile is enlarging or if there are other concerning symptoms, a doctor may evaluate the head with an imaging study to rule out *hydrocephalus* or a *brain tumor*.

Malabsorption. When the intestine is not performing its job of digesting food. The result is a watery, foul smelling diarrhea. Some causes of chronic malabsorption are *celiac disease* and *cystic fibrosis*. This deserves to be checked out.

Malrotation. A congenital abnormality in the development of the intestines. The abnormal position creates a problem with blood flow to the intestines as well as potential for obstruction of food transit. Newborns with this problem have vomiting, constipation, and abdominal pain. Treatment is surgical.

Masturbation. A normal behavior of exploring one's sexual organs. Both boys and girls do it.

Meningitis. Inflammation of the tissues that line the brain and the spinal cord. This can be caused by a virus, bacteria, or by tuberculosis. Symptoms include: headache, vomiting, TRUE IRRITABILITY (i.e. unconsolable), bulging fontanelle (soft spot), fever, neck stiffness, seizures, *petechiae*. This is a medical emergency.

Metabolic disorder. A broad term that describes disorders in breaking down foods (see metabolic storage disease below). These disorders are different than endocrine disorders, which involve abnormal levels of body hormones (e.g. thyroid disease, diabetes, adrenal disease).

Metabolic Storage Disease (Inborn Errors of Metabolism). A group of diseases that all cause an inability to break down certain food products. As a result, byproducts of metabolism accumulate. In some of these disorders this accumulation goes to body parts (liver, heart, brain, kidney, eye) causing permanent damage or even death. The most common storage diseases are test-

glossary

ed for on the state metabolic screens (**PKU, galactosemia**).

Microcephaly. The technical term for a small head. Head size is often heredi-tary. Families with small heads have small headed babies. However, if a child's head size percentile is plateauing or decreasing, an imaging study may be done to look for **craniosynostosis**.

Milk protein allergy. Milk contains protein, sugar, and fat. Some babies (about 1%) have an allergy to the protein component that causes inflammation and irritation of the intestine lining. This leads to diarrhea that can be mixed with blood or mucous. A significant percentage of babies who are allergic to milk protein are also allergic to soy protein. The good news—most kids outgrow this problem.

Mongolian Spots. A bruise like discoloration found on the buttocks of darker pigmented newborns. These spots fade over several years. No treatment is needed.

Murmur. See **heart murmur**.

Nasolacrimal Duct Obstruction (blocked tear duct). Babies have narrow tear ducts that lead out to the corner of the eyes. Occasionally, the tube gets clogged. Tears, which are usually watery, get thick from being backed up. The result—goopy fluid that comes out of the eyes. This can happen inter-mittently for the first year of life. You can help open up the duct by mas-saging gently just below the corner of the eye near the nose. I usually refer patients to an eye doctor if this is happening beyond a year of age. The dif-ference between blocked tear ducts and pink eye (infection) is that the eye is not red or irritated.

Nevus Flammeus (Stork bite, angel kiss). These are newborn birthmarks locat-ed at the nape of the neck, eyelids, and forehead. They are bright pink in color. The marks on the face fade over the first year of life. The marks on the neck can last forever. These marks are not associated with cancer.

Neural tube defects. A congenital abnormality of the brain/spinal cord devel-opment. Many of these disorders can be detected prenatally via an abnor-mal AFP test or an ultrasound. These disorders vary in severity. The most severe form is lack of brain formation (anencephaly). The least severe form is **spina bifida occulta** (see **sacral dimple**), where there is completely normal nerve function.

Neurofibromatosis (NF). A genetic disorder (gene defect) that causes tumors of the tissue covering nerves. Babies are often born without symptoms, although some will have three or more **cafe au lait spots** at birth. As a child grows, he develops numerous (more than five) cafe au lait spots and freck-les in the armpit and groin areas. The tumors on the nerves grow later and can be seen as large bumps under the skin. Most of these tumors are benign (not cancerous), but can occur in dangerous places (e.g. eye, ear, brain, kid-ney). Children with this disorder are seen regularly by a number of doctors. FYI: The diagnosis of NF is not made on the presence of cafe au lait spots alone—this is only one of several symptoms and signs. Most children with a few cafe au lait spots do not have NF.

Night Terrors. Disrupted sleep event where a child over eighteen months of age awakens, appears to be very frightened, but is unresponsive to your soothing. The child has no recall of the event the next morning. These events usually occur in the first third to the first half of the night and are brought on by being overtired or stressed.

Nocturnal enuresis. The official name for bedwetting. It is not abnormal for a child to continue urinating in bed/in a diaper until a child is seven years of age.

Nursemaid's elbow. The unofficial term for an elbow injury common in toddlers. If a child's arm gets jerked or pulled, the forearm bone dislocates (subluxates) from the elbow. The child will keep his arm in a resting position and refuse to lift his hand up. It is easily fixed with a quick office procedure.

Obstructive Sleep Apnea. Disrupted sleep due to tonsil and/or adenoid enlargement. This interferes with a child's breathing at night. Children with this disorder wake up several times a night to catch their breath, but have no recall of the awakenings. Classically, there will be noisy breathing, followed by a pause (apnea), then a large breath. Some children have *sleep disordered breathing* without the pause (apnea) for the same reasons. Either way, these children sleep very poorly at night and have daytime sleepiness and/or behavior issues as a result.

Orbital cellulitis. A serious infection that involves the tissue surrounding the eye. It is caused by a sinus infection that spreads into the area. Symptoms include: limited eye motion, bulging of the eyeball, eyelid swelling, eye pain, and fever. This is the reason that doctors want to see children who have eyelid swelling and a fever.

Orthotic. A custom made shoe insert designed by a podiatrist to provide arch support for people who are flat-footed. The AAP does not currently recommend orthotics for babies and young children.

Otitis media. Literally, middle ear inflammation. Acute otitis media refers to an active infection that came up shortly before it is diagnosed in the office. Serous otitis media (or otitis media with effusion) refers to residual fluid that remains after the active infection is over.

Otitis externa. (Otherwise known as swimmer's ear) Literally, external ear inflammation. This is really an infection of the skin that lines the ear canal. It is caused by water that pools in the ear canal and allows germs to grow. Symptoms include pain with touching the ear itself, swelling and redness of the canal, and sometimes a fever. This is uncommon in kids who don't swim underwater yet.

Paraphimosis. The foreskin gets stuck behind the head of the penis in an uncircumcised boy. This causes lots of swelling and pain.

Pathologic Heart Murmur. See *heart murmur.*

Penile adhesions. The head of the penis sticks to the shaft skin. In boys who are circumcised, it is important to visualize the edge of the head at diaper changes and clean the area of any debris (smegma). If the skin starts to get stuck together, try gently pulling down at the base of the penis to separate the area.

glossary

GLOSSARY

? ?

Perforated eardrum. The natural occurrence of a middle ear infection that causes a small hole in the eardrum to evacuate the pus that is under pressure. It is the equivalent of a pimple popping and draining. Pus and blood will be seen draining out of the ear canal.

Pervasive Developmental Delay (PDD). A disorder of development that falls into the category of Autism Spectrum Disorders. Children with PDD are higher functioning and capable of limited social interactions. They may also have more language skills than those who are severely affected.

Phenylketonuria (PKU). A metabolic disorder routinely tested on the state metabolic screen. It is a genetic defect in an enzyme that breaks down phenylalanine. The incidence is one in 10,000. People with this disorder need to have a special diet. See *metabolic storage disease*.

Phimosis. Inability to pull the foreskin of an uncircumcised boy's penis back. In severe cases, circumcision is necessary to fix the problem.

Pneumonia. Lung inflammation caused primarily by infection. Both viruses and bacteria can cause pneumonia. The tiny air sacs (alveoli) fill up with pus and prevent air exchange. Symptoms include fever, cough, chest pain, and respiratory distress.

Port wine stain. This is a large, red/purple, flat birthmark that occurs on one side of the face or limb. These do not fade over time and are mostly a cosmetic issue. If the birthmark covers the eyelid, a child is evaluated for glaucoma. Any time it occurs on the forehead or eye, a child is also evaluated for a brain abnormality (*Sturge-Weber syndrome*).

Posterior urethral valves. A congenital defect of the formation of the urethra (tube that connects the bladder to the outside). There are valves that normally push the urine (pee) outwards. In this condition, the valves push the urine backwards into the urinary tract. This is rare, and only occurs in boys.

Post-tussive emesis. The Latin words for 'after-cough' vomiting. Babies and young children have overactive gag reflexes. So a forceful cough might bring up lunch. All vomiting in children is not due to an upset stomach.

Preauricular pits and tags. Minor congenital defects of the formation of the external ear. The pits are due to remnants of a cyst that occurred prior to birth. Pits are rarely associated with hearing disorders. The tags are extra pieces of skin. If severe, these can be removed for cosmetic reasons.

Pseudostrabismus. The false appearance that a child looks cross-eyed or has a lazy eye due to the child's facial structure. Babies and young children are often referred to a pediatric ophthalmologist for concerns of a lazy eye (*esotropia, amblyopia*) and are ultimately diagnosed with this benign entity. But it is better to be on the safe side and check out any concerns.

Pyelonephritis. An infection of the kidneys. In an acute infection, a child has fever, back pain, and pain with urination. Infants under six months of age with a bladder infection routinely get admitted to the hospital because there is a greater risk of the infection extending into the kidneys.

Respiratory Distress. This is the term used to describe a child who is air-hungry. If a child cannot successfully get enough oxygen in with each breath, he will breathe faster, heavier, and use chest wall muscles to get as much air in as possible. This equates to a child who is panting, grunting, flaring his nostrils, and retracting (sucking in of the ribcage).

Restless Leg Syndrome. This describes uncontrolled leg movements that are associated with pain. The symptoms happen while the legs are at rest (within 30 minutes of going to bed) and resolve once the legs are moved. RLS occurs more commonly in adults, but can occur in children. Stretching exercises before going to bed and taking iron supplements may reduce the symptoms.

Retinopathy of Prematurity. Children who are born prematurely (31 weeks gestation or less, or under three pounds at birth) are at risk for having an immature retina in the eye. This immaturity can lead to defective blood vessel growth.

Retractions. The term used to describe the sucking in of the ribcage when a child has *respiratory distress*. Retractions occur when the body starts using the chest wall muscles to pull more air in with each breath. With phone encounters, we will ask you to look at how your child is breathing to tell us if he has retractions.

Rickets. Malformation of growing bones in children most commonly due to Vitamin D deficiency. Vitamin D is necessary for calcium to be deposited into the bone (which makes them hard). Bones will form with a bent shape because they are softer than they should be.

Ringworm. See *fungal infections* in Appendix D.

Sacral dimple. This is a tiny divet, or dimple in the lower portion of the back. These can be associated with a minor abnormality of neural tube development called spina bifida occulta. The L5-S1 vertebrae bone is slightly abnormal but the spinal cord (nerve) is formed normally. Most children with sacral dimples are unaffected and do not need evaluation or treatment.

Seborrhea. (Also known as dandruff, cradle cap) A skin problem that causes greasy, flaky, and sometimes red skin in areas where "sebaceous glands" reside—typically the scalp, ears, beside the nose, eyebrows. Many babies are afflicted with this and outgrow it, but this can continue into childhood. Teenagers can also get seborrhea and have it for a lifetime. Treatment includes anti-dandruff shampoos, low potency steroid creams/lotions, and vegetable oil to loosen up the flakes in the scalp.

Sensory Processing Disorder. A constellation of behaviors stemming from an inability to process and adapt to stimuli of the five senses. Children with this disorder have trouble with activities of daily living and social encounters (aversion to textured foods, dislike of socks and tags on clothing, avoidance of messy activities, avoidance of being touched...) Diagnosis occurs most frequently in pre-school or school aged children.

Serous otitis media. Fluid in the middle ear space. This fluid can be present several weeks to months after an acute infection (i.e. ACUTE otitis media). This fluid is sterile (free of bugs), but has the potential to get re-infected.

Antibiotics are not usually necessary or helpful to clear the fluid.

Shingles. A reactivation of the chickenpox virus, named varicella-zoster virus (VZV). Because this virus is a member of the Herpes Virus family, it lives indefinitely in the host it has infected. It will lie dormant and potentially reactivate at any time. Shingles is a cluster of small blisters that erupt along a nerve line (dermatome). Instead of being itchy like chickenpox, they are burning and painful. While the lesions are present, a person is mildly contagious for spreading the VZV virus to others who are not immune (by disease or vaccination).

Sickle cell anemia. A hereditary abnormality of the red blood cell structure, causing impaired oxygen carrying capacity and increased destruction of the red blood cells.

Sinusitis. See Infections, Chapter 16.

Skin tags. These are tiny pieces of raised skin that can occur anywhere on the body. In the newborn, they are most frequently found in front of the ear (*preauricular tag*) or on the vagina. They are not problematic and require no intervention.

Sleep apnea. See *obstructive sleep apnea.*

Sleep Disordered Breathing. Children with large adenoid/tonsil tissue have frequent night wakenings to allow them to breathe in a reclined position. By definition, these children do not have pauses (apnea) while they sleep. However, SDB still results in a poor night's sleep. Standard treatment is surgical removal of the adenoid/tonsils.

Solo or solitary play. When a child plays alone and independently.

Spina Bifida. A congenital abnormality of the spinal cord development. There is a spectrum of severity of the defect. Most severe defects cause paralysis of the legs and body parts supplied by the affected nerves (bowel, bladder function). The incidence of spina bifida is decreasing as more women are taking pre-natal vitamins (folic acid) during pregnancy. See *neural tube defects.*

Stevens-Johnson Syndrome. A serious allergic reaction that can be fatal.

Strawberry Hemangioma. A birthmark made of a collection of blood vessels. The vessels grow and enlarge for the first few years of life, therefore the birthmark gets bigger. The good news—the vessels shrink up and disappear, usually by age five years. Surgery is usually not done to remove these. However, laser therapy may be helpful for lesions on the eyes, nose, or lips.

Stridor. A squeaky, high pitched noise with breathing in that can be heard without a stethoscope. In newborns, it is usually caused by *laryngomalacia*. In any other situation, it is a sign of respiratory distress at the level of the throat. Children with severe *croup* infection have a very swollen airway if they have stridor. If your child has stridor, call your doctor immediately.

Stork bites see *nevus flammeus.*

Sturge Weber syndrome. A serious disorder that includes brain abnormalities in combination with a port wine stain on the face. Brain atrophy, seizures, and paralysis can occur.

Supranumerary nipple (accessory nipple). These are extra, nonfunctional nipples found along the same vertical line as the nipples themselves. They are not problematic. They can be removed for cosmetic reasons.

Toddler's Diarrhea. This is watery stool due to excessive juice intake. The juice contains concentrated sugar (whether it be natural juice or a juice drink). The sugar pulls water into the poop, making it very loose.

Tongue-tied See *ankyloglossia*.

Transient Synovitis. Formerly called *Toxic Synovitis.* This is a benign inflammation in the tissue that lines the joint space (the synovium). It causes hip pain and a limp that resolves on its own in a few days.

Transmitted upper airway noise. Noise that comes from the nose that is heard and felt in the lungs. When there is a moderate amount of nasal congestion (snot) in the nose, the air going through it makes a loud noise as it passes through. Since babies and young children don't know how to blow their noses, this is often a unique occurrence in this age group.

Tuberculosis. (Known as TB. Previously known as "consumption"). Infectious lung disease that causes nodules in the lungs, but can spread to the lymph nodes and brain. The scary part of the disease is that people can be infected or be "carriers" of the infection without showing symptoms. People with active infection classically have fever, cough, weight loss, night sweats, and blood in the mucus they cough up. Although TB is less common than it used to be, it occurs in urban populations and immigrants from Asia, Africa, and Latin America. Recommendations for TB screening (PPD) varies among communities, but is usually required for public school entry.

Umbilical hernia. See *hernia.* These are very common in newborns, particularly African American babies. The size of the hernia can be quite large, but the intestine almost never (I've had one patient) gets stuck (incarcerated). These are caused by weak abdominal muscles which will get stronger as the baby starts using them. Most of these hernias resolve on their own. If the hernia is still present by age two, I'll refer a child to a pediatric surgeon for repair. Old Wives Tale: You do not need to bandage the hernia or place a coin on it to make it go away. Your baby will fix the problem himself when he starts doing Ab crunches.

Undescended testes. Failure of the male sex organs to descend into the scrotum in the newborn male. (In fetal development, they grow in the pelvic area, then travel down to the scrotum.) Often, the testes will come down on their own by six months of life. If they don't, a surgical procedure is performed to affix the testes in the scrotum. Testes in the pelvis are at slightly higher risk for testicular cancer, and make it awfully difficult to perform a monthly self-testicular exam in that location.

Urethral meatal stenosis. This is a narrowing in the exit of the tube that lets urine out. It is rare, but occurs most commonly in circumcised males. It can be caused by inflammation or as a complication of circumcision. It results in a poor urine stream or spraying of urine.

Uric acid crystals. A waste product found in the urine. When the urine is concentrated (low water volume), the uric acid will pull itself out of the urine solution and can be found in crystal form in the diaper. It looks like brick dust and tends to alarm parents who think it is blood. It is an indication of dehydration—so aggressive hydration is the only treatment.

Urinary tract infections (UTI). An infection in the urinary bladder. It is difficult to diagnose a bladder infection in toddlers because they may not complain that it burns when they urinate. Sometimes fever and irritability are the only symptoms. It is a good idea to obtain a urine specimen on young children who have a fever with no obvious source of infection.

Vaginal discharge. Newborn girls often have vaginal discharge due to fluctuating hormone levels. Older girls who have vaginal discharge prior to puberty need to be evaluated for infection.

Vaginitis. This is the catch-all phrase to describe redness and irritation in the vaginal area. Most of the time, it is due to poor hygiene when a little girl is wiping herself after using the bathroom. It can also be set off by skin irritants, like bubble bath, sitting in a wet bathing suit, or wearing tights frequently. Treatment includes bathing in warm water, using a barrier cream on the area, and air drying.

Ventricular Septal Defect (VSD). The most common type of congenital heart defect (abnormal formation of the heart in the fetus). In this defect, a hole is present in either the muscle wall or tissue between the two large chambers (ventricles) of the heart. A murmur is detected due to the blood flow that crosses between the chambers. Most of these holes close on their own with no medical intervention. Children with VSD's are followed by pediatric cardiologists until the hole closes.

Vesicles. Pinpoint, fluid filled blisters seen classically with chickenpox, shingles, and herpes infections. In chickenpox, these lesions appear in crops over a period of a few days.

Vesicoureteral reflux (VUR). An abnormality in the urinary tract system that causes urine to track backwards towards the bladder and kidneys. This urine is not sterile, thus these children are predisposed to bladder and kidney infections.

von Willebrand Disease. A genetically inherited bleeding disorder that affects both the platelets and the blood clotting chain reaction. People with this disorder have frequent, excessive nosebleeds, easy bruising, and heavy periods.

Whooping cough. *See pertussis in Chapter 16, Infections.*

Yeast infection. *See thrush, yeast diaper rash in Chapter 16 Infections.*

References for this section are footnoted in Appendix F.

REFERENCES
Appendix E

Q. How do I know if an Internet site has reliable medical information?

Here are a few thoughts:
1. Find out who has created the website. Is there contact information?
2. What is the purpose of the website?
3. Who are the experts giving the advice?
4. What references are cited? Citations should be listed from scientific journals.
5. Be suspicious of information that is opinionated or seems biased.
6. Be suspicious of products that are touted as cure-alls or miracles.

Q. What's the best search engine to use to research a medical problem?

Google is great to find the number of the local pizza palor or just about anything else online . . . except medical info. Google a disease, condition or other medical term and you're likely to get a list of results that are too general . . . or sites with the term in their title. The *Wall Street Journal* spotlighted these sites as better bets for finding targeted medical info:

◆ *Healthline.com*: A cool flow chart lets you navigate between treatment, diagnosis and risk factors.
◆ *WebMD.com*: Search for a medical condition and you'll find a news archive, reference library and more. (Dr B is partial to this site as she's served as the child health expert for it.)
◆ *Mamma.com*: FAQ's on this site help you zero in on a problem; this site also has graphics from the government's MedlinePlus site.
◆ *Pub Med. ncbi.nlm.nih.gov/pubmed/* Known as "PubMed," this is the ultimate online resource for free access to medical research studies. Most articles only offer a partial description of the study and its results (called an abstract), and usually they are written in technical, medical jargon. So you may or may not know if the study is actually a reputable one with significant results. But if there is a topic you are interested in, Pub Med is a good starting point to see research trends.

Find a good online source for toddler health info? Let us know—see the Contact Us page at the back of this book.

Good books to have in the house

Alternative Therapies
Kemper, K. *The Holistic Pediatrician*. New York: HarperCollins, 2002.

Child Development/Behavior/Discipline
Brazelton, T. *Touchpoints* 2nd Ed. DeCapo Press, 2006.

Davis, L. *Becoming The Parent You Want to Be*. New York: Broadway Books, 1997.

Phelan, T. *1-2-3 Magic: Effective discipline for Children 2–12*. 3rd ed. Glen Ellyn, Il: ParentMagic, Inc. 2004.

Developmental Differences
Greene, RW. *The Explosive Child: A New Approach for Understanding and Parenting Easily Frustrated, "Chronically Inflexible" Children. 3rd ed.* New York: HarperCollins, 2010.

Kranowitz, CS. *The Out-of-Sync Child: Recognizing and Coping with Sensory Processing Disorder. 2nd Ed.* New York: Penguin Putnam, 2006.

Sleep
Ferber, R. *Solve Your Child's Sleep Problems*: Completely revised and updated. New York: Fireside, 2006.

Mindell, J. *Sleeping Through the Night, Revised Ed.* Collins, 2005.

Weissbluth, M. *Healthy Sleep Habits, Happy Child*. New York: Fawcett Books, 2005.

Vaccinations
Humiston, S. *Vaccinating Your Child. Questions and Answers for the Concerned Parent*. Atlanta: Peachtree, 2003.

Offit, P. *Vaccines: What You Should Know.*, 3rd ed. New York: Macmillan, 2003.

Reliable web sites

For starters, go to our website at Toddler411.com for a wealth of useful information, a visual library of rashes and diseases, parent chat room, and links to reliable websites (several of which are listed below). We also suggest you sign up for our free e-newsletter for updates on infant health news.

Allergies

American Academy of Allergy, Asthma, and Immunology	aaaai.org
American Lung Association	lungusa.org
Food Allergy Network	foodallergy.org
Allergy and Asthma Network	aanma.org
Asthma and Allergy Foundation of America	aafa.org

Alternative Therapies/Herbal remedies

National Center for
Complementary and Alt. Medicine   nccam.nih.gov
Longwood Herbal Task Force   www.longwoodherbal.org
UCSF Complementary- Alt. Med   library.ucsf.edu/collres/reflinks/cam

Cancer

National Cancer Institute   cancer.gov/cancer_information
American Cancer Society   cancer.org

Carseats

Children's Hospital of Philadelphia   chop.edu/carseat
National Highway Traffic Safety Administration   nhtsa.gov
American Academy of Pediatrics   aap.org
National Safe Kids Campaign   safekids.org

Childcare

National Association for the Education of Young Children   NAEYC.org
Child Care Aware   childcareaware.org
Healthy Kids, Healthy Care   healthykids.us

Child Development

Centers for Disease Control   cdc.gov/actearly
Zero to Three   zerotothree.org
Easter Seals   easterseals.org
Born Learning   Bornlearning.org
American Speech Language and Hearing Association   Asha.org
National Stuttering Association   nsastutter.org
Autism Science Foundation   autismsciencefoundation.org

Diabetes

American Diabetes Association   diabetes.org
Juvenile Diabetes Research Foundation International   jdrf.org

Emergency Care

Emergency Medical Services for Children   emscmn.org

Gastrointestinal problems (stomach/intestine)

North American Society for Pediatric Gastroenterology   naspgn.org
and Nutrition

General medical information

American Academy of Pediatrics   aap.org
Food and Drug Administration   fda.gov
Keep Kids Healthy   keepkidshealthy.com
Kids Health   kidshealth.org

references

WebMD   webmd.com
Mayo Clinic   mayoclinic.com
National Institutes of Health   nlm.nih.gov
Medscape   medscape.com
Centers for Disease Control   cdc.gov

Heart defects

American Heart Association   americanheart.org
Cincinnati Children's Hospital cincinnatichildrens.org/heartcenter/encyclopedia/

HIV in children

U.S. Dept. of Health and Human Services   aidsinfo.nih.gov/

Lung Problems

American Lung Association   lungusa.org
Cystic Fibrosis Foundation   cff.org
American Academy of Allergy, Asthma, and Immunology   aaaai.org

Nervous System/Seizure disorders

American Academy of Neurology   aan.com
Epilepsy Foundation   epilepsyfoundation.org

Nutrition

Centers for Disease Control   cdc.gov
American Dietetic Association   eatright.org
U.S. Dept of Agriculture   mypyramid.gov

Parenting

Baby Center   babycenter.com
Baby Zone   babyzone.com
Parenthood.com   parenthood.com
Parents Magazine   parents.com

Sickle Cell Disease

Sickle Cell Disease Association of America, Inc.   sicklecelldisease.org

Skin Disorders

Johns Hopkins Hospital   med.jhu.edu/peds/dermatlas
National Eczema Association   nationaleczema.org
disorders

Travel Health

Centers for Disease Control   cdc.gov/travel/index.htm

REFERENCE

Vaccinations

Johns Hopkins School of Public Health	vaccinesafety.edu
World Health Organization	who.int/en/
Immunization Action Coalition	immunize.org
National Network for immunization info	immunizationinfo.org
Vaccine Adverse Event Reporting System	vaers.hhs.gov
Centers for Disease Control	cdc.gov/nip
Children's Hospital of Philadelphia	vaccine.chop.edu

National Organizations

There is a support group for virtually every medical disease and syndrome. The organizations below should be able to link you to a specific organization to meet your particular needs.

American Academy of Pediatrics
141 Northwest Point Blvd., Elk Grove Village, IL 60007
Phone: (847) 434-4000; Web: www.aap.org

Centers for Disease Control and Prevention
1600 Clifton Road, Atlanta, GA 30333
Phone: (800) 311-3435; Web: www.cdc.gov

Easter Seals
230 West Monroe St., Suite 1800, Chicago, IL 60606
Phone: (800) 221-6827 x7153; Web: www.easter-seals.org

March of Dimes Birth Defects Foundation
1275 Mamroneck Ave., White Plains, NY 10605
Phone: (888) 663-4637; Web: www.modimes.org

National Center on Birth Defects and Developmental Disabilities
4770 Buford Highway, N.E., Atlanta, GA 30341
Phone: (770) 488-7150; Web: www.cdc.gov/ncbddd

ZERO to THREE: National Center for Infants, Toddlers, and Families
2000 M Street NW, Suite 200, Washington, DC 20036
Phone: (202) 638-0851; Web: www.zerotothree.org

references

REFERENCE

Growth Chart: Boys (Birth to 36 months)

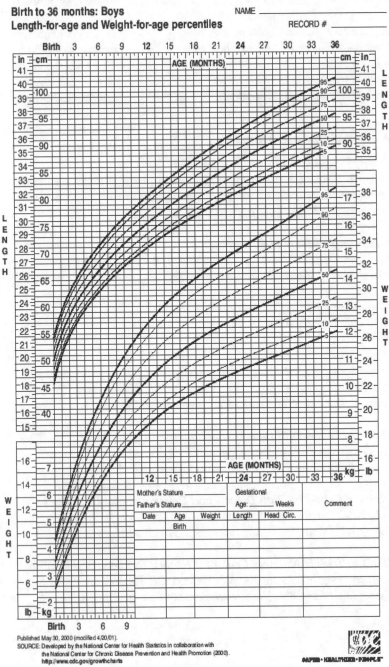

Published May 30, 2000 (modified 4/20/01).
SOURCE: Developed by the National Center for Health Statistics in collaboration with
the National Center for Chronic Disease Prevention and Health Promotion (2000).
http://www.cdc.gov/growthcharts

REFERENCE

Growth Chart: Girls (Birth to 36 months)

Birth to 36 months: Girls
Length-for-age and Weight-for-age percentiles

NAME _____

RECORD # _____

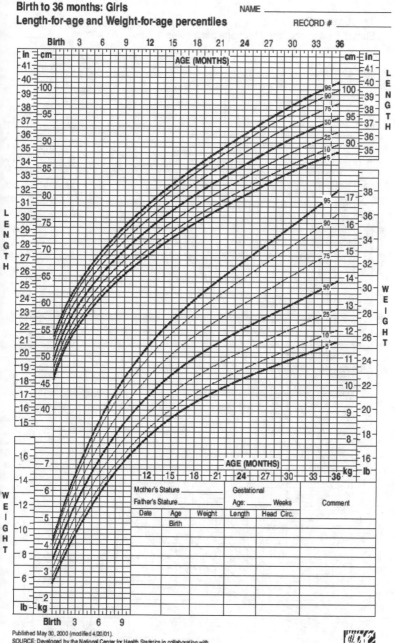

Published May 30, 2000 (modified 4/20/01).
SOURCE: Developed by the National Center for Health Statistics in collaboration with
the National Center for Chronic Disease Prevention and Health Promotion (2000).
http://www.cdc.gov/growthcharts

SAFER • HEALTHIER • PEOPLE

references

REFERENCE

Boys age 2 to 20, Growth Chart

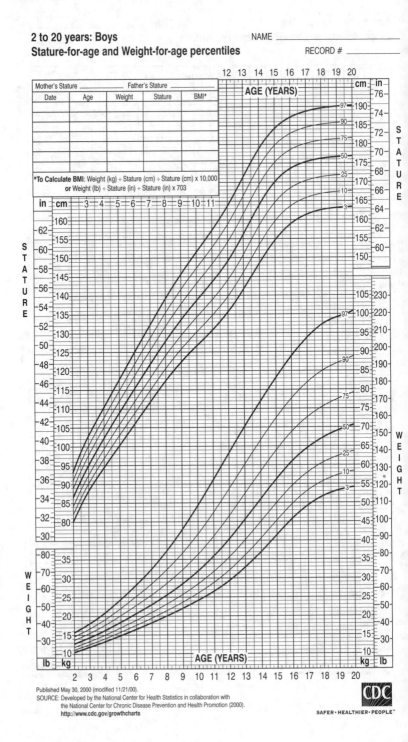

2 to 20 years: Boys
Stature-for-age and Weight-for-age percentiles

NAME _____

RECORD # _____

Published May 30, 2000 (modified 11/21/00).
SOURCE: Developed by the National Center for Health Statistics in collaboration with
the National Center for Chronic Disease Prevention and Health Promotion (2000).
http://www.cdc.gov/growthcharts

SAFER · HEALTHIER · PEOPLE™

Boys age 2 to 20, Body Mass Index

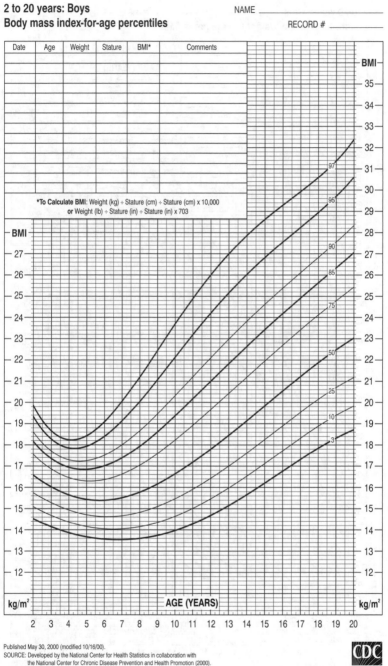

Published May 30, 2000 (modified 10/16/00).
SOURCE: Developed by the National Center for Health Statistics in collaboration with
the National Center for Chronic Disease Prevention and Health Promotion (2000).
http://www.cdc.gov/growthcharts

SAFER · HEALTHIER · PEOPLE™

references

Girls age 2 to 20, Growth Chart

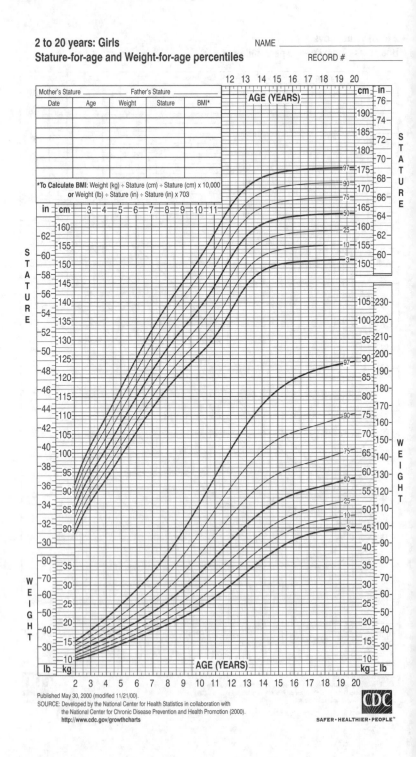

REFERENCE

Girls age 2 to 20, Body Mass Index

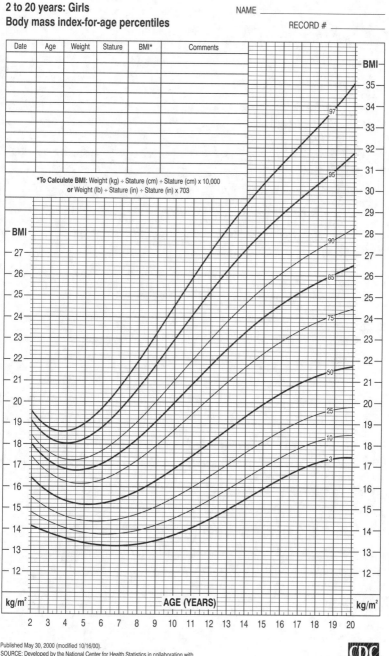

2 to 20 years: Girls
Body mass index-for-age percentiles

NAME _____

RECORD # _____

Date	Age	Weight	Stature	BMI*	Comments

*To Calculate BMI: Weight (kg) ÷ Stature (cm) ÷ Stature (cm) x 10,000
or Weight (lb) ÷ Stature (in) ÷ Stature (in) x 703

AGE (YEARS)

Published May 30, 2000 (modified 10/16/00).
SOURCE: Developed by the National Center for Health Statistics in collaboration with
the National Center for Chronic Disease Prevention and Health Promotion (2000).
http://www.cdc.gov/growthcharts

CDC
SAFER・HEALTHIER・PEOPLE™

references

Footnotes
Appendix F

Chapter 2: Discipline

1. Adapted from Kurcinka, MS: *Raising Your Spirited Child: A Guide for Parents Whose Child Is More Intense, Sensitive, Perceptive, Persistent, Energetic.* Harper, 1998.
2. Briggs DC. *Your Child's Self-Esteem: Step by Step Guidelines for Raising Responsible, Productive, Happy Children.* Main Street Books, 1975.
3. Adapted from Davis L. etal. *Becoming the Parent You Want to Be.* New York: Broadway Books, 1997.
4. Mortweet SL, etal. Coping Skills for the angry/impatient/clamorous child: A home and office practicum. Contemporary Pediatrics June 2004: 43-55.
5. Mortweet SL. See Footnote 4.
6. Dillon S. Helping young children use problem solving to resolve their conflicts. Parent Newsletter, University of Texas at Austin, Priscilla Pond Flawn Child and Family Laboratory; April 2003.

Chapter 3: Milestones

1. Levine MD, etal. *Developmental-Behavioral Pediatrics, 2nd Ed.* Philadelphia: WB Saunders, 1992.

2 a) Scott DT. Premature infants in later childhood: some recent followup results. Semin Perinatol 1987;11(2): 191.
  b) Barlow JR, Lewandowski L. Ten-Year Longitudinal Study of Preterm Infants: Outcomes and Predictors. Syracuse University, American Psychological Association conference, August 2000.

3.
  a) Levine MD, etal. *Developmental-Behavioral Pediatrics, 2nd Ed.* Philadelphia: WB Saunders, 1992.
  b) Adapted from Frankenburg, WE, Dodds, JB. The Denver Developmental Assessment (Denver II). University of Colorado Medical School, Denver, 1990.
  c) Brown FR III, etal. *Neurodevelopmental Evaluation: The Physician's Diagnostic Role in Learning Disabilities In: Diagnosis and Management of Learning Disabilities: An Interdisciplinary/*

Lifestyle Approach, 2nd ed. San Diego: Singular Publishing Group, 1992.

d) Capute AJ, etal: Linguistic and auditory milestones in the first two years of life. Clin Pediatr 1978;17:847.

e) Feigin JZ. Clinical features; evaluation, and diagnosis of learning disabilities in children. In: UpToDate, Rose, BD (Ed), UpToDate, Waltham, MA, 2006.

4.
a) Brainerd C. *Piaget's Theory of Intelligence.* Englewood, NJ: Prentice-Hall, 1978.

b) Levine MD. See Footnote 2.

5. Gaensbauer T, Sand K. Distorted affective communications in abused, neglected infants and their potential impact on caretakers. J Am Acad Child Psychiatry 1979;18:236.

6.
a) psychology.about.com

b) Levine MD. See Footnote 1.

7. Agin MC. The "late talker"—when silence isn't golden. Contemporary Pediatrics Nov 2004; 21: 11.

8. Kavanaugh JF, Truss TJ: Learning Disabilities: Proceedings of the National Conference. Parkton, MD: York Press, 1988.

9. Filipek PA, Accardo PJ, etal: Practice parameter: Screening and diagnosis of autism: Report of the quality standards subcommittee of the American Academy of Neurology and the Child Neurology Society. Neurology 2000;55:468.

10. a) Rice T. Emergent literacy including language development. In: UpToDate, Rose, BD (Ed), UpToDate, Waltham, MA, 2006.

b) Coplan J. Normal Speech and language development: An overview. Pediatrics Rev 1995; 16:91.

c) Genessee F, etal. Language differentiation in early bilingual development. J Child Lang 1995;22:611.

11. Zebrowski PM. Developmental stuttering. Pediatric Annals 2003;32 (7) 453-458.

12. Anderson J. Discipline techniques for the 2 year old. Contemporary Pediatrics. 26(6) 2009. 70-1.

Chapter 4 Is this Normal?

1. Levine MD, etal. *Developmental-Behavioral Pediatrics, 2nd Ed.* Philadelphia: WB Saunders, 1992.

2. Levine MD. See Footnote 1.

3. Levine MD. See Footnote 1.

4. Kubler-Ross E. *On Death and Dying.* New York: Macmillan Publishing, 1969.

5. Jolley PD. University of Texas at Austin, Child and Family Development Lab.

Chapter 5: Play & Preschool

1. Eaton MM. Presentation at the Society for Research in Child Development, April 2005.

2. Spiegel A. Creative play makes for kids in control. National Public

Radio, February 28, 2008. www.npr.org/yourhealth

3. Goldberg E. Parenting magazine, March 2005.

4. University of Texas at Austin, Priscilla Pond Flawn Child and Family Lab School.

5. Adapted from www.bornlearning.org.

6. Dawson G, etal. Randomized, controlled trial of an intervention for toddlers with autism: the early start Denver model. Pediatrics. 2009. DOI: 10.1542/peds.2009-0958

7. Adapted from: Colman L, Ed. Reading development list: what books to choose, and what sequence to read them in, for children from preschool through first grade. Institute of Reading Development, Inc. 2005.

8. Goodwyn SW, Acredolo LP, etal. Impact of symbolic gesturing on early language development. Journal of Nonverbal Behavior 2000; 24; 81-103.

9. Scholastic Assessment Test.

10. Shannon MW. Minimizing lead exposure. American Academy of Pediatrics News 2008; 29(1); 1-11.

11. Levine MD, etal. *Developmental-Behavioral Pediatrics, 2nd Ed.* Philadelphia: WB Saunders, 1992.

12. Mistry KB, etal. Children's television exposure and behavioral and social outcomes at 5.5 years: does timing of exposure matter? Pediatrics 2007; 120 (4); 762-769.

13. Marland SP Jr. Education of the Gifted and Talented, Vol 1. Report to the Congress of the United States by the US Commissioner of Education. Washington DC, US Govt. Printing Office 1972.

14. Levine. See footnote 11.

15. National Institute for Early Education Research. Web: Nieer.org.

16. Steele KM. The Mozart Effect. An example of the scientific method in operation. Psychology Teacher Network. Nov-Dec. 2001.

17. Huston AC. Mothers' time with infant and time in employment as predictor of mother-child relationships and children's early development. Child Development, March/April 2005;76(2): 467-482.

18. Multiple Pathways to Early Academic Achievement, NICHD Early Child Care Research Network, Harvard Educational Review 74 (2004): 1-29.

19. Pediatrics 2005;115(1);187-192.

20. U.S. Dept of Health and Human Services: aspe.hhs.gov/hsp/ccquality-inds02

Chapter 6: Challenges

1. Lahey BB, Pelham WE, Loney J, et al. Three-year predictive validity of DSM-IV attention deficit hyperactivity disorder in children diagnosed at 4-6 years of age. Am J Psychiatry 2004; 161:2014.

2. Krull K. Evaluations and diagnosis of attention deficit hyperactivity disorders in children. In: UpToDate, Rose, BD (Ed), UpToDate, Waltham, MA, 2006.

3. National Initiative for Children's Healthcare Quality. Web: nichq.org.

FOOTNOTES

4. McCann D, etal. Food additives and hyperactive behaviour in 3-year-old and 8/9-year-old children in the community: a randomised, double-blinded, placebo-controlled trial. Lancet. 2007 Nov 3;370(9598):1560-7.

5. National Institute of Neurological Disorders and Stroke. Autism Fact Sheet. www.ninds.nih.gov/disorders/autism/detail_autism.htm.

6. Centers for Disease Control, NCBDDD cdc.gov/ncbddd/features/counting-autism.html accessed April 12, 2010.

7. cdc.gov/ncbbbddd/dd/mr3.htm

8. Grinker R. Unstrange Minds: Remapping the World of Autism. Basic Books; New York: 2007.

9. Grinker R. See footnote 8.

10. The autism epidemic: fact or artifact? JAA Child Adol Psychiatry;2007;46;721-30.

11. The autism epidemic: fact or artifact? JAA Child Adol Psychiatry;2007;46;721-30.

12. DSM–IV, 2000.

13. Nature Genetics 2003;34:27-29.

14. Arking DE, etal. A common genetic variant in the neurexin-superfamily member CNTNAP2 increases familial risk of autism. American Journal of Human Genetics; Jan 2008.

15. Johnson CP, etal. Identification and evaluation of children with autism spectrum disorders. Pediatrics; 2007;120(5):1183-215. www.pediatrics.org/cgi/doi/10.1542/peds.2007-2361

16. Reichenberg A, etal. Arch Gen Psychiatry. 2006;63;1026-1032.

17. Mills JL, etal. Elevated levels of growth-related hormones in autism and autism spectrum disorder. Clinical Endocrinology; 2007;67(2):230-7

18. Institute of Medicine, 2004. Web: iom.edu

19. Limperopoulos C, etal. Positive Screening for Autism in Ex-preterm Infants: Prevalence and Risk Factors. Pediatrics, Apr 2008; 121: 758 - 765.

20. Marianne Barton, Diana Robins, Deborah Fein. Modified Checklist for Autism in Toddlers. 12/18/06 dbpeds.org

21. Autism Society of America. Web: autism-society.org.

22. Elder JH. GFCF diet in autism: results of a preliminary double blind clinical trial. J Aut Dev Disorder;2006;Apr 36(3) 413-20.

23. Myers S. etal. Management of children with autism spectrum disorders. Pediatrics, Nov 2007;120:1162 - 1182.

24. Myers S, etal. See footnote 23.

25. Myers S, etal. See footnote 23.

26. TACAnow.com accessed March 2008.

27. Myers S, etal. See footnote 23.

28. Myers S, etal. See footnote 23.

29.

a) Attention-deficit and disruptive behavior disorders. In: *Diagnostic and Statistical Manual of Mental Disorders, 4th ed*, Text Revision, American Psychiatric Association, 2000.

b) Krull K. See Footnote 2.

30. Levine MD, etal. *Developmental-Behavioral Pediatrics, 2nd Ed.*

Philadelphia: WB Saunders, 1992.

31. National Eye Institute, National Institute of Health.

32. Kranowitz CS. *The Out of Sync Child: Recognizing and Coping with Sensory Integration Dysfunction*. New York: Penguin Putnam, 1998.

33. Levine MD. See Footnote 30.

34. Levine MD. See Footnote 30.

35. National Institute on Deafness and Other Communication Disorders, National Institute of Health. www.nidch.nih.gov/health/voice/apraxia.asp

36. National Institute on Deafness and Other Communication Disorders, National Institute of Health. www.nidch.nih.gov/health/voice/auditory.asp

37. Levine MD. See Footnote 30.

Chapter 7: Toilet Training

1. Blum NJ etal. Relationship between age at initiation of toilet training and duration of training: a prospective study. Pediatrics 2003; 111(4);810-814.

2. Wolraich ML. (ed). *Diagnostic and Statistical Manual for Primary Care Child and Adolescent Version*. Elk Grove Village, Il: American Academy of Pediatrics, 1996.

Chapter 8: Sleep

1. Chervin RD, etal. School performance, race, and other correlates of sleep-disordered breathing in children. Sleep Medicine 2003; 4(1):21-7.

2. Redwine L, etal. Effects of sleep and sleep deprivation on interleukin-6, growth hormone, cortisol, and melatonin levels in humans. J Clin Endocrinol Metab 2000;85:3597

3. Lumeng JC, etal. Shorter sleep duration is associated with increased risk for being overweight at ages 9 to 12 Years. Pediatrics, Nov 2007; 120: 1020 - 1029.

4. http://www.webmd.com/content/article/115/111949.htm

5. Iglowstein I, etal. Sleep Duration from Infancy to Adolescence: Reference Values and Generational Trends. Pediatrics 2003;111;302-307.

6. Pohl CA, etal. Putting sleep disturbances to rest. Contemporary Pediatrics 2002;19(11):74-96.

Chapter 9 Growth

1. Behrman RE. Ed. *Nelson Essentials of Pediatrics*. Philadelphia: WB Saunders, 1990.

2. Behrman RE. See Footnote 1.

3. Bernbaum JC. *Primary Care of the Preterm Infant*. St Louis: Mosby, 1993.

4. Baird J, etal. Being big or growing fast: systematic review of size and growth in infancy and later obesity. British Medical Journal, 2005; doi: 10.1136/bmj.38586.411273.E0.

5. Francis LA, etal. Parental weight status and girls television viewing,

snacking, and body mass indexes. Obes Res 2003;11:143-51.

6. Study Links Produce Prices to Obesity. Wall Street Journal, October 06, 2005.

7. Wall Street Journal. See Footnote 6.

8.

a) Fernandez JR, etal. Waist Circumference Percentiles in Nationally Representative Samples of African American, European American, and Mexican American Children and Adolescents. J peds 2004:145;439-44.

b) Metabolic Syndrome. Contemporary Pediatrics, Dec 2006. 23 (12).

9. Rolls BJ. The super sizing of American: portion size and the obesity epidemic. Nutr Today 2003;38;42-53.

10. Bowman SA, etal. Effects on fast food consumption on energy intake and diet quality among children in a national household survey. Pediatrics 2003; 113:112-118.

11. Seeyave DM, etal. Ability to delay gratification at age four years and risk of overweight at age 11 years. Arch Ped Adol Med 163(4) Apr 2009. 303-308.

12. Reilly JJ, etal. Early life risk factors for obesity in childhood: cohort study. British Medical Journal 2005 June 11; 330 (7504): 1357.

13. Reilly JJ, etal. Total energy expenditure and physical activity in young Scottish children: mixed longitudinal study. Lancet 2004 Jan 17;363(9404):211-2.

Chapter 10 Nutrition

1.

a) Robertson J, Shilkofski N (Ed). *Harriet Lane Handbook, 17th Edition, A Manual for Pediatric House Officers.* Philadelphia: Mosby, 2005.

b) Food and Nutrition Board, National Research Council: Dietary Reference Intakes: Energy. Washington, DC, National Academy Press, 2004.

2. Young LR. *The Portion Teller: Smartsize Your Way to Permanent Weight Loss.* New York: Morgan Road Books, 2005.

3. Young LR. See Footnote 2.

4. Kleinman RE (Ed). *American Academy of Pediatrics, Pediatric Nutrition Handbook, 5th Ed.,* Elk Grove Village, IL: AAP, 2004.

5. Lanou AJ, etal. Calcium, dairy products, and bone health in children and young adults: a reevaluation of the evidence. Pediatrics 2005;115:736-743.

6. Kleinman RE. See Footnote 4.

7. Kleinman RE. See Footnote 4.

8. Food and Nutrition Board, Institute of Medicine, National Academies, 2002.

9. Daniels SR, etal. Lipid screening and cardiovascular health in childhood. Pediatrics 122(1) July 2008. 198-208.

10. Wall Street Journal, June 24, 2003, p D4.

11. Mandel D. Fat and energy contents of expressed human breast milk in prolonged lactation. Pediatrics 2005;116: e432 - e435.

12. Food and Nutrition Board, Institute of Medicine, National Academies, 2002.

13.

a) Omega-3 Oil: Fish or pills? Consumer Reports, July 2003.

b) Painter K. Got Omega 3? Not so much. USA Today, Nov 12, 2007

Chapter 11: Food Tricks & Treats

1. Wardle J, et al. Modifying children's food preferences: the effects of exposure and reward on acceptance of an unfamiliar vegetable. Eur J Clin Nutrition 2003;57(2):341-8.

2. Saarilehto S, et al. Growth, energy intake, and meal pattern in five-year-old children considered as poor eaters. J Pediatrics 2004 Mar;144(3):363-7.

3. Fox MK, etal. Feeding Infants and Toddlers Study: What Foods Are Infants and Toddlers Eating? Journal of the American Dietetic Association 2004; 104 (1): S22-30.

4.

a) Sampson HA: Food allergy. J Allergy Clin Immunol 2003; 111(12): 540-547.

b)

   foodallergyinitiative.org/section_home.cfm?section_id=17&sub_section_id=4

5. American Academy of Pediatrics, Committee on Nutrition. Pediatrics 2000;106 (2):346-349.

6. foodallergyinitiative.org/section_home.cfm?section_id=17&sub_section_id=4

7. Sicherer SH. Etal. Prevalence of peanut and tree nut allergy in the United States determined by means of a random digit dial telephone survey: a 5-year follow-up study. J Allergy Clin Immunol. 2003 Dec;112(6):1203-7.

8. American Academy of Allergy and Immunology. Web: aaaai.org.

9. Sicherer SH. Clinical implications of cross-reactive food allergens. JACI. 2001 Dec;108(6):881-90.

10.

a) JACI 114(1) July 2004.

b) JACI 2005;115;1291-96.

11. Wood RA. The natural history of food allergy. Pediatrics 2003; 111(6): 1631-1637.

12. The Raw Deal on Sushi. Living, May/June 2001.

13. Kleinman RE (Ed). *American Academy of Pediatrics, Pediatric Nutrition Handbook, 5th Ed.*, Elk Grove Village, IL: AAP, 2004.

14. Dyslipidemia, Pediatric News, August 2003, p3.

Chapter 12: Hygiene

1. Fradin MS. Comparative efficacy of insect repellent against mosquito bites. New England Journal of Medicine 2002; 347: 13-18.

2. Wall Street Journal, May 20, 2003, PD8.

3. Medical University of South Carolina's Children's Hospital web site.

4. Parents Magazine. October, 2005.

5. Begley S. Fluoridation, cancer: did researchers ask the right questions? Wall Street Journal, July 22, 2005 issue.

6.

a) Cook-Mozaffari P. Cancer and fluoridation. Community Dent Health. 1996 Sep;13 Suppl 2:56-62.

b) Gelberg KH, Fitzgerald EF, Hwang SA, Dubrow R. Fluoride exposure and childhood osteosarcoma: a case-control study. Am J Public Health. 1995 Dec;85(12):1678-83.

c) Bucher JR, Hejtmancik MR, Toft JD, et al. Results and conclusions of the National Toxicology Program's rodent carcinogenicity studies with sodium fluoride. International Journal of Cancer 1991; 48(5):733–737.

Chapter 13: The Other End

1. Nurko S. etal. Managing Constipation: evidence put to practice. Contemporary Pediatrics;18(12):56-65.

2. Williams CL. Importance of dietary fiber in childhood. JADA, October 1995.

3.

a) Nurko, S. etal. See Footnote 1.

b) Robertson J, Shilkofski N (Ed). *Harriet Lane Handbook, 17th Edition, A Manual for Pediatric House Officers.* Philadelphia: Mosby, 2005.

4. Gonzales ET. Approach to the child with nocturnal enuresis. In: UpToDate, Rose, BD (Ed), UpToDate, Waltham, MA, 2006.

5. Boston Children's Hospital Gynecology Clinic, 1995.

6. Friedman AL. Acute UTI. What you want to know. Contemporary Pediatrics 2008; 25(10): 68-75

7. American Urological Association: Pediatric VUR Clinical Practice Guidelines Panel. Report on the management of VUR in children. 1996.

8. Shaikh N, etal. Clinical features and diagnosis of urinary tract infections in children. In: UpToDate, Rose, BD (Ed), UpToDate, Waltham, MA, 2006.

9. AUA. See Footnote 7.

10. Gonzales ET. See Footnote 4.

11. Schmitt, B. Nocturnal enuresis: finding the treatment that fits the child. Contemporary Pediatrics Sept 1990; 70-97.

12. Lifschitz C. Clinical manifestations and diagnosis of gastroesophageal reflux in children. In: UpToDate, Rose, BD (Ed), UpToDate, Waltham, MA, 2006.

13. Tomlin J, etal. Investigation of normal flatus production in healthy volunteers. Gut 1991 Jun;32(6):665-9.

14. Abraczinskas D. Intestinal gas and bloating. In: UpToDate, Rose, BD (Ed), UpToDate, Waltham, MA, 2006.

15. Chitkara D, etal. Lactose intolerance. In: UpToDate, Rose, BD (Ed), UpToDate, Waltham, MA, 2006.

Chapter 14: You & Your Doc

1. American Academy of Pediatrics, Committee on Practice and Ambulatory Medicine, (RE 9535), 2000.
2. Pediatrics 1998;101(6):1072-1078.
3. American Academy of Pediatrics, Parenting Q and A, Feb 2007.
4. American Academy of Pediatrics, 2008, Recommendations for Preventive Pediatric Health Care.

Chapter 15 Vaccines

1. Offit P. Addressing parents' concerns: do multiple vaccines overwhelm or weaken the infants' immune system? Pediatrics 2002;109:124.
2. Ramnarance C. The truth about vaccines and autism. IVillage.com, September 2009.
3. Schuval S. Avoiding allergic reactions to childhood vaccines (and what to do when they occur). Contemporary Pediatrics 2003; 20(4): 29-53.
4. Pickering LK, Ed. *Red Book: 2003 Report of the Committee of Infectious Diseases. 26th ed.* Elk Grove Village, IL: American Academy of Pediatrics, 2003.
5. Pickering LK. See Footnote 4.
6. Dept of Health and Human Services. Epidemiology and Prevention of Vaccine-Preventable Diseases, January 2007.
7. MMWR 2/29/08 57 (08): 203-206
8. Lancet 2004;363:747-750, 820-824.
9.
a) D'Souza Y, Fombonne E. No evidence of persisting measles virus in peripheral blood mononuclear cells from children with ASD. Pediatrics 2006 Oct 118 (4) 1664-75,
b) Uchiyama T, etal. MMR vaccine and regression in autism spectrum disorders: negative results presented from Japan. J Autism Dev Disorder. 37, 210-217, 2007.
10. Honda H, etal. No effect of MMR withdrawal on the incidence of autism: a total population study. Journal of Psychology and Psychiatry. 2005 Jun;46(6):572-9. doi: 10.1111/j.1469-7610.2005.01425.x
11. Advisory Committee on Immunization Practices, October 26, 2005.
12. Dagan R. Universal toddler hepatitis A virus (HAV) vaccination: an opportunity for the elimination of population disparity in disease incidence. Abstract G-409. ICAAC, Dec 16, 2005.
13. Pickering LK. See Footnote 4.
14. Gardner P, etal. Immunization of adults. N Engl J Med 1993 Apr 29;328(17):1252-8.
15. MMWR 4/23/10. Vol 59 (15);462.
16. EPA. Mercury study report to Congress: Vol 4: An assessment of exposure to mercury in the US; 1997. www.epa.gov/mercury.
17. Schechter R, Grether JK. Continuing increases in autism reported to California's developmental services system: mercury in retrograde. *Arch Gen Psychiatry.* 2008 Jan;65(1):19-24

18. American Academy of Pediatrics Technical Report: Mercury in the environment: implications for pediatricians. Pediatrics 2001; 108 (1):197-205.

19. Communicable Disease Surveillance Center, London.

20. Thompson WW, etal. Early Thimerosal exposure and neuropsychological outcomes at 7 to 10 years. NEJM 2007;357;1281-1292

21. McCarthy J. Louder Than Words: A Mother's Journey in Healing Autism. New York, Dutton. 2007.

22. Offit P. Pediatrics 2003;112 (6):1394-1401.

23. Dept of Health and Human Services, Agency for Toxic Substances and Disease Registry, ToxFAQ's for Aluminum, Sept 2006.

24. Dept of Health and Human Services, Agency for Toxic Substances and Disease Registry, ToxFAQ's for Formaldehyde, June 1999.

Chapter 16: Infections

1. Pickering LK, Ed. *Red Book: 2003 Report of the Committee of Infectious Diseases. 26th ed.* Elk Grove Village, IL: American Academy of Pediatrics, 2003.

2. Pickering LK. See Footnote 1.

3. Klein J. Epidemiology; pathogenesis; diagnosis and complications of acute otitis media. In: UpToDate, Rose, BD (Ed), UpToDate, Waltham, MA, 2006.

4. Rosenfeld RM, etal. Clinical efficacy of antimicrobial drugs for acute otitis media: metaanalysis of 5400 children from thirty-three randomized trials. Journal of Pediatrics 1994;124:355-67.

5. Hoberman, A, Paradise, JL, Reynolds, EA, Urkin, J. Efficacy of Auralgan for treating ear pain in children with acute otitis media. Arch Pediatr Adolesc Med 1997; 151:675.

6. Paradise JL, etal. Developmental outcomes after early or delayed insertion of tympanostomy tubes. N Engl J Med 2005 Aug 11;353(6):576-86.

7. Pichichero, ME. Complications of streptococcal tonsillopharyngitis. In: UpToDate, Rose, BD (Ed), UpToDate, Waltham, MA, 2006.

8. Leder K, etal. Giardiasis in Children. In: UpToDate, Rose, BD (Ed), UpToDate, Waltham, MA, 2006.

9. Behrman RE. Ed. *Nelson Essentials of Pediatrics.* Philadelphia: WB Saunders, 1990.

10. Silverberg NB. A practical approach to molluscum contagiosum. Contemporary Pediatrics (24) 9: Sept 2007.

11. Petersen RL. West Nile Virus infection. In: UpToDate, Rose, BD (Ed), UpToDate, Waltham, MA, 2006.

Chapter 17 Diseases

1. Behrman RE. Ed. *Nelson Essentials of Pediatrics.* Philadelphia: WB Saunders, 1990.

2. Viljanen M, Savilahti E, Haahtela T, Juntunen-Backman K, Korpela R, Poussa T, Tuure T, Kuitunen M. Probiotics in the treatment of atopic eczema/dermatitis syndrome in infants: a double-blind placebo-controlled trial. Allergy 2005 Apr;60(4):494-500.

3. Fleischer DM, etal. The natural history of tree nut allergy. J Allergy

Clin Immunol, 2005, Nov;116(5):1087-93.

4. Golden, DB etal. Outcomes of allergy to insect stings in children, with and without venom immunotherapy. N Engl J Med 2004 Aug 12;351(7):668-74.

6. American Academy of Orthopedic Surgeons Web: orthoinfo.aaos.org.

7. Shinnar, S, Berg, AT, Moshé, SL, et al. Risk of seizure recurrence following a first unprovoked seizure in childhood: A prospective study. Pediatrics 1990; 85:1076.

8. McNeil, DE, Cote, TR, Clegg, L, Mauer, A. SEER update of incidence and trends in pediatric malignancies: acute lymphoblastic leukemia. Med Pediatr Oncol 2002; 39:554.

9. Silverman, LB, Gelber, RD, Dalton, VK, et al. Improved outcome for children with acute lymphoblastic leukemia: results of Dana-Farber Consortium Protocol 91-01. Blood 2001; 97:1211.

10. Adapted from Robertson J, Shilkofski N (Ed). *Harriet Lane Handbook, 17th Edition, A Manual for Pediatric House Officers.* Philadelphia: Mosby, 2005.

11. Behrman RE. See Footnote 1.

12. Mallare, JT, Cordice, CC, Ryan, BA, et al. Identifying risk factors for the development of diabetic ketoacidosis in new onset type 1 diabetes mellitus. Clin Pediatr 2003; 42:591.

13. MacEwen, CJ, Young, JD. Epiphora during the first year of life. Eye 1991; 5(5):596.

14. Wenzler, DL, Bloom, DA, Park, JM. What is the rate of spontaneous testicular descent in infants with cryptorchidism?. J Urol 2004; 171:849.

15. Robertson J. See Footnote 9.

17. Gold, BD, etal. Diagnosis and management of GERD in children and adolescents. Contemporary Pediatrics 2005 Sept; 22(9) supplement.

18. J Allergy Clin Immunol. 2003;112(3):513-517.

19. NAEPP Expert Panel Report: Guidelines for the diagnosis and management of asthma, 2002.

20. Limb, SL, etal. Irreversible lung function deficits in young adults with a history of childhood asthma. J Allergy Clin Immunol. 2005 Dec; 116(6):1213-9. Epub 2005 Nov 2.

21. Behrman RE. See Footnote 1.

22. National Institutes of Health, press release, March 8, 2005.

23. National Institutes of Health, press release, March 8, 2005, Environmental Protection Agency. www.epa.gov/iaq/asthma/hcprofessionals.html.

24. Weitzman M, etal. Maternal smoking and childhood asthma. Pediatrics 1990;85:505.

25. Metry D. Epidemiology; pathogenesis; clinical features; and complications of hemangiomas of infancy. In: UpToDate, Rose, BD (Ed), UpToDate, Waltham, MA, 2006.

Chapter 18: Environmental Health

1. Woodruff TJ, etal. Trends in environmentally related childhood illnesses. Pediatrics 2004;113(4):1133.

footnotes

2. Pollution in Newborns, Environmental Working Group, July 2004.

3. Etzel RA. Environmental risks in childhood. Pediatric Annals 2004 July; 33:7.

4. American Academy of Pediatrics Committee on Environmental Health. In Etzel RA (Ed). *Pediatric Environmental Health, 2nd ed.* Elk Grove Village, IL: American Academy of Pediatrics, 2003.

5. Woodruff TJ. See Footnote 1.

6. Woodruff TJ. See Footnote 1.

7. National Academy of Science. Web: nas.edu.

8. Etzel RA. See Footnote 4.

9. Canfield RL, etal. Intellectual impairment in children with blood lead concentrations less than 10 mcg/dl. NEJM 2003 Apr 17;348(16):1517-26.

10. American Academy of Pediatrics. See Footnote 4.

11. American Academy of Pediatrics. See Footnote 4.

12. www.foodnews.org/ Environmental Working Group.

13. American Academy of Pediatrics Committee on Environmental Health. See Footnote 4.

14. American Academy of Pediatrics Committee on Environmental Health. See Footnote 4.

15. American Academy of Pediatrics Committee on Environmental Health. See Footnote 4.

16. American Academy of Pediatrics Committee on Environmental Health. See Footnote 4.

17. Sathyanarayana S, etal. Baby Care Products: Possible Sources of Infant Phthalate Exposure Pediatrics, Feb 2008; 121: e260 - e268.

18. National Institute of Health, 2005 Report http://ntp.niehs.nih.gov/ntp/roc/toc11.html

19. Shea KM, etal. Pediatric exposure and potential toxicity of phthalate plasticizers. Pediatrics 2003;111(6):1467-1474.

20. Consumer Reports, May 2003. http://www.consumerreports.org/cro/health-fitness/get-the-lead-out-of-the-garden-hose-503.htm

21. a) Calderon RL, etal. Consequences of acute and chronic exposure to arsenic in children. Pediatric Annals 2004 July; 33(7):461-466.
b) Response to requests to cancel certain chromated copper arsenate wood preservative products and amendments to terminate certain uses of other CCA products. 68 Fed Register 17366 (2003) http://www.epa.gov/fedrgstr/EPA-PEST/2003/April/Day-09/p8372.htm.

22. Newburger J, etal. Diagnosis, treatment, and long-term management of Kawasaki Disease: a statement for health professionals from the Committee on Rheumatic Fever, Endocarditis, and Kawasaki Disease, Council on Cardiovascular Disease in the Young, American Heart Association. Pediatrics 2004;114(6):1708-1733.

23. American Academy of Pediatrics Committee on Environmental Health. See Footnote 4.

24. a) American Academy of Pediatrics Committee on Environmental Health. See Footnote 4. b) Environmental Protection Agency.

25. American Academy of Pediatrics: Screening for Elevated Blood Lead Levels, Pediatrics 1998 June;101(6):1072-1078.

26. Kheifets L, etal. The sensitivity of children to electromagnetic fields. Pediatrics 2005 August;116(2): e303-313.

27. Hardell L, etal. Pooled analysis of two case-control studies on use of cellular and cordless telephones and the risk for malignant brain tumors diagnosed in 1997-2003. Int Arch Occup Envir Health, Mar 16, 2006.

28. No change in brain tumor incidence during a time when cell phone usage increased. JNCI. 2009 101: NP; doi:10.1093/jnci/djp444

29. Kheifets L. See Footnote 26.

30. Kheifets L. See Footnote 26.

31.

a) Toxic effects of indoor molds. AAP Committee on Environmental Health. Pediatrics 1998;101 (4 pt1):712-714.

b) Etzel RA. See Footnote 4.

c) Centers For Disease Control, November 2004. http://www.cdc.gov/mold/pdfs/stachy.pdf

Chapter 19 First Aid

1. American Academy of Pediatrics, Committee on Pediatric Emergency Medicine, January 2001.

2. Centers for Disease Control Morbidity and Mortality Weekly Report. Managing Acute Gastroenteritis Among Children. November 21, 2003; Vol. 52 / No. RR-16.

3. Chowdhury HR, etal. The efficacy of bismuth salicylate in the treatment of acute diarrhea and the prevention of persistent diarrhea. Acta Pediatrica 2001;90(6): 605-610.

4. Fleisher GR, etal. *Textbook of Emergency Medicine, 3rd ed.* Baltimore: Williams and Wilkins, 1993.

5. Schmitt BD. Pediatric Telephone Advice, 3rd ed. Hagerstown, MD: Lippincott Williams and Wilkins, 2004.

6. Dauser RC. Minor Head Injury. In: UpToDate, Rose, BD (Ed), UpToDate, Waltham, MA, 2006.

7. Schunk JE. Radial head subluxation: epidemiology and treatment of 87 episodes. Ann Emerg Med 1990; 19:1019.

8. American Academy of Pediatrics: *Caring for our Children. National Health and Safety Performance Standards: Guidelines for Out-of-home Child Care Programs, 2nd Ed.* Elk Grove Village, IL: American Academy of Pediatrics, 2002.

9. Boulder Daily Camera, Caldara: More than a kernel of truth in the kid's ear January 22, 2006.

Appendix A: Medications

1.

a) Murphy JL, Ed. *Prescribing Reference for Pediatricians*: Spring-Summer 2006. New York: Prescribing Reference, Inc., 2006.

b) Lexi-Comp. In: UpToDate, Rose, BD (Ed), UpToDate, Waltham, MA, 2006.

footnotes

2. Shared PJ, Berfman DA: The effect of inhaled steroids on the linear growth of children with asthma: A meta-analysis. Pediatrics 2000;106 (1): E8.

3. Irwin RS, etal. Diagnosis and management of cough executive summary: ACCP Evidence-Based Clinical Practice Guidelines. Chest 2006; 129: 1S-23S.

Appendix B: Alternative Meds

1. The Dietary Supplements Health and Education Act of 1994.

2. Lexi-comp. In: UpToDate, Rose, BD (Ed), UpToDate, Waltham, MA, 2006.

3. Kemper KJ. *The holistic pediatrician. A pediatrician's comprehensive guide to safe and effective therapies for the 25 most common ailments of infants, children, and adolescents. 2nd ed.* New York: Harper Collins, 2002.

4. Lexi-comp. See Footnote 2.

5. Lexi-comp. See Footnote 2.

6. Lexi-Comp. See Footnote 2.

7. Lexi-comp. See Footnote 2.

8. mayoclinic.com

9. Johnson BC, etal. Probiotics for the prevention of pediatric antibiotic-associated diarrhea. Cochrane Database Syst Rev. 2007 Apr 18;(2):CD004827.

10. Paul I, etal. Effect of Honey, Dextromethorphan, and No Treatment on Nocturnal Cough and Sleep Quality for Coughing Children and Their Parents. Arch Pediatr Adolesc Med. 2007;161(12):1140-1146.

Appendix C: Lab Work

1. Gunn VI, etal (Eds). *The Harriet Lane Handbook: A Manual for Pediatric House Officers, 16th Ed.* Philadelphia: Mosby, 2002.

2. Kushner I. Acute phase proteins. In: UpToDate, Rose, BD (Ed), UpToDate, Waltham, MA, 2006.

3. Loeb S. (Ed). *Clinical Laboratory Test: Values and Implications.* Springhouse, Pennsylvania: Spring House, 1991.

Appendix D: Glossary

1.

a) Behrman RE, Kliegman R. Nelson Essentials of Pediatrics. W.B. Saunders, 1990, Philadelphia.

b) Urdang Associates. *The Bantam Medical Dictionary.* New York: Bantam, 1981.

c) Cloherty JP, Stark AR. *Manual of Neonatal Care, 3rd ed.* Boston: Little Brown, 1992.

d) Shelov SP. *Your Baby's First Year.* New York: Bantam, 1998.

? ?

INDEX

INDEX

? ?

INDEX

index

index

index

web site

Have a question about

Toddler 411?

Want to make a suggestion?

*Discovered a great tip
you'd like to share?*

Contact the authors, Denise Fields and Ari Brown:

◆ Email: authors@Toddler411.com

◆ Follow us on Twitter or post to our Facebook
fan page!

What's online?

 Subscribe to our blog at Toddler411.com. Read
the latest news and studies on toddler health!

 Follow us on Twitter! Twitter.com/Baby411

 Become a fan on our Facebook page!
Facebook.com/expecting411

 Join in the conversation with our popular
message boards at Toddler411.com

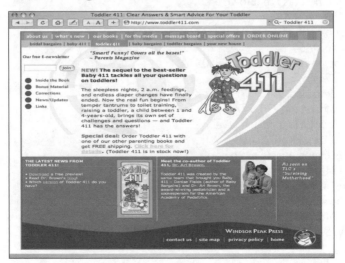

Money BACK GUARANTEE

If this book doesn't save you at least

One

co-pay for a doctor's visit, then we'll give you a complete refund on the cost of this book!

We guarantee Toddler 411 will let you skip at least one doctor's visit for a minor problem with your toddler! Yes, this book will save you AT LEAST one co-payment (typically $15 to $50)!

If it doesn't, just send the book
and your mailing address to

**Windsor Peak Press
436-R Pine Street
Boulder, CO, 80302.**

If you have any questions, please call
(800) 888-0385.

Look at all those other parenting books in the bookstore—no other author or publisher is willing to put their money where their mouth is! We are so confident that *Toddler 411* will save you money that we guarantee it in writing!